Effective Legal Research

Editorial Advisory Board

Little, Brown and Company
Law Book Division

Effective Legal Research

Fourth Edition

Miles O. Price, B. S., B. L. S., LL. B., LL. D.
Late Law Librarian and Professor of Law Emeritus, Columbia University

Harry Bitner, A. B., B. L. S., J. D.
Law Librarian and Professor of Law Emeritus, Cornell University

Shirley Raissi Bysiewicz, B. A., J. D., M. S. L. S.
Professor of Law and Law Librarian, University of Connecticut

Little, Brown and Company
Boston Toronto

Library of Congress Catalog Card No. 78-69772

Fourth Edition

HN

Published simultaneously in Canada by Little, Brown & Company (Canada) Limited

Printed in the United States of America

To
F. J. P., A. B.,
and S. J. B.

Summary of Contents

Appendixes

Table of Contents

Chapter 4 | Legislative Histories of Federal Statutes

Chapter 5 | Indexes and Tables for Work with Federal Statutes

Chapter 6 | Treaties and Other International Acts of the United States

Chapter 7 | Federal Administrative Law

Chapter 8 | Federal Court Rules and Rules of Federal Administrative Agencies

Chapter 9 | State Legislation, Administrative Law, and Court Rules

Chapter 10 | Law Reports: Rationale, Format, and Use as Precedent

Chapter 11 | Law Reports: Decisions of Federal and State Courts

Chapter 12 | Law Reports: The National Reporter System

Chapter 13 | Law Reports: Selective and Special-Subject Systems

Chapter 14 | Law Reports: Tabular Means for Finding

Chapter 15 | Law Reports: Index and Search Books

Chapter 16 | Digests

Chapter 17 | Legal Encyclopedias

Chapter 18 | Citators

Chapter 19 | Treatises and American Law Institute Restatements of the Common Law

Chapter 20 | Legal Periodicals

Chapter 21 | Dictionaries; Words and Phrases; Maxims

Chapter 22 | Form Books; Appeal Papers; Directories

Chapter 23 | Loose-Leaf Services and Topical Reports

Chapter 24 | United Kingdom Materials

Chapter 25 | Canadian Materials

Chapter 26 | Australian Materials

Chapter 27 | New Zealand Materials

Chapter 28 | South African Materials

Chapter 29 | International Law

Chapter 30 | Coordinating the Research Techniques

Chapter 31 | Automated Legal Research

Chapter 32 | Standard Legal Citation Forms

Appendixes

Foreword to the Law Student

According to England's King George III, a lawyer is not a person who knows the law, but one who knows where to find it. This is not entirely so, but let us assume for the moment that it is. The lawyer finds the law principally in books housed in law libraries, so that a lawyer and a law library are inseparable.

Law books, as you may have already observed, are as multitudinous as they are voluminous. Their contents are revealed in still another voluminous host of specialized books of index, which the lawyer consults regularly in attempting to find the law. Once he has succeeded in his search, he is then able to perform another function of the lawyer; namely, evaluating the law and utilizing his conclusions in counseling clients and persuading courts. Hence, the well-equipped lawyer is one who, first of all, is thoroughly familiar with the tools of his profession. He has a priceless advantage over the one less so equipped.

What is true of the lawyer in this respect is even more so of the law student. He is in a strange world in his first year of law school. However much or little he may have read books in his undergraduate days, he has no choice in law school. He must live with a high, wide and sometimes frightening mountain of reading materials. At first they may seem to be put together in such an illogical manner as to defy successful attack. But the lawyer's very necessity of finding the law has brought order out of this seeming chaos by calling forth from the publishers the guides, indexes and other means of approach to the law not found so abundantly in any other literature.

It is the function of courses in the use of law books to acquaint law students, as embryonic lawyers, with the tools of their profession. As such, these courses truly epitomize the "bread and butter" approach in the law school curriculum.

Preface to the Fourth Edition

The authors of this edition have endeavored not only to update the material but to expand the coverage and to provide greater clarity by reorganizing and rewriting various parts of the text. Miles O. Price remains very much a part of this publication.

Five new chapters have been added and one has been divided into two. The five new ones are on Australian Materials, New Zealand Materials, South African Materials, International Law, and Automated Legal Research. The former chapter on English and Canadian Materials is now divided into two separate chapters, United Kingdom Materials and Canadian Materials. Appendix III, Abbreviations, has been made more definitive with substantial additions to the list.

The authors wish to express their special appreciation to the following individuals for their important contributions to the fourth edition: Professor Albert P. Blaustein, Dale Alan Diefenbach, Dorothy Dropick, Mary Fisher, Judith Lahey, Marlene McGuirl, William Matthews, Robert Oakley, Meira G. Pimsleur, Nicholas Triffin, and Ruth Van Demark. Special acknowledgment is made to our families and our library staffs for their patience and support. We also wish to acknowledge our indebtedness to many individuals for their contribution to the previous editions.

We wish to thank the following publishers for permission to use materials from their publications: William G. Brown, Government Printer, Perth, Western Australia; Butterworth & Co. of Australia, of Canada, of Great Britain, and of New Zealand; Canada Law Book Co.; The Carswell Co.; Commerce Clearing House, Inc.; Mrs. Mary Price Franco; The Law Book Co., Australia; Lawyers Co-operative Publishing Co.; Mead Data Central; Queen's Printer for Canada; Shepard's Citations, Inc.; Sweet & Maxwell, Ltd.; West Publishing Co.; and H. W. Wilson Co.

Harry Bitner
Shirley Raissi Bysiewicz

A Note on Exhibits in the Text

Effective
Legal Research

1 | Introduction

§1.1. Law books and their use as affected by the nature of the law.

Lawyers and law students cannot function away from a working law library because the law books which contain the statutes and judicial opinions are the basic source materials of the law. The law library also contains many reference works and indexes which aid in finding and interpreting the law and appraising its authority.

Because of the mutable nature of the law, law books differ greatly from books in other disciplines. The continual changes in the law, combined with the demands of litigation and legal research, necessitate prompt publication and supplementation and more precise indexing than is generally found in other disciplines.

A practical definition of the law is that it is the aggregate of rules recognized and acted upon by courts of justice. In the Anglo-American system, these rules are found both in legislation and in the common law embodied in the decisions of the courts. Changes in the law may occur slowly through a process of growth and synthesis as social conditions change. Common-law rules are thus gradually modified by judicial decisions. Changes may also be sudden and drastic, as in the overruling of a long established judicial precedent, or in the enactment of a statute changing a common-law rule.

Legislation is the product of legally constituted bodies authorized to make rules governing future conduct. These rules are binding within the competence and jurisdiction of the body creating them. None of these rules remains constant. They are subject to interpretation by courts to determine their meaning and may be further amended, repealed, or extended by the particular body which promulgated them.

Thus there is an enormous and constantly changing mass of decisions, legislative enactments, and administrative rules from which the lawyer must speedily and accurately extract the law applicable to a specific problem so that the action of the court to which the problem is presented can be predicted with some degree of certainty and the lawyer can develop the best and most cogent arguments. The task is immeasurably increased because these decisions, as made, and these rules, as enacted, are not published in a subject or classified arrangement but, instead, by jurisdiction and date of decision or enactment.

§1.2. Aim of the search: Authority.

Authority alone is that which is capable of binding a court on a given issue. Its discovery, therefore, underlies and motivates all legal research. Accordingly, practically all law books are either repositories of authority, indexes to authority, or some means of appraising the present value and status of authority. Anything which a court says or cites in its opinion as leading to its decision in a given case is authority of a kind, but the weight which it is to be accorded varies. Some is only persuasive and may be disregarded; other authority is mandatory and must be heeded.

Some legal writers classify legal authority as primary or secondary. Primary authority consists of legislation and judicial decisions which are either mandatory or persuasive. All other legal writings are secondary authority and can only be persuasive. It is, nonetheless, simple and accurate to place all legal authority within the framework of the two categories, mandatory and persuasive. Law books that do not fall in one of the two categories have no authority at all but are merely indexes and tables to aid in finding and appraising authority.

1. *Mandatory authority*. Mandatory authority is authority which the courts must heed, although, under certain circumstances discussed below, they may find reasons for not following it. It is found both in statutes and in judicial decisions.

a. *Legislation as mandatory authority*. Legislation includes the constitutions, laws, and treaties enacted by formal legislative bodies, as well as the rules and regulations enacted and promulgated by municipalities, administrative bodies, and courts. Legislation in effect in the jurisdiction where enacted is mandatory within the jurisdiction, but legislation enacted or promulgated in one jurisdiction lacks any authority, even persuasive, before a court in any other jurisdiction. Where legislation is in conflict with an existing common-law rule in the jurisdiction, the latter is superseded. Outstanding examples of legislation completely superseding and replacing common-law rules are the widespread enactment of workmen's compensation laws, termination of the common-law liability of a husband for his wife's torts, and the abolition of the old "heart balm" suits for breach of promise of marriage.

b. *Judicial decisions as mandatory authority.* Judicial decisions may be mandatory authority depending upon the facts and issues of the case, the jurisdiction in which it was decided, and the court which decided it. Where a previous case involved identical issues and was decided in the same jurisdiction by a higher court or the same court, the holding of the previous decision constitutes mandatory authority. When a court of competent jurisdiction hands down a decision, that decision establishes a precedent binding upon the court rendering it and upon courts subordinate to it until and unless it is reversed on appeal to a higher court or is overruled by the same court in a later case, or the subject matter is changed by statute. Subordination binds the lower court; a policy of uniformity binds the court making the decision. A higher court has both the right and the duty to overrule a former decision which it now deems, for any reason, to have been erroneous or to be inapplicable to present conditions. When the status of a decision as authority is affected by later decisions or legislation, that fact is noted in a citator, described in Chapter 18.

2. *Persuasive authority.* Persuasive authority does not command in the same way that mandatory authority does. Because of the cogency of its reasoning, the high standing of the court deciding it, or the eminence of its author, persuasive authority may tend to sway a court even though it is in no way binding upon it.

a. *Legislation as persuasive authority.* Legislation on a given subject is not even persuasive authority in another jurisdiction which lacks any legislation on the subject. Nonetheless, judicial interpretation of similar legislation from another jurisdiction can be persuasive. This is particularly true in cases of first impression. When, for example, an issue arising from a newly enacted statute reaches a court, there is of necessity no binding precedent from within the forum which dictates how the court must interpret the statute. In such cases, a well-considered decision on a similar statute from a court of another jurisdiction may, by force of its good reasoning, be highly persuasive even though it is in no way binding or imperative. When a court in one jurisdiction does follow the reasoning of another state court and reaches the same conclusion, then such an out-of-state decision is classified as persuasive authority. Furthermore, the legislation of other states may well be considered persuasive where the constitutionality of a new statute is challenged and is in issue, and the courts of other states have construed like legislation.

In addition to the decisions of foreign jurisdictions interpreting similar legislation, there are authorities relating to legislative enactment and promulgation which courts find persuasive in construing statutes, rules, and regulations. Documents such as congressional journals and administrative reports may serve a persuasive function when they illuminate the legislative history and background of a statute and indicate legislative intent. Similarly persuasive may be the reports of law revision commissions, judicial councils, and the opinions of the attorneys general related to a statute in issue before the court.

b. *Judicial decisions as persuasive authority*. Judicial decisions from the same or other jurisdictions which are not binding on a court may nonetheless be persuasive authority if (1) they are from coordinate courts of the same jurisdiction (from, for example, one or more of the Circuits of the United States Court of Appeals or of the court Departments of the Appellate Division of the New York Supreme Court); or (2) they involve dicta from any court in any jurisdiction (see below); or (3) they are from courts of another jurisdiction and the reasoning is cogent and pertinent to the instant case. New York courts, for example, cite Texas decisions and American courts cite English decisions — but only as persuasive support for their own views. When a court in one jurisdiction is compelled by the nature of the case before it to interpret the law of another, conflict of laws rules dictate that the precedential decisions of that other jurisdiction construing its own laws are controlling upon the forum court. The forum court may avoid the precedent, however, if it can find distinguishing facts, issues, or policies.

c. *Dicta as authority*. Dicta are remarks, made by a court in an opinion, concerning a rule of law not necessarily involved in the case or essential to its determination. They are for background or illustration and are not adjudications. (See §10.7 for a discussion of this point.) Theoretically, such dicta have no authority since their subject matter, by definition, is not raised and considered in the decisions in which they appear. In actual practice, well-considered dicta are often persuasive, some so much so that after many years their original status as dicta is often overlooked or forgotten, and they are cited as authority.

d. *Secondary authority: treatises, encyclopedias, Restatements of the American Law Institute, law review articles*. Commentaries on the law by authors not acting at the time in a judicial capacity, sometimes called "secondary authority," may nevertheless be highly persuasive. Although they are only statements of the opinion of their authors, based upon their analysis of legislation and judicial decisions and, as such, not binding in any way upon the courts, they are frequently cited by the courts in their opinions and in other legal writing. Depending upon the prestige of the author and/or the publication as well as the reasoning and cogency of the analysis, such commentaries can be a highly persuasive factor in influencing the outcome of a court's decision.

3. *Mandatory and persuasive authority between federal and state judicial decisions*. While the doctrine of the subordination of lower to

higher courts applies to and establishes binding authority within both the federal court and the state court systems, it does not similarly control the relation of authority between the courts of the two systems. A decision of the United States Supreme Court interpreting federal legislation, including the Constitution, is binding on state and federal courts alike as to the principle stated. In matters of local state law, interpretation involving no federal constitutional issues, a United States Supreme Court decision is binding only on federal courts and not on state courts. Conversely, the pronouncements of the highest state courts construing their own law are binding on federal courts unless a federal constitutional question is involved. In the absence of rulings by the highest state courts, neither those of intermediate courts nor those of state trial courts (which do not publish or index their reports) are binding precedent upon federal courts. *King* v. *Order of United Commercial Travelers*, 333 U.S. 153, 68 S. Ct. 488, 92 L. Ed. 608 (1948). For a discussion of the relation between federal and state courts, see IB Moore, Federal Practice ¶9.402[1] (2d ed., Albany, N.Y., Bender, 1974).

§1.3. Role of stare decisis in law book making.

The significance of the various degrees and kinds of authority stems from the rule of stare decisis which, under our common-law system, largely controls judicial decisions. A brief statement of this rule — also see §10.7 — is that, under a precise set of facts, "a deliberate or solemn decision of a court or judge, made after full argument on a question of law fairly arising in a case and necessary to its determination, is an authority or binding precedent in the same court, or in other courts of . . . lower ranks within the same jurisdiction, in subsequent cases where the very same point is again presented. . . ."[1] The aim of the doctrine is certainty.

The doctrine functions somewhat like a graph upon which every decision in point is represented as a dot. When a figurative line is drawn through all of these dots, a curve or trend of decision is discernible which enables the lawyer to predict with some degree of certainty judicial action upon a similar set of facts in the future. The curve or trend is the statement of a legal principle, distilled from the decided cases and applicable in future cases.

The doctrine of stare decisis makes current updating imperative in law book publishing since the latest decision and the most recent statutory enactment must be considered in the determination of any legal question or issue. The latest reported case, instead of following the line of the previous decisions, may deviate one way or the other,

1. D. H. Chamberlain. The Doctrine of Stare Decisis (N.Y., Baker, 1885), p. 19.

or even reverse its field and head in the other direction. A new statute may modify or repeal an old decision or even abolish an entire line of decisions. Law publishing, therefore, is geared to high speed distribution of law reports, statutes, and their indexes.

§1.4. Law book features.

Primary legal authority is usually published — at least initially — in chronological order. Within each jurisdiction statutes are printed in order by date of enactment, and judicial decisions appear roughly according to the date on which the opinion was handed down. Because the legal researcher is usually interested in authority on a particular subject, there are certain features of law books which assist the searcher in finding the material needed even though it is not published in classified or subject order.

1. *Tables and other features*. When consulting a law book, the user should first ascertain the subject matter and time period covered by the volume. Taking a moment to examine the overall organization of the volume will also provide insight for effective use of the material.

a. The *title page* indicates who wrote or edited the book, what it is about, and the date of publication.

b. *Tables of Contents* provide guidance about the organization of the book and will alert the researcher to the various tools and features of that particular volume or set.

c. *Tables of Abbreviations* are frequent and useful features and should always be sought when the researcher does not know or cannot ascertain the meaning of a particular abbreviation.

d. *Tables of Cases* are the most nearly universal of all law book features and list all cases in the volume by the name of the plaintiff or appellant.

e. *Tables of Statutes Construed* and *Tables of Cases Cited* are forms of citators found in many law books.

f. A *list of Words and Phrases Judicially Defined* is a useful tool for locating exactly how the courts have construed and defined specific words and phrases.

g. The bound volumes of the National Reporter system also contain a *digest* in miniature, providing, in effect, a subject index to the cases contained in that volume. The larger digests are elaborate indexing tools for large numbers of cases and form the lawyer's most necessary tool for extracting the rules of case law.

h. *Transfer* or *parallel conversion tables* are found in most books where there is a change from one form of statute to another (for instance, from the session law to the compiled, subject matter arrangement) or where there is more than one series of law reports (for instance, the official and unofficial series of law reports).

2. *Publication dates and supplementation*. Because the latest statute or decisions may substantially affect a legal rule, the date of a statute or case, a treatise, encyclopedia, or citator is one of the most important aspects of legal research. Outdated authority is not only unhelpful but also potentially dangerous. The legal researcher should, therefore, acquire the habit of checking both the date of publication and the dates covered by the material in the book. Every effort should then be made to update the material and ascertain whether there is later authority on the same point of law.

Most law books try to keep up with the latest developments. They are geared to speed of original publication and to frequency of supplementation. Because new material may often totally revise or repeal much that is in the main volume, the legal researcher should always ascertain whether the desired material is covered by the main work or by a supplement. The supplement might be a "pocket part" inserted in the back of the main volume, a separate supplementary pamphlet, or some other device for staying up-to-date. Whichever method of supplementation is used, it will usually be keyed to the main volume to facilitate the identification of later material. The legal researcher should develop the habit of checking the main volumes and the supplements, and making certain that all the latest developments have been located.

3. *Tools for using law books to find and appraise the law*. Statutes and reported cases are by far the best and most promptly indexed of all professional literature; yet, without sophisticated means for assessing the law, one would be helpless in one's search for the law. With them it is possible to extract the legal principles set forth in every reported American case to within a few days; to find such a case by its name, its subject matter, and its place of publication; and to tell whether it is still good authority. This can also be done for statutes and for English and Canadian material. Tools for using law books include the cumulative and comprehensive indexes, tables, digests, and citators accompanying major collections of reports and statutes as well as treatises, legal encyclopedias, periodicals, dictionaries, and form books. Their makeup and use are described in this book. They are the necessary tools of your profession.

§1.5. State legal research guides.

Some states have guides and manuals specifically for use in legal research in their own state. The following states have law finders:

CALIFORNIA has three books: Fink, *Research in California Law*, 2d ed. (Buffalo, N.Y., Dennis & Co., Inc., 1964); Greenberg, *Intro-*

duction to California Law Finding, 1st ed. (Monterey, Calif., Why Not Creations, 1977); and Henke, *California Law Guide*, 2d ed. (Los Angeles, Calif., Parker & Sons, 1976).

FLORIDA: The researcher consults French, *Research in Florida Law*, 2d ed. (Dobbs Ferry, N.Y., Oceana Publications, 1965).

ILLINOIS: Two books may be consulted: Davies, *Research in Illinois Law* (Dobbs Ferry, N.Y., Oceana Publications, 1954); and Jacobs, Brast, Hess & Sprowl, *Illinois Legal Research Sourcebook* (Chicago, Ill., Illinois Institute for Continuing Legal Education, 1977).

LOUISIANA: Consult Wallach, *Louisiana Legal Research Manual* (Baton Rouge, Louisiana State University Law School, 1972).

MICHIGAN: See Beer, *An Annotated Guide to the Legal Literature of Michigan* (Lake Orion, Mich., Wayne State University, 1973).

NEW MEXICO: Consult Poldervaart, *Manual For Effective New Mexico Legal Research* (University of New Mexico Press, 1955).

NORTH CAROLINA: Consult Kavaas and Christensen, *Guide to North Carolina Legal Research* (Buffalo, N.Y., W. S. Hein & Co., Inc., 1973).

PENNSYLVANIA: See Surrency, *Research in Pennsylvania Law*, 2d ed. (Dobbs Ferry, N.Y., Oceana Publications, 1965).

SOUTH CAROLINA: Consult Mills and Schultz, *South Carolina Legal Research Methods* (Buffalo, N.Y., W. S. Hein & Co., Inc., 1976).

TENNESSEE: Consult Laska, *Tennessee Legal Research Handbook* (Buffalo, N.Y., W. S. Hein & Co., Inc., 1977).

TEXAS: Consult two guides, Boner, *A Reference Guide to Texas Law and Legal History: Sources and Documentation* (Austin, University of Texas Press, 1976); and Lebowitz, *Legal Bibliography and Research: An Outlined Manual on the Use of Law Books in the Texas and Federal Courts*, 2d ed. (Austin, Tex., published by Lebowitz, 1957).

WISCONSIN: See Knudson, *Wisconsin Legal Research Guide* (University of Wisconsin, 1962).

§1.6. Computerized legal research.

A revolutionary method which uses the computer to search primary legal documents has been developing over the past decade. The first commercially available system, on line to the general public, was LEXIS, developed by the Mead Data Central Corporation. West Publishing Company also has a computerized retrieval system, WESTLAW, which uses the familiar headnotes which West has always employed to index cases. In addition, many other systems are available for limited classes of users or for special purposes. FLITE —

Federal Legal Information Through Electronics — is, for example, a system sponsored by the Department of Defense and is available to anyone working for them or on a defense contract. JURIS is a system developed by the Department of Justice.

Computerized research as well as other automated methods of search are explained more fully in Chapter 31, Automated Legal Research.

2 | Types and Importance of Legislation

§2.1. "Conventional" and "subordinate" legislation and their importance.

Of the two types of primary authority, legislation has come to play the dominant role. Where a century ago the search for the law began with an examination of decided cases, today such a search begins with the determination of the applicable legislation. Only after that determination is made does the search turn to cases. The unprecedented enactment of wide-ranging legislation during the last hundred years is responsible for this shift in emphasis. This shift is dramatically reflected in the kinds of cases heard by the Supreme Court. In 1875, more than 40 percent of the controversies reaching the Supreme Court involved common-law litigation. Today, nearly every case heard by the Court is a case of statutory construction.

1. *Conventional legislation*. This type of legislation is the product of legislative action. It includes not only the statutes enacted by the United States Congress and the state legislatures but constitutions as well. In addition, treaties and interstate compacts are also a kind of direct legislation which, while not initiated by legislatures, require their approval. In some states, municipal ordinances are also regarded as conventional legislation, i.e., as "local laws." In other states, such ordinances are viewed as delegated, subordinate legislation.

2. *Subordinate legislation*. This type of legislation is authorized by conventional legislation which delegates legislative powers to other branches of government. The rules and regulations of administrative bodies, the executive orders and proclamations of the President and

state governors, the municipal ordinances in states, and the rules of the various courts are various types of subordinate legislation. The most important subordinate legislation is promulgated under the authority of *specific* enabling legislation. Much subordinate legislation, however, stems from the inherent power of an administrative or judicial body to establish rules for the transaction of its business. On the whole, this subordinate legislation is extremely important and has given rise to a species of law books, particularly the loose-leaf services, which were unknown to earlier generations of lawyers.

§2.2. Classes of conventional legislation and their authority.

While this chapter deals with conventional federal legislation, nearly everything in it applies to conventional state legislation as well.

1. *The Constitution as conventional federal legislation*. Constitutions form the basic law in a given jurisdiction. They establish the legal framework of a government, delegate powers and responsibilities, and define rights and liberties.

The United States Constitution was adopted in 1789 and, for all practical purposes, marks the beginning of federal legislation. The Constitution specifically provides for federal legislation in art. I, §8, cl. 18; art. I, §7, cl. 2; and art. VI, cl. 2. Judicial interpretation of these three provisions restricts the designation "law" to three categories of legislation: the act, the joint resolution, and the treaty. Interstate compacts are approved by acts of Congress or by joint resolutions and are also law. Reorganization plans are not formally designated as law. Nonetheless, when they are approved under the terms of a reorganization act, such plans have the force of law.

2. *Conventional federal legislation below the constitutional level*. Conventional federal legislation is comprised of acts, treaties, interstate compacts, and three kinds of resolutions: joint, simple, and concurrent. Because they involve congressional action, reorganization plans are also considered a type of conventional federal legislation. As noted in §2.1, treaties and interstate compacts are hybrid legislation since they also require the action of an agency outside of Congress. Acts and resolutions are further classified as "private" or "public" depending upon whether they affect individuals and/or specific groups or the public generally. Legally, however, there is no distinction since all acts and joint resolutions, whether "private" or "public," have the force of law.

a. *Conventional legislation having the force of law*.

1. *Acts of Congress*. Acts are the most common form of congressional legislation. They are referred to as bills in the house in which they originate. Bills are designated simply as H.R. 8238 (for House of Representatives) or S. 19 (for Senate) of the respective Congresses.

See Exhibit 1 below. After passage as bills by the originating house, they are called acts upon introduction or re-introduction in the other house. Bills become acts of Congress when they have passed both houses, have been prepared for the President's signature, and then have been either approved by the President or passed over a veto by a two-thirds vote of quorums present in *both* houses.

2. *Joint resolutions*. Of the three kinds of resolutions — simple, concurrent, and joint — only the last one has the force of law. Like acts, joint resolutions must be passed by both houses. All joint resolutions, except those proposing a constitutional amendment, must be signed by the President. Joint resolutions on the federal level differ from acts only in their enacting clause ("Resolved" as opposed to "Be it enacted") and in the frequent prefacing of a joint resolution with a preamble. See Exhibit 2. Unlike the situation in some states where resolutions occupy a lesser status, both acts of congress and joint resolutions are designated as law on the federal level.

3. *Treaties*. Treaties are the formal agreements made between two or more sovereign nations. They originate in the executive branch but require the approval of two-thirds of the Senate in order to be law. They are, therefore, conventional federal legislation. Treaties are discussed in Chapter 6.

4. *Interstate compacts*. Like treaties, interstate compacts are formal agreements initiated outside of Congress. Interstate compacts are negotiated between two or more individual states. They are sanctioned by art. I, §10, cl. 3 of the Constitution which states that "No state shall, without the Consent of Congress, . . . enter into any agreement . . . with another state . . ." The compacts themselves are not enacted by Congress as a separate form of federal legislation but are created by the states concerned. What Congress does is to give its consent by an act or joint resolution or by its approval of a state constitution embodying the compact. Consent may also be inferred from congressional acts recognizing the validity of the agreement. Approval may be given either before or after the states have entered into their compact. The compact is effected by parallel enactments by the several state legislatures involved. Such compacts are commonly used to settle boundary disputes and to provide for various kinds of cooperative state action, particularly in the development of natural resources and of interstate transportation facilities. As public laws, the texts of compacts are in the United States Statutes at Large and in the session laws of the states concerned; the consents of Congress are printed in the United States Code Congressional and Administrative News. Not being of general interest, compacts are not codified in the U.S. Code. A list of all interstate compacts entered into before 1956 is contained in Interstate Compacts, 1783–1956, published by the Council of State Governments.

86TH CONGRESS
2D SESSION

H. R. 12262

IN THE HOUSE OF REPRESENTATIVES

MAY 17, 1960

Mr. SANTANGELO introduced the following bill; which was referred to the Committee on the Judiciary

A BILL

To amend section 353 (3) of the Immigration and Nationality Act.

Be it enacted by the Senate and House of Representatives of the United States of America in Congress assembled, That section 353 (3) of the Immigration and Nationality

---

86TH CONGRESS
2D SESSION

S. 3230

IN THE SENATE OF THE UNITED STATES

MARCH 18, 1960

Mr. BUTLER introduced the following bill; which was read twice and referred to the Committee on the Judiciary

A BILL

To amend section 35 of title 18 of the United States Code so as to increase the punishment for knowingly giving false information concerning destruction of aircraft and motor vehicles.

Be it enacted by the Senate and House of Representatives of the United States of America in Congress assembled, That section 35 of title 18 of the United States Code is

Exhibit 1

86TH CONGRESS
2D SESSION

H. J. RES. 541

IN THE HOUSE OF REPRESENTATIVES

JANUARY 6, 1960

Mr. LOSER introduced the following joint resolution; which was referred to the Committee on the Judiciary

---

JOINT RESOLUTION

Authorizing and requesting the President to set aside and proclaim the Tuesday following the second Monday in June of each year as "National Fraternal Day".

Resolved by the Senate and House of Representatives of the United States of America in Congress assembled, That the President is authorized and requested to issue a

---

86TH CONGRESS
2D SESSION

S. J. RES. 196

IN THE SENATE OF THE UNITED STATES

MAY 23, 1960

Mr. MAGNUSON introduced the following joint resolution; which was read twice and referred to the Committee on the Judiciary

---

JOINT RESOLUTION

To provide for the designation of June 20, 1960, as "National Academy of Television Arts and Sciences Day".

Resolved by the Senate and House of Representatives of the United States of America in Congress assembled, That the President is authorized and requested to issue a

Exhibit 2

5. *Reorganization plans*. Reorganization plans begin as delegated legislation. The President is given the power to reorganize executive agencies by means of a general authorizing statute. Depending on the provisions in the enabling statute, plans must be submitted to one or both houses of Congress for direct legislative action. If Congress does not act to veto the plan, it automatically becomes law. Because reorganization plans are more accurately understood as subordinate administrative legislation, they are discussed in Chapter 7.

b. *Conventional legislation not having the force of law*.

1. *Simple resolutions*. These have no legislative effect outside the house in which they originate. They concern only the business of the one house passing them. Creation and appointment of committees (other than joint, which are created by concurrent resolution), inquiries addressed to government departments, and directives to an investigating committee (other than a joint committee) are by simple resolution.

The text of many but not all simple resolutions as passed is found in the Congressional Record for the day of passage, and they are also printed in the Journal of the house passing them. They are indexed in the Congressional Record index and, by subject only, in the Congressional Record Daily Digest. See Exhibit 3.

2. *Concurrent resolutions*. Unlike simple resolutions, concurrent resolutions are passed by both houses. Unlike joint resolutions, they are not signed by the President and do not have the force of law. Concurrent resolutions are not binding on either house until agreed to by both. They are primarily used to create and appoint joint committees and to arrange for joint sessions of the two houses. In addition, they are frequently used to recall a bill from enrollment, subsequent to passage by both houses but before presidential approval, for correction. Concurrent resolutions are also used as an expression of policy to disapprove reorganization plans submitted by the President. Concurrent resolutions are printed in the United States Statutes at Large, and their passage through Congress is indexed in the Congressional Record and the Congressional Record Daily Digest. See Exhibit 4.

c. *Pre-Constitutional period federal legislation*. Federal legislation begins with the Constitutional period in 1789, but there was legislation under the Articles of Confederation from 1784 to 1788 which preceded the adoption of the Constitution. The enactments were called Ordinances and are to be found in the Journals of the Continental Congress. The Ordinance of 1787 is significant today because it set up the governmental and legal system of the states north of the Ohio River and had a profound effect upon the laws of many of the states then called the Northwest Territory. It is printed in all editions of the United States Code and in the compiled statutes of some of the above states.

86TH CONGRESS
2D SESSION

H. RES. 399

IN THE HOUSE OF REPRESENTATIVES

JANUARY 6, 1960

Mr. CANNON submitted the following resolution; which was considered and agreed to

RESOLUTION

Resolved, That the Clerk of the House inform the Senate that a quorum of the House is present and that the House is ready to proceed with business.

V

86TH CONGRESS
2D SESSION

S. RES. 205

IN THE SENATE OF THE UNITED STATES

JANUARY 6, 1960

Mr. DIRKSEN submitted the following resolution; which was considered and agreed to

RESOLUTION

Resolved, That the Secretary inform the House of Representatives that a quorum of the Senate is assembled and that the Senate is ready to proceed to business.

V

Exhibit 3

86TH CONGRESS
2D SESSION

H. CON. RES. 443

IN THE HOUSE OF REPRESENTATIVES

JANUARY 6, 1960

Mr. McCORMACK submitted the following resolution; which was considered and agreed to

---

CONCURRENT RESOLUTION

Resolved by the House of Representatives (the Senate concurring), That the two Houses of Congress assemble in the Hall of the House of Representatives on Thursday, January 7, 1960, at 12:30 o'clock postmeridian, for the pur-

86TH CONGRESS
2D SESSION

S. CON. RES. 80

IN THE HOUSE OF REPRESENTATIVES

FEBRUARY 10, 1960

Referred to the Committee on House Administration

CONCURRENT RESOLUTION

Resolved by the Senate (the House of Representatives concurring), That there be printed for the use of the Committee on Armed Services one thousand additional copies of part 1 of the hearings held by that committee on an inquiry

Exhibit 4

d. *Confederate States of America legislation, 1861–1865.* The Confederacy legislated throughout its existence and because this legislation was the subject of litigation, it is mentioned here.

3 Publication of Conventional Federal Legislation

§3.1. Federal Constitution.

The Federal Constitution is readily available in many editions. It is found in general encyclopedias, reference works, official and unofficial compilations of federal and state statutes, constitutional law treatises, and the biennial House and Senate Manuals. Because the Constitution, more than any other piece of legislation, requires interpretation, an annotated edition which digests the cases construing the Constitution is indispensable in legal research. There are three comprehensive annotated editions in common use.

1. *Library of Congress edition.* The Constitution of the United States of America; Analysis and Interpretation, Annotations of Cases Decided by the Supreme Court of the United States to June 29, 1972 (1973, Supp. 1976).

This is a useful edition for those seeking a good basic knowledge of the Constitution rather than every case which has construed it. It is in effect an encyclopedic treatment of the Constitution. It contains a "literal print" of the text and amendments, convenient for those who need only the bare text. A useful feature is a detailed account of the ratification of the several amendments by the various states. The Constitution is then annotated, word for word. This edition is virtually a Constitutional history, annotated to the leading cases. Under each clause or section is set forth not only the current interpretation but also a history of the legal route which the courts have traversed in arriving at their present interpretation. The range of source materials in the annotations includes citations to and quotations from both federal and state court decisions, as well as commentaries and treatises, arguments of counsel, and occasionally federal statutes. A unique citator function is performed by three tables: (1) federal and (2) state acts held unconstitutional in whole or in part by the Supreme Court and (3) earlier Supreme Court decisions subsequently overruled. This edition is an updating and partial reorganization of the Corwin edition of 1952.

2. *United States Code Annotated Edition*. Published by the West Publishing Company, the United States Code Annotated devotes several volumes to the Constitution and annotations to it. The annotations in these volumes are all-inclusive and encompass not only all relevant Supreme Court holdings, but also relevant lower federal and state court decisions. There are annotations to other relevant material such as opinions of Attorneys General of the United States, presidential executive orders and proclamations, Board of Tax Appeals and Tax Court decisions, encyclopedias, and law review articles. The annotations in the United States Code Annotated further include references to the West Key Number System. The United States Code Annotated is updated both by pocket supplements as well as by frequent interim service pamphlets which refer to the most recent cases.

3. *United States Code Service edition*. Originally published as the Federal Code Annotated by Bobbs-Merrill, this edition of the United States Code has been acquired by the Lawyers Co-operative Publishing Company and is being republished as the United States Code Service. Like the U.S.C.A., its structure parallels that of the United States Code. Two of its volumes are devoted to the Federal Constitution. They provide annotation not only to the leading cases in point but to federal and state decisions, codified and uncodified laws, and treaties which relate to a particular section or clause. Current supplements to these volumes are published as pocket parts. In addition to annotations to primary legal authority, there are also references to secondary authorities such as American Jurisprudence and the American Law Reports, law review articles, and advisory opinions. Because of their thoroughness, the United States Code Annotated and the United States Code Service provide the necessary means by which the attorney can ascertain the scope of the law of the Constitution as it relates to the precise problem being researched.

4. *Other annotated editions of the Constitution*. In addition to annotations to their own constitutions, some states provide annotations to the Federal Constitution in their statutory compilations. These annotations to the Federal Constitution are to the decisions of the particular state's own appellate courts. The student using these

annotations must always remember that, in interpreting the Constitution, the Supreme Court is the ultimate authority. The Federal Constitution is also found annotated in Columbia University's Legislative Drafting Research Fund's Constitutions of the United States, National and State (1974).

§3.2. Slip laws.

The first officially published form of congressional legislation is in a separate pamphlet for each law. This pamphlet is called a slip law. It is the same text form which is later bound and indexed for each year as the United States Statutes at Large. The purpose of slip law publication is speed. Slip laws are published in two series, as Public and Private laws, together containing both the acts and joint resolutions of the Congress. Through the Seventy-sixth Congress (1939–1942), the Public and Private Joint Resolutions were published as two series, separate from the acts, but they have since been merged as public and private laws.

Public and private laws have equal legal status as law. The student, however, is likely to be little concerned with private legislation which includes, for the most part, legislation passed for the benefit of an individual or group and which is not of direct or immediate interest to the government or to the public. Assignment as "public" or "private" is a matter of editorial discretion on the part of the Editor of Laws of the Administrator of General Service. A slip law is shown with numbered arrows pointing to its various parts in Exhibit 5.

The information given above "An Act" is for index or identification purposes only and is not a part of the enactment. As such it is useful and is repeated when published in the Statutes at Large. Until the issuance of the bound volume of the Statutes at Large — usually about fourteen months (can take up to 3 years!) after the slip law publication — the law and bill numbers together are the law's identification tag.

In the example below, the margined editorial annotation (15) has been part of the slip laws since mid-1951. It corresponds to a similar comment which has always appeared in the United States Statutes at Large edition. The Statutes at Large citation (8) given for an act is subject to correction in the printed volume but is usually accurate. Prior to the Ninety-fourth (1975) Congress, Statutes at Large citations were found in the margin and indicated when a statute would be continued on the next page. In citing from a slip law, the Statutes at Large citation should be given. This is a matter of convenience since slip laws are not readily available and are soon replaced as primary authority by the Statutes at Large edition.

91 STAT. 1420 (9) → PUBLIC LAW 95-196—NOV. 19, 1977 ← (12)

(8)

(10) → **Public Law 95-196**
95th Congress

An Act ← (1)

(2)

Nov. 19, 1977
[H.R. 2770]

(11)

To amend section 142 of title 28, United States Code, relating to the furnishing of accommodations to judges of the courts of appeals of the United States. ← (3)

U.S. courts of appeals, judges, accommodations.

(15)

(4) → *Be it enacted by the Senate and House of Representatives of the United States of America in Congress assembled,* ← (14) That section 142 of title 28, United States Code, is amended by adding the following ← (13) sentence at the end thereof: "The limitations and restrictions contained in this section shall not be applicable to the furnishing of accommodations to judges of the courts of appeals at places where Federal facilities are available and the judicial council of the circuit approves.".

(5)

(6) → Approved November 19, 1977.

(7) → LEGISLATIVE HISTORY:

HOUSE REPORT No. 95-748 (Comm. on the Judiciary).
SENATE REPORT No. 95-579 (Comm. on the Judiciary).
CONGRESSIONAL RECORD, Vol. 123 (1977):
Oct. 31, considered and passed House.
Nov. 4, considered and passed Senate.

1. Kind of legislation (here an Act).
2. Preamble.
3. Popular name or short title (see §5.3).
4. Enacting clause; "Resolved" in a resolution.
5. Example of the type of statutory amendment which inserts additional text. See §9.9 for a discussion of "perpetual revision" statutory amendment.
6. Approval date. If effective on a different date, that date is specified in the Act. When passed over the President's veto or without presidential approval, that is indicated.
7. Legislative history. New, beginning with 88th Congress (after 1963).
8. Statutes at Large citation for the Act as it will appear in bound form.
9. Law number.
10. Congress number.
11. Bill number.
12. See 6.
13. United States Code citation of the act being amended.
14. The first section of any act is unnumbered, but in legal writing it is nonetheless cited as "Section 1."
15. Editorial matter in the margin.

Exhibit 5

Prior to the Eighty-fifth (1957) Congress, chapter numbers were used to indicate the order of approval of bills during a session of Congress. Chapter numbering was consecutive, with public and private laws in a single series. These chapter numbers will still be found in the Statutes at Large covering Congresses preceding the Eighty-fifth. Now, all *public* laws are numbered consecutively in order of approval in *one* series, with *private* laws similarly numbered in *another* series.

It is still important to note that, through the Seventy-fourth (1935) Congress, all bills and their resulting enactments were renumbered at the beginning of each *session* of a two-year Congress, so that not only the number of the Congress but also the session were necessary parts of the citation. Since the Seventy-fifth Congress in 1937, however, all bills and acts have been numbered consecutively through an entire Congress.

Public laws are available as slip laws from the United States Government Printing Office. They are also published unofficially in the United States Code Congressional and Administrative News and in the United States Code Service Advance Service. The United States Code Congressional and Administrative News is published by West semi-monthly when Congress is in session and monthly during congressional recesses. The United States Code Service Advance Service is published on the twentieth of each month by Lawyers Co-operative. Both compilations are published in pamphlet form. Pamphlet issues of the United State Code Congressional and Administrative News are cumulated into an annual volume; those of the United States Code Service Advance Service are not. Like the official government slip laws, these unofficial pamphlet issues are available about three weeks after a law's enactment. Because they are bound pamphlets instead of individual pieces of paper, they are more convenient to use. Laws of great importance are frequently published in the unofficial United States Law Week within a week of approval. In addition, relevant federal legislation is often supplied shortly after enactment by loose-leaf services which deal with specialized areas of law such as tax, labor, securities, etc. Even when such legislation is not published, the publisher will supply subscribers with copies of particular legislation upon request.

Courts take judicial notice of official prints of slip laws without their certification as positive law. 1 U.S.C. §113 (1970).

§3.3. United States Statutes at Large.

Slip laws representing the federal laws enacted during a session of Congress are cumulated into a permanent bound set known as the United States Statutes at Large. This is the first permanent version of federal legislation.

1. *Contents of the Statutes at Large*. Beginning with volume 65 in 1951, the Statutes at Large have contained only public and private laws, joint and concurrent resolutions, proclamations (but not executive orders) of the President, reorganization plans, and Constitutional amendments. The treaties and executive agreements of international import, once published in the Statutes at Large, are now printed in a series called United States Treaties and Other International Agreements.

2. *Use of the Statutes at Large and its status as legal authority*. As was noted in Chapter 2, the lawyer's search for the law begins with a

1. For an exception to this, see 84 Stat. 198-1 (1970).

determination of appropriate legislation. Frequently such legislation is in the form of public law. As the primary source for federal public law, the Statutes at Large serves three main functions.

a. As *best evidence*. With the exception of sections of the United States Revised Statutes which are still in force and almost one-third of the United States Code titles which have been enacted into positive law, the Statutes at Large are the "best evidence" to be cited in legal writing. The titles of the Code not reenacted into positive law are only prima facie law. This means that, if the form of the law found in the Code is at variance with that in the Statutes at Large, the Statutes at Large version governs. This was underscored by the court in *Royers, Inc.* v. *United States*, 265 F.2d 615, 618 (3d Cir. 1959), when it reversed a judgement which had been based upon the Code text. The court stated:

> We do not know what source of United States law is used in the Commissioner's office but we would be surprised if they were not the same as that commonly used by a judge, namely, United States Code or United States Code Annotated. The mistake, therefore, is perfectly natural. But no one denies that the official source to find United States laws is the Statutes at Large and that the Code is only prima facie evidence for such laws.

In legal writing of all types, unless a statute has been reenacted as positive law in a code which thereby repeals it in its original form, it would be cited as a Statute at Large and cited with its popular name title. (E.g., Hatch Summers Act, 52 Stat. 584 (1938) — Additional Judgeships Act.) The United States Code citation is usually added merely for the convenience of those who have only the Code form at hand and not the Statutes at Large. The section numbers cited in legal writing are those of the *original act, not of the Code*, unless the Code section has been reenacted as positive law, expressly repealing the original act from which derived. The Code is so much more convenient to use that law students tend to forget that, with the exception of the titles which have been reenacted into positive law, the Code is only prima facie the law.

b. As *the original form of the act*. If the original form of an act — including the numbering of its sections — is desired, then the researcher must look to the Statutes at Large, not to the Code. Not only is the section numbering between the two versions often different, but also, the ordering of the sections frequently does not correspond. While there are tables converting the original act and its sections to the corresponding Code title and sections, use of these tables commonly leads to error in the transfer.

c. As *a source for uncodified acts*. Many acts are not deemed to be of "public, general and permanent interest" and are never codified.

Some acts, such as revenue acts, are only partly incorporated into the United States Code. These uncodified acts can always be located in their statutory form in the Statutes at Large and the United States Code Congressional and Administrative News.

3. *Form of the Statutes at Large*. The material in the Statutes at Large is copied verbatim from the original acts, reorganization plans, etc. The public and private laws are reprints of the slip laws, except that the identification material (bill number, etc.) is in the margin instead of at the top of each separate act. See Exhibit 6.

a. *Public law numbers*. The public law number indicates the chronological order of approval of the laws of each Congress by the President or passage over a veto. The first number stands for the Congress and should always be given when citing by public law number. Public Law 86-366, therefore, is never Public Law 366 since every Congress has a Public Law 366. Private laws are also numbered consecutively in their own series.

b. *Index material in the margin*. This material, as with slip laws, is intended for identification and index purposes. It includes the bill and public or private law numbers and the date of approval. The approval date is the one used in citing federal acts. Also in the margin are rubrics comparable to the headnotes of a case. Like headnotes, they index the matter in the adjoining paragraphs. They may save much time when the searcher is interested in only one or a few sections of a long act and does not know the section number. They also identify by exact citation amended acts mentioned in the adjoining text only by name or date and save the searcher from recourse to transfer tables.

c. *Tables and Index*. Preceding the Table of Contents of each volume is the authentication of legislation contained in it. This is a common feature of statute volumes. It is a statement indicating the authority of the publication of the laws printed therein. Then follow the List of Public Laws (or Private, in another table) Contained in this Volume, by number, title, approval date, and page where printed. A list of reorganization plans, if there are any, is also included. *This is the place to search when the citation is to the law by law number* for the respective Congresses. Beginning with volume 77, there is a Guide to Legislative History of Bills Enacted Into Public Law which is arranged by *public law number* and, for each law, gives the approval date, bill number, committee report numbers, and dates of congressional consideration and passage. Each annual volume has its *own subject index*.

Beginning with volume 70, the Eighty-fourth Congress, second session (1956), the tables were greatly expanded in the separate Table of the Laws Affected by the enactments in each volume. The first table appeared as a separate pamphlet for volume 70. The table for volume

156 PUBLIC LAW 86-73—JUNE 30, 1959 [73 STAT.

Public Law 86-73

June 30, 1959
[H. R. 2256]

AN ACT

To amend chapter 37 of title 38, United States Code, to provide additional funds for direct loans; to remove certain requirements with respect to the rate of interest on guaranteed loans; and for other purposes.

Veterans. Home, farm and business loans. 72 Stat. 1203.

Be it enacted by the Senate and House of Representatives of the United States of America in Congress assembled, That section 1802(d) of title 38, United States Code, is amended by (1) striking the word "or" before "(2)" in the first sentence thereof, and (2) inserting before the period at the end of such sentence a comma and the following: "or (3) by any Federal Housing Administration approved mortgagee designated by the Federal Housing Commissioner as a certified agent and which is acceptable to the Administrator".

72 Stat. 1205. Guaranties.

SEC. 2. Paragraph (1) of section 1803(c) of title 38, United States Code, is amended (1) by striking out ", but the rate of interest so prescribed by the Administrator shall not exceed at any time the rate of interest (exclusive of premium charges for insurance, and service charges if any), established by the Federal Housing Commissioner under section 203(b)(5) of the National Housing Act, less one-half of 1 per centum per annum"; and (2) by striking out "4¾ per centum per annum" and inserting in lieu thereof "5¼ per centum per annum".

68 Stat. 591. 12 USC 1709.

72 Stat. 1206. Restrictions.

SEC. 3. (a) Section 1804(b) of title 38, United States Code, is amended by adding at the end thereof a new sentence as follows: "The Administrator may also refuse to appraise any dwelling or housing project owned, sponsored, or to be constructed by any person refused the benefits of participation under the National Housing Act pursuant to a determination of the Federal Housing Commissioner under section 512 of that Act."

68 Stat. 610. 12 USC 1731a.

72 Stat. 1206.

(b) Section 1804(d) of title 38, United States Code, is amended by adding at the end thereof a new sentence as follows: "The Administrator may also refuse either temporarily or permanently to guarantee or insure any loans made by a lender or holder refused the benefits of participation under the National Housing Act pursuant to a determination of the Federal Housing Commissioner under section 512 of that Act."

68 Stat. 610. 12 USC 1731a.

72 Stat. 1214. Direct loan revolving fund.

SEC. 4. Section 1823(a) of title 38, United States Code, is amended by inserting immediately after the second sentence the following new sentence: "In addition to the sums authorized in this subsection the Secretary of the Treasury shall also advance to the Administrator such additional sums, not in excess of $100,000,000, as the Administrator may request, and the sums so advanced shall be made available without regard to any limitation contained in this subsection with respect to the amount which may be advanced in any one quarter annual period."

Approved June 30, 1959.

Exhibit 6

71 and those following were published as part of each volume. The cumulated Laws Affected Tables for volumes 70 to 84 were published separately in 1971. The tables include Amendments and Repeals of Prior Laws. They are arranged by date of approval in the following order: General Legislation, Revised Statutes, Internal Revenue Codes, Positive Law Titles of the United States Code (with parallel tables to their precodification sections), Positive Law Titles of the

District of Columbia Code, the Canal Zone Code, Reorganization Plans, Veterans Regulations, Executive Orders and Proclamations, and Treaties and Other Agreements. These tables give what Shepard's Citations (see Chapter 18) calls the "subsequent legislative treatment" (amendments and repeals) of the statutes listed. The treatment is not, however, comprehensive. Although enactments from 1789 are listed, enactments affected are only for the period covered by the list consulted.

§3.4. Unofficial publications of federal legislation and their forms.

1. *United States Code Congressional and Administrative News.* This publication contains all the public laws passed by each session of Congress as well as executive orders (which, as noted, are generally not printed in the Statutes at Large) and proclamations. The United States Code Congressional and Administrative News has been published since the first session of the Seventy-seventh Congress in 1941 and, as with the Statutes at Large, is bound and indexed according to congressional sessions.

While the Statutes at Large text of a public law is the authoritative text to cite, United States Code Congressional and Administrative News indexes only partially duplicate and significantly supplement those found in the Statutes at Large. It is, for example, possible to trace major bills enacted by their titles to their Public Law designation. Similarly, one can locate the United States Code Congressional and Administrative News citation (and from it the Public Law number and the Statutes at Large citation) from an act's popular name. Unlike the Statutes at Large, there are indexes by number to executive orders and proclamations. Finally, while the Statutes at Large lists laws affected by their date of enactment and Statutes at Large citation, the United States Code Congressional and Administrative News indexes amendments and repeals according to United States Code titles.

2. *Federal Code Annotated Public Laws and Administrative Materials 1954–1969.* Facsimiles of public laws, proclamations, and executive orders were at one time also bound by congressional session and published by the Federal Code Annotated in their Public Laws and Administrative Materials. These materials were last published as a volume for the second session of the Ninety-first Congress in 1970. These cumulative editions of congressional enactments have been discontinued since the acquisition of the Federal Code Annotated by the Lawyers Co-operative.

§3.5. Locating a particular federal statute in the Statutes at Large.

Since no general index to all permanent federal legislation exists, the tables found in the Statutes at Large and the United States Code Congressional and Administrative News are indispensable tools in locating a particular federal statute. The index or table one uses depends upon the information one has.

If one has a Statutes at Large citation (e.g., 89 Stat. 477), one simply goes to the volume (89) and page (477) cited. If the Public or Private Law number is known, then its subject matter, date of enactment, and Statutes at Large citation is most easily ascertained by consulting the List of Public Laws or List of Private Laws located at the beginning of the appropriate Statutes at Large volume (the appropriate volume, in turn, is located by reference to the congressional session during which the law was enacted and is designated by the first digits of the law's number). If only the congressional session and the House or Senate bill's number is known, the public or private law number is most readily determined by use of the List of Bills Enacted into Public Law or List of Bills Enacted into Private Law which are also located at the beginning of each Statutes at Large volume. If one knows only the popular name of an act or its actual title as well as the session of Congress in which it was enacted, then the United States Code Congressional and Administrative News can supply the references to the public law number (in the case of the titles of major bills enacted) or to the United States Code Congressional and Administrative News page number (with popular acts). Some, but not all, of these titles and popular names are also found in the subject index of the Statutes at Large. Finally, if one wishes to locate legislation which has been enacted during a particular session and which relates to a specific field (such as Education), then the Statutes at Large subject index for that session is the fastest means for finding such legislation and its Statutes at Large citation.

§3.6. Statutory compilations.

1. *Need for compilations.* As was seen above, the session law forms of conventional legislation such as the Statutes at Large are the "best evidence" in published form of federal and state enactments which have not been reenacted into a code form, expressly repealing the session law form. The session law forms are not, however, the forms most frequently consulted by lawyers and students. There are four sound reasons for this. First, all federal and most state session laws are printed in volumes which are arranged not by subject but chronologically by date of enactment. Secondly, session laws include pri-

vate acts and acts which have only a narrow application. Thirdly, session laws take up a great deal of room. The fourth and most important reason why attorneys and students prefer statutory compilations to session law forms stems from the fact that most enactments are repealed or amended or expire by some date or event limitation within themselves but then extended. Current status of a previous enactment cannot be determined by reference to the session law form of initial enactment.

As a result of this subsequent legislative amendment, repeal, or extension, lawyers and students are, after only a few sessions of a given legislature, faced with a hopeless mass of legislation, the extent, meaning, and operative force of which is not possible to determine. A lawyer cannot operate under such conditions. For this reason, the laws of public general interest in force must be republished in a usable arrangement constantly updated by reference to later legislation. This is done in several ways and the publication is referred to generically as revisions, consolidations, compilations, and codes. These terms are not, however, legal words of art and have no definite meaning as applied to a compilation form.

In the United States, both federal and state legislation are commonly compiled by omitting repealed and temporary acts, incorporating the changes made by amendments, and then combining and rewriting as necessary the remaining acts or parts of acts in a classified subject order. This is the form found not only in the United States Revised Statutes and the United States Code but in most state compilations as well.

2. *Legal authority of statutory compilations*. The legal authority of statutory compilations varies. This authority is usually shown in compilations by an enacting clause covering the reenactment or by a certificate of a legislatively employed commission that the text is a true copy which may be offered in evidence. Compilations which are reenacted into "positive law" repeal and supersede the sessions laws from which they are derived. At the other extreme are compilations which have no legal authority other than that conferred by a private publisher's job well done. Still other compilations have been "certified as true copies" of the original by a commission or a state official. If not reenacted as positive law by the legislature itself and if merely compiled by a commission delegated to do the job, compilations are only prima facie the law, rebuttable in case of textual variance by reference to the original session laws. The matter of statutory authority is extremely important. It is so vital that, unless there has been a formal reenactment of the compilation, the careful lawyer cites the original session law form with the compilation title and section numbers in parenthesis for the convenience of the reader.

3. *Types of compilations distinguished*. The multiplicity of compilation designations and their indiscriminate use has led to a great deal

of confusion. Frequently, the terms "Revised Law," "Compiled Laws," "Consolidated Laws," and "Codes" are used interchangeably to describe the same type of law collection. These terms were defined by the noted English authority on legislation, Courtenay Ilbert, in his *Mechanics of Lawmaking* (London, Froude, 1901). Paraphrased, they are:

Revised Laws originally meant the elimination of superseded or dead statutes, and the reprinting, verbatim, of those remaining in force, in chronological order, without comment or annotation. This is the form of the English *Statutes Revised*.

Compiled Laws are also verbatim copies of the original text, but arranged by broad subject (as pamphlet editions of veterans' laws, patent laws, and the like), published without annotation and usually not indexed.

Consolidated Laws, by the Ilbert definition, are by far the most common type of American statutory collections, under whatever name. In this form, a survey of existing and past statutory law is made by a legislatively appointed commission. Provisions in force are preserved (and often rewritten to some extent) and arranged according to an elaborate subject classification scheme with detailed indexes, parallel reference tables, and other aids to their use. The acid test of their status as authority is whether they are merely "authenticated" as true copies of the original laws or whether they have been *reenacted* in their consolidated form, expressly repealing the original statutes from which derived. The fact that the publication is "official" is irrelevant; most statutory compilations of this kind are published under official auspices either by the legislatures concerned or by arrangement with a commercial publisher.

Codes, as defined by Ilbert, are rare or nonexistent in the United States, though common in Civil-law countries. Theoretically, for each code all existing statutory and case law is distilled into a statement which then comprises the entire law: if it is in the code, it is law; if not there, it is not law. In the United States, the nearest approximation of a true code occurs in an area such as procedural, criminal, or probate law where great precision of definition is required. The Louisiana Code is another example. Such uniform state laws as the Uniform Commercial Code are "codes" only in that they attempt to restate the essence of statutory and case law.

4. *United States Revised Statutes*. This is the only compilation of the "public general laws of permanent interest" covering federal legislation which the Congress has ever reenacted as positive law. Its title is Revised Statutes of the United States . . . in Force on the First Day of December, One Thousand Eight Hundred and Seventy-Three (1875). In it, the mass of existing legislation from 1789 on was carefully analyzed; laws of temporary, private, or local interest and parts

of laws which were of such limited interest were discarded; the remainder was arranged in classified order, rewritten as necessary, and reenacted as law which repealed and superseded the Statutes at Large from which it was derived. This revision aroused much dissatisfaction because of its errors and the feeling that the revisers had, in many instances, exceeded their authority. As a result, a second edition was published in 1878.

a. *Legal status of the first and second editions*. Despite its age, much of the Revised Statutes is still the law of the land, either as enacted or, more commonly, as amended by later enactments. Usually the lawyer or law student learns of the existence of a Revised Statute upon which a current United States Code is based from the parallel citation to authority which accompanies the Code section. It is the unrepealed sections of the Revised Statutes, not the Code sections derived from them, which are, however, the best authority. Many sections of the Revised Statutes are still very much alive. The first edition was reenacted as the law, repealing and superseding the Statutes at Large sections on which it was based. In citing it, therefore, it is neither necessary nor proper to cite the Statutes at Large sections which are no longer in force. Later amending acts should, of course, be cited.

Where it corrects the errors in the first, the *second edition* of the Revised Statutes has a different status. The new sections or parts are, as published in the second edition, only prima facie the law, rebuttable by reference to the amending statute published in the Statutes at Large from which derived. Because of the way corrections and repeals are printed in the second edition, however, there is no difficulty in determining which is which. As shown in Exhibit 7, the distinction is made by the use of brackets [ ] and italics. Material contained in the first edition but later repealed is bracketed in italics,

216 TITLE XIV.—THE ARMY.—CH. 1.

Civil employment prohibited.

5 July, 1838, c. 162, s. 31, v. 5, p. 260.
27 *Feb.*, 1877, c. 69, *v.* 19, *p.* 243.

SEC. 1224. [*Officers of the Army on the active list shall not be separated from their regiments or corps for employment on civil works of internal improvement, nor be allowed to engage in the service of incorporated companies, or be employed as acting paymaster, or disbursing agent of the Indian department, if such extra employment require that he be separated from his regiment or company, or otherwise interfere with the performance of the military duties proper.*] [No officer of the Army shall be employed on civil works or internal improvements, or be allowed to engage in the service of any incorporated company, or be employed as acting paymaster or disbursing-agent of the Indian Department, if such extra employment requires that he shall be separated from his company, regiment, or corps, or if it shall otherwise interfere with the performance of the military duties proper.] [See § 2062.]

Exhibit 7

and the repealer cited in italics in the margin. New material is bracketed, however, in roman type. In consulting the second edition, therefore, particular attention should be paid to the brackets and to italicized matter, whether in the text or the margin.

b. *Form and makeup of the Revised Statutes, 1875.* The arrangement is in 74 titles, and most titles are further subdivided into two or more chapters. The sections are numbered consecutively, from Section 1, Title 1, to Section 5601, Title 74. This useful feature simplifies citation since only the section number is required. The margins contain identification and index material: the subject matter of the section, the Statutes at Large citation from which the section was derived (and, in the second edition, later repealing or modifying statutes), and some citations to cases interpreting either the original statute or the Revised Statutes section. There is a *subject index*. There are indispensable *parallel transfer tables* from the original statute to its Revised Statutes number. These tables serve also as *tables of repeals* of statutes reenacted in the Revised Statutes.

c. *Tracing a Revised Statutes section into the United States Code.* Many Revised Statutes have been incorporated in the Code. Table II of the Code — Revised Statutes 1878 — shows which ones have been incorporated and where in the Code they can be found. A "Status" column in this table indicates whether or not the section has been eliminated or repealed. Thus, R.S. §2938 became 19 U.S.C. §378, but the "Status" column of the table shows that it has been repealed.

d. *Repeals of Revised Statutes sections.* The "Status" column in Table II lists repealed Revised Statutes sections, whether or not they were ever in the Code. Table II in the Code and its counterparts in the United States Code Annotated and the United States Code Service provide the only direct means of tracing a Revised Statutes section into its corresponding Code section or of determining whether a given section is still in force. The only alternative way of doing this is a piecemeal, session by session search through the Table of Laws Affected in the Statutes at Large beginning with volume 70. Once, however, a Code section number is found through the above table, it may be Shepardized as a Code section in the usual manner.

5. *United States Code: Official edition.* As a practical matter, the lawyer consults the United States Code (cited as U.S.C.) more often than any other form of federal statute. If only the text of the section is desired, then the official, unannotated edition of the Code is sufficient. If, however, decided cases which are in point and which interpret a particular Code section are needed, then an annotated edition of the Code must be consulted in order to determine which cases should be read in full.

a. *Authority of the Code.* The Code is the current, official "consolidation and codification of all the general and permanent laws of the

United States . . . in force." [Preface to United States Code (1970).] The Code is, in other words, an arrangement by subject of the existing federal legislation of a public and permanent nature from 1789 to the present. It excludes repealed and expired acts, acts not of general interest, and all but a few private acts.

Treaties are not included except as editorial matter which is needed to explain a Code section. Nineteen of the forty-nine United States Code titles have been reenacted into positive law by Congress. The other thirty titles are prima facie evidence of the law. The presumption is that they are the law, and that presumption is rebuttable only by the production of prior unrepealed acts of Congress at variance with the Code. The nineteen titles which have been reenacted as positive law are designated by asterisks in the table of Code titles found at the beginning of each Code volume.

b. *Editorial selection of statutes included.* Inclusion of legislation in the Code is purely an editorial matter under the supervision of a committee of the House of Representatives. Other editorial features are compiled under contract by a commercial publishing firm employed by the committee. Code sections included in one edition may be omitted from the next or changed from one title of the Code to another by editorial fiat. Consequently, the date or supplement number of the Code edition should be cited to avoid possible textual confusion. When an act included in the Code affects more than one government agency, a section may be repeated entirely in several Code titles. Names of agencies which are not pertinent to the particular title are, however, omitted.

c. *Editorial notes in the Code.* Printed with the Code but not technically a part of it, is various editorially added material, some of which is shown in Exhibit 8. This material, set in fine print beneath the respective Code sections to which it is applicable, aids in the understanding of those sections. Notes often refer to uncodified parts of a statute from which a Code section was derived. Others may explain the effect of the parenthetical citations to authority following each section or group of sections, may cross-reference to related Code sections, or comment upon a transfer of agency functions under a reorganization plan — perhaps printing the reorganization plan in full.

d. *Tables of contents to Code titles.* Each of the forty-nine titles (numbered one to fifty; Title 34 was incorporated into Title 10 in 1956) is preceded by a table of contents consisting of a table of chapters in that title by number and caption. In addition, at the beginning of each chapter there is a similar, expanded table for that chapter.

e. *Section numbering in the Code.* Unlike the Revised Statutes, the Code does not have consecutively numbered sections throughout the

Page 197 TITLE 5.—EXECUTIVE DEPARTMENTS—OFFICERS—EMPLOYEES § 778

63 Stat. 864, to give effect to former provisions of section 778 of this title.

1 → **§ 778. Administration by Secretary of Labor; delegation of powers.**

2 → Sections 751–756, 757–791 and 793 of this title shall be administered by the Secretary. The Secretary is authorized to delegate to any officer or employee of the Department of Labor any of the powers conferred upon him by said sections. (As amended

3 → Oct. 14, 1949, ch. 691, title II, § 205 (a), 63 Stat. 864; 1950 Reorg. Plan No. 19, § 1, eff. May 24, 1950, 15 F. R. 3178, 64 Stat. 1271.)

AMENDMENTS

4 → 1949—Act Oct. 14, 1949, cited to text, amended section generally to give effect to section 3 of 1946 Reorg. Plan No. 2, cited to text, which abolished the United States Employees' Compensation Commission and transferred its functions to the Federal Security Administrator.

TRANSFER OF BUREAU, APPEALS BOARD, AND FUNCTIONS

The Bureau of Employees' Compensation, established within the Federal Security Agency by Agency Order 58 of July 16, 1946, set out under this section, was, together with its functions, transferred to the Department of Labor to be administered under the direction and supervision of the Secretary of Labor, and the functions of the Federal Security Administrator, and of the Federal Security Agency, with respect to such Bureau and with respect to employees' compensation (including workmen's compensation), were transferred to the Secretary of Labor, all of such functions, except those not included in the transfer, to be performed by such Secretary or, subject to his direction and control, by such officers, agencies, and employees of the Department of Labor as he shall designate, by section 1 of 1950 Reorg. Plan No. 19, cited to text and set out below. Section 2 of such Plan transferred to the Department of Labor the Employees' Compensation Appeals Board which had also been established within the Federal Security Agency by said Agency Order 58, and transferred the functions of the Federal Security Administrator, with respect to such Board, to the Secretary of Labor. Such section 2 further provided that said Board shall continue to have authority to hear and, subject to applicable law and the rules and regulations of the Secretary of Labor, to make final decision on appeals taken from determinations and awards with respect to claims of employees of the Federal Government or of the District of Columbia.

REORGANIZATION PLAN NO. 19 OF 1950

15 F. R. 3178, 64 Stat. 1271

EMPLOYEES' COMPENSATION FUNCTIONS

§ 1. BUREAU OF EMPLOYEES' COMPENSATION

The Bureau of Employees' Compensation of the Federal Security Agency, together with its functions, is transferred to the Department of Labor and shall be administered under the direction and supervision of the Secretary of Labor. The functions of the Federal Security Administrator, and of the Federal Security Agency, with respect to the Bureau of Employees' Compensation and with respect to employees' compensation (including workmen's compensation) are transferred to the Secretary of Labor: *Provided*, That there are not transferred by the provisions of this reorganization plan (1) any function of the Public Health Service; (2) any function of the Federal Security Agency or the Federal Security Administrator under the Vocational Rehabilitation Act, as amended (including the function of assuring the development and accomplishment of State rehabilitation plans affecting beneficiaries under the Federal Employees' Compensation Act); nor (3) the function of developing or establishing rehabilitation services or facilities. The functions transferred by the provisions of this section shall be performed by the Secretary of Labor or, subject

1. Section number.
2. Text proper, showing an example of "rewriting" in the Code: the original act reads "This Act shall be administered by the Administrator."
3. Statutory authority for the Code section, including a reorganization plan. This section is an example of "perpetual revision," in which the latest amendment cited combines all the earlier forms in one current superseding enactment. The parenthetical citation affords an accurate means of determining the exact section of the original act (§205a here) from which the Code section was derived. This may also be done through Table I(b), "Statutes Included," of the Code.
4. Editorial matter, identified by it smaller type than the Code proper.

Exhibit 8

entire work. Instead, the material is divided into titles such as Agriculture, Patents, Transportation, etc. For each title, the section numbers begin again with section 1. There is, for example, a 1

U.S.C. §1, a 29 U.S.C. §1, and so on. A citation to a section of the Code must, therefore, include the title number. Depending upon the amount of material in a given title, it may be subdivided by: (1) Title, (2) Part, (3) Chapter, and (4) Section. In a citation, only the title and section numbers, along with the edition date or supplement number and date, need be given. E.g., 25 U.S.C. §1302 (1970).

f. *Text of Code sections*. Sections are copied from the original enactment but often with changes such as those in Exhibit 8 above. The changes, except as noted below, are of form, not of substance. Introductory words of the act, such as "Provided," or "That," which begin the original statute section may be omitted. Code title and section numbers are substituted in the body of the text for the official title and sections of the act when the latter are mentioned in the act. Substantive provisions, such as tariff rates, of some statute sections may be altered by a presidential executive order under an enabling statute with the changes incorporated in the Code sections. Again, often only parts of a statute are included, rather than the entire statute. Reorganization plans, such as that in Exhibit 8, are frequently the basis of agency title or function changes in the Code text. It is important to note that statutory authority is cited in parentheses at the end of each Code section or group of sections. Such authority may be congressional acts or joint resolutions, presidential executive orders, or reorganization plans.

g. *Index and tables for the Code*.

(1) *Subject index*. The subject index is voluminous. It covers legal concepts, government agencies, fact situations, and catchwords involved in statutes. There is also a table of acts by popular name — e.g., the National Labor Relations Act — whether or not they are or ever were in the Code. It is one of the best of such tables for federal legislation.

(2) *Tables of statutes included or repealed, and of Code titles revised in later editions of the Code*. The Tables volume of the Code contains six parallel reference tables which are invaluable in federal statutory research. These tables are included, in substantially identical form, in the United States Code Service and in the United States Code Annotated. Table I covers Revised Titles (those titles of the Code which have been revised since the original adoption of the Code) showing the former and the new section numbers and indicating any omissions or repeals of the original sections. Table II consists of Revised Statutes sections, whether or not they ever were in the Code; the Code title and section of those in the Code; and their present status (whether in a revised title, eliminated, or repealed). Table III indicates Statutes at Large incorporated in whole or in part in the Code with, in parallel, the Code title and section and the present status of the enactment. Tables IV, V, and VI cover, respectively, Executive Orders, Proclamations, and Reorganization Plans.

Special tables for repeals of Revised Statutes sections and Statutes at Large have been dropped. The repealing information which they contained is now incorporated in the Status columns. The tables are described more fully, with exhibits, in §5.6 of this manual.

h. *New editions and supplements to the Code.* The first edition of the Code appeared in 1926. Some editions have been issued every six years. Cumulative supplements are issued annually.

6. *United States Code: Unofficial, annotated editions.* As a practical matter, the lawyer using the Code will consult an annotated edition so that the judicial interpretation given the individual Code sections can be determined. While both the text and the editorial material are substantially the same in the official and annotated editions of the Code, each section of the annotated Codes is followed by digests of judicial decisions and of the opinions of Attorneys General interpreting it. In addition to providing a section's legislative background, the annotated editions also supply references to appropriate sections of the Code, to legal encyclopedias, to law review articles, and to law reports. The annotated editions thus combine the functions of a statutory digest with those of a citator. The lawyer is informed both of a statute's meaning and of its present value as authority.

a. *United States Code Annotated.* Published by the West Publishing Company and cited as U.S.C.A., the United States Code Annotated is the oldest, continuous annotated edition of the Code.

(1) *Text of the U.S.C.A.* The text of the U.S.C.A. is identical to that of the official edition. Each has the same section numbering and substantially the same notes and other editorial material pertaining to legislative history and related Code sections. Because supplements to the U.S.C.A. are published with greater frequency and speed than Code supplements, a variance between U.S.C.A. pocket parts and official supplementation sometimes occurs. The U.S.C.A. tables and indexes often contain material not yet printed in the official edition but which will be incorporated into it when the annual cumulative supplement to the Code is published. So that its use will be more convenient and its revision less cumbersome, the U.S.C.A. is published in many small volumes. Each Code title is contained in one or more volumes. The Constitution encompasses several volumes. The subject as well as the title number of each volume is printed on its binding.

(2) *Material in the U.S.C.A. not found in the official editions of the Code.* The verbatim texts of pertinent statutes are printed for some Code titles. For example, the revenue acts, in their original session law form, from 1924 to date, are printed as a supplement to Title 26, the Internal Revenue title. For some titles, particularly those which have been revised as a result of substantial legislative changes, there

may be an historical or critical essay by a member of the bar which explains the probable impact of the new legislation or a congressional committee report which contains explanatory revisers' notes. Annotated court rules are in a separate volume. Indexes and tables are substantially the same as those of the official edition. However, some titles have additional indexes.

(3) *Annotations in the U.S.C.A.* The annotations are said to digest every opinion interpreting each Code section from both official and unofficial federal and state law reports and the opinions of the Attorneys General of the United States. The digest paragraphs following each Code section are arranged according to a subject scheme which may be very elaborate when the section has been frequently interpreted by the courts. Where there have been many interpreting cases, an alphabetical subject and fact index is provided for each such section for greater convenience in locating decisions involving specific points of law or fact situations. Statutes constantly change, and when Code titles are revised and renumbered they are often greatly expanded. An extreme example of this was in the Internal Revenue Code of 1939; approximately 900 sections of the earlier statutes covered were expanded to 5011. When this occurs, annotations to the old, renumbered sections are transferred to the comparable revised section in the new edition. Occasionally there is no comparable section in the revision so that old editions of annotated statutes are often saved to preserve the source of decisions formerly in point.

(4) *Indexes and tables for the U.S.C.A.* Since West Publishing Company also prepares the indexes and tables for the official Code edition, the indexes and tables found in the U.S.C.A. are very similar to the official. Not infrequently, however, there are additional entries in the U.S.C.A. indexes and tables which are not found in the official. As a result, it may be worthwhile to consult the unofficial tables and indexes if a search in the official edition has been fruitless.

(5) *Supplementation and recompiled volumes.* One substantial advantage of the private, annotated editions of the Code over the official ones is the much greater frequency of supplementation. The U.S.C.A. is supplemented by a pamphlet service, published three times a year, which cumulates at the end of the year into annual pocket parts. The supplements contain new enactments in their Code form and supplement the annotations, tables, and indexes of the complete U.S.C.A. Except for the annotations, the U.S.C.A. may be said to be supplemented during sessions of Congress by the bimonthly issues of the United States Congressional and Administrative News. This promptly prints the public laws as approved as well as conversion tables from the session law form of enactment to the Code form. When new legislation of a particularly important character is enacted, a special pamphlet edition, confined to that act and in

Code form, may be issued by the U.S.C.A. within a few days of the enactment. Such pamphlets will contain all revisers' notes and other editorial matter. This has been done for entire titles when reenacted into positive law; e.g., Title 5.

Recompiled replacement volumes are printed as needed, as, for example, whenever the pocket parts become unwieldy in size or when a massive legislative revision of the subject matter of the title has taken place. The recompilation combines all existing pocket supplement material for a given title or part into one or more new volumes which in turn are supplemented by later pocket parts and the pamphlets issued three times a year. Whatever the form of supplementation, the matter supplemented is indicated on the title page. There is, therefore, no reason for the searcher to omit any of the units necessary for a complete search. This connecting-up is a typical law book publishing technique. *Always look at the publishing date and indicate coverage of any unit or pocket part consulted in any law book.*

b. *United States Code Service (formerly, Federal Code Annotated).* First published in 1936, the Federal Code Annotated (F.C.A.) replaced an earlier annotated edition of the Code. In 1970, the Federal Code Annotated was acquired by the Lawyers Co-operative Publishing Company. Renamed the United States Code Service (U.S.C.S.), the old F.C.A. series is being expanded and supplanted by the new service.

(1) *Text of the U.S.C.S.* Like the F.C.A. before it, the United States Code Service prints the text of the original Statutes at Large enactment rather than the text of the Code sections which have been reworded by the Code's compilers. Where significant rewording has occurred, the rewording is placed in brackets with an explanatory note to alert the reader of the variance. Because the original language of an enactment is found, references within a Code section are to Statutes at Large citations. The parallel Code section and number, however, are found in brackets following the Statutes at Large section number.

(2) *Material in the U.S.C.S. not found in the official edition of the Code.* The Magna Carta is printed in the volumes of organic laws. Uncodified laws, treaties, and proclamations (i.e., legislation never placed in the Code) are annotated in a separate volume. The arrangement of statutes and treaties is chronological with separate tables for each category. United States court rules are in separate volumes.

(3) *Annotations in the U.S.C.S.* While annotations in the Federal Code Annotated included legislative background, digests of judicial decisions and Attorney General and Judge Advocate opinions, references to presidential executive orders and proclamations, and occasional law review citations; the United States Code Service annotates

each section of the Code in terms of its history, ancillary laws and directives, other Code sections, other Lawyers Co-operative publications and law review articles in addition to case law and opinions. Those volumes of the F.C.A. not yet supplanted by the U.S.C.S. have pocket supplements which follow the old F.C.A. format.

(4) *Indexes and tables.* Consisting of five volumes, the U.S.C.S. General Index amplifies and updates the official U.S.C. indexes. It covers added, amended, and repealed laws, court rules, executive orders, and proclamations and is supplemented by annual pocket parts.

(5) *Supplements of the U.S.C.S.* The U.S.C.S. is supplemented not only by the annual pocket supplements but by a Later Case Service, published twice a year, and by the U.S.C.S. Advanced Service pamphlets described in §3.2.

c. *U.S.C.A. and U.S.C.S. compared.* While both the U.S.C.A. and the U.S.C.S. provide a similar service, they do not exactly duplicate each other. Because it is published by West, the "Library References" found in the U.S.C.A. are to Corpus Juris Secundum and the West Key Digest System. The U.S.C.S. "Research Guide," on the other hand, refers the researcher to appropriate articles and annotations appearing in Lawyers Co-operative publications such as American Jurisprudence 2d and the American Law Reports. Annotations to decisions and opinions in the U.S.C.A. are much more extensive, more precisely indexed, and less selective than those found in the U.S.C.S. Unlike the U.S.C.A. which only sometimes includes such information, the U.S.C.S. lists titles and sections of the Code of Federal Regulations which are derived from or related to a particular Code section. The U.S.C.S. also provides a comprehensive listing of law review articles which deal with a given Code section. In addition to the statutory history found in both editions, the U.S.C.A. provides, where available, references to the appropriate United States Code Congressional and Administrative News volume which, in turn, contains the legislative history of the statute. Generally speaking, the U.S.C.A. and the West system are best used for ascertaining the scope of all applicable case law pertaining to a Code section. The U.S.C.S. is best used for locating articles, regulations, and selected annotations. While reference to both annotated editions can frequently be rewarding, either edition can be used by itself.

§3.7. Authority of statutes as publications: A summary.

Even though the authority of the various forms of statutes has been described in the discussion of their publication, it is both useful and convenient to summarize that authority at this point.

1. *Slip laws*. Slip laws are properly citable as authority only until the Statutes at Large or state session laws containing them are published. This matter is largely academic, however, since the slip law form of federal enactments and those in the United States Code Congressional and Administrative News and the U.S.C.S. Advance Service all contain the Statutes at Large citation. The permanent or Statutes at Large form of the citation can, therefore, be made from the slip law.

2. *Statutes at Large and state session laws*. These are cited as such until and unless they are expressly repealed by a later codifying statute and reenacted into positive law. After that they are no longer in force and so should no longer be cited as present authority. On the other hand, when such a reenacted code section has later been amended or a new section added, both the code and the amending session law should be cited with "as amended by" following the reenacted code citation. Where, as is the case with two-thirds of the United States Code titles and most of the state statutory compilations, the statute has been made part of a compilation which is only prima facie the law — that is, it is only certified as a true copy of the session law form — and not reenacted into positive law, cite the session law form as it is found in parentheses at the end of the code section cited, followed by the compilation form. Thus, Act of Jan. 11, 1971, §1, 84 Stat. 2048, 7 U.S.C. §2011 (1970). You are then citing your "best evidence" first, followed by the convenient but not the best form.

3. *United States Revised Statutes*. Simply cite the Revised Statutes, without the statute from which derived. The original statute was repealed with the enactment of the compilation and is, therefore, no longer in force. If it has since been amended, cite the R.S. section "as amended by" the amending statute. If the R.S. section has been included in a later codification of its material into positive law — i.e., in a reenacted Code title — it was repealed by that codification and should no longer be cited. Repeals of Revised Statutes sections are noted in tables in all editions of the United States Code.

4. *United States Code*. The official statement of the congressional committee under whose auspices the Code is compiled is found in the Preface to each volume of each edition and cumulative supplement of the Code. It states that "no new law is enacted [by it] and no law is repealed. It is prima facie the law. It is presumed to be the law. The presumption is rebuttable by production of prior unrepealed Acts of Congress at variance with the Code." In other words, this compilation, though official, has not been reenacted as a whole by Congress as was the Revised Statutes which expressly repealed those acts or parts of acts from which it was derived. On the other hand, it was the original intention of Congress when authorizing the Code of

1926 to take up its titles one by one and reenact them piecemeal as positive law, as it had done wholesale with the Revised Statutes. To date, about a third of the titles have been so treated. Those reenacted are listed at the beginning of each Code volume or supplement and in the tables in the latest volume of the Statutes at Large.

Reenacting a Code title is done by an act of Congress. In order to avoid confusion between the section numbering of the act reenacting the title and those of the Code reenacted, the section numbers of the *codifying act* itself, as published in the Statutes at Large, are spelled out in abbreviated form (as Sec. 2, Sec. 3), while those of the reenacted *codified title* of the Code as printed in that act are designated by the symbols (as §1, §2, etc.). The entire codified and reenacted title is set out in the single, unnumbered Section 1 of the codifying act. Section 2 and following of the codifying act itself, as distinct from the reenacted Code title, consist of saving clauses, the repealers of prior legislation, etc., but are not part of the Code title at all. In order to understand this legislative technique better, the student will do well to examine Pub. L. No. 86-682, 74 Stat. 578 which reenacted Title 39, Postal Service, into positive law.

In citing the Code, first cite the Statutes at Large volume and section from which it was derived, followed by the Code citation, unless the Code title has been reenacted into positive law. Section 2011 of Code Title 7 is cited Act of Jan. 11, 1971, §1, 84 Stat. 2048, 7 U.S.C. §2011 (1970). Where, however, the section cited has been reenacted into positive law, the session law from which it was derived has been repealed and should not be cited. Amendments, however, should be cited as such. Thus, "39 U.S.C. §28, as amended by . . . "

Unless the Code title has been reenacted into positive law, citation of statutory material in legal writing is to the original statutes with parallel references to the Code. However, the work of the codifiers is so well done that the Code has largely supplanted the statutes which are the real authority. Nevertheless, the proper citation form is a mark of a careful lawyer.

4 | Legislative Histories of Federal Statutes

§4.1. The need for legislative histories.

No matter how carefully they are drafted, congressional enactments are seldom completely free of ambiguity. In interpreting statutes, courts frequently resort to a statute's legislative history to determine its real meaning and application. As the place and importance of statutory construction has developed and grown in the past hundred years, the need for legislative history has similarly developed and grown. In 1948, Mr. Justice Robert Jackson observed that the

> . . . custom of remaking statutes to fit their histories has gone so far that a formal Act, read three times and voted on by Congress and approved by the President, is no longer a safe basis on which a lawyer may advise . . . [a] . . . client or a lower court decide a case. This has very practical consequences for the profession. They must consult all the committee reports on the bill, and on all its antecedents, and all that its supporters and opponents said in debate, and then predict what part of the conflicting views will likely appeal to a majority of the Court . . . [34 A.B.A.J. 535, 538 (1948)].

This development has very practical consequences for the law student as well. Law school courses demand extensive and intensive work with statutes so that students will learn both a statute's substantive content and be trained in the techniques of statutory research and evaluation.

§4.2. Types of legislative history.

There are two types of legislative history. The first involves a bill's progress in Congress, from its introduction to its final passage, rejection, or abandonment. By following every step of a bill's progress, it is possible to ascertain the status of a pending bill at a given time. The second type of legislative history relates to the congressional intent underlying an enactment and its meaning. By determining the intent and meaning, the lawyer can convince a court of the soundness of a given statutory construction. This determination is made by means of evidence gathered from hearings held and reports made by committees in charge of the particular legislation and from the floor debates on it which are found in the Congressional Record. A major activity in many law firms and governmental agencies today is the recording of every detail bearing on legislative intent behind the laws in which their clients or their agencies may be concerned.

§4.3. Steps in the passage of a bill through Congress.

How Our Laws Are Made, by Charles J. Zinn, Law Revision Counsel of the House Committee on the Judiciary, provides an excellent brief description of this process. The Senate publication, Enactment of a Law: Procedural Steps in the Legislative Process by the Secretary of the Senate and the Senate Parliamentarian also details the legislative process. Both publications are frequently revised and available from congressmen and senators upon request. As outlined in Zinn, a bill may take any of the following steps before becoming federal law:

1. *The bill is introduced.* The bill is usually drafted by experts employed by the respective houses of the legislature for that purpose. Several private agencies specialize in bill drafting, and many states now have bureaus which members of their legislatures may consult for expert advice on the techniques and factual backgrounds involved. Revenue bills in the Congress must originate in the House of Representatives, though this restriction is often avoided by "riders" attached to Senate bills. When introduced the bill is first dropped into the "hopper," then read by title, given a serial or bill number, assigned to its proper legislative committee, and ordered to be printed. At this point few bills in the House are read even by title.

2. *The bill is considered in committee.* Ninety percent of bills introduced are not considered in committee at all but die without further action. When the standing or special committee of the house in which the bill is introduced does decide to study and report the bill, it

may hold public hearings on it. At this time those who are interested are invited to advocate or oppose it in person or through briefs or both. The committee then submits to the Congress a printed report recommending passage or nonpassage of the bill. This committee report states the reasons for committee recommendations and is important in the lawyer's search for legislative intent.

3. *The bill is placed on the calendar.* The calendar — whether of the House or Senate or of individual committees of either house — shows the order of business. When a bill is reported out of committee, it is placed on the calendar of the house where it was introduced. In the House, "bills raising revenues, general appropriation bills, and bills of a public character directly or indirectly appropriating money or property" are placed on the *Union* calendar. Here are placed most public bills. There is also, however, a House calendar for public bills not raising revenue or appropriating money or property. Bills may be removed from these calendars if there is no objection by a member and placed on the *Consent* calendar. If there is still no objection, bills on the Consent calendar are passed without debate by unanimous consent when brought up for consideration. In this manner about 90 percent of all enacted bills are passed. The *Private* calendar is for bills for claims against the United States and private immigration bills for the admission of non-quota immigrants. When a bill's turn is reached on the calendar, it is read in full, section by section, unless, as is usually the case, the reading is dispensed with by unanimous consent and the entire bill is printed in the Congressional Record. It is then debated. This is the critical stage of a reported bill.

4. *Third reading of the bill, and vote.* The bill is then read for a third time, by title, and voted upon. Ninety percent of all enacted bills are voted by unanimous consent. After passage in one house, the bill is sent to the other house for action.

5. *Procedure in the other house.* After passage of the bill in one house, much the same procedure is followed in the other house, where, however, the "bill" is designated as an "act." If the bill is amended in the second house, it is returned to the first after passage for further consideration.

6. *Conference procedure.* In case of disagreement between the two houses on any part of the bill, each house appoints a conference committee to determine its final form. Conferees may compromise differences, but no new matter may be added by them nor may provisions already agreed upon by both houses be altered. Conference reports are then submitted to each house together with the printed conference bill which retains its original number. The conference report is printed in the house in which the bill originated and occasionally in the other house also. To the practicing lawyer it is useful to know that most conference reports on public bills are also printed

in the unofficial United States Code Congressional and Administrative News and are readily accessible there. Conference reports may be debated but not amended. Many, however, are accepted without debate, and the bill is passed by unanimous consent. Conference bills are usually printed in the Congressional Record at this point.

7. *The bill is signed by the Speaker and the Vice-President.* After passage of a bill by both houses, it is signed, regardless of the originating house, first by the Speaker of the House of Representative and then for the Senate by the Vice-President. It is then "engrossed" or copied — a process which sometimes involves error — and forwarded to the President for approval.

8. *The approval or veto of the bill by the President.* A bill becomes law upon approval by the President, which may be by signature or by failing to veto it during ten days within a session. A veto is affirmative when the President returns a bill to Congress with a message of disapproval; it is a "pocket veto" when the President fails to sign a bill which was received less than ten days before adjournment of Congress. An affirmative veto can only be overidden by a two-thirds vote of a quorum voting in both houses, an event which seldom occurs. The President thus possesses a strong negative power over legislation.

9. *The fate of bills at the end of a Congress.* Bills which have not become law at the end of a Congress die and must be introduced anew in a subsequent Congress if further action is desired. They retain their status from session to session of the same Congress, however. Treaties pending in the Senate remain in the Foreign Relations Committee until disposed of, an action which may take many years (see CCH Congressional Index Treaty Table.)

§4.4. Materials for legislative histories.

1. *Before the bill is introduced.* Legislation usually evolves from a demonstrated need. This need or desire may be shown by the pressure of interested groups or, increasingly, develops as the result of legislative investigation into various areas of the law to see if changes are advisable. The results of these preliminary investigations are usually published as Hearings.

2. *The bill in its various forms.* For the form of a typical bill see Chapter 2. All bills have serial or bill numbers assigned at the time they are introduced. Bills are numbered consecutively through an entire Congress and not renumbered beginning with each session. The bill number, important for tracing the legislative history and status of a bill through Congress, identifies the bill and all hearings and reports on it. The number also appears, as has been seen, as an identification tag on the slip law and in the Statutes at Large.

Identical or "companion" bills may be introduced simultaneously in each house in order to speed passage through Congress. Amendments to bills are each printed separately in the Congressional Record. When such amendments are accepted by the committee in charge of a bill, the bill is then reprinted. In this reprinted bill, matter to be omitted from the original bill has a horizontal line through it, and new matter is printed in italics. When there have been so many amendments offered that original content is lost, the bill may be scrapped in favor of an entirely new one which embodies all agreed-upon changes. It is then called a "clean" bill.

a. *Publication and distribution of bills*. Bills are printed and distributed individually as slip bills. These may be obtained by subscription from the Government Printing Office or individually from congressional committees. *Committee prints:* These are especially prepared for the committees in charge of the respective bills and are obtainable only, if at all, from committee members. They often show in parallel columns, section by section, the provisions of the bill as compared to existing statutes, together with notes giving the purpose of changes made by the new bill. They are thus excellent for showing legislative intent. *Hearings print of a bill:* The bill is always printed as a part of the record of a hearing held on it. *Congressional Record print of a bill:* The Congressional Record prints the text of some bills in original or amended form. Such printing is a matter of editorial discretion. *Resolutions in bill form:* These are printed and distributed in slip form as introduced. Concurrent and simple resolutions are printed in the Congressional Record and, as passed, in the House and Senate Journals. Concurrent resolutions are printed in the Statutes at Large.

b. *Synopses of bills*. The Digest of Public General Bills and Resolutions has been prepared by the Library of Congress since the 74th Congress (1935) "to furnish in the form of a brief summary, the essential features of public bills and resolutions and changes made therein during the legislative process." Each issue shows the status of all bills acted upon and lists public laws and resolutions enacted with corresponding bill numbers. The digests are often quite full and, short of the full text of a bill, provide the best information relating to its content. It is available in most law libraries. Beginning with the 90th Congress (1967), the scope of the Digest was considerably enlarged, especially the information in the subject-index. There are five cumulative issues a year, with biweekly supplementation. The cover page shows which bills are covered. The Digest is a status table for bills of the current session which have been acted upon, with date reported, report number, and date of passage in each house. Private bills are listed but not summarized. Code sections affected are noted. In the subject-index, measures acted upon are starred (*), and some popular-name acts are listed. There is also an author (sponsor) index.

The Commerce Clearing House Congressional Index (described in §4.5.2b) lists and indexes public general bills. Usually it gives only the title of a bill. Sometimes, a brief digest is found.

3. *Committee hearings*. Hearings are held by legislative committees in order to acquire information about the need for new legislation or to permit proponents or opponents of pending bills to state their views. Thus hearings may relate to specific pending bills or they may be held pursuant to a House or Senate resolution calling for the investigation of some condition which may require corrective legislation. Advance notice of hearings is given in the Daily Digest of the Congressional Record. Not all reports of hearings are printed. The CCH Congressional Index and the Daily Digest History of Bills Enacted table (through vol. 107 only) tell which hearings were printed, as does the Monthly Catalog of Government Publications. Although elaborate briefs and even entire books are reprinted in some of the hearings, a great deal of the text consists of impromptu and biased statements of opinion, and the whole must be read with this in mind. Nevertheless, they are important and frequently used in legislative histories. They are available in most law libraries.

4. *Committee reports and memoranda*. Like committee hearings, reports of legislative committees may relate to pending legislation or they may have to do with the possible need of corrective legislation for which no bills have yet been introduced. Each report bears an identifying serial number, as H. Rept. No. 19, 81st Cong., 1st Sess., or S. Rept. No. 163, 72d Cong., 2d Sess.

a. *Reports on pending bills*. Each bill reported to the House or Senate by the committee in charge is accompanied by a report setting forth the recommendation of the committee that the bill should or should not pass and giving the reasons for it. In some cases there may be a dissenting or a minority report. The Legislative Reorganization Act of 1946 gave each committee a professional staff and adequate clerical help. Since then committee reports have tended to be highly factual studies of the background of the bills and the reasons for new legislation. The official prints of committee reports are somewhat difficult to obtain. The unofficial United States Code Congressional and Administrative News prints either the House or Senate Committee report, whichever the editor deems more useful, on bills of general interest enacted into public law.

b. *Reports of exploratory and investigating committees*. Congressional committees are continually investigating such widely divergent topics as small business, subversive activities, juvenile delinquency, baseball, monopoly, and the like, to discover whether or not corrective legislation is needed. The reports of these investigations are often embodied in what, in effect, are extensive treatises on the subject matter involved. Their considerable intrinsic value means that they go beyond their intended purpose of aiding Congress. Examples of such reports are Congress and the Monopoly Problem: Fifty-six Years of Antitrust Development, 1900–1956, in 662 pages; and Documentation, Indexing, and Retrieval of Scientific Information; a Study of Federal and Non-Federal Science Information Processing and Retrieval Programs, in 283 pages.

c. *House and Senate Documents*. "Documents," so called, contain reports of congressional investigatory committees other than those printed as the committee "Reports" described above and presidential messages. Communications which governmental agencies frequently send to Congress relating to pending bills are printed as documents and, usually, in the Congressional Record as well.

5. *Legislative debates and proceedings*. Since 1774, there has been some sort of unofficial publication of the minutes and debates of Congress. The Congressional Record and its Daily Digest and the House and Senate Journals are current publications of congressional proceedings. Prior to 1873 and the first publication of the Congressional Record, congressional minutes and debates were published in the Annals of Congress (1789–1824), the Register of Debates (1824–1873), and the Congressional Globe (1833–1873). These earlier publications are the sources of the legislative histories of enactments prior to 1873.

a. *Congressional Record*. This newspaper is probably the most useful single publication for the purpose of legislative history. Published daily during sessions of Congress, Monday through Friday except on days following a congressional recess, it is supposedly a full and faithful record of all that takes place in Congress. It is not that. Members of Congress may revise their remarks made on the floor before publication in the Record. It is, however, substantially accurate and covers the following:

Introduction of all bills, resolutions, and amendments
Debates, supposedly verbatim, but subject to revision
Text of many bills and joint resolutions; simple and concurrent resolutions are printed as passed
Presidential messages
Treaties, when debated

In addition, there is an appendix in which may be printed communications from government departments concerning pending legislation in which they are interested, extensions of remarks supposed to have been made by Congress on the floor but in fact never made, and such miscellaneous material as a poem by the six-year-old son of a member's constituent.

Index to the Proceedings. Issued every ten days and cumulated *annually*, it comprises a combined Index to the Proceedings and a

History of Bills and Resolutions for both House and Senate. Entries are by subject matter of pending legislation and by congressman. The latter entries cover every bill and amendment offered and every motion or remark made on the floor. The History of Bills and Resolutions is probably the most widely available status table there is for legislation. It is also a finding guide to the text of simple and concurrent resolutions as passed. All bills and resolutions are listed by number, with title, and every action taken on them noted, up to and including approval by the President or passage over his veto. If action occurs during the second session of a Congress on a bill introduced during the first session, the complete history of the bill is found by consulting the table for the first session.

It is difficult, however, to follow debate on a bill through the "History" because it usually only lists the first page where a bill was taken up on the floor but ignores pages skipped because of intervening motions or "yielding" by a congressman debating the bill. Checking debates fully is a laborious task.

A specimen entry is shown in Exhibit 9. The paging of the daily edition of the Congressional Record and of the Daily Digest differs from that of the bound volume. Since congressmen are permitted to revise their remarks prior to the final printing, the text may also differ. *In legal writing, cite the bound volume if available; otherwise, give the volume, page, and exact date of the daily issue.* The same material, for example, is cited from the daily edition as 94 Cong. Rec. 9917 (daily ed. Aug. 4, 1948) and from the bound volume as 94 Cong. Rec. 9761 (1948).

H.R. 8601—To enforce constitutional rights, and for other purposes.
Made special order (H. Res. 359), 5192.—Debated, 5199, 5295, 5441, 5635, 5752, 5807, 6009, 6159, 6277, 6369.—Amended and passed House, 6509.—Referred to Senate Committee on the Judiciary with instructions, 6452.—Reported with amendments (S. Rept. 1205), (S. Rept 1205, pt. 2), 7187.—Debated (in lieu of H.R. 8315), 6931, 6945, 6954, 7023, 7049, 7051, 7053, 7129, 7137, 7208, 7213, 7219, 7244, 7312, 7343, 7344, 7354, 7401, 7408, 7409, 7417, 7448, 7497, 7536, 7558, 7563, 7578, 7728, 7746, 7763, 7803.—Amended and passed Senate, 7811.—Pursuant to H. Res. 503 House concurs in Senate amendments, 8491.—Examined and signed, 8574, 8581.—Presented to the President, 8677.—Approved [Public Law 449], 9796.

Exhibit 9

HISTORY OF BILLS ENACTED INTO PUBLIC LAW (86TH CONG., 2D SESS.)—Continued

Title	Bill No.	Date introduced	Committees—hearings		Date reported		Report No.		Page of Congressional Record of passage		Date of passage		Public law	
			House	Senate	House	Senate	House	Senate	House	Senate	House	Senate	Date approved	No.
To set aside certain lands in Oklahoma for the Cheyenne and Arapaho Indians.	H.R. 816	Jan. 7, 1959	IIA	IIA	May 25, 1959	June 20	378	1617	9461	14221	June 1, 1959	June 24	Sept. 14	86-791
Relating to the disposition of certain U.S. lands in Alaska.	S. 3267	Mar. 23	IIA	IIA	Aug. 29	June 21	2196	1628	18762	14669	Aug. 31	June 28	Sept. 14	86-792
To protect farmers making certain land use changes under the Great Plains conservation program against loss of acreage allotments.	S. 3533 (H.R. 12849)	May 11	Agr	Agr	Aug. 18	June 29	2100	1773	18406	15619	Aug. 30	July 2	Sept. 14	86-793
Authorizing a compact between Maryland, Virginia, and the D.C. for the the regulation of mass transit in the metropolitan area.	H.J. Res. 402	May 27, 1959	Jud*	Jud*	May 18	Aug. 23	1621	1906	11750	19000	June 2	Sept. 1	Sept. 15	86-794
To provide a temporary suspension of duty on heptanoic acid.	H.R. 12659	June 15	WM	Fin	June 29	Aug. 25	2033	1913	15813	17857	July 2	Aug. 26	Sept. 15	86-795
Relating to holding world sport parachuting championships at Orange, Mass.	H.J. Res. 723	June 1	FA		Aug. 26		2169		18387	18587	Aug. 30	Aug. 31	Sept. 15	86-796
To promote fish and game conservation and rehabilitation in military reservations.	H.R. 2565	Jan. 15, 1959	MMF*	IFC	Aug. 5, 1959	May 27	767	1492	6132	13995	Mar. 21	June 23	Sept. 15	86-797
Authorizing grants-in-aid to nonprofit institutions to strengthen health research programs.	H.R. 10341	Feb. 10	IFC*		Aug. 26		2174		18394	18593	Aug. 30	Aug. 31	Sept. 15	86-798
To establish a price support level for milk and butterfat.	S. 2917	Jan. 27	Agr*	Agr*	Aug. 29	June 15	2182	1592	18748	16784	Aug. 31	Aug. 19	Sept. 16	86-799
To amend the Tariff Act of 1930 to place bamboo pipestems on the free list.	H.R. 10841	Mar. 2	WM	Fin	July 1	Aug. 25	2079	1912	15814	18602	July 2	Aug. 31	Sept. 16	86-800

* The starring of printed items is discontinued. See page 62.

NOTE.—The bill in parentheses is companion measure.

TABLE OF COMMITTEE ABBREVIATIONS

AE	Joint Committee on Atomic Energy	EdL	Education and Labor	IIA	Interior and Insular Affairs	PW	Public Works
Aer	Aeronautical and Space Sciences	FA	Foreign Affairs	IFC	Interstate and Foreign Commerce	RAdm	Rules and Administration
Agr	Agriculture	FR	Foreign Relations	Jud	Judiciary	R	Rules
App	Appropriations	Fin	Finance	LPW	Labor and Public Welfare	SA	Space and Astronautics
AS	Armed Services	GO	Government Operations	MMF	Merchant Marine and Fisheries	VA	Veterans' Affairs
BC	Banking and Currency	HA	House Administration	POCS	Post Office and Civil Service	WM	Ways and Means
DC	District of Columbia						

Exhibit 10

b. *Daily Digest of the Congressional Record.* This is a supplement contained in each issue of the Congressional Record but cumulated at the end of a session into a separate bound volume. It is a sort of newspaper within a newspaper for the legislators' use, enabling them to brush up quickly on what went on the day before and what is scheduled for today and for tomorrow. It notes bills introduced the preceding day and bills and resolutions reported or passed. It also contains a résumé of business transacted, of committee appointments, votes, and debates, and of committee hearings scheduled or held. The first issue of each month contains a cumulative statistical survey of the business transacted by Congress to date and a table of appropriation bills passed. In addition to cumulating the daily indexes, the annual index has a useful table of bills enacted into public law during the session and a History of Bills Enacted Into Public Law in which the bill title and number, date of introduction, hearings held, date reported, committee report number, and Congressional Record page noting passage and approval are arranged by law number. See Exhibit 10 *supra*.

There is also a subject index which serves as a status table for each bill and resolution acted upon during the session. A typical index entry follows. Page references are to the Daily Digest, which in turn refers to the pertinent Congressional Record pages. See Exhibit 11.

c. *House and Senate Journals.* These record the proceedings and votes of each house with the debates omitted.

d. *Presidential messages.* Messages from the President are printed when they suggest the need for new legislation or they veto bills passed and submitted for approval by the Congress. Since 1873 they have been printed in the Congressional Record and the House and Senate Journals (veto messages are only in the Journal of the house in which the bill originated), as House or Senate Documents, and, since 1939, selected ones in the unofficial United States Code Congressional and Administrative News.

LIBRARY SERVICES ACT (H.R. 9812, H.R. 12125, S. 2830)
Committee, Senate D263, 283
Senate D298
Committee, House D156, 176, 180, 255, 260, 274, 318
House D453
Public Law 86–679

Exhibit 11

§4.5. Aids in compiling legislative histories.

1. *Official*. Two of the three official sources have already been described.

a. *The Digest of Public General Bills and Resolutions*. See §4.4.2b above.

b. *Congressional Record*. See §4.4.5a–b above.

c. *Legislative calendars*. Calendars are the third official source of legislative histories. Each house and almost every standing committee has its own calendar. They contain excellent status tables which give much information and are frequently and promptly published.

Calendars of the House of Representatives and History of Legislation is the title of perhaps the single most useful tool for the tracing of the legislative history of either a House or Senate bill. It is cumulative and appears daily during term time, except on the day following a day when the House was not in session. It is free and lists bills which have been reported or passed by either the House or Senate. The following are its regular features.

Bills in conference. These are listed by *date*, not bill number. Information includes the title of the bill, conference report number, and action taken by each house. For bills through conference, the same information is given along with the public or private law number and date of approval.

55

NUMERICAL ORDER OF BILLS AND RESOLUTIONS WHICH HAVE PASSED EITHER OR BOTH HOUSES, AND BILLS NOW PENDING ON THE CALENDAR

Complete history of all actions on each bill follows the number in chronological order. For subject of bill see index, using index key following bill number in this section

NOTE.—Similar or identical bills, and bills having reference to each other, are indicated by number in parentheses

No.	Index Key and History of Bill

HOUSE BILLS

H.R. 10.—Self-Employed Individuals Tax Retirement Act of 1961. Reported from Ways and Means May 9, 1961; Rept. 378. Union Calendar. Rules suspended and passed House June 5, 1961. Reported in Senate Sept. 13, 1961; Finance; Rept. 992.

H.R. 29.—Merchant Marine Academy, appointing of U.S. nationals. Reported from Merchant Marine and Fisheries Aug. 15, 1961; Rept. 918. Union Calendar. Passed House Aug. 21, 1961. Reported in Senate Aug. 24, 1961; Commerce; Rept. 785. Passed Senate Aug. 29, 1961. Approved Sept. 6, 1961. Public Law 87-199.

HOUSE BILLS—Continued

H.R. 132.—Education by television. Reported from Interstate and Foreign Commerce Aug. 21, 1961; Rept. 999. Union Calendar............Union 411

H.R. 157.—Playa del Rey Inlet and Harbor, change name. Reported from Public Works Aug. 28, 1961; Rept. 1052. House Calendar. Passed House Sept. 6, 1961.

H.R. 176.—Judicial Conference of the United States, representation. Reported from Judiciary July 10, 1961; Rept. 680. Union Calendar. Passed House July 17, 1961. Reported in Senate Sept. 7, 1961; Judiciary; Rept. 887. Passed Senate Sept. 11, 1961.

Exhibit 12

Numerical Order of Bills and Resolutions Which Have Passed Either or Both Houses, and Bills Now Pending on the Calendar. This is a status table shown in Exhibit 12.

This is one of the best status tables and the most frequently issued of the cumulative tables. There is also a separate status table of major bills by number, title, and steps through Congress. Other features are the union, House, private, and consent calendars; a list of public and private laws and resolutions enacted; and a subject index to the calendars.

Final Edition for a Congress. This issue is prepared after the final adjournment of a Congress in readiness for the convening of the first session of the next Congress. It is a useful source of legislative history for a given Congress because, unlike the History of Bills and Resolutions issued by the Congressional Record, its complete résumé of actions on all House and Senate bills comes out before the next session convenes. Only bills on which there was committee or house action are included. The History of Bills and Resolutions, on the other hand, lists all bills whether or not they were acted upon and covers only a single *session* of Congress. The final legislative calendar edition for a Congress has an index and a complete statistical résumé of the activities of the last five Congresses. There is also a Status of Major Bills table for each session of Congress covered. Vetoes are noted.

2. *Unofficial*. Three of the most frequently consulted publications are unofficial. Two of them publish official legislative documents of various kinds. As is typical of private law publications, they are characterized by prompt publication.

a. *United States Code Congressional and Administrative News*. This periodical is both accessible and indispensable for keeping the reader abreast of current federal legislative documents. In one place, it supplies verbatim copies of federal legislative materials less easily or promptly found in official form. It is useful because it collects not only current federal direct and subordinate legislation but legislative histories in the form of congressional committee reports. It is issued semimonthly during sessions of Congress and cumulates into annual volumes which correspond in coverage to Statutes at Large volumes. In each issue, some or all of the following can be found:

(1) *Public laws of general interest in verbatim text*. This is one of the most convenient forms in which to find such public laws. Statutes at Large citations are included.

(2) *Congressional committee reports*. For the public laws of general interest published in this periodical, at least one committee report is printed. Whether the House or the Senate report is published depends upon the editor's judgment of which is more useful. This is

the "Legislative History" referred to in parentheses preceding the text of the corresponding public law printed in the same pamphlet issue.

(3) *Presidential messages, proclamations, and executive orders, verbatim.*

(4) *Federal court rules as amended, verbatim.*

(5) *Administrative rules and regulations.* A selection of rules, regulations, and proposed regulations is printed. Of particular general interest are those of the Internal Revenue Service and of the Immigration and Naturalization Service and those relating to Social Security.

(6) *Tables.* These largely duplicate those in the United States Code Annotated. Since they are issued semimonthly during sessions of Congress, they serve as supplements to the U.S.C.A. tables. These tables cumulate each issue. As a result, they cover the entire session of Congress to date and are of great value in checking the present status of congressional legislation of a given term. They cover: (a) public laws enacted so far during a session with Statutes at Large citations; (b) United States Code classification assigned to public laws or parts of them incorporated in the Code which are printed in the current pamphlets; (c) United States Code sections affected — whether amended, repealed, etc. — by new legislation; (d) bills enacted into law by bill number; (e) proclamations and executive orders, listed by number, date, and title.

The above tables are so useful that the student should examine them carefully and become familiar with them and their uses.

(7) *Index to all material printed during the session.* This is a cumulative index, covering the entire session to date, so that it is necessary to consult only the latest pamphlet issue of the periodical.

(8) *Index-Digest of Bills Introduced.* The yellow pages of each issue are a status table which is omitted from the bound volumes. Its purpose is to point up legislative highlights of the preceding half month in Congress.

(9) *Annual cumulated volumes.* At the end of each session of Congress, the material in the pamphlet issues of the United States Code Congressional and Administrative News is cumulated into bound volumes under the preceding categories. The bound volumes serve some of the purposes of the Statutes at Large: they are supplements to Code tables, convenient repositories of committee reports on newly enacted public laws, and a collection of selected administrative rules and presidential documents.

b. *Commerce Clearing House Congressional Index.* This is perhaps the most frequently used index to the current legislative history material of a Congress. It is in loose-leaf form, taken from diverse official sources, and arranged and published to be more usable than the official indexes. Purely an index, it contains no texts or abridgments of bills, committee reports, or debates. As is typical of loose-leaf services and reporters, some of its separate indexes are chronological and in two parts (one for the material as a whole, the second for supplementing the first by reference to the latest bills). A *complete coverage thus requires consultation of both indexes.* As is also true of all loose-leaf services, there is a sheet with a tab at the beginning of this service which tells in detail what is contained in it and how to use it. Following these instructions will save the user time and ensure better results than blind hunting. The following are the major features of the Congressional Index:

(1) *Pending public measures indexed.* These are covered under such headings as Headline Legislation, Name Bills (as the Landrum-Griffin bill), Companion Bills, and by subject. Bills acted upon are indicated by an asterisk. The sponsor of the bill is also listed. Only public bills are indexed.

(2) *Bills and resolutions.* These are listed by number.

(3) *Bill status tables.* Though the House Calendar (see §4.5.1c) is more complete and current in its coverage, this is perhaps the most convenient of all legislative status tables to use. Only *reported public bills* are covered, but for them, every congressional action is shown. Approved bills for the current session are indicated by a large star. Information is given about hearings on bills listed, and committee reports are noted along with the serial number of the reports.

(4) *Special reports.* Those not relating to pending bills are listed.

(5) *Public laws enacted so far during the session.* These are listed by number and subject.

(6) *Treaties pending at the beginning of each session.* These are listed with any action taken indicated.

(7) *Members of Congress listed.* Biographical information is given, including committee assignments. This is useful when writing to a member for information or copies of publications. The same information is given in the Congressional Directory, an official publication issued for each session of Congress.

(8) *Voting records of each member of Congress given.* This table covers a member's action on any bill subject to a roll-call vote. Listing is (a) by bill number and (b) by member, thus showing both who voted for and against a given bill and how a given member voted on all roll-call bills.

c. *Congressional Information Service (CIS).* CIS, which began publication in 1970, is one of the most comprehensive sources of legislative materials and information available today. It has basically three components: (1) the monthly, quarterly, annual, and multiple-year cumulative indexes, (2) the monthly and annual abstracts, and (3) the CIS Microfiche library.

The CIS indexes index the following publications on a monthly basis:

(1) *Hearings*. CIS indexing of congressional hearings is virtually complete. Each monthly issue indexes and abstracts all hearings published during the previous month. Note, however, that substantial delays may occur between the hearing date and the publication date.

(2) *Committee prints*. CIS attempts to be as comprehensive as possible in indexing and publishing these, except that individual bills and amendments issued as committee prints are published in a separate CIS service.

(3) *House and Senate Reports*. CIS indexes and publishes all reports except reports on private bills and reports on ceremonial or housekeeping measures.

(4) *Documents*. CIS indexes and publishes all congressional documents as they are issued except documents containing annual reports already issued in separate departmental editions and documents compiling strictly ceremonial material.

(5) *Executive reports and documents*. CIS coverage is complete and current.

(6) *Special publications*. CIS attempts to cover all "apparently useful" special publications which they "are able to locate."

(7) *Public Laws*. The abstracts volume of the CIS annual issue contains a legislative history for each Public Law enacted during that year. These histories frequently index materials which date back to other years and congressional sessions but which are related to the law as passed. In some cases, however, not all the legislative history material for a law has been published by the end of the year. Therefore, it is important to check later issues of CIS for revised legislative histories. The CIS legislative histories are particularly useful in that they cover more than one year, and they refer the researcher to documents, hearings, and events which are not published or indexed in the Congressional Record history of bills and resolutions. The CIS legislative history, supplemented by Congressional Record history, will form an excellent basis for a full legislative history of Public Acts.

The CIS materials are easily accessed through the index volumes which contain a subject index as well as an index of titles, bill numbers, report numbers, and document numbers, and an index of committee and subcommittee chairmen. All these indexes will refer the user to an accession number composed of a letter followed by two numbers. The letter refers to the issuing body of Congress (House, Senate, or joint). The first number refers to the committee or subcommittee with which the document is associated. These numbers never change, so that a description of the entire product of a committee can be found listed under that number in each CIS volume. The second number is an accession number and is used to distinguish between documents in the abstract volume. Numbers following a decimal point in the second number refer to a particular witness in, or segment of, the document indexed. Thus in 1977, accession number S181-44.19 referred to hearings before the Senate Appropriations Committee (S180 through S184). The number "44.19" refers to the 19th item of testimony in the 44th volume of hearings from that committee, abstracted in 1977. Using the accession number, the researcher can go directly to the microfiche edition of the document (which is filed by accession number) or to the CIS abstracts volume where a complete bibliographic citation, description, and abstract of the document will be found.

d. *The Federal Index* began publication in 1976 by Predicasts, Inc., Cleveland, Ohio. It indexes administrative rules and regulations, House and Senate Bills, Congressional reports and hearings, roll calls, and executive orders by using the federal government services. Citations are provided to the Code of Federal Regulations, U.S. Code, House and Senate Bills, and the Weekly Compilation of Presidential Documents.

The user may go directly to the Table of Contents which lists the major headings or may look up the subject in the alphabetical guide.

§4.6. Compiling a legislative history.

In larger law firms and in many governmental agencies, the compiling of legislative histories relating to a client's or agency's interests is a major activity involving extremely detailed data collection and indexing. While ordinarily having a more circumscribed interest in a specific bill, the law student must nevertheless understand the procedure and the techniques involved.

A person compiling a history of federal legislation has a wide variety of materials from which to choose. The procedure followed and the materials used will depend upon the precise objective of the search.

1. *Finding the specific bill.* Frequently the law student wishes to trace the history of a pending bill. For this it is necessary to collect the bills — House, Senate, and companion — in both their original and amended forms. These bills may be found, verbatim, filed by Congress and session, in some law school libraries. They can also be located in abstract form in the *Digest of Public General Bills*.

2. *Status tables.* Once the bill has been located, it is necessary to consult a status table to see what, if any, action has been taken on the bill since its introduction. There are many status tables which are available in various publications. The most complete of these is the History of Bills and Resolutions which is found in the fortnightly

Congressional Record and supplemented daily in part by the Daily Digest of the Congressional Record. This History cumulates in an annual index volume to the Congressional Record which covers each session of Congress. Because it covers *all introduced bills and resolutions, both public and private, whether or not there has been further action*, it is also the most complete federal status table to be found. Other status tables cover only bills which have at least been reported out of committee and thus exclude 90 percent of all bills ever introduced. The Congresssional Record History notes every action of any kind relating to all bills from their introduction to their approval as laws or their final rejection. With the exception of the House Calendar, other status tables do this only for public bills which have been acted upon.

An excellent status table, kept up-to-date by weekly loose-leaf supplements, is in the CCH Congressional Index. This table also notes the votes of each member on pending legislation. A too-little-known but excellent status table is in the legislative Calendars of the House of Representatives which also covers Senate bills. This is a daily, cumulative index by bill number which lists every action to date on the bill. If your law school library does not have this index, it can probably have the school's name placed on a free mailing list.

3. *Legislative intent*. The searcher who is also concerned with what Congress probably intended by the legislation it enacted must have access to the hearings of legislative committees, committee reports, and the pre-enactment House and Senate floor debates. Hearings may have been held before the bill's introduction in order to determine whether or not legislation was needed. Hearings may also have been held after the bill was introduced. These later hearings would have been held so that individuals, foundations, governmental agencies, or any other interested parties could oppose or favor the bill by means of personal testimony or by submitted briefs which could be incorporated later into the text of the hearing. Reference to some status tables or the annual table of public laws in the Daily Digest index volume discloses whether or not the hearings have been printed. If they are printed (and many are not), they can probably be found through the law school library. Reports of legislative committees are also available in most university libraries. Reports, however, are more easily located in the United States Code Congressional and Administrative News or the CIS.

Debates in Congress are a most fruitful source of legislative intent. They are reported at length in the Congressional Record which in turn is indexed fortnightly by an index which cumulates into an annual index. The index is by subject matter, introducer of the bill, and by bill number and shows every action on the bill or resolution introduced.

4. *Finding the bill number of a law*. It often becomes necessary to

trace the legislative history and intent of an existing law. To do this it is first necessary to learn its bill number. This may be done easily by two methods.

a. *Statutes at Large or slip laws.* Both official and unofficial U.S. Congressional Code and Administrative News slip law and statute publication gave the bill number preceding the text of the statute.

b. *From indexes.* When only the subject of a law is known, the above citations are obtained through the statute subject index. A more laborious method is to trace the law through the table in the annual volume of the Congressional Record Daily Digest which, under the public law number, gives the desired information. The CCH Congressional Index table of enacted laws may be similarly used but neither of these methods would be employed if the slip law or Statutes at Large were available.

By the use of these same tables the searcher can find (1) committee reports on the subject matter of the legislation; (2) hearings; (3) debates on the floor of Congress; and (4) presidential messages setting forth reasons for vetoing such a bill. If lucky, the searcher may find a committee print of the bill in which, in parallel columns, are found the legislation existing when the bill was introduced and corresponding provisions of the bill being researched. The committee print may also give the committee's rationale. When there has been extensive revision of existing legislation, as was the case when the patent laws were revised and reenacted into positive law as Title 35 of the United States Code, the revisers' notes may be published in full. This was done for some Code titles by the United States Code Annotated.

5. *Law office or governmental agency procedure.* Compiling histories here is a continuing chore involving much of the following routine.

Digest the Congressional Record and Federal Register (described in Chapter 7) daily, reporting on all legislation of interest to the agency or firm, noting new bills, the progress of previously noted bills, and new or proposed regulations touching agency or clients' activities.

For each new bill of interest, start a file; until the bill becomes a law or dies, initial entries are made on a large index card providing for the following information: bill number, companion and related bill numbers, name of introducer, title and subject matter of bill, hearings, action in Congress (dates, pages in Congressional Record where committee reports are noted), presidential action, public or private law number. All bills, hearings, reports, congressional documents, and Congressional Record clippings of debates are collected along with the act as finally approved.

From the index card you prepared, make a calendar or table of contents in final form, numbering each item in the margin. Collect, arrange by number all material listed, in order, and bind or file for permanent preservation.

FIRST SUPPLEMENT SURPLUS APPROPRIATION
RESCISSION ACT, 1946
Public Law 301 — 79th Congress
Ch. 30 — 2d Session
*(H.R. 5158)
Approved February 18, 1946.

An act reducing certain appropriations and authorizations 1
Communication from the President transmitting . . . (H. Doc. 394) 2
H.R. 5158 as introduced . . . and referred . . . January 17, 1946 3
H.R. 5158 as reported in House, January 29, 1946 4
Report . . . to accompany H.R. 5158 . . . (H. Rept. 1500) 5
H.R. 5158 as passed House January 30, 1946, and referred 6
H.R. 5158 as reported in Senate with an amendment, Feb. 4, 1946 7
Report of Senate committee . . . (S. Rept. 919) 8

REFERENCES IN THE CONGRESSIONAL RECORD 9

1946

Jan. 17.	H.R. 5158 introduced . . . and referred	p.117
Jan. 29.	H.R. reported in House . . . (H. Rept. 1500)	p.571
Jan. 30.	H.R. 5158 considered in House	p.605, 606-7, 611
	Passed House	p.619
	Proposed Reductions in Appropriations	p.616
	Proposed Reductions in Contract Authorizations	p.617
Jan. 31.	H.R. 5158 referred to Senate Committee on Appropriations	p.368
Feb. 8.	H.R. 5158 considered, amended, and passed by Senate	p.1181
Feb. 13.	H.R. 5158 signed by the Speaker of the House	p.1328
	Signed by the President pro tempore of Senate	p.1281
	Signed by the President	p.1328
	Approved by the President February 18, 1946; became Public Law 301	

APPENDIX A.

H.R. 4103, a bill reducing certain appropriations. . . . [the history of this companion bill is given as above]

* This bill supersedes H.R. 4103 . . . and H.R. 4407 . . . H.R. 4407 . . . was vetoed . . . because it contained a rider to return . . . See appendixes for histories on H.R. 4103 and H.R. 4407.

H.R. 5604, a bill reducing or further reducing . . . was reported in the House on February 27, 1946.

Exhibit 13

Cross-references should be made to all companion and related bills, and the same process followed with regard to them.

Above, in Exhibit 13, is part of a very simple legislative history, greatly abridged both as to number and fullness of entries, printed through the courtesy of its compiler, Minnie Wiener, while Librarian of the General Services Administration.

5 Indexes and Tables for Work with Federal Statutes

§5.1. Subject indexes to statutes generally.

A facility in the use of indexes and tables is an indispensable element in the successful use of statutes. This is true because the content and form of statutory law are constantly changing as a result of new legislation, amendment, repeal, and judicial interpretation. Subject indexes, transfer tables, annotations, and citators are the tabular means by which the student and lawyer are kept abreast of the changing form and content of legislation.

Statutory indexes are less complete and less satisfactory than their case law counterparts. Unlike statutory indexes, word indexes to decided cases cover not only every legal principle but every fact situation found in every recorded case. The indexes incorporate the actual situations which have been brought to the court for decision. Statutory indexes, on the other hand, only embody the hypothetical situations which were envisioned by the law makers and specifically included by them in the text of the enactments. The statutory indexes do not encompass the facts of cases which have actually interpreted statutes. Their coverage, therefore, is considerably less detailed than is the coverage of cases interpreting statutes contained in the word indexes of case law digests.

Each volume of the Statutes at Large covers the enactments of one congressional session and indexes all the laws contained in it. Because of the subsequent amendment, the repeal and death of statutes, these indexes are of little value in ascertaining the present state of statute law. In order to ascertain the present status of a particular statute, it is necessary to consult the indexes and tables supplied with statutory compilations.

§5.2. Subject indexes to federal statutes.

Because the Statutes at Large subject indexes are necessarily limited to the enactments of a particular session of Congress, they do not present an accurate picture of the entire field of federal legislation. The subject indexes to the United States Code, the United States Code Annotated, and the United States Code Service, on the other hand, cover all general public laws of permanent interest in force at the time of publication. They are the indexes most commonly used by lawyers. Two indexes, one by Beaman and McNamara and the other by McClenon and Gilbert, together index by subject all federal laws of general public interest in force from 1789–1931. Along with the 1873 and 1878 subject indexes found in editions of the Revised Statutes and those found in earlier Code editions, these indexes are valuable for historical research.

1. *Constitution*. The Constitution is indexed separately in all editions of the United States Code and in separate annotated editions of the Constitution. It is also separately indexed in some state statutory compilations.

2. *All federal statutes ever enacted*. There is no general index with this wide coverage.

3. *All private federal laws ever enacted*. No cumulative index of present value exists, but these laws are indexed in the individual volumes of the Statutes at Large.

4. *All public federal laws ever enacted*. There is no cumulative index of this kind covering all public laws. Such laws are indexed in the individual volumes of the Statutes at Large.

5. *All general public laws of a permanent nature ever enacted*. The two indexes noted above which attempted the indexing of all general

public laws are the Index Analysis of Federal Statutes (1789–1873), compiled by Middleton G. Beaman and A. K. McNamara, and the Index to the Federal Statutes (1874–1931), compiled by Walter H. McClenon and Wilfred C. Gilbert. All public, general, and permanent federal legislation, whether or not in force at the time the indexes were compiled, is covered by these indexes. Because the Index to Federal Statutes was not updated after 1931, it and the Index Analysis of the Federal Statutes are of limited current value. Both indexes are invaluable, however, for tracing the history of earlier legislation. It is possible, for example, to follow the history of federal legislation concerning banks, courts, railroads, etc., from the earliest enactments through 1931.

6. *General public laws of a permanent nature in force.* This is the most common type of statutory subject index for federal compilations of public laws. Every statutory compilation has such an index. Although many sections of the United States Revised Statutes are still in force, its index is of limited interest because the section still in force and subsequent amendments are incorporated into and indexed by the United States Code. Lawyers ordinarily will consult the subject index in either an annotated or an unannotated edition of the United States Code. This type of index must be used with an awareness that *only acts actually in force as incorporated in the compilation indexed* are covered. For earlier codified material, since repealed, superseded, or expired, the index to the latest edition of the compilation still containing such enactments must be consulted. Also, some statutes indexed may since have been amended, repealed, or superseded; thus the searcher is required to look at the latest pamphlet supplements of the compilations or to Shepard's United States Citations to make certain that the present picture is complete and accurate.

7. *United States Code.* The indexes to the Code, either in the official, unannotated edition or in the privately published, annotated editions, are the currently useful indexes of the type which index permanent federal laws of a public general nature. It is important to note that *all material printed in the Code volumes is indexed, editorial matters as well as Code sections.* Entries are both by large topic (as Agriculture, Patents), by governmental agency (as Department of Agriculture, Court of Claims), and by fact or catchword (as High Schools, Jurisdictional Amount), all integrated in a single alphabetical order as in a dictionary. Acts by popular name are occasionally indexed, but there is a separate and more complete table of such acts in all Code editions. The Federal Rules of Civil and of Criminal Procedure are indexed, as are those of some courts. Agency rules of practice which prescribe the conduct of business before these agencies are often printed in the Code as appendices; when this is done, they are indexed.

The United States Code Annotated indexes are prepared by the compilers of the United States Code indexes and the indexes are substantially identical; occasionally, however, the U.S.C.A. indexes are somewhat fuller in content, and it may therefore be wise to search them when the official edition indexes fail. Recompiled volumes of the U.S.C.A. have their own separate indexes, but the general index, since it covers overlapping subject matter from all titles of the Code, is often more satisfactory to use. The United States Code Service has both a general index and one for each volume. In using the Code indexes, it must always be remembered that the citations are to Code titles and sections, not to the original or Statutes at Large form of enactment.

§5.3. Popular-name tables for federal acts.

Many acts (such as the G.I. Bill of Rights) are known by their popular names. Every edition of federal statutes has an index which lists or incorporates popular names of enactments. This is done either by a separate table for popular names, or, less frequently, without a separate table by popular-name entries in the general subject index. The following are the most frequently used popular-name tables.

1. *Shepard's Acts and Cases by Popular Names, Federal and State, 1968*. Supplemented cumulatively by an annual paperback, this publication includes a popular-name listing for both federal and state acts. In the case of federal acts, citations are given to United States Code and to the Statutes at Large. See Exhibit 14.

Hou — FEDERAL AND STATE ACTS CITED BY POPULAR NAMES

Housing Act (Shipping Board)
U. S., Mar. 1, 1918, c. 19, 40 Stat. 438

Housing Act (State)
Del. Code of 1953, Title 31, §4101 et seq.
Kan. Laws 1933, Ch. 225

Housing Law (State Board)
Pa. 1937 Pamph. Laws 1705, No. 359

Housing Act of 1961
U. S. Code 1964 Title 12, §§371, 1701 et seq.
U. S. Code 1964 Title 15, §§631, 633, 636
U. S. Code 1964 Title 40, §§461, 462
U. S. Code 1964 Title 42, §1401 et seq.
June 30, 1961, P. L. 87-70, 75 Stat. 149

Housing Act of 1964
U. S. Code 1964 Title 12, §1703 et seq.

Exhibit 14

2. *United States Supreme Court Reports; Lawyers' Edition, Index to Annotations Volume, Table of Statutes by Popular Name*. This table is one of the best lists of its kind and is published by Lawyers Co-operative Publishing Company. It has an Index to Annotations and

an Annotation History Table. The supplementation of this table is by annual pocket parts.

3. *United States Code popular-name tables*. Both the official and the unofficial editions of the Code contain popular-name tables which include statutes which at any time have been part of the Code. Since all statutes are not codified, however, the United States Code tables are not as comprehensive as Shepard's or the United States Supreme Court Reports, Lawyers' Edition Tables.

4. *United States Statutes at Large Tables of Laws Affected*. Each cumulation of this title publishes a List of Popular Name Acts Affected by the enactments of the Statutes at Large in the period covered. There is no separate popular-name table in the Statutes at Large volumes. Such titles are, however, usually found in the general subject index.

5. *Current-year tables by popular name*. Shepard's United States Citations, the United States Code Annotated, and the United States Code Service all issue yearly supplements. The United States Code Congressional and Administrative News has a popular-name table which is cumulated once a month. The CCH Congressional Index lists Names, Bills, Headline Legislation, and acts by the official short title which is given in the preamble. The general index of United States Law Week and the American Digest System's Descriptive-Word Index frequently list litigated statutes by popular name.

§5.4. Bill status tables.

The importance of these tables for tracing the history of individual bills and resolutions and for determining their current congressional status cannot be underestimated.

1. *Coverage of bill status tables: All bills introduced*. Status tables generally ignore unreported bills, estimated at 90 percent of the total introduced. Omission of a bill from a cumulative status table indicates that it was never reported out of committee.

a. *Congressional Record History of Bills and Resolutions*. This is the one status table which lists *all* bills and resolutions. As introduced, they are indexed in the fortnightly noncumulative indexes to the Congressional Record. Thereafter they are listed only when action is taken on them during the period covered by the index. At the end of each session, all this information is cumulated in a History of Bills and Resolutions for, respectively, the House and the Senate, in which *every bill and resolution introduced*, whether acted upon or not, is listed, and its legislative history given. This is the only complete status table for congressional legislation widely available, and it is a good one.

2. *Coverage of bill status tables: Bills acted upon.*

a. *Congressional Record Daily Digest.* The subject index of bills acted upon serves as a status table. See §4.4.5b.

b. *CCH Congressional Index.* This table lists reported public bills only; for them, every action taken is reported. See §4.5.2b.

c. *Digest of Public General Bills.* This publication (see §4.4.2b) digests bills which have been acted upon and serves as a status table for them. The final issue for each *session* of a Congress is a very useful tool, giving at once rather good abridgments of bills acted upon and noting any action taken in Congress on them.

d. *House of Representatives Calendars.* The daily Numerical Order of Bills and Resolutions Which Have Passed Either House, and Bills Now Pending on the Calendar, as noted in §4.5.1c, is a very good status table of reported bills, private as well as public, for both House and Senate. The Final Edition for a Congress, since it covers an entire Congress instead of only a session (as does the Congressional Record History of Bills), is one of the most useful single status tables.

3. *Procedure in using bill status tables.*

a. *Bill number and Congress known.* When only the bill number and congressional session are known, the searcher need only check that number in a current status table in order to determine what, if any, actions have been taken on it and the dates and nature of such actions. Some tables note the publication of hearings and reports (with the report number). Which table to use depends upon its availability, latest date of coverage, and whether the searcher is interested only in the bill's status in Congress or also wishes to check debates and amendments offered on the floor of Congress. If texts of debates are required, direct citations to them can be found in the Congressional Record History of Bills and Resolutions indexes. Citations in the fortnightly indexes refer to the pages of the unbound daily editions. This paging differs from that of the bound volumes to which the annual index provides references. For the period between Congressional Record indexes, the searcher can check the Daily Digest caption noting Chamber Action, House and Senate.

b. *Bill number and Congress not known.* If the bill is pending and the subject matter is known, any of the status tables listed above should turn up its number. If the bill is known to have been enacted into law and its subject matter or the Public Law number is known, the law can be found through means described in Chapters 3 and 4, such as the subject indexes of the United States Code Congressional and Administrative News, the Statutes at Large, and the CCH Congressional Index. In the margin of each of these, the bill number is shown.

c. *Introducer's name is known.* If the introducer's name is known, the bill number can best be found through the subject index of the Congressional Record and in the CCH Congressional Index.

d. *Searching all required units of tables*. As a matter of routine, the searcher makes certain that *all* pertinent units of indexes consulted have been examined. Thus the fortnightly indexes of the Congressional Record's History of Bills and Resolutions list only bills *as introduced* and, thereafter, any *subsequent* action during a *session* of Congress. In this and other status tables, absence of a bill number in the table means no action has been taken on it. Since the History of Bills and Resolutions fortnightly index is not cumulative, a complete search during a session requires examination of each such fortnightly unit. Because the History of Bills and Resolutions annual cumulation covers only a session of a Congress, a complete search of a bill acted upon but not enacted into law during the first session requires also a search of that bill in the second or later session indexes.

The same procedure as to the latest index is routine for the other status tables listed above, except that the House of Representatives Calendars cover an entire Congress, not just one session.

§5.5. Parallel conversion tables: Bill or chapter number to law number and vice versa.

If the slip law is available, conversion is easy since all the information appears on the face of the law. When, however, the slip law is not available, other means must be used to translate a bill number to a law number, a law number to a Statutes at Large citation, or a law number to a United States Code title and section. There are tables to perform most of these tasks for public laws.

1. *Bill number to public law number*. That is, for example, *from* H.R. 6538, 81st Congress *to* Public Law Number 495 of the same Congress. This information is found as follows:

a. *Face of the slip law or Statutes at Large*.

b. *Status tables*.

c. *United States Code Congressional and Administrative News*. The table of Senate and House Bill Enacted gives this information.

2. *Public law number to bill number*. That is, *from* Public Law Number 496, 81st Congress, *to* H.R. 6538 of the same Congress. The information is found as follows:

a. *On the face of the slip law*.

b. *On the face of the Statutes at Large*. In the Statutes at Large volumes public law numbers are indexed from the List of Public Laws, arranged by law number.

c. *Digest of Public General Bills: Public Laws table*.

d. *Daily Digest of Congressional Record:* annual History of Bills Enacted into Public Law, arranged by law number.

e. *United States Code Congressional and Administrative News:* Table of Public Laws.

f. *CCH Congressional Index:* Enactments by Public Law number.

g. *House Calendar.* Tables of Laws.

3. *Bill or law number to chapter number.* That is, *from* H.R. 6539, 81st Congress, Public Law Number 495, *to* Chapter 139, 81st Congress, 2d Session. Beginning with the 85th Congress, chapter numbers have been abandoned. Formerly they appeared on the face of the slip law or Statutes at Large.

4. *Bill or law number to Statutes at Large.* That is, *from* the above bill and law number *to* 64 Stat. 96. The information is found as follows:

a. *On the face of the slip law.* The Statutes at Large citation has appeared here since mid-1951.

b. *Statutes at Large: List of Public Laws.*

c. *United States Code Congressional and Administrative News or U.S. Code Service.* In the slip law reprint and in the Table of Public Laws.

5. *Bill or public law number to Revised Statutes or Code.* That is, *from* H.R. 451, Public Law 86-171, 86th Congress, *to* 33 U.S.C. §933 (Supp. I, 1959). The information is found as follows:

a. *United States Code Congressional and Administrative News tables.* In the Table of Classifications, which is arranged by public law number.

b. *All editions of Revised Statutes or U.S. Code.* This requires the additional step of translating the bill or law number into the Statutes at Large citation, as in par. 4 *supra.* The equivalent Revised Statutes or U.S. Code citation is then found through the tables of statutes included in the compilations.

§5.6. Parallel transfer tables from one form of statute to another: Publication and use.

In statutory research it is frequently necessary to translate a citation from one form to another. By means of a parallel transfer table, it is possible to translate a Statutes at Large citation to its corresponding United States Code title and section. The tables found in both the official and the private annotated editions of the Code are complete and simple to use. Time will be saved and trouble avoided if the simple techniques needed to use these tables are learned. With the exceptions noted below, Code tables in all editions are substantially the same.

1. *United States Code Tables.*

a. *Table I. Revised Titles.* This parallel table indicates new numbering and revisions of Code titles which have been reenacted into positive law. The former section is given and is followed by the new section or sections. See Exhibit 15a below.

b. *Table II. Revised Statutes 1878.* This parallel table lists all Revised Statutes sections, even if they were never in the United States Code, and gives their present status. It is possible, therefore, to determine whether or not a Revised Statutes section is now in force and its use as authority for Code sections. R.S. §18 is, for example, shown to be 2 U.S.C. §1a, while R.S. §74 was repealed without having attained Code status. This and similar tables in the United States Code Annotated and the United States Code Service provide the only tabular means of updating Revised Statutes sections as such. Once a Revised Statutes section is found to be still in force and its present Code section is determined, it is possible to Shepardize that Code section in the usual manner through Shepard's United States Citations. See Exhibit 15b below.

c. *Table III. Statutes at Large included in the Code.* This table lists statutes which are included in the Code by date of enactment, Statutes at Large volume and page, and by chapter and section number through the 84th Congress and by Public Law number starting with the 57th Congress. Previous Code tables which were entitled Statutes Repealed and Statutes Eliminated are now incorporated in this table under the "Status" column. See Exhibit 15c.

d. *Tables IV to VI. Executive Orders, Proclamations, and Reorganization Plans Included in the Code.* Presidential documents such as executive orders, proclamations, and reorganization plans which in any way affect or implement Code sections are listed by date together with citations to the sections so affected or implemented. See Exhibit 15d.

e. *Repeal tables.* Repeal tables were found in official editions of the Code prior to 1958. They are no longer included in the Code and are, as noted above, incorporated in the "Status" columns of Tables II and III.

2. *United States Code Annotated.* Since the tables of the United States Code are compiled by the editors of the United States Code Annotated, the tables found in the U.S.C.A. are substantially the same as those in the official Code. They appear in a main volume and a cumulative supplement volume. They are further updated by the Cumulative Tables in the United States Code Congressional and Administrative News.

3. *United States Code Service.* In terms both of content and of order, United States Code Service tables are much like those in the official edition. Positive law titles are listed parallel to the original Code form. There is a table of acts by popular names but no tables of executive orders, proclamations, or reorganization acts. Supplementation is by annual pocket parts, Later Case Service Pamphlets.

TABLE I—REVISED TITLES

The following tables represent those titles of the United States Code that have been revised and renumbered since adoption of the Code in 1926. These tables show where former sections of the revised titles have been incorporated in this edition of the Code.

Title		Page	Title		Page
1.	General Provisions	9799	17.	Copyrights	9811
3.	The President	9799	18.	Crimes and Criminal Procedure	9812
4.	Flag and Seal, Seat of Government, and the States	9800	23.	Highways	9815
6.	Official and Penal Bonds	9800	26.	Internal Revenue Code of 1954	9816
			28.	Judiciary and Judicial Procedure	9827

• • •

TITLE 1—GENERAL PROVISIONS

[*This title was enacted into law by Act July 30, 1947, ch. 388, § 1, 61 Stat. 633. This table shows where sections of former Title 1 have been incorporated in revised Title 1*]

Title 1 Former Sections	Title 1 New Sections	Title 1 Former Sections	Title 1 New Sections	Title 1 Former Sections	Title 1 New Sections
1	1	27	107	54	204
2	2	28	108	54a	205
3	3	29	109	54b	206
4	4	29a	110	54c	207
5	5	29b	111	54d	208
6	6	30	112	55	209

Exhibit 15a

TABLE II—REVISED STATUTES 1878

Showing where sections of the Revised Statutes of the United States of 1878 will be found in this edition of the United States Code.

Abbreviations

Rep.—Repealed. Where "Rep." appears in the status column following a U.S.C. reference an explanation of the repeal can be found under such U.S.C. title and section. Where no U.S.C. reference appears the Rev. St. section was repealed prior to the adoption of the United States Code (1926) or for other reasons was not included in the Code but was subsequently repealed.

Rev. T.—Revised Title. Where "Rev. T." appears in the status column the U.S.C. reference is to title and section where the Rev. St. section was originally allocated in the U.S.C. To locate the Rev. St. section in the U.S.C. new title, see the Table (Pages 9799 to 9841, this volume).

Elim.—Eliminated. Where "Elim." appears in the status column following a U.S.C. reference the reason for the elimination of the text can be found under such U.S.C. title and section.

I.R.C. '39—Internal Revenue Code of 1939. Where I.R.C. '39 appears in the status column, it is an indication that the provision was repealed or otherwise superseded by the Internal Revenue Code of 1939.

R.S.	U.S.C.			R.S.	U.S.C.			R.S.	U.S.C.		
Sec.	**Tit.**	**Sec**	**Status**	**Sec.**	**Tit.**	**Sec.**	**Status**	**Sec.**	**Tit.**	**Sec.**	**Status**
1	1	1	Rev. T. 1	74	----	----------	Rep.	152, 153	3	41, 42	Rev. T. 3
	--	--	I.R.C. '39	75—78	----	----------	Rep.	154	3	44	Rev. T. 3
2—5	1	2—5	Rev. T. 1	79	44	321		155	3	45	Elim.
6	1	31	Rev. T. 1	80	2	131		156, 157	----	----------	Rep.
7—11	1	21—25	Rev. T. 1	81	2	132		158	5	1	
12, 13	1	28, 29	Rev. T. 1	82	2	132a		159	5	2	
14—17	--	--	Rep.	83	2	134		160	5	3	Elim.
18	2	1a		84	2	135		161	5	22	

Exhibit 15b

TABLE III—STATUTES AT LARGE

Showing where the Acts of Congress will be found in the United States Code

Abbreviations

Rep.—Repealed. Where "Rep." appears in the status column following a U.S.C. reference, an explanation of the repeal can be found under such U.S.C. title and section.

Rev. T.—Revised Title. Where "Rev. T." appears in the status column, the U.S.C. reference is to title and section where the section of the Act of Congress was originally allocated in the U.S.C. To locate the section of the Act in the U.S.C. revised title, see the Tables (Pages 9799 to 9841, this volume).

Elim.—Eliminated. Where "Elim." appears in the status column following a U.S.C. reference, the reason for the elimination of the text can be found under such U.S.C. title and section.

Exec.—Executed. Where "Exec." appears in the status column, it is an indication that the provisions are directory and that Codification changes in the text of various sections have been made in the Code as a result of such directions.

I.R.C. '39.—Internal Revenue Code of 1939. Where I.R.C. '39 appears in the status column, it is an indication that the provision was repealed or otherwise superseded by the Internal Revenue Code of 1939.

				U.S.C.		
2 Stat.	**Chapter**	**Section**	**Page**	**Title**	**Section**	**Status**
1802—May 3	51	5	193	24	11a	Rep.
1814—Dec. 1	7		248	44	88	
1820—Feb. 10	11	14, 15	543	--		I.R.C. '39
1822—May 7	96	3	692	40	307	Elim.
1836—July 4	352	4	111	43	5	Elim.
1837—Mar. 3	33	1	163, 164	43	5	Elim.
9 Stat.						
1846—Aug. 6	84	5	55	--		I.R.C. '39
1850—Sept. 28	80		515	34	868	Rev. T. 10

Exhibit 15c

TABLE IV.—EXECUTIVE ORDERS

This Table lists the Executive Orders that implement general and permanent law as contained in U.S.C.

Exec. Ord. Date	Exec. Ord. No.	U.S.C. Title	U.S.C. Sec.
1918			
May 11	2859	36	253 nt
1929			
Oct 1	5200	7	452 nt
1941			
June 14	8785	12	95a nt
July 26	8832	12	95a nt
Dec 9	8963	12	95a nt
26	8998	12	95a nt

TABLE V.—PROCLAMATIONS

This Table lists the Proclamations that are referred to in U.S.C.

Proc. Date	Proc. No.	U.S.C. Title	U.S.C. Sec.
1938			
Oct. 25	2307	16	450r nt
1939			
Jan. 25	2320	16	441c nt
Sept. 5	2348	50 App	Prec 1 nt
	2350	50 App	Prec 1 nt
8	2352	50 App	Prec 1 nt
	2353	50 App	Prec 1 nt
10	2359	50 App	Prec. 1 nt
Nov. 4	2374	50 App	Prec. 1 nt
1950			
Mar. 24	2879	26	4731 nt
Oct. 6	2906	50 App	454 nt
Dec. 16	2914	50 App.	Prec. 1 nt
28	2915	50 App.	454 nt
1951			
June 22	2931	50 App	2314 nt
Aug. 1	2935	19	1362 nt
31	2942	50 App	453 nt
Oct. 12	2948	19	1318 nt
25	2950	50 App.	Prec. 1 nt

TABLE VI.—REORGANIZATION PLANS

This Table lists the Reorganization Plans that are set out in U.S.C.

Statutes at Large Section	Statutes at Large Vol.	Statutes at Large Page	U.S.C. Title	U.S.C. Section
		1939 Plan No. 1		
All	53	1423	5	133t nt
		1939 Plan No. 2		
All	53	1431	5	133 nt
		1940 Plan No. 3		
All	54	1231	5	133t nt
		1950 Plan No. 5		
All	64	1263	5	133z—15, 591 nts
All	64	1265	16	792 nt
		1950 Plan No. 6		
All	64	1263	5	133z—15, 611 nts
		1950 Plan No. 8		
All	64	1264	5	133z—15 nt

Exhibit 15d

4. *Use of parallel tables from one form of statute to another.*

a. *Slip laws to Statutes at Large.* The general Statutes at Large citation is given at the bottom of the slip law.

b. *Slip laws to United States Code; Statutes at Large to United States Code.* That is, for example, *from* Act of July 15, 1965, §9(b), Pub. L. No. 89-74, 79 Stat. 234 *to* 21 U.S.C. §321 (1970).

Depending upon the date of a statute's enactment, the transfer from slip law or Statutes at Large citation is made in one of two ways. If the statute is a recent one and not yet included in the United

States Code annual tables, the transfer to the corresponding Code section is made by using the Table of Classifications in a current United States Code Congressional and Administrative News pamphlet. If the statute was enacted before the publication of the current United States Code annual tables, the transfer is made by using the United States Code Table III, the United States Code Annotated Chronological Tables, or the United States Code Service Key to United States Statutes at Large.

c. *Statutes at Large to Revised Statutes*. That is, for example, *from* Act of Sept. 3, 1789, ch. 1, 1 Stat. 65 *to* R.S. §161.

The table which must be used to make this transfer is found in the Reference Index to the Revised Statutes. It is entitled "From Statutes to Sections in the Revised Statutes."

d. *Revised Statutes to the United States Code*. That is, for example, *from* R.S. §4178 *to* U.S.C. §46 (1970).

Table II of the Code lists all sections of the Revised Statutes which have ever been incorporated into the Code.

e. *Revised Statutes to the Statutes at Large; United States Code to Statutes at Large*. This information is given in the text of the compilation itself. In the Revised Statutes, the original Statutes at Large citation is shown in roman type in the margin of the page. In the Code, a section's statutory authority is found in parenthesis at the end of the Code section or a group of sections. See Exhibit 8.

f. *Executive acts affecting Code sections*. Presidential executive orders, proclamations, and reorganization plans frequently affect legislation already incorporated in Code sections or cited in notes following such sections. Code Tables IV-VI list executive instruments along with the section affected or implemented. See Exhibit 15d.

g. *Executive acts: Finding statutory authority for*. Many executive orders and proclamations are issued under authority of specific enabling acts. Table V in Title 3A of the Code of Federal Regulations, Statutes Cited as Authority for Presidential Documents pairs the executive act with its statutory authority.

§5.7. Original and compiled forms of statutes distinguished: A summary.

Because compilations of legislation of general public interest which are arranged by subject are more convenient to use than the slip or session law form, they are frequently used exclusively. It must be remembered that compilations are usually only prima facie evidence of the law and that the original form is still the real and "best" authority. In legal writing, therefore, the session law form of a statute should be cited. The compilation can be cited only if the particular Code title has been reenacted as positive law and the original session law expressly repealed. As a result, the statutory provision that human labor is not a commodity is cited as Section 6 of the Clayton Act, Act of Oct. 15, 1914, ch. 328, §6, 38 Stat. 731, 15 U.S.C. §17 (1970) and never merely as 15 U.S.C. §17 (1970). If the original act has not been amended, the Code text of an individual section is probably identical to that of the original. The arrangement of the sections within the Code is not identical, however, so it is always safer to check with the original both to verify the text and, if necessary, to determine the section arrangement of the original.

§5.8. Finding the earliest publication of new enactments.

Both official and unofficial slip laws generally are a new enactment's fastest form of publication. Sometimes, however, the promptest form of publication is by loose-leaf services which are described in detail in Chapter 23.

§5.9. Finding a particular federal statute.

This may be done in a variety of ways depending upon the information available.

1. *By subject*. Subject indexes are available, both for bills pending in Congress and for enacted legislation. Indexes to the status tables described in §5.4 enable the searcher to find bills when their subject matter is known. Although there is no cumulative index for private law, such laws are indexed by subject matter in the individual Statutes at Large volumes in which they are printed.

Public laws are normally located through a subject index of public general laws in force, such as those found in statutory compilations. If the law, even though a public law, was not of sufficient general interest or permanency to be incorporated in a compilation such as the United States Code, there are only two types of subject indexes available. Neither of these is very satisfactory.

Found in the individual volumes of Statutes at Large, the first type only indexes material contained in the volume and is not cumulative. If the date of the enactment or the approximate date is known, the search is narrowed to the volumes of that date. The other index is of all public general laws which had at any time been in force through 1931. This is the McClenon and Gilbert index, described §5.2.5. As the coverage of this index extends only through 1931, it must be supplemented for later years by searching the volumes of the Statutes at

Large covering 1932 to date. Certain broad subjects by category, such as appropriation acts for the various government agencies, railroad legislation, etc., are listed under those headings in the Shepard's Citations and the United States Supreme Court Reports, L. Ed., popular-name tables. In any search, care must be taken that all applicable statutes are consulted, as more than one may be pertinent to a given set of facts.

In searching multi-volume unofficial editions of the United States Code, the indexes to individual titles are more convenient to use than the much larger general index to the entire Code. The search, however, should not be restricted to them. This is because legislation very often overlaps so that a given topic may be covered by more than one title of the Code. This is particularly true where adjective and substantive law impinge upon one another. Often what seems logically to be substantive law is covered wholly or in part by a procedural provision in a different Code title. The general index to the whole body of the law covered by the Code should be consulted because it coordinates these various overlapping entries.

2. *By title*. Many acts, such as the Taft-Hartley Act, the G.I. Bill of Rights, etc., are known and cited by their popular name. The popular-name indexes described in §5.3 give the various forms of citations under these names.

3. *By bill, law, or chapter number*. Tracing an act when this information is known is described in §§5.5 and 5.6. Because bill and law numbers are renumbered at the beginning of each Congress, the number of the Congress or the approximate date of the act is a necessary part of the data. As was noted, chapter numbers have not been assigned since the close of the eighty-fourth Congress. When they were used, chapter numbers were renumbered with each congressional session. These necessary data are printed on each slip law and in the margin of the Statutes at Large.

4. *Transfer tables from one form of statute to another*. See §5.6.

5. *Treaties*. As will be described in Chapter 6, treaties are indexed both by number and by subject.

6. *Statutes no longer in force*. The only complete coverage is through search of the indexes of all volumes of the Statutes at Large. Indexes to compilations all omit private laws, uncodified laws as well as temporary, repealed, and superseded laws. They index only public general laws in force, excluding appropriation acts. A law indexed in one compilation may be omitted from a later one because it is no longer in force.

Search normally begins with the index of a compilation of laws in force. If the desired law is not found there, a game of legal ticktacktoe ensues. The searcher works back through various editions until the one containing the statute is found. If the law is found in the 1964 Code but not in the 1970 edition, a table of repeals in the 1969 supplement will show when and by what act the law was repealed. Whenever a law is found in a compilation, each section will contain a reference to the original session law from which it was copied. For indexes to all public and general acts from 1789 to 1931, see the Beaman and McNamara and the McClenon and Gilbert indexes described in §5.2.5.

§5.10. Work with the United States Revised Statutes.

Since much of the law contained in the Revised Statutes is still in force, this compilation must not be overlooked. This is true even though it covers only codified laws in force on December 1, 1873. Although seldom seen, the volume containing this compilation should still be checked if the text of its sections is cited as authority for sections of the United States Code which have not been reenacted into positive law and which base their text on Revised Statutes sections. Its makeup and use are described in Chapter 3. Revised Statutes sections which have been incorporated in the United States Code are listed in Table II of the Code. Those which have been repealed, whether or not they were ever in the Code, are also listed in Table II of the Code.

§5.11. Work with the United States Code.

The makeup of the Code and its indexes were described in Chapter 3. It is the form of federal statute most used by the lawyer even though the original Statutes at Large will be cited in legal writing as authority if the particular title cited has not been reenacted as positive law. Which edition of the Code — official unannotated or unofficial annotated — to consult depends largely upon whether only the text of a section is wanted or whether case annotations are also required.

1. *Official editions of the Code.* If only the text of a Code section is wanted, the official edition is more convenient than the unofficial annotated editions since it is not buried in page after page of digest paragraphs of cases interpreting it. Notes, tables, and indexes are largely the same in all editions. Except for the smaller initial cost of the official edition, however, the advantage lies with the unofficial editions. These are the editions customarily used by lawyers.

2. *Unofficial annotated editions of the Code.* As was seen in Chapter 3, the added value of the unofficial editions lies in their case

digests interpreting each section of the Constitution and Code as well as in their more frequent supplementation.

3. *Finding the required Code sections.* When a specific Code section is desired but the citation is to a slip law or to the Statutes at Large, the researcher must use the indexes and tables noted in the description of the Code (§3.6.5) and in the Chapter and Law Number Tables (§5.5) and the Parallel Tables for Statutes From One Form to Another (§5.6). Care must be taken to ensure that the proper volume is consulted. It is necessary to note the publication date of the volume or supplement in order to ascertain whether it covers the desired dates and to make sure that the sequence of parts is complete.

§5.12. Citators for federal statutes.

Having found a statute section in point, the lawyer must then determine two things: (1) whether the section is still in force and in the form found (not amended, repealed, or superseded by later legislative action) and (2) whether it has been construed by a court of competent jurisdiction. Elaborate devices called citators or citation books aid the lawyer here. They are described in Chapter 18.

§5.13. Elementary considerations in work with statutes.

The following is an informal checklist of the things the searcher should ask when embarking upon the solution of a statutory problem.

By far the most important item on the checklist is to determine what is wanted. Is it the text of a bill which is desired or, rather, an indication of its present status in Congress? Is the intent of Congress in enacting a given piece of legislation wanted and, if so, what are the available means of ascertaining such intent? Is a particular statute or section sought? In its original or codified form? What is the authority of the form of a given statute as legislation? What is known about the statute — its date, subject matter, bill or law numbers? Are case or other annotations wanted, or just the text? Has a governmental agency regulation been amended since its promulgation? Once the desired goal has been determined, the rest is largely a matter of knowing the resources of statutory publication.

The next important factor in an efficient search is ensuring that the right materials are used. Does the publication date of the volume being consulted exclude the particular statute, regulation, or annotation sought? Are all the required units and supplements available? Is it certain that the statute is still in force, or should an earlier compilation be consulted?

Finally, has the statute been fully Shepardized, using materials and techniques described in Chapter 18?

6 Treaties and Other International Acts of the United States [1]

§6.1. Importance of treaties and other international agreements in law practice.

Many persons think of the treaty as an esoteric thing which evokes images of high protocol peace conferences. Treaties have, however, extremely practical application. A treaty might, for example, govern the disposition of the effects of a deceased Greek national domiciled in Iowa, the extradition to Missouri of a criminal from the Netherlands, the right of a Chilean to sue in a New York court on a contract, or the validity of a California statute prohibiting certain aliens from holding real property in that state. As long as the nationals of one country travel to, do business in, or choose to live in another country, the treaty defining their rights will be not only of diplomatic interest, but of personal interest as well. Most of the cases interpreting treaties are not from federal courts but, rather, arise in state courts. The Treaty of March 2, 1899, with the United Kingdom, has, for example, been adjudicated twenty-one times, sixteen of those times by state courts. Domestically, the relations of the United States with most of the American Indians are still governed by treaty and

1. The authors acknowledge the valuable assistance of the late Mrs. Florence Zagayko, international law librarian of the Columbia University Law Library, in the preparation of this chapter.

agreement. The recent and successful efforts of Indian tribes to establish water, mineral, and land rights on the basis of treaty obligations are evidence of the importance of these domestic treaties and agreements.

§6.2. Place of treaties and other international agreements in the legislative hierarchy.

Whether or not treaties and executive agreements are properly to be considered as conventional legislation is academic. As a practical matter, they are viewed as interchangeable for many purposes and are treated as such here. Basic to an understanding of the makeup and function of treaty and international materials is an awareness of the political and legal theory underlying such materials.

1. *"Treaty" and "executive agreement" defined.* Article II, Section 2 of the Constitution provides that "[t]he President . . . shall have the Power, by and with the consent of the Senate, to make treaties, provided two thirds of the Senators present concur. . . ." The term "treaty" denotes an international compact concluded by the President with a foreign power, with the approval of the Senate. It may, however, be designated as a treaty, convention, protocol, contract, or by another term. "Executive agreements" are entered into by the President with a foreign state, as the United States representative to foreign nations, and require no action by the Senate. These agreements arise under the authority of specific acts of Congress, such as those which appoint the President as a fact finder with the power to act. They may also be agreements entered into purely under the constitutional powers possessed by the President as the chief executive of the United States.

2. *As the law of the land: Under international law.* Both treaties and executive agreements are contracts between the United States and foreign nations having requisite power to carry out the terms thereof. At international law — the law of nations — they are equally binding. While such an international pact may be invalid as part of the municipal law of the United States, it may still be binding as a contract between the United States and the other signatory. This is true both of executory treaties which require congressional legislation for their effectiveness and of self-executing treaties which require no such legislation. Under later decisions, it seems to be true of executive agreements as well.

3. *As the law of the land: Under municipal law.* A formal treaty, negotiated and signed by the President and approved by the Senate, has the force of a federal statute. Article VI of the Constitution provides that ". . . all Treaties made, or which shall be made, under the Authority of the United States, shall be the supreme Law of the

Land; and the Judges of every State shall be bound thereby, any Thing in the Constitution or Laws of any state to the contrary notwithstanding." A court has said: " . . . there is no principle of law more firmly established by the highest court of the land than that, while a treaty will supersede a prior act of Congress, an act of Congress may supersede a prior treaty. The latest expression controls, whether it be a treaty or an act of Congress." *United States* v. *Thompson*, 258 Fed. 257, 268 (D. Ark. 1919). Like any other statute, a treaty is subject to constitutional limitations and to judicial review, but the courts strive to avoid finding repugnance. It has been said that no treaty has ever been held unconstitutional. Executive agreements may be upheld as the law of the land, even when opposed to the internal policy of a sovereign state. They are probably not, however, the "law of the land" to the extent that they can supersede an act of Congress, except when made under the authority of a later act. To this extent, at least, they are not interchangeable with treaties.

§6.3. Publication of the international acts of the United States.

1. *Press releases*. The first publication of a treaty or executive agreement may be in the form of a mimeographed press release of the Department of State, but not all agreements are so published. It is usually issued at the date of signing, which, in the case of a formal treaty, is in advance of its presentation to the Senate for approval and its later ratification by the President, (Note the nomenclature: The Senate "approves" or "recommends ratification" of treaties; the President then "ratifies.") The text may be preceded by a departmental statement tracing the history of the agreement.

2. *Department of State Bulletin*. Statements concerning the negotiation, signing, ratification, etc., of treaties are published in this weekly Bulletin, and texts of exchanges of notes and of some treaties, if issued as press releases, sometimes accompany them. This information is catalogued in a tardily published annual index.

3. *Senate Executive Documents*. Treaties must be sent to the Senate for confirmation. These treaties, along with messages from the President and the Secretary of State, are (if not classified) published as Senate Executive Documents. When published, a Senate Executive Document is designated by a letter and is always cited by that letter and the number and session of the Congress during which it was received. A Senate Executive Report, on the other hand, is published by the Senate Foreign Relations Committee and is designated by a number. Both Senate Executive Documents and Senate Executive Reports have been compiled by Mariana G. Mabry in her Checklist

of Senate Executive Documents and Reports . . . 1947–1970.[2] Access to Senate Executive Documents and Reports from 1970 to date can be found in the Congressional Information Service described in Chapter 4.

4. *"Slip law" form*. The next form of publication is comparable to the slip law. In this form treaties are listed in the official Monthly Catalog of Government Publications and may be purchased separately from any series in which they may appear. There have been three numbered series of these slip agreements, all issued by the Department of State.

a. *Treaty Series*. The first series was the Treaty Series — cited as T.S. — and bibliographically it is a peculiar series. It began in January 1908 with number 489 and, through number 814, published both formal treaties and executive agreements. Beginning with number 815 through number 994, which ended the series, only formal treaties were published. The issues preceding 489 were unnumbered as published and were finally published as a set between 1968 and 1976 in Treaties and Other International Agreements of the United States 1776–1949 (par. 6 *infra*).

b. *Executive Agreement Series*. Before 1921, some executive agreements were included in the Treaty Series mentioned above, but others were to be found only in such sources as Foreign Relations of the United States, the volumes of Malloy (par. 8 *infra*), particularly in volumes 2 and 4, or in press releases. From October 1, 1929, through March 16, 1945, executive agreements were published as the Executive Agreement Series — cited as E.A.S. — ending with number 506, when the combined series described below was resumed. Executive agreements concluded before 1950 can now be found in Treaties and Other International Agreements of the United States 1776–1949 (par. 6 *infra*).

c. *Treaties and Other International Acts Series*. This series cited as T.I.A.S. — began with number 1501 in December 1945. This number was arrived at by adding the 994 numbers of the Treaty Series to the 506 of the Executive Agreement Series. It was inaugurated to make available in a single series the texts of treaties and other instruments (such as constitutions and charters of international organizations, declarations, agreements affected by exchanges of diplomatic notes, etc.) establishing or defining relations between the United States and other countries." Official prints are judicially noticed as positive law without certification. 1 U.S.C. §113, as amended by Public Law 89-497, 80 Stat. 271.

These three series are indispensable for intensive work with current United States Treaties and executive agreements. They present the

2. Austin, Texas, University of Texas, 1970.

full texts of the various acts, both in English and in any foreign language involved, and include the President's proclamations, if any, of these acts. The title page gives the title and critical dates.

d. *Unofficial treaty publication*. Both the United States Code Annotated and the United States Code Congressional and Administrative News publish a limited number of formal treaties and executive agreements which, in the words of the publisher,

> affect U.S. Code provisions of a relatively permanent duration and general interest. . . . In 1956, an informal agreement was reached whereby the State Department representative would suggest treaties and agreements or references thereto for inclusion — final determination as to use and form would be made by the editorial department of the publishers. . . . For examples of full-text coverage . . . the following may be pointed out:
>
> Title 17, §9 — Unesco Universal Copyright convention.
>
> Title 22, §287, note — Agreement between United Nations and U.S. on U.N. Headquarters.
>
> Title 22, §1372, note — Revised agreement between U.S. and Philippines.[3]

International Legal Materials: Current Documents, a bimonthly publication of the American Society of International Law, photo-offsets original current treaties and related documents.

Tax Treaties is a Commerce Clearing House loose-leaf reporter. It prints the full text of the United States treaties covering income and estate taxes.

5. *Statutes at Large publication*. Treaties were published in the Statutes at Large from volume 8 (which included treaties from 1776 to 1845) through volume 64, covering 1949. From volume 47 (1931–1933) through volume 64, executive agreements of international import were also included. All treaties and executive agreements found in Statutes at Large volumes between 1776 and 1949 have been consolidated and indexed in Treaties and Other International Agreements of the United States 1776–1949 (par. 8 *infra*).

6. *United States Treaties and Other International Agreements*. This series — cited as U.S.T. by volume, page, and year — takes the place of the former publication of treaties and agreements in the Statutes at Large. It is also the annual, bound form of publication of the Treaties and Other International Acts Series, beginning with T.I.A.S. number 2010, January 27, 1950. Each volume is indexed by both country and subject. There are usually several volumes a year.

7. *League of Nations and United Nations Treaty Series*. Although the United States never became a member of the League of Nations, most of the international acts of the United States from 1920 through 1945 were published in the League of Nations Treaty Series. They are

3. West Publishing Company letter to the authors of October 17, 1960.

now published in the successor United Nations Treaty Series and, in addition, have been included in Treaties and Other International Agreements of the United States 1776–1949 (par. 6 *supra*). Both the League of Nations and the United Nations series are well indexed by cumulative indexes which are now published for each fifty volumes.

8. *Other collections of United States treaties*. Until 1976, there was no comprehensive, consolidated publication of treaties and agreements between and among the United States and other governments which were concluded and entered into before 1950. Until then, William H. Malloy's Treaties, Conventions, International Acts, Protocols and Agreements Between the United States of America and Other Powers [4] was the most important compilation for the period covered. Volume 3 of Malloy, covering the years 1910–1923, was compiled by C. F. Redmond and is often cited as 3 Redmond; similarly, the fourth and final volume, covering 1923–1934, was compiled by Edward J. Trenwith and is often cited as 4 Trenwith. Issued by the Department of State, David Hunter Miller's compilation of Treaties and Other International Acts of the United States of America[5] was discontinued after covering only the period through July 1, 1863.

Four times the length of Malloy, Treaties and Other International Agreements of the United States 1776–1949[6] was published by the Department of State under the direction of Charles I. Bevans. Volume 1 appeared in 1968, and volume 13, the final volume, was published eight years later. Volumes 1 to 4 contain, in chronological order, the English texts or official translations of multilateral agreements signed by the United States between 1776 and 1949. Volumes 5 through 12 are arranged alphabetically by country and contain bilateral agreements between the United States and each country. Each volume is indexed by country and subject, and the final volume indexes the entire series. In addition to treaties, the series includes postal arrangements, agreements printed in the Executive Agreements series, and other agreements not found in the Malloy volumes.

9. *Indian treaties*. Indian treaties from 1778 to 1842 were originally collected and published in volume 7 of the Statutes at Large. Indian treaties and agreements concluded after 1842 appear in regular volumes of Statutes at Large. Together with laws relating to American Indians, they were compiled by Charles J. Kappler in Indian Affairs, Laws and Treaties,[7] and are well indexed. The work is best used in conjunction with Felix S. Cohen's Handbook of Federal Indian Law[8] which was first published in 1945 and reissued in 1971.

4. Washington, D.C., U.S. Gov't Printing Office, 1910–1938, 4 vols.
5. Washington, D.C., U.S. Gov't Printing Office, 1931–1948, 9 vols.
6. Washington, D.C., U.S. Gov't Printing Office, 1968–1976, 13 vols.
7. Washington, D.C., U.S. Gov't Printing Office, 1904–1941, 5 vols.
8. Albuquerque, N.M., University of New Mexico Press, 1971.

§6.4. Lists and subject indexes of international acts.

The best index to international acts is a set compiled and edited by Igor I. Kavass and others, entitled U.S. Treaties and Other International Agreements Cumulative Index 1776–1949 and its companion volumes known as the U.S.T. Cumulative Index 1950–1970 and its 1971–1975 Supplement. This set indexes all known U.S. treaties and international agreements by number, chronologically, by country, and by subject. Additional information can be pieced together with the aid of certain lists and indexes.

1. *Treaties in Force.* By far the most essential and useful for various purposes is the list Treaties in Force, published annually since 1950 by the Department of State. As the title indicates, it includes only treaties in force. Part I of the list contains bilateral treaties, arranged by country and, under country, by topic. Citations are given to texts as published in the various sources: Statutes at Large, U.S.T., T.I.A.S., United Nations Treaty Series, Treaties and Other International Agreements of the United States 1776–1949, Malloy, etc.

2. *Numerical lists.* A numerical list of the T.S., E.A.S., and the T.I.A.S. through December 1950 (T.I.A.S. number 222) is in United States Treaty Developments, Appendix II. The publication of this loose-leaf service was suspended on that date. This is a good list and is still useful because it gives not only the titles of the treaties, but also cross-references to other citations of the texts in the Statutes at Large, Miller, Malloy, etc. More recent numbers of the T.I.A.S. are listed numerically only in the cumulative catalogs of the Publications of the Department of State. While these publications are primarily subject catalogs, they include indexes by series number.

3. *Alphabetical indexes by subject and country.* Analytical subject indexes for treaties and agreements concluded and entered into before 1950 are bound individual volumes of Treaties and Other International Agreements of the United States 1776–1949 for each volume as well as in the cumulative index volume. Before its publication, the only detailed analytical index to United States treaties was published in 1931 and is entitled the Subject Index of the Treaty Series and the Executive Series, July 1, 1931. This index covers only T.S. numbers 1 to 839 and E.A.S. numbers 1 to 18 for which there is also a numerical list with citation to the Statutes at Large. Subject indexes in the volumes of U.S.T. since 1950 are analytical.

An old list of Treaties in Force, 1941, can also be useful because of its classified arrangement and its subject index. It was the last such list before the first annual Treaties in Force was published in 1950.

Volume 4 of Malloy has an alphabetical index by subject and country and is one of the most convenient indexes using this approach for the period covered. It is a cumulative index to the four volumes of Malloy, covering the years 1789–1937.

A List of Treaties and Other International Agreements Contained in the United States Statutes at Large is printed in 64 Statutes at Large, Part 3 (1953), which is the last volume of the Statutes at Large to contain international acts. It is a list by country, and under each country the acts are arranged alphabetically by topic. Citations are given to series number, if any, as well as to the Statutes at Large. Indian treaties found in volumes 7 to 18, inclusive, of the Statutes at Large are not included.

The only up-to-date alphabetical lists are those in the latest Treaties in Force, and in each volume of U.S.T. A special list on copyright relations is published as an appendix to Treaties in Force.

4. *Lists of treaties submitted to the Senate*. Information concerning actions on treaties by the Senate is found in several publications. The two Lists of Treaties Submitted to the Senate, 1789–1937, are chronological lists of treaties which give the date of submission to the Senate, the Senate document number, and type of action taken by the Senate, whether acceptance, acceptance with reservation, rejection, withdrawal by the President, no action, or submission only for information. Footnotes give further details on some of the treaties. A useful list of dates of all sessions of Congress is appended. A similar treaty list without the notes is published in 4 Malloy, but covers only 1789 to 1937. Senate Executive Documents and Reports from 1947–1970 are found in Mabry's checklist, §6.3.3 *supra*. It was intended that United States Treaty Developments, *infra*, would continue giving the information on treaties pending before the Senate, but this publication has been suspended. The only convenient compilation now of such information is in the Commerce Clearing House Congressional Index in its section on treaties pending in the Senate during the current session. This list gives the status of such treaties, whether in committee, reported out, ratified, or rejected, and gives references to published hearings and reports. The Calendar of the Senate Committee on Foreign Relations also has such a list, but it is less convenient to use and not generally available.

5. *Treaties by popular name*. Several lists translate the popular name of a treaty (as the Hay-Pauncefote or Ashburton-Webster, etc.) into its official Statutes at Large or other citation. Malloy and Kavass do this in their indexes, as does Shepard's Acts and Cases by Popular Names. Similar lists in the United States Code cannot be satisfactorily used for treaties.

6. *Citators for international acts*. Treaties and executive agreements of international import are federal statutes. As such, they are subject to much the same process of amendment, repeal or extension

as are other federal statutes. They are interpreted by the federal and state courts in the same manner. Consequently, the lawyer will ordinarily Shepardize them through Shepard's Citations as noted below. To a limited extent, however, there are other means of Shepardizing when Shepard's itself is unavailable.

a. *United States Treaty Developments*. The best citator for developments occurring during the period 1944–1950 was the Department of State loose-leaf service bearing this name. For each international act it gave, in one place, the following information: ". . . notes respecting the date and place of signature, effective date, duration, citations to text, signatories, ratifications, adherences, accessions, reservations, amendments, extensions, terminations, authorizing and implementing legislation, executive action, administrative interpretations, opinions of the Attorney General, court decisions, and other relevant action." It is most unfortunate that this admirable publication was discontinued. It is still useful for the period covered.

b. *Subsequent legislative history of treaties*. The present status of treaties in force is indicated by three publications.

(1) *Treaties in Force*. This annual publication notes the revision or termination of articles or clauses of treaties still in force and lists amending, extending, or supplementing treaties. Treaties which have been completely terminated, whether by expiration, denunciation, or replacement, are not included in the list.

(2) *Shepard's United States Citations*. These citators are described in detail in Chapter 18. If the treaty or agreement was published in the Statutes at Large before 1950, any revision, amendment, supplementation, extension, or termination of the treaty or agreement is noted in the United States section, exactly as it is for any other uncodified United States statute. When the United States Treaties and Other International Agreements was inaugurated in 1950, Shepard's Citations added a special table for U.S.T. citations. This table includes citations in federal courts, in later Statutes at Large or U.S.T. volumes, and in the Journal of the American Bar Association, even if only the name of the treaty is found in the case, statute, treaty, or article. State editions of Shepard's Citations also cover the U.S.T. as well as state cases involving treaties before 1950.

It is important to note in Shepardizing treaties that their listing in Shepard's United States Citations and in the state Shepard's Citations as well, is, as with all uncodified federal acts, by date and not by volume and page of the Statutes at Large. Specifically, they are listed by the *date when signed*. For example, a treaty with France on double taxation was signed on October 18, 1946, ratified by the President on June 18, 1948, and proclaimed on October 27, 1949. This treaty was not noted in Shepard's United States Citations until in the 1956–1960 red-paper supplement, in which it was listed as an act of October 18,

1946, the signing date. Shepardizing treaties and agreements published in U.S.T., beginning with 1950, however, is simple, since in both Shepard's United States Citations and the state Shepard's Citations they are listed by volume and page of U.S.T., as 6 U.S.T. 4117.

(3) *Department of State Bulletin*. This weekly publication reports all current treaty action in its section on treaty information. From 1929 to 1939 such information was published separately in the Department's Treaty Information Bulletin and is covered by two cumulative indexes.

c. *Judicial history of treaties in federal courts*.

(1) *U.S. Treaty Developments*. During its short life, this publication was the simplest source of such information. See §6.4.6a *supra*.

(2) *Shepard's United States Citations*. Since it covers all treaties to date which are printed in the Statutes at Large or in United States Treaties and Other International Agreements, this is the tool most lawyers prefer to use in researching both judicial and subsequent legislative history. Only cases from federal courts are indexed. Even so, *all* federal cases mentioning the treaty are listed and not just those cases directly construing it.

(3) *United States Code Service*. This edition of the United States Code has a separate volume entitled Annotations to Uncodified Laws and Treaties which, as the title indicates, includes treaties and other agreements of international import. The citing cases include both federal and state cases but are limited only to those cases actually construing the treaty. Even if a treaty has not been construed by a court, it nonetheless will be listed.

(4) *Supreme Court Reporter*. Beginning with volume 28 (1901), this Reporter has a Table of Statutes Construed which includes treaties. State court cases construing treaties are listed as well as those of the Supreme Court. In 1974 this table terminated.

d. *Judicial history of treaties in the state courts*. Each state Shepard's Citations has a section citing federal statutes construed by the courts of the state covered. This section includes treaties and executive agreements as published either in the Statutes at Large or in United States Treaties and Other International Agreements. As noted above, the U.S. Code Service cites state cases construing treaties even when they have not been appealed to the United States Supreme Court. Another source of information about state court construction of treaties is in the table of Statutes Construed in the National Reporter System volumes. In these tables, treaties interpreted are listed, following Statutes at Large citations, under Treaties, Conventions, and International Agreements. Treaties are more often construed by state than by federal courts.

7. *Indian treaties and agreements*. Federal and state relations with the American Indians are still largely regulated by treaty and agree-

ment. This is particularly true in the areas of land use and condemnation. Indian treaties and agreements are annotated by federal and state cases in the Annotations to Uncodified Laws and Treaties volume of the United States Code Service where they are arranged first by date and, under that, alphabetically by tribe. The most complete statutory citation of Indian treaties, agreements, and statutes to 1943 is in the reissued Handbook of Federal Indian Law[8] by Felix S. Cohen. Use a List of Treaties and Agreements Made by Indian Tribes with the U.S., by the Institute for the Development of Indian Law, Washington, D.C., 1973.

8. *Digests of international law.* There have been five United States digests of international law. These, in essence, are digests of treaties, court decisions interpreting them, and other official documents, together with a great deal of explanatory comment.

a. *A Digest of International Law. . .*[9] Edited by John Basset Moore, this digest is still an indispensable analysis of international law from the point of view of the United States as it is embodied in official documents. Volume 8 comprises an index by subject, country, person; a list of cases cited; and a list of documents cited.

b. *A Digest of the International Law of the United States.*[10] This digest was compiled by Francis Wharton. Although it is now largely superseded, it is the standard digest. The supplement to the third volume consists of material omitted from the first edition because of inadvertence or new developments after that edition went to press.

c. *Hackworth's Digest of International Law.*[11] Greene H. Hackworth edited this digest. It is an analysis of international law as applied by the United States and is based upon material made available since the publication of Moore. While the order and style of treatment are the same, the material in Moore is not duplicated in this later work. Volume 8 is a general index and table of cases.

d. *Whiteman's Digest of International Law.*[12] Marjorie M. Whiteman's Digest of International Law in turn succeeds, but does not duplicate, Hackworth. Cross-references are, however, made to Hackworth and preceding digests in footnotes at the beginning of each chapter. Because of World War II and the resulting growth of international law, topics covered by Hackworth are greatly expanded by Whiteman. The rapid post–World War II growth in technology has led to the addition of new topics such as air space and outer space. There are many other new headings such as "interdependent independent states." Emphasis is placed on the ever-changing nature and

8. Albuquerque, N.M., University of New Mexico Press, 1971.
9. Washington, D.C., U.S. Gov't Printing Office, 1906, 8 vols.
10. 2d ed., Washington, D.C., U.S. Gov't Printing Office, 1887, 3 vols. and appendix.
11. Washington, D.C., U.S. Gov't Printing Office, 1940–1944, 8 vols.
12. Washington, D.C., U.S. Gov't Printing Office, 1963–1973, 15 vols.

definition of international law. Whiteman's work is considerably more than a digest or paraphrase of rules. There are, for example, copious digest quotations from Department of State publications, U.N. Security Council resolutions, conventions, etc. All of these quotations are tied together by the compiler's editorial comment. The digest consists of fifteen volumes. Volume 15 is a comprehensive index of the entire series.

e. *Digest of United States Practice in International Law.*[13] The 1973 edition of this digest marked the first appearance of this annual publication. The first two volumes were edited by Arthur W. Rovine and published by the Department of State; the Digest of United States Practice in International Law is a continuation of Whiteman's Digest of International Law. The third volume was edited by Eleanor C. McDowell. As its title indicates, the series concentrates on United States practice of international law. Each volume of the series chronicles developments in international law for the particular year under fifteen headings such as International Law in General, the Individual in International Law, State Representation, Law of the Sea and International Waterways, International Economic Law, Environmental and Health Affairs. According to Editor Rovine, "[a]ll sources of international law making have been included. The reader will find material from treaties, executive agreements, legislation, Federal regulations, Federal court decisions, testimony and statements before Congressional and international bodies, diplomatic notes, correspondence, speeches, press conference statements, and international memoranda."

9. *Dates of treaties and other international acts.*

a. *Date of treaty.* There are or may be five critical dates in the progress of a formal United States treaty to adoption: the date of the *signature* by plenipotentiaries of the powers concerned, the date of the *approval* by the Senate by a two-thirds vote of those present, the date of *ratification* by the President, the date of the *exchange of ratification*, and the date of the President's *proclamation* of the treaty. The *date when signed* is that by which a formal treaty is cited by the Department of State and by international lawyers and the date by which it is listed in Shepard's Citations. The *effective date*, unless otherwise indicated in the treaty itself, is the date of United States ratification by the President (or, if exchange of ratifications is called for, that date). The effective date can almost always be determined from the printed text. Even though the effective date frequently is specified in the body of the treaty itself, that date is not, for domestic purposes, binding upon United States courts. In published treaties, the effective date is usually also indicated at some point extraneous to the body of the treaty itself, as in a syllabus or on the title page.

13. Washington, D.C., U.S. Gov't Printing Office, 1974 to date.

b. *Date of executive agreement*. The date of an executive agreement is the date on which it is signed. Since such agreements do not require Congressional consent, the *effective date* of an executive agreement is the one stated in the agreement itself. These dates are indicated on the face or title page of, or in a syllabus to the printed publication as well as in the official indexes.

§6.5. Working with the international acts of the United States.

To the lawyer or law student, working with treaties and executive agreements is likely to be less satisfactory than working with other forms of legislation. In the first place, there is no one single series which publishes all treaties and international acts. Tracing changes in form or status of these acts and determining their judicial interpretation both require consulting more than one citator in some instances.

The procedure followed in researching treaties depends largely upon whether or not the researcher is a municipal lawyer working in a conventional law library or an international lawyer with access to an international law collection which includes the various treaty series. As noted earlier, state courts more often construe treaties in connection with some local matter, than do the federal courts. Most Anglo-American law libraries have some volumes on international law. Even so, most lawyers feel more at home with conventional law books. The municipal lawyer prefers to consult the Statutes at Large and its successor, United States Treaties and Other International Agreements, for the publication of international acts. The international lawyer, on the other hand, tends first to turn to the various other treaty collections, such as the Treaty Series, Executive Agreement Series, Treaties and Other International Acts Series, Malloy or Miller, or those of the League of Nations or United Nations. The municipal lawyer is familiar with Shepard's Citations, the international lawyer with the various official publications of the Department of State described in this chapter.

A municipal lawyer usually knows a treaty by the effective date when ratified by the President and not by the date of the signing. The international lawyer as well as the compilers of most of the citation books think of the treaty in terms of the date of signature. Fortunately, this conflict poses no problem if the treaty is in United States Treaties and Other International Agreements since references in Shepard's Citations are by volume and page of that series.

1. *Finding the text of an international act of the United States*.
   a. *For the municipal lawyer*.
      (1) Statutes at Large (through list in volume 64) or through U.S.C.S. volume for uncodified statutes.

(2) Treaties in Force (latest annual list) gives citations to all treaty collections.
(3) Separate volumes of U.S.T. (consulting index in Kavass, see §6.4).
(4) U.S. Code Congressional and Administrative News (for some treaties).
(5) CCH Congressional Index (for Senate document numbers of treaties before the Senate and not published elsewhere).

b. *For those with access to international law collections.*
(1) Treaties in Force (latest, annual cumulative edition). If citation is not found there, use Kavass, Cumulative Index to Treaties and Other International Agreements of the United States 1776–1949 and its companion volumes. See §6.4 *supra*.
(2) Publications of the Department of State (through the semiannual indexes of this cumulative catalog for treaties not found elsewhere, those not yet in force, etc.).

c. *Special aids for translating citations when date, country or title of treaty is unknown.*
(1) If searcher has the citation to series number (T.S., E.A.S., T.I.A.S.) only, see §6.4.2, Numerical lists.
(2) If a citation is to popular name only, see §6.4.5, Treaties by popular name.
(3) If citation is to Statutes at Large only, it is possible to find other citations through:
(a) List in 64 Stat. B1104 where all international acts published in the Statutes at Large through 1949 are listed by country.
(b) Subject List of Treaties, 1931. (Statutes at Large citations are conspicuously placed in the right-hand column of the numerical list, and generally they occur more or less in order so that a reference to a T.S. number may be obtained. It is possible in the Numerical List of Treaties in Treaty Developments to carry this through 64 Stat.)
(4) If a citation is to U.S.T. only, there is so far no direct means to translate to other forms of citations; if a treaty has been cited in a case, it can be tracked down through Shepard's Citations or, if construed by a state court, through the appropriate state Shepard's Citations.

2. *Shepardizing international acts.*
a. *Information on the status of a treaty.* See §6.4.6.
(1) Consulting the latest Treaties in Force, plus checking

the Department of State Bulletins after that date, gives the best record of the status of treaties in force.

(2) Lawyers usually prefer Shepard's Citations (the section of United States Statutes at Large Not in United States Code or, for acts beginning with 1949, the following section of United States Treaties and Other International Agreements). The Treaties in Force method is quicker; the Shepard's Citation method brings the search down to a later date.

b. *Judicial citation or interpretation of an international agreement by United States or state courts.*

(1) Shepard's Citations: Shepard's United States Citations, for federal court cases, and the various state units for state court cases are the best places of search.

(2) United States Code Service uncodified laws volume for both federal and state cases.

(3) Digest of United States Supreme Court Reports, Lawyers' Edition, for some Supreme Court cases only.

(4) Supreme Court Reporter, Statutes Construed tables for both federal and state court cases.

(5) National Reporter System, Statutes Construed tables, in each individual volume, for both federal and state cases.

(6) State Shepard's Citations for state cases, including those appealed to the federal courts.

(7) U.S. Treaty Developments, for action during 1944–1948, is probably the best source for the years covered.

3. *A simple treaty problem.* Decedent, a resident of Wisconsin, makes the President of the Federal Republic of Germany his residuary legatee, the funds to be used for charitable purposes in Germany. Wisconsin levies an inheritance tax, but the President of Germany resists, claiming exemption under a treaty of friendship and commerce with the United States. Wisconsin asserts that the treaty does not apply.

a. *Finding a treaty which might apply.* The latest edition of Treaties in Force lists under Germany a treaty of friendship and commerce, of December 8, 1923, modified on June 3, 1953, and in part replaced by a treaty of October 29, 1954, and cites four different series in which the treaty and its modifications were published. Being of an earlier date than 1950, the 1923 treaty will also be listed in the table in 64 Stat. B1107–1182. Reading the treaties, you discover that you are interested in Section 1 of the 1923 treaty and in Article 29, Section 2 of the 1954 treaty. Search of the Wisconsin Statutes Annotated reveals that the Wisconsin statute in point is W.S.A. 72.04(1), and that annotations digest a number of cases by Wisconsin courts interpreting that section — so many that it might take some time to determine the one which you are interested in. To check further, you search Shepard's Wisconsin Citations, because its quarterly supplementation brings it closer to date than the annotated statute supplements. You know that the 1923 treaty was published in the Statutes at Large, so in the Wisconsin Shepard's Citations you search the section covering United States Statutes at Large Not in the United States Code, where you find that the treaty has been construed by the Wisconsin Supreme Court in 5 Wis. 2d 363, 92 N.W.2d 819 (1958).

The 1953 and 1954 modifications of the treaty, being of later date than 1949, are published in United States Treaties and Other Agreements, and so you search that section of the Wisconsin citator covering U.S.T. where you are cited to the same case. As a further check, you then search Shepard's United States Citations in the same manner for cases construing the treaty. There you are cited to the same Wisconsin case, even though it has not yet been appealed to the United States Supreme Court. You will note that the state court's interpretation of the treaty is covered in both the United States and Wisconsin Shepard's Citations units. You search all units of these two Shepard's Citations, including all bound and unbound supplements. Then you bring your search several weeks beyond the latest Shepard's Citations by consulting the Statutes Construed tables in the advance sheets of the Supreme Court Reporter and the North Western Reporter (which reports Wisconsin cases), covering later cases than those found in the latest Shepard's supplements. A lengthy comment is in 1960 Wis. L.R. 74.

7 | Federal Administrative Law

§7.1. Administrative rules and regulations.[1]

1. *Impact and functions of administrative law.* Administrative agencies were called by Mr. Justice Robert H. Jackson, a "veritable fourth branch of Government," in his dissent in *F.T.C.* v. *Ruberoid Co.*, 343 U.S. 470, 487; 72 S. Ct. 800, 805; 96 L. Ed. 1081, 1089 (1952).

Administrative law is based on a common-sense recognition that government's business must be transacted efficiently and that Congress must, therefore, delegate some of its authority to the agencies and people who actually transact that business. The authority delegated is administrative, legislative, and judicial. Various agencies of the executive branch of government are given rule-making power as well as the preliminary power to make and enforce the decisions under the rules.

2. *Scope and basis of administrative regulation.* Administrative law or sublegislation includes rules and regulations made by the President and state governors, the heads of lesser government agencies, and the courts. Some of these rules are promulgated by virtue of the inherent power of an agency. Generally, these rules and regulations concern matters of orderly procedure within the agency on the transaction of its business. Most sublegislation, however, is promulgated by authorization and direction of specific legislation. This legislation delegates

1. See §4.5

the necessary administrative powers to the designated officers and agencies.

§7.2. The President as lawmaker.

Both indirectly and directly, the President is an important lawmaker. Indirectly, the President's veto is a type of legislative power. A Presidential veto is rarely overridden and fear of it prevents the passage of those bills likely to be vetoed. The President also legislates directly. Within the very wide Constitutional limitations imposed by the doctrine of separation of powers, Congress may authorize the President, among other things, to conclude reciprocal trade treaties with other nations, raise or lower tariff rates, withdraw public lands from private entry, fix certain prices, and realign or create new federal agencies below the rank of department. Much of the President's rule-making power is delegated to various executive agencies under the President's jurisdiction. This is done under the authority of the Act of August 8, 1950, ch. 646, 64 Stat. 419, 3 U.S.C. §§301–303 (1970 ed.). Under the Constitution, the President has wide power over foreign relations and is also Commander-in-Chief of the Armed Forces.

1. *Forms of Presidential legislation*. They include executive agreements, which are discussed in Chapter 6, reorganization plans and proclamations and executive orders.

a. *Reorganization plans*. In effect, these are Presidential orders which go into effect unless disapproved by either house of Congress within a stated time which, under present law, is sixty days. Under these plans, the President may combine, shift, and even abolish designated agencies of the executive branch of the government which are below the rank of department. The reorganization plan is an old device, but its frequent use is a modern innovation. As offered by the President, it is printed in the Congressional Record, as a House and Senate document, in the Weekly Compilation of Presidential Documents, and in the unofficial United States Code Congressional and Administrative News. These are the usual places of publication of *plans proposed but not yet approved*, as well as those which are later approved (by Congress' failure to disapprove). When approved, they are printed in the Federal Register on the day after their effective date. The Code of Federal Regulations prints them as Presidential documents in Title 3. They appear in the Statutes at Large, in the appendix to Title 5 of the U.S.C., and in annotations to the codified sections of the enabling acts under which they were issued. Because it is the only place where *all approved reorganization plans, of whatever date, are collected*, the appendix to Title 5 is where the search normally begins. Furthermore, Title 5 is the only place where all pertinent documents, such as the enabling act, text of the plan, Presidential messages pertaining to the plans, any necessary executive orders implementing them, historical and revision notes, and editorial notes and cross-references for all plans in force can be found. The transfer of the function of one governmental agency to another by a plan is, together with all necessary editorial matter, noted in a Transfer of Functions note. The Transfer of Functions note is found in the reorganization plan under the agency to which the functions were transferred and usually contains references to the appropriate Code title and section. Plans may also be traced in *Shepard's United States Citations* under the Statutes at Large citation.

b. *Proclamations and executive orders.* A great deal of authority, especially when it has been delegated by Congress by means of specific legislation, is exercised by the President in Presidential proclamations and executive orders. They can vary in importance from an order authorizing the appointment of a minor government employee without regard to Civil Service rules, to one establishing a war emergency agency, such as the Office of Price Administration during World War II. Proclamation No. 3355, of July 6, 1960, "Determining the Cuban Sugar Quota," has had, for example, great effect on our foreign relations. Revocation, revision, or amendment of an executive order is by another executive order. There is no difference in legal effect between a proclamation and an executive order.

(1) *Indexes to Presidential Executive Orders.* Presidential Executive Orders from 1862 to 1938 (numbers 1 to 8030) are indexed in Volume II of Presidential Executive Orders by Clifford L. Lord (et al.), Hastings House, N.Y., 1944. Volume I of the same work contains a chronological list of those orders. Some orders issued prior to the numbering of the series are indexed by subject, intermixed with other messages and papers of the Presidents, in Volume X of Messages and Papers of the Presidents, 1789–1897, by James D. Richardson, U.S. G.P.O., Washington, D.C., 1898. More recent orders are indexed in the Federal Register, in the Weekly Compilation of Presidential Documents (which began publication on August 2, 1965), in Title 3 of the Code of Federal Regulations (beginning with Executive Order 7316), and in the U.S. Code Congressional and Administrative News. When an executive order has directly affected a United States Code section, it is also indexed as a statute in the general index of the Code. This, however, seldom occurs.

(2) *Publication of Presidential Documents.* Some Presidential messages and papers from 1789 to 1897 are published in Richardson's work cited above. More recent Presidential documents are published in the Federal Register and in the Weekly Compilation of Presidential Documents (starting August 2, 1965). Proclamations are published in the Statutes at Large. All Presidential documents are published in the

unofficial United States Code Congressional and Administrative News.

§7.3. Publication of administrative rules:[2] The Federal Register System.

Under the Federal Register Act of 1935, as amended by the Administrative Procedure Act of 1946, no person is bound by the terms of an administrative federal rule of general application unless that person has actual notice or unless the rule has been published in the Federal Register. Established pursuant to the act, the Federal Register is the most inclusive repository of federal administrative legislation. The publications comprising this system are the Federal Register, the Code of Federal Regulations, the Weekly Compilation of Presidential Documents, the U.S. Government Manual, and the Public Papers of the Presidents of the United States.

1. *Federal Register.* The Federal Register publishes the literal text of administrative documents which are promulgated under law. The validity of these documents depends upon such publication. The Register is published on each day following a government working day. In effect, it is the daily supplement to the Code of Federal Regulations. It began publication on March 14, 1936.

a. *Content of the Federal Register.* The following documents are required or authorized to be filed and published: (1) Presidential proclamations and executive orders of general interest in the numbered series as well as any other documents which the President submits or orders to be published; (2) every document which is issued under administrative authority which prescribes a penalty or a course of conduct, confers a right, privilege, authority or immunity, or imposes an obligation, and which is relevant or applicable to the general public, to the members of a class, or to the persons of a locality; (3) documents or classes of documents required by an Act of Congress to be filed and published; (4) other documents which are deemed by the Director of the Federal Register to be of sufficient interest. The text as published in the Federal Register is prima facie evidence of the original text and evidence of the filing. Courts are required to take judicial notice of it. The Federal Register covers only Presidential orders and administrative regulations. It does not include the rules of Congress or of courts.

b. *Arrangement of Material in the Federal Register.* The first few pages of the Federal Register are devoted to (1) a schedule of the days

2. The authors acknowledge with thanks the valuable suggestions made on the Federal Register System by Mr. D. C. Eberhart, former Director, Office of the Federal Register. Please see The Federal Register; What It Is and How To Use It, published by the Office of the Federal Register, National Archives and Records Services, GSA. GPO Washington: 1978.

on which federal agencies will publish documents, (2) a telephone listing to provide additional information and assistance, (3) reminders of rules going into effect and dates of meetings and public hearings, (4) a table of contents, (5) a list of the Code of Federal Regulations (CFR) parts which have been affected by that daily publication of the Federal Register, and (6) a cumulative listing of the CFR parts which have been affected by the month's Federal Register publications. The major portion of the Federal Register is composed of (7) the published federal documents, followed by (8) a listing of the Sunshine Act meetings (since March 1977).

The published federal documents are arranged under four principal headings: Presidential Documents, Rules and Regulations, Proposed Rules, and Notices.

(1) *Presidential Documents* — Proclamations and executive orders are published in this section of the Federal Register.

(2) *Rules and Regulations* — Rules and regulations are arranged in the Federal Register according to the numbered titles of the Code of Federal Regulations (C.F.R.). Rule revision and change occur frequently.

> (a) *Rules of Practice*. Such rules prescribe the procedure which must be followed in transacting business before administrative agencies. If in force at the time of the title's revision, the rules printed in the Federal Register are reprinted in the Code of Federal Regulations. Some are also printed in the United States Code. In addition, most agencies print their own rules separately and will send them free on request. Frequently, however, such pamphlets are not kept up to date. The most complete and current collection of practice rules is that published in Pike and Fischer's Administrative Law, Second Series. Some of the loose-leaf services described in Chapter 23 also print agency rules of practice which are pertinent to their subscribers. Treatises on such subjects as taxation or patents frequently print the rules of practice as appendices.
>
> There is no general heading for Rules of Practice in the index to the Federal Register. Often they are not even listed under the agency concerned. When they are listed, they have been indexed under such odd headings as Organization and Procedure.

(3) *Proposed rules* — Before the adoption of new rules or changes to existing rules, the proposed rules or rule changes are published in the Federal Register in a separate section. These are published in advance of adoption so that those who are affected may register protests or suggest changes. Such proposed changes are listed in the List of Sections Affected.

(4) *Notices* — Along with notices of meetings, agreements filed for approval and notices of opinions and orders, changes in statements of agency organizations are often printed in the notice section.

c. *Federal Register Index*. The Federal Register Index consists of a table of contents arranged alphabetically by agency and selectively by subject. Next to the alphabetical entry in this selective table of contents is the page number of the Federal Register which contains the particular item. The Federal Register Index is published monthly, quarterly, and annually.

In the back of each Federal Register Index is a Cumulative List of Parts Affected, *infra*.

2. *Code of Federal Regulations*. (Cited C.F.R.) The code bears the same relation to the Federal Register as the United States Code does to the Statutes at Large by including rules *actually in force* at the time a particular volume of the C.F.R. is published. If, as is frequently the case, there has been more than one change in a rule during the year, only the form in force at the time of republication is printed in the C.F.R. If the intermediate form or forms of the rule must be located, it is necessary to consult the Federal Register.

The C.F.R. is not as inclusive as the Federal Register in some other aspects: (a) Most descriptions of agency organization are omitted in favor of digests of the statements which are found in the United States Government Manual. Citations to the full statements in the Federal Register are, however, given. (b) Many miscellaneous rules are omitted from the C.F.R. or cited in it only by reference. Some lengthy rules are incorporated by reference only. (c) Even though they often contain statements useful to the public concerned, preliminary statements of policy reasons for the adoption of certain rules are omitted. (d) Proposed rules are omitted.

a. *Format of the Code*. Like the United States Code, the C.F.R. is divided into fifty titles. The first five titles concern government organization. The remaining titles are arranged alphabetically. Even though the internal organization is quite different and the section numbers do not in any way coincide, many of the titles correspond in number to those of the United States Code.

The basic subdivision is into chapters, parts, and sections. The chapters usually bear the names of the agencies administering the rules which are included. The section numbers are formed from the part numbers, plus a decimal point and a subsection. Thus §202.13 is subsection number 13 of Part 202. A full citation would include the title and the section number, e.g., Rules Tariff, 14 C.F.R. §221.102 (1977).

The C.F.R. is revised annually with titles 1 to 16 revised as of January 1; titles 17 to 27 as of April 1, 28 to 41 as of July 1, 42 to 50 as of October 1. When the C.F.R. chapter becomes unwieldy, the chapter will be completely revised.

b. *Current status and statutory basis of Code sections*. It should be emphasized that the C.F.R. is a compilation of rules actually in force at the date of revision. Any sections which have been amended, superseded, terminated, or repealed during the calendar year covered by the annual pamphlet are cited in a brief note, together with the page in the Federal Register printing the original.

A List of Sections Affected at the back of each C.F.R. volume cites all sections of regulations which were affected either directly or indirectly during any preceding calendar year. A separate C.F.R. volume covers the period 1949–1963. Statutes which are the authority for the rules are cited with the rules in the C.F.R. The rules' first place of publication — which is usually in the Federal Register — is also cited.

The C.F.R. Finding Aids section of the index volume contains a table of statutory authority and United States Code authority for the corresponding C.F.R. sections. A second table of value, Presidential Documents Included or Cited in Currently Effective Rules, has been discontinued pending further study. Exhibit 18 is an example of this Table, last revised as of January 1, 1976, and is retained in this edition because it may still be of value in legal research.*

c. *Code of Federal Regulations Index*. There has been great change and improvement in the C.F.R. indexing. Although agency entries are not neglected, the present stress is on catchwords rather than agency. The index is now more like a digest descriptive-word index. It is smaller than the old General Index and is issued annually in pamphlet form.

d. *Cumulative List of C.F.R. Sections Affected*. The Cumulative List of C.F.R. Sections Affected covers regulatory changes published in the Federal Register that have affected the Code of Federal Regulations since the last revision of each volume. Changes in regulations are shown by title, chapter, and section. The Federal Register page where the change appears is provided, as well as a one- or two-word description of how the sections, chapters, etc., are affected. Proposed changes are carried by title and part only, with the Federal Register page where the proposal appears. This publication also includes a Parallel Table of U.S.C.–CFR citations, and a Table of Federal Register Pages and Dates.

3. *Weekly Compilation of Presidential Documents*. The third member of the Federal Register System, the Weekly Compilation of Presidential Documents, has been published each Monday since August 2, 1965. The issues contain Presidential items released up to 5:00 P.M. of the preceding Friday, such as proclamations, executive orders, press conferences, speeches and letters, and memoranda to other members of the executive branch.

An Index of Contents appears at the beginning of each issue. At the end, a Cumulative Index to Prior Issues covers all items from the

*Table II — Presidential Documents — has been suspended. Exhibit 18 is an example of the former table.

beginning of the calendar quarter. Cumulation begins anew with each quarter. Thus, quarterly indexes are published in issue numbers 1, 14, 27, and 40 of each year. There are also separate semiannual and annual indexes. Publication of the C.F.R. and the F.R. is being updated by the use of computer technology. The formats of these indexes may change to provide more detailed information for the user.

4. *United States Government Manual.* An understanding of the mechanics of the government, the names of officials, an awareness of the statutory authority and limitations of a government agency are often of great assistance in beginning a search. The Government Manual's purpose is to keep its users abreast of the current organization, functions, and major personnel of government agencies and of selected quasi-official agencies and international organizations. It prints digests of the more complete statements already printed in the Federal Register. For each agency, it sets forth its mode of creation and its authority — whether under statute, executive order or reorganization plan — and its organization, including major personnel, organization charts, and functions. It is an annual publication.

a. *Index.* There are name, subject, and agency indexes. Appendices include Executive Agencies and Functions . . . Abolished, Transferred, or Terminated Subsequent to March 4, 1933, commonly used abbreviations and acronyms and standard Federal regions. This index is the best starting place to look for determining the statutory origin, organization, functions, and principal personnel of government agencies. Personnel is also covered in a separate index.

5. *Public Papers of the Presidents of the United States.* The last unit of the Federal Register System is the Public Papers series. This is a series of bound volumes, issued annually beginning with the Truman administration in 1945 and continuing through the terms of subsequent Presidents. Their function is to provide a uniform and systematic publication of the Presidential messages and papers essential to an understanding of the laws and the administrative rules of the year covered.

Included in each volume are the State of the Union address, budget and economic messages, and other formal communications to the Congress. Also included are the President's news conferences, Presidential addresses and informal remarks, letters to congressional leaders and to the heads of federal agencies, all "statements by the President," and the public record of meetings with foreign leaders.

All items published in the Public Papers are first published in the Weekly Compilations. Starting with the Public Papers of the Presidents: Jimmy Carter, 1977, for the first time, the full text of executive orders, proclamations, announcements of appointments, and nominations of administration officials is included. In other words, all material printed in the Weekly Compilations of Presidential Documents is now covered by the Public Papers of the Presidents.

Whenever possible, the text is based on original sources. All items are in the public domain, usually by virtue of release by the White House Press Office. Each annual volume is separately indexed.

a. *Index*. Each volume contains a complete subject index. Names of persons and places are listed alphabetically together with analytical entries covering the text of all items. Special categories group classes of items, such as "Veto Messages" or "Statements by the President."

§7.4. Conversion tables.

Conversion tables make it possible (1) to determine what rules have been promulgated under the authority of a given statute, proclamation, or executive order; (2) to determine the statutory basis of any rule; (3) to determine what changes have been made in the form of any established rule; and (4) to some extent, to Shepardize Presidential proclamations and executive orders as well as some administrative regulations. Examine Tables and other lists of the C.F.R. Index Volume, and of each volume in which research is done.

1. *Statute to rule*. As *from* 49 U.S.C. §921 *to* 19 C.F.R. §333. Conversion is made by Table I in the Finding Aids section of the index volume of the C.F.R. It is arranged by United States Code citation, with parallel citation to the C.F.R. rule for which the United States Code is cited as authority. Exhibit 16 gives examples.

Table I—Authorities 8 U. S. C. 1362

United States Code	Code of Federal Regulations
8 U. S. C. 1228	8 CFR Part 212
	Part 231
	Part 235
	Part 238
1229	8 CFR Part 231
	Part 239
	Part 280
1251	8 CFR Part 223a

Exhibit 16

2. *Statute to executive order or proclamation*. In Table 5 of 3A C.F.R. there is a table entitled Statutes Cited as Authority for Presidential Documents. See Exhibit 17.

3. *Presidential proclamations, orders, or reorganization plans to C.F.R.* As *from* Executive Order No. 11012 *to* 41 C.F.R. 101-6000.

United States Statutes at Large—Continued

Date	Citation	Title of Act	Document
1960			
Sept. 13	Joint Res., 74 Stat. 898	National Forest Products Week.	Proc. 4399.
1961			
Apr. 7	75 Stat. 43	Law Day, U.S.A.	Proc. 4364.
Sept. 4	[75 Stat. 424], as amended	Foreign Assistance Act of 1961.	EO 11841.
Do	Sec. 503(a) [75 Stat. 435], as amended.	do	Memorandum of May 20, 1975.
Do	Sec. 504(a) [75 Stat. 436], as amended.	do	Memorandums of June 30, 1975.
Do	Sec. 506(a) [75 Stat. 436], as amended.	do	Memorandum of Jan. 10, 1975.
Do	Sec. 614(a) [75 Stat. 444], as amended.	do	Memorandums of Apr. 25, May 9, 1975.

Exhibit 17

Table II of the now discontinued C.F.R. "Finding Aids" volume lists these Presidential documents by number with their subject matter, C.F.R. title and section number, and comment concerning the nature of the reference. See Exhibit 18. See also §7.3.2b.

4. *Presidential proclamations, orders or reorganization plans to United States Code.* As *from* Executive Order No. 11,788 *to* 12 U.S.C. §1904. This is done, not through a Federal Register System Table, but through Tables IV–VI of the United States Code, and similar tables in the United States Code Annotated and United States Code Service.

5. *Code of Federal Regulations to statutory or Presidential authority.* As *from* 16 C.F.R. §2226.0 *to* 38 Stat. 721, 719; 15 U.S.C. §46, 45; 20 Fed. Reg. 613.

a. *Footnote citation to authority.* Authority is cited for C.F.R. sections, either as a footnote for a single section or as a note preceding a group of sections. See Exhibit 19.

b. *Title 3 table of first edition of C.F.R.* A table in Title 3 of the first edition of the C.F.R., arranged by the C.F.R. title and section number, gives in parallel columns the proclamation or executive order included or cited in the regulation. No statutory authority is cited, and this table was omitted from all supplements and from the second edition, since the same information now accompanies the text of each regulation. Thus Title 3 of the first edition should be retained for reference purposes.

Finding Aids — Table II—Presidential Documents

E. O. No.	Date	F. R. Citation	Subject	Reference	Comment
	1962	**27 F.R.**			
11012	Mar. 27	2983	Performance of certain functions under secs. 1(a) and 1(b) of Administrative Expenses Act of 1946.	41 CFR 101–6.000 Subpart 101–6.1	Cited in text. Cited as authority and in text.
11016	Apr. 25	4139	Authorizing award of Purple Heart	32 CFR 882.25 49 CFR 1.46	Cited in text. Cited in text.
11017	Apr. 27	4141	Providing for coordination with respect to outdoor recreation resources and establishing the Recreational Advisory Council.	32 CFR 263.2	Cited in text.
11021	May 7	4409	Administration of trust territory of Pacific Islands by Secretary of Interior.	32 CFR 761.3	Cited in text.
11030	June 19	5847	Preparation, presentation, filing and publication of Executive orders and proclamations.	15 CFR Ch. XX, App. A	Cited in text.
11035	July 9	6519	Management of Federal office space	41 CFR 101–18.101 Subpart 101–19.8 101–20.001, 101–20.103–1	Cited in text. Cited as authority. Cited in text.
11037	July 20	6967	Amendment of sec. 12 of Executive Order 6260 of Aug. 28, 1933, as amended.	31 CFR Part 54	Cited as authority.
11038	July 23	7003	Continuing in effect Executive Order No. 10945 of May 24, 1961, relating to Administration of Export Control Act of 1949, as amended.	15 CFR Parts 368–399	Cited as authority.
11041	Aug. 6	7859	Peace Corps; continuance and administration in the Department of State.	1 CFR App. A, XXII–1.2 22 CFR Parts 302–305	Cited in text. Cited as authority.
11046	Aug. 24	8575	Authorizing award of Bronze Star Medal	32 CFR 882.25 49 CFR 1.46	Cited in text. Cited in text.

Exhibit 18

Chapter XIV—Commodity Credit Corporation § 1421.430

the provisions of the note, shall be paid by the producer to the county office which approved the loan, unless the deficiency is one which will be assumed by CCC pursuant to the terms of the note.

§ 1421.406 Farm storage interim loan rate.

The farm storage interim loan rate for Flue-cured tobacco shall be that set forth in the annual crop year supplement.

Subpart—1976 Crop Flue-Cured Tobacco Farm-Stored Loan Supplement

AUTHORITY: Secs. 4 and 5, 62 Stat. 1070, as amended (15 U.S.C. 714 b and c); Secs. 101, 107, 301, 401, 405, 63 Stat. 1051, as amended (7 U.S.C. 1441, 1445, 1421, and 1423).

SOURCE: 41 FR 36807, Sept. 1, 1976, unless otherwise noted.

§ 1421.420 Availability.

A producer desiring a farm storage loan on his eligible Flue-cured tobacco stored in Alabama, Florida, Georgia, North Carolina, South Carolina, and Virginia must request a loan at the county ASCS office not later than November 1, 1976.

tobacco security the loan. (2) Delivery, as directed by CCC, during a period of approximately 1 week beginning immediately after the close of the 1976 auction marketing season to a cooperative association designated by CCC of a quantity of Flue-cured tobacco eligible for price support having a settlement value equal to the outstanding principal balance of the loan.

(b) Notwithstanding the provisions of § 1421.23 of the general regulations, no deduction for storage charges will be made if the tobacco is delivered during this period. The association will advise producers of the time and place at which the tobacco is to be delivered in liquidation of farm storage loans and will determine the settlement value of the tobacco delivered on the basis of the grade and quality thereof as determined by the inspection service of the Agricultural Marketing Service, USDA.

§ 1421.424 Delivery charge.

Notwithstanding the provisions of § 1421.11 of the general regulations, there shall be no delivery charge on the

Exhibit 19

6. *Changes in form or status of published rules: Revisions revocations.* Tables performing somewhat the role of the Shepard's Citations legislative history notations are necessary and have been provided.

a. *Shepard's Citations.* If a rule is cited in connection with a Statutes at Large or Code section in a judicial decision, it is covered as a Statutes at Large or Code section in Shepard's United States Citations. That, however, rarely occurs. Presidential proclamations, reorganization plans, and executive agreements may be identified through Tables IV–VI of the United States Code and the comparable tables in the unofficial editions of the Code. The procedure is to consult the table of Presidential documents which is included in the Code and then to Shepardize the Code section with which the document is identified.

b. *National Reporter System Tables of Statutes Construed.* Presidential proclamations and executive orders as well as administrative regulations which have been the subject of litigation are covered by the tables which are found both in the advance sheets and in the bound volumes of the National Reporter System.

c. *United States Supreme Court Reports, Lawyers' Edition, Desk Book.* Supreme Court decisions construing the orders and rules noted above are covered in the Table of Federal Laws, Rules and Regulations Cited and Construed.

CHAPTER XII—STATISTICAL REPORTING SERVICE
(AGRICULTURAL STATISTICS)
DEPARTMENT OF AGRICULTURE

PART 1300—PEANUT STATISTICS

Sec.
1300.1 Scope of regulations.
1300.2 Definitions.
1300.3 Persons required to submit reports; forms to be used; where available.
1300.4 Time when reports are due.

AUTHORITY: The provisions of this Part 1300 issued under sec. 6, 49 Stat. 1899; 7 U.S.C. 956.

SOURCE: The provisions of this Part 1300 appear at 23 F.R. 2375, Apr. 11, 1958. Redesignated at 28 F.R. 4788, May 14, 1963.

§ 1300.1 Scope of regulations.

Under the act of June 24, 1936, as of the United States who is authorized to exercise the powers and to perform the duties of the Secretary of Agriculture under the act.

§ 1300.3 Persons required to submit reports; forms to be used; where available.

(a) The following persons are required to submit monthly reports, as follows:

(1) Peanut cleaners, shellers, crushers and manufacturers of crude peanut oil, peanut cake and meal are required to report on Form C. E. 6-18 "A", Peanut Stocks and Processing Report, inventories, receipts and disposition of

Exhibit 20

d. *Loose-leaf services*. Commercial loose-leaf services not only note changes in form, such as amendments and revocations of rules, but cite and discuss decisions concerning them.

7. *Determination of the present form of a federal rule or regulation*. This is one of the most important and frequent tasks the worker with federal administrative rules and regulations has to perform. Because of the monthly day-to-day cumulation of the List of Parts Affected which is found in each issue of the Federal Register, it is a less laborious task now than it was formerly.

It should be emphasized that the C.F.R. is a compilation of rules actually in force at the date of publication of the annual compilations. Any sections which have been amended, superseded, terminated or repealed during the calendar year covered by the annual pamphlet are cited therein in a brief note, together with the page in the Federal Register printing the original. See Exhibit 20 *supra*.

The search normally begins with the volume of the appropriate title of the C.F.R. containing the desired rule or regulation. Then the pamphlet entitled *LSA: List of CFR Sections Affected* is consulted by CFR title, chapter, part, and section. It is cumulated quarterly. See Exhibit 21. Then check the *Cumulative List of C.F.R. Parts Affected* appearing in the front of the latest daily issue of the Federal Register

List of Sections Affected

All sections in this volume of the Code of Federal Regulations which were affected by documents published in the Federal Register since January 1, 1964, are enumerated in the following list. Entries indicate the nature of the changes effected. Page numbers refer to Federal Register pages.

For the period before January 1, 1964, see the "List of Sections Affected, 1949–1963," which is published in a separate volume.

1964

17 CFR	29 F.R. Page
Chapter I:	
150.10	
Added	15571
Chapter II:	
200.11	
(b) amended	11579
200.15	
Revised	5276
200.18	
Revised	15282
200.20	
Revised	15282
200.21	
Amended	5276

17 CFR—Continued	29 F.R. Page
Chapter II—Continued	
201.7	
(e) revised	9487
201.8	
(b) and (c) revised	9487
201.9	
(d) revised	9487
(b) redesignation as (b)(1); (b)(2) added	13422
201.11	
Heading and (d) and (e) revised	3567
(d) and (e) revised	9488
201.12	
Heading and (a) revised	3567
(d) added	9488

Exhibit 21

for changes published after the monthly LSA pamphlet coverage. See Exhibit 22. For example, you may be researching a problem in the beginning of October; first you checked the CFR title; second, you checked the LSA pamphlet for September and the quarterly pamphlet; third, you checked the latest daily issue of the Federal Register in October. If in your research the LSA pamphlet was for August, remember to check the last September issue of the Federal Register for the *Cumulative List of C.F.R. Parts Affected* as well as the latest October daily issue of the Federal Register.

8. *Citators for rules: subsequent judicial history*. Changes in form of rules which would correspond to the conventional citators' "legislative history" notations were discussed in the preceding section. To find the "judicial history" (that is, the interpretation or construction of such a substantive rule by a court) is, with very few exceptions, virtually impossible, or at least impracticable, by tabular means.

§7.5. Other sources of federal rules publication.

Printed copies of regulations and rules of practice are distributed by some federal agencies. These publications cover the agency's own

CUMULATIVE LIST OF CFR PARTS AFFECTED DURING APRIL–JUNE

The following numerical guide is a list of parts of each title of the Code of Federal Regulations affected by documents published during April–June.

1 CFR

Ch. I.......... 13865, 18535, 23701
305.......... 27507

PROPOSED RULES:
465.......... 23583

3 CFR

DETERMINATIONS:
April 22, 1978.......... 17789

EXECUTIVE ORDERS:
11126.......... 14431
11189.......... 21315
11195.......... 21315
11832.......... 14431
11861.......... 21315
11888.......... 15127
11902.......... 20947
11903.......... 20949
11972.......... 20949
11993.......... 20949
11995.......... 21315
12022.......... 15133
12050.......... 14431, 19811
12051.......... 15131

3 CFR—Continued

PROCLAMATIONS—Continued
4567.......... 18533
4568.......... 19999
4569.......... 20215
4570.......... 20473
4571.......... 21313
4572.......... 21999
4573.......... 23553
4574.......... 25413
4575.......... 25987

REORGANIZATION PLANS:
No. 1 of 1978.......... 19807

4 CFR

331.......... 16149, 24819
401.......... 24820
402.......... 24820
403.......... 24820
404.......... 24820
405.......... 24820
406.......... 24820
407.......... 24820
408.......... 24820

7 CFR—Continued

300.......... 26411
301.......... 15607, 25135
401.......... 14638, 14639, 15319, 18536, 18537, 19337, 26561
410.......... 20781
414.......... 16693, 18537
656.......... 26277, 27158
719.......... 18159
724.......... 16310, 19338, 28429
725.......... 19339
726.......... 19339
728.......... 28430
730.......... 16968, 26412
775.......... 28431
795.......... 19339, 16968
905.......... 17797, 20475, 24821
907.......... 14435, 15407, 16697
908.......... 14435, 15407, 16698, 17935, 19193, 19643, 20218, 21636, 22330, 23701, 24822, 25789, 26689, 28169
910.......... 14303, 14640, 15608, 16968, 17798, 18160,

Exhibit 22

particular activities. Loose-leaf services do the same for the subject matter covered by them. The most complete current unofficial publication of Presidential proclamations and executive orders is in the United States Code Congressional and Administrative News, which also publishes some administrative regulations of general interest.

§7.6. Administrative agency rulings and opinions.

Written opinions and orders through which administrative agencies construe and apply the laws and regulations they administer parallel in form those of conventional courts. Though less formal, the procedure of agencies and their quasi-judicial tribunals closely resembles that of conventional courts.

1. *Scope of administrative rulings*. The rulings of a given agency may relate only to the internal affairs of the agency itself in the transaction of its business or may regulate the relations of the government with private citizens or of citizens with each other. On the one hand, a ruling may be an office opinion or memorandum which means it is effective only regarding matters which relate to internal procedure. The chief law officer of the federal or state government may, on the other hand, lay down advisory interpretations for outside application. Opinions of the Attorney General are such interpretations. Decisions and orders effective outside the government proper range from patent grants and public utility rate regulations to regulatory decisions under specific statutes.

2. *Publication of administrative agency rulings*. Many agencies publish their rulings. When printed in full, they so closely resemble reported court decisions in form that they require little additional comment here. They may appear in any or all of the following forms.

a. *Press releases*. These are ordinarily mimeographed and circulated to newspapers and others interested within a day or two of the decision. They commonly contain a brief statement of facts which is followed by a paraphrase of the arguments of counsel, an abridgment of the opinion, and the decision.

b. *Advance sheet reports of decisions*. These reports give either long abridgments of the full opinion or, more commonly, the complete decision and order, minus a syllabus but with all footnotes. There is some serial designation by which they may be cited. Usually this includes the volume number of the report series in which the decision will eventually appear and a case number. Page numbers of printed reports are undetermined when advance sheet reports are distributed. As a result, an advance sheet decision of the N.L.R.B. would be cited 97 N.L.R.B. No. 72.

c. *Printed slip decisions*. These are generally in the final and complete form which will be found in the later-published bound cumulations. Such publication is not common.

d. *Advance sheet pamphlets and bulletins.* The content and frequency of rulings in this form vary from agency to agency. Some contain both agency and court decisions. Only agency decisions and rules of practice, dockets of impending hearings, etc., are found in others.

e. *Bound volumes of agency rulings.* The preliminary unbound form of an agency ruling is almost always superseded by a bound volume, duplicating in all essential features the bound volumes of court reports.

f. *Unofficial publication of agency rulings.* The impact of administrative law is such that those affected, or their attorneys, must have speedy access to all aspects of it — the law, the rules and regulations, and decisions. Loose-leaf services which cover such areas as labor law, trade regulations, taxation, public utilities law, environmental law are the best answer to this need. At the end of a given period, the decisions reported in these services may be cumulated and bound. This is done for labor, tax, environmental law, utilities, trade regulation decisions, energy, and many other areas.

Legal periodicals frequently publish federal or state (or both) court and agency adjudications. For state regulatory agencies these may be the best or even the only printed reports available. Examples of such periodicals publishing such adjudications are: the Public Utilities Fortnightly and the Federal Communications Bar Journal.

g. *Administrative law digests.* Court decisions involving administrative law are digested under appropriate subject headings in conventional case digests covering these courts.

(1) *American Digest System.* (See §16.5.) Cases involving administrative law are collected, beginning with the Fifth Decennial in the Administrative Law and Procedure title. These are, however, only court decisions and not agency rulings. Since not all material deemed by the searcher as classifiable under this title may in fact be digested here, the searcher should still consult the Descriptive-Word Index.

(2) *Agency special-subject digests.* Most official and unofficial publication series of agency rulings have digests of some kind. Often it is only the index digest found in each bound volume, so that a complete coverage requires the examination of numerous single volumes. Some federal agencies cumulate this digest material at irregular intervals and, for the periods covered, such digests are extremely useful. The most useful digests of official agency decisions are apt to be commercial ones. Such are the Consolidated Digest of Decisions Under the Interstate Commerce Act,[3] and supplements covering decisions

3. Fowler, Ind., H. C. Lust Co.

from 1887 to date, and the Lois G. Moore, Tax Court Digest and annual pocket supplements.[4]

More common are the digests which are part of unofficial editions of agency rulings. Examples are the cumulative digests of the United States Patents Quarterly and the Labor Relations Cumulative Digest and Index of the (unofficial) Bureau of National Affairs.

(3) *Pike & Fischer Administrative Law Service.*[5] This is a service for the procedural, not the substantive, aspects of administrative law. While it covers the decisions of six federal courts and twenty-four administrative agencies (beginning with 1948), the approach is to procedure generally, rather than to specific agencies. The four-volume Consolidated Digest covers both series, and has annual pocket supplements. Beginning with the Second Series of the Service in 1951 there are annual bound volumes of new cases, collecting reports of both court and agency decisions on administrative procedure. All material is keyed to the Administrative Procedure Act, but its scope is somewhat wider. Current Material (loose-leaf) contains the text and headnotes of current opinions and decisions of courts and agencies. A loose-leaf Desk Book contains the digests of current cases not yet incorporated in the Consolidated Digest supplements, the text and legislative history of the Administrative Procedure Act, the text of other relevant acts, and the rules of practice of some twenty-four agencies. There is also a newsletter.

h. *Citators*. Shepard's Administrative Citations, which began in 1967, covers decisions and orders of selected federal administrative agencies. Commercial loose-leaf services may also offer citator information.

4. Indianapolis, Ind., Bobbs-Merrill, 1951 to date.
5. Albany, N.Y., Matthew Bender & Co., 1941–1948, 5 vols.; New York, Pike & Fischer, Second Series, 1952 to date. Decisions, Digest, Current Material, Desk Book.

8 Federal Court Rules and Rules of Federal Administrative Agencies

§8.1. Function, authority, and nomenclature of rules of court and administrative agencies.

Rules of practice govern both the procedure of getting into a court or before an administrative agency and the conduct of business when there. They assist in the proper and expeditious transaction of business. They are so important that failure to proceed in accordance with them may be an automatic bar. Successful practice before government agencies like the Patent Office or the Interstate Commerce Commission often depends more upon a thorough knowledge of their rules of practice than of the substantive law involved.

1. *Rule-making power generally*. There has been much question whether and to what extent the power to make court rules resides in the legislatures or in the courts themselves. The courts stress their inherent powers and assert that the doctrine of separation of powers in this country limits the legislatures' control. The weight of judicial authority is that the courts do have inherent power to make reason-

able rules. On the other hand, the rules must conform to and be subordinate to legislation which is constitutional in the jurisdiction where enacted. Significantly, the federal rules of civil procedure (effective September 16, 1938) and of criminal procedure (effective February 1, 1941), written for the guidance of the district courts, were promulgated under an enabling act of Congress.

2. *Authority of rules of court.* Rules of court which are not inconsistent with enactments of the legislature have the force and effect of statutes. Any rule inconsistent with a statute is inoperative. Rules prescribed for district courts by the United States Supreme Court by virtue of 18 U.S.C. §3771 and 28 U.S.C. §2072 (1970) supersede existing statutes repugnant to them. Rules of court made and published are said to have the force of law and are binding on the court and the parties to the action. *District of Columbia* v. *Roth,* 18 U.S. App. D.C. 547, 553 (1901).

3. *Nomenclature of rules of court.* Rules of court may be called rules of practice or rules of procedure. The term is often used interchangeably with federal or state codes of procedure which are direct enactments of the legislature not promulgated by the courts. Even though adopted by the courts pursuant to a legislative directive, the court rules in some jurisdictions are incorporated into the procedural codes. The distinction should be maintained, however, between a code of procedure enacted by law and the rules of the court operating under that code and implementing it.

§8.2. Federal court rules.

The statutory authority for federal court rules has been noted above. The Supreme Court of the United States has promulgated rules for its own court and the separate lower federal courts. The civil procedure and criminal procedure rules are for use in federal district courts and the admiralty rules for use in admiralty cases.

1. *District court rules and Courts of Appeals rules for individual courts.* The federal court rules promulgated by the Supreme Court are for the general guidance of the courts. Since the individual Courts of Appeals in their circuits and the federal district courts throughout the country encounter special local conditions and circumstances, these courts are empowered by 28 U.S.C. §2071 (1970) to make their own special rules, not inconsistent with the rules of general application laid down for them by the Supreme Court. Such rules as are promulgated by the several circuits are easily found, but those of the district courts are not. See §8.4.

§8.3. Rules of practice of quasi-judicial agencies and their tribunals.

Agency rules prescribe procedure before examiners or other agency officials in the transaction of business before their agencies and for appealing from adverse office decisions to one or more quasi-judicial tribunals within the office. Knowledge of the rules and compliance with them are presumed, and many agencies have their own administrative bars which regulate the admission and conduct of agents or attorneys representing clients before them. While qualifications for admission to some of these administrative bars consist only of evidence of good character, they are very strict for such agencies as the United States Patent Office. Agency rules of practice affect two aspects of administrative procedure, both of which can be illustrated by Patent Office practice.

The first aspect regulates the routine operation of getting the applicant's business done in the Office: the form of application for a patent, the oath and fees, correspondence with the Office concerning the application, and the like. The second provides for appeal from an adverse decision of patent examiners to the quasi-judicial tribunals of the Office. From these tribunals an appeal lies to the Court of Customs and Patent Appeals, which ranks as a United States Court of Appeals.

Administrative agencies promulgating rules of practice include such agencies as the Interstate Commerce Commission, the Tax Court (an administrative agency, not a true court), and the Federal Trade Commission. While procedure before these quasi-judicial tribunals is apt to be somewhat less formal than in the courts, it is nonetheless parallel in most respects. The rules are often detailed and voluminous, occupying as many as 150 pages of text for some agencies. The power to promulgate rules of practice is granted federal agencies by Section 3a of the Administrative Procedure Act. They are published in the Federal Register.

§8.4. Availability of published court and agency rules.

1. *Federal Register*. Federal agency rules are not binding upon persons affected unless they have actual notice or unless the rules have been published in the Federal Register. This official newspaper, described in Chapter 7, was established for the publication of administrative rules and orders of general effect. Court rules are not published in the Register, because courts are not administrative agencies. At the end of each year, rules which were originally published in the Federal Register are cumulated in the Code of Federal Regulations, described in §7.3. They are not court rules.

2. *Court or agency distribution.* Many courts and quasi-judicial administrative agency tribunals distribute their rules in pamphlet form, free on application. Aside from the Federal Rules Service which is an unofficial publication described in §8.5, this is often the only source for local federal district court rules.

3. *In statute compilations.* Federal court rules are printed in the United States Code. They are found there by using the general index. The U.S.C.A. and the U.S.C.S. both publish court rules. With the exception of local court rules, rules for specific courts as well as the general rules are included. The rules of practice of some of the quasi-judicial administrative tribunals are printed and indexed. Much historical and other editorial matter is supplied; in addition, the U.S.C.A. and the U.S.C.S. annotate the rules to cases and Attorney Generals' opinions.

4. *In law reports.* Except for the rules of the Courts of Appeals and of individual district courts, federal court rules and their amendments are printed in the United States Reports, the Supreme Court Reporter, and the Supreme Court Reports, Lawyer's Edition. A unit of the National Reporter System, the Federal Rules Decisions prints federal court rules of general application and their amendments which are promulgated by the Supreme Court.

Shepard's United States, Federal, and state Shepard's Citations cover court rules and indicate where in the law reports they are printed.

5. *In loose-leaf services.* The Federal Rules, described below in §8.5, collects texts of local federal district court rules. On the whole, this is the most convenient compilation of such rules. Agency rules are published in Pike & Fischer's Administrative Law Service which is described in §7.6.2g(3).

6. *In commentaries on the rules.* Separate treatises on the rules and encyclopedias of procedure which comment on the rules also include the texts of rules. Local practice books commonly print the text of rules in effect in their jurisdiction.

7. *In volumes collecting the rules.* Federal court rules, including those of the circuits of the Courts of Appeals, but not those of the individual district courts, are published as separate volumes of the United States Supreme Court Reports Digest[1] and the United States Supreme Court Digest.[2] The Federal Court Rules Annotated[3] is an annotated manual which includes state court decisions on federal court rules.

8. *Finding lists of court and agency rules.* The index below refers to the paragraphs in §8.4 in which the places of publication of the men-

1. Rochester, N.Y., Lawyers Co-operative Publishing Co.
2. St. Paul, Minn., West Publishing Co.
3. Indianapolis, Ind., Bobbs-Merrill Co., Inc., 2d ed., 1963, 2 vols.

tioned rules are noted directly or by implication. The relative values of these sources are largely a matter of the frequency and fullness of supplementation.

Administrative Agencies, 1, 2, 3, 5
Admiralty, 2, 3, 5, 7
Civil procedure, federal, 3, 4, 5, 6, 7
Copyright, 2, 3
Court of Claims, 2, 3, 7
Courts of Appeals, local rules, 2, 3, 5
Criminal procedure, federal, 3, 4, 5, 6, 7
Customs Court, 2, 3, 7
District Courts, local rules, 2, 3, 5
District of Columbia Court of Appeals, 2, 3, 7
Emergency Court of Appeals, 2, 3, 7
General Orders in Bankruptcy, 3, 4, 7
Military Appeals Court, 2, 3, 7
Tax Court of the United States, 2, 3, 7

§8.5. Decisions construing court rules.

Decisions of federal, state, and quasi-judicial tribunals construing their rules of procedure are usually printed in the same law reports that cover the decisions of such tribunals generally. There are, however, two special reporters which print only decisions which construe federal court rules.

1. *Federal Rules Decisions*. The decisions of federal courts construing rules of civil and criminal procedure are printed in this unit of the National Reporter System. The decisions appearing in this series are only those which have not been printed in the Federal Reporter or the Federal Supplement. Each advance sheet and bound volume of this reporter, however, cites the cases in all federal courts construing each rule. Articles on the federal rules are printed or reprinted from other sources in this reporter.

2. *Federal Rules Service*. This is a loose-leaf service, published by Pike & Fischer, which is devoted entirely to decisions construing the federal rules of civil procedure. In one unit it combines the functions of a law reporter, a digest, and a citator. Usually the material for a period is cumulated annually into a bound volume of decisions. Indexing is from the beginning of the service in 1939. A second series began in 1958.

The service is organized around a copyrighted device called the Federal FindeX. It serves somewhat the same functions for this service as the copyrighted Key Number of the West Publishing Company for case digests generally. The service is organized around the FindeX and comprises a weekly news release, a cumulative table of cases, the text of federal decisions construing the rules, the Local Court Rules in Force, a word index giving a fact approach, and a Federal Rules Service Digest covering all federal court cases decided since the adoption of the Federal Rules of Civil Procedure in 1938. As already noted, the Local Court Rules collection is the most convenient repository of the local rules of the various federal district courts. The Digest is arranged by Rule number.

§8.6. Citation books for court rules.

Court rules are treated as statutes in citators. That is, two aspects of such rules are or may be covered: (1) amendments to and repeals of existing rules are noted along with additional new rules; and (2) cases construing the rules are cited and, in some citators, digested.

1. *Shepard's United States, Federal and state Citations*. Shepard's United States, Federal and all state citations of the Shepard's Citations treat court rules as they do statutes by noting changes in text and by citing to cases construing the rules. Comments on the rules by law journals within the jurisdiction and several representative ones chosen at large from other jurisdictions are also noted. As with other forms of statutes, cases annotating earlier forms of rules are, as far as possible, brought over to annotate the corresponding current form. The place of publication in the official reports of the jurisdiction in which the latest revision of the rules is published is also noted.

2. *Statutory compilations printing rules of court*. Amendments, repeals, and new rules are customarily noted. Annotated editions of statutes digest decisions construing each rule.

3. *Commentaries on the rules*. These serve some of the purposes of the citator. Unlike citators, however, they usually are not in tabular form.

4. *Loose-leaf services*. The Federal Rules Service FindeX is a citator.

5. *Tables of Statutes construed*. In all National Reporter System advance sheets and bound volumes there are tables which cover the interpretation of court rules. These tables are not, however, cumulative and cover only each particular volume.

6. *United States Supreme Court Bulletin*. This is a Commerce Clearing House loose-leaf publication which, among its other functions, annotates Supreme Court rules.

§8.7. Suggested routine for search of court rules.

1. *Finding the rules of a given court or agency*. The rules will be found either as a part of a statutory compilation covering the appropriate jurisdiction or in a separate manual of court rules. If there is doubt, consult the list in §8.4.8. Rules of quasi-judicial tribunals are often part of the rules of practice of the agency served. If of general application, the practice rules for federal agencies are published in

the United States Code of Federal Regulations. The Federal Register and the Code of Federal Regulations are described in Chapter 7.

2. *Ascertaining the latest form of a rule.* The current form of a court rule will ordinarily be found through the supplementary service to annotated editions of the statutes or in the editorial notes in unannotated editions. The Shepard's Citations unit notes amendments, repeals, and additions to the rules, and cites the official law report in which court rules are published. Both the National Reporter System advance sheets and the Federal Rules Service current supplementary sheets print federal court rules and amendments of general application.

Finding the latest form of a federal administrative rule is somewhat more complicated. It is done through the Code of Federal Cumulative List of C.F.R. Sections for the Code of Federal Regulations and for each issue of the Federal Register. See §7.4.7.

3. *Finding citations to decisions construing a rule.* This may be done through Shepard's Citations, the table of Statutes Construed in the National Reporter System, annotated rules which are usually found in annotated statute compilations, the Federal Rules Service, and, as commentaries, in treatises covering the rules.

4. *Finding a textual discussion of a rule.* There are many ways of doing this. Probably practice books are the best. For example, Moore's Federal Practice[4] and Wright's Federal Practice and Procedure[5] discuss at length all the federal rules of civil procedure with exhaustive comment based upon the cases. Shorter treatments do the same thing to a lesser extent. Local practice books cover the law of a state or region and include court rules. Law reviews are a source of learned discussion of court rules. The Federal Rules Decisions prints or reprints articles on various aspects of the Federal Rules of Civil Procedure.

4. Albany, N.Y., Matthew Bender & Company, Inc., 1975–
5. St. Paul, Minn., West Publishing Co., 1969–1977.

9 State Legislation, Administrative Law, and Court Rules

§9.1. Similarity to federal legislative forms.

What has been written in this book about conventional federal legislation and its publication is essentially true also of state legislation. Differences relate to the chronological period covered, frequency of statutory compilations, and availability of legislative history sources. Long before the establishment of the Union in 1776, the colonies had published their legislation regularly. The lawyer and law student are, however, seldom concerned with colonial legislation. Legislation dating from 1776 is readily available, both in session law and compiled forms. The states have been less conservative than the United States in compiling their statutes in subject arrangement. In most states, there have been many editions of session laws and compilations. Although most states publish some sort of status table during legislative sessions, legislative history sources are notable by their absence. Until recently, only a minority of states published compilations of administrative regulations similar to those of the Code of Federal Regulations. Now, however, well over two-thirds of the states and territories have such compilations in varying forms. State court rules are published in various forms by all the states and territories.

§9.2. Constitutions.

State constitutions are published in statutory compilations. When, as is frequently the case, there have been several different constitutions, all are published.

Research with constitutions is facilitated by (1) Constitutions of the United States, National and State (Dobbs Ferry, N.Y., Oceana Publications, Inc., 1962, 2 vols., loose-leaf), which publishes the full text of the *latest* constitutions and amendments, with brief notes on the history and sources of each constitution; (2) Index of State Constitutions (2d ed., Edwards, New York, 1959), which is very detailed; (3) A Selective Bibliography on State Constitution Revision; Compiled by Balfour Halevy (New York, 1963); and (4) A Selective Bibliography on State Constitutional Revision; Compiled by Myron Fink for the New Mexico Constitutional Revision Commission (September, 1966) (which is, in effect, an updating of Halevy for 1963–1966).

1. *Amendments to state constitutions*. Amendments are frequent. Their text is printed in all state statutory compilations. As submitted to the voters in most states, the text of proposed amendments is printed in the session laws and referenced in Shepard's Citations for the respective states. Since most amendments so submitted are not ratified, a careful check must be made of the status of proposed amendments. Shepard's Citations state units cover constitutions just as they do other legislation and include amendments as well as proposed amendments and their adoption. Citations to later revisions and amendments of state constitutions are given in the biennial Book of the States which is published by the Council of State Governments, with a list of recent treatises and documents.

2. *Judicial history of state constitutions*. Constitutions are covered by the various kinds of citators described in Chapter 18, including Shepard's Citations, certain Supreme Court digests, and the Table of Statutes Construed in all units of the National Reporter System.

§9.3. State session laws.

Every state publishes its session laws under such titles as Acts and Resolves, Laws, Public Laws, Acts and Joint Resolutions, etc. These are not legal words of art, but all designate the enactments of the state legislature concerned at a regular or special session. Regular session periods are held annually or biennially and are supplemented by special sessions necessitated by emergency conditions in war, times of financial stress, etc. Usually, the laws of a special session are combined with those of a regular session in a single volume.

1. *Slip laws.* Very few states officially publish their laws. For an increasing number of states, however, the publisher of the annotated edition of the state statutes publishes an advance sheet, "session law service," in which the latest enactments are printed in session law form. This is in addition to the pamphlet supplements to the compiled statutes which contain the latest annotations to cases interpreting statutes existing in code form.

2. *Session laws proper.* Enactments — public, private, and local laws and resolutions — are usually published in a single volume. Some states, however, publish local, public, and private laws in separate volumes. Usually the resolutions — which in some states lack the force of law — follow the acts and are separately numbered. In some states the current enactments are published in classified order (as in Kansas) and follow the classification of the statutory compilation. By far the greater number, however, arrange the session laws in the bound volumes in chronological order, by date of approval, as in the United States Statutes at Large.

a. *Content of session law volumes.* All have subject indexes and tables of chapters or acts in numerical order. Many session law volumes have tables of statutory revisions or code titles and sections amended and repealed. Other tables may include amendments and repeals of uncodified laws, allocation of session laws into the state code, bills maturing into laws during the session, and data concerning the legislature and legislators.

b. *Unofficial editions of session laws.* In connection with the publication of their annotated laws and current pamphlet law service, the commercial publishers employed by some states compile volumes of the laws enacted during a session and include allocation tables to the compilation as well as texts of communications by state officials or private institutions or individuals favoring or opposing legislation enacted during the sessions. Since these volumes usually precede the publication date of the official session laws by several months and since the communications are at least some aid in legislative history research, they can be extremely useful.

c. *Authority of session laws.* See §9.9.

§9.4. State statutory compilations.

State compilations follow in form and content the United States Code pattern of "public general and permanent" laws, arranged by subject. Their status as legal authority varies from state to state depending upon whether they have been reenacted as positive law or are only certified copies of the original session laws. They are variously called Codes, Revisions, Compilations, Consolidations, General Statutes, or Statutes, according to the preference of the legislatures. These are not, however, legal words of art and their status depends upon the authority conferred upon them by the legislature in each case.

1. *Status of the compilations as law*. See §9.9.

2. *Content of state compilations: Statutes and court rules*. All the state statutes needed by the lawyer in practice are included. These comprise statutes of public general and permanent interest, omitting obsolete material, appropriation acts, and statutes of no general interest. Court rules are commonly included. Constitutions, federal and state, together with pre-statehood organic charters, are usually found at the beginning of the compilation. The Magna Carta is frequently found here. Uncodified laws, usually relating to the business of government, may be published in a separate volume, as are McKinney's New York Unconsolidated Laws.

3. *Content of state compilations: Editorial matter and case annotations*. Editorial matter in *official compilations* is likely to be a brief notation of the origins of the various statute sections with an occasional cross-reference to or note of amendment or repeal. These notes are likely to be of limited value and for most purposes must be supplemented by an unofficial annotated edition. This is particularly true when the searcher is tracing the history of a statute section, its evolution from the original session law, and its subsequent amendment.

a. *Editorial matter*. This usually includes the derivation of each statute section from its earlier forms with occasional excerpts from revisers' notes which explain why changes were made. Pertinent law review articles may be cited, as well as legal encyclopedia and American Law Reports comment. Essays on the law of the state by members of the local bar are found in some annotated editions. Some compilations print a compilation of rules of practice of official and unofficial boards in addition to statutory forms.

b. *Case annotations*. These vary from none at all to complete case digests which cover both federal and state courts and the opinions of the state attorney general. West Publishing Company and affiliated company editions copy or paraphrase, without the Key-Number, National Reporter System case headnotes. The classification schemes for state statutory compilations frequently change, sometimes radically, between editions. In such instances, case digests under the old classification system are taken over into the new if there is a place there for them. It sometimes happens, however, that a presumably obsolete old section is omitted altogether in the new. The old annotations are then dropped entirely. This only occurs when a provision has been entirely repealed and has not merely been shifted to another part of the statute classification.

4. *Indexes to state compilations*. See §9.6.

5. *Parallel conversion tables from one form of statute to another*. Conversion tables for federal legislation have been discussed in §§5.5 and 5.6. The functions of state statutory conversion tables are identical, but the problems involved are greater because of more frequent changes in the statutory form of state legislation. Classification schemes, for example, are not merely changed, but often completely revamped. The parallel conversion table is thus even more important for state than for federal legislation.

The table's purpose is to enable the searcher to trace an earlier session law or compilation form of legislation into its place in the current compilation and to determine if it is still law. Tracing backward to the legislative antecedents of a current code section, as in the United States Code, is done through the citations to authority following each compilation section. As amended by later enactments, the current compilation is covered by Shepard's Citations.

The lawyer or student, however, often is cited to an earlier form. So that this form can be Shepardized, it must be translated into the present form which is covered by Shepard's. This is often a difficult process, since the pertinent section may have been repealed with no provision for its subject matter to be found in the new classification scheme. Thus, while the conversion tables are indispensable, they do not always cover all enactments cited in earlier cases. If the earlier Shepard's Citations are available, the earlier cases may then be found. If they are not available, the searcher must then go through obsolete editions of state compilations for any case annotations that might be found there.

a. *Types of state statutory conversion tables*. The most useful but seldom found type of table traces the original session law through all earlier compilations to the current one. Arranged under the session law citation, this type of table notes, in addition to the latest classification designation, sections no longer in the compilation because they have been repealed or are obsolete. A more common type lists only those session laws which have at any time been codified. An example of the first type is shown in Exhibit 23 from the New Mexico Statutes Annotated (1953).

The more common conversion table goes back from the current compilation to one or more earlier revisions. The most elaborate one of this type is for the Iowa Code Annotated (1951), as shown by Exhibit 24.

Tracing the original session law into the revision carries the searcher back to the table of statutes included in the *earliest revision*

TABLE OF CORRESPONDING SECTIONS

Ch.	Section	Herein	Ch.	Section	Herein	Ch.	Section	Herein
45	1	73-15-8	76	5	67-11-5	97	15	75-13-15
	2	Sep. Cl.		6	67-11-6		16	75-13-16
	3	Rplg. Cl.		7	67-11-7		17	75-13-17
	4	Emer. Cl.		8	67-11-8		18	75-13-18
46	1	14-5-1, n.		9	67-11-9		19	75-13-19
	2	Sep. Cl.		10	67-11-10		20	75-13-20
	3	Rplg. Cl.		11	67-11-11		21	75-13-21
	4	Emer. Cl.	77	1	R. 1953,		22	Sep. Cl.
47	1-5	Appn.			ch. 138, § 123		23	Emer. Cl.
48	1	Temp.		2–6	R. 1953,	98	1	Spec.

Exhibit 23

TABLE 2

CORRESPONDING SECTIONS

Abbreviations

Om. - - - - - Omitted
R. - - - - - - Repealed
R.C.P. - - - Rules of Civil Procedure
Rep.Cl. - - - Repealing Clause
Sav.Cl. - - - Saving Clause
Sep.Cl. - - - Separability Clause
U. - - - - - - Unconstitutional

Code 1924 Sec.	Code 1927 Sec.	Code 1931 Sec.	Code 1935 Sec.	Code 1939 Sec.	I.C.A. and Iowa Code Sec.
1	1	1	1	1	1.1
2	2	2	2	2	1.2
8	3	8	3	3	1.3
4	4	4	4	4	1.4
	4–a1	4–a1	4–a1	4.1	1.5
	4–a2	4–a2	4–a2	4.2	1.6
	4–a3	4–a3	4–a3	4.3	1.7
	4–a4	4–a4	4–a4	4.4	1.8
			4–f1	4.5	1.9
			4–f2	4.6	1.10

Exhibit 24

following the session law's enactment. If such revision is not available, recourse must be had to the subject index of the current edition. This is a necessarily inexact process.

In New York there is, at present, no tabular means by which the searcher may trace a session law into the Consolidated Laws if the subject matter of the law is not known. This is a tabular blind spot; however, session laws enacted prior to 1909 may be traced into the consolidated laws by means of Birdseye's Annotated Consolidated Laws, N.Y., Banks Publishing Co., 1909, vol. 6.

After reenacting a compilation as positive law, some states do not follow it up by later compilations of the same authority, but instead adopt compilations which are only prima facie the law. This happened with the United States Revised Statutes (enacted into positive law) and the United States Code (prima facie the law except as to individual titles later reenacted). Some state codes like the Mississippi Code carry the latest positive law compilation into the current prima facie revision and indicate in it the disposition of session laws enacted since the latest positive law compilation. See Exhibit 25.

Pt 1 — 1942 CODE TO 1972 CODE — **Table A**

Code 1942 §§	**Code 1972 §§**	**Code 1942 §§**	**Code 1972 §§**	**Code 1942 §§**	**Code 1972 §§**
7605-23	59-9-73	7623-27	59-17-57	7667	77-7-243
7605-23	59-9-75	7623-28	59-17-47	7668	77-7-245
7605-23	59-9-81	7623-29	59-17-5	7669	77-7-19
7605-24	59-9-83	7623-30	S	7670	77-7-171
7605-25	59-9-3	7623-31	E	7671	77-7-181
7605-26	59-9-1	7624	59-19-1	7672	77-7-183
7605-26	59-9-3	7625	59-19-3	7672	77-7-185
7605-27	S	7626	59-19-5	7673	77-7-119
7605-41	59-11-1	7627	59-19-7	7673	77-7-121
7605-42	59-11-3	7628	59-19-9	7673-01	77-7-123
7605-43	59-11-5	7629	59-19-11	7673-02	77-7-125
7605-44	59-11-7	7630	59-19-13	7674	77-7-53
7605-45	E	7631	59-19-15	7675	77-7-261
7606	59-13-1	7632	77-7-1	7676	77-7-55

Exhibit 25

b. *Subsequent amendments, repeals, etc.* With a few exceptions, conversion tables enable the searcher to trace the provisions of a session law or earlier compilation into the latest compilation. These tables include information concerning subsequent legislative action.

6. *Supplementation of state statutory compilations.* Few state official compilations are supplemented at all. The searcher is thus relegated to unofficial editions for later information. Supplementation is otherwise typical of law books generally and consists of annual pocket parts, cumulative bound supplements, recompiled individual volumes, etc. Because of its frequency, the most satisfactory type is by advance sheet service which supplies the text of new session laws together with tabular material giving their statute classification, citations to repeals, amendments, etc. This information supplements

tables in the bound set. Since it may print legislative material not otherwise readily available, the student should be acquainted with the supplementation available for a needed state's compilation. The supplementation may include governors' messages and recommendations concerning pending legislation as well as similar documents from other official and unofficial bodies.

Noting the date of publication. This must be done with any statutory material to assure that the full sequence or original parts and all later supplementation are covered.

§9.5. Municipal charters, ordinances, and codes.

The creation of municipal corporations is a function of the state legislature. The modern practice is to enact a general law setting up standards and conditions for the creation of such corporations and then to assign the duty to some officer or official body to determine whether these have been met in specific instances. Incorporation may also be by special act if not forbidden by the state constitution or by the adoptión of a home rule charter in states permitting such charters.

1. *Charters*. The charter granted by the legislature constitutes a limited delegation of its power over the government of the area covered. In form, it may follow a special or general statute; or it may be one selected from among a number of legislatively authorized forms (optional charters); or the commission or city manager form may be adopted. The charter is the city's fundamental document and is judicially noticed by the courts. Unless contrary to the state constitution, the legislature may amend or repeal a municipal charter. Constitutional or home rule charters may, in some states, be amended by a vote of the electors.

2. *Ordinances*. These are the local laws of the municipalities, enacted by the duly constituted board of aldermen, council, or commission, under authority delegated by the state legislature, and are for application within the narrow limits of its jurisdiction. An ordinance must be in writing and enacted according to all the prescribed formalities. It may be in furtherance of the police power of the municipality and prescribe penalties for its violation; it may grant franchises and special privileges; it can be for the improvement of the physical facilities of the corporation, for the doing of public works, or for abatement of nuisances; it may correspond to a code of laws laying down rules for the conduct of public business. If duly enacted, an ordinance is as binding upon those concerned as the general laws of the state are upon its citizens.

In some states, a general statute provides for enactment by the state's cities, counties, and villages of local laws which are in effect ordinances but are published with the session laws of the state, often in separate volumes. In many localities, ordinances are referred to as resolutions.

In states where there is an "upstate" community overshadowed by a "downstate," overwhelmingly large city, the legislature is likely to keep more than usually close control over the ordinances of the metropolis. An example is New York City which operates under a home rule charter but is governed by means of a huge administrative code enacted by the state legislature and amended by subsequent acts of that legislature.

3. *Citators for charters and ordinances*. Charters and ordinances are amended, repealed, and adjudicated just as conventional legislation is and are covered by the usual statutory citation books. The coverage is incomplete, however, because of the failure of the municipalities to provide the necessary information concerning amendments and repeals.

a. *Shepard's Citations*. In all state Shepard's Citations, charters and ordinances, their amendment, repeal (with the above noted limitation), and adjudication are covered. Because most ordinances are not numbered and must, therefore, be cited by subject and date, there is a separate index of ordinances in some state citators. Otherwise, the tabular treatment in Shepard's Citations is exactly the same as it is for other statutes.

b. *National Reporter System*. The Table of Statutes Construed in the regional units cites charters, but apparently not ordinances, construed by cases in the various jurisdictions.

c. *Lawyers' Edition of the United States Reports*. City ordinances and codes construed by the Supreme Court of the United States are covered in the tables of the Lawyers' Edition of the United States Reports.

§9.6. State statutory indexes.

1. *Subject indexes to state statutes*.

a. *All laws ever enacted in a state*. As with federal statutes, no state has an index covering all of its statutory enactments; some states have partial indexes. New York, for example, has the General Index to the Laws of the State of New York, 1777–1901. Each session law volume of a state has its own subject index. These indexes are not cumulative.

b. *All public laws presently in force*. Such an index, in a single listing, would index codified, uncodified, and procedural laws. The nearest present approximation to such an index is the Larmac Consolidated Index to the Constitution and Laws of California, but this does not index private laws or appropriation acts.

c. *All public general laws presently in force*. Every general state statutory compilation has such an index. All are patterned after the United States Code index. In some states the constitution and the procedural laws are together in one index and substantive laws in another index. This can be confusing.

In using an index of laws in force to trace a particular enactment when the date is unknown, it is necessary to start with the current index and work back and forth through indexes to earlier editions until an entry covering the desired law is found. When found, the section of the statute will tell from what session law it was derived so that the original text may be found. When the citation to source is only to another, earlier edition of the statutory compilation, that compilation must be searched for the desired session law citation.

d. *Indexes to laws of more than one state*. There is no such index covering current public general laws. From 1925 to 1948 the Library of Congress published a State Law Index. Partial coverage is often found in indexes to limited compilations which are usually made by government agencies or in treatises. These are noted in §9.10. Useful bibliographies of multi-jurisdictional references to compilations, legislation, and statutes arranged by subject can be found in Appendix A of Margaret Howell's A Bibliography of Bibliographies of Legal Material, N.J. Appellate Printing Co., Inc., Woodbridge, N.J., 1969, and in John S. Schultz, Comparative Statutory Sources, W. S. Hein Co., N.Y., 2d edition, 1978.

2. *Popular name indexes to state statutes*. As separate tables, state popular name statutory indexes are uncommon. Some of the general indexes to state compilations do occasionally note statutes by popular name as entries in their normal place in the combined alphabet. The Iowa Code Annotated, for example, has a separate table. Shepard's Citations for each of the states have popular name tables for statutes, and, in addition, state statutes are cited by popular name in Shepard's Acts and Cases by Popular Names.

3. *Parallel conversion tables from one form of state statute to another*. See §9.4. The problem is more difficult in work with state statutes than with federal because in most states there have been many different editions of statutory compilations which have radically changed the numbering systems of the sections or entirely discarded the old system. This makes it difficult or impossible in many cases to match up the old statute section with its current form.

a. *Session law to code*. Transfer tables of this kind are uncommon, both in session laws and in official editions of the codes. They are, however, fairly common in the private annotated editions.

b. *Code to session law*. Code sections cite the original session law from which derived, so that if the code section is found, the rest is simple. The citation is commonly in parentheses at the end of the text of the section, but may be in small print below it. If, as often occurs, the citation to authority is merely to an earlier compilation, then that compilation must be searched for citation to the session law source.

c. *Code tables translating from one edition to another*. Most state statutory conversion tables make it possible to trace an older section number into the current form, or the reverse, as described in §9.4.5.

4. *Bill status tables*. The chapter and law numbers of an act are noted on the face of the session law as published and in tables in each session law volume. Many state legislatures or other state agencies publish status tables during a session which are often cumulated and also printed at the close of a session. For some states, during the sessions of the state legislature there are private services which indicate the progress of a bill through the legislature.

§9.7. Citation books for state statutes.

The conventional forms are Shepard's Citations and, also for judicial interpretations, the Tables of Statutes Construed in the various units of the National Reporter System, described in Chapter 12. The tables of amendments and repeals of existing legislation by new laws which are found in each volume of most state session laws are of limited utility because they are not cumulative. Annotated statutes give judicial history by indicating what the courts have done in construing the legislation printed in them.

§9.8. Legislative history and intent.

Unlike congressional history and intent, state legislative history and intent are difficult to determine. While some states do distribute bills upon application, most states do not. Digests of pending state legislation are more common and may be subsequently cumulated. These digests constitute a bare outline of a statute's legislative history. Only California, Maine, and Pennsylvania have legislative journals which record actual legislative debate and parallel the Congressional Record in form and content. The legislative journals for the other states are merely minutes of the sessions and record little more than a bill's introduction and the final vote. In some of the states having unofficial legislative services for annotated statutes, information relating to pending legislation is available. This information often includes the reports of the commissions and administrative agencies proposing and opposing pending legislation. Not all states have legislative services which are so comprehensive. In these states, state law librarians or legislative reference librarians are frequently the only source of legislative intent. Communication with them may elicit governors' messages, legislative committee reports, and other legislative material, some or all of which is in manuscript form and is otherwise unavailable.

Perhaps the most fruitful source of background information on state legislation is found in the reports and bulletins of the numerous state law revision commissions, legislative research bureaus, legislative councils, and state university bureaus of government and public administration. State law librarians or legislative reference librarians are again the best sources for such material.

§9.9. Authority of state statutes.

1. *Session laws.* Unless and until superseded by a codification which has been reenacted into positive law, expressly repealing the session law from which derived, state session laws are "best evidence" of the laws in printed form. Compilations not so reenacted are merely prima facie the law, certified as true copies and receivable in evidence, but rebuttable in case of repugnance of texts by reference to the original session law from which derived. Some states, like New York, have "perpetual revision" of code sections, in which each enactment amending or adding to a section is enacted as positive law by the session law itself. Thus, "Section 211 of the General Corporation Law is amended to read as follows: . . . ." In that form of enactment, the latest amendment supersedes all that has gone before, and is the definitive form of the statute. In such cases, the session form of citation is seldom used, but only that of the consolidation. For example, the above, in New York, would not ordinarily be cited as New York Laws 1956, Chapter 381, but as New York General Corporation Law §211.

Even state compilations which have been reenacted as positive law are usually unannotated or only sparsely annotated in the official edition and are not frequently supplemented. As a result, they are not of as much use to the lawyer as are unofficially published, annotated editions. In practice, therefore, the lawyer consults an unofficial edition if available. Unless the preferred unofficial code contains statutory language not included in the latest official code, the official edition is cited as authority in legal writing. In New York and California, statutory compilations are cited by the name of the publishers, McKinney (New York) and West (California).

2. *Statutory compilations.* The status of state compilations of the laws as legal authority varies from state to state, depending upon whether they have been reenacted as positive law or are only certified

as true copies of the original session laws, entitled to be received in evidence, but rebuttable by the original session law in case of repugnance of texts.

a. *Enactment of the compilation into positive law.* This reenactment of the compilation makes it the highest form of authority. It supersedes the original session law from which derived and expressly repeals that law. It is something *the legislature has done directly*, not acting through a commission or the Secretary of State. *The test is the presence or absence of an enacting clause.* If it has a clause such as "It is enacted by the General Assembly as follows," or "Be it enacted," it is of the highest authority. Later amendments to its sections are cited as such; that is, the compilation is cited by title and section, "as amended by" the amending session law. An exception is the "perpetual revision" type of amendment noted under Session Laws, *supra*, in which the amending session law either entirely supersedes the section amended or adds a new section. In such cases, the amendment may be said to be cumulative in effect, the latest form superseding all earlier ones.

b. *Official compilation of laws in force, in classified order, but without reenactment as positive law.* This is the United States Code form and the one commonly adopted by the state compilations. The resulting text is prima facie the law, rebuttable by reference to the original form from which derived. No new law is enacted by the compilation nor old one repealed by it. Usually the legislature delegates the work of compilation to a state reviser by means of a revision statute.

Students often confuse positive law and prima facie the law compilations with official and unofficial compilations. An official compilation is merely one put out under governmental auspices of some kind — either directly published by the government or sponsored by it. It may or may not be positive law or only prima facie the law. The United States Code, for example, is fully official since it is published under the auspices of the Congress and printed by the Government Printing Office. Almost two-thirds of it, however, is only prima facie the law. The Wisconsin legislature authorizes a "reviser" to compile a subject arrangement of the laws which is published by the state. This is certainly official, but, since it is merely an editorial job by an appointed agent of the legislature and not reenacted as such by the legislature, it is only prima facie the law. See § 3.7.

c. *Unofficial and annotated edition of an official compilation.* Official publications tend to be sporadic, seldom revised, and sparsely annotated. After publication, therefore, they become out of date and of diminishing value to the lawyer. The private publisher remedies this with an annotated edition, frequently supplemented, which the lawyer uses to the exclusion of the official edition, except to cite the latter as authority in legal writing (see par. b *supra*).

d. *Entirely unofficial compilations.* Purdon's Pennsylvania Statutes is, from beginning to end, an unofficially published, classified arrangement of the laws of Pennsylvania. It has no official status of any kind, but is so well done that it is cited by and to all courts. It is a typical annotated edition of the statutes. The student should bear in mind that in citing Purdon's, P.L. does not mean Purdon's but Public Law of Pennsylvania.

3. *Municipal ordinances.* These are delegated legislation, in that the state legislature has empowered the municipal authorities to enact certain measures for the governance of their corporate areas. To the extent that they do not exceed this authority, municipal ordinances are binding upon those subject to them. The same is true of local laws.

§9.10. Subject collections of statutes covering more than one jurisdiction.

One of the most frequent calls from law students is for collections of the laws of all states on various subjects. Although there have been some attempts at supplying this need, it is simply too great a task. As a result, there is no general collection of present value. When such compilations are made for a specific subject, they are likely to suffer from two weaknesses: (1) the compilers have included the obvious laws but failed to include many which have an important peripheral effect and (2) the collections are not kept up to date. There is no royal road for the researcher in working with such statutes, and the safest procedure is to make a careful and laborious search of the statutory compilations of all states in the particular legislative area. The collections which have been made vary greatly in treatment. Some print the entire text of the legislation. Others merely provide digests or paraphrases of legislation with citations given to the full text.

1. *Directories paraphrasing laws.* The Martindale-Hubbell Law Directory[1] paraphrases, at considerable length, business and family laws of all states and most foreign countries and is kept up by annual new editions. They are described in Chapter 22.

2. *Compilations on one subject only.* Such collections are occasionally made by official agencies, may be included as an important part of treatises, or may be published by foundations.

3. *Trade or professional organization compilations.* Various organizations sometimes provide compilations of statutes or abridgments of them for their members.

1. Summit, N.J., Martindale-Hubbell Law Directory, Inc.

4. *Uniform Laws Annotated*. The Uniform Laws are promulgated by the National Conference of Commissioners of Uniform State Laws to meet the need for uniformity between states in the areas of business, domestic relations, and criminal law. One such law, the Negotiable Instruments Law, has been adopted by all states, with or without modifications. Some have yet to be adopted by any state. The annual Handbook of the Conference lists adopting states by name. Furthermore, because adopting states have to fit the law into their own classification schemes and cannot therefore ordinarily enact the Uniform Laws in either the same sequence or with the same section numbers, there is a parallel conversion table from the Uniform Act sections to those of each state adopting it. Enacting statutes of the various states are cited with dates of adoption. Tentative drafts of laws not yet promulgated by the Conference as well as the texts of certain obsolete uniform laws are printed in the Handbook. The Uniform Laws can be Shepardized as such through the National Reporter System tables of Statutes Construed and, in Shepard's Citations, by means of the state statute adopting them.

The Uniform Laws Annotated is a typical annotated compilation. It has one or more laws to each volume and is kept up to date by annual pocket supplements. In 1976 a Master Edition which includes expanded coverage of the Uniform Commercial Code was published.

Uniform Commercial Code. Dating from 1952, this Code, in effect, supersedes most prior Uniform Laws on commercial law. By 1976, it had been adopted, with modifications to suit local practice, by 49 states, the District of Columbia, and the Virgin Islands. States adopting it have provided parallel references from Code sections to their own corresponding state sections. There are available from several sources reprints of the "official" edition, with parallel reference tables from superseded Uniform Laws and with invaluable compilers' explanatory "Comments." Many state annotated statutes have issued special U.C.C. pamphlets with explanatory notes and, in some, annotations to the decided cases. A voluminous literature on the Code has sprung up. Much of it renders preceding publications, including some treatises, obsolete. There are several loose-leaf services covering the Code.

5. *Current state session laws pertaining to business*. The CCH Advance Session Laws Reporter is a loose-leaf reporter offering speedy publication of verbatim texts of current session laws "of general business interest." There is one binder for each state. Laws are listed by bill number and are subject-indexed.

6. *Comparative statutes*. John S. Schultz in Comparative Statutory Sources, W. S. Hein Co., N.Y., 2d edition, 1978, lists comparative statutory provisions on specific topics, e.g., blue-sky laws, garnishment of wages, interest rates.

§9.11. State administrative law.

1. *Importance*. State administrative law has a far greater impact on the average citizen than federal administrative law does. The barber, the nurse, the teacher, the plumber — all practitioners of the many trades or professions subject to licensing — anyone who uses electricity and telephone or drives an automobile, the farmer selling milk, the laborer injured on a job or out of work — all these and many more are affected in one way or another by rules, regulations, rate schedules, and decisions of state administrative agencies and commissions.

2. *State administrative rules and regulations*. There is a significant development in the availability of administrative law materials in the states. Approximately three-quarters of the states have administrative codes. Some states that do not have an administrative code do publish an index of regulations in force. Most state licensing or regulatory agencies and commissions publish the regulations governing licenses and distribute them free. Similarly tax and equalization boards, workmen's compensation hearing officers and similar boards usually print their regulations. It is to be hoped that all the states will soon continue their efforts to systematically compile and publish their rules in a way similar to that of the Federal Register System.[2]

3. *State administrative agency opinions and decisions*. State agency decisions follow the pattern of the federal agency decisions, but official publication of them is somewhat rare, except in the instances discussed below.

a. *Attorney General's opinions*. The advisory opinions of the chief law officer of the state usually follow closely the form and technique of a judicial opinion. When they comment on cases or statutes, they are noted in some of the state Shepard's Citations units as "citing cases." They are similarly noted in the annotated statutes in some states. Every state publishes its attorney general's decisions. Since March 1937, the Council of State Governments has published a Digest of Opinions of Attorneys General. Formerly weekly, now monthly, it has an annual index.

b. *Public utilities commission decisions*. State public utilities commissions approve or initiate rate schedules, grant certificates of convenience and necessity, and issue orders to effectuate their decisions. The opinions and orders closely follow the form of judicial opinions and are usually published in conjunction with the routine periodical reports of the respective commissions. Public Utilities Reports, First

2. Tseng & Pederson, *Acquisition of State Administrative Rules and Regulations*, 28 Ad. L. Rev. 277, 278 (1976).

and Second Series,[3] have published both court and agency decisions. There is an annual digest.

c. *Loose-leaf services*. The most convenient, expeditious, and complete collection of state administrative rules and decisions on any given subject is usually in loose-leaf services. As described in Chapter 23, they cover such varied topics as labor, insurance, taxation, and public utilities.

§9.12. State court rules.

State courts follow much the same procedure as the federal in promulgation of rules not inconsistent with the constitution and enactments of the state legislatures. Since 1939, many states have adopted rules of procedure modeled after the federal rules. The Federal Rules Service Digest contains comparative tables of such state rules and the corresponding federal rules upon which they are based and points out the differences existing between them.

State court rules are printed in the official editions of the law reports of about two-thirds of the states, though in a few states only amendments are printed. Rules are printed in the advance sheets, but not in the bound volumes of the National Reporter System units, and in most cases, furnish the promptest available printing of these rules. ("Statutes Construed" Tables cite them.) In addition, state court rules are found in more than half of all state statutory compilations.

§9.13. Legal research guides and court guides.

For state legal research guides see Chapter 1, §1.5.

For a brief guide to each state court system, including maps showing judicial divisions, the researcher may use *The American Bench*, 1979, published by Reginald Bishop and Associates, Inc. Minneapolis, Minnesota.

For a more comprehensive guide, research is facilitated by the use of *Federal and State Court Systems — A Guide*, by Fannie J. Klein, 1977, published by Ballinger Publishing Company, Cambridge, Mass. It includes a chapter on state courts with a Table of Courts for all the states, the District of Columbia, Guam, and Puerto Rico. Another

3. Washington, D.C., Public Utilities Reports, Inc.

chapter treats more fully the selected state court systems of: Alaska, California, Colorado, the District of Columbia, Hawaii, Illinois, Massachusetts, New York, and Puerto Rico. Bibliographies are also furnished for these selected states.

10 Law Reports: Rationale, Format, and Use as Precedent

§10.1. Importance of law reports.

What a lawyer wants most is a case squarely on point, decided by a court of competent jurisdiction, which has not been reversed on appeal but which is still standing as good legal precedent. The most important material in a reasonably complete American working library is, therefore, its collection of published reports of judicial decisions, English, Canadian, and American. Except for statutes and the tools for their use, practically all other books in a law library are case reports or the means for unlocking the store of rules found in such reports or for ascertaining whether the rule of law of a given case is still good law. Elaborate machinery for making these printed reports accessible is necessary because the bound reports are organized by decision dates, not by subject matter. Legal purists maintain that, because a statute's meaning is fixed and determined only by a judicial decision construing it, case law is the only legal authority.

§10.2. Definition and purpose of a law report.

A printed law report is not the minutes of a trial. It does not record the evidence, examination, cross examination, and other proceedings before the court. It is, instead, ". . . the production of an adequate record of a judicial decision on a point of law, in a case heard in open court, for the subsequent citation as a precedent. A law report is a report of law and not of fact. Only the issues and the facts relevant to the point of law should be recorded, since every judgment is founded on a decision of fact."[1]

"The purpose of a law report is the exposition of the law. It should show the parties, the nature of the pleadings, the essential facts, the arguments of Counsel, the decision, and the grounds for the judgment."[2]

§10.3. What judicial decisions are reported.

With some exceptions, the printed law reports found in law libraries are of appellate cases. An appellant case is one appealed from a trial court or from an intermediate appellate court on a point of law to correct an error which the appellant believes was detrimentally committed in the court below. The exceptions are the printing of selected cases from the federal district courts and the United States Customs Court, all of which are trial courts, and of those of some lower courts in a few states such as California, New York, and Pennsylvania. Even in these courts, the cases reported have to do with the weight or admission of evidence, pleadings, or other matters of law rather than of fact. Not even all appellate cases are reported. Reported cases are confined to those which make new law or are of general interest to the public. Cases which are merely routine are excluded. The selection of cases to be reported and printed is usually a matter of editorial discretion on the part of the reporter.

The value of decisions of state trial courts as precedents is dubious; it is practically nonexistent if the reports are not printed but are of record only in the clerk's office of the court where decided. See South Carolina Court of Common Pleas for Spartansburg County, Judgment Roll No. 33,454, July 10, 1946; *King* v. *Order of United Commercial Travelers*, 333 U.S. 153, 68 S. Ct. 488, 92 L. Ed. 608 (1948). The main reason for this is that such unprinted reports are in effect secret. They are not available to the profession generally but are found only in the clerk's office and are likely to be upset on appeal.

Selective printing of reports excluded too many cases which should have been reported and was one of the reasons for the establishment

1. Moran, The Heralds of the Law, London, Stevens, 1948, pp. 13, 14.
2. Great Britain, Lord Chancellor's Department, Report of the Law Reporting Committee, London, H.M.S.O., 1940, p. 3.

of the National Reporter System which publishes many thousands of otherwise unreported appellate decisions.

§10.4. Reporting judicial decisions.

Contrary to English practice, opinions of American courts are read from the bench instead of being delivered orally. In the United States, there are official reporters who are responsible for making a record of all proceedings, including the opinion and judgment of each case. Some reports are designated as official and others, unofficial. The difference between the two is that the official are published under statutory direction and the unofficial usually are not. Both use identical texts of opinions and judgments which are supplied by the courts. Editorial matter such as tables, indexes, and, usually, headnotes are, however, different between the official and unofficial. Both official and unofficial reports may be cited in court, but courts prefer citation in parallel to unofficial reports. The official is to be cited first, followed by the unofficial. Thus, *Wynn* v. *Sullivan*, 294 Mass. 562, 3 N.E.2d 235 (1936).

1. *Unofficial law reports*. The principal advantages of unofficial law reporting are the greater speed of publication and the inclusion of reports which the editors deem worthy of publication, but which the official reporter did not.

Before the National Reporter System was instituted, the publication of the official reports lagged behind the actual decision from one to three or four years. This played havoc with the rule of stare decisis, because the latest cases were unavailable. In its "advance sheets," the National Reporter System publishes state and federal reports weekly and Supreme Court reports biweekly.

Other advantages of unofficial reporting are the selection of cases, across jurisdictional lines, which the editors deem of general interest to the profession and their extensive annotation to cases in all jurisdictions. Special-subject series, like public utilities, labor, taxation, etc., are published for lawyers interested in those fields.

2. *"Star paging" of unofficial edition*. Paging in unofficial editions is seldom identical to that of the official. This is because, while the opinion text is identical, editorial features are different and usually the type style and size of page are not the same. The lawyer, however, may find it necessary to cite the exact page of the official, even though only the unofficial is available. The device of "star paging" is employed to make this possible. It indicates the precise word or letter on one page of the official with which that page ends and the one with which the next page begins. Thus:

. . . of competition. From
*464
its findings, the Com- . . .

Here, the last word on page 463 was "from" and the first on 464 was "its."

Some of the older reports have been reproduced in facsimile, making the star paging device unnecessary. Because all National Reporter System reports except the Supreme Court Reporter are printed before the official reports, the only National Reporter System report to have star paging is the Supreme Court Reporter.

§10.5. Law reports cited by the name of the reporter.

Until the middle of the nineteenth century, law reports were named after the particular publishers such as Hun, Pickering, and Brevard, regardless of the name of the jurisdiction reported. The multiplicity of meaningless personal names caused so much confusion that the practice was abandoned and the name of the jurisdiction became an integral part of the series title.

Official series existing at the time this change took place renumbered all their volumes consecutively from the earliest ones on.

At that time, the ninety volumes of the United States Reports which report Supreme Court cases from Dallas through Wallace and the ninety-six Massachusetts Reports which reported Williams through Allen were renumbered. Confusion has nevertheless resulted in citing these early "nominatives." One reason for the confusion lies with the renumbered volumes. Cases in these volumes predate the renumbering and therefore cite all other cases in their old form as nominatives. Another reason for the confusion stems from the conservatism of lawyers. They just prefer the original form. Thus, 90 U.S. is still cited as 90 U.S. (23 Wall.), but 91 U.S. is not 1 Otto (its reporter), but 91 U.S., because that is where the renumbering occurred and Otto and his successor were never cited by their names. A similar procedure was followed for state nominative reports.

In bibliographic manuals on law books such as Price and Bitner's Effective Legal Research (Prentice-Hall, Inc., 1953) and in Shepard's Citations for the United States Reports and for some of the early state nominatives, parallel tables from the nominative citation to the renumbered volumes are provided.

Those early series which had ceased publication when renumbering became the rule were not renumbered and are still cited by the name of the reporter. Since their titles are always abbreviated in citations, tables of abbreviations are necessary in order to identify the reports. Digests and encyclopedias of law frequently contain tables of abbreviations. A comprehensive table of abbreviations is found in Appendix III of this book.

§10.6. Parts of a reported case.

A reported case may consist of the following parts:

1. *Title*. The title or case name designates the parties, such as *Smith* v. *Jones*, In re *Pimsleur*, *Matter of Cohen*, *People* v. *Clarence* (a criminal case), *The Elizabeth* (an admiralty case, giving the name of the vessel involved), or *United States* v. *34 Cases of Square-face Gin*.

The plaintiff's name usually precedes the defendant's name in the case title; but, in some courts, the order is reversed on appeal when the defendant in the court below has lost and becomes the "Plaintiff in Error" in the court above. Tables of cases customarily follow the official case designation in listing cases; but a growing number of case tables are also by "Defendant-Plaintiff." This listing enables cases to be found when only the defendant's name is known.

2. *Docket number*. When a case is filed in the court clerk's office, it is assigned a serial number, called a docket number, which serves as an identification tag in its progress through the court. This number is usually printed in a law report following the title of the case. The term of court and the dates of argument and decision are also noted here.

3. *Headnote or syllabus*. This is an extremely important index to the law which is found in the reported opinion. It is the foundation of the case digests which enable the lawyer to find cases in point in the United States — if they exist — from 1754 to date. The headnote is made up of brief statements of the law involved in the reported case. Each paragraph usually comprises a single sentence. The headnote may be either a purely propositional statement of legal principle or a factual statement containing sufficient facts to tie it to the case reported. In some states, it is written by the judge or court. When this is the case, it will usually bear the notation "syllabus by the court." In most states it is usually written by the reporter. The official headnote by the reporter differs in text from that of the unofficial. The unofficial is generally more detailed. Where, as in Georgia, Ohio, and Oklahoma, the court is required by law to write a syllabus, it is the personal statement of the law by the judge. The National Reporter System reports customarily carry both the syllabus of the court, if any, and their own. Their syllabus also numbers the individual paragraphs of the headnotes in boldface type to correspond to numbers in the text of the opinion. This makes finding the text state-

ments upon which the headnote paragraphs are based easier and quicker. These boldface type numbers should not be confused with the Reporter Key Number which is also attached to each headnote paragraph and which is a classification number employed in compiling case digests.

With the possible exception of the syllabi by the courts, headnote paragraphs are not authority but only indexes to it. They contain both the reasoning leading inevitably to the holding — the ratio decidendi — and the dictum, which is useful background material in the opinion but not necessary to the decision. The case itself must be read if the headnote points to it as possible precedent to be relied upon.

4. *Statement of facts of the reported case.* Formerly, a statement of facts preceded the opinions of most courts. It is now seldom found except briefly at the beginning of the opinion itself. New York official reports still have it, however, as does the American Law Reports Annotated, an unofficial, selective case series.

5. *Statement of how the case arose.* A brief statement of how the case came to the court which is deciding it is found in practically all published case reports. It may precede the opinion or, more often, be in the opinion itself as a statement by the court preceding its discussion of the issues. Such a statement is important because how a case arose often affects its value as precedent. A case, for example, appealed on a prayer for a preliminary injunction is unlikely to be authority on the merits of a point of substantive law even though such a point may be discussed as background for the decision. Such discussion would be dictum, perhaps persuasive but not mandatory.

6. *Names of counsel.* These are found preceding the opinion. Counsel are often willing to supply inquiring lawyers or law students with briefs. They may also be willing to detail the arguments, the questions asked by the courts, and other possible factors influencing the decision and affecting its value as precedent. Law students sometimes take advantage of this in preparing moot court briefs.

7. *Synopses of briefs of counsel.* These once preceded the opinion, but are seldom found any more. Today they are found only in A.L.R. and L. Ed. Supreme Court reports of decisions.

8. *Opinion of the court.* This is the heart of the law report to which all else, except the actual decision with which the report closes, is incidental and subsidiary. In it the court explains why it decided as it did. The opinion begins with a statement of the facts involved, sufficient to establish the issues, the parties concerned, and the relief sought. Errors charged to the court below are detailed. Judicial technique then usually applies the method of the syllogism, as classically expressed by Professor Eugene Wambaugh: "(1) When the circumstances surrounding the parties are thus and thus, the rights of the

parties are thus and thus; (2) in this particular case such circumstances do surround the parties; (3) in this particular case the other circumstances are not material; and (4) in this particular case the rights of the parties are as indicated in the first proposition. (In the phraseology of logicians, the first of these propositions is the major premise, the second and third taken together are the minor premise, and the fourth is the conclusion.)"[3]

Following this technique, the opinion commonly consists of a general statement of the points of law involved. This is likely to be pure dictum. The law is then applied to the specific circumstances of the case being decided. The statement of law involves the reasoning or ratio decidendi which, in turn, is the statement of an underlying principle leading inevitably to the decision. It is this last which is most prized by the lawyer seeking judicial precedents.

Opinions of the court may be unanimous. Or there may be concurring opinions when the concurrer agrees with the result but not with the reasoning to it. Dissenting opinions are the minority's statement of its reasons for disagreeing. Per curiam or memorandum decisions report routine decisions. They commonly lack any statement of the reasoning behind them, which thus somewhat diminishes their value as precedent. Frequently, when a written opinion has been read, but the court orders only the decision to be printed, the National Reporter System report of the case supplies the headnotes to the opinion as actually delivered and the case is thus digested.

9. *Decision of the court*. This is the court's statement that the decision below is "Affirmed," "Reversed," that "There is no error," etc. This is what the court *does*, as distinguished from what it *says* in its opinion. The decision is final, but the opinion as delivered by the court may be revised and, occasionally, even withdrawn before publication.

§10.7. Stare decisis in case law.

1. *The doctrine defined*. The theory of Anglo-American law is *stare decisis et non quieta movere*, "to adhere to precedent and not to unsettle things which are settled." This means that the principle underlying the decision in one case will be deemed of imperative authority, controlling the decisions of similar cases in the same court and in lower courts within the same jurisdiction, unless and until the decision in question is reversed or overruled by a court of competent authority.

A single decision does not necessarily create a precedent to be followed. Since decisions of trial courts may be appealed to higher courts and probably are not the best evidence of the rule of law laid

3. The Study of Cases, Boston, Little, Brown and Co., 1892, p. 16.

down, decisions which are relied upon as precedent are usually those of appellate courts. A detailed discussion of the rule of stare decisis on the weight of the decisions of various hierarchies of courts is found in 1 B Moore, Federal Practice ¶10.402 (2 ed. 1974).

2. *Res judicata distinguished.* Res judicata has nothing to do with precedent. It merely operates as an estoppel between the parties to a specific case, so that ". . . a right, question of fact distinctly put in issue and directly determined by a court of competent jurisdiction, as a ground of recovery cannot be disputed in a subsequent suit between the same parties or their privies." *Southern Pacific Ry.* v. *United States*, 168 U.S. 1, 48, 18 S. Ct. 18, 27, 42 L. Ed. 355, 377 (1897).

3. *Reasons for the doctrine.* Following is Chancellor James Kent's statement:

"A solemn decision upon a point of law arising in any given case, becomes an authority in a like case, because it is the highest evidence which we can have of the law applicable to the subject, and the judges are bound to follow that decision so long as it stands unreversed, unless it can be shown that the law was misunderstood or misapplied in that particular case. If a decision has been made upon solemn argument and mature deliberation, the presumption is in favor of its correctness, and the community has a right to regard it as a just declaration or exposition of the law, and to regulate their actions and contracts by it. It would, therefore, be extremely inconvenient to the public, if precedents were not duly regarded and implicitly followed. It is on the notoriety and stability of such rules that professional men can give safe advice to those who consult them; and people in general can venture with confidence to buy and trust, and to deal with each other. If judicial decisions were to be lightly disregarded, we should disturb and unsettle the great landmarks of property. When a rule has been once deliberately adopted and declared, it ought not to be disturbed unless by a court of appeal or review, and never by the same court, except for very cogent reasons, and upon a clear manifestation of error; and if the practice were otherwise, it would be leaving us in a state of perpetual uncertainty as to the law."[4]

4. *Analysis of the doctrine of stare decisis.*

a. *The point must have been raised and considered.* This must have been done both by counsel and court. If raised by counsel but not treated by the court, it is not a precedent.

b. *Identity of essential circumstances.* No two cases are identical. Nonessential circumstances such as parties, time, and place, may be stripped from a fact situation so that a case may be used as precedent. When, however, the elimination of an element changes the legal principles involved, the case is no longer "like" the original, and the elimination cannot be supported.

4. 1 Commentaries on American Law, 14th ed., Boston, Little, Brown and Co., 1896, p. 476.

c. *Doctrine of the case*. There must be a rule in the case without which that case could not have been decided as it was. This rule must be of general application to the class of cases under consideration.

d. *Ratio decidendi or reasoning*. This is the legal reasoning of the court which leads inevitably and necessarily to the decision. It is a statement of a doctrine precisely applicable to the case being decided and necessarily involved in the decision. As reasoning from a rule to its specific application, it is broader than the decision.

e. *Dictum*. Dictum is an expression of opinion concerning the state of the law. The legal issue discussed is not necessarily raised by the case and its resolution is not necessary for the decision. Dicta are not regarded as precedents within the rule of stare decisis because, not having been at issue before the court, they have not been argued by counsel or investigated fully. Only the specific case before the court is the basis of a precedent. Well-considered dicta, nevertheless, are often highly persuasive and are frequently cited. When this is done, however, it should be with full awareness.[5]

5. *Illustrative case*. The opinion in *Hoffman* v. *Le Traunik*, 209 F. 375 (N.D.N.Y. 1913), illustrates the distinction among dictum, *ratio decidendi*, and decisions. It is also a good example of the decisive effect on precedent of the manner in which a case reaches the appellate court. This particular opinion is also proof that an opinion need not be dull.

In Equity. Suit by Aaron Hoffman against Sam Le Traunik, for alleged infringement of copyright in the use of monologues. On motion for preliminary injunction pendente lite. Denied.

P charged D, a burlesque comedian, with using copyrighted monologues. The opinion reproduced one monologue and discussed certain similarities of D's material; it then proceeded as follows: [See Exhibit 26 below.]

Casting the proposition extracted from the excerpt in Exhibit 26, in the form of a syllogism, we have:

(1) Preliminary injunctions will not issue except in the clearest cases. [A general rule.]

(2) Where, on a motion for a preliminary injunction, complainant makes affidavit one way, defendant the other; and the substantive issue will be tried on its merits within two months; no public interest being involved; and the damage to the complainant will not be very serious, no clear and satisfactory case is made. [Illustrating the rule.]

(3) Therefore, these conditions existing here, the motion for a preliminary injunction to restrain D from using his monologues is denied.

All that is said above by the court about copyright and infringement is dictum and not required for the decision. The case decides

5. Paraphrased from Wambaugh, The Study of Cases, Boston, Little, Brown and Co., 1892, pp. 16 et seq. passim.

378 209 FEDERAL REPORTER

378 HOFFMAN V. LE TRAUNIK

It may be proved on the trial that the complainant originated all these expressions, and the court may be of the mind that no one but the author and his licensees should be permitted to use them; but, so long as the defendants aver under oath that they were not new with complainant but common property and used on the stage prior to the writing of complainant's monologues, it seems to me that a preliminary injunction should not issue. No public interest is involved, and the damage to the complainant will not be very serious. The answers are served, and a term of court will be held at Albany February 10th, when the suit can be tried if the parties desire.

[2] To be entitled to be copyrighted, the composition must be "original, meritorious, and free from illegality or immorality." And "a work, in order to be copyrighted, must be original in the sense that the author has created it by his own skill, labor, and judgment, without directly copying or evasively imitating the work of another." However, "a new and original plan, arrangement, or combination of materials will entitle the author to a copyright therein, whether the materials themselves be new or old."

[3] But here the defendants have not copied substantially the plan, arrangement or combination of materials found in complainant's monologues or in any one of them. Conceding literary or artistic merit in the complainant's monologues growing out of some original matter combined with old matter in a new and an original plan, arrangement, or combination, the defendants do not infringe, not having used that plan, arrangement, or combination, unless they have abstracted and used some of the complainant's new matter and so much of it as to authorize the finding that there has been a copying or a taking.

"Copying the whole or a substantial part of a copyrighted work constitutes and is an essential element of infringement. It is not confined to literal repetition or reproduction but includes also the various modes in which the matter of any work may be adopted, imitated, transferred, or reproduced with more or less colorable alteration to disguise the piracy. But, on the principle of de minimis non curat lex, it is necessary that a substantial part of the copyrighted work be taken." 9 Cyc. 939, 940.

If there is any piracy in this case, it consists in the taking and use of these isolated expressions or "gags," as they are called, and to constitute infringement it must be established by the complainant that they were original with him. The burden is on him to show this, and with complainant making affidavit one way and the defendants the other, and a sworn answer also interposed, a clear and satisfactory case on such a subject is not made for the drastic use of a preliminary injunction.

The motion is denied, but the defendants must be ready for trial at the Albany term of this court or the motion may be renewed on the same and additional papers.

Exhibit 26

nothing on the merits of any copyright infringement issue, but, for reasons given, refuses a preliminary injunction.

§10.8. Publication of law reports: Promptness and format.

1. *Promptness of publication and the rule of stare decisis.* Application of the rule of stare decisis demands access to the latest cases if the lawyer is to advise a client properly. This is because any late case may affirm, modify, or overturn an existing rule of law. Accordingly, case law publishing is geared to both speed in publishing the case report itself and speed in printing all indexes and other tools necessary for their effective use.

2. *Chronological arrangement of published law reports.* Law reports are published when decided and are so arranged in the publications making them available to lawyers. Exceptions to this rule are cases published in a few special-subject periodicals and special-subject law reports series such as those for labor, public utilities, taxation, etc. Because of this chronological arrangement, elaborate indexes such as case digests, legal encyclopedias, and treatises are necessary to enable the lawyer to find the law in the approximately four million American cases reported to date and in English cases.

3. *Slip decisions.* Some courts, both federal and state, issue slip decisions on their decision days or close to them. Each such decision is in the form of a separate pamphlet, with complete text but no syllabus or headnote. Unofficial slip decisions for the Supreme Court of the United States are published in the CCH United States Supreme Court Bulletin, a weekly loose-leaf service, and in the United States Law Week. In each case, the reports are facsimile reprints of the official decision. Ordinarily they reach their subscribers in from one to five days after a decision date.

4. *Advance sheets.* Outstanding examples of speed in law publishing are the advance sheets. Each is a pamphlet collecting all reports decided within the jurisdiction or jurisdictions covered by the individual advance sheet which have been reported since its preceding issue. All units of the National Reporter System are covered by advance sheets and there are official editions for the Supreme Court of the United States and for several state courts.

Advance sheets appear weekly for the National Reporter System, (semimonthly for the Supreme Court Reporter), as opposed to an average of once a year for the official bound reports. Since the page and volume numbers of all National Reporter System advance sheets are the same as those of the cumulated volumes, citation to them is identical to citations to the bound volumes—i.e., the same volume and page.

The National Reporter System advance sheets are the epitome of law book format, containing, as they do, almost every typical feature. They have tables of cases, tables of statutes construed, words and phrases of legal meaning as defined by the courts in the reports printed in the respective sheets, law reports, and a digest which cumulates progressively into the digest in the bound volume of the Reporter, into the General Digest covering all Reporter units, and eventually into the Decennial Digests.

a. *Corrections in advance sheets.* Because of their speed of publication, advance sheets are subject to error. Furthermore, a judge writing an opinion can, at any time prior to final publication in bound form, withdraw it for revision or even from publication entirely.

5. *Legal newspapers and periodicals publishing law reports.* Daily newspapers such as the New York Law Journal and comparable journals in other large cities usually publish highly selective reports of cases decided within the jurisdiction served by them. The publication may be a full report or, usually, a full report minus the headnote, or an abridged report. Practitioners' periodicals of less frequency of publication also publish law reports. Although the chief value of such reports is their promptness of publication, they also publish reports not printed elsewhere. Thus the New York Law Journal publishes some reports not published in the New York Miscellaneous Reports or in the New York Supplement.

6. *Loose-leaf services publishing law reports.* Special-subject series of reports in labor, tax, public utilities, and other regulatory fields are found in loose-leaf services. The reports, which appear first in loose-leaf form to be inserted in the service's binders, are, for some series, collected later and published in bound volumes.

7. *Bound volumes of law reports.* All the forms of law reports described above have as their principal asset speed of publication. For convenience of finding and use, however, the bound volume, which is the final form of publication of law reports, is superior and is the form commonly found and consulted on library shelves. For the material published in each individual volume, it contains the tables, digests, and other features mentioned above for advance sheets. Often, as noted in Chapters 8 and 9, it prints court rules and amendments.

8. *Governmental agency publication of law reports.* Governmental agencies, particularly those having quasi-judicial functions, collect and bind both judicial and quasi-judicial decisions affecting them and the laws they administer. An example is the Federal Communications Commission Reports. While these agency decisions vary in format and authority, they tend to resemble decisions of formal courts.

11 Law Reports: Decisions of Federal and State Courts

§11.1. The federal court system as it affects law report publication.[1]

The complexity of the federal court system is reflected in the multiplicity of series reporting the decisions of the courts comprising it. At the present time, there is a three-tiered hierarchy of federal constitutional courts as well as several specialized statutory or legislative courts. In addition, there are courts for the insular possessions of the United States. These were, however, reduced in number and jurisdiction with the admission of Alaska and Hawaii to statehood and Puerto Rico to commonwealth status.

The lowest courts in this federal hierarchy are the district courts which are general trial courts of original jurisdiction. There is at least one federal district court in each state, and in many states there are two or more. The district courts for the District of Columbia, Guam, Puerto Rico, the Canal Zone, and the Virgin Islands also have local jurisdiction which is analogous to that of state courts. This was true of the district courts of Alaska prior to statehood. Appeal from the district courts ordinarily lies to the Courts of Appeals, but, in some instances, is directly to the Supreme Court.

1. The United States Court (H. Doc. No. 233, 86th Cong., 1st Sess., 1959) in 12 pages describes the United States court system. Fannie J. Klein, Federal and State Court Systems (New York, N.Y., Institute of Judicial Administration, 1976) in 320 pages outlines the federal and state court systems and their relation to each other, with special reference to the courts of New York State. Both publications contain schematic diagrams of court systems.

The second rung of federal courts is composed of the Courts of Appeals, formerly the Circuit Courts of Appeals. These courts hear appeals from the district courts mentioned above. There are eleven numbered circuits geographically covering the United States and its insular possessions. The territorial jurisdictions and their circuit numbers are shown on a map printed in each Federal Reporter advance sheet and bound volume. Because appeals from them lie directly to the Supreme Court, several other courts also rank, for certain purposes, as courts of appeal.

The Court of Appeals for the District of Columbia ranks as a court of appeals, and there are, in addition, three statutory courts from which appeals lie directly to the Supreme Court. These are the Court of Customs and Patent Appeals, the Emergency Court of Appeals, and, as of 1960, the Court of Claims.

There were various other categories of federal trial and intermediate appellate courts before 1880, which were reported in so many different series that it would be impossible for the lawyer to have them all. For practical purposes, the cases so reported have been combined in a series entitled Federal Cases, described in §11.3.

At the top of the ladder is the Supreme Court of the United States — its official title, commonly shortened to United States Supreme Court or, simply, Supreme Court. In addition to a limited original jurisdiction which includes suits between the states, it hears appeals from the Courts of Appeals and from some classes of district court decisions.

The statutory or legislative courts described in §11.5 occupy a status somewhat different from that of Constitutional courts. This difference in status is discussed at length in 1 Moore, Federal Practice ¶10.4 (2d ed. 1974) and in other works on federal practice.

1. *Inclusiveness of publication of federal court decisions.* Not all decisions of any federal court, even those of the Supreme Court, are reported. On the other hand, all written and nearly all per curiam decisions of the Supreme Court are reported either officially or unofficially. This is true also of the reports of the intermediate appellate courts and those of the special courts. Only selected decisions of the district courts are published.

§11.2. United States Supreme Court reports.

All decisions for which there are written opinions are published both in the official United States Reports and in the unofficial Lawyers' Edition and Supreme Court Reporter. Most but not all per curiam reports of decisions are also printed. Many which are not in the official series are reported in the two unofficial series. Per curiam decisions are of a routine nature and, for the most part, simply note the probable jurisdiction of the Court, extend the time for filing various petitions, fix the compensation of special masters, permit the filing of briefs as amici curiae, and relate to similar matters which do not affect the merits.

1. *Opinions of Supreme Court Justices in chambers*. Each Supreme Court Justice is assigned to a circuit of the Courts of Appeals and, as such, sits in chambers to hear petitions and motions of various kinds such as those for stays of execution, continuances of bail pending appeal from conviction, etc. While the opinious rendered are usually brief, some are not. A notable example of the latter is the opinion of Mr. Justice William O. Douglas in granting a stay of execution to Julius and Ethel Rosenberg from their conviction of espionage. 73 S. Ct. 1152, 1173, 97 L. Ed. 1607, 1629 (1953). The Douglas opinion in chambers in the Rosenberg case was printed as an appendix to his dissent in the order vacating the stay of execution. 346 U.S. 273, 313 (1953). The practice of printing these opinions began privately in 1950 in the Supreme Court Reporter and the Lawyers' edition. Starting with volume 396 they are published in the United States Reports. They are discussed by Frederick Bernays Wiener in 49 Law Library Journal 2 (1956) and by Marian Boner in 65 Law Library Journal 213 (1972).

2. *Slip decisions*. A slip decision is one in which each separate report is a separate pamphlet, handed down during term time. Because it lacks headnotes and may be corrected in text later, its only virtue is speed of publication. It does contain the docket number, the title (as *Chamberlain* v. *Pierce)*, how it came to the Court (as by writ of certiorari, etc.), and the date of the decision, together with the text of the opinion and of the decision. The official edition includes both written and per curiam decisions and is mailed from the Government Printing Office in Washington to subscribers. It reaches them anywhere from two days to two weeks after decision date. Facsimile editions are published unofficially in the CCH United States Supreme Court Bulletin and in the United States Law Week described later in this section. These unofficial editions reach their subscribers somewhat earlier than the official edition. Loose-leaf services frequently mail decisions of outstanding interest to their subscribers on decision day.

3. *Advance sheets*. Advance sheets are published during term time for the official United States Reports, the Lawyers' Edition, and the Supreme Court Reporter. Since the volume numbering and pagination are identical with those of the bound volumes into which the respective series cumulate, the advance sheets are cited as bound volumes, not as advance sheets.

4. *United States Reports*. This is the title of the official edition of the reports of the Supreme Court of the United States, a series nominally dating from 1774 but actually reporting Supreme Court

cases only from the August term of 1791. It is a typical law report series with advance sheets, called Preliminary Prints, which appear at irregular intervals varying from a month to six weeks during term time. The lag from decision to receipt date may be up to two months so that the searcher should seek a slip decision if time is of the essence.

As noted in §10.5, the first ninety volumes of the reports, entitled Reports of Cases Argued and Adjudged in the Supreme Court of the United States, are still cited by the names of their official reporters even though they were renumbered as volumes 1 through 90 in 1875. Beginning with volume 91 in 1876, the series title was changed to United States Reports, its present title. The first ninety volumes are cited by the renumbered volume with the reporter name given in parenthesis. The 1872 Slaughter-House cases are, for example, cited as 83 U.S. (16 Wall.) 394 (1872). Below is a transfer table from the reporter citation to the renumbered consecutive volume citation:

Reporter	*Nominative Citation*	*United States Reports*	*Dates Covered*
Dallas	1–4 Dall.	1–4 U.S.	1790–1800
Cranch	1–9 Cr.	5–13 U.S.	1801–1815
Wheaton	1–12 Wheat.	14–25 U.S.	1816–1827
Peters	1–16 Pet.	26–41 U.S.	1828–1842
Howard	1–24 How.	42–65 U.S.	1843–1860
Black	1–2 Black	66–67 U.S.	1861–1862
Wallace	1–23 Wall.	68–90 U.S.	1863–1874
United States Reports		91–date	1875–date

5. *Lawyers' Edition of the Supreme Court Reports*. This unofficial edition covers the entire series of reports of the Supreme Court from its volume 1 to date. It contains many decisions not reported originally in the early official volumes. The report text is that of the official volumes, except that errors in the official ones are pointed out and parallel statutory and case citations are supplied when lacking in the official.

The editorial matter, however, is quite different. In the Lawyers' Edition, Second Series, a rather full summary of each case precedes the report of the case itself. The headnotes are by the publisher's staff and are keyed to the Digest of the U.S. Supreme Court Reports, L. Ed., described in §16.9.3. Through them, annotations of cases involving similar legal principles are found. The principal difference between this series of United States reports and others is that most of the cases are carefully and often elaborately annotated in the manner of the American Law Reports Annotated (A.L.R.) which is published by the same firm.

An annotation like those in the Lawyers' Edition takes up the points of law involved in a decided case, notes or discusses all cases in point, and indicates the general rules applicable, majority and minority rules, jurisdictional factors, and the impact of the present case upon the existing law. Extensive tables of federal and state statutes construed by the Supreme Court are included in each volume for that volume, thus performing some of the functions of a conventional citator. They are cumulated in volume 14 of the Digest of the United States Supreme Court Reports, L. Ed.

Since volume numbers and pagination of the Lawyers' Edition are different from those of the official United States Reports, a parallel cross-reference table in each volume references the official citation to the Lawyers' Edition. The Lawyers' Edition publishes, without written opinions, some decisions not officially reported. Along with the occasional reports of Justices in chambers sitting as Circuit Judges, per curiam orders comprise most of these reports.

The first series of the Lawyers' Edition ended with 351 U.S. Reports. Beginning with the first volume of the Second Series, briefs of counsel and annotations are printed in a separate section at the end of each bound volume (covering usually three volumes of official U.S. Reports). Briefs of counsel and annotations are printed in a separate section so that pagination and citation of the advance sheet will be identical to that of the bound volume. The annotations are similar to the A.L.R. annotations discussed in Chapter 13 and are often elaborate. The annotation of the *in rem* case entitled *A Book Named "John Cleland's Memoirs of a Woman of Pleasure"* v. *Attorney General of Massachusetts* (383 U.S. 413, 86 S. Ct. 975, 16 L. Ed. 2d 1, (1966)), the Fanny Hill case, occupies twenty-six pages of discussion of the right of free speech and the press, indexed in detail, and cross-referenced to A.L.R. annotations and American Jurisprudence sections in point.

6. *Supreme Court Reporter*. The coverage of this unit of the National Reporter System dates from 106 U.S. (October Term, 1882) to the present. It is a typical Reporter, with the usual features which include the Key-Numbering of headnote paragraphs. Advance sheets appear semimonthly, with the subscriber receiving them ten days to three weeks after the decision date. The bound volumes into which the advance sheets cumulate are "star-paged" to the official. While the text of the opinions is identical to that of the official edition, corrections in the official edition may be pointed out and additional per curiam opinions printed. The headnotes and other editorial matter are different, however, and are written by the publisher's own editorial staff.

In addition to features common to all Reporters, the Supreme Court Reporter also includes, as adopted, all federal court rules and amendments, except local ones of federal district courts, and has tables of rules construed by cases reported. A transfer table from official to Reporter citation is supplied, and in each advance sheet and bound volume, there is a digest, identical in classification with that of the American Digest System (§16.5), which covers the reports published in the advance sheet or bound volume. A Statutes Construed table, described in §12.3, is significant because it cites state court decisions interpreting federal statutes.

7. *Services covering the United States Supreme Court.* Three services cover the work of the Supreme Court. Two of them print the slip decisions unofficially.

a. *Journal of the Supreme Court.* This is a daily, official publication, issued during term time, which notes business which is transacted by the Court, such as the admission of attorneys to practice, orders handed down, etc. Decisions of the Court are not included. Because it lacks an index, search in it is difficult. It is reprinted in the United States Law Week described *infra.*

b. *CCH United States Supreme Court Bulletin.* Mailed to subscribers on decison day, this loose-leaf reporter provides elaborate coverage of the business of the Supreme Court. It contains: (1) a statement of all official actions taken by the Court for the preceding week; (2) facsimile reprints of decisions and orders which usually reach subscribers before the official prints; (3) a subject index to cases on the docket or decided during the term; (4) a table of cases on the docket; (5) rules of the Supreme Court; (6) the docket, with a summary of docketed cases; (7) a weekly United States Supreme Court Docket with highlights of recently docketed cases and cases awaiting decisions; and (8) a tentative calendar for arguments before the Court. This is a very detailed status table for the Supreme Court and a repository of slip decisions for the current term.

c. *United States Law Week.* This is a periodical service. Two important sections are devoted to the work of the Supreme Court and the printing of facsimile copies of its latest decisions. Mailed on decision day, it usually reaches the New York area, for example, with its Supreme Court news and case reports the next day. It contains the complete docket, summaries by topic of cases on it, and a Review of Supreme Court's Work. The Review is a unique treatment of various aspects of the Court's work. Exhaustive arguments of the more important cases recently heard by the Court and awaiting decision, in addition to questions by the Court, are presented for various categories of cases. Frequently, the term's cases awaiting decision are reviewed.

The indexes to the Supreme Court sections of the United States Law Week are elaborate, by subject, case, and docket number, and are cumulated at irregular four-to six-week intervals during the term, with a final cumulated issue at the end of the term.

The services mentioned above give a detailed picture of the pending work of the Supreme Court, the docket, the cases argued and awaiting decision, and the text of the term's decisions to date.

§11.3. Lower federal court reports.

It is commonly said that the decisions of the federal courts below the Supreme Court have not been officially reported. Rather, they have appeared only in a multitude of unofficial series before 1880 and in units of the unofficial National Reporter System since then. This is, however, only partly true. Each of the eleven circuits of the Court of Appeals, the Court of Appeals for the District of Columbia, and the special courts of appeal noted in §11.5 prints and distributes its slip decisions. Unfortunately, these decisions for the numbered circuits of the Courts of Appeals are not bound for distribution and few libraries have them. Reversing the usual practice — that the unofficial reports print decisions not officially reported — the above slip decisions *may print per curiam decisions not printed in the unofficial Federal Reporter*. The special courts of appeal are said to prefer citation to their own official reports rather than to the unofficial. All courts, however, accept citations to the unofficial only. This is generally law review practice as well. One reason is the very practical one that the unofficial reports are much more generally available in law libraries than are official reports.

1. *1789–1880 Federal Cases*. During the period preceding the establishment of the Federal Reporter in 1880, some 233 different reporters at various times printed lower federal court decisions. This was an impossible situation for the practicing lawyer. Between the years 1894 and 1897 a new series, Federal Cases,[2] appeared. It combined and reprinted the original, diversely published cases. This set is now used to the exclusion of the original reports it reprints.

a. *Arrangement of Federal Cases*. The arrangement of cases is not chronological, as in other reports, but by title and an arbitrary case number. That is, Case No. 1 is *The Aalesund*, Case No. 26 is *Acker* v. *The Rainbow*, Case No. 18,222 is *In re Zug*, etc. By the time the last volume was ready for printing, ninety-one additional cases were found which were put in an alphabetically arranged supplement in the last volume and, continuing the consecutive numbering, were given numbers 18,223 to 18,313. This necessitated a table of cases to take care of the two alphabets. As nearly as possible the cases included were copied verbatim from the originals together with the original citations, the court deciding the case, the decision date, and

2. St. Paul, Minn., West Publishing Co., 1894–1897, 30 vols.

a headnote. Unreported cases cited to certain points in other decisions are noted by title, e.g., 30 F. Cas. No. 17,856. This case is not reported textually in Federal Cases, but, because it is cited for certain points of law in 2 Wharton's Digest 408–410, Federal Cases reprints the Wharton Digest statements of these points.

b. *Citation of cases printed in Federal Cases*. As in all series in which there has been a change in numbering or other designation, cases citing the reprinted cases before the change in numbering was made cite the original form. It is, therefore, necessary to translate these citations into the Federal Cases citation. If the citation contains the case name, it is only necessary to go to Federal Cases and the 18,222 cases arranged in the main alphabet by case number. If the case is not found there, the 91 "Additional Cases" arranged by name in the appendix must be searched. If, however, the citation is only to the original series volume and page, then a "blue-paper" parallel transfer Table of Citations, shown in Exhibit 33, must be used to find the Federal Case location. Thus, 2 Benedict's (2 Ben.) U.S. District Court Reports 76 is Federal Case No. 15,627. [The full citation would be: *United States* v. *Lot of Leaf Tobacco*, 26 Fed. Cas. 996 No. 15,627 (E.D. N.Y. 1867).]

2. *1880 to date: National Reporter System reports*. With the exception of the special courts described in §11.5, the reports of lower federal courts from 1880 to date which are generally consulted are the units of the National Reporter System entitled the Federal Reporter, the Federal Supplement, and the Federal Rules Decisions. There are technically no official reports for these lower federal courts other than those designated by them as official. Some technically unofficial reports can be said to have semi-official status.

The Judicial Conference of the United States which regulates administrative matters concerning the federal courts has, for example, forwarded requests to the West Publishing Company concerning the content of its Reporters of federal courts and may be said to have thereby conferred at least a semi-official status. Specifically, on March 11, 1960, the Conference approved the following resolution: "Resolved, that the Judicial Conference of the United States approve a request by the United States Court of Claims that its opinions be published hereafter in the Federal Reporter, 2d Series."

These Reporters are typical units and contain all the features common to the National Reporter System.

a. *Federal Reporter*. From its beginning in 1880 through volume 60, Second Series (October Term, 1931), the Federal Reporter reported cases from the federal district courts and the then Circuit Courts of Appeals as well as selected cases, principally tax cases of the United States Court of Claims. With the beginning of the Federal Supplement, the Federal Reporter reported only cases decided by the intermediate courts of appeals; that is, the Courts of Appeals, the Court of Appeals for the District of Columbia, United States Court of Custom and Patent Appeals and the patent, trade-mark, and customs cases from the United States Emergency Court of Appeals. With the above exceptions, all written opinions of the federal courts below the Supreme Court are said to be reported. Since the status of the Court of Claims has been changed to allow appeal directly to the Supreme Court, its decisions are, beginning with volume 276, second series, again reported in the Federal Reporter. Cases reported for this court are principally tax cases. There are weekly advance sheets for this Reporter.

b. *Federal Supplement.* This Reporter covers the federal district courts beginning with the October Term, 1932. Volumes 1 to 181 of this series cover the Court of Claims from October, 1932 to March, 1960. As noted above, the Court of Claims is once again reported in the Federal Reporter as of 1960, with weekly advance sheets.

c. *Federal Rules Decisions.* This Reporter reports decisions construing the federal rules of civil and criminal procedure. Most of these decisions are from the federal district courts and are not reported elsewhere. The Federal Rules Decisions began publication in 1940 following the adoption of the Federal Rules and is a typical National Reporter System unit, except that it also prints speeches and articles on federal practice. These are indexed in each volume of the set (for that volume). There are, in addition, occasional cumulative indexes. These have appeared in volumes 12, 20, 30, 40, and 50. Federal rules are annotated to the cases published in standard report series. New revisions and amendments of court rules are printed as adopted. There are monthly advance sheets.

§11.4. "Consent" decisions in antitrust cases.[3]

In its prosecution of antitrust cases, the Department of Justice Antitrust Division frequently negotiates what are called "consent decrees" under which the party proceeded against agrees to take or to desist from certain action. These decrees currently are published in the CCH Trade Regulation Reports, first in loose-leaf form and later in cumulated, bound form. The Department included them in a compilation of Decrees and Judgments in Federal Anti-trust Cases, July 2, 1890–January 1, 1918. This compilation has been brought up through 1949 by means of four additional volumes which are not sold to the public. The LEXIS data bank contains consent decrees and consent orders from the Federal Trade Commission beginning in 1970.

3. The authors acknowledge with thanks the assistance of Marie L. Resweber of the Department of Justice Library; now retired.

§11.5. Lower federal courts for which there are official reports.

There are official reports, printed by the government, for all the special federal courts or quasi-judicial tribunals listed below. In form these reports are typical law reports. Although the courts concerned prefer to be cited to their own official reports, it is both proper and customary to cite instead the National Reporter series in which they are reported.

1. *Court of Claims*. Now a constitutional court by Act of September 3, 1954, ch. 1263, §39(a), 68 Stat. 1240, 28 U.S.C. §171 (1970), it has jurisdiction to hear statutorily defined claims against the United States, and its decisions have been reported in the Federal Reporter and Federal Supplement as noted above. There are official slip decisions and there have been two consecutive series of official reports which cover from 1855 to date.

2. *Court of Customs and Patent Appeals*. This is a legislative court which hears appeals from the Customs Court and Patent Office tribunals and, on questions of law, from certain findings of the United States Tariff Commission. Its decisions are officially reported in two separate, parallel series, the Court of Customs and Patent Appeals Reports (Patent Cases) and the Court of Customs and Patent Appeals Reports (Customs Cases). Its patent decisions up to 1967 were reported in the official Commissioner's Decisions, but are now reported primarily in the unofficial United States Patents Quarterly. The Federal Reporter also publishes United States Court of Customs and Patent Appeal Decisions.

3. *Customs Courts*. Even though it was called a true court of the United States in *Brooks* v. *Mandel-Witte, Inc.*, 84 F.2d 922 (2d Cir. 1932), *cert. denied*, 286 U.S. 559 (1932), there has been some confusion concerning the status of this court. It was formerly the Board of General Appraisers of the Treasury Department, but was transformed into a legislative court by the Act of May 28, 1926, c. 411, §1, 44 Stat. 669, 19 U.S.C. §405a (1970).

4. *Emergency Court of Appeals*. This is a legislative court having limited jurisdiction to hear cases reviewing orders of the Emergency Price Control Administration and successor agencies. Its decisions were reported in the Federal Reporter. For a history of its nineteen years, see 299 F.2d 1 (1962).

5. *Court of Military Appeals*. Despite its name, this is not a court, but a quasi-judicial tribunal which, for administrative purposes, is located in the Department of Defense. Together with the holdings and decisions of the Judge Advocates' General Boards of Review, these are cumulated into the unofficial Courts-Martial Reports.[4]

4. Rochester, N.Y., Lawyers Co-operative Publishing Co., 1951–1952 to date.

Lawyers Co-operative also publishes the Decisions of the U.S. Court of Military Appeals. In 1978 West's Military Justice Reporter began publishing the Opinions of the U.S. Court of Military Appeals and Selected Opinions of the Courts of Military Review and the Trial Courts.

6. *Tax Court of the United States*. This also is an independent executive agency, not a true court. Its decisions are officially reported in advance sheets and cumulated in bound volumes. Loose-leaf tax services print and annotate the reports.

§11.6. Digests of cases decided in federal courts.

The reported cases of all federal cases are digested in the conventional case digests which are described in Chapter 16.

§11.7. Citators for federal court reports.

These are described in Chapter 18.

§11.8. State court reports.

Every state has its system of courts with a supreme court — by whatever title — at the top. Some, like California, Illinois, Indiana, Missouri, Ohio, and New York, have intermediate appellate courts as well. In some states, for example, New York, Ohio, and Pennsylvania, selected reports of certain courts of first instance are printed.

1. *Official state reports*. Once every state had an official court report to which its courts preferred to be cited. Their number is now diminishing, and there is a trend toward discontinuing the official reports and relying, instead, upon reports published by private publishers. The following states have discontinued the publication of official reports: Alabama, Alaska, Delaware, Florida, Iowa, Kentucky, Louisiana, Maine, Mississippi, Missouri, North Dakota, Oklahoma, Tennessee, Texas, Utah, and Wyoming.

A count at the end of 1978 showed that the official law reports of nearly 25 states were prepared for publication, wholly or in part, by the West Publishing Company, Callaghan, Equity, Bancroft-Whitney, Harrison, Hirschfield, Pantagraph, Michie, Review, Law Abstracts, Bryan, or the Lawyers Co-operative Publishing Company. In some instances, one or more editorial features of, for example, the National Reporter System are incorporated into the series. In series such as Wyoming's Wyoming Reporter, the official form has been totally discarded and replaced by National Reporter System volume numbering and format. While few states publish slip decisions, there are many advance sheets. The citation form for state law reports is discussed in Chapter 32.

2. *Unofficial editions of state reports.* The distinction between official and unofficial state reports is significant only in that state courts prefer, sometimes as specifically indicated by their rules, to be cited to the official reports rather than to the unofficial. In legal writing, the official, if published, should be cited first with the unofficial citation following in parallel. The unofficial reporters print many reports of decisions not printed in the official. This often bothers the first-year law student, who has been quite properly instructed always to cite the official and who, in some instances, can find an unofficial but no official report of a case.

There are several means of determining whether there ever was an official report for a given case. The table of cases in a digest covering the appropriate jurisdiction will give citations to all forms of standard reports — official, National Reporter System, and A.L.R. If the table of cases was printed before the official volume was published, however, this test fails. Another and usually the most accurate check is through the regional Shepard's Citations — Atlantic, Southwestern, etc. If it fails to cite the official report in addition to the unofficial, then, subject to the recent case reservation, there is no official report.

3. *Digests of state and territorial cases.* In one form or another the reported decisions of all federal and state appellate courts and of some courts of first instance from 1658 to date are said to be covered by conventional digests. These are described in Chapter 16.

4. *Legal encyclopedias covering individual states.* Legal encyclopedias generally are described in Chapter 17. Both the Lawyers Cooperative Publishing Company and the West Publishing Company issue encyclopedias covering the law of some of the individual states.

12 Law Reports: The National Reporter System

§12.1. Scope.

The National Reporter System (or the Regional Reporter System) is a privately published edition of law reports. It covers the appellate courts of all states, and some state courts of first instance and all true federal courts but the Customs Court. In addition, there are two special series, the New York Supplement for the courts of record of New York and the California Reporter for the lower courts of California. It is by far the most comprehensive of all unofficial report series, and, as noted in §11.8, a growing number of states have abandoned their own official reports, choosing to rely instead on the National Reporter System which began in 1879 with the North Western Reporter and, within a decade, had spread to all the courts indicated above. Two of the more recent series are the Federal Rules Decisions, added in 1940, and the California Reporter, begun January 4, 1960. The Federal Rules Decisions reports federal court decisions which construe the federal rules of civil and criminal procedure for the district courts and which are not printed in either the Federal Reporter or the Federal Supplement.

Intermediate state appellate courts have not always been reported. The Illinois Appellate Court reports appeared for the first time in the 1936 North Eastern Reporter which printed cases reported in volume 284 of the official reports.

1. *State editions.* State editions of the regional reporters are a rather recent innovation. The Atlantic, North Eastern, North Western, Pacific, South Eastern, South Western, and Southern units of the System are called regional reports, as distinguished from the Supreme Court Reporter, Federal Reporter, Federal Supplement, and Federal Rules Decisions which cover federal courts. In the text of the state editions, the text of the regional Reporter is unchanged, and all tables and other subsidiary features are included. There are, however, additional tables, on colored paper, for the individual state reported in that particular Reporter. Thus the Massachusetts edition of the North Eastern Reporter has a table showing the sections of Massachusetts General Laws of 1932 (the latest edition reenacted as positive law) amended or repealed by the Massachusetts legislature during the session of the current year. There are also parallel conversion tables from the official Massachusetts Reports to the corresponding North Eastern Reporter citation, from the Massachusetts Advance Sheets of the current year to the North Eastern Reporter, and from the North Eastern Reporter citation to the official Massachusetts Reports citation.

2. *Court reports and years covered by Regional Reporters and Regional Reporter digests.*[1]

Atlantic Reporter (1885 to date): *52 Connecticut; 12 Delaware (7 Houston); 6 Delaware Chancery; *77 Maine; *63 Maryland; *63 New Hampshire; *47 New Jersey Law; *40 New Jersey Equity; *108 Pennsylvania State; *102 Pennsylvania Superior; 15 Rhode Island; 58 Vermont; District of Columbia, 31 A.2d (1942).

Atlantic Reporter Digest (cases from 1764 to date): All Connecticut, Delaware, Maine, New Jersey, and Rhode Island cases from the earliest time as reported in standard reports; Maryland, New Hampshire, Pennsylvania, and Vermont cases only from 1 Atlantic Reporter to date.

California Reporter (1960 to date): Supreme Court, Courts of Appeal, Appellate Department Superior Court. Begins with 53 Cal. 2d 187; 176 Cal. App. 2d 1, but includes some cases in 175 Cal. App. 2d.

New York Supplement: 1 New York (Court of Appeals), 1847 to date; lower courts of record (including the Appellate Divisions), 1888 to date.

North Eastern Reporter (1885 to 1971): *112 Illinois; 284 Illinois Appellate; 102 Indiana; 1 Indiana Appellate; 139 Massachusetts; 99 New York; 43 Ohio State; 20 Ohio Appellate.

North Eastern Digest (cases 1817 to 1970): All Indiana cases from

1. The asterisk indicates that only part of the volume is covered.

the earliest time as reported in standard reporters. Illinois, Massachusetts, New York, and Ohio cases only from 1 North Eastern Reporter to 1970 when publication ceased.

North Western Reporter (1883 to date): 1 Dakota; 51 Iowa; 41 Michigan; 26 Minnesota; 9 Nebraska; 1 Nebraska Unofficial; 1 North Dakota; 1 South Dakota; 46 Wisconsin.

North Western Digest (cases 1836 to date): All North Western Reporter cases from the earliest time as reported in standard reporters.

Pacific Reporter (1883 to date): 1 Alaska, 348 P.2d; 1 Arizona; 64 California; 1 California 2d; 1 California 3d; 1 California Appellate; 1 California Appellate 2d; 1 California Appellate 3d; 2 California Unreported; 7 Colorado; 1 Colorado Appellate; 44 Hawaii in 351 P.2d; 2 Idaho; 30 Kansas; 1 Kansas Appellate; 4 Montana; 17 Nevada; 3 New Mexico; 1 Oklahoma; 1 Oklahoma Criminal Appeals; 11 Oregon; 3 Utah; 1 Washington; 2 Washington Territory; 3 Wyoming.

Pacific Digest (cases 1850 to date): All Pacific Reporter cases; see also California Reporter, *supra*.

South Eastern Reporter (1887 to date): *77 Georgia; 1 Georgia Appellate; *96 North Carolina; *25 South Carolina; *82 Virginia; 29 West Virginia.

South Eastern Digest (cases 1729 to date): All South Eastern Reporter Cases.

Southern Reporter (1887 to date): *80 Alabama; 1 Alabama Appellate; *22 Florida; 104 Louisiana; 39 Louisiana Annotated; 9 Louisiana Appellate; 64 Mississippi.

Southern Digest (cases 1809 to date): All Southern Reporter cases and also early decisions of Florida prior to Southern Reporter.

South Western Reporter (1887 to date): 47 Arkansas; *84 Kentucky; *8 Kentucky Law Reporter; 1 Kentucky Decisions; 89 Missouri; *93 Missouri Appellate; *84 Tennessee; 16 Tennessee Appellate; 66 Texas; 21 Texas Appellate; 1 Texas Civil Appeals; 31 Texas Criminal Reports; 4 Willson Civ. Cas. Ct. App. (Texas).

South Western Digest (cases 1887–1958): only from volume 1 of the South Western Reporter to volume 309 of the South Western Reporter, Second Series, inclusive, except all Texas prior to South Western Reporter, Suspended with 309 South Western Reporter.

Supreme Court Reporter (1882 to date): 106 United States Reports to date.

United States Supreme Court Digest (1754 to date): All cases from 2 U.S. (2 Dall.) to date.

Federal Reporter (cases 1880 to date): U.S. Circuit Court to 1912 (when abolished); U.S. Circuit Courts of Appeal (1891 1948), continued by Courts of Appeals (Sept. 1, 1948 to date); U.S. District courts to 1932; U.S. Commerce Court, 1910–1913 (entire life); U.S. Court of Customs and Patent Appeals (Patent Cases), 1929 to date; U.S. Court of Claims 1930–1932, 1960 to date; U.S. Court of Appeals for the District of Columbia Circuit, 1919 to date.

Federal Digest (1754 through 1938 term): Federal courts, except Customs Court; includes cases from all federal courts for Alaska and Hawaii and the United States Court of Appeals for the District of Columbia.

Modern Federal Practice Digest (1939 term to 1961): Continues the Federal Digest. Pocket supplements attempted to keep the series up to date, but these have become unwieldy and have necessitated a new series.

The Federal Practice Digest 2d is a new series being published which supplements the Modern Federal Practice Digest.

Federal Supplement (1932 to date): U. S. District Courts; U. S. Court of Claims, 1932–1960.

Federal Rules Decisions (1940 to date): Federal court decisions, not reported elsewhere, which interpret the federal Rules of Civil and Criminal Procedure.

§12.2. Rationale of the National Reporter System.

The National Reporter System is described in considerable detail in a free pamphlet distributed by the publishers, the West Publishing Company. What follows is intended only to point out several important features of the system.

1. *Speed of publication as exemplified by the advance sheets*. Proper application of the rule of stare decisis or precedent requires the speedy availability of the latest reports of decided cases in point. At the time the National Reporter System was inaugurated in 1879, the official state reports made a farce of this rule, because they were published from one to several years after the decision date. The situation has improved little since then. This is because law report publication is expensive. In most states, there are not enough cases decided during a year to justify the publication of more than a single volume. The contribution of the National Reporter System here was to collate the reports of several contiguous states in order to provide sufficient text to justify the expense of publishing them weekly. The result was the "advance sheet," published weekly for the system except the semimonthly Supreme Court Reporter and the monthly Federal Rules Decisions. Each advance sheet issue is a reporting and digesting system in miniature which covers the cases in it. Each has all the features which later cumulate into the bound volume of the appropriate Reporter.

2. *Combining the reports of contiguous states*. An underlying rationale of the regional reporters is that the law in certain large groups of contiguous states is similar and reflects interests common to all states in the group. The states in the North Eastern or Atlantic Reporter areas may, for example, operate under quite different rules of water law than do those in the Pacific Reporter area.

3. *Reporting more cases than reported in the official reports*. Not all the reports of cases decided in any court are published. Whether or not they are is, for most courts, a matter of editorial discretion on the part of the official reporter. In most jurisdictions, if the official reporter decides that a given case is merely routine and adds nothing to the state of the law, such a case is not reported. While recognizing that only a few important cases failed to be reported as a result of official editorial discretion, the National Reporter editors still believed that too few cases were being published. Accordingly, they have printed thousands of cases not officially reported. The Supreme Court has questioned the value as precedent of unreported cases because of their unavailability to the public and likelihood of appeal. Regional Reporters have added a good bit of otherwise neglected authority to the literature by their policy.

It must be emphasized that just because certain Regional cases have not been officially published, their authority as precedents is in no way diminished.

4. *Key number system*. While the copyrighted Key Number logotype ⚿ is no more a classification device than is a section symbol, it does serve to identify the elaborate classification system of points of law in the decided cases which is the basis of the West Publishing Company system of digests. By this system, the individual headnote paragraphs of the cases reported in federal and appellate courts from 1897 to date are readily found. Furthermore, by means of conversion tables to the earlier Century Digest, cases back to 1658 can be located. The philosophy and application of the Key Number system and its application to digests are described in Chapter 16.

§12.3. Content of material in the National Reporter System.

1. *Opinions and headnotes*. Since, as a matter of public record, courts provide the written texts of the opinions they read in open court, these are identical with those of the official reports, with two occasional exceptions: (a) The court may, at any time up to the printing of its opinions in the official reports, revise them. Sometimes such reports have even been withdrawn and others submitted. This is caught in the National Reporter System before the bound volume is

CITY OF TOLEDO v. JOHNSON Ohio 675
50 N.E.2d 675

72 Ohio App. 46
CITY OF TOLEDO v. JOHNSON, Appellant.

Court of Appeals of Ohio, Lucas County
June 1, 1938.

1. Criminal law ⚷304(21)

Court of Appeals cannot take judicial notice that the "number game" is a "game or scheme of chance" or gambling.

See Words and Phrases, Permanent Edition, for all other definitions of "Game of Chance" and "Number Game"

2. Gaming ⚷94(1)

In a prosecution for operating a "number game" as a game of chance for money in violation of ordinance, there must be proof that a number game is such a game or scheme of chance or gambling in absence of statute or ordinance recognizing the number game as being in such classification.

3. Gaming ⚷98(1)

Where there was neither statute nor ordinance defining the number game as a game of chance for money, and court was unauthorized to take judicial notice that the number game is a game of chance, evidence that defendant was maintaining the number game was insufficient to sustain a conviction under ordinance of maintaining a game of chance for money.

At the left of this page is a typical application of the Key-Number to a National Reporter System case report, taken from 50 N. E. 2d 675 (1938). (Where it is available at press time, the official citation is supplied, as here, rendering the use of conversion tables to find such citation unnecessary. Such is the time lag of official reporting, however, that this official citation is usually undetermined when the bound *Reporter* volume is made up.) The example is from a state requiring the court to prepare a syllabus, and so the two sets of headnotes, official and *Reporter*, afford an opportunity to compare headnote writing techniques. Usually there are more *Reporter* paragraphs than official, and the *Reporters* try to connect each note as directly as possible to the case reported, by including facts. Each note is a single sentence. In some cases a *Reporter* headnote is given, even though the opinion is not printed as part of the report, as in *Schmidt v. Langer*, 336 Ill. App. 158, 83 N. E. 2d 35 (1948).

In the example, the bold-face numerals (**1, 2, 3**) are not part of the headnote or Key-Number classification, but refer to like numerals, in brackets [**1**], in the text of the opinion, where the headnoted rule is stated. Criminal Law ⚷ 304(21) is the Key-Number, each such number always being composed of *both a word or words (the main topic heading), and a number (indicating the sub-topic)*. In the digest at the back of the *Reporter* in which our case is printed, this subhead is defined as *Evidence: Judicial Notice, Presumptions, and Burden of Proof: Nature of certain games and terminology thereof*. This particular paragraph, verbatim, is printed in 13 *Fifth Decennial Digest* 668, along with six other paragraphs on the same topic, from six states. It is also printed in the *North Eastern Reporter Digest* under the same classification. By means explained in Chapter 19 like cases in point, if any, from 1658 to date may be found through this same Key-Number.

676 Ohio **50 NORTH EASTERN REPORTER, 2d SERIES**

Syllabus by the Court.

1. A court may not take judicial notice that a "number game" is a game or scheme of chance or gambling.

2. In order to sustain a conviction on a charge of unlawfully engaging "in a game of chance for money, to wit, number game," in violation of an ordinance making it unlawful to engage in a game of chance, there must be proof that a "number game" is a game or scheme of chance or gambling, there being no such "game of chance" recognized by statute or ordinance as a "number game."

George Johnson was convicted of engaging in a game of chance for money, and he appeals.—[Editorial Statement]

Exhibit 27

printed and the revised text is printed. Such revision seldom occurs. (b) The Reporter editors may discover errors in their reports. While covering the same material, the headnotes of the Reporter and those of the official reports do not exactly coincide either in the number of paragraphs or in the text. There are apt to be more paragraphs in the Reporter than in the official edition. These serve as the basis of the infinitely detailed American Digest System classification. Where, as directed by law in some states, the court writes its own headnotes stating the law of the case, the National Reporter System regards them as part of the official text of the decision and prints them along with its own headnotes. In National Reporter reports, the headnotes are numbered to correspond to numbers in the text of the opinion where points of law are found. See Exhibit 27.

2. *Words and phrases*. The courts' definitions of either words of common usage or legal terms of art which are stated in their opinions are collected in each advance sheet and bound volume of the Reporter. They are then taken from them to form a very large dictionary of such definitions. This is described in Chapter 21.

3. *Court rules*. New rules, revisions, and amendments are printed in the appropriate Reporter units at their time of adoption.

4. *Tables of cases*. There are two case tables in the bound volumes of all units except those of the Supreme Court Reporter which reports the cases of only one court. The first table, in a single alphabet, lists all cases in all the states or federal circuits which are covered by the Reporter. Then, as a further convenience, when the individual state or federal court is known, there is a second index by state or circuit. The advance sheet tables of cases, however, are all in a single alphabet.

5. *Tables of statutes construed*. Found in each advance sheet and bound volume, these tables serve an interim citator function. They list conventional and subordinate legislation which has been construed by the courts in the cases reported. Their use as citators is described in Chapter 18.

6. *Digests*. Each advance sheet and bound volume contains a digest in miniature, formed from the Key-Numbered digest paragraphs of cases reported in it.

7. *Miscellaneous features*. Judges in the courts reported are listed in each bound volume by jurisdiction. Judicial Highlights are occasionally found in advance sheets. There is a "synopsis of state and federal cases of current interest and importance."

§12.4. Citation books for the National Reporter System.

Shepard's Citations covers all Reporter units. These are described in Chapter 18.

§12.5. Parallel transfer tables from official to National Reporter citations or the reverse.

These tables are described in §14.5.

13 Law Reports: Selective and Special-Subject Systems

§13.1. Annotated reports systems.

1. *Rationale.* The annotated reports system is a device which enables the legal researcher, whether practicing attorney or student, to pick the brains of an expert editorial staff as an aid to problem solving. It is based upon two assumptions: first, that out of the thousands of new cases reported each year there are some which are of interest to lawyers of all jurisdictions, not just to those in the one in which the case was decided; second, that these same lawyers will find useful a careful and precise listing of all American cases in point along with a discussion based upon them of the points of law involved, the majority and minority rules, and the impact of the annotated case upon the law. There is also a recognition of the fact that a case in point in one jurisdiction, even if not mandatory authority, may be highly persuasive when cited to the courts in another jurisdiction. Comprising but a small fraction of the total cases in all jurisdictions, the cases have undergone expert selection and annotation and merit consideration by lawyers everywhere.

2. *Selective case series, past and present.* At various times, there have been some eight principal selective reports series in the United States. Only the American Law Reports Annotated (cited as A.L.R.) and A.L.R. Federal are currently published. The earlier series were

not annotated to any important degree, and their purpose was to make available to lawyers a limited selection of cases of interest in all jurisdictions. In the days before law libraries were as complete and accessible as they now are, this served an important function.

Three early series, known collectively as the "Trinity Series," were the American Reports, American Decisions, and American State Reports. These printed a selection of American Cases from the earliest times through 1911. They were not truly annotated cases but did contain some notes helpful to the lawyer at the time. American and English Annotated Cases (1906–1911) merged into American Annotated Cases (1912–1918), and Lawyers Reports Annotated was published in two series from 1888 to 1918. As their titles indicate, they were annotated, but their annotation varied in degrees of completeness and fell short of the fullness of the present A.L.R. and A.L.R. Federal. All of these competing series were merged in 1918 into the current American Law Reports Annotated. Of these early law reports series, only the Lawyers Reports Annotated (L.R.A.) serves a presently useful purpose, and the others are now seldom found on law library reading room shelves. The only current value of these series is that they print the text of a decision. It is, however, better for the searcher to go to the American Digest System table of cases and find the official citation and read the report from it since it is the series which must be cited in legal writing. Though of diminishing value, Lawyers Reports Annotated is on the reading room shelves of most law school libraries.

3. *American Law Reports Annotated (cited as A.L.R.).* This reporter prints and annotates cases from 1918 to date in three units: A.L.R., First Series, in 175 volumes, covers from 1918 to 1947; the Second Series (A.L.R.2d), in 100 volumes, from 1947 to 1965; and A.L.R. Third Series (A.L.R.3d), from 1965 to date.

a. *Selection of cases for A.L.R. reports.* Cases from all American jurisdictions are selected. While Supreme Court cases were not excluded from early A.L.R. Reports, very few were ever included and later reports ceased including them at all, because all such cases are printed in the annotated Lawyers' Edition of the Supreme Court reports which is issued by the same publishers. Supreme Court cases which are reported in A.L.R. tend to be those of interest to lawyers whose principal practice is in state courts. Before 1969, many United States Courts of Appeals reports were printed in A.L.R. Since then, federal court cases have been annotated in A.L.R. Federal (see par. 4 below).

Cases for inclusion and annotation are selected on the basis of their utility to the profession, not because they are leading cases. They may be broken down into broad categories of subject matter:

(1) *Cases lending themselves to an exhaustive treatment of an*

important subdivision of the law of a major topic. Such subject matter might include a subdivision of contracts or torts, which the editors feel needs to be brought more up-to-date than has been done in legal encyclopedias or treatises. An example is the 113-page annotation in 55 A.L.R. 6 on the "implied or apparent authority of an agent to purchase or order goods or merchandise."

(2) *Cases treating limited areas of the law which are not covered at all or are covered insufficiently in other law books.* Examples of this type are annotations such as the 305-page annotation in 164 A.L.R. 8 on "liability for accidents at street or highway intersection as affected by reliance upon or disregard of traffic sign, signal or marking"; the 63-page annotation in 55 A.L.R.2d 129 on "liability for injury or death from electrification of guy wire"; the 28-page annotation in 57 A.L.R.2d 569 on "rights of fishing, boating or bathing or the like in inland lakes"; the 58-page annotation in 65 A.L.R.2d 342 on "carbon copies of letters or other written instruments as evidence"; or the 155-page annotation in 100 A.L.R.2d 16 on apportionment of damages caused by successive impacts of motor vehicles.

Sometimes a group of cases illustrating different aspects of a single topic will be annotated in a single A.L.R. volume. Examples are the four annotations in 68 A.L.R.2d on group insurance termination (totaling 257 pages) and the three in 13 A.L.R.3d on a union's rights regarding members' dues and fines (totaling 53 pages).

b. *Content of A.L.R. reports.* A.L.R. is composed of selected cases each followed by a comprehensive annotation which provides a useful analysis of the legal issues contained in that preceding case. Every opinion is printed in full from the official text. Parallel official, Regional Reporter, and A.L.R. are cited. The decision is summarized at some length in the Second and Third Series, as illustrated by Exhibit 28 below. The subject of the annotation is noted. Headnotes are written by the editors, but any "syllabus by the court" is regarded as part of the official record of the case and is printed verbatim. The headnotes are classified according to the Permanent A.L.R. Digest classification. A.L.R. is coordinated with the text of American Jurisprudence, the legal encyclopedia published by the Lawyers Co-operative, which is largely based upon A.L.R. cases. Conversely, there are Am. Jur. cross-references to A.L.R. annotations. As with National Reporter cases, headnotes are numbered and keyed to corresponding numerals in the text of the opinion. A.L.R. is one of the very few remaining report series in which the statement of facts and summaries of arguments of counsel are supplied.

c. *The A.L.R. annotation.* The varied subject matter of A.L.R. annotations has been indicated above. Unlike some earlier ones, all A.L.R. cases are now annotated. Annotations vary in length from a half-page note to an encyclopedic treatment of 300 pages or more.

1355

EDYTHE B. BURNS, Appt.,
v
ROBERT H. BURNS, Respt.

Montana Supreme Court — February 2, 1965
145 Mont 1, 400 P2d 642, 13 ALR3d 1355

SUMMARY OF DECISION

In divorce proceedings in the Sixth District Court, Sweet Grass County, Montana, George J. Allen, J., both parties sought a divorce. The trial court's judgment consisted of a decree of divorce granted to each party, and an award of child custody and alimony to the wife.

On appeal by the wife, the trial court's judgment was affirmed by the Supreme Court of Montana, which, in an opinion by Doyle, J., held, inter alia, that when the trial court in a divorce action wherein both parties sought a divorce found that both parties established grounds for divorce, and further found that the legitimate objects of marriage were destroyed, it could, in its discretion, award a divorce to both parties, notwithstanding statutory provisions for the denial of a divorce upon showing recrimination.

John C. Harrison, J., and Adair, J., dissented.

HEADNOTES

Classified to ALR Digests

Divorce and Separation § 62 — divorce to both parties — recrimination statutes

1. When the trial court in a divorce action wherein both parties seek a divorce finds that both parties have established grounds for divorce, and it further finds that the legitimate objects of marriage have been destroyed, it may, in its discretion, award a divorce to both parties, notwithstanding statutory provisions that divorces must be denied upon showing recrimination, and that recrimination was a showing by the defendant of any cause of divorce against the plaintiff, in a bar of the plaintiff's cause of divorce.

[Annotated]

Divorce and Separation § 87 — propriety of alimony award — divorce awarded to both parties

2. An award of alimony to a wife in her divorce action wherein the husband also

SUBJECT OF ANNOTATION

Beginning on page 1364

Power of court to grant absolute divorce to both spouses upon showing of mutual fault

Exhibit 28

An annotation is organized in much the same manner as a case digest or legal encyclopedia topics described in Chapters 16 and 17. It tends to proceed from the general to the specific and often discusses procedure and remedies. For A.L.R.3d, this discussion is found in a section of the annotation titled "Practice Pointers." The Introduction defines the limits of the annotation, states broadly the existing law, and points out the main and subsidiary topics to be considered. Often earlier annotations or materials are referred to. Then, as in a digest or encyclopedia, the main topic is broken down into increasingly narrow subtopics. Each of these is considered in turn with majority and jurisdictional rules stated and analyzed and with discussion of supporting cases. Variation and departures from the various rules and the reasons for them are pointed out. Where the result depended upon a statute, that fact is noted. The final structural breakdown of an A.L.R. annotation is into numbered sections. These have an important subsidiary function because they are used to keep the annotation up-to-date by references to later cases in point. Later cases supplementing annotations are noted differently in each of the A.L.R. series. The various aids for updating are described in par. f below and in Exhibits 30 and 31.

Preceding each annotation of substantial length is an alphabetical index. This index may consist of several pages of catchwords relating both to legal principles and to fact situations (e.g., Discretion of the court, Store account book, Boating accident) noted in the text. The Word Index, described below, offers one of the most fruitful approaches to the law. A Table of Jurisdictions Represented in the annotation is also provided for Second and Third Series annotations.

These features of an A.L.R. annotation are illustrated by Exhibit 29.

d. *Authority citation in A.L.R. annotations.* All American cases in point are said to be considered in the annotation in addition to occasional British cases. Following the statements of the general rules, all cases in point are cited by jurisdiction. For the textual analyses following the general statements, individual supporting cases, including the case being annotated, are analyzed, and majority and minority rules and variations are stated and discussed. Although there are no formal headnote case digests, the cases cited as authority are discussed at some length in many instances and are, in effect, digested. Citation is by jurisdiction and by means of a typography which makes locating a jurisdiction simple. The series name part of a report citation is printed in boldface type, as 43 **Del.** 494. As a further aid, a table of jurisdictions cited in each annotation precedes the annotation, a feature begun with 57 A.L.R.2d.

There are no advance sheets. Because it takes time to prepare the annotation, the cases fully reported in A.L.R. are usually over a year

ANNOTATION

LIABILITY OF PARTICIPANT IN TEAM ATHLETIC COMPETITION FOR INJURY TO OR DEATH OF ANOTHER PARTICIPANT

by

Donald M. Zupanec, M.A., J.D.

§ 1. Introduction

[a] Scope

This annotation[1] collects those cases in which the courts have discussed the question whether, and under what circumstances, a participant in a team athletic competition[2] can be

1. Insofar as the instant annotation treats matters discussed in the annotation at 7 ALR2d 704, that annotation need no longer be consulted.

TOTAL CLIENT-SERVICE LIBRARY® REFERENCES

4 Am Jur 2d, Amusements and Exhibitions §§ 86, 98; 57 Am Jur 2d, Negligence § 284

1 Am Jur Pl & Pr Forms (Rev Ed), Amusements and Exhibitions, Forms 81–96

22 Am Jur Proof of Facts 287, Football Injuries

2 Am Jur Trials 2, Investigating Particular Civil Actions; 7 Am Jur Trials 213, Contact Sports Injury Cases

ALR Digests, Amusements § 11

L Ed Index to Annos, Amusements; Assault and Battery

ALR Quick Index, Amusements, Exhibitions, Shows, and Resorts; Assault and Battery; Negligence

Federal Quick Index, Amusements and Exhibitions; Assault and Battery; Negligence

Consult POCKET PART in this volume for later cases

1300

Exhibit 29

old by publication. For this reason, parallel A.L.R. citation is often omitted from another publisher's digest tables of cases, which are frequently made up before the selection of a case for annotation is made. The digest table of cases is, accordingly, not always a reliable test of whether or not a case has been published in A.L.R. A more certain method is to check the A.L.R. Tables of Laws Reported or the appropriate unit of Shepard's Citations in the cumulative red-paper supplement or later bound volume. See §18.4.2g.

e. *Utility and citation of A.L.R. annotations.* The annotated cases do not cover legal or fact situations as inclusively as does a digest; too few cases are annotated for that. On the other hand, since all cases in point are said to be considered in the annotations themselves, the subject matter covered is much wider than the limited number of annotations might indicate. The annotations are so carefully done that they are widely used by both practicing lawyers and law students. If these searchers can find annotations in point and update them by supplements or other means, they have had preliminary, arduous tasks of case-finding and analysis done for them. Annotations are particularly effective in analyses of narrow subjects not yet adequately treated in textbooks or encyclopedias. They are also effective when a new decision has upset an old rule, and treatises and encyclopedias have not yet adequately discussed its probable effect. The annotation may treat at considerable length a facet of a subject only touched on in passing in textbooks. An example is the two successive annotations by W. E. Shipley in 16 A.L.R.2d 3 and 393 (1951) on the topics of (1) excessive and (2) adequate damages for personal injuries not resulting in death. Together, these two annotations occupy 453 pages and consider 162 types of injury. Their subject indexes alone extend to fifteen pages.

Annotations are not themselves authority but only indexes to authority. In citing the annotation, the *page upon which the annotation begins, not that of the reported case,* is the one to give. Supplementary references in the A.L.R. Blue Book of Supplemental Decisions, the A.L.R.2d Later Case Service, and the A.L.R.3d pocket part supplements are to the annotation, not to the reported and annotated case.

Annotated cases are cited in federal court briefs or in law reviews only as cases, not as annotations, but are frequently cited for their annotations in state courts. The proper form of citation is as follows:

> *King* v. *Superior Court,* 108 Ariz. 492, 502 P.2d 529, 60 A.L.R. 3rd 172 (1972). [when cited as a case]
>
> *King* v. *Superior Court,* 108 Ariz. 492, 502 P.2d 529, 60 A.L.R. 3rd 172 (1972). *See* Annot., 60 A.L.R.3rd 176, 197 (1974). [meaning that part on page 197 of an annotation which begins on page 176 and was written in 1974]

f. *Supplementing A.L.R. annotations by later cases in point.* Cases cited as authority for A.L.R. annotation sections are the latest available at press time. Later cases do, however, continue to appear. The searcher must be made aware of them if the search for authority is to be complete and up-to-date.

A.L.R., First Series, takes care of this with its Blue Book of Supplemental Decisions for Annotations in American Law Reports. To the extent that it notes these later cases in point, it is a citator. All annotations are listed in the Blue Book by A.L.R. volume and the page upon which the annotation starts and not the page upon which the annotated case begins. Under it are cited all later cases in point by jurisdiction. See Exhibit 30.

56 ALR SUPPLEMENTAL DECISIONS 158

56 ALR 527-529

Supplemented 83 ALR 147, and 120 ALR 511.✦

56 ALR 532-533

Supplemented 107 ALR 1463.✦

56 ALR 543-577

Allen v. T. & P. R. Co. (CA La) 195 F2d 545.
Merlino v S. P. Co. 132 Cal App2d 58, 281 P2d 583.
Murphy v A. T. & S. F. R. etc. 139 Cal App2d 792, 294 P2d 458.
Keturosky v. I. H. B. R. Co. 1 Ill App2d 88, 116 NE2d 410.
Keystone-Fleming Transport v T. (Tex Civ App) 277 SW2d 202, error dismd.
Pope v. E. M. R. C. Corp. (W Va) 75 SE2d 584.
Boyce v N. U. Co. (Wyo) 297 P2d 820.

56 ALR 601-645

U. S. v M. (CA3rd) 229 F2d 830 (citing anno).
United States v N. (DC Pa) 128 F Supp 805 (citing anno).
Hilton v A. (Va) 96 SE2d 151 (citing anno).

56 ALR 647-655

Supplemented 91 ALR 1055.✦

56 ALR 701-702

Kinner v. S. (Idaho) 262 P2d 994.

56 ALR 721-722

Advisory Opinion to the Covernor (Fla) 88 So2d 131.
Advisory Opinion to the Governor (Fla) 95 So2d 603.
State ex rel. Stadter v. P. (Or) 251 P2d 123.

56 ALR 727-729

Graham v. P. (Colo) 248 P2d 730.
White v. P. (Colo) 249 P2d 823.
People v. G. 415 Ill 47, 112 NE2d 133.
People v. B. 415 Ill 329, 114 NE 2d 370.

Exhibit 30

If the number of supplemental cases in point become unwieldy, a supplemental or superseding annotation is often compiled which incorporates all these cases and comments on them. As noted in Exhibit 30, such supplemental annotations are indicated by a star under the citation to the original annotation, and searches for future cases are made under the starred citation, not under the original citation. Because the Blue Book list of additional citations is by case only, with no indication of which section of the annotation it applies to, determining whether a given additional case cited in it is pertinent involves a slow and laborious matching up if there are very many cases cited. The Blue Book has been published in five "permanent" volumes covering later supplementing cases through 1975. These, in turn, are kept up-to-date by a pamphlet Blue Book Service which is issued annually. The Blue Book service is confined entirely to supplementing cases annotated in A.L.R., First Series.

Second Series Annotations are updated by a separate set of volumes known as the A.L.R.2d Later Case Service. Each of these volumes is arranged by volume and page of annotation affected and is further updated by annual pocket parts.

The annotations in the Third Series are kept up-to-date with annual pocket parts in each volume of A.L.R.3d. The arrangement is also by the volume and the page of the annotation affected. See Exhibit 31.

The A.L.R.2d Later Case Service and the A.L.R.3d pocket parts are a great improvement over the Blue Book in two respects. As in the Blue Book, all annotations for which later cases in point are cited are listed by volume and page of annotation. There, however, the

AMERICAN LAW REPORTS

THIRD SERIES

1978 Supplement

VOLUME 69 ALR3d

69 ALR3d 22–86

§ 1 [69 ALR3d 24]

[b] Related matters

Admissibility under state law of hospital record relating to intoxication or sobriety of patient. 80 ALR3d 456.

Admissibility of police reports under federal business records act (Federal Rules of Evidence, Rule 803, and predecessor amendments). 31 ALR Fed 457.

§ 3 [69 ALR3d 32]

Also holding or recognizing that hospital records are generally admissible in criminal prosecutions under provisions of business entry statutes:

NJ—State v Martorelli, 136 NJ Super 449, 346 A2d 618.

NC—State v Wright, 29 NC App 752, 225 SE2d 645 (citing annotation).

Tenn—Graham v State (Tenn) 547 SW2d 531.

Tex—Moton v State (Tex Crim) 540 SW2d 715.

Wash—Bradley v Maurer (1977) 17 Wash App 24, 560 P2d 719.

69 ALR3d 104–112

§ 1 [69 ALR3d 105]

[b] Related matters

Admissibility under state law of hospital record relating to intoxication or sobriety of patient. 80 ALR3d 456.

Admissibility of police reports under federal business records act (Federal Rules of Evidence, Rule 803, and predecessor amendments). 31 ALR Fed 457.

Failure To Inform Patient of Nature and Hazards of Surgery. 8 Am Jur Proof of Facts 2d 145.

§ 3 [69 ALR3d 108]

Admission of reports from other doctors which contained opinions which were not disputed as to factual information relating to acts, conditions, and events were admissible within business records exception. Bradley v Maurer (1977) 17 **Wash** App 24, 560 P2d 719.

69 ALR3d 122–482

§ 1 [69 ALR3d 130]

[b] Related matters

Construction and effect of will provisions not expressly mentioning payment of death taxes but relied on as affecting the burden of estate or inheritance taxes. 70 ALR3d 630.

Construction and effect of provisions in nontestamentary instrument relied upon as affecting the burden of estate or inheritance taxes. 70 ALR3d 691.

Construction and effect of will provisions relied on as affecting payment of real or personal property taxes or income taxes. 70 ALR3d 726.

Construction and application of statutes apportioning or prorating estate taxes. 71 ALR3d 247.

Remedies and practice under estate tax apportionment statutes. 71 ALR3d 371.

§ 4 [69 ALR3d 186]

[c] Intention as derived from language of instrument in light of surrounding circumstances; extrinsic evidence

See Estate of Bryner **(Pa)** 345 A2d 706, infra § 39[a].

[c] Meaning of words

See Estate of Bryner **(Pa)** 345 A2d 706, infra § 39[a].

Exhibit 31

resemblance ceases. The cases are not merely listed by jurisdiction. Instead, they are listed, where pertinent, under the *precise section number* of the annotation which they supplement. The citation is, then, by A.L.R., 2d or 3d volume, page, and *section number*, together with the title heading of that section. In addition, each listed supplemental case is digested and commented upon, sometimes at considerable length. Where later cases present distinct new subject matter, new sections and headings are added. Where an A.L.R.2d annotation has been supplemented or superseded by a later one, that fact is noted by a statement. Thus, 13 A.L.R.2d 191–252 is supplemented in 58 A.L.R.2d 865. An Annotation History Table in the A.L.R. Quick Index lists annotations in A.L.R. First, Second and Third Series. Thus, 160 A.L.R. 1406 is superseded by 43 A.L.R.2d 632. First Series case annotations may still be traced through the Blue Book (see Exhibit 30) or through the historical table in the A.L.R. Quick Index.

There may be more recent supplementation through the National Reporter System's Key Number system advance sheets and West's General Digest reporting or digesting cases later than those cited in the A.L.R. Annual Later Case Service. Thus, if the searcher knows either the name of a supplemental case or its subject matter and finds the report in the National Reporter System, the pertinent Key Number classification for the point of law can be determined, National Reporter System advance sheets and the General Digest reporting or digesting later cases can be consulted, and the search can be brought beyond the Later Case Service to within a very few weeks of the latest decision.

g. *Citators for selective cases*. Neither L.R.A. nor A.L.R. cases are covered as such in Shepard's Citations. Rather, they are Shepardized under their official and National Reporter System citations. Shepard's Citations will note that if a case has been discussed or merely cited in annotation, that annotation will be cited. Then by referring to the annotation, other cases in point, more recent and more pertinent may be located. If the name of the case is known, its citation forms may be found in the usual way through the American Digest System table of cases or through the tables of cases for L.R.A. or A.L.R. in their respective digests. Because they do note later cases in point with annotations, the Blue Book, the A.L.R.2d Later Case Service, and the A.L.R.3d pocket parts also serve as citators.

4. *A.L.R. Federal*. Patterned after A.L.R., Third Series, the first volume of A.L.R. Federal was published by Lawyers Co-operative in 1969. The series was undertaken because of the growing importance of federal regulation and litigation to the practicing lawyer. In it, leading decisions of federal courts are reported and annotated. Pertinent statutes, rules, and regulations are analyzed, and procedural forms are supplied where appropriate. Each volume is supplemented by an annual pocket part, and the entire series is indexed by the Federal Quick Index which, in addition to A.L.R. Federal, covers all federal matters in the three A.L.R. series, Am. Jur. 2d, and the other Lawyers Co-operative publications.

§13.2. Approaches to the law through L.R.A., A.L.R., and A.L.R. Federal.

There are three approaches, standard for all digests and the tools for their use: the table of cases, the fact approach through the descriptive-word index, and the analytic approach through topic analyses in the digest or, for A.L.R., 2d and 3d, and A.L.R. Federal, in the Quick and Federal Quick Indexes. These approaches are generally described in §30.1. Specific A.L.R. aids are described below:

a. The Complete Digest of Lawyers Reports Annotated 1888–1918. This conventional digest is now little used.

b. Permanent Digest of American Law Reports Annotated. This otherwise conventional digest, covering volumes 1 to 175 of A.L.R., First Series, stresses A.L.R. annotations, but the points of law digested are wider in scope, and there are more of them than in the annotations. This is because, while all points in an A.L.R. case are fully digested, only a few closely connected ones are annotated. Thus, *Egner* v. *States Realty Co.*, 170 A.L.R. 500, has twenty-nine headnotes (all reflected in the Digest). But only the first six, relating to the termination of partners' agency by partnership dissolution, are the subject of the annotation and are so indexed in the Word Index. The function of the usual descriptive-word index is performed by the Word Index to Annotations and the Quick Index, below. This 12-volume set includes a table of cases by plaintiff and defendant names.

c. The A.L.R.2d 1 to 100 Digest, Cases and Annotations, covering the 100 volumes of the Second Series, is a typical case digest as described in Chapter 16. Access to the law is through the table of cases (by both Plaintiff and Defendant), the scope note and cross-references to and from pertinent topics, and the Word Index and the Quick Index described below.

d. The A.L.R. Word Indexes to Annotations, covering together the first two series of A.L.R., are the usual point of departure in an A.L.R. search. They are the descriptive-word indexes to the annotations, with references to the annotations, not to the digests. The first two volumes of the index cover A.L.R.2d 1–75 in one alphabet. A.L.R.2d volumes 76 to 100 are covered by yet another single alphabet in volume 3. They are easily distinguishable on the shelves by their bright red binding.

e. A.L.R. Quick Index to Annotations. A.L.R. First, Second and Third Series are now covered by new A.L.R. Quick Indexes.

The Quick Indexes are designed to combine most of the functions of the digest and of the descriptive-word index. References are to the more accurate exact titles of the annotations, rather than the former cryptic subject-condensation type of entry. The pocket supplement has a table of cases (by plaintiff only) of the latest cases to date. A new feature is the Annotation History Table, referred to above. The publishers indicate that the Quick Index may supplant both the former A.L.R. Digest and the Word Index to Annotations format.

§13.3. Special-subject reporters.

Several series of law reports select decisions relating to special and limited subjects in which their subscribers are interested. They may collect labor, tax, public utilities, trade regulation, or bankruptcy cases, and usually the cases contained in them are also published in the regular official and unofficial reports series. Occasionally, however, as in the antitrust consent decisions in the CCH Trade Regulation Reports, they make available material not otherwise printed for general distribution. Most such current series are issued as loose-leaf services, collecting and binding in permanent form the reports first printed in the services in loose-leaf form.

§13.4. Loose-leaf reporting services.

These are described in Chapter 23.

14 Law Reports: Tabular Means for Finding

§14.1. Need for tables.

If all case reports from all jurisdictions were published in a single, all-inclusive series arranged in alphabetical order by case name, there would perhaps be little need for tables as aids to finding individual case reports. They are not, however, so published. There have been many hundreds of different, parallel series in which, with the exception of Federal Cases, the reports are printed in chronological, not alphabetical, order by jurisdiction. Tables to aid in locating cases are therefore indispensable.

§14.2. Copying case citations fully and accurately.

Always copy down the very fullest information about each case you read and select for reference. When you have a law report in front of you, giving the name of a case and the citation in at least one form, or when you have in front of you some other kind of law book giving a citation to a case in which you are interested, do not skimp in setting down the information identifying it. The five seconds you save in writing down an abridged and hasty citation may cost you many minutes of detective work before the correct citation is found.

For example, if the case is *Bordy* v. *Smith*, 150 Neb. 272, 34 N.W.2d 331, 5 A.L.R. 250 (1948), write all that down while you have the actual report or other law book citing it open in front of you.

There are at least two sound reasons for this. First, if you or the person whose citation you are copying has made an error in it somewhere, each element of that complete citation can be an important clue. If all elements — title, official and unofficial reporter volume and page, and date of decision — were written down, some are bound to be correct and will lead speedily to the correct full citation. Second, if the official report containing your case is off the shelf at the time, you have the citation to the unofficial and vice versa, and you have given yourself two chances to find the case. Or, if you are citing the case to somebody else and you do not know which reporter — official or unofficial — is available, you have, as a matter of courtesy, provided three citations and have not forced the other person to use a parallel conversion table.

§14.3. Tables of abbreviations.

In order to save time and space, legal writers employ many hundreds of abbreviations in their citations of case series, statutes, encyclopedias, etc. Some of these are obvious, like U.S., Harv. L. Rev., but many are not and would be incomprehensible without tables of abbreviations to identify them. Such tables are available in digests, loose-leaf services, citators, dictionaries, encyclopedias, etc. A comprehensive table of abbreviations is found in the present edition of Effective Legal Research, by Price, Bitner, and Bysiewicz, in Appendix III.

§14.4. Tables of cases.

Almost every law book which prints or cites cases has a table of cases. The table of cases approach to legal research is one of the most fruitful of all, but because full utilization involves case tables or some materials not yet studied in this book, its detailed discussion is postponed to Chapter 30.

§14.5. Parallel citation tables from official reports and reverse.

As already noted, law reports may be published officially or unofficially in various and usually duplicating forms such as the National Reporter System, selective annotated case series, special-subject series, or loose-leaf services. Reports from more than 200 different series were, for example, combined in the single Federal Cases.

Because few libraries have all forms of every report, and because, even if the official is at hand, the searcher may desire to utilize the Key Number approach to a digest through a National Reporter System headnote or to see if a case has been annotated in A.L.R., parallel citation tables from one form to the other are supplied by law publishers. These permit the translation from the official to the unofficial or the reverse. Thus, *from* 41 Ohio App. 169 *to* 180 N.E. 659; or *from* 139 So. 509 *to* 19 La. App.; or *from* 150 Neb. 272, 34 N.W. 2d 331 *to* 5 A.L.R.2d 250. There are several means of doing this. Which means is best at a given moment depends upon the circumstances.

The parallel listing of cases in case tables is in this form: official citation first, Regional Reporter next, then selective case series if any: *Kritzer* v. *Moffat*, 136 Wash. 410, 240 P. 355, 44 A.L.R. 681 (1925). Some tables include the date of decision, some do not. In legal writing it should always be included because it is an important element of the case cited.

1. *Tables of cases*. Because these tables arrange cases alphabetically by name or title, the name of a case is a prerequisite to their use. All such tables have a listing by plaintiff-defendant; increasingly, there is also a defendant-plaintiff listing, either in a separate table or combined in the same alphabet with the plaintiff-defendant list. The American Digest System Decennial Digests have only a plaintiff-defendant table, but other National Reporter System digests, as well as the digests of other publishers, have defendant-plaintiff listings.

Most plaintiff-defendant tables give the complete parallel citations *as known on the date the tables were compiled*. This reservation is necessary because sometimes the table may have been compiled before a case listed was selected for annotation by A.L.R. The A.L.R. citation would then be omitted though, in fact, the case is annotated in that series. Similarly the official citation may not have been published at the time the table was compiled. This occurrence, however, is more rare. A further advisable check on this is through Shepard's Citations.

156 TEXAS REPORTS

Tex.	S.W.2d		Tex.	S.W.2d		Tex.	S.W.2d		Tex.	S.W.2d		Tex.	S.W.2d		Tex.	S.W.2d	
Pg.	Vol.	Pg.	Pg.	Vol.	Pg.	Pg.	Vol.	Pg.	Pg.	Vol.	Pg.	Pg.	Vol.	Pg.	Pg.	Vol.	Pg.
1	291	673	139	293	488	238	294	385	329	294	795	455	295	901	561	297	817
7	291	697	148	293	484	252	294	377	334	295	890	456	295	894	570	297	811
18	291	721	154	293	493	252	293	841	340	295	412	467	296	233	574	297	813
28	291	926	158	293	758	267	295	654	365	295	408	474	296	517	580	298	108
36	291	693	168	293	753	269	294	712	371	295	405	484	297	112	584	298	119
44	291	677	176	293	639	277	294	706	376	295	902	488	296	757	587	298	93
61	291	689	185	293	736	282	294	705	382	295	642	492	296	750	593	298	[illegible]

Exhibit 32

2. *Official citation to unofficial citation*. For example, *from* 142 Tex. 589 *to* 180 S.W.2d 135.

a. *National Reporter Blue Book*. This transfer table is "[a] complete table showing volume and page of the Reporter for every case found in the corresponding state [and United States Supreme Court] reports." As seen in Exhibit 32, it is a very simple table which lists the official report by volume (above the line) and page (below the line) with the unofficial Reporter citation in parallel. The Blue Book is in units covering, respectively, years to 1928, 1929 to 1936, 1937 to 1948, 1949 to 1960, 1961 to 1970, with cumulative pamphlet supplements.

b. *State Blue and White Books*. The need for them having largely ceased,[1] these are no longer published. There was a separate book for each state, sold for use only in the state covered. For the one state only, a Blue Section was a counterpart of the National Reporter Blue Book and translated the official state report citation to the unofficial. The White Section reversed this process by translating the unofficial citation to the official.

c. *State editions of Regional Reporter advance sheets*. For states such as Massachusetts which have special editions of the advance sheets, a colored-sheet table is provided in each advance sheet which translates from the official to the unofficial. Conversely, there are tables translating from the unofficial to the official.

d. *Original report series to Federal Case citation*. A blue-page table in the digest volume of the series makes this conversion—for example, *from* 1 Ben. 15 *to* 27 F. Cas. No. 16,510. This table is shown in Exhibit 33.

Vols. 1–30.] TABLE OF CITATIONS.

BANNING & ARDEN'S PATENT CASES—Cont'd.

Vol. 5, Ban. & A.—Cont'd.

Page.	F. C. No.	Page.	F. C. No.
484 (2 F. 899)........	—	572 (3 F. 222)........	—
486 (3 F. 338)........	—	575	17,579a
488 (3 F. 335)........	—	577 (3 F. 143)........	—
491 (2 F. 855)........	—	584 (3 F. 151)........	—
509 (3 F. 95).........	—	586 (3 F. 298)........	—
511 (3 F. 636)........	—	590 (3 F. 509)........	—

BENEDICT'S UNITED STATES DISTRICT COURT REPORTS.

Vol. 1, Ben.

Page.	F. C. No.	Page.	F. C. No.	Page.	F. C. No.
1..........	5,339	225..........	13,202	397..........	17,474
8..........	2,617	226..........	6,416	398..........	7,892
15..........	16,510	228..........	1,556	402..........	6,189
19..........	4,472	234..........	12,218	406..........	8,577
19 (note)..	8,412	241..........	14,012	407..........	1,543
23..........	2,642	264..........	9,796	408..........	11,834

Exhibit 33

e. *Shepard's United States and state citations*. If either the official or the unofficial citation is known, it is very simple to translate from

1. Letter dated April 8, 1959, from West Publishing Company to one of the authors.

MASSACHUSETTS REPORTS Vol. 174

—570—	Vol. 174	6MQ(2) 20	—129—	195Mas[2]115	—212—	259Mas [2]462
s 54NE 257		16MQ(5)224	s 54NE 338	196Mas [2]20	s 54NE 539	265Mas [8]386
177Mas[1]193		—68—	33ALR [1]748n	197Mas[2]483	s 75AS 300	267Mas [2]522
180Mas [1]19	—1—	s 54NE 358	—132—	199Mas[1]572	s161Mas 558	269Mas 393
180Mas[1]147	s 54NE 339	s176Mas 433	s 54NE 502	201Mas[1]300	j184Mas[1]155	275Mas [5]335
184Mas[1]129	178Mas [4]63	183Mas[1]556	206Mas [5]68	d204Mas [2]27	d226Mas[1]491	228US [8]274
190Mas [1]83	194Mas[4]180	186Mas 42	231Mas[5]581	215Mas [1]35	100AS 520n	57LE [8]833
192Mas [1]44	210Mas[7]156	195Mas 54	14Lns 102n	f219Mas [1]90	45Lns [1]305n	33SC [8]460
193Mas [1]66	211Mas[4]133	210Mas[1]298	—144—	219Mas [2]91	AC'18D 5n	229US[12]377
206Mas [1]79	226Mas[8]453	—74—	s 54NE 490	250Mas[1]371	—216—	57LE[12]1235

Exhibit 34

one to the other by means of the appropriate Shepard's Citation unit. Depending upon which unit must be consulted, this is now done in two ways. In the older Shepard's units (easily recognized because they do not stand as tall on the shelves as later ones), this translation was made by an "s" immediately following the page citation. The "s" meant the "same case in the other series." Thus, in the Massachusetts case in Exhibit 34, 174 Mass. 212, the "s" refers to the same case printed in 54 N.E. 539 and 75 American State Reports 300.

In the parallel citation in Exhibit 34, the "s 161 Mas 558" refers to the same case at its first hearing before the Supreme Judicial Court while the "174 Mas 212" is the rehearing of that case. Thus "161 Mas 558" is not a parallel citation to 174 Mass. 212 as are 54 N.E. 539 and 75 Am. St. R. 300.

In the taller, more recent compilations of Shepard's Citations, the parallel translation is done in another manner, and the "s" has a different meaning. This is illustrated in Exhibit 35.

UNITED STATES SUPREME COURT REPORTS Vol. 362

— Or —	Formula-	s363 US 858	f190 FS 681	f283 F2d 485	—574—	s 3 LE 76	195 FS 751
364 P2d1011	tion-Trial	s 4 LE1739	— CA2d —	f286 F2d 922	(4 LE963)	s 79 SC 66	4 A3 667s
—456—	Court Dis-	s 80 SC1605	12 CaR334	('61 MC	(80 SC909)	s361 US 803	23 A3 1419s
(4 LE874)	cretion	('61 MC	67 NM 246	1135)	s350 US 971	s 4 LE 53	—901—
(80 SC874)	366 US 322	1923)	354 P2d 537	288 F2d 806	s100LE 843	s 80 SC 50	No. 130
s361 US 874	6 LE 322	s264 F2d 289	11 A3 646s	('61 MC	s 76 SC 444	s362 US 99	(80 SC608)
s 4 LE 113	81 SC1248	s286 F2d 875	—539—	1172)	s359 US 924	s 4 LE 584	s361 US 808
s 80 SC 137	j366 US 372	s155 FS 442	(4 LE941)	290 F2d 398	s 3 LE 627	s 80 SC 543	s 4 LE 57
s 6 NY 788	j 6 LE 351	('58 MC978)	(80 SC926)	('61 MC	s 79 SC 610	s257 F2d 885	s 80 SC 62
s188 S2d 184	j 81 SC1274	192 FS 450	s361 US 808	1087)	s359 US 951	s161 FS 702	s361 US 947
s159 NE 677	Sherman	('61 MC712)	s 4 LE 57	290 F2d 430	s 3 LE 759	s164 FS 107	s 80 SC 400
s 6 NY 881	Act-Vio-	Nav. Wat.	s 80 SC 70	('61 MC	s 79 SC 741	—609—	s363 US 817
s188 S2d	lation-De-	Obstruc-	('59 MC	1177)	s258 F2d 937	(4 LE1009)	s 4 LE1157
[1001	cree-Ade-	tions-In-	2665)	d291 F2d 97	cc276SW533	(80 SC960)	s 80 SC1245
s160 NE 128	quacy of	dustrial	s265 F2d 426	j291 F2d 98	Hab. Corp.	s 86 Az 275	s265 F2d 825
	Relief	Solids-In-		291 F2d 419	Sentence	s345 P2d 202	s148 FS 106

Exhibit 35

In the listing of 362 U.S. 456, the parallel citations to the Lawyers Edition and the Supreme Court Reporter, respectively, are in parenthesis. The "s's" preceding 361 U.S. 874 (and, in parallel, 4 L. Ed. 2d 113 and 80 S. Ct. 137) and the various New York reports are references to the same case at various stages of litigation, both in the Supreme Court and in the New York courts from which it was appealed. They do not refer to the identical report in 362 U.S. 456.

The parallel citation in Shepard's Citations is given only in the paperbound supplements which lead up to the first bound volumes following the listing of the case and in that first bound volume following the publication of the report cited. It is not repeated in later supplements or bound volumes. If one form of citation is known, Shepard's Citations is perhaps the most satisfactory parallel translation table from official to unofficial or vice versa.

f. *Official to A.L.R. citation*. The last volume of the *Later Case Service 2d* has such a table. The official Shepard's unit, however, makes the translation by means of the "s" or parenthetical citation to the case when it has been published in A.L.R.

3. *Unofficial citation to official citation*. For example, *from* 281 P. 728 *to* 75 Utah 6.

a. *Shepard's Reporter Citations*. This procedure is precisely the reverse of that described above for translating from official to unofficial citation and is carried out through the Reporter Citations. The Regional Reporter Citations will reveal that there are many cites to cases in the reporters for which there are no official reports. This is probably the most nearly infallible test for such non-publication of an official report corresponding to a given decision.

b. *State editions of Reporter advance sheets*. Those states for which there are special state editions of National Reporter advance sheets provide, in each advance sheet, a colored-sheet table which translates from the National Reporter to the official.

Whenever the official form of citation has been determined by the time the bound volume of the National Reporter is published, it is included, preceding the case name in the National Reporter. Usually, the National Reporter is printed before the official citation is known.

15 Law Reports: Index and Search Books

§15.1. Need and kinds of indexes and search books in case law.

Although, as far as is known, nobody has ever made a complete and accurate count of published reports of American judicial decisions, there are said to be in existence approximately four million of them, with over 30,000 being added each year. Assuming, conservatively, that for each of these cases there are six headnote paragraphs, these statements of principles of law involved in the decided cases would mount up to over 18 million, with annual additions of over 180,000. The law reports to which these headnote paragraphs apply are published in chronological, not subject, order.

The need for some workable device or devices to enable the lawyer to locate among this enormous, growing, and unclassified mass of statements those which are in point and to appraise the value as precedent of the cases in which they were made or decided, is obvious. To meet this need several different kinds of law books have been developed. Generically they are called indexes and search books. They include case digests, treatises, encyclopedias, annotations, restatements of the law, legal periodicals, dictionaries, form books, loose-leaf services, and citation books. They are the necessary means which the lawyer must employ to find, appraise, and apply legal authority.

§15.2. Authority of index and search books.

Under the definition of authority in Chapter 1, treatises, encyclopedias, annotations, restatements of the law, and legal periodicals may, to the extent that they are cited by the court, be designated as persuasive authority. Judges frequently cite them because of the excellence and completeness of their analyses of the statutes and cases which *are* mandatory authority. Since no court would be bound by any statement of the law in them, such persuasive authorities themselves are in no sense mandatory. No matter how excellent the reasoning and cogent the conclusions, they are only unofficial statements unless delivered from the bench as part of an opinion. While undoubtedly persuasive in many cases, they are cited because the citer approves and adopts them as a convenient analysis and statement of that which is authority.

Accordingly, a judge holding that a certain rule is as stated in American Jurisprudence, Corpus Juris Secundum, Wigmore, or a Columbia Law Review article by Chafee is merely saying that the editors or authors of the works cited above have read and analyzed the cases and statutes carefully and have written down a statement of the law extracted from them which the judge believes to be a proper interpretation of this authority. In light of the frequency with which these secondary materials are cited by the courts, the distinction is perhaps academic. It does, however, exist and should always be kept in mind. The primary function of secondary materials is to direct the searcher to the sources relied upon.

Search books, indexes such as digests and the various tables and other tools aiding in their use, and citation books have no authority of any kind under any definition. The statement of a rule of law in a digest cannot be accepted as applicable to a given situation without careful study of the case digested. Index books are not an end in themselves, but only a means to an end. As such they are indispensable.

A detailed and, at times, highly critical analysis of such secondary materials as annotations, encyclopedias, and treatises is by Professor John Henry Merryman in Authority of Authority, 6 Stanford L. Rev. 613-673. While directed specifically at authority cited by the California Supreme Court, it has general applicability.

See also §1.6, Computerized legal research.

Most publishers of law search books and indexes, such as West, Lawyers Co-operative Publishing Company, and Shepard's Citations, publish and distribute free, elaborate, and graphically illustrated descriptions of their publications and how to use them. They are very helpful.

16 | Digests

§16.1. Function of digests.

The case digest is the lawyer's indispensable tool. It is a detailed subject index to the law as set forth in the reported cases. Its text is composed, without connecting comment, of headnote paragraphs which

C.A.Ky. 1964. Where petitioner, who contended that conduct of clerk of state court had denied him rights under equal protection and due process clauses, was provided by Kentucky rules with adequate post-conviction procedure to seek determination of such question, but he had not attempted to obtain relief thereunder, he was not entitled to federal habeas corpus. U.S.C.A.Const. Amend. 14; KRS 203.340; RCr Ky. 11.42; CR Ky. 60.02.—Jones v. Davis, 336 F.2d 594.

C.A.Md. 1963. State prisoner had exhausted available state remedies before petitioning for habeas corpus in federal District Court, where prisoner, after his Maryland conviction, appealed directly to Court of Appeals of Maryland on ground of insufficiency of evidence and then unsuccessfully sought in a post-conviction proceeding to raise constitutional question as to use at trial of evidence obtained through allegedly unlawful search. 28 U.S.C.A. § 2254; U.S.C.A.Const. Amends. 4, 14.—Walker v. Pepersack, 316 F.2d 119.

Exhibit 36

form the syllabi or headnotes of the published law reports. In the American Digest System, described in §§16.5 and 16.6, these paragraphs are, for cases reported in the National Reporter System, the actual Key-Numbered headnote paragraphs which have been taken from the various Reporters and to which citator material showing the subsequent judicial treatment of the cases has been added. Exhibit 36 shows two digest paragraphs from the Seventh Decennial Digest.

The reports of the cases from which these headnotes are taken are arranged in their respective bound volumes in chronological order by date of decision, not in subject order. To form the digest it is necessary to arrange these millions of headnote paragraphs by subject, using an elaborate classification scheme which brings headnotes of similar cases together. Although the subject classification schemes employed by the various publishers of digests differ from each other in detail, they are so similar to each other in organization and effect that only the American Digest System need be described here.

§16.2. Distinguishing features of digests.

The digest is a collection of separate paragraphs, each of which is related to its counterparts only because it belongs in the same subject class and states a similar principle of law. These paragraphs are linked together by no editorial comment on the case or cases involved—i.e., there is no synthesis of rules from a group of cases and no statement of the jurisdictional rules, historical developments, majority and minority views, etc., as there would be in a treatise, encyclopedia, or law review article. Each stated rule is there on its own. The digest thus leaves to the reader the task of determining for each statement its present place within the hierarchy of decisions on the point and its applicability to a specific problem. This presupposes possession of all skills and techniques necessary for the digest's proper use; that is why the digest is peculiarly the lawyer's tool.

In using this tool, however, even the lawyer must be constantly on the alert to note the law's changes, both by decision and by statute. When a decision or line of decisions seriously modifying or overturning the existing rule is digested and the digest paragraph takes its place under the proper digest classification, no statement is made in the digest itself of the probable effect of this new decision or decisions on existing law, and the older, perhaps overruled or modified decisions can be relegated to their proper place only by the searcher. The digest will not assist in the reappraisal.

An example is the 1942 case of *Williams* v. *North Carolina*, 317 U.S. 187, 63 S. Ct. 407, 143 A.L.R. 1273 (1942). This case expressly overruled the 1906 case of *Haddock* v. *Haddock*, 210 U.S. 563, 26 S. Ct. 525, 50 L. Ed. 867 (1906), which had, for a generation, been settled law on the full faith and credit involving matrimonial domicile. There was, however, no editorial comment in the digest to this effect. Indeed, the old *Haddock* case digest paragraphs and the digests of many cases following its doctrine are still in the digest. This illustrates the necessity of reading and relying upon the authority of a decided *case*, not merely the *digest* of the case.

§16.3. Authority of digests.

It follows that a digest is not authority of any kind, even persuasive, but only a guide or index to finding such authority. There is no presumption that the rule of law as stated in a digest paragraph is the rule of the case digested. This is particularly true because not only reasoning and actual holding are digested, but pure dictum as well. An editor can only rarely compress in the conventional digest's single-sentence paragraph the entire rule of the case, including the fact situation, how the case arose, relevant statutes, and the other factors which determine the value of a case as authority. There is no indication in the digest paragraphs whether the rule of law stated in a given paragraph is holding, reasoning, or dictum; and, in practice, the majority of cases taken from the digest by the searcher will have to be discarded as unsuitable after careful examination. Human errors are another factor affecting the use made of digests. While errors occur only infrequently, they do occur. The inadvertent omission of a "not" may cause the digest to state exactly the reverse of the rule of the case. The digester may also have misunderstood the case, particularly if a technical or scientific rule was involved.

§16.4. Scope of digests.

Digests vary greatly in scope. The American Digest System is the most comprehensive of all in its coverage. Since the National Reporter System reports many cases not elsewhere covered, the American Digest System also digests cases not elsewhere digested. Other digests cover various federal, regional, and state units of the National Reporter System, individual courts such as the Supreme Court and the Court of Claims, or single topics such as patents, labor relations, or taxation.

§16.5. American Digest System.[1]

The American Digest System is said by the publisher to cover all standard law reports from appellate courts rendering written decisions

1. St. Paul, Minn., West Publishing Co.

from 1658 to date. It also digests selective opinions from certain courts of first instance, including those of the federal district courts and some lower state courts.

1. *Units of the American Digest System.* The system is composed of the Century Edition and the Decennial Digests, and is supplemented by the bound volumes and monthly pamphlet issues of the General Digest. These units are shown in the table in Exhibit 37.

TABLE
SHOWING PERIOD OF TIME

COVERED BY EACH UNIT OF THE

AMERICAN DIGEST SYSTEM

TOGETHER WITH

VOLUMES OF DIGEST WHERE TABLES OF CASES WILL BE FOUND

YEARS	DIGEST UNIT	TABLE OF CASES WHERE FOUND
1658–1896	Century	First Decennial, vols. 21–25
1897–1906	First Decennial	First Decennial, vols. 21–25
1907–1916	Second Decennial	Second Decennial, vol. 24
1916–1926	Third Decennial	Third Decennial, vol. 29
1926–1936	Fourth Decennial	Fourth Decennial, vol. 31
1936–1946	Fifth Decennial	Fifth Decennial, vols. 48–49
1946–1956	Sixth Decennial	Sixth Decennial, vols. 35–36
1956–1966	Seventh Decennial	Seventh Decennial, vols. 37–38
1966–to date	General Digest, Fourth Series	General Digest, vol. 1–to date

Exhibit 37

Note that each Decennial begins and ends in midyear and in a year whose final digit is a six. It covers terms of court and not the calendar year. The table shown is to be found immediately following the title page of each bound volume of the General Digest into which the Reporter advance sheets cumulate and which, in turn, cumulates into the Decennials.

The Century Edition, the predecessor of the Decennials, covers the years 1658–1896. Its class subdivisions are called sections as in other digests and do not correspond precisely in coverage to the Key Numbers adopted in the First Decennial and continued to date. As is shown in Exhibit 43, a parallel conversion table in volume 21 of the

First Decennial translates from the Century section numbers to the Decennial Key Numbers.

The Decennials, as their name indicates, cumulate every ten years from the General Digest. The General Digest is first a monthly pamphlet which cumulates approximately every four months into a bound volume and is then superseded every ten years by the Decennial compiled from it. Each National Reporter System advance sheet has its own Key Number digest in miniature for cases printed in it. This miniature digest cumulates each month in the pamphlet General Digest. The routine of a complete American Digest System search, therefore, may carry through the Century, the Decennials,

REPORTERS AND REPORTS

COVERED BY

SIXTH DECENNIAL DIGEST

REPORTER OR REPORT	From	To
Atlantic	46 A.2d 1	121 A.2d 728
Federal	153 F.2d 305	230 F.2d 792
Federal Rules Decisions	5 F.R.D. 108	18 F.R.D. 517
Federal Supplement	64 F.Supp. 233	138 F.Supp. 959
New York Supplement	60 N.Y.S.2d 185	149 N.Y.S.2d 896
North Eastern	65 N.E.2d 417	133 N.E.2d 256
North Western	21 N.W.2d 881	75 N.W.2d 840
Pacific	166 P.2d 593	295 P.2d 400
South Eastern	37 S.E.2d 1	92 S.E.2d 88
Southern	25 So.2d 57	86 So.2d 368
South Western	192 S.W.2d 577	288 S.W.2d 320
Supreme Court	66 S.Ct. 686	76 S.Ct. 558
Alaska	10 Alaska 1	15 Alaska 688
U. S. Court of Customs and Patent Appeals	33 C.C.P.A. Customs 1	41 C.C.P.A. Customs 246
U. S. Court of Claims	103 Ct.Cl. 1	131 Ct.Cl. 800
Hawaii	37 Hawaii 1	40 Hawaii 738

Exhibit 38

the bound and unbound General, and the various advance sheets later than the latest General pamphlet.

a. *Table showing reports digested in each unit*. In order to pinpoint a search chronologically, it is necessary to make sure that all pertinent report volumes have been covered in the digest consulted. This is easily done for the General Digest and the Decennials, beginning with the third Decennial, by a table on the page following the table of contents in each volume. As may be noted in Exhibit 38, not only are all the National Reporter System units digested in the present Decennials, but official reports as well.

2. *Classification scheme of the American Digest System*. The seven great subdivisions of the rules of law expounded in the cases — that is, the law of persons, property, contracts, torts, crimes, remedies, and government — are expanded into chapters or main topic headings such as "Abandonment," "Aviation," "Chattel Mortgages." These may be said to correspond to the division of a treatise into chapters, except that the order of placement in the digest is alphabetical by chapter heading instead of by logical progression of subjects. These headings correspond to the lawyer's conventional conception of the divisions of the law as taught in law school. A list of these main topics is found in the front of every volume of the digests, beginning with the Fourth Decennial, and the breakdown affords a useful elimination process for topics to be or not to be searched. For example, there is no topic or subtopic for conflicts of laws, and the cases involving conflicts, which are scattered through the various main topics, are best found through "Conflict of Laws" in the Descriptive-Word Indexes of the digest.

3. *"Scope-Note" and Analysis*. Each main topic of the digest has a "Scope-Note" and "Analysis." Beginning with the Seventh Decennial Digest, the "Scope-Note" was expanded and replaced by a "Subjects Included" and a "Subjects Excluded and Covered by Other Topics" listing. See Exhibit 39.

a. *"Scope-Note."* The subject matter treated and not treated by a particular topic can be easily determined by glancing at the "Subjects Included" and "Subjects Excluded and Covered by Other Topics" listings. In addition, related topics digesting the same subject matter are also specifically referenced in the "Subjects Excluded and Covered by Other Topics." The "Scope-Note" found for topics in the first six decennial digests lists the subject matter covered in a given main topic and only by implication excludes subject matter not treated. Use of these devices avoids waste of time in searching appropriate topics.

Suppose, for example, a guardian and ward problem relates to the marriage or divorce of the ward, a trust for the ward, or workmen's compensation awards. A searcher will soon discover that these topics

GUARDIAN AND WARD

SUBJECTS INCLUDED

General guardianship, particularly of the persons and estates of infants, by nature or under parental or judicial appointment

Rights, powers, duties, and liabilities of guardians in respect of the persons and property of their wards

Legal proceedings relating thereto

SUBJECTS EXCLUDED AND COVERED BY OTHER TOPICS

Guardians ad litem and special guardians, see INFANTS, MENTAL HEALTH and other specific topics

Infants and their property, matters irrespective of guardianship, see INFANTS

Insane or otherwise incompetent persons, guardianship of, see DRUNKARDS, MENTAL HEALTH, SPENDTHRIFTS

For detailed references to other topics, see Descriptive-Word Index

---

Analysis.

I. GUARDIANSHIP IN GENERAL, ⚷1–7.

II. APPOINTMENT, QUALIFICATION, AND TENURE OF GUARDIAN, ⚷8–27.

III. CUSTODY AND CARE OF WARD'S PERSON AND ESTATE, ⚷28–74.

IV. SALES AND CONVEYANCES UNDER ORDER OF COURT, ⚷75–115.

V. ACTIONS, ⚷116–136.

VI. ACCCOUNTING AND SETTLEMENT, ⚷137–165.

VII. FOREIGN AND ANCILLARY GUARDIANSHIP, ⚷166–172.

VIII. LIABILITIES ON GUARDIANSHIP BONDS, ⚷173–182.

I. GUARDIANSHIP IN GENERAL.

⚷1. The relation in general.
2. Power to control guardianship.
3. What law governs.
4. Guardians by nature.
5. Guardians in socage.
6. Volunteer and de facto guardians.
7. Estoppel to deny guardianship.

Exhibit 39

are not digested under "Guardian and Ward." Since the "Subjects Excluded and Covered by Other Topics" listing does not mention them, the searcher must either look under the main topics "Marriage," "Divorce," "Trusts," or "Workmen's Compensation," or look in the Descriptive-Word Index, described in par. e, page 204 under "Guardian and Ward" and its subentries under the above subjects.

b. *Analysis*. This device splits the main topic into workable smaller concepts by which a searcher skilled in the law is able to arrive speedily at the proper Key Number. In any fairly large topic, the main analysis is subject to further breakdown into subanalyses and even into sub-subanalyses. In such large topics as "Evidence," "Internal Revenue," and "Patents," there may be as many as 2500 subdivisions or Key Numbers. It is this detailed analysis, leading to the appropriate Key number, that forms the basis of the so-called "analytical approach" to the case law which is described in §16.6.

c. *Application of the Analysis to other Key Number digests.* All National Reporter System case reports syllabi or headnote paragraphs are Key-Numbered. The Key Number assigned is uniform throughout the West Publishing Company digests so that when a pertinent Key Number is found in any Reporter case, similar subject matter will be found under it in any West digest. Under an identical Key Number, cases from all jurisdictions which involve the same subject matter are digested in all Decennial units, in the monthly General Digest units, in the regional digests, and in all West state digests. Cases decided as long ago as 1896 are included.

Cases decided before mid-1896 are digested in the Century Digest, covering from 1658 to 1896. Since the *section* numbers of the Century Digest do not agree precisely with the Decennial Digest *Key Numbers*, a simple additional step is necessary to find the earlier cases corresponding to those digested under, for example, "Conversion 🔑 21." A boldface cross-reference immediately under the Key Number heading in both the First and Second Decennials cites the appropriate Century Digest section number or numbers. Thus the Key Number above is covered in the Century Digest by §§56–65. An example of this cross-reference is shown in Exhibit 44.

Although the digests mentioned as part of the West system are substantially uniform in makeup, a given West state digest may contain additional features of local interest; the same is true, of course, of digests by other publishers. There are individual state digests for nearly every state.

4. *Digest paragraphs.* Because they contain the statement of rules of law from decided cases, the digest paragraphs themselves are the meat of the digest. They are arranged by subject under the Key Number classification. Under each Key Number, the paragraphs are arranged by jurisdiction and, under jurisdiction, by date of decision. Through the Fifth Decennial, this date was given in boldface type with the digest paragraph. These dates were omitted in the Sixth Decennial Digest. They are found, however, for most cases in the Seventh Decennial Digest and for all cases in the Eighth Decennial Digest.

United States Supreme Court cases come first; then come Courts of Appeals cases, followed by those of the federal district courts, alphabetically by state district; then state court cases, alphabetically by state, with the digest paragraphs in each state arranged in the descending order of court rank. These digest paragraphs differ only slightly from the original syllabi or headnotes of the reporter cases from which they are taken. In the digest, they often contain additional citator information (affirmances, reversals, etc., on appeal) which was not available when the case was first printed and digested. See Exhibit 40.

5. *Auxiliary tables and indexes*. Because digests are so voluminous and complex, they require a variety of tables and indexes in order to be usable. American Digest System tables and indexes are typical of all others and are described below.

a. *Table of cases*. The table of cases provides one of the most effective approaches to the law because, as shown in Exhibit 40, it lists for each case all Key Numbers under which that case has been digested. Thus, when a case has been cited in, for example, a law review article or another case, recourse to the table of cases will lead through the Key Number listings to all other cases in point. A more effective use of the tables of cases approach is to go to the actual case in the National Reporter System to determine the exact Key Number pertinent to your research.

Each digest unit has its own table of cases with a listing like that in Exhibit 40.

> **Lane v. Endicott Johnson Corp,** Sup, 75 NYS2d 171, aff 274 AppDiv 833, 80 NYS2d 639, app den 274 App Div 855, 82 NYS2d 387, aff 299 NY 725, 87 NE2d 450, cert den 70 SCt 243, 338 US 892, 94 LEd 548—Arb & Aw 36; Labor 263, 433, 436, 453; Mast & S 3(2).

Exhibit 40

It will be noted that, in addition to listing the pertinent Key Numbers under which the digest paragraphs are classified, later court action, if any, on the *identical* case is noted. To this limited extent, the Decennial tables serve as case citators. Also see Exhibit 41.

This table's citator function is supplemented by the monthly table in the General Digest which is shown in Exhibit 42.

The case tables always give the National Reporter System citation. Up until 1966, if at the time the Decennial table was prepared for press, the official report and the A.L.R. reports had been published, their citations were included. Unfortunately, these reports, with their volume and page numbers, were frequently not then available so that the alternative citations may be lacking, and after 1966, parallel cita-

TABLE OF CASES

ABBREVIATIONS

aff	affirmed	mod	modified
am	amended	rearg	reargument
cert	certiorari	reh	rehearing
den	denied	rev	reversed
dism	dismissed	transf	transferred
foll	followed	vac	vacated
gr	granted		

References are to Digest Topics and Key Numbers

A

A v. B, Ark, 233 SW2d 629—Adop 7, 14.

A A Bennett, Inc v. Minneapolis Gas Co, CAMinn, 227 F2d 665. See Arena Co v. Minneapolis Gas Co.

Aaberg v. People, Colo, 183 P2d 260—Larc 40(2), 68(1); Sales 11, 208.

A A Bush, Contractor v. Watkins, Miss. 80 So2d 19. See Bush v. Watkins.

Aaby v. Better Builders, Minn, 37 NW 2d 234—Mech Liens 5, 157(4, 5), 290(4); Trial 401.

Aaby v. States Marine Corp, CANY, 181 F2d 383, cert den 71 SCt 66—Ship 38, 42(1, 7), 58(2½).

Aaby v. States Marine Corp, DCNY, 80 FSupp 328, aff 181 F2d 383, cert den 71 SCt 66—Ship 38, 42(1), 51 (7), 58(1, 2½).

A Arena & Co v. U S, DCCal, 103 F Supp 505—Evid 574; Int Rev 951.

Aarnes v. Aarnes 172 La 648, 135 So 13—Divorce 411, 416(2).

Aaron v. Agwilines, Inc, DCNY, 75 F Supp 604—Courts 274(13), 276; FedCivProc 492, 500.

Aaron v. Bay Ridge Operating Co CANY, 162 F2d 665, mod 68 SCt 1186, reh den 69 SCt 10 and Huron Stevedoring Corp v. Blue 69 SCt 11—FedCivProc 2281, 2744; Labor 1278.

Aaron v. Bay Ridge Operating Co, CANY, 204 F2d 88. See Addison v. Huron Stevedoring Corp.

Aaron v. Bay Ridge Operating Co, DCNY, 69 FSupp 956. See Addison v. Huron Stevedoring Corp.

Aaron v. Bay Bridge Operating Co, DCNY, 96 FSupp 142. See Addison v. Huron Stevedoring Corp.

See Com ex rel Aaron v. Court of Quarter Sessions of Westmoreland County.

Aaron's Estate v. C I R, CA3, 224 F 2d 314—Int Rev 1000.

Aarons v. Board of Medical Examiners, CalApp, 176 P2d 706, subsequent opinion 187 P2d 8—Phys 4.

Aarons v. Local 32-E, Bldg Service Emp Intern Union, Sup, 52 NYS2d 262—Labor 455, 456, 482; Mast & S 7.

Aarons v. U S, CAMo, 200 F2d 828—Courts 361; Land & Ten 200.74, 200.76; War 219, 220.

Aaronson v. U S, CAMd, 175 F2d 41—Crim Law 29, 59(5), 200(3); Larc 27; Rec S Goods 6.

Aaronson Bros Paper Corp v. Fishko, Sup, 144 NYS2d 643, aff 146 NYS2d

Exhibit 41

TABLE OF CASES

References are to Digest Topics and Key Numbers

A

Abel v. Board of Works of City of Elisabeth, NJSuperAD, 164 A2d 764—App & E 169, 170(1), 181, 756, 757(1), 773(2); Courts 82, 85(1); Judgm 665, 715(1, 3); Zoning 29, 153, 193, 484, 653, 654, 743.

A B Lewis Co v. Robinson, TexCivApp, 339 SW2d 731—Corp 498; Evid 543(4), 553(1); Plead 139; Princ & A 169(3); Sales 477(5), 481; Tresp 45(5), 67; Trial 395(7).

Absher v. Illinois Cent R Co, Ky, 339 SW2d 874—Judgm 185.3(17); Mast & S 78.4(1); Trusts 105.

Acker v. Karosen, Sup, 207 NYS2d 16. See Leventhal v. Acker.

Alford v. Emory University, Ga, 116 SE2d 596—Plead 214(1); Tax 242 (2), 498.

Allen v. Coal Operators Cas Co, La App, 124 So2d 344—Evid 574; Work Comp 1420, 1652.

Allen v. Travelers Ins Co, LaApp, 124 So2d 367—Work Comp 64, 105, 110, 111, 134, 155, 159, 1319.

Allison v. Ely, Ind, 170 NE2d 371—App & E 882(11); Autos 181(2), 244(20), 245(24); Trial 176.

Allison v. Unemployment Compensation Bd of Review, PaSuper, 165 A2d 125—Social S 388, 584, 655, 662, 665.

Amato v. R R Heywood Co, AD3d, 206 NYS2d 626—Work Comp 1509.

Ambrose v. Singleton, Colo, 356 P2d 253—Wills 840.

Archer-Daniels-Midland Co v. Paull, DCArk, 188 FSupp 277—Bankr 145 (1), 146, 150, 152; Contracts 28(3), 322(3), 350(1); Damag 40(2), 125; Joint Adv 8.

Archuleta v. Landers, NM, 356 P2d 443—App & E 919; Judgm 460(4); Jury 25(2), 28(3, 9); Proc 96(4); Quiet T 35(3), 36, 37(1); Ven & Pur 242.

Argroe v. Marinaccio, NJSuperAD, 164 A2d 809—Work Comp 662, 766.

Argroe v. Morris Plains Amoco Service Station, NJSuperAD, 164 A2d 809. See Argroe v. Marinaccio.

Aris Gloves, Inc v. U S, CustCt, 188 FSupp 50—Cust Dut 10; Notice 9.

Arkansas Real Estate Co v. Fullerton, Ark, 339 SW2d 947—App & E 262

Exhibit 42

tions to official state reports were omitted. The Decennial case tables, therefore, are not always the best means by which to determine the parallel citations — official, unofficial, and A.L.R. — for a given case. If only the unofficial cite is given, take it and check the appropriate Shepard's Regional Citations which will give the official and A.L.R. cites if available.

The Decennial case table is supplemented by the monthly General Digest pamphlets. Like the pamphlets, the table of cases cumulates every four months in the General Digest volume and every ten years in the new Decennial series.

Advance sheets list the cases reported in each issue. Depending upon the period to be covered, then, a complete table of cases search may include the Decennials, the bound volumes of the General Digest since the latest Decennial, the monthly pamphlet issues since the latest bound volume of the General Digest, and the advance sheets of the appropriate reports for the month subsequent to the latest pamphlet issues of the General Digest.

The same case may be listed several times in a table, each appearance representing a different stage of the case's progress through the courts. In such a listing, the case on appeal to the Supreme Court of the United States is listed first even though it was decided later than some of the state actions. Thus, *Kalb* v. *Luce*, a Wisconsin case, is listed six times in the Fifth Decennial table of cases because of a variety of appeals and hearings which culminated in an appeal to the United State Supreme Court. In searching the table, therefore, care must be taken to ascertain the final disposition of the case being searched. This is particularly true of a case decided in a year ending with the digit 6 because the Decennial coverage follows the court term period of that year; a case decided in April 1946 might be listed in the Fifth Decennial while one decided in October would be in the Sixth Decennial.

The name of a case may be changed on appeal if the defendant in the case below lost and appeals to a higher court. Thus *Colver* v. *Skeffington* in the federal district court may be listed as *Skeffington* v. *Colver* in the table of cases covering the U.S. Court of Appeals report of that case.

(1) *Defendant-Plaintiff case tables*. Decennial Digest case tables are Plaintiff-Defendant tables only. Most digest tables, including many by West, now also have Defendant-Plaintiff tables where the cases are listed alphabetically by defendant last names. Usually these tables refer back to the Plaintiff-Defendant table.

(2) *Popular-name case tables*. Beginning with the table of cases volume of the Second Decennial Digest, each table of cases volume has a table of cases which are known or cited by popular name, such as the *Apex* case and the *Danbury Hatters* case. These tables give the

same information as the other case tables described above do. For other popular-name tables, see §30.1e.

b. *Parallel transfer tables from Century to Decennial Digest or reverse.* The Century Digest, covering the years 1658 to mid-1896, is classified by *section numbers;* the Decennials are organized by *Key Numbers.* To facilitate search, however, there are parallel conversion tables from the Centennial to the Decennials so that, having found a Centennial section number, the searcher can easily find the equivalent Key Number in the Decennial. Pink-paper Tables of Key Number Sections for Century Digest are found in volume 21 of the First Decennial. These cite parallel Century topic and section numbers and corresponding Decennial Key Numbers. Thus "Contribution 20" of the Century is equivalent to "Contribution ⊶ 9(5)" of the Decennial.

CENTURY DIGEST SECTIONS WITH CORRESPONDING KEY-NUMBERS A 51

CONTRIBUTION

Cent. Sec.	Dec. & Key No. Sec.	Cent. Sec.	Dec. & Key No. Sec.	Cent. Sec.	Dec. & Key No. Sec.	Cent. Sec.	Dec. & Key No. Sec.	Cent. Sec.	Dec. & Key No. Sec.	Cent. Sec.	Dec. & Key No. Sec.	Cent. Sec.	Dec. & Key No. Sec.
1	1	5	3	9	5	13	7	17	9(3)	18	9(2)	21	9(6)
2	2	6	5	10	6	14	9(1)		Lim. of Act. 49(1-8)	19	9(4)	22	9(8)
3	4	7	5	11	6	15	8			20	9(5)		
4	4	8	5	12	6	16	Eq. 44						

Exhibit 43

Going from Key Number in the Decennial to section number in the Century is even simpler. In both the First and Second Decennials, there is a "See" reference beneath each boldface Key Number which indicates the corresponding Centennial section number.

If the Century Digest must be researched for a case found in the Third or later Decennials, the searcher simply takes the Key Number reference into the Second Decennial where the "See" reference to the Centennial will be found. With the exceptions noted below for new or expanded Decennial main topics, it is thus a simple mechanical matter, once a case in point is found and its Key Number or section numbers in point ascertained from the headnote paragraphs, to work back and forth through both the Centennial and Decennials, finding all cases in point from 1658 to date.

c. *Key Number changes: Tables of new or expanded classification of topics.* Law changes, and digest classifications change with it. In the Sixth Decennial, there were eight new or expanded topics; the Seventh and Eighth Decennials each contain four more. Because they require one additional step, these topics constitute an exception to the rule that, once having found a Key Number in point, the

🔑21. Operation and effect.
See 11 Cent. Dig. Conversion, §§ 56-65.

Effect on right to maintain partition, see Partition, 🔑21.

Exhibit 44

searcher merely needs to check all units of the American Digest System under that Key Number to find all other cases in point. When such changes are made in the Key Number classification, the editors reexamine all reported cases, regardless of date or original Key Numbers or sections. The classification scheme of the new topic is then developed, and all pertinent cases are reclassified under the new topic. The digest paragraphs are then republished in the next pocket parts of the various state, regional, and federal digests. They are then published in the next General Digest volume and are eventually merged into the next Decennial Digest. Having found the Key Number "Negligence 🔑 105" in the headnote of the Pacific Reporter aviation case, *Montijo* v. *Samuel Goldwyn, Inc*. 113 Cal. App. 57, 297 P. 949 (1931), it is not, for example, possible to go directly to the digest of the case and those of similar cases under the same Key Number in the Sixth and later Decennials. This is because digests of all aviation cases of whatever date have been reclassified in the Sixth Decennial under the new topic "Aviation." To find the new Key Number of the *Montijo* case, the searcher must consult the Sixth Decennial Table of Cases for the *Montijo* case. There it is discovered that the new Key Number covering the assumption of risk or the contributory negligence of a stunt aviator is "Aviation 🔑 152."

"Workmen's Compensation" in the Fourth Decennial and "Administrative Law and Procedure" in the Fifth Decennial were new topics which were published with a special table of cases. All cases collected under the new topic, together with their newly assigned Key Numbers, were listed. Having the name of an earlier case, the searcher needed only to consult this supplementary table of cases which supplied the new Key Number.

The current Decennial Digest practice is to *list all cases, old and new, of whatever date*, which are collected in the new or expanded digest topic, *in the general table of cases for the Decennial unit in which the new topic first appears*. For example, the names of all aviation cases of whatever date, reported through mid-1956, are listed in the Sixth Decennial table.

In either situation—whether a special table of cases is provided or all cases of whatever date are listed in the general table of cases for the particular decennium in which the new topic appears — there is just the one additional step of going forward from the old to the new Key Number through the table of cases in the Decennial for the decennium in which the new or expanded topic first appeared.

As a rule *there is no cross-reference table from the former Key Number to the new one*. This leaves it to the alertness of the searcher to discover that the old Key Number is no longer appropriate and to search in the case tables of later Decennials under the old case name for the current Key Number.

Parallel transfer tables between the old and new Key Numbers have been provided, however, in the Seventh, Eighth, and following Decennials for revised and new topics. Tables from the new to the old and from the old to the new Key Numbers are provided.

d. *Key Number tables in the General Digest*. Not published with the Fourth Series, these tables are once again being published with the Fifth General Digest Series. They cumulate in the bound volumes of the General Digest Descriptive-Word Index and are supplemented at irregular intervals by a pamphlet, Cumulative Table of Key Numbers. The tables are designed to avoid the necessity of searching through as many as thirty interim General Digest volumes which may contain no digests under a given Key Number. In Exhibit 45, for example, the Key Number "Abandonment 7" appears only once, in volume 5, in the first eight volumes of the General Digest. It would, therefore, be fruitless to search the other volumes.

e. *Descriptive-Word Index*. This is an enormous dictionary-like table, listing in alphabetical order words and phrases describing the fact situations arising in the cases reported during the given period covered by a unit of the American Digest System.

Thus, if your case involves tomato paste adulteration, for example, you can find the principle involved through this table under "Tomato

TABLE OF KEY NUMBERS

GENERAL DIGEST, VOLUMES 1–8 5th SERIES

A Time Saver for Locating The Latest Cases

Example: Having found a proposition of law under the topic Licenses 🔑24, refer to the same topic and Key in this table which will show that other cases appear in the General Digest, Fifth Series, Volume 1. Search is therefore unnecessary in Volume 2 of the General Digest, Fifth Series.

ABANDONMENT	ABDUCTION	ACCOUNT	ACKNOWLEDGMENT
🔑	🔑	🔑	🔑
2—1, 2, 3, 5, 7	12—3, 4, 6	1—1, 4, 7	1—2, 5
3—1, 2, 3, 5		5—3	4—1
4—1, 7	ABORTION	6—7	5—1, 3, 6
5—1, 3, 8		7—7	38—4
7—5	1—1, 2, 3, 4, 5, 6, 7, 8	8—6	39—4

Exhibit 45

Paste." Or you may be interested in such terms as "war surplus," "sudden stopping," a tractor clutch gone wrong, etc. Worms-in-jam cases may be found under both "Worms" and "Jam."

In addition to the above catchwords, this table breaks up each of the main topics of the Digest into workable, alphabetically arranged fact situations.

To provide for flexibility and ease in finding pertinent Key Numbers through the various units of this table, there is a great deal of duplication and overlapping of entries. Thus a situation involving a passenger injured in a jumpy plane during rough weather is covered in the main topic headings of "Aviation" and "Carriers," and is also found in the fact situation entries "Airlines," "Airplanes," "Passengers,"etc.

The tables for the first two and second two Decennials were combined, but each subsequent Decennial has had its own table. Each bound volume of the General Digest supplementing the latest Decennial has its own blue-paper Descriptive-Word Index, and for every ten volumes of the General Digest during a decennium there is a blue-cloth supplement.

Every case digest, by whatever publisher, has an index, under whatever name the publisher chooses to give it. It is the means employed in the fact approach to the law described in §21.4.4 and §30.1.4.

§16.6. Techniques for using the American Digest System.

1. *Preliminary problem analysis*. First, analyze the facts of your situation. Clear away deadwood and restrict your consideration to those elements necessary to the solution of the problem:

What parties are involved?
How did the case arise, how did it find its way to this court?
What is the subject matter — tort, contract, crime?
Is a statute involved?
What is the cause of action?
What remedy is sought?

Not all these elements are likely to be vital in any single problem. In a contract case the fact that the plaintiff is an infant may be controlling,while it might be of no importance in a tort. Whether a case involves the admissibility of evidence, want of jurisdiction, or an improper charge to a jury may determine the applicability of digested cases to the problem at hand. A case decided on a statute is unlikely to be a useful precedent if there is no statute involved. Nor can a prayer for a preliminary injunction lead to a decision on the merits of a substantive fact situation.

2. *Approaches to the law through the digest*. There are four ways to find cases in point through the American Digest System or any other standard digest. While simple, the specific examples given in the discussion below illustrate the reasoning and routines to be followed in using these various techniques. The student should remember, however, that in actual practice a case exactly on point concerning the facts and the law of a problem is uncommon. Generally the lawyer must be content with a reasonably analogous fact situation which is applicable to the rule of law involved. Very often the cases in several different Key Number classifications must be fully searched before the right one is found.

a. *Table of cases approach*. This is one of the most effective and the simplest approaches to the law. When a footnote in a treatise, encyclopedia, casebook, or law report cites a case in point, you can trace the case by name in the table of cases. This leads you immediately to the Key Numbers under which your case has been digested and, through them, to all other cases in point. Again, it should be noted that the more effective technique is to go to the actual case in the Reporter in order to determine the exact Key Number most relevant to your research. If, however, you do not know the date of the case, it may be necessary to search through several Decennial Digest units. See §16.5c.

Since the table of cases technique can be used with nearly all books which print or discuss law reports and since there are a number of common problems which arise out of all of them, the technique is described in greater detail in Chapter 30, Coordinating the Research Techniques.

b. *Fact or Descriptive-Word Index approach*. Legal questions arise out of fact situations. Accordingly, all digests provide exhaustive indexes to the fact situations found in the reported cases. The one in the American Digest System, the largest in size and scope, is called the Descriptive-Word Index. Using this index, the searcher for Key Numbers in point analyzes the pertinent facts of a case, determines one or more words which tie in significantly with the legal consequences involved, and is led to the desired Key Numbers.

Thus a dining car waiter whose duties require the polishing of silver sues the railroad under a Workmen's Compensation statute because of resulting dermatitis. Various facts call for attention: dining car, waiter, silver polish, railroad, workmen's compensation, and dermatitis, among others. Of these, "Railroads" and "Workmen's Compensation" are main topics in the Digest, legal words of art or legal concepts. The others are strictly fact words or catchwords. The least common denominator of these various words is "dermatitis," and under it in the Descriptive-Word Index, Key Numbers in point will be found. Although additional steps may be required to locate them, the same Key Numbers in point or a cross-reference to the appropriate heading will also be found under some of the other words above.

WORKMEN'S COMPENSATION
DERMATITIS, SEE DERMATITIS

The Descriptive-Word Index is an enormous dictionary-type affair. In it words and terms are arranged, not systematically by legal concept, but in a single, great alphabet. Both catchwords and main topic heads are found. The arrangement under the main topic heads — which are almost always legal words of art — is largely by catchwords, as in the "Workmen's Compensation" example above, rather than by legal concepts. Thus catchwords like "Dermatitis," "Quonset Huts," "One-legged Race" are found under the main legal topic involved and as separate entries. The problem below, illustrated in Exhibit 46, is taken from the Fifth Decennial Digest and shows how the fact-index approach works.

(1) *Problem illustrating the fact approach.* A woman brings an action to recover for injuries received when she jumped from a stalled automobile at a railroad crossing and was struck by one of a line of boxcars which was suddenly discovered to be backing toward the automobile. Several main topics are involved here — railroads, torts, negligence, automobiles, and damages — but they are all very large, and the analysis leading to the desired point is not very obvious. Two special facts are, however, present: the accident occurred at a railroad crossing and a train backed into the plaintiff at the crossing. Since the totality of crossing accidents is greater than those caused at such crossings by backing trains, "backing" is determined to be the smallest significant fact, the least common denominator. Examination of "backing" in the Fifth Decennial Digest Descriptive-Word Index leads to the subentry "Trains," with a further subdivision under "Crossing accidents," where fact situations are noted with pertinent Key Numbers. See Exhibit 46.

The Descriptive-Word Index so meticulously picks out applicable fact situations, however, that the desired Key Numbers could also have been found less directly through several different entries under "Automobiles," "Crossings," "Railroads," etc.

The above is purely a catchword problem, depending upon the unusual factor of "backing" for its easy solution. In some instances, however, no such decisive catchword is available, and a closer scrutiny of the facts must be made. Such scrutiny requires examination of the detailed alphabetical analyses under the main topics in the Descriptive-Word Index. For example, the guest knowingly riding in an automobile driven by an intoxicated driver is consequently injured in an accident and seeks recovery. The significant words here are

BACKING (Cont'd)

TRAILER into highway, contributory negligence of motorist. Autos 245(67)

TRAINS—

Contributory negligence of motorist crossing. R R 327(1), 333(1)

Crossing accidents, R R 310

Absence of license signals as negligence as jury question. R R 350(8)

Amendment of pleading affecting limitations. Lim of Act 127(14)

Contributory negligence of—

Automobile guest. R R 350(21)

Motorist, reliance on precautions on part of railroad. R R 330(1–3)

Gross negligence. R R 310

Instruction, conformity to pleadings and issues. R R 351(2)

Last clear chance. R R 338

Question for jury. R R 350(8)

Darkness. R R 350(26)

Proximate cause. R R 350(32)

Pleading cause of action under last clear chance doctrine. R R 344(10)

Duty as to lookout for employees in yard. R R 369(3)

Exhibit 46

"passenger," "guest," "intoxicated driver," and "automobile," and under these words, directly or indirectly, the proper Key Numbers can be found. Proper legal analysis, however, shows that the real point at issue is the passenger's contributory negligence in knowingly riding with an intoxicated driver. Under the main topic of "Contributory Negligence," the pertinent Key Numbers are given under half a dozen subheads—"Automobiles"; "Intoxicated Driver, driving with"; "Guest, driving with intoxicated host"; "Intoxicated Persons, riding with"—with cross-references to other pertinent topics. The proper Key Number is thus speedily found.

Since there is a different Descriptive-Word Index for each Decennial, common sense must be employed in using them. For example, few people were purchasing radios and automobile tires on the installment plan between 1896 and 1916, the period covered by the Descriptive-Word Index for the first two Decennials. A search in this unit for a case involving such transactions would probably be useless. Such a search in the next unit, covering the Third and Fourth Decennials during the next twenty years, would, however, be fruitful. Similarly, atomic energy was not involved in any cases digested in the Fifth Decennial, but the Descriptive-Word Index covering later periods does include such entries.

In searching the Descriptive-Word Index, remember that the Index for the latest Decennial is supplemented by a blue-paper supplement for each volume of the General Digest and that, for every ten volumes of the General Digest, these paper supplements are cumulated into a bound volume.

c. *Analytical or topical approach*. It is often quicker to find the Key Numbers in point through legal analysis than by the fact approach.

Having a set of facts but no case in point and with no salient catchword pointing to the Descriptive-Word Index, how is the pertinent Key Number to be found analytically?

First, a preliminary analysis should be made to determine whether the problem is one of persons, property, contracts, torts, crimes, remedies, or government. The next step will further break your problem down into a much smaller subdivision of the law such as admiralty, damages, husband and wife, or tenancy. These logically belong to one of the subjects in the list of Digest Topics found in the front of each volume of the Decennials since the Fourth. Most topics are fairly obvious. For example, an insurance contract leads to "Insurance" rather than to "Contracts" because insurance is a smaller and more workable subdivision of the law of contracts. Similarly, a problem on the admissibility of evidence falls within the topic "Evidence." Others may not be so obvious and require more careful analysis. The proper recipient of the proceeds of a deceased's life insurance might be a problem in insurance, equity or marshalling of assets. Perhaps your pertinent Key Numbers can be found under all these topics. In this the "Subjects Included," "Subjects Excluded and Covered by Other Topics," and "Analysis" at the beginning of each main topic help. The following is a simple, but typical, example of how the analytical approach works.

(1) *Problem illustrating the analytical approach*. Your client occupies a loft building for manufacturing purposes. Some goods have been damaged by the overflow of water from that part of the same building occupied by and under the control of the defendant. The defendant admits the overflow. Damages are involved, but liability must first be established. Since the parties are both tenants of a building, the Digest topic "Landlord and Tenant" is consulted. Checking the main analysis of that topic enables the searcher to discard all subtopics but "VII. Premises, and Enjoyment and Use Thereof," shown in Exhibit 47.

Most large topics such as "Landlord and Tenant" also have a subanalysis which further breaks down the main topic. A check of subtopic VII in the subanalysis leads to an examination of "E. Injuries from Dangerous or Defective Conditions." See Exhibit 48.

This subanalysis is valuable because it aids in the ultimate Key Number analysis. The subanalysis under E suggests Key Numbers ⚷ 163 and ⚷ 166, especially ⚷ 166(9). Searching under this Key Number, backward to the first Decennial and forward through the General Digest bound volumes and blue monthly pamphlets,

29-5th D—197

LANDLORD AND TENANT

Scope-Note.

INCLUDES nature and incidents of estates for years and tenancies from year to year, at will, or at sufferance; leases and agreements for the occupation of real property in general, the relation between the parties thereto, and their rights and liabilities as between themselves and as to others incident to such relation; and remedies relating thereto.

Matters not in this topic, treated elsewhere, see Descriptive-Word Index.

Analysis.

Exhibit 47

17—3d Dec.Dig.,Page 1139 LANDLORD AND TENANT

VII. Premises and Enjoyment and Use Thereof—Continued.

(E) INJURIES FROM DANGEROUS OR DEFECTIVE CONDITION.

⚿162. Nature and extent of landlord's duty to tenant.
163. Mutual duties of tenants of different portions of same premises.
164. Injuries to tenants or occupants.
164 (1). Injuries due to defective or dangerous condition of premises in general.
164 (2). Injuries due to failure to repair.
164 (3). Injuries due to negligence in making repairs.
164 (4). Injuries due to unlighted passageways.
164 (5). Liability for injuries to subtenant.
164 (6). Liability of landlord as dependent on knowledge of defects.
164 (7). Notice to or knowledge of tenant as to defects.
165. Injuries to employé of tenant.
165 (1). Injuries due to defective or dangerous condition of premises in general.
165 (2). Injuries due to failure to repair.
165 (3). Injuries due to unlighted passageway.
165 (4). Liability of landlord as dependent on knowledge of defects.
165 (5). Failure to guard dangerous places.
165 (6). Operation or condition of elevators.
165 (7). Notice to or knowledge of tenant as to defects.
166. Injuries to property of tenant on premises.
166 (1). Nature and extent of the duties of landlord and tenant respectively.
166 (2). Injuries due to defective condition of premises in general.
166 (3). Injuries due to failure to repair.
166 (4). Injuries due to negligence in making repairs.
166 (5). Injuries due to defective water pipes or drains.
166 (6). Injuries due to negligent acts of landlord.
166 (7, 8). Injuries due to negligence of third persons in general.
166 (9). Injuries due to negligence of cotenant.
166 (10). Liability of landlord as dependent on knowledge or notice of defects.
167. Injuries to third persons and their property.
167 (1). Duties of landlord and tenant to third persons.
167 (2). Injuries due to defective or dangerous condition of premises in general.

Exhibit 48

locates all cases in point from 1896 to date. A search of "Landlord and Tenant ⚿ 166(9)" in the Second Decennial leads to a notation in boldface type stating that this subject matter is collected in the Century Digest, covering cases back to 1658, under "Landlord and Tenant §§657 and 658." Covering the bound volumes of the General Digest, the Table of Key Numbers shown in Exhibit 45 discloses the only volumes of that digest which include any cases under ⚿ 166(9). This makes it unnecessary to search any other interim volumes for cases in point. A complete search would also include the advance sheets not yet covered by the monthly pamphlet of the General Digest.

d. *Words and phrases approach to the law.* Courts are often called upon to define words or terms, the meanings of which are in dispute. These judicial definitions are printed as headnote paragraphs in the reporter and then collected in alphabetical order in a dictionary of many volumes, called Words and Phrases. The words so defined may be legal words of art like "fine," "forced heir," or "forgery," but frequently consist of words in common use like "flat stones," "flax," "flight crew," or "food." Such dictionaries and the approach to the law through them are discussed in Chapter 21.

3. *Progress from unit to unit of the Digest for full coverage*. In practice, most lawyers are likely to begin their search with the General Digest and work backward to the First Decennial and from there to the Century. It should be remembered that a full search may include: (1) the Century Digest; (2) all Decennial Digests; (3) all bound volumes and monthly pamphlets of the General Digest; and (4) National Reporter System advance sheets to date.

§16.7. Digests of lesser scope than the American Digest System.

Nearly all the reported cases digested in the American Digest System are also included in less comprehensive digests. A few digests, like Clark's Digest Annotator[2] for certain New York lower court cases, cover cases not included in the American Digest System organization; no detailed description of them individually is needed. Some of their specialized features, however, are pointed out below. If you know how to use one digest, you know how to use them all.

§16.8. Digests of cases decided in the federal courts.

As stated earlier, all reported cases with few exceptions are covered by the American Digest System. If, however, only a federal court decision in point is being sought, considerable time is saved by searching a digest whose coverage is wholly confined to federal cases. Together, three digests cover all the federal courts. Several other digests which cover individual courts combine to effect complete coverage.

1. *Federal Digest, Modern Federal Practice Digest, and West's Federal Practice Digest 2d*.

a. *Scope of coverage*. All federal constitutional and legislative courts of record are covered. The Federal Digest, 1940 edition, is the repository of the federal case law through the year 1938. This set includes only permanent bound volumes and is not supplemented. When new federal rules governing district courts in civil and criminal matters

2. Boonton, N.J., Kimball-Clark Publishing Co., 1938 to date.

were promulgated in 1938 (the Criminal Rules became effective in 1941), federal practice was changed radically. The publishers of the Federal Digest felt that there should be a clean break between the older digested cases and the newer ones and, consequently, inaugurated the publication of the Modern Federal Practice Digest. All pamphlets and pocket parts since have supplemented only the new digest. Pocket supplements have made the Modern Federal Practice Digest unwieldy and so a third digest, Federal Practice Digest 2d, is being published.

The Descriptive-Word Index for the Modern Federal Practice Digest covers all federal case law from the earliest times to date and supersedes the Descriptive-Word Index for the Federal Digest.

Thus, with the completion of the Modern Federal Practice Digest, all federal case law is covered in:

(1) Federal Digest bound volumes, not including the bound cumulative supplements and Descriptive-Word Indexes, but including the tables of cases. All cases through 1938 are here.

(2) Modern Federal Practice Digest, for cases beginning with 1939 to 1961.

(3) The Federal Practice Digest 2d, supplementing the Modern Federal Practice Digest and supplemented by quarterly pamphlets and annual pocket parts.

Certain administrative tribunals such as the Tax Court of the United States bear the title "court" but are not true courts. They are not covered in these digests. The reports of the federal courts of Alaska and Hawaii, which, during the territorial period, also served some of the functions of state courts, and the United States Court of Appeals for the District of Columbia, a circuit of the United States Court of Appeals, are covered. Cases originating in Puerto Rico, now a commonwealth, are reported in the Federal Supplement and Federal Reporter.

The Federal Digest, Modern Federal Practice Digest, and the Federal Practice Digest 2d are typical of the Key Number digests described earlier in this chapter. They have the usual descriptive-word index, case tables, and lists of adjudicated patents and trademarks. They also have some features not found in the Decennials. There is a Defendant-Plaintiff case table in addition to an index to words and phrases judicially defined in the digested cases. Court rules construed are listed in a separate table.

New or expanded topics usually appear in these digests before they do in the Decennials. For example, in the Seventh Decennial there is no main topic "Products Liability." Although it was later incorporated in the Eighth and will be incorporated in succeeding Decennials, this topic appeared in the Modern Federal Practice Digest as soon as it was announced.

b. *Steps in a complete search of reported federal cases.*

(1) *Cases decided through 1938.* The search here is in the Federal Digest unless the pertinent topic has been expanded or superseded by a new topic in the Modern Federal Practice Digest. In that case, the procedure in §16.5.5c, *supra*, must be used.

(2) *Cases decided from 1938 to date.* The cases from 1938–1961 are digested in the Modern Federal Practice Digest. The hard-bound covers 1939–1961. Paperback supplements to the Modern Federal Practice Digest continue until the completion of the Federal Practice Digest 2d. From 1961 to date, the researcher uses Federal Practice Digest 2d.

(3) *New topics in Modern Federal Practice Digest.* Many main digest topics either have been started as new topics (e.g., Securities Regulation and Products Liability) or have been greatly expanded since the beginning of the Federal Digest. These new or expanded topics constitute exceptions to the rule that Key Numbers cover identical material in all Key Number digests. The modified search procedure for them has been described in §16.5.5c, *supra*.

(4) *Search for latest cases in the General Digest and reporter advance sheets.* Since supplementation of the Federal Practice Digest 2d is only quarterly, a digest search may include two additional steps to produce the latest cases: examination of the monthly General Digest pamphlets later than the latest quarterly digest supplement, and of the advance sheets of the various reports covering still later cases. An accurate check of the reports covered in the regional units is supplied by the tables at the beginning of each quarterly and annual digest supplement and of each monthly General Digest issue. These tables give the precise volume and page citation to the reports digested in each supplement.

2. *State digests digesting federal court reports.* State digests commonly digest all federal court decisions involving their state or cases on appeal to the Supreme Court of the United States from their respective state courts.

3. *Supreme Court of the United States cases.* Supreme Court cases are digested both in the American Digest System and in the Federal Digest, Modern Federal Practice Digest, and the Federal Practice Digest 2d, but there are two special digests for the Supreme Court alone.

a. *Digest of the U.S. Supreme Court Reports, L. Ed.* This is an excellent digest, in twenty volumes, published by the Lawyers Cooperative Publishing Company with cross-references to that company's American Law Reports Annotated, American Jurisprudence, and Lawyers' Edition of Supreme Court Reports. Although it is a typical case digest, with the usual tables and indexes, it has some special features of its own.

(1) *Table of cases.* This table is in a single alphabet for plaintiff-defendant, defendant-plaintiff, and popular name (e.g., *Hot Oil* case). References to additional cases and discussions in point are made in it through citations to American Jurisprudence and American Law Reports Annotated. Annotations in the Lawyers' Edition are indexed in a separate volume. Dissenting and separate concurring opinions are separately listed in the tables. The Table of Federal Statutes by Popular Name (e.g., Morrill Act, Taft-Hartley Act) is a very useful tool. Words and phrases judicially defined are not listed in the Tables volume, but under "Words and Phrases" in the digest proper as a main topic of the digest.

(2) *Court rules.* Rules covering all federal courts (but not those covering specific district courts) are printed in two separate volumes. Another volume is devoted to the Federal Rules of Evidence adopted in 1975.

(3) *Citator information.* Some information not readily available elsewhere can be found here. Digest paragraphs, for example, note whenever a point of law digested has been modified or commented upon by a subsequent Supreme Court decision and include the holding of the later case. These digests are kept up to date by annual pocket parts. The extensive Table of Cases Affirmed, Reversed, Reheard, Etc., in volume 14 covers rehearings in the Supreme Court of both federal and state lower courts' cases. The arrangement is by the volume and page of the report being reconsidered and not by case name. The exact disposition of the case by the Supreme Court is noted. This table supplies one of the speediest means of determining whether or not a specific federal or state case or group of cases has been appealed to the Supreme Court as well as the disposition of the case or cases there. A complete search here would cover the table in volume 14, its annual pocket supplement, and the later bound volumes (but not the advance sheets) of the Lawyers' Edition.

b. *United States Supreme Court Digest.* A West Publishing Company Key Number digest, this has the various features of such digests, such as tables of cases, of words and phrases judicially defined, and of cases listed by popular name as well as a descriptive-word index. Court rules for all but the individual district courts are printed. Both the digest paragraphs and the table of cases give available citator information regarding actions on appeal.

4. *Digests covering lower federal courts.*

a. *Federal Cases.* The digest to Federal Cases is of no current interest as a digest, but it is useful for its conversion table which translates the original citations of the lower federal court cases up to 1880 to the Federal Cases citation, as, for example, from 7 Blatchf. 555 to Fed. Cas. No. 602.

b. *Federal Digest, Modern Federal Practice Digest, and Federal Practice Digest 2d.* These three digests cover all federal courts of record, past and present. They are described in §16.8.1, *supra*.

c. *Court of Claims Digest.* Covering cases from 1855 to date, this West digest is used like any other Key Number digest.

d. *Customs Court Digest.* This digest covers all Customs Court decisions and those of the Court of Customs and Patent Appeals from 1910 to date. For customs reports there are also small, officially published digests. Since so much of the Customs Court's function relates to the interpretation of the law of specific types of imports, the Words and Phrases section of this digest is useful. Such terms as "shrines," "bricks," "regulus of copper" are defined.

e. *Digests for "courts" which are not true courts.* There is a Tax Court Digest.[3] The Tax Court is not a true court but an administrative tribunal. Similarly, the United States Military Court of Appeals, though nominally a court under Article 67 of the Code of Military Justice, is an agency of the Department of Defense. Its decisions are published, and there is a Citator and Index for the first twenty-five volumes and one for every five volumes beginning with the twenty-sixth. These are not true digests but are "index-digests" with descriptive-word analysis under broad subject headings.

§16.9. State and territorial court digests.

In one form or another, the reported decisions of all federal and state appellate courts and those of some courts of first instance, from 1658 to date, are covered by conventional case digests. The American Digest System covers state courts. State and territorial courts are also covered by regional reporter digests (e.g., Atlantic, Pacific) and, for most states, and the territories before statehood, by separate digests for each political division.

1. *Regional Reporter digests.* These are typical Key Number digests. The South Western Reporter Digest and The North Eastern Reporter Digest have been discontinued. The coverage of the other regional units varies from the beginning of the reporter (about 1880) to date for some, to complete statehood coverage for others. See §12.1.

2. *Individual state digests.* The West Publishing Company publishes separate digests for nearly all of the fifty states, and others are

3. Indianapolis, Ind., Bobbs-Merrill Co., 1952 to date.

in preparation. Other publishers cover other states. For your own purposes, check with your law librarian to see which states are covered by individual digests in your library.

The West state digests are Key Number digests with the digest paragraphs taken from the American Digest System (which means, in effect, from the regional reporter advance sheets with such added citator information as was available when the state digest went to press). For most states there are also local materials which are not found in the American Digest System. Examples are the enumeration and history of all New York state courts and the description of their reports found in 2 Abbott's New York Digest and the Table of Statutes Construed in the Massachusetts Digest Annotated.

There are many state digests other than those which are published by West, and some of them, by permission, copy the Key Number classification without the key symbol. Their composition, tables, and methods of use so nearly coincide in all significant respects with other digests that the lawyer or student who can work with one digest is soon at home with them all. All of these digests emphasize their local character. The Indiana Decennial Digest is keyed to Burns's Indiana Statutes which, in turn, is keyed to the Digest. In addition to some other citator data, Page's Ohio Digest has a separate alphabetical table of Cases Judicially Noticed. Callaghan's Wisconsin Digest cites A.L.R. annotations. local practice treatises, and all law review comments on Wisconsin cases.

Jointly published by the West Publishing Company and the Lawyers Co-operative Publishing Company, Abbott's New York Digest employs the Key Number classification of the former company and refers to pertinent A.L.R. annotations of the latter. Volume 2 of the Consolidated (first) Edition lists and describes all New York courts and their reports. Two other New York digests cover selected lower court opinions of the First and Second Judicial Departments of New York (the greater New York metropolitan area). While most of these opinions are also published in official and regional reporter system reports, a legal newspaper, the New York Law Journal, publishes some opinions not found in other report series. A New York case search covering cases decided in the lower courts of the First and Second Departments may, therefore, require a search of New York Law Journal cases. Also covering such cases is Clark's Digest Annotator (1937 to date) which appears monthly and cumulates into an annual bound volume. It has its own classification scheme, table of cases, and subject-matter index. Along with selected First and Second Judicial Department reports, the New York Law Journal includes some digests of New York Court of Appeals and Appellate Division cases and of United States Supreme Court and Courts of Appeals decisions.

§16.10. Coordinating the digest with other case-finders.

While most comprehensive and generally useful, digests are not the only case-finders. Treatises, legal encyclopedias, legal periodicals, annotations, and citators are also fruitful sources of cases in point and provide starting points for searchers.

The simplest technique for coordinating the various indexes to cases in point is to find a single case and go on from there. This starter case may be found in a treatise, law review article footnote, legal encyclopedia, or another case. Then, either by checking a Key Number digest table of cases or by going directly to the reporter containing the case, Key Numbers in point are found. With the name of the case you may find, through the Index to Legal Periodicals tables beginning with 1917, that the case has been discussed in a law review article or case comment. Through the parallel citations of your case in case tables or footnotes or by means of a search in the A.L.R. case table, you will discover whether your case has been the subject of an A.L.R. annotation. These annotations are also cited in American Jurisprudence, a legal encyclopedia discussed in the next chapter. Further checking with Shepard's Citations, described in Chapter 18, will reveal citations to any appeals of your case as well as to other cases which have cited it as precedent. It is a snowballing process which starts from one or more cases in point and rapidly builds up.

It is also a process which turns up more chaff than wheat, requiring the examination and discarding of many useless cases before you find those which are helpful. It is a process which demands the use of all of your skills and discriminatory ability to appraise and to cull the cases found.

17 | Legal Encyclopedias

§17.1. Function, scope, and content of legal encyclopedias.

Ideally the legal encyclopedia includes the following material: (1) a complete and integrated statement of all applicable law; (2) citation to relied-upon authority, which may include not only references to cases in point but also digests of cases and excerpts from standard treatises and American Law Institute Restatements; (3) exhaustive analytical and subject indexes; and (4) frequent supplements, in which the main text may be rewritten in view of cases later than those forming the basis of the original discussion.

The encyclopedia is best used as a starting point in a search for the law. By supplying the reader with an elementary statement of the law applicable to his or her problem, the encyclopedia gives the searcher a valuable frame of reference. Those cases cited as supporting the text and selected by the searcher for reading are placed in their proper perspective by the encyclopedia.

The text in the encyclopedia begins with a general and elementary statement of the law, proceeds to a more detailed consideration of all aspects of the substantive law concerned, and ends with a discussion of the available remedies. Special-subject encyclopedias commonly contain annotated substantive and procedural forms. The encyclopedia provides a useful starting point in a search. It serves the double purpose of giving searchers a good treatment of topics of which they are relatively ignorant and of refreshing their familiarity with other subjects. By citing its authority the encyclopedia serves as a case-finder. Once searchers have cases in point, the whole field of search through the digests, treatises, legal periodicals, annotated cases, and citation books is opened up to them.

Since the primary purpose of the encyclopedia is to help judges decide and lawyers to win cases, it is similar to the practitioners' textbook in that it expounds upon the law *as it is*. The persons for whom it is designed are often not concerned with the history of the past or speculation as to the future of the law; if desired, these can be gleaned from scholarly treatises or law review articles on history or jurisprudence. The encyclopedia resembles student books, however, in that (1) it is careful to state and explain majority, minority, and jurisdictional rules, and (2) its statements of the law begin with an elementary exposition of each point covered.

§17.2. Authority of legal encyclopedias.

An encyclopedia is not a primary (binding) authority; no court is bound in any way to regard its statements of the law as precedent. An encyclopedia functions instead as a well-indexed general description of the law as set forth in the decided cases upon which its statements are based. On the other hand, legal encyclopedias are frequently cited with approval in judicial opinions—not as authority in themselves, but as containing well-reasoned statements of the rules of law as extracted from the cited cases relied upon.

§17.3. Form of legal encyclopedias.

Like the conventional treatise, the encyclopedia states the law in literary form as extracted from the authorities cited. Like the digest, the encyclopedia is alphabetically arranged by topics under a classification system similar to that of the digest (even to the scope-note, analysis, and subanalysis). The scope-note is an eliminator. By stating briefly what is covered by a topic it also tells by implication what is not covered. The searcher who uses the scope-note thus avoids wasting time. The analysis may be compared to an unusually detailed table of contents. Most encyclopedias consist of approximately 400 alphabetically arranged treatises, which vary in length from a few lines to hundreds of pages. They resemble the digest in that they have a descriptive-word index. Although no general encyclopedia has a table of cases, some of the special-subject ones do. The typical page of an encyclopedia resembles those of law books generally; the text discussion is found above the line and is supported by citations below the line to authority relied upon.

§17.4. Advantages and disadvantages of the encyclopedia form.

The encyclopedia aims to be a one-set library and may represent a considerable saving of both cost and space over a collection of individual treatises covering the same aggregate of legal topics. It probably covers the totality of the law more precisely and leaves fewer gaps than such a collection of treatises would. Continuity of editorial policy assures that changes in the law will be reflected and that there will be regular and complete supplementation. Consequently, in theory the encyclopedia is never out-of-date by more than the time between annual supplements. The comprehensive indexes may frequently offer a better guide to the body of the law than the sum total of the indexes of individual treatises.

On the other hand, the compilation of an encyclopedia is such an enormous task that it extends over many years. It took sixteen years to complete American Jurisprudence 2d and twenty-four (including time spent in compiling a general index) for Corpus Juris Secundum. Although the supplements note the changes which occur over such a long period of time, a complete rewriting of affected topics to reflect these changes in the law lags.

In addition, lawyers often fail to understand that the general statements of law found in a legal encyclopedia represent the beginning, rather than the end, of the research process. Frequently, the generalized statement may be inapplicable in particular fact situations. Thus, searchers must always examine the authorities cited in support of textual statements in order to determine their accuracy for particular situations.

§17.5. The two current general legal encyclopedias.

A general legal encyclopedia aims to cover all topics, both substantive and adjective, of our American law. There are two current general legal encyclopedias: American Jurisprudence Second[1] (cited as Am. Jur. 2d) and Corpus Juris Secundum[2] (cited as C.J.S.). While their scope of coverage is identical, their approaches differ somewhat. Their similarities and differences are outlined briefly here,[3] as a pre-

1. San Francisco, Cal., Bancroft-Whitney Co., Rochester, N.Y., Lawyers Co-operative Publishing Co., 1962–1977, 82 vols. and 6 General Index vols., with Table of Statutes and Rules Cited. Annual cumulative pocket supplements, recompiled volumes, and topic supplementation through New Topic Service as required.

2. Brooklyn, N.Y., American Law Book Co., 1936–1958, 101 vols. and 5 General Index vols. Annual cumulative pocket supplements and recompiled volumes as required.

3. This outline was suggested by Professor Albert J. Blaustein, of the Rutgers University School of Law, South Jersey Branch, whose students have found it useful.

liminary to more detailed descriptions of each encyclopedia separately.

1. *Basic differences between the two encyclopedias.* Policy differences in compiling the two encyclopedias are stated as follows by the publishers themselves·

> *American Jurisprudence Second:* ". . . a modern comprehensive text statement of American law (state and federal) completely revised and rewritten in the light of modern authorities and developments. . . ."
>
> *Corpus Juris Secundum:* ". . . a complete restatement of the entire American law as developed by all reported cases."

2. *Mutual characteristics outlined:*

Characteristics	*Am. Jur. 2d*	*C.J.S.*
Multivolume	82 text volumes	101 text volumes
Arranged alphabetically by topic	More than 430 topics with the New Topic Service	433 topics
Descriptive-word indexes	Six-volume General Index, plus index in each volume for topics covered in that volume.	Five-volume General Index, plus index in each volume for topics covered in that volume.
Table of cases; table of statutes	No table of cases; Tables of statutes (U.S. Code, uniform laws and court rules) are in each volume, and compiled into a separate volume.	No table of cases; no table of statutes.
Scope-note, analysis	Yes, as in a digest	Yes, as in a digest
Dictionary functions	Definitions through general index	Definitions through special index of words and phrases following main text in each volume, and in alphabetical order in main text volumes.
Supplementation	Annual pocket parts; replacement vols.; New Topic Service.	Annual pocket parts; replacement vols.

§17.6. American Jurisprudence.

This legal encyclopedia, the predecessor of American Jurisprudence Second (Am. Jur. 2d), has been entirely superseded by Am. Jur. 2d as a legal text and should no longer be read as a statement of existing law.

§17.7. American Jurisprudence Second (Am. Jur. 2d).[4]

Am. Jur. 2d has now entirely superseded Am. Jur. The Am. Jur. 2d text uses such of the older Am. Jur. text as required no change, but much of the text has been rewritten or expanded in order to cover recent developments in the law. Cases and other references later than Am. Jur. have been added; new topics are introduced as necessary. A cross-reference table in each Am. Jur. 2d volume leads from sections in Am. Jur. to the corresponding but usually differently numbered sections in Am. Jur. 2d.

This encyclopedia aims at complete coverage of both adjective and substantive law of general application, as modified by statute. It also serves a dictionary function in defining legal maxims and words and phrases.

1. *Scope of citation to authority*. Am. Jur. relies heavily upon cases printed in the annotated, selective cases series. While Am. Jur. 2d does not attempt to cite all cases in point and still cites A.L.R. annotations, it cites many more non-A.L.R. cases than did Am. Jur., including foreign ones. Pertinent American Law Institute Restatements are quoted or cited. Am. Jur. 2d places considerable emphasis upon federal statutes, the Uniform Laws (including the Uniform Commercial Code), court rules, and articles in legal periodicals and treatises.

2. *Arrangement of material; supplementation as affecting indexes and tables*. The arrangement resembles that of the digests we have already studied. Unlike the digests (which are a collection of self-contained paragraphs independently stating principles of law without any connecting comment), the text of the encyclopedia discusses these principles in literary form, with citations to the cases and other materials relied upon as authority. There are more than 430 main topics or separate treatises, arranged alphabetically by broad topic. The New Topic Service consists of new topics developed after the alphabetical bound volume was published. If the topic warrants treatment in depth, additional pamphlets or bound volumes are printed covering topics such as the Pension Reform Act and the Federal Rules of Evidence. Just as in a digest, analyses and subanalyses precede the text and form the basis of the analytical approach to the law through the encyclopedia.

New cases causing changes in the law are reflected in the encyclopedias by annual cumulative pocket supplements to each text volume. In time, these pocket supplements become unwieldy, and a "recompiled" volume is issued. The publishers incorporate the supplementary material in this volume and rewrite the original text as necessary.

4. See the publisher's The Living Law, for a detailed account of Am. Jur. 2d and its use.

3. *Subject indexes to Am. Jur. 2d; the fact approach to law.* These indexes correspond to the descriptive-word indexes to A.L.R. digests and others, as described in Chapters 15 and 16.

For Am. Jur. 2d there are four different index units, and it is important to keep them straight. They are:

a. *General Index.* This index, published in 1977 and 1978, covers all of Am. Jur. 2d. It is a vast alphabetically arranged index to the material in the Am. Jur. 2d text proper. Like the descriptive-word index of a digest, it includes in a single alphabetical arrangement of entries three different categories: (1) main topics, a list of which is at the front of every text volume; (2) large subjects, such as "Unemployment Compensation," which are not main topics in the encyclopedia, with alphabetically arranged catchword subentries thereunder; (3) catchword entries, such as "adjudges," "after maturity," "bad woman" (incidentally there was no catch phrase entry for "bad man"). Maxims are listed under the maxim itself (e.g., *De minimis non curat lex*).

As in a digest descriptive-word index, there is extensive duplication of subject entries in the indexes, to lead the searcher more speedily to the object of his search — which is a main topic head and a specific section number under it, corresponding in function to the Key Number — without too much analytical effort on his part.

For example, if the searcher seeks a discussion of the effect of the completion of a bill of lading by filling in blanks, he can find the same reference under the main topic "Carriers," subhead "Completing"; under the large subject of "Bills of Lading," subhead "Blank"; and under the catchwords of "Blanks and Blank Instruments" and "Complete or Completeness." There are many cross-references from topics not used to topics used. The typography of these cross-references tells its own story, as explained in a page following the title page of each index volume. This page, Explanatory Illustration, should be read.

Dictionary function of General Index. The General Index does not itself define maxims and words and terms. Instead, it refers to the text where they are defined. The use of the index is necessary because neither maxims nor words defined are to be found in alphabetical order in the main text. For example, "bay" is defined in "Waters §385"; "certified public accountant" in "Accountants §1" of Am. Jur. 2d.

b. *Recompiled volumes' separate indexes.* When a volume is recompiled and republished, the old section numbers of the original volumes are sometimes superseded, so that the General Index may no longer apply for their subject matter. The indexes in the recompiled volumes wholly supersede, for their precise subject matter, the bound volume of the General Index covering a specific title. For all material later than the date of the General Index, the pocket supplements of the General Index must be consulted for peripheral material in volumes of Am. Jur. 2d. Broad references to articles in the Am. Jur. New Topic Service will also be found in pocket supplements to the General Index.

A main function of the General Index is to coordinate citations to discussion of a given topic in all titles. For example, while the material on divorce and separation is covered generally in a volume devoted to that subject, many peripheral aspects of this subject matter are commented upon in other titles, as "Adoption," "Adultery," "Appeal and Error," and "Income Taxes."

c. *Am. Jur. 2d indexes to each volume*. Each volume is separately indexed. There are cross-references from matter treated in other topics. There is also a Table of Parallel References in the front of each volume, from Am. Jur. sections to those of Am. Jur. 2d, from which, also, the reverse transition from Am. Jur. 2d to Am. Jur. is easily made.

d. *Pocket supplements*. Am. Jur. 2d pocket supplements are annual and cumulative. The reader is advised to read the detailed Explanatory Note in the front of each supplement, which cites later cases, calls attention to new principles of law, and notes the addition of new sections and of new text material.

4. *Analytical approach*. This approach to Am. Jur. 2d is precisely the same as in a digest. The outline or table of contents of "Divorce and Separation" is in nineteen subtopics, each subtopic being further subdivided into the ultimate sections under which the subject matter is discussed. Scanning this outline speedily turns up the information shown in Exhibit 49.

5. *Table of cases approach not available*. Since the Am. Jur. system has no table of cases, this valuable approach to the law is not available.

6. *Table of Statutes and Rules Cited*.[5] Am. Jur. 2d also includes a separate volume entitled "Table of Statutes and Rules Cited." These tables show, by reference to title and section, where provisions of the United States Code Service are cited in Am. Jur. 2d. In addition, citations to the following in Am. Jur. 2d are also noted: the Uniform Laws, the Federal Rules of Civil and Criminal Procedure, Federal Practice Rules, and the Federal Bankruptcy Rules and Bankruptcy Official Forms.

Use of the Table of Statutes and Rules Cited is extremely easy. Simply look up the particular title and section in which you are interested. The topic of Am. Jur. 2d references and the section are given.

5. San Francisco, Cal., Bancroft-Whitney Co., Rochester, N.Y., Lawyers Co-operative Publishing Co., 1977, 1 vol. with a cumulative pocket supplement.

24 Am Jur 2d DIVORCE AND SEPARATION

XIII.—Continued
D. TEMPORARY ALIMONY (§§ 548–570)
E. SUIT MONEY, COUNSEL FEES, AND COSTS (§§ 571–599)
F. PERMANENT ALIMONY (§§ 600–707)
G. ENFORCEMENT OF JUDGMENT, DECREE, OR ORDER (§§ 708–771)

XIV. CUSTODY, SUPPORT, AND PATERNITY OR LEGITIMACY OF CHILDREN
A. CUSTODY OF CHILDREN (§§ 772–826)
⟶ B. SUPPORT OF CHILDREN (§§ 827–875)
C. DETERMINATION OF PATERNITY, LEGITIMACY, OR LEGITIMATION OF CHILD (§§ 876–878)

XV. OPERATION AND EFFECT (§§ 879–882)

b. MODE AND AMOUNT OF ALLOWANCE; ALLOWANCES FOR SPECIFIC PURPOSES

§ 837. Mode of allowance; award of property
§ 838. — Trust to secure child support
§ 839. Amount of allowance
§ 840. — Mother's or child's means or earning capacity
§ 841. — Effect of agreement or stipulation of parties
§ 842. Awards for education and other specific purposes
⟶ § 843. — College education

Exhibit 49

If an asterisk appears next to the Am. Jur. 2d section number, this reference is to the Am. Jur. 2d pocket supplement. See Exhibit 50.

In addition to this separate volume which cumulates all references to statutes and rules, each of the 82 volumes contains a Table of Statutes Cited which lists all citations in that volume of the United States Code Service, Federal Rules and Uniform Laws. The New Topic Service of Am. Jur. 2d contains similar statutory tables for each new topic and a supplement which updates these statutory tables.

The Table of Statutes and Rules Cited volume and each individual volume's table of statutes are updated through cumulative pocket supplements.

7. *The Desk Book*. Another feature of Am. Jur. 2d is the Desk Book: Historical and Legal Documents, Facts, Tables, Charts, and Statistics of Special Interest to Attorneys.[6]

6. San Francisco, Cal., Bancroft-Whitney Co., Rochester, N.Y., Lawyers Co-operative Publishing Co., 1962, 659 pp., with a cumulative pocket supplement.

TABLE OF STATUTES

UNITED STATES CODE SERVICE—Continued

Title and section	*Am Jur 2d title and section*
15 USCS—Cont'd	
§ 77b(3)	Securities Regulations—Federal §§ 79, 90*
§ 77b(4)	Securities Regulations—Federal § 75
§ 77b(6)	Securities Regulations—Federal § 120
§ 77b(7)	Securities Regulations—Federal § 17; Securities Regulations—State § 1
§ 77b(8)	Securities Regulations—Federal § 115
§ 77b(9)	Securities Regulations—Federal § 168
§ 77b(10)	Securities Regulations—Federal § 168
§ 77b(11)	Securities Regulations—Federal §§ 8, 8*, 9*, 76
§ 77b(12)	Securities Regulations—Federal § 78
§ 77c	Public Securities and Obligations § 218; Securities Regulations—Federal § 35
§ 77c(a)(1)	Securities Regulations—Federal § 36
§ 77c(a)(2)	Securities Regulations—Federal §§ 37, 38
§ 77c(a)(3)	Securities Regulations—
15 USCS—Cont'd	
§ 77c(b)	Bankruptcy §§ 348, 348*; Securities Regulations—Federal § 49
§ 77c(c)	Securities Regulations—Federal § 49
§ 77d	Securities Regulations—Federal § 96
§ 77d(1)	Securities Regulations—Federal §§ 3, 8, 97
§ 77d(2)	Securities Regulations—Federal § 102
§ 77d(3)	Securities Regulations—Federal §§ 8, 100
§ 77d(3)(A)	Securities Regulations—Federal § 100
§ 77d(3)(B)	Securities Regulations—Federal § 100
§ 77d(3)(C)	Securities Regulations—Federal § 100
§ 77d(4)	Securities Regulations—Federal §§ 8, 101
§ 77d(5)	Securities Regulation—Federal § 96*
§ 77e	Bankruptcy §§ 1308, 1329, 1357, 1555; Securities Regulations—Federal § 120*
§ 77e(a)	Securities Regulations—

Exhibit 50

This is a data book for lawyers. In addition to containing a complete listing of titles in Am. Jur. 2d, it is divided into seven parts, as follows: Part I prints the text of sixteen classic documents (the Constitution, Magna Carta, United Nations Charter, etc.); organization charts of federal government agencies; officers and addresses of the principal federal administrative agencies; and a great deal of similar data for the states, territories, and possessions. Part II concerns the federal and state courts, their organization, and statistics regarding civil and criminal cases. Part III relates to the legal profession: ethics, bar admission procedure, accredited law schools, American Bar Association organization, and the number of lawyers in the United States (by states and by sex). Part IV prints the text of ancient English statutes and tabulates a wide variety of statutory materials across state lines (voting qualifications, limitations periods for common actions, marriage and divorce laws, Uniform Laws, etc.). Part V is devoted to statistical matters, such as financial and mathematical tables, tax and annuity computation tables, mortality tables, price index charts, foreign exchange and foreign money, weights and measures, weather, population, and skid-speed charts for automobiles. Part VI is a table of American and major British law reports and of common abbreviations of legal materials (such as law reports, statutes, and periodicals). Part VII, Miscellaneous Records, gives such information as where to write for vital statistical records of the various states, tables of descent and distribution, mail time between cities, number of days from any day in one month to the same day in any other month, etc.

A subject index is provided towards the end of the Desk Book. In addition, cumulative pocket supplements keep the data found in the Desk Book up-to-date.

§17.8. Corpus Juris.

This legal encyclopedia, the predecessor of Corpus Juris Secundum (cited as C.J.S.), has been entirely superseded by C.J.S. as a legal text and should no longer be read as a statement of existing law. Therefore it will not be described here. The cases and other authorities cited in the original C.J. volumes are, however, still cited by reference in the text and footnotes of C.J.S., so that the encyclopedia often retains its place on law library shelves entirely for the sake of these citations.

§17.9. Corpus Juris Secundum.

This general legal encyclopedia aims to be at once "a complete restatement of the entire American law, as developed by all reported cases," an annotated legal dictionary, and an annotated dictionary of legal maxims.

1. *Scope of citation to authority in C.J.S.* The publishers claim to cite all cases in point. In addition, C.J.S. cites and often quotes pertinent American Law Institute Restatements provisions, treatises and law review articles. The theory of legislation and of statutory construction generally is treated. Where a statute is involved in a decision cited as authority, that fact is mentioned in the footnote citation of the case. No attempt is made, however, to treat local statutes generally; that is left to local practice books. Where statutes significantly affect the body of an area of law, their effect is analyzed in the main text. While there is no intention to serve as local practice books, the fundamentals of procedure are covered in detail.

The totality of citations to authority in C.J.S. includes also the cases cited by its predecessor, C.J., but the text of C.J. is entirely superseded by the C.J.S. text and should not be read. All citations in found in the cases where the positive law of the domicile makes void certain kinds of marriages by its citizens although celebrated elsewhere, and although they would otherwise be valid where celebrated, in which case such a marriage is held to be void not only in the domiciliary state,[29] but in every other state.[30]

For an extended discussion of the foregoing and an exhaustive collection of the authorities, the C.J. S. title Marriage § 4, also 38 C.J. p 1276 note 24–p 1279 note 45, should be consulted.

A distinction should be made at this point between the creation and existence of the marriage status and the incidents attached thereto. Hence while a foreign contracted marriage will be recognized everywhere, the rights and duties flowing therefrom will be governed by the law of the place where the parties are[31] or by some law other than that of the state creating the status, depending upon the nature of the problem involved.[32] Appropriate sections of the title Husband and Wife should be consulted for the treatment of the law governing the particular rights growing out of the marriage relation.

See § 16 c infra for a discussion of the foregoing rules in so far as they involve the capacity of the parties to enter into the marriage status. See § 20 e infra for a discussion of the law governing the formal requisites of a marriage.

d. Parent and Child

While ordinarily the relation of parent and child is governed by the law of the domicile of the parent having custody, any state in which a minor child is found has jurisdiction to determine questions of custody and control in the interest of the child.

As stated in the C.J.S. title Parent and Child § 1, also 46 C.J. p 1220 note 3, the term parent and child indicates the relation existing between husband and wife or either of them and their legitimate offspring. It is a status, not a property right.[33]

A Conflict of Laws problem involving this relationship may arise when the right to, and jurisdiction to determine, the custody and control of a minor child is involved. While basically the domicile of the parent having custody of the child is the place which has control of the status of parent and child, because the domicile of the parent is that of the child, see the C.J.S. title Domicile § 12, also 19 C.J. p 411 note 29, only such state having the right to adjudicate any change in the relationship,[34] because every state has an interest in the welfare of children within its confines, the law of the domicile of the parents is not necessarily a factor in determining questions of the custody and control of a child,[35] the state within which the child is found

Mass.—Atwood v. Atwood, 8 N.E.2d 916.
N.Y.—In re Seymour, 185 N.Y.S. 373, 113 Misc. 421.
Okl.—Eggers v. Olson, 231 P. 483, 104 Okl. 297.

29. Mass.—Atwood v. Atwood, 8 N.E.2d 916—Hanson v. Hanson, 191 N.E. 673, 287 Mass. 154, 93 A.L.R. 701.
N.Y.—Bell v. Little, 197 N.Y.S. 674, 204 App.Div. 235, modifying 189 N.Y.S. 935, and affirmed 143 N.E. 726, 237 N.Y. 519—Bays v. Bays, 174 N.Y.S. 212, 105 Misc. 492.
Okl.—Eggers v. Olson, 231 P. 483, 104 Okl. 297—Ross v. Bryant, 217 P. 364, 90 Okl. 300.
Wis.—Lyannes v. Lyannes, 177 N.W. 683, 171 Wis. 381.

Prohibiting evasion of local law

The legislature can declare out-of-state marriage of Massachusetts residents void in Massachusetts, if marriage was consummated in another state to avoid provisions of Massachusetts laws forbidding marriage in Massachusetts.—Atwood v. Atwood, Mass., 8 N.E.2d 916.

Law of domicile governs

Where citizens of one state go to another state, and there contract a marriage prohibited by the statutes of the former state governing public policy as to persons competent to enter into such status, and return forthwith to the place of domicile, the validity of their marital status, when drawn in question therein, will be determined by the law of domicile under the rule that the law, n t of the place of contract, but of the domicile of the parties, governs.—Ross v. Bryant, 217 P. 364, 90 Okl. 300.

"**A marriage which is against the law of the state of domicil** of either party, though the requirements of the law of the state of celebration have been complied with, will be invalid everywhere in the following cases: (a) polygamous marriage, (b) incestuous marriage between persons so closely related that their marriage is contrary to a strong public policy of the domicil, (c) marriage between persons of different races where such marriages are at the domicil regarded as odious, (d) marriage of a domiciliary which a statute at the domicil makes void even though celebrated in another state."—Restatement, Conflict of Laws § 132.

30. Mich.—People v. Steere, 151 N.W. 617, 184 Mich. 556.
Wis.—Hall v. Industrial Commission, 162 N.W. 312, 165 Wis. 364, L.R.A. 1917D 829.

31. Wis.—Forbes v. Forbes, 277 N.W. 112, 226 Wis. 477.
12 C.J. p 459 note 25.

32. S.D.—Calhoun v. Bryant, 133 N.W. 266, 271, 28 S.D. 266.

"We believe a substantially correct statement of the proposition is that the law of the state where the marriage is consummated establishes the 'relationship' of one to the other as husband and wife or parent and child which is universally recognized, but that the mere incidents flowing from that 'status' or relationship are controlled by the law of the domicile of the parties or the situs of the property."—Calhoun v. Bryant, supra.

33. Pa.—In re Rosenthal, 157 A. 342, 103 Pa.Super. 27.

34. Iowa.—Kline v. Kline, 10 N.W. 825, 57 Iowa 386, 42 Am.R. 47.
Minn. State v. Larson, 252 N.W. 329, 190 Minn. 496.
N.Y.—Finlay v. Finlay, 148 N.E. 624, 240 N.Y. 429.
Tex.—Lanning v. Gregory, 99 S.W. 542, 100 Tex. 310, 10 L.R.A.,N.S., 690.

35. N.Y.—Finlay v. Finlay, 148 N.E. 624, 240 N.Y. 429, 40 A.L.R. 792.

911

Exhibit 51

the C.J.S. Annotations volumes, issued annually until the completion of C.J.S., have been incorporated in C.J.S. and should not be consulted. The method of citing C.J. cases in C.J.S. is shown in Exhibit 51.

2. *Arrangement of material in C.J.S.* Since the internal arrangement of C.J.S. is like that of the Decennial Digests described in Chapter 16 (except that C.J.S. has no table of cases), little needs to be added here.

Unlike the digest, C.J.S. carefully extracts the rules of law from the decided cases and other authorities cited below the line in a typical C.J.S. page and states the law in literary form. There are 433 different treatises of varying length in C.J.S. which are arranged alphabetically from "Abandonment" to "Zoning." C.J.S. also serves a function not covered by the Decennials. It defines words and phrases and maxims.

The Scope-Note, Analysis and subanalyses function similarly in both digest and C.J.S. The titles for the same subject matter in the Decennials and C.J.S. occasionally are different (e.g., "Agency" in C.J.S. and "Principal and Agent" in the Decennials); more frequently the titles are identical. C.J.S. has, however, many additional titles not found in the Decennials, such as "Architects," "Barratry," "Business Trusts," "Conflict of Laws." In a topic in which a statute is influential (e.g., "Forgery" or the "Statute of Frauds"), the parallel in analysis is striking. The encyclopedia and the digest differ chiefly in analysis in that the encyclopedia always starts out with an elementary introduction, for which there is no parallel in the digest.

As in a conventional textbook the subject is developed in C.J.S. in logical fashion, from the general to the specific and to the remedial or procedural. The ultimate subdivision of subject matter in C.J.S. is the section, which corresponds in that respect to the Decennial Key Number. Each section begins with a paragraph in boldface type. This briefly distills and summarizes the applicable law. The encyclopedia then expands into a full treatment of the subject in the following text, with citations to authority. This is a helpful device, somewhat analogous to the headnote paragraphs in a case report or to the boldface type statements in the Hornbook series of student texts, such as Prosser on Torts.

The analytical solution of the problem of overflowing water in the loft, on page 209, is precisely the same in C.J.S. as in the Decennials, as examination of 52 C.J.S. §§423 and 432 will demonstrate.

3. *Page format of C.J.S.* A typical C.J.S. page is shown in Exhibit 51. In the specimen page the boldface paragraph "d. Parent and Child" summarizes the conflicts rule, which is then expanded in the rest of this subsection. Points to be emphasized in the notes are also in boldface. The topic ("Conflict of Laws") and the section (§14), page (911), and note numbers (33 to 35) are keyed to similar notations in the cumulative annual supplements, where later citations to authority on the precise points of law referred to are found under the same numbers. The supplementary citations may so modify the law

as to require the rewriting of the original text in the pocket supplements.

Authority is customarily cited below the line — though sometimes also in the main text — and is often a direct quotation from an opinion, an A.L.I. Restatement, a treatise, or a reporter headnote. This authority may include citations (both in the main text and in footnotes) of earlier cases and comments cited below the line in C.J. Cross-references to other pertinent titles in C.J.S. are also given.

4. *Dictionary and words and phrases function of C.J.S.* Maxims and legal words and terms are defined. However, it is much more convenient to consult a one- or two-volume conventional legal dictionary for these definitions than the 101 volumes of C.J.S. or the 82 volumes of Am. Jur. 2d. On the other hand, the encyclopedia definitions are more completely annotated and kept more up-to-date than are those in the dictionaries.

Maxims (such as *Discretio est scire per legem quid sit justum*) are listed and defined in their regular alphabetical order in the respective volumes of C.J.S. In addition all volumes containing a subject index also have at the back a section of Words and Phrases and Maxims in This Volume, which directs the searcher to the exact page where a definition is found in that volume. Maxims are not always listed in the General Index to C.J.S.

Legal words and terms as defined in C.J.S. are found in two ways: first, through the General Index in regular alphabetical order as in any dictionary; second, through the list in the back of each volume covering definitions in that volume. These two sources complement each other. For example, under "Discretion" in the General Index we learn that the word is defined in titles "Appeal and Error," "Federal Courts," "Internal Revenue," and in volume 27 at page 289, under "Discretion." In the latter volume, under the subhead "In Phrases," many other phrases employing the word "discretion" are defined, such as "legal discretion" and "political discretion." Unfortunately this Words and Phrases list is not updated in the pocket supplements.

Some definitions, with their citations to authority, are exhaustive. For example, "At" and "Public" occupy seventeen and sixteen pages, respectively.

5. *Indexes for C.J.S.* At first glance the indexing of C.J.S. and its supplementation may seem complicated, but actually it is not. Here is how it works.

There are two indexes: (1) the General Index, with its annual cumulative pocket supplements, and (2) the title indexes, one for each of the 433 C.J.S. titles as listed at the beginning of every volume of the set. Of these two indexes, the really *basic coverage is through the title indexes*, which the General Index coordinates and supplements. An index search, then, includes consultation of both the indexes mentioned above.

a. *Title indexes*. Each of the 433 main C.J.S. topics or titles is separately indexed in the volume in which it is printed, with one exception. When a title begins in one volume and is completed in another, it is indexed only in the final volume containing that title. These indexes are referred to in the General Indexes as "title indexes."

The title indexes are the most important subject indexing of C.J.S. Any index search should start with them for matter up to the date of publication. For example, if the searcher is interested in notice as an element of fraudulent conveyances of corporate property, he or she should first consult the index to "Corporations" in volume 20 of C.J.S., subtitle "fraudulent conveyances," for any material up to 1940, the publication date of the C.J.S. volume covering that subtopic. For material from 1940 to date in this subtopic, the searcher would look in the General Index and its annual pocket supplements under the same title and subtitle. There will be no additional index entry if the materials later than 1940 are only cumulative in effect and make no new law. If there are additional cases in point, they will be noted in the pocket supplement (not an index but a systematic noting of new material) in volume 20, containing the main text treatment of the topic. No additional entry is made because the new cases are precisely covered by the same title, subtitle, and section designations as in the original text volume. Later citations will be noted in the index, however, whenever they constitute new law or for some other reason require additional comment or rewriting.

The title index coverage is limited to material in the actual title indexed, with cross-references to material in other titles. If, as frequently happens, *another title* does contain material pertinent in any way to the subject matter of this title, it can be found through the General Index. For example, the index to "Wills" in 97 C.J.S. covers only material contained in volumes 94 to 97 of C.J.S. on the topic of wills. In it there are no cross-references to materials involving wills in other titles. Thus, the General Index complements the title index. While specific legacies, devices and gifts, for example, are covered generally in "Wills" and indexed in volume 97 of C.J.S., an executor's or administrator's powers and duties under the will are discussed in the title "Executors and Administrators." The General Index, under "Wills — specific legacy, devise or gift" refers the searcher *generally* to the "title index to Wills," which is in volume 97, but for the powers and duties of executors and administrators, the reference is to the specific sections in "Executors and Administrators" covering the desired subtopic.

b. *Recompiled volume indexes*. When the bulk of the pocket part supplementary material or substantial changes in the law of a given C.J.S. title require it, the entire title is rewritten to incorporate new material and to note the changes. The recompiled title or titles found in the expanded, recompiled volume are then reindexed and the original volume with its index discarded.

c. *General Index and its functions*. The five-volume General Index covers all of the C.J.S. titles. Topics not constituting "titles" are also covered in detail as in other descriptive-word indexes (e.g., Rivers and Streams, Social Rights and Standing). Separate words or phrases (e.g., "soapstone," "sweat," "uncut diamonds," and "vending machines") are listed in their regular word order as in a dictionary.

There is an additional table of Words and Phrases and Maxims in This Volume, at the back of each text volume just preceding the title indexes. In total, these separate indexes include more words and terms than are found in the General Index in the alphabetical listing of separate words. Maxims may be both in the General Index and in their proper alphabetical order in the text volumes.

The General Index has two principal functions. First, it is a title-finder. Second, it is a coordinator of subject entries which are found in two or more different titles. This is illustrated by Exhibit 52.

"Security," which is not a C.J.S. title, is covered generally by the indexes to the four titles mentioned in the General Index, as illustrated by Exhibit 52. The searcher should thus examine the title indexes in the text volumes covering "Chattel Mortgages," "Costs," "Mortgages," and "Principal and Surety." Items related to security which are covered to some extent in other titles than these are made

SECURITY
Generally, see **Title Index to**
Chattel Mortgages
Costs
Mortgages
Principal and Surety
Abandonment, discharge of indemnitor by, **Indem § 40, p. 635**
Accord and satisfaction, new or additional security, **Accord § 25**
Account stated,
Given to settle, **Acct St § 44**
Taking security on settlement affecting right to impeach, **Acct St § 51**

Exhibit 52

specific entries under "Security" in the index (e.g., "Indemnity §340," "Accord and Satisfaction §25").

Thus, a student interested in a wife's power to acquire a separate domicile for divorce purposes would normally start his or her index search in the detailed index to "Divorce" in volume 27B of C.J.S. He or she would *also*, as a part of the search, consult the General Index to C.J.S. for two reasons: first, for references to new material since 1959, the publication date of volume 27B; second, for references to other pertinent titles and sections such as, for example, "Domicile §12," page 26.

6. *Tables in C.J.S.*

a. *Table of cases or Table of statutes not supplied.* There are no tables of cases or tables of statutes in C.J.S.

b. *Table of abbreviations.* At the front of each volume of C.J.S. there is a table of abbreviations of reports, treatises, and legal periodicals cited as authority. Although this is by no means a complete table of abbreviations, it is useful as such beyond the immediate confines of C.J.S. itself.

c. *Volumes and pages of reports covered by the annual cumulative pocket supplements.* These tables are found in each pocket supplement. If students want to supplement their encyclopedia search by going to the digest or reporter advance sheets for later cases, the pocket supplement tables will tell them exactly what volumes and pages of each standard report are covered in the C.J.S. supplement. Thus, students are able to know the specific volumes and pages of reports which must be checked in order to update an encyclopedia search.

7. *Supplementation of C.J.S.* There are three forms of supplementation.

a. *Annual cumulative pocket parts.* The text material in the C.J.S. volumes is updated by annual cumulative pocket parts. These supplementary entries are keyed to the original text of the bound volume by having exactly the same volume, title, section, page and footnote numbers. Matching up the original text and the supplement is done very simply. For example, to bring up to date the text and corresponding citations to authority for the topic "Commerce §142," note 99, which is on page 971 of volume 15 of C.J.S., it is necessary only to go to the pocket supplement of volume 15, under "Commerce §142," page 971, note 99, where later citations in point are collected. See Exhibit 53.

When later decisions in point are merely cumulative in effect and do not change the law, no added comment is made in the supplements, even though hundreds of new cases have been cited for a single footnote, as in "Conspiracy §93(1)," footnote 79. Every later case

§ 142 COMMERCE **15 CJS 104**
Page 512

Grandfather proceedings
U.S.—Sims Motor Transport Lines, Inc. v. U. S., D.C.Ill., 183 F.Supp. 113, affd. 80 S.Ct. 1076, 362 U.S. 637, 4 L.Ed.2d 1019.

99. U.S.—Schenley Distillers Corporation v. U. S., supra, n. 97—I. C. C. v. Isner, D.C.Mich., 92 F.Supp. 582.

Since the publication of Corpus Juris Secundum the case cited therein has been reversed and the court has been held not required to determine whether applicant is entitled to a certificate under other provisions of the Motor Carrier Act of 1935.[99.1]

99.1 U.S.—U. S. v. Maher, Or., 59 S.Ct. 768, 307 U.S. 148, 83 L.Ed. 1162, reh. den. 59 S.Ct. 831, 307 U.S. 649, 83 L.Ed. 1528—A. E. McDonald Motor Freight Lines v. U. S., supra, n. 97—A. B. & C. Motor Transp. Co. v. U. S., D.C.Mass., 69 F.Supp. 166.

In this example, the added text material shows that the cases relied upon in the original note have been reversed, states the new rule, and cites the reversing case, together (in note 99.1) with later cases in point. C.J.S. is thus to a limited extent a citator. Although C.J.S. makes such comments as this, often at considerable length, its policy is not to speculate (in the manner of law reviews) on the *probable* effects of new rulings or statutes.

Exhibit 53

in point is said to be cited and, if necessary, commented upon in the supplements. Where, however, the later cases have modified the law as stated in the original C.J.S. text, these changes in the law are noted in the pocket part supplements. An example of extensive rewriting in the supplements is in the "Bankruptcy" title, in which statutory amendments since publication of the "Bankruptcy" volumes have substantially changed the law.

A table at the front of each pocket supplement lists the volumes and pages of reports covered in the supplementary materials.

b. *Recompiled volumes*. Where the mass of supplementary decisions makes a pocket part unwieldy, or where extensive changes have been made in the law covered by one or more titles included in a C.J.S. volume, a new volume is issued. The text of the original volume is rewritten as necessary, and added materials are incorporated into the new volume. The original volume is then discarded; the expanded volumes inherit the original volume's number, plus additional "A" or "B" numbered volumes as required. Thus, original volume 27 comprised "Discovery" through "Domesticated" and included the large title of "Divorce." The law relating to divorce was so greatly changed by later decisions that a revision of the whole title was necessary; the expanded material in old volume 27 is now contained in new volumes 27, 27A, and 27B. The respective titles in the recompiled volumes are completely indexed anew. These indexes, rather than the General Index, should be a starting point for a descriptive-word search in these titles.

c. *General Index pocket parts*. The General Index is supplemented by annual cumulative pocket parts.

§17.10. State legal encyclopedias.

The publishers of Am. Jur. 2d have brought out state "Jurisprudence" legal encyclopedias, e.g., California, New York, Ohio, Texas, which parallel Am. Jur. 2d in purpose but emphasize the law of a single state (as influenced by federal law, of course). Other publishers have similar state legal eyclopedias.

§17.11. Special-subject legal encyclopedias.

These are really very large textbooks (some are twenty or more volumes) which cover their subject matter (insurance, automobiles, corporations, oil and gas, federal and state procedure, etc.) in great detail. Most of them differ from the general legal encyclopedia in that they have tables of cases; annotated legal forms are also a common feature. They are essentially case-finders with a running commentary on the law covered. While there are descriptive-word indexes, the analysis of topics at the beginning of each title is ordinarily not as detailed as in the general encyclopedias or digests.

§17.12. Techniques of using legal encyclopedias.

As noted earlier in this chapter, the general legal encyclopedia serves both as a text commentary on the law and as a case-finder. The searcher who knows little or nothing about a topic of law can find in the encyclopedia an elementary statement of the law. Lawyers can refresh their memory of legal fields in which they have become rusty by using the legal encyclopedia. They can also find the applicable rules covering any topic, substantive or procedural, set out in the most detailed manner.

A worker seldom can complete a job with the use of only a single tool; neither can a lawyer. So far in this book, we have studied tools of various kinds, including annotations, digests, and encyclopedias. A lawyer would probably use all these in a search and also some legal tools we have not yet discussed. The following illustrative problem employs some of the necessary techniques of integrating the materials studied so far.

1. *Problem*. At the time of their marriage, H took out a $15,000 life insurance policy in favor of W as named beneficiary. There was a double indemnity provision in case of accidental death. The policy also provided that "In the event of death of any beneficiary before insured, the interest of such beneficiary shall vest in the insured"; and "Double indemnity death benefits shall not be payable if death resulted . . . from having been engaged in aviation or aeronautics." H and W were killed in the crash of a regularly licensed carrier airplane

in which they were passengers. What are the rights of the administrators and of the estates of H and W? The insurer denies liability for double indemnity, on the ground that as an airplane passenger H was "engaged in aviation or aeronautics." His administrator claims that the "death of beneficiary before insured" provision entitled him to the proceeds, because of a presumption of H's longer survival in case of death by common disaster. Since both problems are solved by similar processes in the encyclopedias, digests, and A.L.R., only the first one will be solved here as an example. In order to prevent duplication, the solution will be approached first by the fact method through C.J.S. and then through the analytical approach in Am. Jur. 2d, with mention of two special-subject encyclopedias and of the digests. Each approach is, of course, equally available to users of any of these encyclopedias.

The insurer denies liability for double indemnity, on the ground that H was "engaged in aviation or aeronautics."

2. *Index approach*. On its face, this might be either an aviation or an insurance problem. A search under Aerial Navigation, however, in the General Index to C.J.S. and in volume 2 of C.J.S. under the same title, reveals that the Aerial Navigation concerns the licensing and operation of airplanes and the liability as between passenger and carrier; insurance as between passenger and insurance company is not covered at all. Therefore, you think of "Insurance" as an index heading. Under this title in the General Index you are referred to the index to the title "Insurance" in volume 46 of C.J.S. This index yields the following applicable entries, all leading to "insurance §938," pages 1085–1086 of volume 45. See Exhibit 54.

INDEXING

Airplanes and aeronautics
  Life insurance, death from engaging in aviation, § 938
Double Indemnity
  Death resulting from particular risks, § 938
  Passenger
    Double Indemnity for death, § 938
    Participating in aviation within exception, § 938
    Public conveyance, death of passenger riding in, § 938
Life Insurance
  Accidental death benefits, § 938
  Aviation, liability for death while engaging in, § 938
Passengers
  Airplane
    Double indemnity clause exception applicable to passenger of, § 938
  Double indemnity for death, § 938

Exhibit 54

Closer analysis of the specific pages cited leads to page 1086, where the precise question involved in the problem is discussed. Footnotes 91 and 92 contain citations to authority from all jurisdictions which have considered it. Normally at this point, the C.J.S. text would refer to earlier cases in point in C.J., but there is no such citation in this example. When the "Insurance" title of C.J. was compiled in 1924, people were not yet riding as passengers in commercial airplanes; consequently there were no cases for C.J. to cite. Turning to the annual cumulative pocket supplement in the back of volume 45, a search under 45 C.J.S. 1086, §938, notes 91 and 92, will reveal any later authorities in point.

3. *Analytical approach*. In solving the same problem through the analytical approach, in Am. Jur. 2d this time, the same preliminary analysis leads to the topic "Insurance." As in digests, under the legal encyclopedia title there first is a main analysis with only the principal chapter headings and references to pages where each main heading is expanded into a detailed subanalysis. The searcher, in scanning the many main headings, discards as inapplicable such headings as "Insurance Companies" "Insurance Agents and Brokers," "Insurable Interest," etc. "XVII: Risks and Coverage," however, seems encouraging. Subdivision "D-1: Aviation or Aeronautics," covering sections 1319 to 1330, seems to be particularly in point. Although perusal of the text under those section numbers gives a good general discussion of the matter of "engaging in" aeronautics, section 1329 seems to be the closest in point. Notes 7 to 11 cite authority and refer to two A.L.R. annotations in point, 155 A.L.R. 1026, 1035 and 17 A.L.R.2d 1041, 1052. The latter annotation lists thirty-eight different exclusionary clauses in insurance policies, where death results from riding in an airplane. Of these, Clause 10 is directly in point and lists and discusses several cases in which the clause was construed.

Later cases are found through the A.L.R.2d Supplement Service and in the pocket supplement to volume 44 of Am. Jur. 2d by the process of matching title, section, page and note numbers with those of the main text. New material may call for a new note to a given section or a revision of it.

Exhibit 55, showing a subanalysis under "Insurance," illustrates the use of the analytical method.

4. *Special legal encyclopedias*. The insurance problem above, and problems in other subject matter for which there are special-subject encyclopedias, are solved in exactly the same two ways as in a general legal encyclopedia. A table of cases approach, unavailable in general encyclopedias, is possible through many special legal encyclopedias as well. The space devoted to a given topic in a special-subject encyclopedia is often considerably more than that in a general legal one. For example, each of two insurance encyclopedias devotes about four

44 Am Jur 2d INSURANCE

§ 1267. Exception of suicide
§ 1268. Statutory provisions

f. DISEASE OR BODILY INFIRMITY

§ 1269. Generally; meaning of "disease" and "bodily infirmity"
§ 1270. Pre-existing disease or infirmity—where not proximate cause
§ 1271. — Where disease or infirmity is proximate or substantial cause
§ 1272. Disease or infirmity resulting from accident
§ 1273. — Effect of exception of liability for disease or specified physical condition
§ 1274. Disease or infection resulting from act voluntarily done or allowed by insured
§ 1275. Burns
§ 1276. Exception or limitation as to hernia
§ 1277. Exceptions as to "fits"

g. MEDICAL AND DENTAL TREATMENT

§ 1278. Generally; death or injury resulting from treatment or operation as "accident" or by "accidental means"
§ 1279. — As a result of use of anesthetics
§ 1280. Provision excluding liability for death or injury from treatment or operation

Exhibit 55

times as much space to our airplane passenger problem as do the general legal encyclopedias. The indexing is also apt to be much more detailed in the special-subject encyclopedia.

5. *Words and phrases approach*. This approach, described for C.J.S. at §17.9.4, is frequently useful when the legal interpretation of a word or term is involved. In our insurance problem the chief point at issue is whether, within the terms of the insurance policy, H was "engaged in aviation or aeronautics." Notes 90 to 92 to "Insurance §938," on page 1086 of volume 45 of C.J.S. concern the construction of that term. The dictionary function of C.J.S. is demonstrated in 30 C.J.S. 698–700, where "engage" is defined as to its various uses. Footnote 80(6) on page 700 defines "engaged in aeronautics," with citations to cases. In Am. Jur. 2d the Words and Phrases section of the General Index does not define the word in our connection, but in the index to "Insurance" in volume 44 the word is defined under "Insurance: Aviation: participation or engagement in."

6. *Integration of annotations and digests with encyclopedias*. Work with A.L.R. annotations has been described in detail at pages 173–180. These annotations often complement the discussion of many points of law in the encyclopedias by considering at length minute aspects touched upon only broadly in the relatively limited space available in encyclopedias and treatises. Annotations are cited directly in Am. Jur. 2d.

The digest, in supplementing the encyclopedia, serves two useful functions. It digests cases in point and thus provides the searcher with much more information than mere citations. Second, because its supplementation is monthly instead of annually, the digest provides more recent information than the encyclopedia. Carrying the search into the advance sheets provides further supplementation as well.

Employing the methods learned in the preceding chapter on digests, the searcher speedily discovers the Key Number "Insurance ⚷ 515.8—Aviation or aeronautics," where he will find all cases in point in the Decennials, the General Digest, and in the reporter advance sheet digest sections.

18 | Citators

§18.1. Functions of citators.

In his The Jerry Giesler Story,[1] the noted Los Angeles trial lawyer relates how in his early days he lost a case when he cited as authority in a trial a case which, unknown to him, had been reversed on appeal. The presiding judge then took him into his chambers and said, "I suggest you regard this as a useful lesson rather than a humiliating experience. Your lesson is: Always Shepardize your case."[2] The judge should have added "and your statute."

1. New York, Simon and Schuster, 1960.
2. The Jerry Giesler Story 282 (1960).

The citator or citation book tells lawyers whether the statutes and cases to be cited by them as authority are in fact valid for that purpose. Through subsequent legislative or judicial action the status of this material as authority constantly changes; there is no assurance that the long-sought-for statute or case exactly in point is of any value whatever when found. The careful lawyer and the student, therefore, check the present value of each authority they consider using.

1. *Evaluating a case as authority*. There are several facets in evaluating the authority of a case, as pointed out below.

a. *Same case on appeal*. A case on appeal may be affirmed, reversed, or modified, or the appeal may be dismissed. There may be rehearings by the same court. All these actions are noted in citators. In Shepard's Citations, the outstanding example of the citation book, this aspect of the citator is called the "history" of the case.

b. *Citation of a case in an action on an entirely different and later case*. Such a citation or action may affect the value of an earlier case as precedent. A court may overrule the earlier case as stating a doctrine no longer valid as applicable to later cases. This in no way affects the *holding* of an overruled case as between the original parties to it, as an appellate decision does. Its action is purely prospective and not retroactive. More frequently, courts may diminish or enhance the value of an earlier case. They may do this by *criticizing*, *distinguishing*, *explaining*, *following*, or *questioning* the holding in the earlier case cited to it. This is what Shepard's Citations calls the "treatment" of the cited case.

2. *"Cited" and "citing" statutes or cases explained*. These terms, frequently employed in legal writing and in this book, require some explanation. A *cited* case or statute in a citator is simply the one which is being Shepardized (see §18.3); in Shepard's Citations this means the volume number of a case above the line near the top of a Shepard's page and the number in boldface type below the line. In a statute it is the enactment, the status of which you are testing as precedent. A *citing* case, on the other hand, is a different case which refers to the *cited* case; in Shepard's Citations this means all the cases listed below the boldface page number noted above. In the Massachusetts case shown in Exhibit 56 *infra*, 296 Mass. 275, with its reporter counterpart, 5 N.E.2d 720, is the *cited* case. Everything else, beginning respectively with 298 Mass. 500, 11 N.E.2d 590, is *citing* material.

Citing material has a wide range. In our Massachusetts example, it includes all Massachusetts and federal court reported decisions construing Massachusetts cases, opinions of the Attorney General of Massachusetts affecting existing cases, law review comments on the cited cases, and annotated reports system comments on Massachusetts cases.

3. *Collecting other cases in point*. Some citators, such as Shepard's Citations, collect additional references of value by listing all cases commenting upon a case known by the searcher to be in point (the *citing* cases commenting upon the *cited* case). Since the courts have regarded a case as worthy of comment by them regarding the point of law involved, such cases may weigh heavily as precedent. By the same token, the cases commenting upon a case in point may themselves have value as precedent. Cases commenting upon a statute may aid the lawyer in ascertaining the statute's meaning.

4. *Providing parallel citations to other standard reports or editions of statutes*. Shepard's câse citations are perhaps the most accurate and complete means of translating from one form of case citation to another. In the Massachusetts example in Exhibit 56, the citator translates from Massachusetts to Northeastern and from Northeastern to Massachusetts.

5. *Court rule publication indicated*. Citators may tell in which volumes of reports court rules and amendments to them are published.

6. *Tables of statutes and cases by popular name*. Statutes and cases are often cited by a popular name (such as the Taft-Hartley Act or the *Hot Oil* case) which must be translated to the official citation before they can be Shepardized. Tables are provided for this purpose. See §30.1.

§18.2. Scope of citators.

In one form or another, citators cover federal and state statutes, adjudicated patents and trademarks, municipal ordinances, standard editions of reported court and administrative agency decisions, Uniform Laws, American Law Institute Restatements (for approximately one-half of the states) and more than 150 legal periodicals.

§18.3. Shepard's Citations.

By far the most complete American citator system, in both geographical scope and fullness of treatment, is Shepard's Citations.[3] It is so well known that it has given rise to the legal words of art, "Shepardize" and "Shepardizing," to describe certain essential operations in assessing the current value of statutes and cases as authority. These terms are used in this book by the express permission of Shepard's Citations, Inc.

1. *Federal coverage*.

a. *Shepard's United States Citations*. Shepard's United States Cita-

3. Colorado Springs, Colo., Shepard's Citations, Inc.

ILLUSTRATIVE CASE

Massachusetts Reports

Vol. 296

—275—

s 5NE 720
s300US 657
s 81LE 867
s 57SC 434
298Mas[2]500
299Mas 410
d300Mas[6]637
e301Mas[1]212
302Mas[3]567
302Mas[6]614
303Mas[4]647
303Mas[3]658
304Mas[4]181
304Mas 189
304Mas 293
304Mas 649
305Mas 235
305Mas 292
306Mas 30
307Mas[1]274
307Mas[3]419
309Mas 447
309Mas[3]567
309Mas 582
309Mas[3]593
309Mas 623
310Mas[3]552
312Mas[6]493
313Mas[1]730
314Mas [4]38
315Mas[3]340
315Mas[4]372
317Mas 56
317Mas[1]508
319Mas 306
320Mas [3]40
322Mas[5]736
323Mas[3]291
324Mas 48
324Mas[8]138
324Mas[7]250
325Mas[3]654
326Mas 627
327Mas[6]361
329Mas 319
330Mas[4]537
331Mas[2]362
331Mas 508
331Mas[1]690
334Mas 61
d334Mas[6]720
301US [8]573
81LE[8]1283
57SC [8]884
89F2d[4]211
e 89F2d[3]380
23FS [8]995
31FS [2]604
38FS 867
39FS [1]666
47FS [1]498
37-38AG 82
'38-39AG 69
'41-42AG135
'42-44AG 5
'53-54AG 63
19BUR663
22BUR 89
25BUR 61
33BUR 4

Citations to the case of Howes Brothers Company v. Unemployment Compensation Commission reported in Volume 296 Massachusetts Reports at page 275 are shown in the left margin as they appear in this volume.

An examination of the history of this case shows that the same case "s" (see tables of abbreviations, *infra*) is reported in 5 Northeastern Reporter, Second Series "NE" page 720. Upon appeal to the United States Supreme Court, a petition for writ of certiorari was denied in 300 United States Reports "US" 657, 81 Lawyers Edition of United States "LE" 867, 57 Supreme Court Reporter "SC" 434. The arrangement of these citations is an example of the grouping that is used wherever there are parallel sets of reports covering the same citing case.

An examination of the treatment of this case indicates that it has been distinguished "d" and explained "e" in subsequent cases in the Massachusetts Reports and Federal Reporter, Second Series.

The first citation is found in 298 Massachusetts Reports "Mas" 500. The superior figure "2" appearing in advance of the citing page number 500 indicates that the principle of law brought out in paragraph two of the syllabus of 296 Mas 275 is also dealt with in 298 Mas 500. If you are especially interested in this paragraph of the syllabus, the citing authorities indicate that this point of law has been cited to in a case reported in 31 Federal Supplement "FS" 604.

There are references analyzed to other paragraphs of the syllabus of the cited case in cases reported in the Massachusetts Reports, United States Supreme Court Reports (three editions), Federal Reporter, Second Series "F2d", Federal Supplement and in the notes of the American Law Reports "ALR". Thus, the citations dealing with a point of law in any particular paragraph of the syllabus may be referred to instantly without examining every citation to the case.

This case has also been cited in the Opinions of the Attorney General of Massachusetts "AG", Boston University Law Review "BUR" and Massachusetts Law Quarterly "MQ".

By reference to the citations to the corresponding decision in the Northeastern Reporter division of this volume, which are reproduced in the right margin it is possible to trace the history and citations to this decision in the parallel Massachusetts decisions in the Northeastern Reporter and in cases in the United States Supreme and lower Federal Courts.

Thus, in the most compact and convenient form, the complete judicial history of every Massachusetts case is shown; where else reported; whether affirmed, reversed, dismissed or modified; and the mode of its citation, whether followed, explained, distinguished, overruled, etc., and the extent to which each of the points decided in the case has been regarded as an authority.

North-eastern Reporter, Second Series

Vol. 5

—720—

s296Mas 275
s300US 657
s 81LE 867
s 57SC 434
11NE [6]590
12NE [4]855
d 15NE[13]818
e 16NE[23]667
19NE[13]814
20NE [8]457
22NE [9]60
22NE [8]61
22NE [1]865
22NE [7]66
23NE [4]136
23NE [5]137
23NE [9]161
23NE [5]668
24NE[18]676
25NE [5]380
25NE 762
27NE [4]268
30NE [2]220
30NE [8]275
34NE 536
34NE[12]537
34NE [7]541
35NE 74
35NE 14
35NE[28]252
39NE [8]107
45NE 472
49NE [1]226
49NE [5]595
52NE [6]571
53NE 109
57NE [15]18
59NE [2]2
65NE [9]532
68NE [4]188
79NE[11]729
81NE [7]558
84NE [7]542
85NE [5]237
85NE 782
92NE 249
96NE [5]147
99NE [7]58
108NE [1]850
115NE[12]730
118NE[18]863
120NE [4]392
122NE [2]358
133NE [5]777
d134NE [[18]898
301US[29]573
81LE[29]1283
57SC[29]884
89F2d[9]211
e 89F2d[7]380
23FS[29]995
31FS[12]604
38FS 867
39FS [2]666
47FS [2]498

tions includes citations to the following material: Supreme Court decisions, United States statutes (both as Statutes at Large and United States Code sections), treaties, and court rules for federal courts. The United States Citations is separated into two divisions: (1) Supreme Court decisions and (2) statutes and court rules. Prior to 1967, this citator covered in its statutes division, certain federal agency decisions now included in Shepard's United States Administrative Decisions.

b. *Shepard's Federal Reporter Citations*. This citator covers the decisions of federal courts below the Supreme Court and is also separated into two divisions. The first division, Federal Cases and Federal Reporter, includes the citations to federal appeals courts' decisions. The second division covers court decisions appearing in the Federal Supplement, Federal Rules Decisions and the Court of Claims Reports. The coverage of the Federal Reporter Citations was radically altered in 1967 by the new Shepard's United States Administrative Citations, which took over some of the Federal Reporter Citations' former field.

c. *Shepard's Federal Labor Law Citations*, which began in 1959, is described at §18.17.3b.

d. *Shepard's United States Administrative Decisions*. This series, inaugurated in 1967, is described at §18.17.3a.

e. *Shepard's United States Patents and Trademark Citations*, which was initiated in 1968, is described at §18.17.3c.

In all, the above federal citations units include fifty-seven different statutory or case series, the precise coverage of which is not always obvious. In order to lead the searcher quickly to the proper Shepard's federal unit, a *Table of Reports in Shepard's United States, United States Administrative, United States Patents and Trademarks, Federal and District of Columbia Editions* is printed near the front of each red-paper supplement to the above-named citators. See Exhibit 60.

2. *State, territory, and District coverage*. Each state (unless West has become the sole reporter) has its own Shepard's unit for official statute and case coverage. In addition, each unit of the West regional reporters (including citators for the California Reporter and the New York Supplement) gives *case* coverage of states included in that region. In 1968, Shepard's Citations began the publication of separate citators for Puerto Rico and the District of Columbia.

§18.4. Shepardizing a case: General considerations.

Ascertaining a case's present status as authority through Shepard's Citations is intrinsically simple. It is made virtually error-proof for anyone who will read the explanatory material at the front of each

ABBREVIATIONS – ANALYSIS
STATUTES

Form of Statute

Amend.	Amendment	No.	Number	Sp	Special Session
Appx.	Appendix	p	Page	St.	Statutes at Large
Art.	Article	¶	Paragraph	Subch.	Subchapter
C or Ch.	Chapter	Pt	Part	Subd.	Subdivision
Cl.	Clause	P. L.	Public Law (United States)	Sub ¶	Subparagraph
Ex. Ord.	Executive Order	Res.	Resolution	Subsec.	Subsection
		§	Section		

Operation of Statute
Legislative

A	(amended)	Statute amended.
Ad	(added)	New section added.
E	(extended)	Provisions of an existing statute extended in their application to a later statute, or allowance of additional time for performance of duties required by a statute within a limited time.
L	(limited)	Provisions of an existing statute declared not to be extended in their application to a later statute.
R	(repealed)	Abrogation of an existing statute.
Re-en	(re-enacted)	Statute re-enacted.
Rn	(renumbered)	Renumbering of existing sections.
Rp	(repealed in part)	Abrogation of part of an existing statute.
Rs	(repealed and superseded)	Abrogation of an existing statute and substitution of new legislation therefor.
Rv	(revised)	Statute revised.
S	(superseded)	Substitution of new legislation for an existing statute not expressly abrogated.
Sd	(suspended)	Statute suspended.
Sdp	(suspended in part)	Statute suspended in part.
Sg	(supplementing)	New matter added to an existing statute.
Sp	(superseded in part)	Substitution of new legislation for part of an existing statute not expressly abrogated.
Va	(validated)	

Judicial

C	Constitutional.	V	Void or invalid.
U	Unconstitutional.	Va	Valid.
Up	Unconstitutional in part.	Vp	Void or invalid in part.

Exhibit 57

clothbound and red-paper-bound Shepard's Citations volume. This material explains the Shepardizing process itself.

1. *Abbreviations.* A page of "Abbreviations-Analysis" explains the meanings of the abbreviations to the left of the various case citations in the citators. See Exhibit 57. Abbreviations used but not explained

in this Analysis are "App'l Pen'g" in Shepard's Federal Reporter Citations and "U.S. Sup. Ct. App'l Pen'g" in the state and other Shepard's Reporter units. These abbreviations are used only in the pamphlet supplements; as soon as the pending appeal has been disposed of, the notation is removed.

2. *Information gleaned from Shepardizing*. In this Shepardizing process the searcher will glean any or all of the following information:

a. *Parallel citation from one report series to another*. (As from official to unofficial or vice versa.) Shepard's Citations provides one of the best means of translating an official citation to an unofficial citation, or the reverse. The parallel citation is supplied, whether or not other cases have later cited the main case.

"Same case in another reported series" is denoted in the older Shepard's Citations by the "s" preceding the case citation. In most of the newer ones it is done by enclosing the case citation in parentheses; the "s" is then reserved for the cited case in another stage of its progress through the courts.

Note that once the parallel citation has been printed in a bound volume of Shepard's, it is no longer given in succeeding supplements.

These parallel citations may also be found by using the National Reporter Blue Book, described in §14.5.2a, or other case tables.

b. *Appellate disposition of the cited case*. This is what Shepard's calls the "history" of the case. Affirmances, reversals, denials of certiorari, or dismissals of appeals are noted.

c. *Courts' citation of the cited case as authority in another and later case*. Under the main or *cited* cases are listed citations to any cases which have subsequently commented on the *cited* case and so affected its status as authority. This is the "treatment" of the *cited* case by the *citing* cases listed.

There may be a significantly long list of citing cases under each cited case. Because lawyers are unable to read every citing case when the list of such cases is extremely long, Shepard's has devised two notations which reduce the number of citing cases a lawyer must check. First, a list of abbreviations is used to describe the treatment given in each instance. Thus, the student or lawyer may quickly learn whether the later case follows, criticizes, explains or overrules the earlier decision.

Second, Shepard's divides topically the citations to the *cited* case. Earlier Shepard's volumes spelled out in the citator itself the topic or point of law discussed by the citing case. Shepard's now employs a reference to the headnote number instead. If lawyers know the headnote covering the point of law in which they are interested, they need not examine citing cases which are assigned to different headnotes. Frequently, however, there are several references which Shepard's has not assigned to a headnote. It is generally advisable to check these references.

Shepard's Citations lists separately each citation to a case even though one citing case may contain several references to the earlier case. When several references are made to the cited case within a few pages of one another and within the same volume of the reporter, this may indicate a thorough discussion of the cited case. Such repeated citations within a single case may be profitably explored.

d. *Courts of other jurisdictions citing the main case.* State citation units do not provide the citations of courts in other states. This information is available through the Regional Reporter units. The citations are to the Regional Reporters and not to the official citing reports. Shepard's Federal Citations and Shepard's United States Citations list the citations of state courts which may be found in the Regional Reporter units or selected official state reports.

e. *Attorney Generals' comments on the cited case in their opinions.* Each state citator lists comments by the state's attorney general upon the cited case. The regional Shepard's unit does not include references to comments by the attorney generals of the states within the coverage of the unit. Shepard's Federal Citations and United States Citations include all references to cited cases made by the United States Attorney General.

f. *Law review comments on the cited case.* Except for articles in the American Bar Association Journal, neither Shepard's Federal Citations, United States Citations, nor the various regional units include citations made by law reviews. State citators, however, include case references made by law reviews of the state in which the decision was rendered. In addition, these state citators note comments made by nineteen prominent law reviews from various sections of the country. For more extensive law review research, see Shepard's Federal Law Citations in Selected Law Reviews.

g. *A.L.R. annotations mentioning the cited case.* A.L.R. annotations which mention the main case are indicated in all regional state and federal units.

§18.5. Shepardizing a case: State Shepard's Citations.

1. *Example.* You have found a case in point, 296 Mass. 275, which you wish to cite as authority. First, however, you Shepardize it to ascertain whether it is still good law.

You consult the various clothbound volumes and the paperbound supplements of Shepard's Massachusetts Citations. To do this you simply find your citation: Volume 296 (in large type above the line near the top of a page in the Shepard's volume), and page 275 (in large boldface type below the line). On the other hand, if your citation is to the unofficial 5 N.E.2d 720, you consult Shepard's Northeastern Reporter Citations, where volume 5, Second Series, is found above the line, and page 720 is found in boldface below the line. The rest of the simple process is described in the instruction page, Exhibit 56 *supra*.

2. *Selecting the proper state Shepard's Unit and Volume*. There is possible difficulty here in only two instances: (1) selection of the proper unit of the New York official case citators, and (2) selection of the report volume number for those states which have renumbered their old "nominative" reports, i.e., reports cited by the name of the reporter instead of by jurisdiction.

a. *New York official reports citators*. Since New York has had ninety different official series of reports from its numerous courts, there are three Shepard's units for this state (in addition to Shepard's New York Supplement Citations, which covers the unofficial series): (1) Shepard's Court of Appeals Citations, (2) Shepard's Miscellaneous Citations, and (3) Shepard's Supreme Court Citations.

A table of New York Reports in Shepard's New York editions, which is located near the front of each red-paper supplement to each edition, lists alphabetically all ninety report series and indicates which Shepard's unit covers each series. Parallel reference tables in Shepard's New York Court of Appeals Citations tell where each Court of Appeals case is printed in the New York Supplement and details all "nominative" series (such as Abbott or Sanford) publishing Court of Appeals reports.

b. *State reports by name of reporter which have been renumbered consecutively*. Until the mid-nineteenth century, most official reports series in the older states were known and cited by the name of the official reporter, such as Pickering, Randolf, or Chipman. This proved so cumbersome that most such series then still current were renumbered consecutively and chronologically in a single numerical series bearing the name of the state only. Shepard's Citations follows the renumbered order. In spite of this renumbering, however, these early nominatives are commonly cited by their original Pickering, Randolf, etc., volume numbers. Whenever this renumbering has occurred, Shepard's Citations provides a cross-reference table (such as the one shown in Exhibit 58) in the front of each appropriate unit. Where these old nominatives have been discontinued and have not been renumbered, they are listed in the table of contents of the appropriate Shepard's units under their names. This is true of many early New York case series, such as Barbour or Lansing.

3. *Comments on a state case by courts of another jurisdiction*. Although a decision in Illinois is not mandatory in Iowa or Oklahoma, it may be highly persuasive there. Well-reasoned and significant opinions by the courts of one state are often cited as persuasive authority by the courts of other states. For example, *Mitchell* v. *Rochester Ry. Co.*, 151 N.Y. 107, 45 N.E. 354 (1896), has been cited by the courts of thirty-five other states. As a practical matter such

MASSACHUSETTS REPORTS, Vols. 18–96

CROSS REFERENCE TABLE

1 Allen	83 Massachusetts	15 Gray	81 Massachusetts
2 Allen	84 Massachusetts	16 Gray	82 Massachusetts
3 Allen	85 Massachusetts	1 Metcalf	42 Massachusetts
4 Allen	86 Massachusetts	2 Metcalf	43 Massachusetts
5 Allen	87 Massachusetts	3 Metcalf	44 Massachusetts
6 Allen	88 Massachusetts	4 Metcalf	45 Massachusetts
7 Allen	89 Massachusetts	5 Metcalf	46 Massachusetts
8 Allen	90 Massachusetts	6 Metcalf	47 Massachusetts
9 Allen	91 Massachusetts	7 Metcalf	48 Massachusetts
10 Allen	92 Massachusetts	8 Metcalf	49 Massachusetts
11 Allen	93 Massachusetts	9 Metcalf	50 Massachusetts
12 Allen	94 Massachusetts	10 Metcalf	51 Massachusetts
13 Allen	95 Massachusetts	11 Metcalf	52 Massachusetts
14 Allen	96 Massachusetts	12 Metcalf	53 Massachusetts
1 Cushing	55 Massachusetts	13 Metcalf	54 Massachusetts
2 Cushing	56 Massachusetts	1 Pickering	18 Massachusetts
3 Cushing	57 Massachusetts	2 Pickering	19 Massachusetts
4 Cushing	58 Massachusetts	3 Pickering	20 Massachusetts
5 Cushing	59 Massachusetts	4 Pickering	21 Massachusetts
6 Cushing	60 Massachusetts	5 Pickering	22 Massachusetts
7 Cushing	61 Massachusetts	6 Pickering	23 Massachusetts

Exhibit 58

out-of-state citing cases are traceable only through their National Reporter System citations. After the development of the Regional Reporter citators, state citators have included practically no citing cases of other states.

a. *Citation of cases decided before the National Reporter System.* Comments by out-of-state courts on cases of the forum are available only through unofficial citations. Since the Regional Reporter dates from 1879, *citing* cases previous to that date cannot be found. *Cited* cases from the very beginning can be found for more than half the states *if* cited unoffiicially at any subsequent date. With three exceptions,[4] citing cases not reported in the National Reporter System will *not* be included in state citators.

Searchers of out-of-state citing cases must confront the following question: How does a searcher know whether to check the Regional

4. Citations to Delaware cases reported in the Atlantic Reporter as cited in all units of the National Reporter System or in vols. 1 to 283 Illinois Appellate Court Reports, vols. 1 to 19 Ohio Appellate Reports or vols. 1 to 101 Pennsylvania Superior Court Reports which were published prior to the time that cases reported in those three series of state reports began also to be reported in the National Reporter System may be obtained by referring to Shepard's Atlantic Reporter Citations.

Reporter or the state citator for out-of-state citing cases? Searchers may make this decision by consulting the state citator of the *cited* case. Immediately before each report series is a table which indicates the extent to which citing cases of various reports are included. Beginning with citations to volume 102 of Indiana Reports, out-of-state citations must be pursued in the Northeastern Reporter, which includes Indiana cases. The following parts of report series are other examples of instances in which the state citators include out-of-state citing cases found in Regional Reporters: California Supreme Court Reports 1–63, Illinois Supreme Court Reports 1–113, Illinois Appellate Court Reports 1–283, and Nebraska Reports 1–8. In order to test your understanding of these difficult concepts, you may wish to explore these and other examples yourself.

If the state Shepard's unit for the report series includes citing cases found in the National Reporter System, these citing cases are listed by the unofficial cite (*not* their official state citation) immediately following the citing cases of the forum. How this is done is shown by Exhibit 59. Thus, 102 Ill. 359 has been cited by 362 Ill. 60 and by other cases, such as 198 N.E. 704 and 106 P.2d 175 (citing cases other than Illinois listed by the unofficial citations).

To summarize briefly: (1) If a state case was decided *before* the National Reporter System's coverage of that state began, any out-of-state citing cases will be found in the state citator; (2) with three exceptions (mentioned in footnote 4, above), *citing* cases not reported in the National Reporter System will not be included in either the state citators or the Regional Reporters; (3) if a state case was decided *after* the National Reporter System began coverage of that state, any out-of-state citing cases will be found in the Regional Reporter covering that state.

b. *Citation of cases reported in the National Reporter System.* Every state Shepard's Citations contains a section listing cases for that state under the regional volume and page number.

Again taking as an example 296 Mass. 275, Shepard's Massachusetts Citations contains a section called Northeastern Reporter (Massachusetts cases), which lists this case under its reporter citation of 5 N.E.2d 720 as a *cited* case. Massachusetts and federal *citing* cases

ILLINOIS SUPREME COURT REPORTS **Vol. 102**

—359—
362 Ill [1]60
198 NE[1]704
106 P2d 175

Exhibit 59

(those cases which have mentioned 296 Mass. 275 in their opinions) are listed under the *cited* case by the unofficial citation. Because the official reports section of a state Shepard's unit lists citing cases by official citation, you would normally wish to translate the unofficial reporter citation (5 N.E.2d 720) to the official citation (296 Mass. 275) by means of the reporter citation's parallel official citation tables. When a case is reported (as many are), only in the unofficial and not in the official report, you will of course find it listed only in the separate regional section in the state Shepard's unit having such a section.

c. *Citation of a state court case by courts of all jurisdictions*. Since the state Shepard's Citations lists only federal court and local court (Massachusetts, in our example) citing cases, the approach to the courts of all jurisdictions must be through the appropriate Shepard's Regional Reporter Citations. In our Massachusetts example, taking the citation 5 N.E.2d 720 into Shepard's Northeastern Citations, you will find there every regional citation of cases mentioning this case, together with the state of the court making the decision. The order of listing these citing cases under the above citation is: United States Supreme Court cases affirming or reversing, Massachusetts commenting or citing cases, cases from other states in the regional unit (Northeastern here), and cases listed alphabetically by state as found in other Regional Reporters.

§18.6. Shepardizing a case: Regional Reporter units of the National Reporter System Shepard's Citations.

The nine Regional Reporters (Atlantic, Northeastern, Northwestern, Southern, Southeastern, Southwestern, Pacific, New York Supplement, and California Reports) cover all standard report series, but coverage is limited to the period from about 1880 to date only. Together with the federal citators described in §18.7, these regional units comprise the National Reporter System Shepard's Citations.

1. *Process employed in Shepardizing*. Shepardizing cases through the Regional Reporter Shepard's Citations is exactly the same as when the state citators are used, but the Regional Reporter citators provide a nationwide citing-case coverage. The results are broader because the unit, in addition to citing cases of the forum commenting upon the case you are Shepardizing, also includes all citing cases in all Regional Reporters. Our main case, 296 Mass. 275, is shown, through the 5 N.E.2d 720 citation in Shepard's Northeastern Reporter Citations, to have been cited by the courts of twenty other states.

No statutes or law review comments are covered by the Regional Reporter citators. A.L.R. annotations are noted, however.

2. *Shepardizing state cases not officially reported.* Regional Reporters print many cases which are not officially reported and thus cannot be Shepardized in the state Shepard's Citations except in the section covering local state cases reported unofficially (e.g., the section of Northeastern Reporter—Massachusetts Cases). The absence of a parallel official citation in its place in a regional Shepard's Citations is almost infallible proof of the lack of an official report. For cases decided after the development of the National Reporter System, the Regional Reporter Shepard's Citations is more complete in its listings than the state Shepard's official section, to the extent of its inclusion of cases unreported officially. Cases antedating the National Reporter System, if commented upon by the Regional Reporters at a later date, are frequently included in the state Shepard's unit, as explained *supra*.

§18.7. Shepardizing a case: Federal units of the National Reporter System Shepard's Citations.

Federal *court* decisions are covered by three different Shepard's units: Shepard's United States Citations, Shepard's Federal Citations, and Shepard's Federal Labor Law Citations (which cover N.L.R.B. decisions, also). Since the series covered by these three units comprise some fifty-seven different ones — not always easily distinguishable from their titles — Shepard's has provided in each red-paper supplement to the above units a Table of Reports covering all federal units (see Exhibit 60).

Table of Reports in Shepard's United States, United States Administrative and Federal Reporter Editions

Abstracted Protest Decisions	Administrative
Abstracted Reappraisement Decisions	Administrative
Abstracts	Administrative
Abstracts, New Series	Administrative
American Bankruptcy Reports	Federal
American Bankruptcy Reports, New Series	Federal
American Maritime Cases	Federal
Appeal Cases, District of Columbia Reports	Federal
Application for Review Decisions	Administrative
Black's Reports (66–67 U. S.)	United States

Exhibit 60

Two other units, Shepard's United States Patents and Trademarks Citations and Shepard's United States Administrative Citations, are also part of Shepard's federal coverage. These two units and Shepard's Federal Labor Law Citations are described in §18.17.3a, c, and b, respectively.

1. *Supreme Court cases*. These are covered by Shepard's United States Citations.

The procedure for Shepardizing Supreme Court cases is similar to the procedure for state citator use. There are some important aspects of Shepardizing Supreme Court decisions which should be mentioned, however. *Citing cases* in Shepard's United States Citations include all state reports, all units of the National Reporter System, A.L.R. annotations, and a wide variety of administrative reports series.

Citations to reports in Shepard's United States Citations are in three parallel series: (1) by United States Reports official citation, (2) by Supreme Court Reporter citation, and (3) by Lawyers' Edition citation. Since the first ninety volumes of the United States Reports are commonly cited by the reporter's name instead of by series volume number, a Parallel Reference Table in the front of the unit translates from the nominative (Dallas, Peters, etc.) to the United States Reports citation as it has been renumbered. To save space, all actual Shepardizing information is given only under the official citation, with the following exception. The unofficial listing of Supreme Court cases shows some cases not officially reported. If such cases have been the subject of action which is covered by Shepard's units, that action is indicated under the unofficial citation only, since there is no place for it under the official.

2. *Lower federal court cases*. Shepard's Federal Citations cover those federal courts below the Supreme Court (including federal courts in the District of Columbia and United States territories) as distinct from administrative agencies having the title but not the full status of a federal "court" and federal court rules above the local federal district court level. Since the coverage of this Reporter citator unit was changed radically in 1967, the comparative table shown in Exhibit 61 should be consulted when you are in doubt.

§18.8. Case citators other than Shepard's Citations.

1. *Digest tables of cases generally*. Through their tables of cases or in their digest paragraphs or both, most case digests state whether the cases digested have been affirmed, reversed, or modified on appeal. This treatment corresponds to the Shepard's "history" of the case.

2. *Digest tables of cases affirmed, reversed, or modified*. Tables in the General Digest list cases which have been affected by later deci-

sions and thus provide the history of cases. The Digest of the United States Supreme Court Reports has a similar table.

3. *Tables of cases judicially noticed*. Several state digests have such tables, arranged as plaintiff-defendant case tables.

4. *Loose-leaf services and reporters as case citators*. Especially in tax and regulatory fields, loose-leaf services perform a citator function. This is described in Chapter 23.

§18.9. Shepardizing legislation: General considerations.

Legislation is somewhat more complicated to Shepardize than cases. Once a case is decided and the opinion published, its form is fixed. Subsequent judicial action may affect its value as precedent but does not affect its form. Statutes, however, change in form. Constitutions are amended or new ones adopted. Session laws are later codified into sections of codes or other compilations, and they are amended or repealed. Codes themselves are revised at intervals.

The function of Shepardizing legislation, therefore, is a dual one: (1) to trace subsequent legislative action on a given law. This may include amendments, repeals, additions, extensions of the term where an act is to end on a given date or event, revisions, etc. (2) To trace subsequent judicial action construing the legislation. This may include decisions as to constitutionality and validity.

§18.10. Shepardizing legislation: Shepard's Citations coverage.

The Shepard's system covers federal and state constitutions, session laws, compiled statutes, city charters and ordinances, and court rules. Subordinate legislation has limited Shepardizing coverage. (See §18.17.)

§18.11. Shepardizing legislation: Arrangement of legislation in Shepard's Citations.

The ability to find the legislation to be Shepardized in the appropriate unit is increased by knowledge of the physical order in which the various types of legislation are arranged in these citators.

The arrangement depends upon the form of the legislation. This form may be changed by legislative action subsequent to the original enactment or promulgation. This is significant principally when a session law (for example, the Statutes at Large in federal legislation) is incorporated in a subject arrangement in a federal or state compilation of public, general and permanent interest, such as the United

States Code and similar state compilations. Arrangement of legislation in Shepard's Citations is as follows:

1. *Constitutions*. The arrangement is by article and section and by amendment and section for the federal Constitution. State constitutions are listed by date of adoption, then by article and section.

2. *Session laws*. The federal form is the Statutes at Large. These are listed by date, chapter (or, beginning with the eighty-fifth Congress in 1957, by law number for the Statutes at Large) and section.

3. *Compilations of statutes*. These are listed by edition or date, then by title and section.

4. *Treaties*. Until 1949, treaties were listed as Statutes at Large, by date of treaty. Thereafter, treaties are listed in a special section in both Shepard's United States Citations and in state Shepard's Citations under United States Treaties and other International Agreements.

5. *Municipal charters and ordinances*. These are arranged alphabetically by municipality and listed thereunder by date and section. There is a subject index of charter provisions and a separate index for ordinances.

6. *Court rules*. The arrangement is by court, date, and section.

7. *Presidential executive acts*. Executive orders, proclamations, and reorganization plans can be Shepardized when they form integral parts of Code sections. To find out whether they are included within the Code, check the tables of Executive Acts included in the tables and volumes of the Code. See also §18.17.

§18.12. Shepardizing legislation: Information supplied by Shepard's Citations.

The information includes notations of subsequent amendments, repeals, etc., by the legislature and judicial action construing the legislation as to constitutionality and validity. This is shown by the illustrative statute in Exhibit 61 *infra*. The abbreviations employed for statutes in this example are explained in the Abbreviation-Analysis: Statutes at the front of every Shepard's unit covering statutes.

§18.13. Shepardizing legislation: The Federal Constitution and conventional legislation in Shepard's Citations.

Shepard's United States Citations covers the Constitution and all conventional federal legislation. In addition, nearly all state Shepard's Citations list decisions of their own courts construing the Federal Constitution and statutes.

ILLUSTRATIVE STATUTES

Mississippi Code, 1942 and Supplement, 1956

TITLE 40

Ch. 3

Div. 1

§ 10109

A1955Ex [p 228 — 1
A1956 p 676

C203Mis 716 — 2
C 35So2d 73
36So2d 142
218Mis 303
63So2d 80
61So2d 276

C337US 664 — 3
C 93LE1618
C 69SC 1264

1955Ex p254 — 5

Div. 3

§ 10146-04

See §10149

Rs1955Ex [p 251§4 — 1

§ 10149

S §10146-04

A1946 p 527 — 1
A1948 p 773
Rp1952 p667

203Mis 715 — 2
35So2d 73
36So2d 142
219Mis 390
68So2d 473
Up43So2d185

Subd. d — 6
203Mis 724
35So2d 75
36So2d 142

Citations to section "§" 10109 of Division "Div." 1 and to § 10146-04 and § 10149 of Div. 3 of Chapter "Ch." 3 of Title 40 of the Mississippi Code of 1942 and Supplement, 1956 are shown in the left margin in the same form in which they appear in this volume.

Where a cited section of the Mississippi Code of 1942 has been superseded by a section in a recompiled volume of that same code, Shepard's Mississippi Citations includes under the superseded section an "S" reference to the superseding section and under the superseding section a "See" reference to the superseded section. Thus the references "S § 10146-04" under § 10149 and "See § 10149" under § 10146-04 indicate that § 10146-04 has superseded § 10149.

Citations to each cited statutory provision are grouped as follows:

1. amendments, repeals, etc. by the Mississippi Legislature;
2. citations by the Mississippi Supreme Court analyzed as to constitutionality or validity;
3. citations by federal courts analyzed as to constitutionality or validity;
4. citations in legal periodicals;
5. citations in Acts of the Mississippi Legislature; and
6. citations to specific subdivisions.

For the purpose of illustration only, this grouping has been indicated by bracketing the citations accordingly. It will be noted that as yet there are no citations in group four.

In indicating the legislative and judicial operation of a cited statute, the letter-form abbreviations shown on page 15 are used.

The first illustrative statute, § 10109 of Div. 1, was amended "A" by acts appearing on page "p" 228 of the General Laws of Mississippi, Extraordinary Session "Ex" of 1955 and page 676 of the Laws of 1956. The section was held constitutional "C" by the Mississipi Supreme Court in a case reported in 203 Mississippi Reports "Mis" 716 and 35 Southern Reporter, Second Series "So2d" 73. Each reference to a citing case as reported in the Mississippi Reports is followed by any cross reference to the same case as reported in the Southern Reporter. The section was also cited by the Mississippi Supreme Court in a case reported only in 61 So2d 276. The United States Supreme Court held the section constitutional in a case reported in 337 United States Supreme Court Reports "US" 664, 93 Lawyers' Edition, United States Supreme Court Reports "LE" 1618 and 69 Supreme Court Reporter "SC" 1264. The section was also cited by the Mississippi Legislature in an act appearing on page 254 of the General Laws of Mississippi, Extraordinary Session of 1955.

The second illustrative statute, § 10146-04 of Div. 3, was repealed and superseded "Rs" by a subsequent act of the Mississippi Legislature.

The third illustrative statute, § 10149 of Div. 3, was amended twice and repealed in part "Rp" by subsequent acts of the Mississippi Legislature. The section was cited in two Mississippi cases and was held unconstitutional in part "Up" by the Mississippi Supreme Court in a case reported only in 43 So2d 185. Subdivision "Subd." d of § 10149 was specifically cited by the Mississippi Supreme Court in a case reported in 203 Mis 724, 35 So2d 75 and 36 So2d 142.

Arranging legislation by date in Shepard's Citations sometimes causes confusion in the United States Citations when (as in treaties, for example) a group of earlier but hitherto unpublished acts are collected in a later volume of the Statutes at Large. Since the date controls the order of listing, the Act of January 23, 1972, c. 5, which is 1 Stat. 229, follows in Shepard's Citations a treaty of July 2, 1791, published in a treaty compilation in 7 Stat. 39.

1. *Constitution*. This is covered by article and section, and by amendment and section. Citing cases in the United States Citations are from the federal courts alone; comments from the American Bar Association Journal and annotations from the Lawyers' Edition and A.L.R. are also noted. State court treatment of the Constitution is covered by the respective state Shepard's Citations.

2. *Statutes at Large*. Shepardizing any session law is quite simple if the law has never been codified in a subject-matter compilation of laws of public, permanent and general interest. The law is to be found in Shepard's Citations by exact date of enactment, chapter or law number, section and Statutes at Large volume and page. The important factor is the date of enactment, however, because under this date all subsequent legislative and judicial action is noted.

Difficulty arises with a session law which (being of public, general and permanent interest) has been incorporated into a subject-matter compilation of such enactments, such as the United States Code or its state counterparts. Shepard's United States Citations covers as Statutes at Large only those enactments of Congress which have never been so incorporated. For those that have been incorporated, the Statutes at Large citation must be translated to the Code form and Shepardized there. For federal laws, this is done through Table III, Statutes at Large, in the Tables volume of the U.S. Code. All state statutory compilations have similar transfer tables from the session law to the compilation form.

Accordingly, the Act of February 21, 1871, c. 62, 16 Stat. 419, can be Shepardized as a Statute at Large because it was never codified. In order to Shepardize such a statute, the searcher must use that part of Shepard's United States Citations entitled United States Statutes at Large (not in United States Code). The Act of February 1, 1876, c. 6, 19 Stat. 2, however, cannot be Shepardized as a Statute at Large because (as an Act of public, permanent and general interest) it was codified as 22 U.S.C. §178, a form of citation found through the above parallel transfer table. It can be Shepardized through that part of Shepard's United States Citations entitled United States Code (1970 edition or later editions as they appear).

a. *Federal and state cases construing the Statutes at Large*. Shepard's United States Citations and state Shepard's Citations cover both federal and state cases construing the Statutes at Large. The state units, of course, note only their own state decisions construing the Statutes at Large.

3. *Revised Statutes.* The United States Revised Statutes are not covered as such by any Shepard's Citations, though many sections are still in force. If (as is the case with most of these sections still in force) they have been integrated with the United States Code, they can be Shepardized under the Code sections for which they are statutory authority. The parallel transfer Table II, Revised Statutes, in the tables volume of the Code gives the Code citation, which can then be Shepardized.

For example, R.S. §1827 is statutory authority for 40 U.S.C. §216 and can be Shepardized as that Code section. If the section to be Shepardized never was in the Code, its session law citation will be found at the end of the section of the Revised Statutes itself and can be Shepardized as a Statute at Large. If the section is no longer in force, that fact can be ascertained from Table II, Revised Statutes, in the tables volume of the Code.

The Statutes Construed Tables in each volume of the National Reporter System cover the Revised Statutes, but these tables are not cumulative. Consequently, a complete search would require examination of every bound volume and each succeeding advance sheet of the reports.

4. *United States Code.* If an enactment has been incorporated in the Code, it can be directly Shepardized only through the *latest form* of its Code citation. Indirectly, however, an earlier Code form can be translated into its present form. The Statutes at Large citation, which is authority for any form of the section, is given in Table III of the U.S. Code, as noted above, together with the present Code section. Furthermore, if the former Code section was in a Code title reenacted into positive law and that title has later been revised so that the old section number is obsolete, Table I in the Code Table volume gives the present section number by which it is now Shepardizable. In all state Shepard's units, citations to Code titles and sections by cases interpreting the law of the forum are covered.

Labor provisions of the Code can be Shepardized through Shepard's Federal Labor Law Citations, which collects all provisions concerning labor regulation. As Code sections, these provisions are also covered by Shepard's United States Citations.

Amendments or other statutory changes occurring before the latest Code edition and Supplement are not shown as such. Changes subsequent to the latest Code supplement appear in the current paperbound Shepard's Citations supplement.

Thus, the Shepard's bound supplement, covering 1968–1974, noted only changes since the 1970 edition of the Code and its Supplement II (1972). The April 1977 red-paper Supplement to 1968–1974 covered later statutory changes through the 1970 Code and its Supplement V (1975). As far as possible, all cases construing the present statute in any of its earlier forms are transferred to the current section. There is not always an exact counterpart of the older form, however. A repealed statute is not so represented.

In practice this Shepard's policy does not cause much difficulty because the searcher is ordinarily interested only in the latest form of enactment. If, on the other hand, searchers do want to trace the earlier forms and the cases construing them, they can usually do so through the "history" comments in an annotated edition either of the United States Code or of the corresponding state compilations.

5. *Treaties*. Through 1949 (64 Statutes at Large), treaties were published as Statutes at Large and can be Shepardized as such in both Shepard's United States Citations and, as construed by state courts, in state Shepard's Citations. Confusion often results because treaties are listed by treaty date (which by no means always coincides with the Statutes at Large publication date). Beginning with 1950, treaties can be Shepardized through the same federal and state Shepard's Citations units in a special section entitled United States Treaties and Other International Agreements, by volume and page of this new treaty series publication. The Statutes Construed Tables in the National Reporter System cover treaties.

Other publications serving a citator function for treaties are discussed in Chapter 6.

6. *State court construction of federal legislation*. State courts construe the Federal Constitution when it affects their own states. Nearly every state Shepard's Citations has a section listing federal legislation construed. Whether a particular state has such a section is always indicated by the Table of Contents of the unit covering the state.

§18.14. Shepardizing legislation: State conventional legislation in Shepard's Citations.

The same difficulties arise in Shepardizing state legislation as in federal, and the method of Shepardizing state legislation is the same.

1. *Session laws*. The current Shepard's Citations practice is to cover as session laws only those laws not incorporated into the state subject-matter compilation. This follows the policy described for the Federal Statutes at Large and the United States Code. Tables of Statutes Construed in Reporter advance sheets cover session laws as such. Some state statutory compilations have tables showing all amendments, repeals, etc., for session laws for varying periods.

2. *Compilations of statutes*. The Shepard's Citations practice is to cover subject-matter compilations of statutes only in their latest form,

as of the date of publication of the particular Shepard's unit or supplement. However, in most states, all citations to cases construing the predecessor form of the statutes are transferred to the new form as far as possible. In practice this causes lawyers little difficulty, since generally they are interested only in the statute in its present form. For most states, tables are provided in the statutory compilations. This enables the searcher interested in an earlier form of statute to translate the present form into the earlier one, though it is not always possible to find an equivalent.

3. *Municipal charters and ordinances*. Municipal legislation is covered by the state Shepard's Citations in a special section which includes a subject index of the legislation construed. The Statutes Construed Tables found in each volume of the National Reporter System also cover charters. For Supreme Court decisions, the Laws Cited and Construed Table of the Digest of the United States Supreme Court Reports provides similar coverage.

Shepard's Ordinance Law Annotations is a six-volume set arranged by topics arising from fact situations. It digests American cases interpreting city and county ordinances.

4. *Uniform state laws*. There is no Shepard's Citation unit covering the Uniform Laws as such. On the other hand, parallel transfer tables in the Uniform Laws Annotated volumes enable the searcher to find the corresponding official state law citation for any section. Once that law has been found, the searcher can Shepardize the law in the usual manner. Shepard's Acts and Cases by Popular Names, Federal and State, permit a similar translation to the official statutory citation which can be Shepardized. The Statutes Construed Tables found in each volume of the National Reporter System cover the Uniform Laws as such, but they are not cumulated from volume to volume.

5. *Interstate compacts*. These can be Shepardized as session laws in the Shepard's Citations of the states concerned. Each state enacts separately, as a conventional session law, the agreed-upon compact. The National Reporter System Statutes Construed Tables and the Laws Cited and Construed Table of the Digest of the United States Supreme Court Reports list the compacts as interstate compacts.

6. *Federal court construction of state legislation*. Nearly all state Shepard's Citations list federal court decisions construing the state's legislation.

§18.15. Shepardizing legislation: Statutory citators other than Shepard's Citations.

Several publications which serve a citator function have been mentioned. They are best used to supplement a Shepard's Citations unit temporarily, until the latest supplement of that unit appears. Some of these publications are described below.

1. *Statutes Construed Tables of the National Reporter System.* Each advance sheet and bound volume of the Regional Reporter contains a table of federal and state statutes construed by decisions printed in that unit. Citation is not confined to decisions printed in the regional unit containing the table, but covers interpretations by decisions reported in other units for the same period. For example, the table in the Atlantic Reporter notes the interpretations of Maryland statutes by all federal courts covered by the Supreme Court Reporter, Federal Reporter, and Federal Supplement; by Maryland courts reported in the Atlantic Reporter; and by other courts reported in other regional Reporters.

The Statutes Construed Tables in the reporters include not only federal and state constitutions, session laws, and treaties but also municipal charters, court rules, Presidential proclamations, executive orders, and uniform laws.

The principal value of this table is that it may temporarily bring your search closer to date for the statutes covered than does Shepard's Citations. This is because the advance sheets bearing the table appear weekly, whereas the most frequent publication of the Shepard's Citations is the six-week period between the issuance of the red-paper supplement and the white-paper supplement. (An exception is the monthly supplementation of Shepard's Federal Labor Law Citations.) The regional table notes only that a statute has been construed by a given case and does not disclose the nature of the action taken. For that information, the cited case must be consulted. Thus, the Statutes Construed Tables perform a more limited role than Shepard's and are best used to supplement the latest Shepard's unit.

These tables are not cumulated.

2. *Table of Laws Cited and Construed of the Digest of the United States Supreme Court Reports.* This table is an adjunct of the Lawyers' Edition of the United States Supreme Court Reports. By means of it, cases can be found construing statutes covered by no other citator. Coverage includes Indian laws and treaties with foreign nations as well as with the United States, the Articles of Confederation, Acts of the Continental Congress and of the Confederate States of America. Treaties and executive agreements with foreign nations, interstate compacts, proclamations and executive orders of the President are covered, in addition to conventional federal and state legislation construed by the Supreme Court. It covers state and territorial statutes in their original forms, which Shepard's Citations no longer does. This table is supplemented by annual pocket parts.

3. *Compiled statutes as citators.* Some official unannotated editions and most annotated editions of statutes may serve a citator function in conjunction with Shepard's Citations by covering forms of statutes which are earlier than the current one treated in Shepard's Citations. A certain amount of the history of each section or group of

sections of a statute is given, and annotations cite or digest cases construing the statutes. Examples are the United States Code Annotated and the United States Code Service.

§18.16. A complete citator search.

1. *Shepard's Citations*. A complete Shepard's Citations unit consists of the following parts: (a) one or more bound volumes; (b) a quarterly red-paper cumulative supplement, which eventually matures into a bound supplement; and (c) for the United States, Federal Citations, Labor Law Citations, reporter units of the National Reporter System and approximately one-half of the state Shepard's Citations, a quarterly white-paper Advance Sheet Edition. The Advance Sheet Edition appears six weeks after the red-paper cumulative supplement. Thus, for units containing this edition, supplementation occurs every six weeks (except for the Labor Law Citations, for which there is a month's interval).

The exact coverage of a complete unit is indicated on the cover of the latest paper supplement, as in Exhibit 62.

The oldest case may be cited, or the oldest statute (if still in force) may be construed by the very latest case. Thus, to Shepardize 1 Mo. 1 completely, each unit of Shepard's Missouri Citations must be searched: the bound volumes, the latest red-paper supplement, and the white-paper Advance Sheet Edition to date. Each unit contains a tabulation of citing cases covered by it: "This Issue Includes Citations in. . . ." It tells you the precise volumes and pages of each citing series included. The latest white-paper supplement will cite the earliest statute or the earliest case, if it has been affected by a current decision.

2. *Statutes Construed Tables*. These tables may supplement the various units of Shepard's Citations and cite later cases construing a given statute than are recorded in the latest Shepard's Supplement. A

WHAT YOUR LIBRARY SHOULD CONTAIN

CASES	STATUTES
1963 Bound Volume	1963 Bound Volume

Supplemented with
September, 1968 Cumulative Supplement Vol. LVIII No. 3
October, 1968 Advance Sheet Vol. III No. 2

DESTROY ALL OTHER ISSUES

Exhibit 62

significant research tool containing such tables is the National Reporter System described in §18.15.

§18.17. Administrative law citators: Subordinate legislation and decisions.

Although coverage for federal administrative decisions is incomplete, Shepard's United States Administrative Citations has widened coverage significantly. Some of the available material is noted below:

1. *Administrative rules and regulations changes.*

a. *List of C.F.R. Sections Affected and List of Sections Affected.* Once the searcher has discovered and read a pertinent administrative rule in the Code of Federal Regulations or the Federal Register, he or she will want to determine if later regulations have affected the pertinent regulation. This may be done through using the List of Sections Affected in the Federal Register and the List of C.F.R. Sections Affected in the C.F.R., which are described in §7.3.

b. *Loose-leaf services.* Some regulatory and tax services note changes in and revocation of rules and regulations. See Chapter 23.

2. *Presidential legislation.* See §7.3.

a. *Proclamations.* In some degree these are covered by (1) Shepard's United States Citations, as Statutes at Large when a proclamation is listed as a statutory source affecting or authorized by a Statute at Large; (2) Shepard's United States Citations when the proclamation is integrated with U.S. Code sections (to be found through Table V of the Code in its Tables volume); (3) National Reporter System's Statutes Construed Tables, which cover the case law on proclamations; (4) Laws Cited and Construed Tables in the Digest of the United States Supreme Court Reports, which notes Supreme Court decisions construing proclamations.

b. *Executive orders.* Since these are not published in the Statutes at Large, they are not directly covered by Shepard's Citations. Many, however, are made integral parts of Code sections by enabling legislation and so are discussed or printed in the notes to the Code sections. Since all such sections are covered by Shepard's United States Citations, the executive order can be Shepardized to the extent that it directly relates to a Code section. Relating an executive order, proclamation or reorganization plan to a Code section is accomplished through Table III of the Code, or through similar U.S.C.A. or U.S.C.S. tables.

Thus, in Exhibit 63, below, if you wish to Shepardize executive order number 6084, the various Code sections of which it is in any way a part are found through the table, and these Code sections are Shepardized. This procedure is indirect and not altogether satisfac-

TABLE IV.—EXECUTIVE ORDERS

This Table lists the Executive Orders that implement general and permanent law as contained in U.S.C.

Exec. Ord.		U.S.C.		Exec. Ord.		U.S.C.	
Date	No.	Title	Sec.	Date	No.	Title	Sec.
1918				1941			
May 11	2859	36	253 nt	June 14	8785	12	95a nt
				July 26	8832	12	95a nt
1929				Dec. 9	8963	12	95a nt
				26	8998	12	95a nt
Oct. 1	5200	7	452 nt				
				1942			
1933							
				Mar. 11	9095	50 App.	6 nt
→ Mar. 27	6084	12	Prec. 636 nt	Apr. 4	9126	50 App.	601 nt
June 8	6161	16	831u nt	May 29	9176	22	Prec. 611 nt
10	6166	5	124-132 nt	30	9177	50 App.	601 nt
July 30	6237-A	50 App.	12 nt	July 6	9193	50 App.	6 nt
Aug. 28	6260	12	95a nt	Aug. 20	9230	5	631a nt
Oct. 25	6359	12	248 nt		9232	50 App.	601 nt
				Nov. 5	9262	50 App.	601 nt

INTRODUCTORY

Ex. Ord. No. 6084. Reorganizing Agricultural Credit Agencies of the United States

Ex. Ord. No. 6084, Mar. 27, 1933, provided in part: . . . It is hereby ordered that:

(1) The functions of the Secretary of Agriculture as a member of the Federal Farm Board, and the offices of the appointed members of the Federal Farm Board, except the office of the member designated as chairman thereof, are abolished.

(2) The name of the Federal Farm Board is changed to the Farm Credit Administration.

(3) The name of the office of Chairman of the Federal Farm Board is changed to Governor of the Farm Credit Administration, and he is vested with all the powers and duties of the Federal Farm Board.

(9) The unexpended balances of appropriations to the Secretary of Agriculture, the Federal Farm Loan Bureau, and the Federal Farm Board for salaries, expenses, and all other administrative expenditures in the execution of the functions herein vested in the Farm Credit Administration shall be transferred to and vested in the Farm Credit Administration as a single fund for its use for salaries, expenses, and all other administrative expenditures for the execution of any or all of such functions without restriction as to the particular functions for the execution of which the same were originally appropriated. All other appropriations, allotments, and other funds available for use in connection with the functions and executive agencies hereby transferred and consolidated are hereby transferred to and vested in the Farm Credit Administration, and shall be available for use by it, for the same purposes as if the Farm Credit Administration

Exhibit 63

tory. Nevertheless, such executive orders can be Shepardized whether the order becomes an integral part of the Code section or is only mentioned in an editorial note to the section.

The Statutes Construed tables in the National Reporter System note whenever an executive order has been construed by the courts; the similar tables of the Digest of the United States Supreme Court Reports L. Ed. do it for Supreme Court cases. "Finding lists" of some loose-leaf services act as citators for pertinent executive orders. See §23.4.

See §7.2 for a discussion of the changes in executive orders.

c. *Reorganization plans*. The same procedure is followed as for proclamations and executive orders. See Table VI in the U.S. Code.

3. *Administrative agency decisions*. Many agency decisions can be Shepardized. Shepard's Citations has several units which cover many series of administrative agency decisions: Shepard's United States Administrative Citations; Shepard's Federal Reporter Citations; Shepard's Federal Labor Law Citations; and Shepard's United States Citations, Patents and Trademarks. To tell which unit covers a specific series, see the Tables in the red-paper supplements, referred to in §18.7 above. The Labor Law unit's coverage is not included in these tables, however.

Loose-leaf services or reporters cover many agency decisions, either through citators arranged by case name or through their table of cases. If a Shepard's unit does not cover the desired series, a loose-leaf service (especially in the tax field) is an effective substitute.

a. *Shepard's United States Administrative Citations*. Begun in 1967, this edition now serves several series formerly covered by Shepard's United States and Federal Reporter units as well as several agency decision series never before Shepardizable. Although Shepard's follows precisely in this unit the demarcation line separating true court from administrative agency, the reader should consult the table in the red-paper supplements in order to determine its precise coverage. *All* reports of agency decisions (whether or not formerly included in other Shepard's units) and all series which previously could not be Shepardized are collected in the bound volumes of the United States Administrative Citations; consequently it is unnecessary to search elsewhere if the desired series is covered.

The publisher has included many cross-reference tables between citations of official agency reports and unofficial reports (such as between the Federal Securities Law Reporter and the official S.E.C. Decisions and Reports). These tables are invaluable if one wishes to convert a citation from the unofficial to the official reports or vice versa. Any cross-references will be found in the first volume published after the cross-reference becomes available; they are not repeated elsewhere.

A preface in this citator describes in detail the coverage of United States Administrative Citations and provides general instructions on its use. In addition, Shepard's has included in the bound volumes some illustrative cases explaining the citation tables and cross-reference tables. Supplementation of this citator occurs quarterly; no white-covered Advance Sheets are issued.

b. *Shepard's Federal Labor Law Citations.* This Shepard's unit, begun in 1959 and supplemented monthly, is a citator devoted entirely to a specific area of administrative law. It contains three distinct sections, as follows:

(1) *Cases.* Decisions and orders of the National Labor Relations Board since its inception receive the usual Shepard's Citations treatment. Federal court decisions after 1935 are listed in the following subsections: United States Supreme Court Reports (Labor Cases); Lawyers' Edition, United States Supreme Court Reports (Labor Cases); Supreme Court Reporter (Labor Cases); Federal Reporter, 2d Series (Labor Cases); Federal Supplement (Labor Cases); Federal Rules Decisions (Labor Cases). Citing cases include those from all federal and state courts, N.L.R.B. decisions, and several unofficial reports series. In addition, citations to the main case are noted if they appear in the following: selected law reviews; annotations of the Lawyers' Edition, United States Supreme Court Reports; labor relations periodicals; and annotations of American Law Reports.

(2) *Statutes.* The Statutes Edition indicates all references to labor provisions of the U.S. Code since 1947 by federal and state courts. A table of Federal Labor Acts by Popular Names or Short Titles provides both a table of labor acts by popular name and a parallel transfer table from the original form of the act to its Code title and section.

(3) *Cross-references.* Another feature of the Federal Labor Law Citations is a cross-reference table from the Decisions and Orders of the N.L.R.B. to the places where they appear in the loose-leaf services or reports of the Bureau of National Affairs, Commerce Clearing House, and Prentice-Hall. In addition, cross-reference tables from the loose-leaf services to the Decisions and Orders of the N.L.R.B. are provided. Cross-references tables from labor law services or reports to court reports are also provided.

c. *Shepard's United States Patents and Trademarks Citations.* This Shepard's unit provides a thorough citator coverage of patents and trademarks. Citations noted include those found in federal and state court reports, federal administrative reports, annotations, and selected law review articles. In addition, cross-reference tables between patent and court reports are provided.

What might be called the history of a patent or trademark (whether declared valid, infringed, etc.) is also covered by the Federal Digest, the Modern Federal Practice Digest, and the Decennial Digests, under "Patents and Trade-Marks" respectively. See §16.8.

4. *Statutes and regulations as construed by federal agencies*. There is little agency coverage of this kind.

a. *Shepard's Federal Labor Law Citations*. As described earlier in this section, this unit covers National Labor Relations interpretations of federal labor acts.

b. *Index Digest and Tables of Statutes, Etc., Cited in Decisions of the Comptroller General of the United States*. Every volume of the Decisions of the Comptroller General of the United States contains an index digest and a table of statutes, opinions of the Attorney General, court decisions, and earlier opinions of the Comptroller General cited in that volume. These tables and indexes are cumulated every five years into the Index Digest of the Decisions of the Comptroller General of the United States.

c. *Agriculture Decisions*. Each bound volume has a citator for statutes, regulations, orders and court decisions relating to matter printed in the Decisions.

d. *Cumulative Bulletin of the Internal Revenue Service*. This is an example of the publication of agency interpretations of an internal or intra-agency nature.

e. *Loose-leaf services*. In tax and regulatory fields these services, through formal citators or through "finding lists" arranged by statute or regulation perform a citator function.

§18.18. Miscellaneous legislation which can be Shepardized.

1. *A.L.I. Restatements*. Approximately one-third of the state Shepard's Citations include state court construction of the Restatements. The best citator for the Restatements is the American Law Institute Restatement in the Courts. It was first published in 1945 covering the years 1932–1944; recently supplements have been issued biannually.

In 1976, *Shepard's Restatement of the Law Citations* was published. It is a compilation of reference cites to the A.L.I.'s Restatement of the Law.

2. *Interstate Compacts*. These are covered in Shepard's Citations as enactments of the states concerned — as session laws but not as a separate type of legislation. The Statutes Construed tables in the National Reporter System cover them as interstate compacts.

3. *Court rules*. See §8.6.

4. *Uniform State Laws*. See §18.16.

§18.19. Legal periodicals which can be Shepardized.

In order to show where articles in legal periodicals have been cited in other law review articles or court decisions, Shepard's Citations began publishing in 1968 its Shepard's Law Review Citations. This publication covers over 150 law reviews and legal periodicals. The coverage includes all articles written since 1947 and cited in later articles from 1957 to date, or in state or federal decisions. The volume is kept up to date by cumulative supplements.

§18.20. Social Sciences Citation Index.

The Social Sciences Citation Index (SSCI), published three times a year and cumulated annually by the Institute for Scientific Information, currently covers the years from 1969 to date; but it has been adding on prior years retrospectively, and its past coverage may expand in the future. The SSCI fully indexes over 1300 social science journals (including over 130 law journals), selectively indexes over 2000 more journals, and consists of three indexes which may be used separately but which gain in usefulness if used together.

1. *The Citation Index*. This index is in three parts. The first part, a personal author index, lists alphabetically by author's name, then by date and title, all cites to that author's work in publications issued during the year covered by the SSCI volume used. Cited works are not restricted to articles, nor is there a length or date requirement for indexing. Thus, books, articles, letters, editorials, etc., dating from Plato to the present, may be found in the citation index if they were cited during the current year. Following this author index there is a "corporate author" citation index. This index is of great use to law researchers because it includes citations to cases, listed alphabetically by the name of the plaintiff. The third part of the citation index lists citations to anonymous works and is also of substantial use to law researchers since all citations to unsigned case notes (among other anonymous works) are listed there alphabetically by the name of the periodical, then by volume and page where the note appears.

2. *The Source Index*. The Source Index of the SSCI lists all the articles indexed in the SSCI during the year covered which cite works listed in the Citation Index. The information given in the Citation Index about citing articles is quite sketchy and serves mainly to direct the researcher to the Source Index which gives the author's full name and joint authors, if any, the full title of the citing article, the journal name, volume, issue number and page number where the citing arti-

cle can be found, the author's address, and, for recent volumes, a list of all the works cited in the article. A second part to the Source Index collects all source authors under their corporate addresses, making it possible to determine at a glance all indexed publications issuing from a particular law school, institute, government bureau, or other corporate entity during a particular year.

3. *The Permuterm Index*. This index takes all significant words in the titles of articles published during the year covered by a particular SSCI volume and indexes them in permuted pairs. Thus, for example, the title "Sex Discrimination Against Women" would be indexed under: Sex-Discrimination, Sex-Women, Discrimination-Sex, Discrimination-Women, Women-Sex and Women-Discrimination. The Permuterm Index enables the researcher to find articles of interest, to the extent indicated by words in the title, even where no eminent authority or original source article is known.

4. *Use of the SSCI*. The efficient use of the SSCI will require a thorough reading of the introductory materials in each volume, as the description given above only skims the surface of the intricacy and sophistication of this publication. The most obvious use, however, is similar to the use of Shepard's as a citator for books, articles, cases and case notes in areas of interest to the researcher. By searching a known author, case name, or case note in the Citation Index, all current references to the researched work can be found. By looking up the referring articles in the Source Index, additional references cited in those articles can be found. Where no author or case is known, use of the Permuterm Index can lead the researcher into source articles whose titles include words related to the subject researched and, again, the Source Index will give references to other articles, cases, and books of potential interest.

19 Treatises and American Law Institute Restatements of the Common Law

§19.1. Treatises.

1. *Functions*. Treatises serve several purposes. A person may use them to refresh his or her memory on the present state of the law covered by the book. Treatises may also be used in the detailed study of an aspect of the law less thoroughly treated elsewhere. In addition, lawyers frequently refer to treatises in order to find citations to leading cases in point which may lead to other cases in point.

As an index to the law, the treatise applies the expert knowledge and research facilities of the author to an exhaustive consideration of the decided cases and statutes. The treatise then sets down an exposition of the law which is founded upon the exhaustive analysis. It thus goes a step beyond the digest, which supplies no comment. The encyclopedia is said to be an alphabetically arranged collection of treatises. According to its scope and purpose, however, the treatise may be expected to do things that the encyclopedia does not usually attempt. It traces the history of the law covered and its development along varying lines. The best treatises are more assiduous than the encyclopedia in pointing out the effect of statutes or of cases overruling a line of earlier cases. Treatises also call more attention than encyclopedias to the fluctuations of the law: trends, needed changes, jurisdictional rules, and majority and minority rules. Unlike the encyclopedia, the treatise frequently contains critical commentary upon the law. Thus it exerts a definite formative influence upon the law. Student books tend to emphasize the elementary exposition of the law and seldom attempt to cite all cases in point. Practitioners' treatises frequently provide for at least annual supplementation.

2. *Authority*. Under a strict definition of authority, treatises are only persuasive and not mandatory. As a practical matter, however, a treatise has authority to the extent that its well-reasoned statements of the law as distilled from the cases and statutes are persuasive. No court, however, is compelled to follow a treatise. When treatises are cited in opinions and briefs (as frequently happens), the judge or attorney citing them has adopted their reasoning as his or her own. Mandatory authority is the product of legislatures and of opinions officially delivered from the bench rather than based on treatises.

Within these limitations treatises may be extremely useful. The law student will find them of great value in providing background in the law and clarification of knotty points of law. Treatises are often cited by both courts and attorneys. While no court is bound by a statement in *Wigmore* or *Williston* or any other treatise, courts are frequently persuaded by a carefully reasoned analysis of a line of cases in a treatise, especially if that analysis has stood up for a number of years.

3. *Varieties*. The variety of treatises is treated at considerable length in Price and Bitner, Effective Legal Research 192–198 (1953); what is said there need only be summarized briefly here.

Treatises are written on every conceivable subject having any relation to the law. They may be classified roughly according to their purpose as histories of law, theoretical works on jurisprudence, commentaries and monographs covering a large or small topic in great detail, and textbooks proper. These categories may overlap in many treatises; authors do not write primarily according to the technical classifications of subject matter.

a. *Student books*. The treatise written primarily for law school use offers an elementary expositon of the principles of the topic covered (such as contracts, torts or insurance) for the purpose of instructing its readers or refreshing their memory. It usually traces the historical development of the topic to some extent, discusses the divergent rules, criticizes cases, and tries to provide a broad picture of the law involved. Often it is a scholarly work providing the best available analysis on the topic treated. The student book makes no attempt to list all cases in point but confines itself to a relatively few leading ones. Theory and trends (elements which are commonly omitted from encyclopedias and practitioners' books) are emphasized. It is an excellent starting point for a brush-up in the subject and for citations of good cases in point. Furthermore, it often supplies the most convenient survey of the more scholarly aspects of a subject. Substantial parts of some student books first appeared as leading articles in law reviews.

Students should not substitute student treatises for a careful reading of their casebook. Student books are helpful, however, in answering students' questions regarding cases or trends in law. The table of cases in such a book serves as a case-finder. In connection with any given course, the student may find, through the table of cases, that many of the cases in his or her casebook are discussed or cited in the student book. Other citations to authority may lead the student to A.L.R. annotations, periodical articles, etc.

b. *Practitioners' books*. Most law books are written neither for students nor scholars but to help practicing lawyers win cases. Accordingly, they emphasize the case-finding function of the treatise and the practical aspects of existing law rather than historical development, theories, or critical comment on the law. They assume more of a background in the law on the part of the reader than does the elementary student book. Some practitioners' books are little more than digests and are thus worthless if not frequently supplemented. They are apt to disappoint the seeker after an adequate picture of the meanderings of the law or the reasons behind them. If they cite all cases in point and extract from them a valid statement of the law as it now stands as a basis for prediction by judge or advocate, they serve their purpose (if they are supplemented frequently enough to keep up with current developments and cases). On the other hand, there is no absolute dividing line between the scholarly books and the practitioners' books. Some of the better books are both.

c. *Cram and bar review books*. The cram book is one which the student, upon graduation from law school, uses as an adjunct to taking his local bar examination. It is an outline of a restricted topic such as criminal law, family law or practice, for a single jurisdiction, and is intended only for review purposes, not as an exhaustive treatment. It mentions local peculiarities of the law, collects a minimum number of outstanding cases and statutes for its jurisdiction, frequently revised to keep up with the latest local developments, but is worthless for general instructional purposes.

d. *Student editions of practitioners' books*. It is not uncommon to extract suitable material from the more scholarly of the comprehensive treatises, and to publish it separately for student use. In such a book most of the citations to cases in the larger work are omitted, and only leading historical cases are cited. An example is Austin W. Scott's Abridgment of the Law of Trusts,[1] in which much of the text but few of the case citations of his scholarly five-volume, The Law of Trusts[2] are put into a single volume. George R. Bogert accomplishes the same result by writing a Hornbook Series Handbook of the Law of Trusts,[3] in which much of the material of instructional value from

1. Boston, Mass., Little, Brown and Co., 1960.
2. 3d ed., Boston, Mass., Little, Brown and Co., 1967, 6 vols.
3. 5th ed., St. Paul, Minn., West Publishing Co., 1973.

his The Law of Trusts and Trustees[4] is compressed into a single volume.

e. *"Local" books*. Many practitioners' books are designed for the lawyers of a specific jurisdiction or area. The most common of these are treatises on the procedure of a jurisdiction or area. Of necessity they are usually supplemented at least annually. They tend to become commentaries on the practice acts and court rules. Another type of local book covers substantive law, such as the New York law of real property or the oil and gas law in the states of the Southwest.

f. *Mechanics of the practice of law*. The law student, in preparing paper work in practice and moot court courses in law school, must know something of the practical side of a lawyer's office activities: how documents are drafted and typed in proper form; how fee contracts are written, etc. Listed below are a few of the many books published for the lawyer but useful as well for the student:

Altman, Mary Ann, and Weil, Robert I., How to Manage Your Law Office. New York, N.Y., Matthew Bender, 1973- , 1 vol. loose-leaf.

American Bar Association Section of Economics of Law Practice, The Lawyers Handbook. Ann Arbor, Mich., Institute of Continuing Legal Education, 1975- , 1 vol. loose-leaf.

Bigelow, Robert P., Law Office Economics and Management Manual. Mundelein, Ill., Callaghan, 1970- , 2 vols. loose-leaf.

Cantor, Daniel J., Managing the Law Office; Organization, Systems, Records and Fees. Mundelein, Ill., Callaghan, 1964.

Shannon, William H., Accounting and the Law. St. Paul, Minn., West Publishing Co., 1957.

Strong, Kline D., Law Office Management. St. Paul, Minn., West Publishing Co., 1974.

g. *Law books for non-lawyers*. Works on law for the engineer, the farmer, the undertaker, the physician or the nurse are generally non-technical discussions of elementary contract and tort law as applied to these professions. These books, usually not intended for use by lawyers, are written to call the attention of the people concerned to some of the legal problems which may confront them. The lawyer may use these books as case-finders. By citing a few cases in point concerning their specialized problems, they afford a starting point in the search through the digests for all cases in point.

h. *Foreign law books for the law student*. Increasingly the practice of American lawyers brings them into contact with foreign law. Because law courses reflect this trend, the student's research often calls for works on foreign law, especially those in the English lan-

4. St. Paul, Minn., West Publishing Co., 1935- , 15 vols.

guage. The law digests in the Martindale-Hubbell Law Directory cover, in digest form, the business and domestic relations laws of most foreign countries. For Latin America, the Pan-American Union synthesizes the laws in matters affecting business in a series entitled "A Statement of the Laws of . . . ," in which each number covers a specific country and each is written by a lawyer native to the country covered.

An excellent source of information regarding publications in English relating to foreign laws are the following by Dr. Charles Szladits, of the Parker School of Foreign and Comparative Law, of Columbia University:

Bibliography of Foreign and Comparative Law: Books and Articles in English. New York, N.Y., Oceana Publications, 1955. Frequently supplemented.

International and Foreign Law Sources for the Business Lawyer, Business Lawyer, April 1960, p. 575.

h. *A.L.R. annotations as treatises*. Recently many A.L.R. annotations have tended to assume the functions of treatises, particularly in their detailed treatment of relatively small areas of broad topics. For example, the annotation in 72 A.L.R.2d 6–183 is a discussion of the "Negligence of Driver of Motor Vehicle as Respects Manner of Timely Application of Proper Brakes." Like a conventional treatise it has an author. It has a very detailed and analytical table of contents, a similarly detailed subject index, and a table of jurisdictions represented by the cases cited. There is also a tendency to publish in a single A.L.R. volume several annotations relating to minute aspects of the same broad topic, such as compromise and settlement, evidence, wills, etc.

4. *Supplementation of treatises*. Most treatises are supplemented annually. The most common type of supplement is the cumulative pocket supplement. A recent development which overcomes some of the disadvantages of other kinds of supplementation is the loose-leaf binder. Loose-leaf binders allow for the preparation and insertion of new pages or pamphlets in their proper places without reissuing the entire work.

5. *Techniques in the use of treatises*. Perhaps the most important factor in utilizing treatises is finding a text which covers the specific problem. In law school libraries, the most frequently used treatises are usually placed on reserve at the loan desk. These and other treatises are indexed in the library's card catalogue, which lists all books in the library by author, title, and subject matter.

Lawyers and students will find useful the various tables and indexes of the conventional treatise. The table of contents fulfills an obvious function and should be examined for the author's analysis. The subject index provides a much more detailed analysis by broad subject and catchword. Readers, however, must realize that indexers may approach a problem differently from themselves, and that considerable ingenuity is often required to find a topic's listing. The table of cases, found in nearly all law books, emphasizes the secondary nature of the treatise. The pages of a treatise are generally composed of text commentary which are supported by citations to authority in the footnotes. In a book on legal history or the philosophy of law, there are comparatively few footnote references. In a student treatise, most of the leading cases in point are cited. In a practitioner's work, substantially all cases in point are cited; footnote references often take up more space on a page than the main text.

The table of cases has two principal functions. First, it leads to the page, pages, or sections in the treatise where the significant points of law in a case are discussed. Second, the case citations in the footnotes on the designated pages give parallel references to standard reports printing the case and thus lead the searcher to annotations or digests of other cases in point.

§19.2. American Law Institute Restatements of the common law.

1. *Function*. Although the Restatements are not treatises, they aim "to present an orderly restatement of the general common law of the United States, including in that term not only the law developed solely by judicial decision, but also the law that has grown from the application by the courts of statutes that were generally enacted and were in force for many years."[5]

They are not codes; instead, they are rules of law which, in the opinion of the Institute, would be applied by enlightened courts in the United States. In determining which rules are included, the Institute considers all factors which a court would consider, such as the weight of precedent and the impact of the rule. The Institute has shown with increasing frequency that it is not bound by the weight of authority; this willingness to espouse "minority rules" has evoked heated discussion.[6] The Restatements attempt to achieve some degree of unity of the rules of the common law among the states. They try to give the judges a statement of the common-law rules

5. Wolkin, Restatements of the Law: Origin, Preparation, Availability, 21 Ohio B.A. Rept. 663 (1940).

6. Compare Wechsler, The Course of the Restatements, 55 A.B.A.J. 147 (1969), in which Wechsler defends the willingness of the Institute to consider other factors in addition to the weight of authority, with Helms, The Restatements: Existing Law or Prophecy, 56 A.B.A.J. 152 (1970), in which Helms attacks current policy.

which has more scholarship and study behind it than are found in the conventional treatise or legal encyclopedia. To the lawyer they give a rule of decision backed by the prestige of the Institute and a high degree of acceptance by the courts. To the student they give a statement of principles, backed by commentaries and numerous illustrative examples to clarify various rules of law.

Most of the work of compiling the Restatements was done by "Reporters" for each topic, persons eminent in their respective fields. These Reporters are assisted by staffs of "advisers." After each group of specialists determined for itself the proper statement of the "best rule" of law in each instance, the tentative draft or parts of it were submitted to the Council of the American Law Institute for debate and final approval. The Reporters have been law teachers of the caliber of Williston, Powell, Hanna, and Beale. The advisers were eminent teachers, practitioners, and judges. No other study of comparable thoroughness and scholarship has ever been made of American law.

2. *Form and scope*. To date, Restatements have been adopted by the Institute for agency, conflicts of laws, contracts, foreign relations, judgments, property restitution, security, torts, and trusts. In addition, a code of criminal procedure and a model code of evidence have been promulgated. In conjunction with the National Conference of Commissioners of Uniform State Laws, a Uniform Commercial Code has been developed; it has been adopted, usually as amended, by many state legislatures.

Each Restatement begins with an introduction, describing the organization and purpose of the Institute, and an elaborate schematic table of contents showing the organization of the material. The treatment of this material closely resembles that of the Hornbook series of treatises. First, there is a boldface statement of principle (which may be more or less elaborately subdivided). This is the Restatement proper. Second, there is a comment for most sections. The comment is designed to explain the meaning of the boldface section and to limit its application. Third, there are illustrations of the various sections and subsections. These correspond to the footnote digests of cases supporting text statements in treatises. Although they do not include citations to cases, any law student will recognize many familiar cases described in the illustrations.

Also included in the Restatements Second are Reporter's Notes which cite cases and secondary authority useful to the searcher. The First Restatements, however, do not contain these Reporter's Notes. Finally, the Restatements Second include an Appendix, which acts as a citator to all written decisions citing the Restatements. The Restatements state only the "best rule" and cite no authority. The rule stated, however, has been found to be applicable in nearly 98 percent of the decided cases mentioning the Restatements since their adoption.

3. *Indexes*. Each Restatement has its own detailed index. There is also a General Index covering all Restatements. This combines the individual indexes in a single alphabetical arrangement and also contains many additional catchwords and cross-references. If the searcher lacks a citation to a specific Restatement topic and section, the combined Index should first be consulted. Although each Restatement has its own index, there is overlapping of subject matter between Restatements, all of which is caught in the combined Index.

4. *Keeping the Restatements up to date*. Although there is no regular supplementation, the Institute attempts to keep Restatements up-to-date. This is done in three ways. First, tentative drafts of proposed changes are circulated to the advisers. These drafts set forth proposed changes and the reasons for and against making them. Second, the Restatement of the Law, 1948 Supplement, published the text of changes adopted up to 1948. Third, most Restatements have been so thoroughly revised as to call for new editions called Restatements Second. Some of these Restatements Second have been revised and enlarged as well. Most changes have been made only to clarify language.

5. *Authority*. The authority of the Restatements is only persuasive; they have been highly persuasive, however. As of April, 1976 over 55,000 appellate decisions had cited the Restatements. Few courts which cite the Restatement explicitly reject the Restatement rule. It would seem that the Restatements are becoming accepted as the authoritative statement of the common law of the United States. On the other hand, many aspects of the law covered by the Restatements have not been covered in state decisions citing them, so that categorical statements should be made with great caution. Courts often fail to mention the Restatements in their decisions.

6. *Shepardizing*. In 1976, Shepard's Citations published Shepard's Restatement of the Law Citations, which notes all citations to American Law Institute Restatements since their inception. Federal citing cases reported in the three series of reports cover United States Supreme Court cases, the Federal Reporter, the Federal Supplement and the Federal Rules Decisions. State citing cases reported in the National Reporter System are covered as well. Finally, selected leading law reviews, the American Bar Association Journal and A.L.R. annotations citing Restatements are noted.

The Restatements are given coverage as well in more than a third of the state Shepard's Citations. For the states covered, this is the best means of completely tracing citations of cases commenting on the Restatements, even though considerably more information is given in the Restatement in the Courts. The state Shepard's which cover the Restatements also cite articles in law reviews published in the states covered, as well as those published in selected law reviews published in other states.

The Restatement in the Courts (which is published periodically and is not cumulated from one volume to the next) is arranged by Restatement — e.g., Agency, Trusts — and section. Citations are in the form of digests of decisions, as in a digest. The first volume in 1945 cited thousands of law review comments also, but these are omitted from the supplements. It should be noted that the 1948 publication is titled Restatement of the Law and gives textual changes up to that date. In addition, this publication contains the 1948 supplement to the Restatement in the Courts.

Thus far Restatements Second have been published for Agency, Conflict of Laws, Foreign Relations, Torts, Trusts, and Property (which has been only partially completed as of 1977). Except for Foreign Relations, these volumes each have Appendix volumes containing digests of cases and citations to law review articles relevant to each section. In addition, the publisher gives cross-references to West and A.L.R. digests. This last feature is not found in the Restatement in the Courts.

State annotations were undertaken by cooperative efforts of the various state bar associations and law reviews in a very ambitious program in conjunction with the Institute. Although annotations for one or more Restatements have been published for nearly all states, and the project is still alive, it has not been kept up very well.

English courts (both trial and appellate) have cited the Restatements, but such citation by English courts is rare.

7. *Glossary of terms defined in the Restatements*. A 68-page glossary of definitions included from all Restatements is printed in the Restatement in the Courts, Permanent Edition (1945), beginning at page 43.

20 | Legal Periodicals

§20.1. Function and authority.

"Today, periodical writing plays a leading part in the shaping of our law. While law reviews exert some influence over legislation and administration, their greatest impact in the formation of law is through the courts. Although objections to judicial reliance on legal periodicals and related sources have erupted in Congress and the press . . . such writing has generally been accepted now for several years as a central part of the judicial process. In 1941 Mr. Chief Justice Charles Evans Hughes characterized legal periodicals as the 'fourth estate' of the law. . . . The growth of legal writing has enlarged the knowledge available to the Court. When they are aware of it, the Justices are compelled to take notice of such writing if they are to base their opinions on the best available knowledge, This is true whether or not counsel in a case takes notice of such sources."[1]

Legal periodicals (especially the law school publications) can be of great assistance to the law student, particularly in the preparation of moot briefs and seminar papers. They often discuss in meticulous and scholarly detail aspects of the law not covered elsewhere. They generally provide these detailed analyses in advance of their publication in treatises.

The legal periodical is also a valuable aid to the practitioner and the foremost outlet of the legal research scholar. It is the most versatile of all the publications in a law library. It is flexible and represents many points of view. It discusses legal topics ranging from the elementary, through the eminently practical, to the most learned and

1. Newland, The Supreme Court and Legal Writings: Learned Journals as Vehicles of an Anti-Trust Lobby, 48 Geo. L.J. 105, 126, 142 (1959).

abstruse. New developments in the law are usually first discussed in legal periodicals and often only there. As a forum for the critical analysis of legal topics it is preeminent. It discusses the law as it was, as it is, as it is tending, and as it ought to be—with a thoroughness rarely found elsewhere.

The authority of legal periodicals is only persuasive. Although they are cited increasingly in courts, they are not mandatory at all. On the other hand, they certainly are persuasive as the "fourth estate of the law."

§20.2. Varieties.

Legal periodicals are published under many auspices and for many purposes. The principal varieties are mentioned below:

1. *Scholarly periodicals, including law school reviews.* Although periodicals of a thoroughly scholarly character (such as the Law Quarterly Review and the Modern Law Review) are independently published, the typical scholarly legal periodical in the United States is the law school review, sponsored by a law school and edited by a student board.

The law student is more likely to be interested in the law school review than in any other type of legal periodical. Such reviews serve as outlets for the scholarly and technically expert writings of teachers, practitioners and judges. The student work in them is closely supervised for quality. Typically such periodicals are divided into four parts.

a. *Leading articles.* About half the total space of any given law review issue is usually occupied by articles by law school teachers, practitioners and judges. These articles are likely to be exhaustive analyses of narrow topics and include full citations to authority. Such an exhaustive treatment of many of these topics is often not found elsewhere.

b. *Notes or Comments section.* Student writers contribute valuable notes and comments on the law. Although usually limited to eight or ten pages in length, some are much longer. Typical of their diverse subject matter are notes on such topics as entrapment, consequences of abstention by a federal court, expropriation of alien property, extraterritorial application of antitrust laws, and government officials' absolute privilege in libel and slander suits.

c. *Recent cases commented upon.* Five or six cases are usually selected from a reading of all advance sheets for a comment by a student writer in each issue of a review. The comments are valuable to the law student because they contain a fairly exhaustive treatment of a minute point of law and explain the meaning of particular cases.

The cases so treated have been indexed since 1917 in the Index to Legal Periodicals and can also be found in the Social Sciences Citation Index.

d. *Book reviews*. While book reviews are useful, the time lag between publication of the book and of the review is frequently so long as to impair their value to the law student.

e. *Special features of law school reviews*. Most law reviews emphasize to some extent the law of their own state or region. Some of these may also serve as an organ of the state bar association. Other law school reviews specialize in a particular aspect of the law. The Louisiana Law Review and the Tulane Law Review emphasize civil law in America. Other reviews, such as those of Notre Dame, St. John's University, and the Catholic University of America emphasize to a limited degree the canon law. Aviation law, tax law, criminal law and labor law are specialties of other law school reviews.

The intramural law school review is a variant which carries nothing but student work. This publication, which is becoming obsolete, is composed entirely of student notes and case comments. The intramural review is designed primarily as an outlet for the best work of students in legal bibliography and legal writing courses.

2. *Topical periodicals*. Several law schools now sponsor more than one law review. Generally, these additional reviews are devoted to a single area of the law. Duke University's Law and Contemporary Problems was the first of these topical law school reviews. Since its inception, the number of such periodicals has increased to more than thirty. In addition, some schools which sponsor only one law review have confined themselves to a single topic (e.g., the University of Louisville's Journal of Family Law).

Topical periodicals cover a wide range of topics. Those schools sponsoring more than one review tend to have a periodical devoted to international law. Other areas of law are well represented in topical periodicals: for example, jurisprudence, family law, business law, computers and law, taxation, civil rights and civil liberties, and constitutional law. These periodicals are especially important resource tools for those specializing in a single area of law.

3. *Professional law reviews*. Some of the best legal periodicals are published by associations of scholarly specialists. For law teachers there are the Journal of Legal Education and the Journal of the Society of Public Teachers of Law. Bar association journals, though usually not of a particularly scholarly character, are important; several are indexed in the Index to legal Periodicals. Various sections of the American Bar Association, such as the section of administrative law, the section of labor law, the section of public utility law, publish periodicals that deal with their special subject matter. Important to practitioners of administrative law are journals like the Journal of the Patent Office Society and the I.C.C. Practitioners' Journal.

4. *Practice periodicals and legal newspapers*. The main function of practice periodicals is to keep practitioners abreast of the legal business transacted in their areas. Commonly these periodicals print court dockets and some law reports of special local interest. Some legal newspapers are designated as the official organs for courts in their areas. Examples of local legal newspapers are the New York Law Journal, Washington (D.C.) Law Reporter, and the Chicago Law Bulletin. Your law school librarian will tell you whether such a legal newspaper is published for your area. In 1978, the National Law Journal and the Law Times started publication as legal newspapers intended for a national audience.

5. *United States Law Week*.[2] The law student and practitioner should, by all means, be familiar with this publication, which has been mentioned in connection with statutes and Supreme Court slip decisions.

a. *Sections of the United States Law Week*. The U.S. Law Week is a loose-leaf (or, rather, a loose-pamphlet) periodical, consisting of an unnumbered federal statutes section and four numbered sections. As stated by the publisher: "The *statute section* is issued only as laws of general interest or importance are passed by Congress." Numbered Section 1, entitled Summary and Analysis, is a four-page news commentary (issued weekly) on developments in law. Section 2 publishes digests and abridgments of selected new federal and state court decisions and of federal agency rulings. Section 3 contains the journal of proceedings of the Supreme Court, summary orders of the Court, cases docketed and a summary of cases recently filed, calendar of hearings scheduled, and special articles on the Supreme Court's work. Section 4 contains the full text of all Supreme Court opinions, which is supplemented by digest headnotes and presented with a cumulative table of opinions for the current term of the Court.

b. *Indexes*. The U.S. Law Week has two indexes. One covers the general developments volume containing statutory section and Section 2. This index cumulates every two months and concludes with a final index issued at the end of each volume. Another index covers Supreme Court Sections 3 and 4. It is issued periodically throughout the term; a final index at the end of the current term covers all developments within the term. The index is by subject, docket number, case name, legislative acts and court rules, patents and trademarks.

§20.3. Abridgments of legal periodical articles.

The Law Review Digest[3] is a bimonthly periodical presenting quite long abstracts of articles from a wide variety of legal periodicals, with

2. Washington, D.C., Sept. 5, 1933 to date.
3. St. Paul, Minn., The Barrister's Press, v. 1– , 1950– .

emphasis on the practical aspects of the practice of law. In addition, there is a subject-matter index covering many articles not digested. An annual index cumulates the bimonthly subject indexes.

There are a number of periodicals abridging articles on special subjects. Commerce Clearing House publishes *Federal Tax Articles*, which is arranged by International Revenue Code section numbers in order to correspond with the CCH Standard Federal Tax Reporter.

These abridgments of periodical articles are helpful resource tools to the busy practitioner having no immediate access to the articles themselves. Because footnotes and significant textual material are often omitted in such condensations, it is advisable to consult the original article whenever possible.

§20.4. Indexes to legal periodicals.

Nearly all legal periodicals publish indexes for each of their volumes. In addition, cumulative indexes for various periods are usually published. Another type of index covers a great many periodicals in a single subject, author, and title alphabet. Because of the great expense involved in compiling and printing, the multiperiodical index is commonly less full than the individual periodical indexes mentioned above or the descriptive-word indexes to the case digests and encyclopedias.

1. *Jones-Chipman Index to Periodical Literature*.[4] The first three volumes of this index cover the period preceding the start of the Index to Legal Periodicals in 1908 and thus are indispensable for their period. The last three are little used in libraries possessing the Index to Legal Periodicals, which is considerably more inclusive in its periodical coverage and is better kept up-to-date. The Jones-Chipman Index is a subject and author index to the principal English language legal periodicals from 1803 to 1937. The arrangement of subject entries is alphabetical by rather large topics. Few notes or case comments and no book reviews are indexed.

2. *Index to Legal Periodicals*.[5] This is the most inclusive index to English language legal periodicals from 1908 to date. More than 375 of the principal American, British and British Commonwealth periodicals, many bar association publications, and some judicial council reports are indexed. Entries are arranged alphabetically by subject under a scheme based (by permission of the West Publishing Company) upon the copyrighted American Digest System scheme.

The indexing policy has varied somewhat over the years. Present policy requires that articles be at least five ordinary pages or two folio

4. Various imprints, 1888–1939, 6 vols.
5. New York, N.Y., H. W. Wilson Co., 1908 to date.

pages in length; case notes, bibliographies, biographies, book reviews and notes on legislation must be at least two ordinary pages or one folio page long in order to be included. Starting with volume 17, references are made to the pages on which the particular article begins and ends. Annual surveys of law (except for national surveys) within a jurisdiction are indexed under the name of the jurisdiction. Case notes of insufficient length to be noted as articles are included at the end of each subject heading under the subheading of "Cases."

Searching through the numerous units of the Index to Legal Periodicals may be laborious and often requires considerable ingenuity. Since not more than two or three subject entries are made for an article (because of the printing expense involved), indexing is not as detailed as it should be. If the searcher knows that a certain article or type of article is published in a given law review, the separate indexes for that law review will provide considerably more detailed indexing than the Index to Legal Periodicals.

The Index to Legal Periodicals is divided into (1) subject and author indexes, (2) book review indexes, and (3) beginning in 1917, case indexes. Prior to September 1961, there were separate subject and author indexes. As of that date they were combined in a single alphabetical index. The names of student authors are omitted (i.e., signatures to case comments). In the case table, cases commented upon in leading articles, notes and case comments are listed alphabetically by the plaintiff's last name. In addition, as of October 1963, many pertinent cases commented upon are cumulated at the end of each subject heading. See the cases listed under "Eavesdropping" in Exhibit 64. Note that the titles of case comments are not given. Thus, the searcher who is interested in only one aspect of a case must search through all listed case comments in order to discover those few which may be pertinent to his or her inquiry. Book reviews have not been indexed by the reviewer's name since 1961; they are currently indexed instead by the surname of the author of the book being reviewed. See Exhibit 65.

The Index to Legal Periodicals cumulated annually through 1925. Beginning with 1926, it has cumulated both annually and triennially. From year to year, the frequency of publication has varied. Presently, a new unbound index is published every month except September. A cumulative index published quarterly reduces the number of indexes a searcher must examine in order to find the most recent publications on a given topic.

3. *Index to Periodical Articles Related to Law.*[6] This index, published quarterly (January to October), covers selected material of legal interest from journals not included in the Index to Legal Period-

6. Dobbs Ferry, N.Y., Glanville Publications, Inc., 1958 to date.

SUBJECT AND AUTHOR INDEX 43

On health care as a legal right: an exploration of legal and moral grounds. W. T. Blackstone. Philosophical justifications, political activity, and adequate health care. A. Soble. More on the right to health care. W. T. Blackstone. Ga L Rev 10:391-418 Wint '76, 11:525-44 Spr '77

Oregon's partial responsibility defense: disposition of the defendant and burden of proof. Willamette L J 13:347-64 Spr '77

Peremptory challenges of judges in the Alaska courts. UCLA-Alaska L Rev 6:269-300 Spr '77

Post judgment garnishment without notice and a hearing is constitutional. Mercer L Rev 28:997-1002 Summ '77

Pretrial release in California: proposed reforms of an unfair system. Pacific L J 8:841-64 Jl '77

Prisoners have no right to procedural due process in interinstitution transfers. Neb L Rev 56:753-64 '77

Problematic definitions of property in multistate death taxation. Harv L Rev 90:1656-81 Je '77

Procedural and substantive rights of parents in child dependency hearings. Gonzaga L Rev 12:505-17 Spr '77

Procedural due process in prisoners' rights: the state giveth and the state taketh away. BU L Rev 57:387-408 Mr '77

Prosecutor's duty to disclose after United States v. Agurs (96 Sup Ct 2392) U Ill L F 1977:690-718 '77

Public officers' personal liability for money damages. M. I. Sikora, jr. Mass L Q 62:31-9 Spr '77

Real property attachment—property or economic interest? Wash L Rev 52:767-89 Jl '77

Restatement of the Roth-Fuentes analysis of procedural due process. W. H. Lawrence. Ga L Rev 11:477-524 Spr '77

Right to defend pro se—Faretta v. California (95 Sup Ct 2525): due process and beyond. Tulsa L J 11:365-96 '76

S.J.C. [S.J.C., Matter of (Tex) 533 S W 2d 746] revisited: the standard of proof in juvenile cases. Baylor L Rev 29:343-56 Spr '77

Standard of proof in involuntary civil commitment proceedings. D. Share. Det Coll L Rev 1977:209-58 Summ '77

Standards of judicial review under the equal protection and due process clauses. S. H. Bice. So Calif L Rev 50:689-718 My '77

Substituted service of process on foreign corporations in Oklahoma: notice and due process. Tulsa L J 12:181-93 '76

Tax sales, due process and severed mineral interests in Oklahoma. Tulsa L J 11:615-26 '76

Tenure rights in contractual and constitutional context. R. C. Brown. J L & Educ 6:279-318 Jl '77

Title IX sex discrimination regulations: private colleges and academic freedom. Urban L Ann 13:107-37 '77

Turner v. General Motors Corp [(Mich) 246 N W 2d 631]: workers' disability compensation—payment of benefits pending final determination on appeal. Det Coll L Rev 1977:415-28 Summ '77

Valentine v. Gray (410 F Supp 1394): incarceration and the right to free enterprise. New England J Prison L 3:549-87 Spr '77

DUNN, Christopher
Govt contracts (B)

DUNNE, Stephen L.
Antitrust law (O)
Legislation—Or (O)

DUPLANTIER, Adrian
Biog (Hubert)

DURAND, Richard M.
Judicial stat (I)
Juries (I)

DURESS

Brainwashing as a defense to criminal liability: Patty Hearst (U.S. v. Hearst, Cr. 74-364-OJC) revisited. D. T. Lunde, T. E. Wilson. Crim L Bull 13:341-82 S-O '77

Duress: an affirmative defense to criminal prosecution. R. L. Vogel. JAG J 29:85-110 Fall '76

DUVAL, Benjamin S., Jr
Education (E)
Right of privacy (E)
Infants (E)

DWYER, Johanna T.
Consumer protect (I)
Food law (A)

DWYER, John L.
Contracts (I)
Domestic relat (I)
Implied trusts (I)

EASEMENTS

Customary and expansible easements: applicability of the rule against perpetuities. Ore L Rev 56:518-33 '77

Perdurable estates. J. D. A. Brooke-Taylor. Convey 41:107-25 Mr-Ap '77

Use of extrinsic evidence to interpret real property conveyances: a suggested limitation. Calif L Rev 65:897-919 Jl '77

See also
Rights of way

EAVESDROPPING

Foreign security surveillance—balancing executive power and the fourth amendment. Fordham L Rev 45:1179-201 Ap '77

Cases

Berlin Democratic Club v. Rumsfeld, 410 F Supp 144
Harv Int L J 18:192-5 Wint '77

ECCLESIASTICAL law

Church and state. Cambrian L Rev 7:11-30 '76

Support orders, church courts, and the rule of *filius nullius*: a reassessment of the common law. R. H. Helmholz. Va L Rev 63:431-48 Ap '77

See also
Churches

Exhibit 64

icals or the Index to Foreign Periodicals and Collections of Essays. Unlike the Index to Legal Periodicals, no page length requirements must be met for inclusion in this index. Number 4 of each volume is cumulative for the year. There is a ten-year cumulative volume for 1958 through 1968 and a five-year cumulative volume for 1969 through 1973. In the future, there will be cumulative volumes every five years. Some periodicals indexed are legal newspapers; others are bar association publications, Most, however, are periodicals in the fields of economics, sociology, and political science, which publish occasional articles relating to law. This index fills a gap in legal periodical indexes and can function as an important research tool in legal research.

4. *Index to Foreign Legal Periodicals and Collections of Essays.*[7]

7. London, Institute of Advanced Legal Studies, University of London, Feb. 1960 to date.

156 INDEX TO LEGAL PERIODICALS

Duffy, J. Healers: the rise of the medical establishment. 1976
ABA J 63:1254+ S '77. J. R. Sakmyster
Dunne, G. T. Hugo Black and the judicial revolution. 1977
Harv L Rev 90:1733-45 Je '77. L. B. Boudin

Edwards, R. G. RICS handbook of community land and development taxation,
Pt2: Development taxation. 1976
BTR 1977:124-7 '77. P. Hobbs
Ehrlichman, J. Company. 1976
ABA J 63:1248+ S '77. R. E. Willy
Emanuelli, C. Les moyens de prevention et de sanction en cas d'action illicite contre l'aviation civile internationale. 1974
DePaul L Rev 25:973-6 Summ '76. R. A. Friedlander
European association for legal and fiscal studies. Branches and subsidiaries in the European Common market: legal and tax aspects. 2d ed. n.d.
L Q Rev 93:472-4 Jl '77. I. S. Stephenson

Fairest, P. B. Mortgages. 1975
Irish Jur 10:197-9 Summ & Wint '75. P. Wylie
Federalist; ed. by J. E. Cooke. 1961
Yale L J 86:1273-85 My '77. M. Diamond
Yale L J 86:1286-96 My '77. J. N. Shklar
Feeney, T. G. Canadian law of wills: probate. 1976
U W O L Rev 15:259-63 '76. A. H. Oosterhoff
Fitzmaurice, J. Party groups in the European parliament. 1975
Brooklyn J Int'l L 3:318-23 Spr '77. I. E. Druker
Forer, L. G. Death of the law. 1975
ABA J 63:1080+ Ag '77. H. J. Berman
Penn BA Q 48:277-80 Ap '77. L. G. Forer
Frankfurter, F. From the diaries of Felix Frankfurter, with biographical essays and notes; by J. P. Lash. 1975
Am J Legal Hist 21:80-3 Ja '77. S. Levinson
Tulsa L J 11:471-5 '76. R. A. Woolery
Friedland, M. L. Access to the law. 1975
Sask L Rev 41:211-13 '76-'77
Friedland, M. L. ed. Courts and trials: a multidisciplinary approach. 1975
Sask L Rev 40:311-14 '75-'76
Friedman, L. M. Legal system: a social science perspective. 1975
Am Bus L J 14:275-7 Fall '76. G. W. Spiro
Friendly, F. W. Good guys, the bad guys and the first amendment: free speech vs. fairness in broadcasting. 1976
BU L Rev 57:419-27 Mr '77. G. Rahdert

Graglia, L. A. Disaster by decree: the Supreme Court decisions on race and the schools. 1976
Ark L Rev 30:571-6 Wint '77. R. E. Knowlton
Houston L Rev 14:955-62 My '77. J. W. Ely, jr
Ohio S L J 38:239-43 '77. M. J. Perry
U Det J Urb L 54:651-65 Wint '77. R. E. Boltz
U Det J Urb L 54:667-71 Wint '77. L. D. Beer
Great Britain. Committee on the future of broadcasting. Report (Cmnd. 6753, 1977)
Modern L Rev 40:460-6 Jl '77. C. Munro and G. R. Sullivan
Great Britain. Law commission. Report on matrimonial proceedings in magistrates courts. 1976
Modern L Rev 40:450-60 Jl '77. D. Bradley
Green, L. C. Law and society. 1975
Sask L Rev 41:197-200 '76-'77. W. H. McConnell
U W O L Rev 15:245-51 '76. R. Martin
Grosman, B. Police command. 1975
Sask L Rev 40:303-6 '75-'76. J. F. Klein
Sask L Rev 40:306-8 '75-'76
Gukiina, P. M. Uganda: a case study in African political development. 1972
Harv Int L J 18:215-17 Wint '77. D. Goldstein

Hahlo, H. R. South African law of husband and wife. 1975
Irish Jur 10:379-81 Summ & Wint '75. P. T. Horgan
Hallman, R. M. Towards an environmentally sound law of the sea. 1974
Ocean Devel & Int L 4:269-96 '77. M. Waldichuk
Hamilton, R. W. Cases on corporations—including partnerships and limited partnerships. 1976
Ky L J 65:764-7 '76-'77. J. B. McAdams
Hardman, J. P. Development land tax. n.d.
BTR 1977:124-7 '77. P. Hobbs
Hargrove, J. L. ed. Who protects the ocean? 1975
Ocean Devel & Int L 4:269-96 '77. M. Waldichuk
Harrington, M. Twilight of capitalism. 1976
Hofstra L Rev 5:957-77 Summ '77. E. M. Abramson
Hay, D. and others. Albion's fatal tree: crime and society in eighteenth-century England. 1975
Am J Legal Hist 21:179-84 Ap '77. R. T. Vann
Heller, P. B. Handbook of federal bank holding company law. 1976
Bus Law 32:1953-4 Jl '77. F. Solomon
Helmer, J. Drugs and minority oppression. 1975
Am J Crim L 4:245-7 '75-'76. S. Udell

Exhibit 65

This quarterly index is the product of the Institute of Advanced Legal Studies of the University of London and of the American Association of Law Libraries. The fourth quarterly issue of each year cumulates the other three into an annual volume. In addition three-year cumulative volumes are published. Articles of at least four pages in length are indexed; book reviews are indexed if they are two and one-half or more pages in length. Cases are not indexed. Indexes include a subject index, an author index, a geographical index and a book reviewers' index. About 360 different periodicals are indexed. The entries are in the language of the periodical indexed, but languages not using the Roman alphabet are transliterated into that alphabet.

Those interested in the Index to Foreign Legal Periodicals and Collections of Essays should consult Blaustein, Manual on Foreign Legal Periodicals and Their Index.[8]

5. *Index to Canadian Legal Periodical Literature.*[9] Those interested in Canadian legal periodicals may prefer this index over the Index to Legal Periodicals. Unlike the Index to Legal Periodicals, it indexes all Canadian legal periodicals and also includes articles of legal interest from other Canadian sources. It also establishes no page length requirements for inclusion.

8. Dobbs Ferry, N.Y., Oceana Publications, 1962.
9. Montreal, Index to Canadian Legal Periodical Literature, 1961 to date.

New indexes are issued every two months and are cumulated annually into a bound index. Every ten years these annual indexes are cumulated. The Index to Canadian Periodical Literature contains separate subject and author indexes as well as a book review index and a table of cases.

6. *Finding the most recent articles.* Frequently there is a delay of more than a month between the time of publication of an article and its appearance in an index. Those wishing to discover the most recent articles pertinent to their problem may consult three sources. The Current Index to Legal Periodicals, published by the University of Washington Law Library and Law Review, issues every week an index covering recent legal publications. Like the Index to Legal Periodicals, the index is arranged alphabetically by subject matter. Thus a searcher who is researching a particular topic can quickly discover whether any pertinent articles have been recently published. A list of periodicals indexed in each issue is given on the first page of the index.

Contents of Current Legal Periodicals[10] does not index recent periodicals by topic. Instead, the table of contents page of each recent periodical is reproduced. At the beginning of each month's issue, the publishers provide a short list of areas of law in which articles have been published recently. The searcher is then referred to the publications which have included articles within each area of law.

The National Law Journal, mentioned in §20.2 above, also has a Weekly Index to Legal Literature as one of its regular features. The index, however, does not claim to be comprehensive and includes articles in particular subject areas coming to the attention of the compiler each week and deemed to be worth reading.

7. *Other legal periodical indexes.* The Index to Federal Tax Articles[11] is a multidisciplinary index which includes accounting and economic journals in addition to legal periodicals. It consists of three volumes (indexing all tax articles from 1913 through mid-1974 by topic and also by author) and a supplement (which includes all articles from mid-1974 to date). This index is an obviously significant research tool for the tax lawyer.

The Annual Legal Bibliography[12] contains a selected list of books and articles received annually by the Harvard Law School Library. Each annual issue is divided into four types of law: common-law jurisdictions, civil law and other jurisdictions, private international law, and public international law. These types of law are subdivided into various areas of law (such as jurisprudence, family law, commercial law, etc.) Thus, a searcher can locate quickly an abundance of

10. Wilmington, Del., Corporation Service Company Publication.
11. Boston, Mass., Warren, Gorham & Lamont, Inc., 1975 to date.
12. Cambridge, Mass., Harvard University Printing Office, 1961 to date.

legal literature on a wide range of topics. Every month (except July, August and September) the Current Legal Bibliography[13] lists new books and articles received by the Harvard Law School Library.

§20.5. Approach to the law through legal periodicals.

Finding an article squarely in point with your needs is usually more difficult than finding cases or statutes, because there are relatively few of the former compared to the number of the latter. The article's coverage is apt to be considerably broader in scope than the searcher's specific problem. Thus the searcher must locate articles which look promising and then read them thoroughly for statements and authorities helpful to his or her particular question. Fortunately, this sifting process is simplified somewhat by the authors' self-indexing techniques once the searcher has found pertinent articles.

Most leading articles are divided and subdivided into small units containing separate subject captions. Commonly the first division of an article is the introduction, which states the problem and gives an historical and perhaps bibliographical summary of the topic. Legal writers are generally meticulous in giving credit to other writers for material used or suggested. Thus the finding of one article reasonably in point frequently leads through its footnotes to the best of the earlier literature. Although this is usually true throughout the whole article, it is especially true at the beginning of an article (where citation to this earlier literature is likely to be collected). When the topic discussed is one upon which comparatively little has been written, especially where a new legal-technological development is involved, this can be a very useful technique. See, for example, Estep, Radiation Injuries and Statistics: The Need for a New Approach to Injury Litigation, 59 Mich. L. Rev. 259 (1960), which cites books, articles, hearings and other documents from a wide variety of legal and non-legal sources.

Because there is an increasing number of specialized periodicals, students are advised to consult their law librarian before undertaking a periodical literature search. The law librarian can familiarize the student with the periodical resources available and the techniques for utilizing them.

1. *Subject indexes*. Unless the searcher already has a direct citation to an article, the search normally begins with a periodical index, as described above. For most research topics, the first index explored will be the Index to Legal Periodicals. Before delving into the corpus of the Index to Legal Periodicals, it is helpful to check the "List of

13. Cambridge, Mass., Harvard University Printing Office.

SUBJECT AND AUTHOR INDEX 143

WILLSEY, Burke W.
Inc tax: deductions—US (C)
Oil and gas (C)
Taxation—US (C)

WILSON, Carol L.
Estate planning (W)
Inherit taxes (W)
Probate law and prac (W)
Trusts and trustees (W)

WILSON, David A.
Forests and forestry (F)
Taxation—Can (F)
Taxation—State (F)

WILSON, James A.
Economics (E)
Fishing: int law (S)
Legislation—US (S)

WILSON, Lawrence C.
Juvenile cts (J)
Legislation—Can (J)

WILSON, Paul E.
Biog (Sutton)

WILSON, Robert F.
Inc tax: deductions—US (T)
Inc tax: partnerships—US (T)
Oil and gas (T)

WILSON, Stephen V.
Crim law (E)
Docs and recs (O)
Fed rules crim proc (O)
Grand jury (O)
Search and seizure (O)
Self-incrimination (O)
Taxation: enforcement—US (O)

WILSON, Thomas A.
Budgets (R)
Economics (R)

WILSON, Thomas E.
Crim responsibility (B)
Duress (B)
Psychiatry (B)
Sentencing (B)

WINNER, Russ
High seas (S)
Int confs (S)
Science (S)
Sovereignty (S)
Treaties (S)

WIRE tapping. See Eavesdropping

WISCONSIN
Term of the Wisconsin supreme court (August

WITTICK, J. J.
Food law (C)

WITTMAN, Donald
Accidents (P)
Economics (P)
Insurance (P)
Penology (P)

WOLKINSON, Benjamin W.
Adm proc—Mich (F)
Ind arb (F)
Pub officials (F)

WOMEN
'Black shift' phenomenon in criminal justice. S. N. Adams. J System J 2:185-94 Wint '76
ERA's last mile: women's work. P. Beyea. Civil Liberties Rev 4:45-9 Jl/Ag '77
Equal rights for women: the role of affirmative action. Sw U L Rev 9:177-215 '77
Impact of legal education on the beliefs, attitudes and values of law students. G. J. Rathjen. Tenn L Rev 44:85-118 Fall '76
Legal position of Irishwomen in the later middle ages. K. Simms. Irish Jur 10:96-111 Summ & Wint '75
Preliminary survey of action to further human rights in the Asian region specifically by the United Nations through its programme of advisory services in the field of human rights. Aust Yearbook Int L 1970/73:51-67 '75
See also
Discrimination: sex
Married women

WOOD, Fred B.
Adm law—US (L)
Automation (L)
Economics (L)
Freedom of inf (L)
Natural resources (L)

WOOD, Norman J.
Discrimintaion: age (M)
Equal protect (M)

WOODLIFFE, J. C.
Continental shelf (I)
Oil and gas (I)
Treaties (I)

WORKMEN'S compensation
Automobile insurance—other insurance clauses which do not purport to reduce uninsured motorist coverage below the statutory minimum are valid, and proceeds from such coverage are payable to widow as administrator of estate without a reduction for the workmen's compensation benefits received by the widow as a dependent beneficiary. Drake L Rev 25: 915-22 '76
Constitutional law—records—workmen's compensation claims must be disclosed under the Texas open records act, but certain data may

Exhibit 66

Subject Headings." See Exhibit 66. If your topic is not given a separate heading, find the headings most pertinent to your topic. Often the publisher will provide helpful cross-reference. See "wire tapping" under Exhibit 66. Because few articles are given more than two subject headings, the articles are listed alphabetically by title rather than being broken down systematically into subtopics. Thus the searcher may have to scan several pages of listings in an effort to locate pertinent titles. An effort has been made to invert titles to the first significant word so that the search is shortened. This cannot be relied upon to pinpoint the subject matter, however; a thorough search requires going down the entire list of titles. Occasionally the title of the article may not reveal the exact subject matter discussed. The searcher must examine such articles to determine whether the desired topic is covered.

In the Index to Legal Periodicals, some large topics such as Constitutional Law have been broken down geographically. For the most part, however, you must follow the cross-references from the large topic to smaller subdivisions. For example, "Evidence: See also

Admissibility of Evidence, Admissions, Burden of proof, Parol evidence, Witnesses, etc." But it is still a laborious task to sift all the titles for one which might be in point. For example, in the 1961–1964 triennial cumulation, there are five pages of citations to articles on a wide variety of subtopics related to patents. Although the rewards of periodical research are often most valuable, they are usually to be earned only through diligence and patience.

As mentioned above, the Index to Legal Periodicals may not index many articles in which you are interested. You therefore will want to examine the Index to Periodical Articles Related to Law and the Social Sciences Citation Index. If there is an index covering the area of law in which you are interested (such as foreign law or tax law), you should consult this index as well. Your topic may have nonlegal aspects which you wish to pursue. If so, you can utilize nonlegal indexes fruitfully. Perhaps the best known of these indexes is the Readers' Guide to Periodical Literature,[14] which indexes many popular and scholarly periodicals. Also useful are the Social Sciences Index[15] and the Humanities Index,[16] which are published quarterly and cumulated annually into bound volumes. Prior to April 1974, these indexes were combined as the Social Sciences and Humanities Index.[17] Finally, you check for recent legal articles in point by utilizing the Current Index to Legal Periodicals, the Contents of Current Legal Periodicals, and the National Law Journal Weekly Index.

2. *Author indexes*. The Index to Legal Periodicals contained separate subject and author indexes prior to the 1961–1964 triennial cumulation; these two types of index entries have been combined since 1961 in a single index. Both before and after the combination of these index entries, the citation has been to the main subject heading under which the authors' articles are indexed. In Exhibit 64, for example, four writings of Lawrence Ebb are indexed. We can find the titles and citations of these publications by referring to the specified subject heading and looking for the title under the letter given. Thus, for example, we discover that he has written an article entitled "Transfers of foreign technology in Latin America," which is indexed under Industrial property, Latin America, and Technology.

3. *Shepard's Citations*. Most state Shepard's Citations cite periodical articles or case comments on particular cases. Earlier practice, however, required that the articles appear in legal periodicals published in the state in which the case was decided. A latter expansion of this purely local legal periodical coverage has resulted in listing

14. New York, N.Y., H. W. Wilson Co., 1900 to date.
15. New York, N.Y., H. W. Wilson Co., April 1974 to date.
16. New York, N.Y., H. W. Wilson Co., April 1974 to date.
17. New York, N.Y., H. W. Wilson Co., 1907 to March 1974. Prior to 1965 this was known as the International Index to Periodicals.

case citations also in the American Bar Association Journal and in nineteen outstanding law reviews from various parts of the country. Federal law citations in the selected law reviews are now covered in Shepard's federal law citations. No similar coverage is found in Shepard's Reporter Citations. But now, for example, Shepard's Pennsylvania Citations show that 387 Pa. 548 was commented upon not only in the University of Pittsburgh Law Review in its own state but also in the Harvard and Virginia Law Reviews as well.

4. *Shepard's Law Review Citations.* In order to show where articles in legal periodicals have been cited in other law review articles or court decisions, Shepard's Citations has published its Shepard's Law Review Citations. This publication presently covers more than seventy law reviews and legal periodicals. The coverage includes all articles written in these periodicals since 1947 and cited in later articles from 1957 to date or in state and federal decisions. Volumes are kept up to date with cumulative supplements.

5. The Social Sciences Citation Index, discussed in §18.20, should also be consulted for citations to articles or books, whenever published, cited in covered publications from 1969 to date.

6. *Table of cases.* A table of cases approach is available through the Jones-Chipman Index, volume 3, page 536, covering 1898 through 1907. It is also available through case tables in the Index to Legal Periodicals from 1917 to date. The individual law reviews index cases commented upon from their first volumes to date. The cases listed are usually only those discussed in individual case comments. But if a case is discussed at length in a leading article or note at a later date, that case is also listed regardless of the date of decision. The Social Sciences Citation Index also indexes case notes and citations to them alphabetically under the plaintiff's name in the corporate author index and under the journal volume and page number in the anonymous author index.

Law students also often find these case comments useful in providing an understanding of cases in casebooks or ones cited by their instructors for outside reading. An important case may be discussed by as many as thirty-five different law reviews.

7. *References from treatises, encyclopedias and annotations.* Legal periodicals are frequently cited in these research materials, especially in footnotes. Reference to the cited legal periodical can often illuminate the thinking of the citer and thus provide the reader with a better understanding of the subject matter.

21 Dictionaries; Words and Phrases; Maxims

§21.1. Function and value of law dictionaries.

Law is a science requiring the precise use of words. The law dictionary is, therefore, indispensable. This is particularly true for beginning law students, who are confronted not only by a relatively new vocabulary but also by unexpected requirements of semantic precision. They cannot afford to be mistaken or hazy as to the exact meaning of legal terminology. Roscoe Pound has written:

> My first advice to the beginner in the study of law has always been to buy a good law dictionary and turn to it constantly. . . . The sure way of acquiring an enduring grasp upon legal terminology is to look up every word as it is encountered in the student's reading, get its meaning concretely in view of the context, and keep up this process until there is an assured conviction that it is no longer necessary.[1]

While unabridged general English language dictionaries define legal words of art, they do not do so with the detail and precision of a good law dictionary. They seldom cite authority for their definitions as frequently as law dictionaries. The law dictionary defines and illustrates the meaning of words, terms, and phrases which are legal words of art or have legal significance. Most of these are English; because the early language of the law was Latin and Law French,

1. Foreword to Ballentine, Law Dictionary with Pronunciations. 3d ed., Rochester, N.Y., Lawyers Co-operative Publishing Co., 1969.

many words from these languages also are defined. Many modern French and Spanish terms are plentiful in the law, too, as well as canon law terms. Most dictionaries cite or quote authority for their definitions; law dictionaries probably do so more than any other, however.

§21.2. Authority.

The law dictionary is not authority; the cases or other sources that it cites may be. On the other hand, to some extent the dictionary may serve as a case-finder through its citation of authority. Thus, the use of legal dictionaries can result in that snowballing process in legal research by which a single case in point so often leads to all similar cases. The "words and phrases" type of dictionary quotes or paraphrases the actual language of the courts in defining words or terms when the meaning of these words is significant in a decision.

§21.3. Scope.

Law dictionaries vary in size and scope from the small pocket glossary or synonym dictionary to those which are almost encyclopedic in their discussion of the law and citation to authority. These latter define more words and cite more authority than any other type of law dictionary. Not surprisingly, they are the kind most commonly consulted by student and lawyer alike.

Maxims, beloved of the old-time lawyer and still encountered, are defined by most law dictionaries and legal encyclopedias. Generally these are found either in special tables or in regular alphabetical order throughout the respective works. Legal encyclopedias serve a dictionary function, as noted in Chapter 17. Tables in most law dictionaries list common abbreviations, English regnal years, mortality and interest tables, etc.

§21.4. Some United States law dictionaries described.

1. *Bouvier's Law Dictionary and Concise Encyclopedia.*[2] At one time this was the best known of all American law dictionaries, but it is now outdated and seldom used. It was first published in 1839. In growing from a dictionary into a small encyclopedia, it became so large that it was somewhat inconvenient to use as a dictionary and too small to serve as a current encyclopedia.

2. 3d revision (8th ed.), Kansas City, Mo., Vernon Law Book Co., 1914, 3 vols.

2. *Ballentine*[3] *and Black*.[4] These are probably the most used American law dictionaries and are semiencyclopedic in scope. Their makeup and functions are those described above and require no additional description here. Both define words, phrases, and maxims with citations to authority and variorum definitions. Law school libraries commonly have one or both of them freely available for consultation.

3. *American Law Institute Restatement Glossary*. This is not a general legal dictionary but instead a glossary of terms defined in the Restatements. It is printed in the Restatement in the Courts, Permanent Edition (1945), beginning on page 43. For a complete description of this glossary, see §19.2.

4. *Words and phrases dictionaries*. Definitions in this type of dictionary are taken from judicial opinions in which the word or phrase is defined by the courts. Sometimes the language is quoted verbatim, but usually it is paraphrased by the compiler. It can be a very useful approach to the law when the meaning of a word or phrase is important. The words and phrases approach is frequently an effective starting point in the search for cases. In effect, the dictionary of this type is a digest of words instead of points of law. See Exhibit 67.

An example is Words and Phrases.[5] This work is kept up to date both by annual cumulative pocket supplements and by the various reporter advance sheets from which the supplements are compiled. Each advance sheet has its own table of words and phrases. Although the reporter bound volumes and reporter digests (but not the American Digest System) also have a table of words and phrases, the reporter and digest tables only list the words without defining them. These words are defined in the headnotes and in the opinions on the pages referred to in the tables in the advance sheets and bound volumes of the reporters.

5. *Dictionary function of legal encyclopedias*. This function is described in §§17.6 and 17.8.

§21.5. British law dictionaries.

1. *Value*. Although our common law and many of our statutes stem from the English tradition, the terminology of British law is often different. For that reason an English law dictionary is a useful adjunct to law study. The semiencyclopedic Jowitt's Dictionary of

3. Law Dictionary with Pronunciations. 3d ed., Rochester, N.Y., Lawyers Co-operative Publishing Co., 1969.
4. Black's Law Dictionary . . . with Guide to Pronunciation. 4th ed., rev., St. Paul, Minn., West Publishing Co., 1968.
5. Permanent edition. St. Paul, Minn., West Publishing Co., 1940–1952. 46 vols. and recompiled vols. See Exhibit 63.

PARALLEL

Parallel or nearly so—Cont'd

theory that the quoted word required that transmission line be equidistant from gas pipe line in its entire course. Valente v. Atlantic City Elec. Co., 101 A.2d 106, 108, 109, 28 N.J.Super. 476.

Railroads

The term "parallel and competing roads," within the meaning of Const.Ky.1891, § 201, prohibiting the consolidation of a railroad with a parallel or competing road, applies to two roads which connect two important cities, and are natural competitors for the traffic between such cities. Louisville & N. R. Co. v. Commonwealth of Kentucky, 16 S.Ct. 714, 719, 161 U.S. 677, 40 L.Ed. 849.

The term "parallel line," in the clause of the Constitution forbidding any railroad corporation to in any way control any other corporation having in its control a parallel or competing line, is not limited in its operation to a railroad completely constructed, but includes a projected road surveyed, laid out, and in the process of construction. Pennsylvania R. Co. v. Commonwealth, Pa., 7 A. 368, 373.

"Parallel railroads," as used in Const. art. 15, § 6, providing that no railroad corporation shall consolidate with any other railroad corporation owning or having under its control a parallel or competing line, etc., means railroads running in one general direction, traversing the same section of country, and running within a few miles of one another throughout their respective routes, and does not include exact parallelism. State v. Montana R. Co., 53 P. 623, 627, 21 Mont. 221, 45 L.R.A. 271.

Exhibit 67

English Law[6] has displaced Wharton's Law Lexicon[7] as the most useful for current purposes. It is especially helpful in the United States for its definitions of medieval legal terms (particularly those from several foreign languages which found their way into English legal usage) and its descriptions of statutes, old courts, and the functions of various officials.

2. *English words and phrases dictionaries*. Stroud's Judicial Diction-

6. London, Sweet & Maxwell, 1959, 2 vols.
7. 14th ed., London, Stephens, 1938.

ary[8] differs from its American counterparts in that it has tables of cases and statutes which are involved in the judicial definitions. In addition to including Scottish, Irish, and Dominion sources, it also lists cases on the construction of repealed statutes. See Chapter 24, §24.11.

3. *Maxims*. As already noted, most law dictionaries and encyclopedias define maxims. Broom, A Selection of Legal Maxims, Classified and Illustrated,[9] is a treatise or commentary based upon maxims.

4. *Development and history of British law dictionaries*. Students interested in this subject should consult Price and Bitner, Effective Legal Research 221–24 (1953).

8. 4th ed., London, Sweet & Maxwell, 1971, 5 vols.
9. 10th ed., London, Sweet & Maxwell, 1939.

22 Form Books; Appeal Papers; Directories

§22.1. Form books.

Drafting legal documents is a test of exact and formal knowledge. The student, when he or she sits down to write out a document for moot court or other problem work in law courses, is beset by doubts. Is this clause too broad; does that proviso properly protect; does this declaration state a cause of action; is the manuscript properly typed?

The form book is indispensable in answering such questions. Your law school library should have a collection of books containing printed forms. In copying or adapting forms, one must make certain that they fit exactly the precise situation for which they are being used. A carelessly adapted form is potentially very dangerous.

1. *Annotated forms*. A form which has not been adjudicated has somewhat the same weak status as an unadjudicated statute. Therefore, it is customary to include in form books those forms which have withstood attack in court. The fact that a form is not annotated does not necessarily condemn it, however. It may be one of such age and universal acceptance that it is protected by a sort of judicial notice. Statutory forms are almost always annotated.

American Jurisprudence Legal Forms Annotated[1] and American Jurisprudence Pleading and Practice Forms[2] are the most elaborate and most closely indexed collections of forms. They are both keyed to

1. 2d ed., Rochester, N.Y., Lawyers Co-operative Publishing Co., 1971–1974, 20 vols. Annual cumulative pocket-part supplements.
2. Rev. ed., Rochester, N.Y., Lawyers Co-operative Publishing Co., 1966–1974, 25 vols. Annual cumulative pocket-part supplements.

the American Jurisprudence encyclopedia as well as to the cases construing individual forms. A checklist of items to look out for in drafting a form is printed at the beginning of each volume of the American Jurisprudence Legal Forms Annotated. Other collections of somewhat lesser scope are described below under Encyclopedic Collections.

2. *Varieties*. Forms are broadly classified as either concerning substantive or procedural law; form books are usually one or the other, though some have both types of forms in them. An example of the latter is Medina's Bostwick,[3] in which three-quarters of the forms pertain to procedure and the remainder to Common Forms of Instruments, which are business forms.

One reason for the separation of form books into distinct volumes is that practice forms change more rapidly than substantive law forms because of changes in practice acts and rules. Thus procedure form books need more frequent supplementation or new editions than do substantive law forms. Most substantive law forms (if not based upon statutes) are of rather general application; that is, many of these forms may be used across jurisdictional lines. For example, many form books, though devoted predominantly to New York forms and case annotations, are published as of general applicability. Others are designed for specific geographical areas where special problems of law (for example, irrigation or oil and gas) may be encountered.

3. *Sources*.

a. *Statutory forms*. Both substantive and procedural statutory forms are commonly printed in state statutory compilations, where they can be found through the general index. Many statutory forms, including a few from foreign countries, are printed in the Martindale-Hubbell Law Directory.

Procedural forms are usually applicable only in one jurisdiction. They are commonly adapted for frequent supplementation or new editions in order to keep abreast of statutory changes. Substantive law forms are much more standard and normally do not call for such frequent revision.

b. *Encyclopedic collections*. The American Jurisprudence forms have been mentioned above. Modern Legal Forms[4] and Nichols, Cyclopedia of Legal Forms, Annotated[5] print both standard and statutory forms, which are annotated to the decisions. They are well indexed and supplemented by new forms and new annotations.

3. Medina's Bostwick Lawyers Manual. 6th ed., New York, N.Y., Matthew Bender & Co., 1954.

4. St. Paul, Minn., West Publishing Co., 1963–1972, 17 vols. Annual pocket supplements and periodically recompiled vols.

5. Chicago, Ill., Callaghan & Co., 1955– , 14 vols. Periodic supplements and recompiled vols.

Topics are arranged alphabetically by broad subject as far as practicable. Within a subject topic, the first forms are usually of broad coverage (long form) followed by shorter forms. Then particular clauses are set forth. For example, you can find forms relating to such minute topics as attacks by a cat, injuries to a toe or heel, or injuries causing embarrassment. Rabkin and Johnson, tax experts, have compiled Current Legal Forms with Tax Analysis,[6] which contains comments upon the tax aspects of the different forms in it.

c. *Topical form books*. Forms relating to a single topic may be published as separate works or as an integral part of a treatise on the subject covered. Examples of the separate topical form book are Collier, Bankruptcy Forms Manual;[7] Bailey and Rothblatt, Complete Manual of Criminal Forms;[8] Bittker, Federal Income Taxation of Corporations and Shareholders: Forms;[9] Wolf and Fletcher, Corporation Forms, Annotated;[10] Klipstein, Drafting New York Wills: Law and Forms[11] (which is especially useful for its checklist of items to be included in drafting a will); and Herzog's Bankruptcy Forms and Practice.[12]

More commonly, however, topical forms are adjuncts of treatises on the topic covered. Moreoever, forms are frequently included in loose-leaf services in order to assist the practitioner. Often their presence in treatises and loose-leaf services is noted by the word "Forms" on the spine of the volume or volumes containing them.

d. *Practice or procedural forms*. Such forms are almost always statutory and thus restricted in scope to a particular jurisdiction, action, or tribunal. They may appear as compilations of forms only. More than one-half of the states are specifically covered by their own procedural form books. Most frequently, however, these forms are published as integral parts of local practice treatises. Many treatises on practice include printed forms, which are usually annotated to the decisions. Treatises on substantive law which are peculiarly the creatures of statutes (such as bankruptcy or patents) usually print procedural forms.

There are many excellent federal practice form books available to the practitioner. Among them are Bender's Federal Practice Forms;[13]

6. Albany, N.Y., Matthew Bender & Co., 1960, 22 vols. Loose-leaf service.
7. 2d ed., New York, N.Y., Matthew Bender & Co., 1963, loose-leaf, 2 vols.
8. 2d ed., Rochester, N.Y., Lawyers Co-operative Publishing Co., 1974, 2 vols. Cumulative pocket supplements.
9. Boston, Mass., Warren, Gorham & Lamont, 1975.
10. 4th ed., Chicago, Ill., Callaghan & Co., 1972– .
11. 2d ed., New York, N.Y., Matthew Bender & Co., 1969, 1 vol. loose-leaf. Cumulative supplements.
12. 5th ed. New York, N.Y., C. Boardman Co., 1974, 2 vols. loose-leaf publication.
13. New York, N.Y., Matthew Bender & Co., 1951 to date. 11 vols. loose-leaf publication.

Federal Procedure Forms, Lawyers Edition;[14] and West's Federal Forms.[15]

e. *Foreign law forms*. Some foreign law forms are printed in the Martindale-Hubbell Law Directory.

f. *Form book for student use*. Professor Kenneth R. Redden, of the University of Virginia Law School, has compiled a Law Student's Form Manual[16] which is useful as an example of how to handle forms even though it is slanted to Virginia law.

4. *Typing legal forms*. A lawyer generally has a secretary trained to type legal papers in correct form, but the law student ordinarily does not. A neat and technically correct paper is important. Several books (such as Horowitz, Lawyers' Manual,[17] McCarty, Law Office Management[18] and the PLI, The Lawyers Secretary, 4th[19]) are available to help achieve this result.

5. *How to use form books*.

a. *Selecting the proper form*. The index to the collection of forms should first be consulted. The analytical tables of contents, often elaborate and systematic, also aid in this search. Supplements should also be searched, especially for procedural forms, where statutory changes are frequent. If a procedural form is copied from a general book of forms, make certain that it is applicable to your jurisdiction. Statutes and appeal papers are good sources to search for procedural forms.

b. *Selecting the applicable clauses*. Most form books, particularly the multivolume type, help the searcher by presenting an introductory or preparatory explanation of the applicability and technique of finding the desired form for each topic. In fitting in particular clauses, avoid the use of inconsistent or contradictory ones. If forms could be safely taken verbatim from a book or a stationery store's stock, the lawyer's function would be greatly reduced. Few forms can be so taken and used, however. Common sense, caution, and professional skill must be employed at all times in adapting forms for a specific set of facts. A form book is never a substitute for sound legal training.

c. *Checklists in the use of forms*. Because nobody has an infallible memory, checklists serve an important function. The careful will-drafter, for example, always has a detailed checklist of items to be included or discussed. This technique is generally applicable to the use of all forms. The most complete list is probably that at the begin-

14. Rochester, N.Y., Lawyers Co-operative Publishing Co., 1975 to date.

15. St. Paul, Minn., West Publishing Co., 1971 to date, 11 vols. Annual cumulative pocket supplements.

16. Charlottesville, Va., Michie Co., 1951.

17. 3d ed., New York, N.Y., Central Book Co., 1953.

18. 3d ed., Englewood Cliffs, N.J., Prentice-Hall, 1955.

19. New York, N.Y., Practising Law Institute, 1972.

ning of each volume of American Jurisprudence Legal Forms Annotated.[20]

Your law librarian can tell you what form books your library has and where to find them.

d. *Manuals for the use of forms.* Several books intended for the legal secretary are also helpful to the law student and the lawyer. Evangeline Sletwold's Manual of Documents and Forms for the Legal Secretary[21] gives general and specific instructions for typing legal documents and provides many actual forms. In addition, it has a good bibliography of form books and their use. Mary Ann Altman's Self-Administering Course for Legal Secretaries ran through ten issues of *Law Office Economics and Management*. Wider in scope than *Sletwold*, it is intended for courses in law offices for instruction of the secretarial staff. Marjorie K. Heller's *Complete Course in Legal Secretarial Practice* is also useful to a lawyer's secretarial staff.[22]

§22.2. Briefs and records on appeal.

In most jurisdictions appellants and appellees must submit to the appellate court printed briefs and transcripts of the record from the court below. These printed papers represent the product of the best legal knowledge and research in authorities on the part of counsel.

1. *Principal functions in a law library.* After they have served their original purpose, appeal papers have two principal functions: (1) Legal researchers with similar problems study them for their analyses, arguments, and supporting authorities. (2) When a pleading used in an appeal paper has withstood attack on appeal, it is frequently studied for form and content by other lawyers in their own practice and by students in preparing moot court briefs.

§22.3. Directories.

Legal directories list lawyers in active practice and give certain information about them. Some general directories list all lawyers within a particular jurisdiction or geographical area; others list lawyers in a specified branch of practice or members of a particular bar association.

1. *Martindale-Hubbell Law Directory.*[23] This directory performs several functions.

20. See note 1, *supra*.
21. 2d ed., Englewood Cliffs, N.J., Prentice-Hall, 1976.
22. Heller, Marjorie K., and Cohen, Betty, A Complete Course in Legal Secretarial Practice, Monarch, N.Y., 1977.
23. Summit, N.J., Martindale-Hubbell, Inc., 1931 to date. Published annually.

a. *Lawyers listed.* Practically all lawyers in active practice are listed. The directory is subdivided by states and lists alphabetically lawyers and firms by city and town. In consulting this directory it is thus necessary to know the state and city of practice of a listed lawyer in order to find his or her name since there is no alphabetical list of lawyers. The dates of birth, of college and law school graduation, and of admission to the bar are given, together with any practice specialty, membership in the American Bar Association, and a "confidential" rating. Professional cards are printed both in the listings for individual lawyers and in a Biographical Section at the end of the main directory for law firms. In the latter the partners' names and some additional data (such as bank references, the nature of the practice, and usually a list of clients) are given. A selection of foreign lawyers is also listed. A special listing is made of lawyers admitted to practice before the United States Patent Office.

b. *Law digests.* Laws of all states and territories and of many foreign countries are digested with citations to the statutes. Particular emphasis is given to business and family laws. The digests are prepared by lawyers in each state or foreign country and are fairly detailed. Special forms of statutory instruments favored in the various jurisdictions are often included, and statutory forms are frequently a part of the text. The federal section is confined to digests of United States copyright, patent, tax, and trademark laws. In many law libraries the Martindale-Hubbell Law Directory is the only readily available source of foreign law.

Uniform and model acts and codes are printed in full in an appendix. The Code of Professional Responsibility is also included in the appendix. In addition, users will find a section on the American Bar Association.

c. *Court information.* The jurisdiction, important personnel, terms and calendars of federal, state, District of Columbia, and Canal Zone courts are given.

2. *United States Lawyers Reference Directory.*[24] This directory provides much of the same information as the one described above. In addition to providing information regarding lawyers in the fifty states, separate sections for state and federal data are added. In the fifty state sections, information regarding the state court system, the state legislature and executive officers, and the state bar association is given. The federal section lists various executive officers, legislators, and federal agencies, in addition to providing valuable federal court information.

3. *The American Bench.* This directory[25] lists judges from all levels of federal and state courts. It has an alphabetical name index which

24. Los Angeles, Calif., Legal Directories Publishing Co., Inc., 1 vol. loose-leaf publication. Published annually.

refers the user to a more complete jurisdictional listing for each judge. Information given includes biographies, office addresses and telephone numbers, brief descriptions of the courts, and maps of their jurisdictional areas.

4. *Miscellaneous legal directories*. Most bar associations, law school alumni associations, and legal fraternities issue directories of their members. These are of interest principally to lawyers rather than law students.

25. Minneapolis, Minn., Reginald Bishop Forster & Associates, Inc. To be published annually.

23 | Loose-leaf Services and Topical Reports

§23.1. Genesis and function.

A loose-leaf service is a publication within a binder which can be readily opened for supplementation. Topical reports appearing in loose-leaf form collect and explain all the law on a single topic in one place. Publishers supplement loose-leaf services very frequently (often once a week) in order to keep lawyers abreast of rapidly changing and important areas of law.

Loose-leaf services have become increasingly important research tools for lawyers. To a great extent, this results from the growing role of federal and state governments in regulating business and personal activities through the use of administrative agencies. The Constitutional amendment authorizing income taxation, world wars, a great depression, a rapidly changing technology, and improved communication methods have triggered extraordinary changes in the laws governing our lives. Traditional legal research tools have often been incapable of meeting the lawyer's demand for quick and easy access to the vast amount of rapidly changing laws, administrative regulations and rulings, court decisions and various other government documents. It is impossible for any lawyer to collect, organize, and digest much of this material promptly and accurately. The loose-leaf service attempts to do this for lawyers. In many respects, it is a legal publisher's embodiment of that colloquial term, the "package deal." It collects data from various sources and reports all pertinent material in a specialized field of law in which the continuous reporting of new developments is necessary. Its special contribution is the coordination and presentation of all the essential data in a highly usable form.

The publishers of loose-leaf services frequently include editorial comment, which is labeled as such and is supported by the latest pertinent authority in all fields.

Although loose-leaf services cover a wide variety of legal topics, lawyers have become increasingly dependent upon them in two instances. First, lawyers often need to have immediate access to critical information or decisions. Thus United States Supreme Court decisions are quickly disseminated through loose-leaf services such as *United States Law Week* (which is published by the Bureau of National Affairs) and the *Supreme Court Bulletin* (published by Commerce Clearing House). Likewise, various loose-leaf services quickly circulate information regarding current statutory developments in Congress.

Second, the sources of authority, (e.g., the regulations and rulings of various administrative agencies, statutes and case law) in many areas of law are frequently not readily available or are found only by using several independent sources. Loose-leaf services collate and organize topically these various authorities so that the attorney's task is simplified. Generally, loose-leaf services are available in many areas of the law in which federal administrative agencies exercise significant authority. These areas include, for example, environmental law, labor law, security regulation, trade regulation, aviation law, food and drug regulation, and taxation.

§23.2. Advantages claimed.

1. *Speed of availability*. The loose-leaf form permits supplementation at will. The text of important statutes may be mailed to subscribers on the day of enactment. When a new statute or regulation makes existing material obsolete, the editors analyze anew the topic or subtopic affected. These new developments are immediately incorporated into the body of the reporter as new pages to replace the outdated one. New statutes, amendments, regulations and proposed regulations are mailed out shortly after approval or promulgation.

2. *Topical consolidation of authority and sources*. Each reporter attempts to be an exhaustive source of information for one field of law. Thus, statutes, court decisions (including those which have not been reported in traditional reporter publications), administrative regulations and rulings, and editorial explanations may be covered in complete detail in one source. The aim of such consolidation is to reduce to a minimum the number of sources which a lawyer must consult. All relevant data is brought together in one unit (often on the same page) and frequently presented with editorial explanations. A common index for the entire loose-leaf service enables the legal researcher to find this data quickly and efficiently.

3. *Cutting across jurisdictional lines*. Often (as in labor law, for example) there is interplay between federal and state statutes and decisions. The service aims to present the composite picture in one place. Thus lawyers are frequently able to discern jurisdictional trends without consulting a number of sources.

4. *Editorial explanations*. The editors endeavor to illustrate, analyze, and show the law in action. They explain apparent inconsistencies and tie the whole together.

5. *Expert and speedy indexing*. Loose-leaf services are indexed, and the indexes are frequently supplemented. Loose-leaf services are most helpful only if one has mastered the use of the index, which functions as a key to the contents of the service. Indexes are described in §23.3.6 below.

§23.3. Basic organization.

Although the organization varies considerably from publisher to publisher and from service to service of the same publisher, certain fundamentals are common to most of them.

1. *Binders*. Each service is delivered to the subscriber in one or more binders, a practice which permits removal of superseded pages and insertion of new ones.

2. *Instructions for use*. Because of the necessity of speedy revision and the diversity of materials covered, loose-leaf services are arranged and constructed in a different manner from most other law publications. The publisher supplies with each service clear and detailed instructions on how to use it. These are carefully set forth with specimen pages and problems. A conspicuous tab at the front of each volume points out these instructions; and a few minutes' perusal of them will save a great deal of time over aimless searching.

3. *Basic text or compilation*. The basic information on the topic covered by a service is usually set forth in a basic text, which is revised at intervals varying with the subject matter. Where the changes in statute and decision are frequent and drastic (as in income taxation), the basic compilation may be revised annually. If, on the other hand, the topic is relatively stable (as in wills or trusts), there is a continual partial revision, with a complete revision only after several years' accumulation of changes.

4. *Arrangement within the basic compilation*. Services are usually based upon regulatory statutes and the rules and regulations promulgated by authority of the statutes. For purposes of quick reference, the basic statute and the accompanying regulations are generally printed in their entirety in one place in the service. Then, following the organic statutes and the regulations comes the basic compilation proper, as noted above. Here the entire text of the statute is broken

down into small, workable subdivisions in a logical scheme of subject arrangement. Each of these subdivisons is accompanied by the pertinent administrative regulations. Editorial commentaries, which are based upon and explain the statutory material, are often included. Accompanying all this are decisions (or digests thereof) and orders interpreting the statutes and regulations. Finally, there are various indexes, tables, and so forth. With each mailing of new material a sort of newsletter is enclosed, pointing out new developments in the field covered by the service.

Two general plans of arranging the basic contents are commonly encountered. The first of these is called the statutory plan because it follows the section sequence of the statute under analysis. This plan is used where the statute in question develops the field logically (as, for example, the Internal Revenue Code).

Where there are numerous statutes of coordinate importance, which often may overlap in coverage (as in labor law or trade regulation), the arrangement is usually by topic with ample cross-references to related topics. Similarly, where the subject matter of the service follows common-law rules closely (as in trusts and estates), the material is developed by subject or topic.

5. *Paragraph number arrangement*. All material is identified and indexed by paragraph number rather than page number. These numbers are not fixed classification notations as in a digest, but merely serial numbers which are usually changed with each new edition of the service. In most loose-leaf services, paragraph numbers are enclosed in brackets to avoid confusion with official numbers assigned to laws and regulations. Each page of the service is also numbered for ease and accuracy in filing.

6. *Indexes*. Subject indexes are a significant tool in the proper use of loose-leaf services. Although they vary greatly from service to service, their format and use are described in detail in each service by how-to-use tabs preceding each of them.

a. *Subject matter coverage*. Depending upon the number of volumes and complexity of the service or the reporter, there may be as many as four or more types of subject indexes: (1) The coordinator of fairly broad topics (called variously the Answer Finder, Problem Solver, or Rapid Finder Index); (2) the basic index to the complete text of the service as compiled at the time the basic text was published; (3) the index to new matter—the supplementary, current index; and occasionally (4) special-subject indexes such as the indexes to substances (heparin sodium, rice bran, fatty acid, etc.) in the CCH Food, Drug and Cosmetics Reporter. The Rapid Finder type of index is usually found only in multi-volume services. Its purpose is the coordination of references to the complete service. It is especially useful when the subject matter in which you are interested may be organized logically under more than one main topic. For example, in the CCH Federal Securities Law Reporter, more than a dozen subtopics are collected under "Registration statements"; thus searchers are able to locate their probable interests very quickly. The basic topical index may cover the entire service and may be the only index to the basic compilation; or it may refer to topics in a more detailed topical index provided for each major subdivision of the service. The index to new matters or the current index is for matters covered by insertion pages in the main text which have been issued after the basic text was published and the basic index compiled. The special-subject index noted above is not common but can save research time when available.

In practice, each index is likely to be used. Searchers might begin with the Rapid Finder (see Exhibit 68), then move to the basic index under the indicated catchword, and finally go to the current matter

10,101

Rapid Finder Index

Paragraph

A

Abandonment losses 1535

Paragraph

Adjustments
amount and method of adjustment 4809-4814

• CCH • 10,223 YEA

Paragraph

Transferees 5649-5660
. fiduciary's personal liability 5662
. liability for tax 5649-5662
. notice of fiduciary relationship . . 5667-5670
. suits to restrain assessment or collection 5778-5779

Transfers to avoid tax, application of excise tax 4896

Transportation costs, employees' 717.03

Traveling expenses, deductibility . . 1350-1354

Treasury bond exemption, trusts or partnerships 972

Paragraph

"Unrelated trade or business" defined 3251-3257

V

Valuation of inventories 2938

Virgin Islands, tax rebates 4370-4372

Voluntary demolition or removal of buildings or equipment, losses . . 1546.012

W

Wagering losses 1580, 1581

Exhibit 68

index. The use of the special-subject matter index will usually be obvious when the need arises. References in all indexes are to the serial numbers of paragraphs rather than pages. The page references are almost always for the use of the person filing insertion pages.

b. *Date covered and supplementation.* Although it is not practicable to revise the basic index every time new material is added, the new material still has to be indexed. The solution is to have two, or sometimes even three, indexes: the index to the whole compilation, which indexes everything up to the time of publication of the service; a supplemental index to later published material; and, in some services, still a third index, to the very latest material. A complete index search would cover all of these. Auxiliary to these supplementary indexes are Cross-Reference Tables or Supplementary Cross-Reference Tables. These tables refer from a paragraph number in the basic compilation to later, relevant supplementary material which is collected in the current material file under a later paragraph number. Thus, if the main compilation of material covers your subject matter under ¶52.101, you can find later material in point, if any, by going to the parallel reference tables under ¶52.101, which will tell you under what paragraph numbers the later material is organized.

c. *Finding lists.* Official material contained in services is usually listed under so-called finding lists. Thus, in a federal tax service these lists give paragraphs covering the respective Internal Revenue Code Sections, the Regulations, court and Internal Revenue Service rulings, etc., as well as Presidential Executive Orders which have affected tax matters. For example, Executive Order No. 10,916 is noted in ¶5209.11 of the CCH Standard Federal Tax Reporter, Revenue Ruling 60-321 is noted in ¶2944.115 and Treasury Decision 6506 is noted in ¶5069B.001. The finding lists also usually contain the table of cases.

d. *Table of cases.* The case tables in services list all orders of any kind affecting a party in addition to court decisions. They also serve a citator function, as noted below.

§23.4. Citator function.

Loose-leaf services often serve an invaluable citator function. Tax and regulatory services note legislative and judicial actions affecting statutes and regulations covered by them and are annotated with judicial decisions and agency rulings. Information concerning administrative regulations and rulings is often unavailable elsewhere. The rulings themselves are listed in case tables which also give the subsequent judicial history of each ruling. Finding lists lead to notations of amendments or repeals of statutes and regulations.

Tax citators in loose-leaf services render a complete citator service for court and Tax Court cases, Treasury decisions and rulings, and pertinent Executive Orders. Commonly, tax citator case tables are divided into two sections: (1) court and Tax Court decisions by case name; and (2) Treasury decisions and rulings, and Executive Orders, by serial number. While the Internal Revenue Code and Treasury Regulations have no loose-leaf citator as such, changes in form are indicated. Case comments and others concerning them are also made in the annotations to the Code sections by which the services are arranged.

§23.5. How to use.

While the approaches to the loose-leaf services resemble closely those to digests, annotated statutes, and legal encyclopedias, each service has its own special features. The best advice, therefore, is to study carefully the "How to Use This Service [or Reporter]" instruction sheets and tabs in the front of each volume or subdivision of the service. This results in a substantial saving of time and in a better understanding of the use of the service than discovering proper usage through a trial-and-error method. A much more complete demonstration of what is involved in the solution of problems is found in these instructions.

Problem. The following simple problem is designed to demonstrate the variety of index tools provided by a typical loose-leaf service (or reporter, as Commerce Clearing House designates its products). For convenience, a number of illustrative exhibits taken from a "Reporter" are shown and keyed to the text. In order to save space, the CCH Standard Federal Tax Reporter is used in this particular problem. Very similar tools and procedures are available through the Prentice-Hall Federal Taxes and the Research Institute of America Tax Coordinator.

Statement of facts. A captain of the Marines was assigned to a Far East post for eighteen months. Her family was not permitted to accompany her. Her quarters were provided, but not the cost of her meals. May she deduct the cost of the meals as traveling expenses away from home?

1. *Index or fact approach*. a. *First step: the basic indexes:* This approach requires the same preliminary problem analysis as the descriptive-word index approach to the digest or encyclopedia. Here the question concerns the situs of the taxpayer's "tax home," which governs her tax liability. In particular, the searcher must discover whether the "temporary-permanent" job exception applicable to United States civilians applies as well to Marine service personnel.

First, consult the green-paper Rapid Finder Index (see Exhibit 68) just preceding the main Topical (or subject) Index of the reporter. This index, a coordinator leading to all subtopics treating a given-fact key word, gives a general coverage of various types of traveling expense deductions.

Since the reference from the Rapid Finder Index is not as detailed as you may need, you now examine the main Topical Index (see Exhibit 69), under Traveling Expenses. There you find many specific expenses noted and a cross-reference to "Meals and Lodging: expense of, deductibility." By checking this cross-reference, you discover several paragraphs that deal with your subject: ¶¶203A, 1350, and 1352.145.

b. *Second step: the basic text*. Going now from the index to the main text, you decide to try ¶1350 first. See Exhibit 70. In Exhibit 71 you find a "CCH Explanation" in subsection ¶1350.021, which discusses traveling expenses in general. This Explanation is a careful editorial explanation of the problems involved. There may also be the full text or digest of pertinent I.R.S. Regulations. Following the Explanation, you find digests of cases of all kinds (memoranda, Tax Court and court decisions, etc.). Preceding these digests for many topics (such as ours) is an alphabetical table of comments leading directly to cases which may be in point. See Exhibit 72.

¶1350.1981 relates to meals and lodgings of service personnel away from home. In this subparagraph we find three cases digested. One of these, *Stidger*, is a Supreme Court decision and is exactly in point (which rarely happens in practice). The digest of *Stidger* cites agency and court decisions and tells where *Stidger* is printed in the CCH U.S. Tax Cases (USTC).

c. *Third step: current matter indexes*. You wonder whether there is any new material in point. Therefore, you consult the Cumulative Index which coordinates new matters with the basic contents. To do this you use the paragraph numbers of the basic contents, which are arranged in order in the Cumulative Index and in its Supplements. The references you wish to update are the CCH Explanation at ¶1350.022 and the decisions involving service personnel at ¶1350.198 and ¶1350.1981.

Reference to these paragraph numbers in the "Current Items to Cumulative Index" shows no entries for the subparagraphs in which we are interested. See Exhibit 73. Checking the main part of the Cumulative Index turns up no additional cases or comments either. Thus, the Supreme Court's decision in *Stidger* is still binding; service personnel, according to that decision, cannot deduct expenses for meals and lodging.

Research by Citator. When you have the name of a case in point, you can also use the citator. See Exhibit 74. The pages in the Citator

6844 **Topical Index**
References are to paragraph (¶) numbers.

TRANSFERS—continued
. sales—see Sales of property
. securities
. . pension trust, to, income to transferor 631.404
. . reorganization 1522.64
. . tax saving as motive 1522.974
. . trustee, to 1522.987
. stock
. . controlled corporations 1522.782
. . losses 1522.83
. stock valuation on 4460.272
. system group, SEC ordering exchanges or distributions, gain or loss recognition 4677
. timber lands, basis 3524.10
. transferor, defined 2543.365
. . transferor's appeal to Tax Court dismissed 5660.054
. transferor's basis
. . capital expenditures v. business expenses 2219.388
. . depreciation accrued 4536.74
. . retransferred stock 2543.309
. . zero basis 2543.368
. trust—see Transfers in trust
. valuation of property transferred, options 4460.169
. will, under, sales of property, gain or loss recognition 4470.50
. worthless accounts, debt transferred to parent corporation 1619.022

TRANSFERS IN TRUST
. after 12/31/20, gain or loss basis 4526; 4530.017
. before 1/1/21 4532
. charitable contributions deduction 1860; 1864.3515
. gain or loss basis
. . allotted Indian lands 4530.025
. . beneficiary of irrevocable trust 4530.03
. . constitutionality 4530.032
. . existence of trust not proved 4530.0341
. . part gift, part sale 4530.037
. . revocable trust 4530.043

TRAVELING EXPENSES—continued
. actor 1350.03
. adjusted gross income 701; 716.03; 716.141
. airline employees 1350.0348
. airplanes 1350.035; 2296.61
. alien 1352.016
. allocation between personal and business purposes 229; 2296.11
. apartment for business use 1350.0353
. armed forces members 717.123
. armed forces reserve members 1350.1275
. author 1350.0357
. automobile expenses—see Automobiles: expenses
. award acceptance 1350.1115
. away from home 1350.021; 1350.022; 1352.01-1352.11
. . allocation between personal and business purposes 2296.12
. baseball players 1350.05; 1352.02
. business and pleasure trip 203.08; 1350.054; 1350.055; 1350.078
. business purpose, necessity of 203.08
. chiropractor, seminar attendance 1350.0839
. circus performer 1352.0287
. claims adjuster 1352.13
. cleaning 1350.021
. clergyman 1350.08
. commuters' fares 1350; 1350.021; 1350.069; 1352.144
. . business calls on way to work 203B
. conditions to be met 1350.022
. congressmen 1350.1225
. . trust fund payment 1350.1296
. constant travel status 1352.03
. construction company employee away from home 1352.132
. construction workers 1352.132; 4934.185
. conventions and meetings 1350.074-1350.084
. deductibility 1342.258; 1350.021
. deductibility, adjusted gross income 701; 716.03
. doctor employed by state 717.066

Topical Index **6659**
References are to paragraph (¶) numbers.

MARRIAGE COUNSELING
. exempt status of organization providing 3033.353
. fees paid 2206.0512

Marriage fees 644.14

Marriage settlement, legal expenses 2006.3273; 2206.162

Married, defined 1239.0867; 5020.62

Marsh Foundation, exemption 3033.26; 3035.05

MARYLAND
. accrual dates of taxes 1449.0661
. estate's income
. . real estate 3605.5209
. ground rents—see also Ground rents 2831.8848
. . deductibility as interest 1415; 1416.015; 1416.187; 4470.0103
. . income from 947.05
. . leases as real estate sales 668.538
. income tax, year deductible 2907.1085
. reservation of ground rent 2831.8848
. state tax liens, priority 5362.804
. taxes imposed by, deductibility 1449.476; 1449.815; 2907.1085
. tenants by the entirety 323.165
. waiver executed after dissolution of corporation 5447.905

MASSACHUSETTS
. accrual dates of taxes 1449.0661
. agreements between husband and wife null 323.05

MAUSOLEUM
. crypts
. . capital asset status 4512.0426
. . contracts to sell 2830.945
. estate tax deduction v. income tax deduction 3621.1477
. income from, taxable income computation 2765.265
. sale of space 2916.685
. . application of installment sale provision 2871.60

Mausoleum space, depreciation 1715.30

Maximum self-employment income 4863

MAXIMUM TAX ON PERSONAL SERVICE INCOME 4842B-4843.30
. computation 4843.02
. consulting fees 4843.20
. deferred compensation 4843.25
. definition of personal service income 4843.015
. dividends undistributed 4843.50
. farmer 4843.30
. foreign source income 4336.0885
. rate 201.13
. tax planning 204.025
. undistributed dividends 4843.50

Mayo fellowship grants 1179.04

MEALS AND LODGING
. compensation v. exempt income, convenience of employer 1187-1191.085
. . airline employee in Alaska 1191.04
. . cash in lieu of meals 1191.01
. . cattle partnership 1191.055

Exhibit 69

'54 Code

(2) in settlement of any action brought under such section 4 on account of such violation or related violation.

The preceding sentence shall not apply with respect to any conviction or plea before January 1, 1970, or to any conviction or plea on or after such date in a new trial following an appeal of a conviction before such date.

(h) CROSS REFERENCE.—

(1) For special rule relating to expenses in connection with subdividing real property for sale, see section 1237.

(2) For special rule relating to the treatment of payments by a transferee of a franchise, trademark, or trade name, see section 1253.

.01 Amended by P. L. 94-455, P. L. 92-178, P. L. 91-172, P. L. 87-834, P. L. 86-779 and P. L. 85-866. For details see the Code Volumes.

.10 **Committee Reports on P. L. 92-178 are at 1972-1 CB 498, 559 and 644.**

.13 **Committee Reports on P. L. 91-172 are at 1969-3 CB 199, 423 and 644.**

.15 **Committee Reports on P. L. 87-834 are at 1962-3 CB 420 and 727.**

.20 **Committee Reports on P. L. 86-779 are at 1960-2 CB 827, 858 and 859.**

.21 **Committee Reports on P. L. 85-866 are at 1958-3 CB 811.**

.22 **Committee Reports on 1954 Code Sec 162 as originally enacted were reproduced at 561 CCH ¶ 1322.10.**

Reg. § 1.162-1 is at ¶ 1329.

• ***Regulations***

[¶ 1350] § 1.162-2. **Traveling expenses.**—(a) Traveling expenses include travel fares, meals and lodging, and expenses incident to travel such as expenses for sample rooms, telephone and telegraph, public stenographers, etc. Only such traveling expenses as are reasonable and necessary in the conduct of the taxpayer's business and directly attributable to it may be deducted. If the trip is undertaken for other than business purposes, the travel fares and expenses incident to travel are personal expenses and the meals and lodging are living expenses. If the trip is solely on business, the reasonable and necessary traveling expenses, including travel fares, meals and lodging, and expenses incident to travel, are business expenses. For the allowance of traveling expenses as deductions in determining adjusted gross income, see section 62(2)(B) and the regulations thereunder.

(b)(1) If a taxpayer travels to a destination and while at such destination engages in both business and personal activities, traveling expenses to and from such destination are deductible only if the trip is related primarily to the taxpayer's trade or business. If the trip is primarily personal in nature, the traveling expenses to and from the destination are not deductible even though the taxpayer engages in business activities while at such destination. However, expenses while at the destination which are properly allocable to the taxpayer's trade or business are deductible even though the traveling expenses to and from the destination are not deductible.

(2) Whether a trip is related primarily to the taxpayer's trade or business or is primarily personal in nature depends on the facts and circumstances in each case. The amount of time during the period of the trip which is spent on personal activity compared to the amount of time spent on activities directly relating to the taxpayer's trade or business is an important factor in determining whether the trip is primarily personal. If, for example, a taxpayer spends one week while at a destination on activities which are directly related to his trade or business and subsequently spends an additional five weeks for vacation or other personal activities, the trip will be considered primarily personal in nature in the absence of a clear showing to the contrary.

(c) Where a taxpayer's wife accompanies him on a business trip, expenses attributable to her travel are not deductible unless it can be adequately shown

Exhibit 70

[¶ 1350]—Continued

that the wife's presence on the trip has a bona fide business purpose. The wife's performance of some incidental service does not cause her expenses to qualify as deductible business expenses. The same rules apply to any other members of the taxpayer's family who accompany him on such a trip.

(d) Expenses paid or incurred by a taxpayer in attending a convention or other meeting may constitute an ordinary and necessary business expense under section 162 depending upon the facts and circumstances of each case. No distinction will be made between self-employed persons and employees. The fact that an employee uses vacation or leave time or that his attendance at the convention is voluntary will not necessarily prohibit the allowance of the deduction. The allowance of deductions for such expenses will depend upon whether there is a sufficient relationship between the taxpayer's trade or business and his attendance at the convention or other meeting so that he is benefiting or advancing the interests of his trade or business by such attendance. If the convention is for political, social or other purposes unrelated to the taxpayer's trade or business, the expenses are not deductible.

(e) Commuters' fares are not considered as business expenses and are not deductible.

(f) For rules with respect to the reporting and substantiation of traveling and other business expenses of employees for taxable years beginning after December 31, 1957, see § 1.162-17. [Reg. § 1.162-2.]

.001 Historical Comment: Proposed 7/10/56. Adopted 4/3/58 by T. D. 6291. Amended 8/27/58 by T. D. 6306 to reflect the adoption of Reg. § 1.162-17.

Traveling Expenses

• • *CCH Explanation*

.021 In general.—Code Sec. 162 (¶ 1320) allows a deduction for traveling expenses incurred while away from home in the pursuit of a trade or business. These expenses include travel fares, meals and lodging, and expenses incident to travel such as the cost of sample rooms, telephone and telegraph, public stenographers, clothes care, etc. Travel expenses are distinguished from transportation expenses in that the latter is a narrower concept and includes only the cost of transporting a person from one place to another in the course of employment, excluding commuting costs, while he is not "away from home" in a travel status. Some examples of transportation expenses are cab fares, bus fares, and the like, as well as a pro rata share of the cost of operating a personal automobile when partially used for business (see ¶ 1354). Meals and lodging are not included among transportation expenses. Both travel and transportation expenses, however, are deductible from gross income in computing the adjusted gross income. (See ¶ 717.01). (Traveling expenses incurred in the production of income under Code Sec. 212—as distinguished from expenses incurred in a trade or business—are also deductible, but, to be deducted, must be itemized on Schedule A of Form 1040, unless they are attributable to the production of rents or royalties. See ¶ 2006.475.)

.022 Requirements.—In order for traveling expenses to be deductible under this Code section, three conditions must generally be fulfilled, namely, (1) they must be reasonable and necessary, (2) they must be incurred while away from home, and (3) they must be

17,012 TRADE OR BUSINESS EXPENSES—Sec. 162 [page 17,007]

• • • *Annotations by Topic*

17,044 TRADE OR BUSINESS EXPENSES—Sec. 162 [page 17,007]

.1921 An airline mechanic's $8-per-day allowance for foreign travel did not exceed the amount expended and, therefore, did not result in taxable income.

Chianese, 9 TCM 627, Dec. 17,784(M).

.1922 Where the expected reimbursement was not made because of the corporation's financial condition, the expenses did not become those of the corporate officer who incurred and paid them.

H. A. Worth, 20 TCM 218, Dec. 24,668(M), TC Memo. 1961-39.

W. Ockrant, 25 TCM 333, Dec. 27,885(M), TC Memo. 1966-60.

.1923 An employee, who did not furnish records of his actual expenses, was denied a deduction of $25 per day in excess of reimbursement for away-from-home expenses incurred while being temporarily reassigned.

S. W. Hennessey, Jr., 28 TCM 1108, Dec. 29,778(M), TC Memo. 1969-209.

.193 **Restoration of reimbursement.**—See ¶ 4837.21.

.198 **Serviceman's expenses** in visiting home and in returning home after his discharge, including the cost of moving his family, are nondeductible personal expenses.

Frederick Tilney, Jr., 12 TCM 92, Dec. 19,451(M).

.1981 A member of the military services is not "away from home" while at his permanent duty station and may not deduct traveling expenses, including meals and lodging, incurred at such location. This is so even though it is not feasible or even permissible for his family to join him.

H. A. Stidger, (Sup. Ct.) 67-1 USTC ¶ 9309, 386 U. S. 287.

Similarly.

J. A. McDonald, 33 TCM 274, Dec. 32,486(M), TC Memo 1974-57.

An Army captain could not deduct the cost of his meals in an officers' mess, a voluntary organization to which he belonged, or the expense of a "striker fee" (janitor service for his living quarters), since he was not "away from home," his place of business being his Army post.

Bercaw v. Com., (CA-4) 48-1 USTC ¶ 9153, 165 F. 2d 521.

¶ 1350.181 Reg. § 1.162-2

Exhibit 72

Current Items to Cumulative Index to 1978 Developments for Reports 40-47

See also Cumulative Indexes at pages 70,251 and 70,301.

From Compilation Paragraph No.			To New Development Paragraph No.
202	.06	*212 Corp.*, TC (¶ 7968H)—Effect of private annuity transaction. *Rewrite* (¶ 8100).	
203C	.06	*Suttle*, TCM—Interest free loan to controlling shareholder is not income	7971B
209	.01	*Suttle*, TCM—Controlling shareholder did not recognize gain on his interest free loan	7971B
225	.05	IRS issues more corporate slush fund guidelines—*Rewrite*	8096
255	.04	Deduction for attorney's fees barred by statute of limitations—*Rewrite*	8078
256		Tax loophole widened by new gift tax decision—*Rewrite*	8077
259	.12	*Quinlivan*, TCM (¶ 7592)—Rental deduction permitted. Gov't on appeal to CA-8 (9/5/78).	
321	.03	*Millette and Associates, Inc.*, TCM (¶ 7753)—Insurance commissions and service fees includible in income. Taxpayer on appeal to CA-5 (9/5/78).	

See also Cumulative Indexes at pages 70,251 and 70,301.

From Compilation Paragraph No.			To New Development Paragraph No.
1332	.1332	*Malmstedt* rem'd CA-4 (¶ 9479)—Commercial development was continuation of business for residential developer. *Rewrite* (¶ 8091). Cert. not authorized.	
	.1332	*Norman*, TCM—Expenses for travel and entertainment expenses disallowed	7970X
1338	.2661	Entertainment expenses of members of Congress—Rev. Rul.	6933V
1340	.2736	*Fixler*, TCM—Deduction denied for lack of substantiation	7972L
	.2767	*Fixler*, TCM—Entertainment expenses not deductible as business expenses	7972L
	.277	*Leon*, TCM—Expenses did not pass directly related or associated with test	7969P
1341	.2546	*Busking*, TCM—A carpenter was allowed a small deduction for tools	7972B
1342	.25	*Kenfield*—Acquiescence announced	6885
	.265	*Busking*, TCM—A carpenter was allowed a small deudction for work clothes	7972B
1344	.316	Medical malpractice claim payments by professional association—Letter Ruling	6971S
1348	.419	*Soelling*, TC—Legal expenses for investment property were capital expenditures	7970L
	.4331	*Bentley*, TCM (¶ 7547) Legal fees paid in stock. Gov't on appeal to CA-9 8/28/78.	
1350	.069	Rev. Rul. 76-453 inapplicable to commuting expenses—P. L.	6934F
	.07	*Crepeau*, TCM—Commuting expenses are nondeductible personal expenses	7970R
	.07	*Duncan*, TCM—Commuting expenses were not deductible	7971H
	.075	*Bodine*, TCM—Cost of attending air traffic controllers convention was nondeductible	7968C

Exhibit 73

STE **92,048** **——CCH——**

- **CA-6**—(rem'g TC), 66-1 USTC ¶ 9168; 355 F.2d 200 (Haserot Est., McK.)

Hempt Bros., Inc., 74-1 USTC ¶ 9188, 490 F2d 1172
Antrim Est., Dec. 28,397(M), 26 TCM 320, T.C.Memo. 1967-60
Lewis, Dec. 28,178, 47 TC 129

- **TC**—41 TC 562; Dec. 26,620; NA. 1966-2 CB 7 (Haserot Est., H. McK.)

Verito, Dec. 27,202, 43 TC 429

Stidger, Howe A. .... ¶ 1350.069, 1350.1981, 1352.01

- **Sup. Ct.**—(rev'g CA-9), 67-1 USTC ¶ 9309; Ct.D. 1914, 1967-1 CB 32; 386 U.S. 287; 87 S.Ct. 1065

Markey, 74-1 USTC ¶ 9192, 491 F2d 1249
Six, 71-2 USTC ¶ 9694, 450 F.2d 66
Jones, 71-1 USTC ¶ 9461, 444 F.2d 508
Sanders, 71-1 USTC ¶ 9260, 439 F.2d 296
Rosenspan, 71-1 USTC ¶ 9241, 438 F.2d 905
Jenkins, 70-1 USTC ¶ 9135, 418 F.2d 1292
Wills, 69-1 USTC ¶ 9401, 411 F.2d 537
Tauferner, 69-1 USTC ¶ 9241, 407 F.2d 243
McKenzie, 76-2 USTC ¶ 9696, 431 FSupp 993
Hess, 71-1 USTC ¶ 9431, 329 F.Supp. 1353
Egan, 71-1 USTC ¶ 9420, 325 F.Supp. 1227
Six, 71-1 USTC ¶ 9213, 322 F.Supp. 547
Edmerson, 70-1 USTC ¶ 9409, DC
Rosenspan, 70-1 USTC ¶ 9323, 316 F.Supp. 194
Six, 69-1 USTC ¶ 9424, 300 F.Supp. 277
Lackey, Dec. 34,500(M), 36 TCM 890, T.C.Memo. 1977-213
Leisner, Dec. 34,488(M), 36 TCM 864, T.C.Memo. 1977-205
Montgomery, Dec. 33,176, 64 TC 175
McDonald, Dec. 32,486(M), 33 TCM 274, T.C.Memo. 1974-57
Lewia, Dec. 31,489(M), 31 TCM 831, T.C.Memo. 1972-168
Carr, Dec. 31,487(M), 31 TCM 826, T.C.Memo. 1972-166
Puckett, Dec. 30,937, 56 TC 1092
Chawlow, Dec. 30,903(M), 30 TCM 770, T.C.Memo. 1971-185
Tucker, Dec. 30,657, 55 TC 783
Lawrence, Dec. 30,292(M), 29 TCM 1004, T.C.Memo. 1970-235
Wine, Dec. 30,236(M), 29 TCM 877, T.C.Memo. 1970-195
DuBrul, Dec. 30,127(M), 29 TCM 531, T.C.Memo. 1970-124
Kennedy, Dec. 29,996(M), 29 TCM 255, T.C.Memo. 1970-58
Michaels, Dec. 29,836, 53 TC 269
Clark, Dec. 29,831(M), 28 TCM 1260, T.C.Memo. 1969-241
Chimento, Dec. 29,755, 52 TC 1067
Baker, Dec. 29,226, 51 TC 243
Chappuis, Dec. 28,886(M), 27 TCM 222, T.C.Memo. 1968-48
Kroll, Dec. 28,864, 49 TC 557
Glogowski, Dec. 28,679(M), 26 TCM 1202, T.C.Memo. 1967-236
McLendon, Dec. 28,481(M), 26 TCM 544, T.C.Memo. 1967-118
Drinko, Dec. 28,475(M), 26 TCM 532, T.C.Memo. 1967-115
Rev. Rul. 75-432, 1975-2 CB 60
Rev. Rul. 73-468, 1973-2 CB 77
Rev. Rul. 67-438, 1967-2 CB 82

- **CA-9**—(rev'g TC), 66-1 USTC ¶ 9161; 355 F.2d 294

Cowger, Dec. 27,940(M), 25 TCM 513, T.C.Memo. 1966-95

- **TC**—40 TC 896; Dec. 26,286

Stiefel, Reuben .... ¶ 3922.39

- **TC**—9 TC 576; Dec. 16,039; A. 1948-1 CB 3

Prizant, Dec. 30,923(M), 30 TCM 817, T.C.Memo. 1971-196
Kates, Dec. 29,235(M), 27 TCM 1423, T.C.Memo. 1968-264
Offord, Dec. 24,874(M), 20 TCM 797, T.C.Memo. 1961-159
Spada, Dec. 17,747(M), 9 TCM 941
Carolin, Dec. 17,023(M), 8 TCM 548
Rood, Dec. 17,013(M), 8 TCM 531
Roberts, Dec. 16,799(M), 8 TCM 60
Pickelsimer, Dec. 16,280(M), 7 TCM 111

Stieff Estate, Charles C. .... ¶ 2831.885, 3644.024

- **BTA**—2 BTA 1109; Dec. 937

Blair, Dec. 5610, 18 BTA 69

Stieff, Gideon N. v. Tait .... ¶ 2831.885

- **CA-4**—(aff'g DC), 1929 CCH D-9172; 1929 CCH Fed. Cts. Vol., page CCA-7151; 31 F.2d 1020
- **DC**—1928 CCH D-8228; 1928 CCH Fed. Cts. Vol., page 7883; T. D. 4204, VII-2 CB 259; 26 F.2d 489

Stiegler, Jr., Rene A. .... ¶ 4639.12

- 23 TCM 412; Dec. 26,686(M); T.C.Memo. 1964-57

Stieglitz, Treiber Co., Inc. .... ¶ 1619.58, 1619.59

- 1 BTA 452; Dec. 172; A. IV-1 CB 3

Stiening, Beryl R., Exrx. (See Rae Est., Walter S.)
Stier, Robert F. E. (See Hollister, Guy)

46 10-18-78 **Current Citator Table—Court, Tax Court and BTA Cases** **90,153**

- **CA-9**—(aff'g TC), 70-2 USTC ¶ 9584; 430 F.2d 679

Cited in:
Loftin and Woodard, Inc., 78-2 USTC ¶ 9645, CA-5

Sterling, Ralph v. Ham .... ¶ 2871.09, 2871.52, 2874.089

- **DC**—3 USTC ¶ 1080; 3 F.Supp. 386

Cited in:
Bostedt, Dec. 35,237, 70 TC —, No. 47
Maddox, Dec. 35,016, 69 TC 854

Sterling Distributors, Inc. .... ¶ 3321.0352

- **CA-5**—(rev'g and rem'g DC), 63-1 USTC ¶ 9288; 313 F.2d 803

Cited in:
Motor Fuel Carriers, Inc. 77-2 USTC ¶ 9661, 559 F2d 1348

Sterman, Leone

- **DC**—Tex, 77-1 USTC ¶ 9357

Stern, Jean F., Transferee .... ¶ 5357.105, 5660.209, 5660.2091

- **Sup. Ct.**—(aff'g CA-6), 58-2 USTC ¶ 9594; Ct.D. 1830, 1958-2 CB 937; 357 U.S. 39; 78 S.Ct. 1047

Cited in:
Stanick, Dec. 35,299(M), 37 TCM 1217 T.C.Memo. 1978-289
Groetzinger, Dec. 34,761, 69 TC 309
Rev. Rul. 78-299, 1978-32, 8

Stern, Maurice M. .... ¶ 1627.241

- **TC**—35 TCM 1061; Dec. 33,965(M); T.C.Memo. 1976-245

Stickell, Jr., Arthur L.

- **DC**—Ill, 78-1 USTC ¶ 9328

Stickney, Charles L. v. Squire .... ¶ 3920.80

- DC, Wash., 51-2 USTC ¶ 9443

Cited in:
Thornberry Constr. Co., 78-1 USTC ¶ 9452, 576 F2d 346

Stidger, Howe A. .... ¶ 1350.069, 1350.1981, 1352.01

- **Sup. Ct.**—(rev'g CA-9), 67-1 USTC ¶ 9309; Ct.D. 1914, 1967-1 CB 32; 386 U.S. 287; 87 S.Ct. 1065

Cited in:
Frank, 78-2 USTC ¶ 9545, 577 F2d 93
Bell, 78-1 USTC ¶ 9123, CtCl Trial Div
Michel, Dec. 34,675(M), 36 TCM 1388, T.C.Memo. 1977-345

Stierhout, Lois K. .... ¶ 4336.0964, 5316.555

- **TC**—24 TC 483; Dec. 21,080; A. 1955-2 CB 9

Cited in:
AVCO Financial Services, 78-1 USTC ¶ 9117, DC

Stiles, Fred M.

- **TC**—69 TC 558; Dec. 34,913; A. 1978-33, 5

Stiner, Carol I. .... ¶ 1342.265, 5770.0517

- **CA-10**—(aff'g unreported DC per curiam), 75-2 USTC ¶ 9762; 524 F2d 640

Cited in:
Peacock, III, Dec. 34,934(M), 37 TCM 177, T.C.Memo. 1978-30

Standard Federal Tax Reports
028—82 **STI**

Exhibit 74

volume list by name all cases decided since 1913 to the current year, with agency or court action, where they are printed in U.S. Tax Cases, and other cases citing them. Searching for still later cases, you consult the "Current Citator Table" which precedes the main citator table. There you find additional cases which have cited *Stidger*. You also check the case table for the current year, which is located in volume nine.

2. *Analytical approach*. This is somewhat more complicated than with digests because the services vary in content and organization of material. As with digests, however, the problem is analyzed through its legal implications rather than by fact or catchword situations.

a. *Tables of contents following permanent tabs*. The function and use of the tables of contents may be compared to the "Analysis" of the case digest. For example, consider the problem of the income deductibility of advertising as a business expense, specifically for promotion or advertising of goodwill. The table of contents for the CCH Standard Federal Tax Reporter lists (under I.R.S. Regulation §1.162–14) the desired subject matter as being treated under ¶1392 of the Reporter. Finding this is made easier by the presence of a "Correlator" which is "a preliminary discussion introducing the subjects covered in this division. Use it for a quick review of the high points. . . ." The text of ¶1392 devotes six pages to a discussion of the problem and includes an "explanation" of the issues, the Commissioner's policy, pertinent regulations, and court and agency decisions. By a similar process, the same matter is found in the Prentice-Hall Federal Tax Service 1976 under ¶11,090.

3. *Table of cases approach*. Tables of cases fulfill the same function in loose-leaf services and reporters as in other law books. Although practice varies somewhat from service to service, the following information may be given:

1. Full citation (including parallel citations, if any, to standard reports series) to the case.
2. Number of paragraph where found in the service.
3. Citator function.
4. In some services (where the basic compilation is frequently revised because of statutory changes) citations to prior-year paragraph numbers in earlier editions of the service at which the case is printed in full.

4. *Finding lists approach*. The finding list is a means by which official material is found in the text of the service. It is a parallel conversion table from an official citation to the paragraph number in the service where the item is printed or discussed. Case tables are usually designated in the services as finding lists.

Statutes, regulations, Presidential Executive Orders or proclamations, attorney generals' opinions, etc., are listed numerically by category if treated in the service. References generally include a citation to the paragraph numbers of the service at which the authorities are discussed or printed.

Finding lists of official materials serve to coordinate information regardless of where the materials are discussed in the service. The value of finding lists is obvious. Statutes are not always printed in a service in the order of their original section numbering, and regulations are commonly printed in connection with pertinent statutes rather than in the order of their original numbering.

Usually, finding lists are in tabular form and follow the official statute or regulation as cited. They are alphabetical, however, when the indexed material is not numbered.

Shepard's Federal Labor Law Citations serves as a finding list. The Cross-References section in this citator shows where the decisions and orders of the National Labor Relations Board are reported and digested in the Bureau of National Affairs labor services and in the CCH and Prentice-Hall labor services and reporters.

Working with finding lists is simple. The searcher merely matches up the official citation of authority (the section number of a part of a law, an article number of a regulation, the series and serial number of a Presidential Executive Order or of an administrative agency order or memorandum) with the number in the finding lists. This directs the searcher to the appropriate paragraph number in the service. Alphabetical finding lists are arranged, of course, as in your dictionary or telephone directory. Not all services have finding lists; publishers label such finding lists plainly so that searchers may quickly discern whether a service contains one.

5. *Special-subject services by state*. Some topics (like taxation, corporations and labor) have separate services or editions. Here the services aim to index and annotate every state statute relating in any way to the main topic. Furthermore, once the pertinent section number for one state is found, a uniform arrangement within each of the states renders it simple to locate similar material in any other state.

6. *Special tax reports*. In the taxation field several publishers periodically produce tax reports that either discuss aspects of tax law or provide information about the latest legal developments in the tax area.

For example, the BNA Tax Management series has produced over 360 Portfolios since 1969. These booklets provide in-depth studies of particular tax issues and are written by tax practitioners who have developed special expertise.

The Research Institute of America publishes *The Tax Coordinator, Weekly Alert*, which serves as a newsletter providing the latest tax news from legislative developments to new judicial decisions, to I.R.S. Letter Rulings. This weekly publication is collected in a looseleaf binder arranged chronologically. CCH and PH have comparable services.

24 United Kingdom Materials*

§24.1. Introduction.

Although the United Kingdom is a unitary state with a general common-law tradition, there are differences in its constituent parts. Northern Ireland's judicial procedure closely resembles that of England and Wales, but there are differences in Parliamentary jurisdiction. Changes in Parliamentary authority with regard to Northern Ireland, initiated in 1972, still remain unresolved. Scots law includes some remnants of Romanistic legal principles, and some of these legal and judicial elements persist today.

Sources and search tools of the legal systems of England, Wales, Northern Ireland, and Scotland are considered together in this chapter. Titles and series which give special consideration to Northern Ireland and Scotland are discussed as necessary.

§24.2. Laws and statutes.

American and English statute forms are similar. Both include what

*This chapter was written by Mary L. Fisher, Law Librarian, General Electric Company, Fairfield, Conn.

may be generally classified as public general and private or personal acts. In addition, United Kingdom statutes include Church Assembly Measures. There are also similarities in the mode of issuance; both governments issue slip laws and session laws. The difference to be noted is that there is no code of laws of the United Kingdom really comparable to the United States Revised Statutes or the United States Code.

1. *Slip laws.* These have been available in varying format since 1484. They are issued by Her Majesty's Stationery Office (H.M.S.O.) as approved, as a separate pamphlet. By the Acts of Parliament Numbering and Citation Act, 1962, all acts passed beginning 1963 are designated by chapter numbers within a calendar year, that is, as 1963, c. 1. Her Majesty's printer makes the texts of the law available also to commercial publishers, who commonly distribute them as part of a law report or other segment of a subscription service.

2. *Session laws.*

a. *Public General Acts and Measures.* English slip laws are cumulated by H.M.S.O. and bound annually in two volumes as Public General Acts and Measures (with title variance).[1] They correspond to the United States Statutes at Large. For each annual compilation, there are alphabetical and chronological lists and a derivation table showing the effects of the current year's legislation, noting repeals, amendments, or other restrictions.

b. *Current Law Statutes Annotated.*[2] Beginning in 1947, this is issued in parts irregularly throughout the year and contains all statutes and Church Assembly Measures passed by the United Kingdom Parliament. Annotations accompany those statutes of general applicability. Arrangement is by chapter, that is, in chronological order. Included with the periodic issues during the year is a cumulative statute citator for the calendar year for statutes of that year and earlier statutes. There is cumulative subject access to this annotated subscription service. References to the debates as reported in Hansard are part of the annotations.

c. *Public General Acts passed by the Parliament of Northern Ireland,* which subsequently received royal assent, were issued annually as Northern Ireland Statutes and Orders in Council Having Effect as Such (with title variance)[3] for the period, 1922 through March 30, 1972, at which time direct rule by Parliament (London) began. Since the passage of the Northern Ireland Acts of 1972 and 1974, laws for Northern Ireland have been published as Orders in Council. Each volume includes tables of acts for the volume and acts affected and a subject index.

1. London, H.M. Stationery Office.
2. London, Sweet & Maxwell.
3. Belfast, H.M.S.O.

d. *Scottish Acts since 1707* are included in Public General Acts and Measures. Public General Statutes Affecting Scotland (with title variance)[4] were issued under authority, 1847 – 1947.

e. *Scottish Current Law Statutes*.[5] Since its inception in 1948, each part, issued irregularly throughout the year, contains full text and annotations of all acts related to Scotland which have received royal assent. Each part includes an index and a cumulative statute citator.

3. *Chronological Table of Statutes*.[6] In this annual cumulative volume prepared under the direction of the Statute Law Committee, United Kingdom statutes since 1235 are listed chronologically by calendar year and chapter thereof. Through 1962 the regnal year is given in brackets. Repeals and modifications of enactments are noted in italics with a reference made to the repealing or modifying act. References to the Acts of Northern Ireland since 1923 are italicized. There is a separate chronological table of the Acts of the Parliaments of Scotland, 1424 - 1707.

4. *Compilations of statutes*. There have been published several chronological collections of statutes dating from the Magna Carta. Those most currently used for reference are described below. Since the establishment of the first Statute Law Committee in 1868, editions also have been prepared. Statute law revision is a process of repealing obsolete or superseded statutes or those which have been repealed by, or are inconsistent with, a subsequent enactment.

a. *Statutes of the Realm*.[7] This is the most complete, accurate, and scholarly edition of the statutes for the period 1225 – 1713. Texts of the statutes are in both language contemporary to the time and modern English. There are many statutes herein long since repealed but of historical importance. Editorial notes accompany many of the statutes. Each volume has its own index. In addition, there are cumulative alphabetical and chronological indexes. The particular present value of these indexes is their access to the statutes of historical importance, which, of course, are not covered by the Index to the Statutes in Force although they are to be found in the Chronological Table of the Statutes.

b. *Acts and Ordinances of the Interregnum, 1642–1660*.[8] This collection covers the period of Cromwell's Commonwealth. Volume 3 contains a chronological list of acts and ordinances, a subject index, and an index of names, places, and things legislated about, together with an essay on the content and validity of legislation of the interregnum period.

4. Edinburgh, Blackwood, 1848–1947. 101 vols.
5. Edinburgh, W. Green.
6. London, H.M.S.O.
7. London, E. Eyre & A Strahan, 1824–1828.
8. London, H.M.S.O., 1911. 3 vols.

c. *The Statutes Revised*,[9] third edition, is a 32-volume official compilation of public general statutes and Church Assembly Measures from 1235 through 1948 as amended and in force at the end of 1948. Acts of exclusive relevance to Northern Ireland and pre-1707 Scots Acts have been omitted. Each volume has its own detailed subject and chronological indexes. There is, however, no cumulative index to the set. Use with this set the annual Public General Acts and Measures, the Chronological Table of Statutes, and the Index to the Statutes, for which see below.

There is an important caveat to be made in consideration of this set. The Statutes Revised had lost currency by the time of publication. Parliament is in process of consolidating many of its enactments, and the first issuance of a new, officially revised edition entitled Statutes in Force began in 1972.

d. *Statutes in Force*.[10] Begun in 1972, the statutes in force are being issued officially in binder format. Existing legislation is being amalgamated and marked for insertion in binders by broad subject arrangement. It is intended that the contents will be a complete permanent edition upon its anticipated completion in 1980. Acts in this edition incorporate amendments to the date appearing on the title page of each fascicle. Notes from the Statutes of the Realm are reproduced as now relevant. Dates of royal assent appear in brackets after the long title of the act. Alphabetical and chronological indexes are issued for subject binder(s) as completed. A consolidated index for the whole is planned upon completion of the set. Currency of the set is to be maintained by issuing new enactments for insertion in binders. Acts extensively amended will be reissued in revised form as replacement texts. An annual cumulative supplement divided by subject parts contains new enactments, acts repealed or revised, and acts grouped elsewhere which affect legislation within the particular subject group.

e. *Statutes Revised Northern Ireland 1301/1800–1948/50*[11] is an official compilation. It is patterned after the English revision.

f. *Acts of the Parliaments* [*of Scotland*] *1124–1707*[12] is the scholarly compilation, and Acts of Scotland 1424 – 1707[13] is the official edition of laws during the period that Scotland was an independent state. In 1707, by the Acts of Union, the Scottish and English Parliaments *per se* ceased, and the Parliament of the United Kingdom, consisting of Scottish and English members, replaced them as a newly formed legal institution. The edition of Public General Statutes Affecting

9. London, H.M.S.O., 1950. 32 vols. & index.
10. London, H.M.S.O.
11. Belfast, H.M.S.O., 1956. 16 vols.
12. Edinburgh, 1844, 1814–1824. 11 vols.
13. 2d. ed. rev., Edinburgh, H.M.S.O., 1966.

Scotland, 1707–1847,[14] covers the transitional period from independence to the first publication of the session laws, which carry the same title and are referenced in §24.2d.

g. *Halsbury's Statutes of England*, third edition.[15] This set classifies and reprints statutes of England and Wales in force which are of public general interest and Church of England Measures under broad, alphabetically arranged titles. Within each title, there is a table of contents which includes an alphabetical list of statutes contained therein, subject cross-references, and a Preliminary Note or introductory essay on the scope and subject matter of the title. Following this, the texts of the acts are printed verbatim. See Exhibit 75. Regulations applicable under sections of an act are cited. Each volume contains a subject index and table of statutes in both alphabetical and chronological sequence. The general index provides cumulative subject access and alphabetical and chronological lists of statutes.

The set is kept up to date by a current statutes service, an annual cumulative supplement, and annual continuation volumes. The current statutes service prints in loose-leaf format the texts and annotations of new enactments and includes a noter-up, which emends the texts of the statutes in the set. The cumulative supplement (see Exhibit 76) consolidates the material in the noter-up segment of the service. The bound continuation volumes contain the Acts and Church of England Measures which received royal assent during the previous year. As such, the continuation volumes supersede the current statutes service for that numbered year. Following the United Kingdom's entrance into the European Economic Community (EEC) in 1972, continuation volume 42A, dealing solely with EEC law, was issued in the format of the general titles described above. Beginning with 1976, cumulative supplement volumes contain material on the EEC.

5. *Indexes to statutes*.

a. *Index to the Statutes, 1235 to date*.[16] This is an official cumulative subject index to public acts in force. It has been issued annually by the Statute Law Committee since 1870. As a companion volume to the Chronological Table, it serves as an index to the third edition of the Statutes Revised and to the annual Public General Acts and Measures thereafter. In recent years, there has been some time lag in its issuance.

b. *Index to the Statutes in Force of Northern Ireland*[17] is patterned after that of the English Index. Coverage is from the United Kingdom Parliament of 1801 through 1972.

14. Edinburgh, Blackwood, 1876. 3 vols.
15. London, Butterworths, 1968 to date. 40 vols. & index & continuation vols.
16. London, H.M.S.O.
17. Belfast, H.M.S.O.

THE OIL IN NAVIGABLE WATERS ACT 1955

(3 & 4 Eliz. 2 c. 25)

ARRANGEMENT OF SECTIONS

An Act to enable effect to be given to the International Convention for the Prevention of Pollution of the Sea by Oil, 1954, *and otherwise to make new provision for preventing the pollution of navigable waters by oil* [6th May 1955]

Oil in Navigable Waters Acts 1955 and 1963. This Act and the Oil in Navigable Waters Act 1963, p. 658, *post*, may, by s. 4 (2) of the Act of 1963, p. 661, *post*, be cited together as the Oil in Navigable Waters Acts 1955 and 1963, and by that provision the Act of 1963 is to be construed as one with this Act.

Oil in Navigable Waters Acts 1955 to 1971. By the Oil in Navigable Waters Act 1971, s. 12 (2), Vol. 41, title Shipping and Navigation, that Act is to be construed as one with the Oil in Navigable Waters Acts 1955 and 1963 (as to which see the preceding note) and the said Acts are to be cited together as the Oil in Navigable Waters Acts 1955 to 1971.

Northern Ireland. This Act applies with modifications; see ss. 23 and 25 (2), *post*.

WHEREAS a Convention entitled "The International Convention for the Prevention of Pollution of the Sea by Oil, 1954" (in this Act referred to as "the Convention of 1954") was signed on behalf of Her Majesty's Government in the United Kingdom in London on the twelfth day of May, nineteen hundred and fifty-four:

And whereas it is expedient to enable effect to be given to that Convention, and otherwise to make new provision for preventing the pollution of navigable waters by oil:

NOTE

International Convention for the Prevention of Pollution of the Sea by Oil 1954. This Convention was the outcome of a Conference held in London from 26th April to 12th May 1954 on the invitation of the Government of the United Kingdom; see Final Act of Conference and text of the International Convention for the Prevention of Pollution of the Sea by Oil 1954 (Cmd. 9197).

Exhibit 75

SHIPPING AND NAVIGATION

(FOR MAIN TITLE, SEE VOLUME 31)

CONTINUATION OF LIST OF STATUTES ON PAGES 1 TO 3 OF MAIN TITLE

Carriage of Goods by Sea Act 1971	Vol. 41, p. 1312.
Oil in Navigable Waters Act 1971	Vol. 41, p. 1330
Shipbuilding Industry Act 1971	Vol. 41, p. 1345
Merchant Shipping (Oil Pollution) Act 1971 ..	Vol. 41, p. 1345
Prevention of Oil Pollution Act 1971	Vol. 41, p. 1361
Harbours (Loans) Act 1972	Vol. 42, p. 1914
Industry Act 1972, ss. 10–12, 16–19, Sch. 3, Sch. 4, Part II	Vol. 42, p. 1917
Merchant Shipping Act 1974	Vol. 44, p. 1415
Industry Act 1975, ss. 23–25, 39 (1), (4), (5), (7) ..	Vol. 45, p. 1748

VOLUME 31

PAGE

Preliminary Note

3 *The Merchant Shipping Acts.* For the Acts which may be cited together as the Merchant Shipping Acts 1894 to 1971, see the Merchant Shipping (Oil Pollution) Act 1971, s. 21 (1), Vol. 41, p. 1360, and the notes thereto.

The Merchant Shipping Act 1974, Vol. 44, p. 1415, is to be construed as one with the Merchant Shipping Acts 1894 to 1971, and references to the Merchant Shipping Acts include references to the Merchant Shipping Act 1974; see s. 23 (1) of that Act, Vol. 44, p. 1438.

The Oil in Navigable Waters Acts 1955 and 1963 were amended by the Oil in Navigable Waters Act 1971, Vol. 41, p. 1330, but all three Acts are repealed by the Prevention of Oil Pollution Act 1971, s. 33, Schedule, *ibid.*, pp. 1396, 1397, which consolidated the legislation relating to oil pollution.

Oil in Navigable Waters Act 1955 (c. 25)

615 The whole Act is repealed and replaced by the Prevention of Oil Pollution Act 1971, s. 33 (1), and Schedule, Vol. 41, pp. 1396, 1397. For the replaced provisions, see the destination table to that Act, *ibid.*, p. 1398.

Merchant Shipping (Liability of Shipowners and Others) Act 1958 (c. 62)

Section 1

647–648 n. *General Note.* For the position, in relation to the distribution of a limitation fund which is paid into court in proceedings for limitation of liability for oil pollution, of a person who is entitled to limit his liability by virtue of this Act, see the Merchant Shipping (Oil Pollution) Act 1971, s. 5 (4) (*b*), Vol. 41, p. 1350, as from a day to be appointed. And as to proceedings in cases of concurrent liabilities of owners and others where the other person is entitled to limit his liability under this Act, see *ibid.*, s. 7 (*b*), *ibid.*, p. 1351, as from a day to be appointed.

648 n. *Order under this section.* The Merchant Shipping (Limitation of Liability) (Sterling Equivalents) Order 1967, S.I. 1967 No. 1725, was revoked and replaced by S.I. 1972 No. 734 (revoked). See now S.I. 1975 No. 1615 (specifying £114·89 and £37·06 as the amounts to be taken as equivalent to 3,100 gold francs and 1,000 gold francs respectively).

653–654 **Section 8**
Sub-ss. (1) and (6) repealed by the S.L.(R.)A. 1974, Vol. 44, p. 1585.

654 **Section 10**
Sub-s. (3) repealed by the Northern Ireland Constitution Act 1973, s. 41 (1), Sch. 6, Part I, Vol. 43, pp. 1213, 1221.

" **Schedule**
Repealed by the S.L.(R.)A. 1974, Vol. 44, p. 1585.

Exhibit 76

6. *Dates of statutes*. Statutes become effective on the date they are given royal assent, unless otherwise specified. Although English statutes are conventionally cited by regnal year, that is, by the year of the sovereign's reign during which they were enacted (1 Geo. V; 15 Vic.), by virtue of the Law Revision Act, 1948 (11 & 12 Geo. VI, c. 62, s. 5), it is legal to cite an act by short title. British practice is increasingly to cite by short title and year only. The volumes of statutes being annual, this is the most convenient form of citation. Nearly all significant statutes since 1875 bear a short title, part of which is the year of passage. However, the regnal year and chapter are usually added in legal writing, especially for statutes passed prior to 1963. A list of regnal years is given below.

Table of Regnal Years of English Sovereigns

King	*Inclusive Dates*
William I Wm.	14 Oct. 1066–9 Sept. 1087
William II	26 Sept. 1087–2 Aug. 1100
Henry I Hen.	5 Aug. 1100–1 Dec. 1135
Stephen	26 Dec. 1135–25 Oct. 1154
Henry II	19 Dec. 1154–6 July 1189
Richard I Ric.	3 Sept. 1189–6 April 1199
John	27 May 1199–19 Oct. 1216
Henry III	28 Oct. 1216–16 Nov. 1272
Edward I Edw.	20 Nov. 1272–7 July 1307
Edward II	8 July 1307–20 Jan. 1327
Edward III	25 Jan. 1327–21 June 1377
Richard II	22 June 1377–29 Sept. 1399
Henry IV	30 Sept. 1399–20 March 1413
Henry V	21 March 1413–31 Aug. 1422
Henry VI	1 Sept. 1422–4 March 1461 (deposed by Edward V)
Henry VI	9 Oct. 1470–about April 1471 (regained throne)
Edward IV	4 March 1461–9 April 1483
Edward V	9 Apr. 1483–25 June 1483
Richard III	26 June 1483–22 Aug. 1485
Henry VII	22 Aug. 1485–21 April 1509
Henry VIII	22 April 1509–28 Jan. 1547
Edward VI	28 Jan. 1547–6 July 1553
Mary M.	6 July 1553–24 July 1554
Jane	6 July 1553–17 July 1553
Philip and Mary Ph. & M.	25 July 1554–17 Nov. 1558
Elizabeth I Eliz.	17 Nov. 1558–24 Mar. 1603
James I Jac. or Jas.	24 March 1603–27 March 1625
Charles I Car. or Chas.	27 March 1625–30 Jan. 1649
Charles II	30 Jan. 1649–6 Feb. 1685

Interregnum		30 Jan. 1649–29 Jan. 1661
James II		6 Feb. 1685–11 Dec. 1688
William and Mary	Wm. & M.	13 Feb. 1689–8 Mar. 1702
Anne		8 March 1702–1 Aug. 1714
George I	Geo.	1 Aug. 1714–11 June 1727
George II		11 June 1727–25 Oct. 1760
George III		25 Oct. 1760–29 Jan. 1820 (Regency 25 Oct. 1810–29 Jan. 1820)
George IV		29 Jan. 1820–26 June 1830
William IV		26 June 1830–20 June 1837
Victoria or	Vic.	20 June 1837–22 Jan. 1901
Edward VII		22 Jan. 1901–6 May 1910
George V		6 May 1910–20 Jan. 1936
Edward VIII		20 Jan. 1936–11 Dec. 1936
George VI		11 Dec. 1936–6 Feb. 1952
Elizabeth II		6 Feb. 1952–

§24.3. Subordinate legislation.

By authority delegated by particular acts of Parliament, ministers of government and departments and agencies responsible to them issue subordinate legislation or regulations called Statutory Instruments. Included in the Statutory Instruments are orders under delegation to the Queen's Council made under the prerogative powers of the Crown and not requiring legislative sanction. Commonly, Parliament in its enabling legislation, provides a check on the exercise of this administrative function by retaining the right to confirm or negate them prior to their promulgation.

1. *Statutory Instruments.*[18] This official edition includes virtually all statutory instruments of general and permanent character and certain Orders in Council. Prior to 1948, regulations were known as statutory rules and orders; the official title of the publication was Statutory Rules and Orders and Statutory Instruments Revised to December 31, 1948. The first three volumes of this set provide both the original form of the instrument and all amendments to it. In subsequent volumes only the current form is given, with footnote citations to the amendments.

Instruments are numbered serially by year. The statutory authorization and the effective date of each instrument are given. The current Statutory Instruments consists of three parts, each comprising several volumes and covering a four-month period. There are tables

18. London, H.M.S.O.

and indexes for each part cumulating annually, which list chronologically instruments in force, the effect of new instruments adopted on parliamentary acts, and/or the effect of the year's legislation on previous instruments.

2. *Statutory Rules of Northern Ireland*[19] have been issued (with title variance) officially since 1922. Rules are printed sequentially. Each volume includes a numerical table of the rules issued during the year, the rules effected, and a subject index. A consolidated index is published triennially.

3. *Index to Government Orders*[20] (with title variance). This is a biennial cumulative subject index. It includes lists of all statutes under which orders have been issued and repealed, with the subject heading under which the order may be found in the index. For access through official sources to the annual volumes not yet covered by this index, use the indexes to Statutory Instruments.

4. *Halsbury's Statutory Instruments*.[21] This unofficial set is conveniently arranged under broad subject titles. Each title contains lists of instruments included, cross-references, preliminary notes or summary essay, and annotations followed by the texts, all in a format similar to that describing Halsbury's Statutes. Currency of the set is maintained by means of a loose-leaf binder containing quarterly additions to the chronological list of instruments, quarterly cumulative additions to the subject titles, keyed to relevant pages in the main volumes, and an annual cumulative supplement which replaces the earlier three issues and incorporates all prior material. Access through the indexes is by either instrument number or subject. The consolidated index volume is revised and reissued triennially. References to Northern Ireland and Scotland are included.

§24.4. Treaties.

British treaties and agreements of international effect (including unratified treaties) are published as Command Papers, all of which appear in the bound volume of the Parliamentary Papers for each session, entitled State Papers. Treaties are indexed in the monthly and annual lists of government publications of Her Majesty's Stationery Office.

Those treaties which are ratified, and most of the agreements and exchanges of notes, are numbered within the Treaty Series,[22] in which a new numbering commences every year. The last treaty series

19. Belfast, H.M.S.O.
20. London, H.M.S.O.
21. London, Butterworths. 23 vols. & index & loose-leaf current binder.
22. London, H.M.S.O., 1892–1967. New series 1968 to date.

number of each year is an index, and the one preceding it is a list of treaty ratifications, accessions, withdrawals, etc., for the current year. Biennial or triennial indexes are also issued within the series itself. The numbered series began in 1892.

British treaties are included also in the collection of British and Foreign State Papers,[23] covering the period from 1812, and in Hertslet's Commercial Treaties.[24] Hertslet was incorporated into British and Foreign State Papers, beginning with volume 116 (1922) of the latter. The first volume of each of these series includes pertinent treaties in force at the time the set was begun. An Index of British Treaties, 1101–1968,[25] compiled by Clive Parry, provides access by country and subject as well as by date.

Treaties relating to the United Kingdom's entrance into the European Community are discussed at §24.8.2.

§24.5. Law reports — historical series.

1. *Year Books*. English law reporting first came into existence toward the end of the thirteenth century. Year Books, so-called because they first appeared as manuscripts grouped by regnal years, are believed to have been transcribed originally by students of the law or practitioners in open court until 1537. Most of the Year Books have now been reprinted under various auspices with extensive scholarly notes. The Year Books profoundly influenced the progress of the law in the 300 years after their writing.

2. *Named reporters*. During the period 1537–1865, there were more than 300 different, sometimes duplicating reports series, known by the name of the transcribing reporter. Among those of greatest historical note are the reports of Plowden and Coke. There was no systematic, successive reporting for the whole period; no single named reporter deals with all the decided appellate cases, nor do all of them combined. The duplication and variance of law reporting was furthered by the fact that any written report signed or initialed by a barrister present when the opinion was delivered orally in court (and usually not from manuscript) or any oral report vouched for by a barrister could then, as now, be cited in court. One may conveniently locate these reports today in the reprint series described below.

3. *English Reports, Full Reprint*.[26] Practically all reports of value for the years 1378–1865 are purported to be found herein. About

23. London, H.M.S.O., 1812 to date.
24. London, Butterworths, vols. 1-19, 1827–1895; H.M.S.O., vols. 20–21, 1898–1925.
25. London, H.M.S.O., 1970. 3 vols.
26. London, Green, 1900–1930. 176 vols. Reprint ed., South Hackensack, N.J., Rothman.

100,000 cases are reprinted verbatim with parallel citations to reports of the case in other series. Some editorial notes are provided. The parallel citations to other reports not printed are in the following form (the S.C. meaning same case in another report):

> *Mayor of Ludlow* v. *Charlton*, 6 M. & W. 815 (1840). [S.C. 10 L.J. Ex. 75; 3 Jur. 657; 8 Car. & P. 242. Followed, *Arnold* v. *Poole Corp.*, 4 Man. & G. 860. Referred to, *Wells* v. *Kingston-Upon-Hull*, 1875, L.R.C.P. 409]

The reprint volumes are arranged by courts — House of Lords, Chancery, Nisi Prius, etc. — and are star-paged to the original so that the exact paging of the original may be cited from the reprint. Many "unauthorized" series of reports were not reprinted at all, but most cases reported in the unauthorized reports were reprinted in the Full Reprint from authorized reports. A wall chart, listing alphabetically all report series reprinted and parallel references to the corresponding volumes of the Reprint, is provided. The chart is usually located adjacent to the library shelves holding the Reprint. There is a two-volume table of cases.

4. *Revised Reports.*[27] This set reprints most of the cases for the period 1785–1865. In general its coverage for these years duplicates that of the English Reports, Full Reprint, but in addition it reprints many collateral (unauthorized) report series not found in the Full Reprint. There is a table of cases and an index-digest.

5. *English Law Reports, Pre-1865.*[28] This is a microform edition of pre-1865 English nominatives which are not printed in the English Reports, Full Reprint, or in the Revised Reports, either because the original set of reports was excluded from the above series, or because the editors of these other series had selected for reproduction another report of a case.

6. *All England Law Reports Reprint.*[29] This is a selection of cases revised and annotated, covering the period 1558–1935, reported in the Law Times Reports and earlier reports, which the editors deemed of general interest and value to present-day practitioners. The reprint is intended to complement the All England Reports, for which see §24.6.2.

Cases originally printed in all the standard reports series for the period covered are included if, in addition to their coverage in the Times Law Reports, such cases were originally printed in one or more other series. That is, if a case was printed both in the Times Law Reports and in a duplicating series, that case can be found by its

27. London, Sweet & Maxwell, 1891–1917. 149 vols.
28. Dobbs Ferry, N.Y., Trans-Media Pub.
29. London, Butterworths, 1968. 52 vols.

case name in this reprint, because the table of cases will give all the parallel citations for each case reprinted.

Texts of the reports are reprinted verbatim; there are extensive headnotes which serve as citators up to the date of publication. The index volume contains an alphabetical list of cases and a comprehensive index to their contents by subject.

§24.6. Law reports — modern series.

Modern law reporting in a form familiar to the legal research evolved in the mid-eighteenth century, but systematic, successive reporting and publishing began in 1865. The court system was simplified principally by the Judicature Acts of 1873, 1875, 1881, and 1950, and the Law Report series, which have closely reflected the changes in court organization, have been altered accordingly. For a brief description of earlier court organization, see Price and Bitner (1953).

The system of courts of the United Kingdom in effect combines in one hierarchy those which in the United States would have separate federal and state jurisdictions. Courts presently in existence may be classified variously, but for purposes here, it is sufficient to outline the upper hierarchy of British courts of general jurisdiction, and to note the existence of some special courts such as the Restrictive Practices Court. At the pinnacle is the House of Lords, which is the final court of appeal in civil cases for all the United Kingdom and in criminal cases for England, Wales, and Northern Ireland. The Judicial Committee of the Privy Council is a special appellate body for final review of the dependencies and some independent members of the Commonwealth. The High Court, the Court of Appeal (London), and the Crown Court comprise the Supreme Court of Justice. The three divisions of the High Court are Chancery, which considers estates, trusts settlements, contractual rights, partnerships; Family, which deals with probate and other matters as the name implies; and the Queen's Bench, which has the broadest jurisdiction, covering most other civil litigation. Admiralty Court cases also come within the purview of the Queen's Bench. The Crown Court hears serious criminal cases tried on indictment with a jury.

1. *Law Reports*.[30] These reports, begun in 1865, comprise the principal body of law reporting for England and Wales. The editor of the Law Reports (monthly) and the Weekly Law Reports is the final arbiter as to inclusion. Cases printed in the Law Reports are those concerning new points of law and those of permanent interest to the legal profession. Cases of temporary interest or merely illustrative of

30. London, Incorporated Council of Law Reporting for England and Wales.

an old principle are omitted from the Law Reports but may be printed as starred cases in the Weekly Law Reports. English judges revise and approve texts of their own decisions prior to publication, and it is customary for the courts to prefer citation to the Law Reports, when a case has been published in one of these series.

Court	*Report Series*
House of Lords	Appeal Cases
Judicial Committee of the Privy Council	Appeal Cases
Supreme Court of Justice	
High Court	
Queen's Bench	Queen's Bench
Chancery	Chancery
Family	Family
Court of Appeal	In one of the above divisional series from which the appeal came
Crown Court	Criminal Appeal Reports (Included in Law Reports Index)
Restrictive Trade Practices Court	Restrictive Trade Practices Reports (Included in Law Reports Index)

It is essential to note from the above table the distinction between Court of Appeal cases, which decisions are located in the divisional series, and the Appeal Cases, a Law Report series of appellate cases heard in the House of Lords and the Judicial Committee of the Privy Council. Similarly, appeals of a case from a magistrates' court (lower court) to a divisional court are reported in the appropriate divisional report series.

The four current Law Report series: Appeal Cases, Queen's Bench, Chancery, and Family (entitled Probate prior to 1972) are issued in monthly parts, the latter two together. Pamphlet issues carry a cumulative table of cases reported. Pink-paper indexes are issued as supplements. Each annual volume contains tables of cases reported and cases, statutes, and statutory instruments judically noticed. For a fuller analysis of subject and tabular access to the contents, see below.

a. *Weekly Law Reports*. In 1953 the Weekly Law Reports, having absorbed the Times Law Reports (1884-1952) and the Weekly Notes

(1850–1952), became the most complete current general English law report series published. Each issue is in two parts. Volume 1 (of each part during each calendar year) includes starred reports which are not intended for inclusion in the Law Reports. These are prepared by barristers and may be so cited, but they are not revised by judges. Volumes 2 and 3 print the reports as they will appear subsequently in the Law Reports, Restrictive Practices Reports, and Industrial Court Reports, except that arguments of counsel, prefacing the Law Reports publication of the decision, are omitted. Weekly Law Reports cases are released approximately three weeks after the date of decision. In each issue there is a cumulative table of cases for the volume to date and a subject digest of cases in that issue. Indexes to volumes 1 to 3 cumulate annually. For fuller analysis of subject and tabular access to the contents, see below.

b. *Restrictive Practices Reports*.[31] The series, begun in 1958 with the creation of the Restrictive Trade Practices Court, reports decisions regarding monopolies, restrictive trade practices, and resale price maintenance. Pamphlets are issued approximately twice yearly. For each volume there is a table of cases and tables of cases, statutes, and instruments judically considered.

c. *Digests, indexes, tables to Law Reports publications*. The Law Reports Digest of Cases and Statutes from 1865 through 1950, when it was discontinued, was an outstanding search tool. It is continued by the Law Reports Index, encompassing the years 1951-1970, and the Red Index, covering the period 1971–1976. Supplementing these are indexes for the current volumes of series described above. Access through the index is by case name or subject. Additionally, there are tables of cases, statutes, statutory instruments, and EEC enactments judicially considered. There are numerous cross-references. The scope of the indexes goes beyond Law Reports and Weekly Law Reports to include cases reported in All England Law Reports and special subject reports covering, for example, tax, local government, and criminal appeal cases.

2. *All England Law Reports*.[32] These weekly reports, which commenced in 1936, have since incorporated the Law Times (1843-January 1948) and the Law Journal Reports (1822-1949). The editors select cases from the House of Lords, the Court of Appeal, High Court, the Restrictive Practices Court, and other superior courts and courts of special jurisdiction, involving new principles of law and cases interpreting established principles in light of modern circumstances. Each case reported is prefaced by a headnote; more extensive editorial notes are sometimes added. Following the headnotes, cross-references are provided to appropriate sections of Halsbury's

31. *Ibid*.
32. London, Butterworths.

Statutes of England, Halsbury's Statutory Instruments, Halsbury's Laws of England, and the English and Empire Digest.

The Consolidated Tables and Index, 1936-1976, in two volumes, provides comprehensive subject reference and tabular access to cases, statutes, and statutory instruments judicially construed, as well as cases affected by subsequent decisions. Supplemental cumulative indexes are issued at regular intervals.

3. *Northern Ireland Law Reports*.[33] These consist of reports of cases in superior courts of Northern Ireland and those on appeal to the House of Lords.

4. *Cases decided in the Court of Session and Also in the Judiciary and House of Lords*.[34] These report Scottish cases as the title indicates. The Court of Session is the superior civil court of Scotland, functioning as both a court of first instance and a court of appeal. Each volume in the above series has a subject index and table of cases. Subject access is most easily achieved through Current Law indexes.

§24.7. Digests.

Digests issued as one element of a set are described with that set. See, for example, Law Reports Digest . . . 1865–1950, §24.6.1c; and All England Law Reports Index, §24.6.2.

1. *English and Empire Digest*.[35] Relevant cases from earliest times and many different series of law reports have been culled and summarized to make this set the most comprehensive digest published. Arrangement of cases in classified order under broad subject titles and chronologically within the topic parallel, in large measure, the organization of material in Halsbury's Laws of England. Titles begin with a summary of their subject scope and content. Each section is keyed to Halsbury's Laws of England, third edition; it includes also cross-references within the Digest to paragraph numbers in other specific volumes. A distinct consecutive number is assigned to each case digest within each title. Digests of English cases precede Irish, Scottish, and other selective Commonwealth cases and are printed in larger type. Appended to English cases are annotations which trace the subsequent judicial history and authority of the cases. See Exhibit 77.

Each volume has its own index and table of cases. In addition, there is a three-volume consolidated table of cases and a two-volume general index of subjects and words and phrases.

33. Belfast, Incorporated Council of Law Reporting for Northern Ireland.
34. Edinburgh, Clark, 1821 to date.
35. London, Butterworths.

THE STATUTE OF FRAUDS [**1339–1355 : *814–*817**] 211

mtged. the house for the purpose of raising money to pay his debts. The Duchess joined with the Duke in covenanting to pay the mtge. debt, but the equity of redemption was reserved to the Duke alone. Upon the death of the Duke in 1892 the Duchess claimed to be entitled to the house subject to the mtge. There was evidence that she had assigned the house to the Duke solely to enable him to mtge. it in his own name, & that it was part of the arrangement between them that he should re-assign to her, which, if he had lived, he would have done:—*Held:* the case fell within the authorities which forbid Stat. Frauds to be used to cover what would amount to a fraud, & consequently the statute could not be successfully pleaded in opposition to the claim by the Duchess.—*Re* MARLBOROUGH (DUKE), DAVIS *v.* WHITEHEAD, [1894] 2 Ch. 133; 63 L. J. Ch. 471; 70 L. T. 314; 42 W. R. 456; 10 T. L. R. 296; 38 Sol. Jo. 289; 8 R. 242.

Annotations:—**Consd.** Hodgson *v.* Marks, [1970] 3 All E. R. 513. **Refd.** Rochefoucauld *v.* Boustead, [1897] 1 Ch. 196; Isaacs *v.* Evans (1899), 16 T. L. R. 113; Tsang Chuen *v.* Li Po Kwai, [1932] A. C. 715; Bannister *v.* Bannister, [1948] 2 All E. R. 133.

1345. Conveyance of interest in land—Whether evidence of trust admissible.]—Where land was paid for with the money of A., parol evidence to show that the purchase was made on behalf of B. was refused.—BARTLETT *v.* PICKERSGILL (1760), 1 Eden, 515; 1 Cox, Eq. Cas. 15; 4 East, 576, n.; 28 E. R. 785.

Annotations:—**N.F.** Rochefoucauld *v.* Boustead, [1897] 1 Ch. 196. **Consd.** Heard *v.* Pilley (1869), 4 Ch. App. 548. **Refd.** R. *v.* Dunston (1824), Ry. & M. 109; James *v.* Smith, [1891] 1 Ch. 384.

1346. —— ——.]—A son conveyed an estate to his father nominally as purchaser, but really as a trustee, & in order that the father, who was in better credit than the son, might raise money upon it by way of mtge., for the use of the son. The father died shortly afterwards & before any money was raised, having by a will, subsequent to the conveyance, made a general devise of all his real estates:—*Held:* the case was within Stat. Frauds, & parol evidence was not admissible to prove the trust.—LEMAN *v.* WHITLEY (1828), 4 Russ. 423; 6 L. J. O. S. Ch. 152; 38 E. R. 864.

Annotation:—**Consd.** *Re* Marlborough, Davis *v.* Whitehead, [1894] 2 Ch. 133.

1347. —— ——.]—LINCOLN *v.* WRIGHT, No. 1341, *ante*.

1348. —— ——.]—Pltf., apprehensive of being indicted for bigamy, which it turned out he was not liable to be, conveyed real property to deft., on a parol agreement to re-transfer when the difficulty had passed. On a bill for a re-transfer, deft. denied the agreement & insisted on Stat. Frauds, the trust not being in writing:—*Held:* this was a case of fraud & the statute did not apply.—DAVIES *v.* OTTY (No. 2) (1865), 35 Beav. 208; 5 New Rep. 391; 34 L. J. Ch. 252; 12 L. T. 789; 13 W. R. 484; 55 E. R. 875.

Annotations:—**Consd.** Booth *v.* Turle (1873), L. R. 16 Eq. 182. **Refd.** Haigh *v.* Kaye (1872), 7 Ch. App. 469; Rochefoucauld *v.* Boustead, [1897] 1 Ch. 196.

1349. —— ——.]—HAIGH *v.* KAYE, No. 1342, *ante*.

1350. —— ——.]—BOOTH *v.* TURLE, No. 1343, *ante*.

1351. —— ——.]—*Re* MARLBOROUGH (DUKE), DAVIS *v.* WHITEHEAD, No. 1344, *ante*.

1352. —— ——.]—It is a fraud on the part of a person to whom land is conveyed, as a trustee, & who knows it to have been so conveyed to deny the trust & claim the land. Consequently, notwithstanding Stat. Frauds, it is competent for a person claiming land conveyed to another to prove by parol evidence that it was so conveyed on trust, & that the grantee knowing the facts, is denying the trust.—ROCHEFOUCAULD *v.* BOUSTEAD, [1897] 1 Ch. 196; 66 L. J. Ch. 74; *sub nom.* DE LA ROCHEFOUCAULD *v.* BOUSTEAD, 75 L. T. 502; 45 W. R. 272; 13 T. L. R. 118; 41 Sol. Jo. 156, C. A.; *subsequent proceedings*, [1898] 1 Ch. 550, C. A.

Annotations:—**Apld.** Hodgson *v.* Marks, [1970] 3 All E. R. 513. **Refd.** Isaacs *v.* Evans (1899), 16 T. L. R. 113; Bannister *v.* Bannister, [1948] 2 All E. R. 133; Lawson *v.* Hosemaster Machine Co., Ltd., [1966] 2 All E. R. 944.

SCOTTISH, IRISH AND COMMONWEALTH CASES

***814.** *General rule.*]—LEES *v.* CONDELL (1853), 1 V. L. T. 176.—**AUS.**

***815.** ——.]—Pltf. sued deft., her husband, for specific performance of an alleged agreement to execute a marriage settlement. Deft. denied that there had been any concluded agreement, & pleaded Stat. Frauds. It was proved that, the negotiations for the settlement having broken down, deft., without the consent of pltf.'s father, or knowledge of the trustees of the proposed settlement, married pltf. & afterwards refused to make a settlement upon her:—*Held:* deft. had not been guilty of fraud so as to take the case out of Stat. Frauds.—HOGAN *v.* HOGAN (1869), 8 N. S. W. S. C. R. (Eq.) 96.—**AUS.**

***816.** ——.]—Stat. Frauds & Mineral Act, B. C., s. 19, will not be allowed to be made instruments of fraud.—ROBERTS *v.* ROBERTS, [1923] 2 W. W. R. 137.—**CAN.**

***817.** *Conveyance of interest in land—Whether evidence of trust admissible.*]—SMITH *v.* BENOR (1913), 24 O. W. R. 521; 4 O. W. N. 985; 10 D. L. R. 824.—**CAN.**

B. Part Performance

LAW. *See* HALSBURY'S LAWS (3rd Edn.), Vol. 8, pp. 109 *et seq.*

CROSS-REFERENCES. *See* Nos. 1335 *et seq.*, *ante* (effect of fraud); as to what amounts to specific performance, generally, SPECIFIC PERFORMANCE, Vol. 44 (Repl.), Nos. 307 *et seq.* As to what contracts applicable, *see* FAMILY ARRANGEMENTS, Vol. 24 (Repl.), Nos. 32 *et seq.* (contract for family arrangement); GUARANTEE & INDEMNITY, Vol. 26 (Repl.), No. 186 (when doctrine not applicable); LANDLORD & TENANT, Vol. 30 (Repl.), Nos. 397 *et seq.* (personal liability of agent), Nos. 467 *et seq.* (extent of doctrine); SALE OF GOODS, Vol. 39 (Repl.), Nos. 157 *et seq.*, Nos. 212 *et seq.* (contract for sale of goods); SALE OF LAND, Vol. 40 (Repl.), Nos. 206 *et seq.* (contract relating to land), Nos. 218 *et seq.* (what constitutes); SETTLEMENTS, Vol. 40 (Repl.), Nos. 219 *et seq.* (contract upon consideration of marriage).

1353. Effect in law.]—BOYDELL *v.* DRUMMOND, No. 854, *ante*.

1354. When equitable doctrine applied—Execution of wholly parol agreement—Not to supply defect in written agreement.]—Where there is a whole agreement by parol & part of it is executed a ct. of equity will decree a specific execution of the whole, for Stat. Frauds does not extend to that; but where there is an agreement by writing executed, you cannot come by evidence to supply any defect in that agreement, which was intended to be part of that agreement but not inserted in it, for that would be to evade Stat. Frauds (*per* CUR.).—BINSTEAD *v.* COLEMAN (1720), Bunb. 65; 145 E. R. 597.

1355. ——.]—Stat. Frauds not pleadable where

Exhibit 77

Currency of the set is maintained by the following means. The blue-banded volume edition is being replaced by green-banded volumes. Within each new green-banded volume, there is a reference adaptor providing tabular reference transfer, as necessary, from the numbering in the blue-banded volumes to the new ones. Continuation volumes covering a five-year period are permanent supplements to the main volumes. Through the system of distinct numbering of each case digest, the history of the case can be followed, and newer cases on the same issue can be located. See Exhibit 78.

An annual cumulative supplement keeps the set current. The volume is consulted as the final step in checking the history and treatment of the case and serves as the latest citator. References therein lead the user back to the continuation volumes as necessary. See Exhibit 79.

2. *Current Law.*[36] The set as a whole is a digest and citator to statutes, statutory instruments, and case law since inception of the work in 1947. It includes also an index to selective English periodical literature and a list of books recently published. Its parts, excepting Current Statutes Annotated, described at §24.2.2b, are analyzed as follows.

a. *Monthly Current Law.* This is a pamphlet advance service for the set. Arrangement is basically in classified format with many subheadings and cross-references. Important cases of the preceding month from the Weekly Law Reports and All England Reports, with citations to them, are digested fully, noting facts, legal principles, dictum, and statutes and cases construed. Cases from many English specialist-subject report series and reports and periodicals of Northern Ireland, Scotland, the Commonwealth, and European Communities are summarized with brevity. Statutes, instruments, and case law restricted to Northern Ireland are digested under the heading, Northern Ireland. Treatment of Scottish law is discussed further below. English statutes and statutory instruments are digested within the subject sections and are also listed separately under the heading, Statutes and Orders. Citations to relevant periodical articles are appended to the classified sections. Monthly Current Law is useful also for identifying recently issued Royal Commission reports and White Papers and for following the status of Parliamentary bills.

b. *Current Law Year Book.* This supersedes the monthly Current Law issues for the year of the title. See Exhibit 80. Year Books for 1947–1951 have been melded into the Current Law Consolidation. Year Book indexes are cumulative through 1976. Master volumes are issued at the end of every five years, giving references to paragraph items in the Year Books covering the five-year span. They do not supersede the Year Books.

c. *Current Law Citator.* This is an annual cumulative citator to both statutory and case law. The case citator provides the history and treatment of every English case reported since 1947, every Northern Ireland, Scottish, or Commonwealth case digested since 1947, every English case considered since 1947, and cases commented upon in

36. London, Sweet & Maxwell.

CONTINUATION VOLUME D: 1971–1975 120

***689a.** *Clause in will.*]—A clause in a will leaving a house & contents to a companion upon condition that she should be living with testatrix at the latter's death is a "sufficient memorandum or note" within the meaning of Statute of Frauds, R. S. N. S. 1967, c. 290, s. 6, to identify an alleged oral agreement in those terms between testatrix & her companion.—JOHNSON *v.* NOVA SCOTIA TRUST CO. (1973), 43 D. L. R. (3d) 222.—**CAN.**

***740a.** *General rule—Terms only partly set out.*]—A written memorandum of an alleged two-year contract of employment, though signed by the employer, is insufficient to satisfy the requirements of Stat. of Frauds, R.S.O. 1970, if it omits any reference to the duration of the contract sought to be enforced.—ACKERMAN *v.* THOMSON AND MCKINNON, AUCHINCLOSS, KOHLMEYER, INC. (1974), 47 D. L. R. (3d) 524; 4 O. R. (2d) 240.—**CAN.**

1162a. Necessity for stating price—No price fixed —Agreement "to negotiate fair & reasonable contract sums".]—A co. represented by T wished to develop a site by building a motel, filling station & hotel. T got into touch with C, a property developer who was well placed to obtain finance for the development. At a meeting between T & C it was proposed that C should introduce someone to finance the development & that T should employ the co. which C represented to construct the bldgs. After that meeting C wrote a letter to T, dated Apr. 10, 1969, stating that he was in a position to introduce to T someone who had access to the necessary finance for the development; C also pointed out that his commercial interest in the matter was that of a bldg. contractor. The letter continued: "Accordingly I would be very happy to know that, if my discussions & arrangements with interested parties lead to . . . a financial arrangement acceptable to both parties you will be prepared to instruct your Quantity Surveyor to negotiate fair & reasonable contract sums in respect of each of the three projects as they arise. (These would, incidentally be based upon agreed estimates of the net cost of work & general overheads with a margin for profit of 5%) which, I am sure you will agree, is, indeed reasonable." On Apr. 28 T wrote to C: "In reply to your letter of Apr. 10, I agree to the terms specified therein, & I look forward to meeting the interested party regarding finance." C introduced a person willing to provide finance for the development. T instructed his quantity surveyor to negotiate with C as to the price for the bldg. works, but agreement with C on the price could not be reached & the negotiations broke down. T then instructed contractors other than C's co. to carry out the development. C's co. brought an action in which they claimed a declaration that there was an enforceable contract to employ them as builders for the development & that T's co. were in breach of contract in employing other bldg. contractors:—*Held:* the letters did not give rise to any enforceable contract between T's co. & C's co. because (1) the price was a matter which was fundamental to the contract. Accordingly there could be no binding contract unless the price had been agreed, or there was an agreed method of ascertaining the price which was not dependent on negotiations between the parties. The letters did not contain any agreement on the price, nor did they provide for any method for ascertaining the price; they amounted to no more than an agreement to negotiate fair & reasonable contract sums; (2) a contract to negotiate even though supported by consideration was not a contract known to the law since it was too uncertain to have any binding force & no ct. could estimate the damages for breach of such an agreement.—COURTNEY & FAIRBAIRN, LTD. *v.* TOLAINI BROS. (HOTELS), LTD., [1975] 1 All E. R. 716; [1975] 1 W. L. R. 297; 119 Sol. Jo. 134, C. A.

***818a.** *Effect in law—Principles applicable—Fraud as essence of doctrine.*]—The principles applicable to the doctrine of part performance are virtually indistinguishable from those to be considered in deciding whether there is an estoppel. The essence of both doctrines is fraud, for it is fraud to mislead another into accepting the existence of a contract & doing acts to his prejudice when harbouring the intention to repudiate the contract. Accordingly, a plea of part performance is not only applicable in an action for specific performance but also in an action for an instalment of purchase money. Acts of part performance may amount to an estoppel in the common law action for an instalment of purchase money & may be used to refute a defence of what in essence amounts to *non est factum*.—CELONA *v.* KAMLOOPS CENTENNIAL (PACIFIC NO. 269) BRANCH, ROYAL CANADIAN LEGION (1972), 31 D. L. R. (3d) 305; [1972] 6 W. W. R. 257. —**CAN.**

***830a.** *When equitable doctrine applied—Act must be unequivocal—& clearly referable to contract.*]—Where a pltf., who alleges an oral contract for the sale of land, has entered into possession & has paid mtge. instalments directly to two mtgees., part performance can successfully be pleaded so as to allow parol evidence to establish the contract alleged. The entering into possession & the making of the mtge. payments are unequivocally referable to the agreement for purchase & sale. This is so even if the narrower interpretation of the doctrine of part performance, which requires the acts relied on to be referable to a specific contract, rather than the broader interpretation, which simply requires the acts relied upon to be referable to some contract involving an interest in land, is the proper interpretation of the doctrine.—TOOMBS *v.* MUELLER (1974), 47 D. L. R. (3d) 709; [1974] 6 W. W. R. 577.—**CAN.**

***849a.** *When equitable doctrine applied—Oral agreement to work on farm—Promise of inheritance.*]—C. orally agreed to leave his farm to applt. in return for the latter's services. Applt. for many years performed valuable & arduous services on which C. fully relied for the operation & management of the farm. C. died intestate & applt. sued the administrator for specific performance of the oral agreement. At trial it was held that his services constituted sufficient part performance to take the agreement out of Statute of Frauds 1676, 29 Car. II, c. 3. On appeal, this decision was reversed on the ground that the services were not sufficiently referable to the agreement sought to be enforced. On further appeal:—*Held:* as applt.'s services were unequivocally referable to the very land in question they were sufficient to constitute part performance of the oral agreement.—THOMPSON *v.* GUARANTY TRUST CO. OF CANADA (1973), 39 D. L. R. (3d) 408; [1974] S. C. R. 1023; [1973] 6 W. W. R. 746.—**CAN.**

***859a.** *Work on land in return for agreement for sale of land.*] —Work done by a son on his father's land does not amount to part performance of an oral agreement for the sale of the land to the son. Such work is equally consistent with an expectation of inheriting the land or a wish to repay the father's generosity as with the agreement sought to be enforced.—ROSS *v.* ROSS, JR. (1973), 33 D. L. R. (3d) 351.—**CAN.**

Part V.—Consideration

***919a.** *Agreement to pay higher price.*]—Where one is bound by agreement to supply goods to another at a certain price, & the other subsequently agrees to pay a higher price, the supply of the goods is not sufficient consideration to support the promise to pay the higher price.—GILBERT STEEL, LTD. *v.* UNIVERSITY CONSTRUCTION, LTD. (1973), 36 D. L. R. (3d) 496; [1973] 3 O. R. 268.—**CAN.**

***945a.** *Promise to perform household services.*]—Pltf. lived in an illicit relationship with one B. for 38 years, during which time she performed housekeeping services for him & spent some of her own money for household necessities. B. orally promised to leave his estate to pltf. but died intestate. Pltf. sued on the promise &, alternatively, for reimbursement of money spent & payment for services rendered:—*Held:* pltf. was entitled to recover no more than moneys spent on funeral, hospital & incidental expenses; with regard to the promise there was no memorandum in writing so as to satisfy Statute of Frauds, nor was there corroboration as required by sect. 13 of Alberta Evidence Act, R. S. A., 1970. As to the second branch of the claim, no implication of law in favour of pltf. could be founded on the fact of cohabitation or the performance of household services; the onus was on pltf. to prove that the services were to be paid for & she had failed to discharge it.—SWAN *v.* PUBLIC TRUSTEE, [1972] 3 W. W. R. 696.—**CAN.**

*** An asterisk indicates a Scottish, Irish or Commonwealth case.**

Exhibit 78

legal periodicals. References are given to the Year Book paragraphs in which the cited or citing cases are digested and to the report citation. See Exhibit 81.

Similarly, the statute citator gives the status of post-1947 statutes, their statutory effect on prior legislation, cases construing post-1947 statutes, and orders and instruments issued pursuant to the statutes.

CUMULATIVE SUPPLEMENT: NOTER UP 66

*408a. *General rule.*]—LAKE ONTARIO CEMENT CO. *v.* GOLDEN EAGLE OIL CO., LTD. (1974).—CAN. *See* Continuation Vol. D.

631. **Refd.** American Cyanamid Co. *v.* Ethicon, Ltd., [1975] 1 All E. R. 504; Fellowes *v.* Fisher, [1975] 2 All E. R. 829.

*473. *Delete whole case.*

*473a. *Fraudulent hoax—Inducement of signature by.*]—GAERTNER *v.* FIESTA DANCE STUDIOS, LTD. (1972).—CAN. *See* Continuation Vol. D.

641. **Refd.** Lloyds Bank, Ltd. *v.* Bundy, [1974] 3 All E. R. 757.

644. *As to* (1) **Refd.** Wales *v.* Wadham, [1977] 2 All E. R. 125.

664. **Refd.** Lloyds Bank, Ltd. *v.* Bundy, [1974] 3 All E. R. 757.

*486a. *Threat of violence.*]—BARTON *v.* ARMSTRONG (1973).—AUS. *See* Continuation Vol. D.

689. **Apld.** Lloyds Bank, Ltd. *v.* Bundy, [1974] 3 All E. R. 757.

*519a. *Arising from special relationship—But not that of husband & wife.*]—HARDING *v.* HARDING (1972).—CAN. *See* Continuation Vol. D.

*519b. *Arising from confidential relationship.*]—TREADWELL *v.* MARTIN (1976).—CAN. *See* Division 2, *post.*

743. **Apld.** Lloyds Bank, Ltd. *v.* Bundy, [1974] 3 All E. R. 757.

*537a. *Gifts to nursing home by patient.*]—PUBLIC TRUSTEE *v.* SKORETZ (1972).—CAN. *See* Continuation Vol. D.

764a. *Banker & customer.*]—LLOYDS BANK, LTD. *v.* BUNDY (1974). *See* Continuation Vol. D.
Apld. Clifford Davis Management, Ltd. *v.* W.E.A. Records, Ltd., [1975] 1 All E. R. 237.

764b. *Composer & business manager.*]—CLIFFORD DAVIS MANAGEMENT, LTD. *v.* W.E.A. RECORDS, LTD. (1975). *See* Continuation Vol. D.

*542a. *Agreement by elderly foreigner.*]—CYMBALUK *v.* LEWICKI (1973).—CAN. *See* Continuation Vol. D.

722. **Refd.** Lloyds Bank, Ltd. *v.* Bundy, [1974] 3 All E. R. 757.

*544a. *Bank knowing of plaintiff's emotional attachment to debtor.*]—MCKENZIE *v.* BANK OF MONTREAL (1976).—CAN. *See* Division 2, *post.*

800. **Apld.** Lloyds Bank, Ltd. *v.* Bundy, [1974] 3 All E. R. 757.

844. **Consd.** Bolton *v.* Mahadeva, [1972] 2 All E. R. 1322. **Refd.** Chappell *v.* Times Newspapers, Ltd., [1975] 2 All E. R. 233.

848. **Refd.** Bolton *v.* Mahadeva, [1972] 2 All E. R. 1322.

848a. *Failure of plaintiff to perform whole contract—Defective performance.*]—BOLTON *v.* MAHADEVA (1972). *See* Continuation Vol. D.

*606a. *No contract for payment—Agreement to render services in consideration of promissee leaving estate.*]—HINK *v.* LHENEN (1974).—CAN. *See* Division 2, *post.*

*613a. *General principles.*]—DONALD DYER REAL ESTATE, LTD. *v.* CREDIT MOUNTAIN LAND CO., LTD. (1975).—CAN. *See* Division 2, *post.*

Part IV.—The Statute of Frauds

860. **Refd.** *Re* Crowhurst Park, Sims-Hilditch *v.* Simmons, [1974] 1 All E. R. 991.

876a. *Agreement to leave money by will.*]—SCHAEFER *v.* SCHUHMANN (1972). *See* Continuation Vol. D.
Refd. Cadogan *v.* Cadogan, [1977] 3 All E. R. 831.

935. **Refd.** Esso Petroleum Co., Ltd. *v.* Mardon, [1976] 2 All E. R. 5.

*671a. *Settlement of action for declaration that land held in trust.*]—MCKENZIE *v.* MCKENZIE (1976).—CAN. *See* Division 2, *post.*

958. **Refd.** Law *v.* Jones, [1973] 2 All E. R. 437.

982. **Refd.** Law *v.* Jones, [1973] 2 All E. R. 437.

*689a. *Clause in will.*]—JOHNSON *v.* NOVA SCOTIA TRUST CO. (1973).—CAN. *See* Continuation Vol. D.

1005. **Refd.** Law *v.* Jones, [1973] 2 All E. R. 437.

1011. **Refd.** Myton, Ltd. *v.* Schwab-Morris, [1974] 1 All E. R. 326.

1060. **Refd.** Steadman *v.* Steadman, [1974] 2 All E. R. 977.

1091. **Refd.** Law *v.* Jones, [1973] 2 All E. R. 437.

*740a. *General rule—Terms only partly set out.*]—ACKERMAN *v.* THOMSON AND MCKINNON, AUCHINCLOSS, KOHLMEYER, INC. (1974).—CAN. *See* Continuation Vol. D.

1141. **Distd.** New Hart Builders, Ltd. *v.* Brindley, [1975] 1 All E. R. 1007.

1148. **Refd.** Law *v.* Jones, [1973] 2 All E. R. 437.

1162a. *Necessity for stating price—No price fixed—Agreement "to negotiate fair & reasonable contract sums".*]—COURTNEY & FAIRBAIRN, LTD. *v.* TOLAINI BROS. (HOTELS), LTD. (1975). *See* Continuation Vol. D.

1173. **Refd.** Law *v.* Jones, [1973] 2 All E. R. 437.

1188. **Refd.** New Hart Builders *v.* Brindley, [1975] 1 All E. R. 1007.

*775a. *Whether special authority necessary—Agency by estoppel.*]—JOHNSON *v.* TERRIER AND TERRIER (1974).—W. INDIES. *See* Division 2, *post.*

1212. **Refd.** Sorrell *v.* Finch, [1976] 2 All E. R. 371.

1222. **Refd.** Law *v.* Jones, [1973] 2 All E. R. 437.

1233. **Refd.** Law *v.* Jones, [1973] 2 All E. R. 437.

1282. **Distd.** New Hart Builders, Ltd. *v.* Brindley, [1975] 1 All E. R. 1007.

1289. **Consd.** Steadman *v.* Steadman, [1974] 2 All E. R. 977.

1303. **Refd.** Steadman *v.* Steadman, [1974] 2 All E. R. 977.

1352. **Apld.** *Re* Densham (Bkpt.), *Ex p.* Trustee of Bkpt. *v.* Densham, [1975] 3 All E. R. 726. **Refd.** Steadman *v.* Steadman, [1974] 2 All E. R. 977.

1367. **Refd.** Kingston *v.* Ambrian Investment Co., Ltd., [1975] 1 All E. R. 120.

1371. **Distd.** Price *v.* Strange, [1977] 3 All E. R. 371.

*818a. *Effect in law—Principles applicable—Fraud as essence of doctrine.*]—CELONA *v.* KAMLOOPS CENTENNIAL (PACIFIC NO. 269) BRANCH, ROYAL CANADIAN LEGION (1972).—CAN. *See* Continuation Vol. D.

*830a. *When equitable doctrine applied—Act must be unequivocal—& clearly referable to contract.*]—TOOMBS *v.* MUELLER (1974).—CAN. *See* Continuation Vol. D.
Add. Citations (after [1974] 6 W. W. R. 577):—(1975), 54 D. L. R. (3d) 160, n.; [1975] 3 W. W. R. 96

*849a. *When equitable doctrine applied—Oral agreement to work on farm—Promise of inheritance.*]—THOMPSON *v.* GUARANTY TRUST CO. OF CANADA (1973).—CAN. *See* Continuation Vol. D.

*859a. *Work on land in return for agreement for sale of land.*]—ROSS *v.* ROSS, JR. (1973).—CAN. *See* Continuation Vol. D.

1388. **Expld.** *Re* Gonin, Gonin *v.* Garmeson, [1977] 2 All E. R. 720.

Part V.—Consideration

1397. **Refd.** D. P. P. *v.* Turner, [1973] 3 All E. R. 124.

1411. **Apld.** Argy Trading Development Co., Ltd. *v.* Lapid Developments, Ltd., [1977] 3 All E. R. 785. **Refd.** *Re* Wyvern Developments, Ltd., [1974] 2 All E. R. 535.

1484. **Distd.** Harris Simon & Co., Ltd. *v.* Manchester City Council, [1975] 1 All E. R. 412.

*919a. *Agreement to pay higher price.*]—GILBERT STEEL, LTD. *v.* UNIVERSITY CONSTRUCTION, LTD. (1973).—CAN. *See* Continuation Vol. D.
Add. Citations:—
affd. (1976), 67 D. L. R. (3d) 606; 12 O. R. (2d) 19.

*920. *Add. Citations (after* 9 D. L. R. (3d) 425):—*on appeal sub nom.* TANENBAUM *v.* SEARS, [1972] S. C. R. 67.

*938a. *Absorption of business losses.*]—MACIVER *v.* AMERICAN MOTORS (CANADA), LTD. (1976).—CAN. *See* Division 2, *post.*

*945a. *Promise to perform household services.*]—SWAN *v.* PUBLIC TRUSTEE (1972).—CAN. *See* Continuation Vol. D.

1577. **Folld.** Harrop *v.* Thompson, [1975] 2 All E. R. 94.

1661. **Distd.** A. R. Dennis & Co., Ltd. *v.* Campbell, [1977] 1 All E. R. 128.

1669. **Distd.** A. R. Dennis & Co., Ltd. *v.* Campbell, [1977] 1 All E. R. 138.

*976a. *General rule—Agreement to settle action for unpaid price—Vendor to accept lesser price & purchaser to return part of land.*]—C. & M. FARMS, LTD. *v.* ROTTACKER FARMS, LTD. (1976).—CAN. *See* Division 2, *post.*

*** An asterisk indicates a Scottish, Irish or Commonwealth case.**

Exhibit 79

See Exhibit 82. There is a separate statutory citator volume for the period, 1947–1971. The current Law Citator is updated by the tables included in the current monthly parts.

To trace legislative and judicial action since 1947, Current Law is a widely used case and statutory citator. A searcher goes to the citator to get reference to Year Book paragraphs, then to the Year Book

C.L.Y. *SHIPPING AND MARINE INSURANCE*

The defendants admitted restricting the navigation but claimed that they were authorised by the 1791 Act. *Held*, (1) on the question of whether later legislation relating to road traffic supported the defendants' contention, each statute can only be interpreted on its own terms and could not be governed by decisions on other statutes with different terms; (2) the duties imposed upon the defendants were to be found only in the 1791 Act and these could not be varied by common law; (3) the Act prohibited the defendants from restricting navigation; (4) the defendants had failed to establish that they were authorised by the 1791 Act to restrict the navigation during the rebuilding of the bridge. Judgment for P. (*Sharpness New Docks and Gloucester and Birmingham Navigation Co.* v. *Att.-Gen.* [1915] A.C. 654 applied: B.O.C.M. SILCOCK *v.* COMPANY AND PROPRIETORS OF SELBY BRIDGE [1976] 2 Lloyd's Rep. 322, Brandon J.

2577. Northern Ireland. See NORTHERN IRELAND.

2578. Offshore installations. See SEA AND SEASHORE.

2579. Oil pollution

OIL POLLUTION (COMPULSORY INSURANCE) (AMENDMENT) REGULATIONS 1976 (No. 154) [8p], made under the Merchant Shipping (Oil Pollution) Act 1971 (c. 59), s. 10 (4); operative on March 7, 1976; amend S.I. 1975 No. 869 with the effect that a certificate for a ship registered in a country which is not a party to the Convention (Cmnd. 4403) is recognised for the purposes under that S.I. if it is issued by or under the authority of the government of Spain.

OIL POLLUTION (COMPULSORY INSURANCE) (AMENDMENT No. 2) REGULATIONS 1976 (No. 857) [8p], made under the Merchant Shipping (Oil Pollution) Act 1971, s. 10 (4); operative on July 26, 1976; amend S.I. 1975 No. 869.

MERCHANT SHIPPING (OIL POLLUTION) (PARTIES TO CONVENTIONS) (AMENDMENT) ORDER 1976 (No. 1039) [12p], made under the Merchant Shipping (Oil Pollution) Act 1971, ss. 19 (2) and 8A (3) as inserted by the Merchant Shipping Act 1974, s. 9; operative on July 30, 1976; amends S.I. 1975 No. 1036 by substituting new first and second Schedules.

PREVENTION OF OIL POLLUTION (CONVENTION COUNTRIES) (ADDITIONAL COUNTRIES) ORDER 1976 (No. 1160) [8p], made under the Prevention of Oil Pollution Act 1971, s. 21 (3); operative on August 23, 1976; recognises a number of countries that have accepted the Convention relating to oil pollution.

OIL POLLUTION (COMPULSORY INSURANCE) (AMENDMENT No. 3) REGULATIONS 1976 (No. 1177) [8p], made under the Merchant Shipping (Oil Pollution) Act 1971, s. 10 (4); operative on September 1, 1976; give effect to the International Convention on Civil Liability for Oil Pollution Damage signed in Brussels, 1969 (Cmnd. 4403).

OIL POLLUTION (COMPULSORY INSURANCE) (AMENDMENT No. 4) REGULATIONS 1976 (No. 1440) [8p], made under the Merchant Shipping (Oil Pollution) Act 1971, s. 10 (4); operative as to regs. 1 and 2 (1) (*a*) on September 27, 1976 and as to the remainder on February 20, 1977, provide, inter alia, for the recognition of certificates of insurance against liability for oil pollution damage caused by ships.

PREVENTION OF OIL POLLUTION (CONVENTION COUNTRIES) (BAHAMAS) ORDER 1976 (No. 2154) [10p], made under the Oil Pollution Act 1971, s. 21 (3); accepts the Bahamas as a Convention Country for the purposes of the prevention of oil pollution at sea.

Orders made under the Merchant Shipping (Oil Pollution) Act 1971 (c. 59), s. 18 (1) and the Merchant Shipping Act 1974 (c. 43), s. 20 (1); extend to the territories listed the provisions of the Merchant Shipping (Oil Pollution) Act 1971, with the necessary adaptations, enabling effect to be given to the International Convention on Civil Liability for Oil Pollution Damage (November 1969); also extend the Merchant Shipping Act 1974, Sched. 1, Pts. I and V, enabling effect to be given to the International Fund for Compensation for Oil Pollution Damage (December 1971):

S.I. 1976 Nos. 53 (Gibraltar) [30p]; 223 (Turks and Caicos Islands) [30p]; 2143 (Falkland Islands) [10p].

2580. Pilotage

PORT TALBOT PILOTAGE (AMENDMENT) ORDER 1976 (No. 1533) [5p], made under the Pilotage Act 1913 (c. 31), s. 7; operative on November 15, 1976;

Y.B.—19

Exhibit 80

paragraphs where the complete material is found. Since the annual Current Citator is kept up-to-date by the monthly issues of Current

HUS CASE CITATOR 1947–76

Husey *v.* London Electricity Supply Corporation [**1902**] 1 Ch. 411 .... *Applied*, 3422
Hussain, *Ex p.* *See* R. *v.* Chief Immigration Officer, Bradford Airport.
— *v.* City of Birmingham. *See* Hussain *v.* Secretary of State for the Environment.
— *v.* Department of Education and Science, *The Times*, February 26, 1975, C.A. .... *Digested*, 75/**1179**
— *v.* Secretary of State for the Environment (1971) 23 P. & C.R. 330; *sub nom.* Hussain *v.* City of Birmingham (1971) 221 E.G. 627, D.C. *Digested*, 72/**3332**
Hussey *v.* Horne-Payne (1874) 4 App.Cas. 311 .... ***Considered***, 65/680. *Applied*, 71/**1347**
— *v.* Minister of Health (**1952**) **3** P. **&** C.R. **275**, Lands Tribunal .... *Digested*, 53/**550**
— ***v.* Mount Charlotte Investments** [1966] I.T.R. **359**; 1 K.I.R. 360, **Industrial Tribunal** .... ***Digested*, 67/1450**
— *v.* Palmer [1972] 1 W.L.R. 1286; 116 S.J. 567; [1972] 3 All E.R. 744; [[1973] C.L.J. 41], C.A. .... *Digested*, 72/**3167**: *Applied*, 75/3365
Hussien (Shaabin Bin) *v.* Kam (Chong Fook) [1970] A.C. 492; [1970] 2 W.L.R. 441; [1969] 3 All E.R. 1626; *sub nom.* Hussein *v.* Kam (Chong Fook), 114 S.J. 35; [86 L.Q.R. 435], P.C. .... *Digested*, 70/**205**
Husson *v.* Husson [1962] 1 W.L.R. 1434; 106 S.J. 737; [1962] 3 All E.R. 1056 .... ***Digested*, 62/2378**
Hutcheson (John) and Others, 1954 S.C. 3; 1954 S.L.T. 33 .... ***Digested*, 54/1636**
Hutchings *v.* Giles [1955] Crim.L.R. 784, D.C. .... *Digested*, 55/**2421**: *Applied*, 62/2643
— *v.* Hutchings (1975) 237 E.G. 571, C.A. .... *Digested*, 76/**1392**
Hutchins *v.* British Railways Board [1974] I.R.L.R. 303; Industrial Tribunal .... *Digested*, 74/**1326**
Hutchinson, *Re*, Holt *v.* Hutchinson [1955] Ch. 255; [1955] 2 W.L.R. 586; **99** S.J. 185; [**1955**] 1 All E.R. **689**; [19 Conv. 229] .... *Digested*, 55/**1037**
— ***v.*** Ackland, LVC/51/1960 [1961] J.P.L. 424; 178 E.G. 899, Lands Tribunal .... *Digested*, 61/**7423**
— *v.* Hutchinson, 63 T.L.R. 645; 92 S.J. 55; [1947] 2 All E.R. 792; [92 S.J. 35; 12 Conv. 231] .... ***Digested*, 4551**: *Applied*, 8851; 56/4002; 66/5819: *Considered*, 4558: *Distinguished*, 4554; 53/1643
— *v.* — [1963] 1 W.L.R. 280; 106 S.J. 836; [1963] 1 All E.R. 1, D.C. ***Digested*, 63/1078**: ***Considered*, 67/1261**
— ***v.* Jauncey** [1950] 1 K.B. **574**; **66** T.L.R. (**Pt.** 1) 195; 94 S.J. 48; [**1950**] 1 All **E.R.** 165; [**14 Conv. 97**], C.A. .... ***Digested*, 8528**: ***Followed***, 8529: *Applied*, 58/**3254**
— *v.* London County Council. *See* Hutchison *v.* London County Council.
— *v.* **London & North Eastern Ry.** [**1942**] 1 K.B. 481 .... ***Applied*, 6858; 56/6043**: ***Considered*, 54/1315; 57/2435; 68/3294**: ***Distinguished*, 58/2293, 2295**
— *v.* McCusker [1973] N.I. 244, C.A. .... *Digested*, 76/**1921**
— ***v.* National Refuges for Homeless and Destitute** Children [1920] A.C. **794** .... ***Distinguished*, 10902**: ***Applied*, 65/4040**
Hutchinson (A. M.) *v.* Electrolux [1976] I.R.L.R. 289, Industrial Tribunal *Digested*, 76/**889**
Hutchinson (Robert) & Co. *v.* British Railways Board [1970] S.L.T. 72, Outer House .... *Digested*, 71/**1714**
Hutchinson & Co. (Publishers) *v.* Turner [**1950**] **W.N.** 462; 66 T.L.R. (Pt. 2) **676**; **94** S.J. **670**; [**1950**] 2 All E.R. **633**; [1950] T.R. 285; 43 **R.** & I.T. **942**; **31** T.C. **495**; [**101** L.J. **74**] .... ***Digested*, 4747**, 4749
Hutchinson Brothers, Appeal, *Re* 1972 No. J12; (1972) 33 Traf.Cas. 116, Transport Tribunal Rd. Haulage Appeals Div. .... *Digested*, 72/**3487**
Hutchinson's Application, *Re*, LP/41/1963 [1964] J.P.L. 422; 190 E.G. 87, Lands Tribunal .... *Digested*, 64/**3123**
Hutchinson's Trusts, *Re* (1882) 21 **Ch.D.** 811 .... *Applied*, 10866–7
Hutchinson's Will Trusts, *Re*, Gibbons *v.* Nottingham Area No. 1 **Hospital Management** Committee [1953] Ch. 387; [1953] 2 **W.L.R.** **872**; [**1953**] 1 **All E.R. 996**; [**17 Conv. 245**]; ***sub nom.*** Hutchinson, ***Re*, Gibbons *v.* Nottingham** Area No. 1 Hospital Management Committee, **97** S.J. **300** .... ***Digested*, 53/460**: ***Considered*, 64/410**: ***Distinguished***, 64/410
Hutchison *v.* Aitchison (1970) 114 S.J. 549; 9 K.I.R. 69 .... *Digested*, 71/**11782**
— *v.* Cocksedge & Co. [1952] 1 All E.R. 696n. .... *Digested*, 52/**367**
— *v.* Hutchison [1951] W.N. 296, D.C. .... *Reported*, **3099**: *Applied*, 52/1090
— ***v.*** London County Council [1951] 2 Lloyd's Rep. 401, C.A.; affirming ***sub nom.*** Hutchinson *v.* London County Council [1951] 1 Lloyd's Rep. 490 .... *Digested*, **6844**
— *v.* Westward Television, *The Times*, December 18, 1976, E.A.T. .. *Digested*, 76/**951**
Hutchison (Cinemas) *v.* Tyson [1970] Crim.L.**R. 350**, D.C. .... *Digested*, 70/**1652**
Huth *v.* Clarke (1890) 25 Q.B.D. 391 .... *Applied*, 5860

544

Exhibit 81

Law in both the English and Scottish editions, it is possible to follow all statutes and cases construed covered by Current Law to date.

1975 STATUTE CITATOR 1972-76

CAP.

1975—cont.

82. **Civil List Act 1975.**
Royal Assent, December 19, 1975.

83. **Northern Ireland (Loans) Act 1975.**
Royal Assent, December 19, 1975.

1976

1. **National Coal Board (Finance) Act 1976.**
Royal Assent, March 4, 1976.

2. **Consolidated Fund Act 1976.**
Royal Assent, March 25, 1976.

3. **Road Traffic (Drivers' Ages and Hours of Work) Act 1976.**
Royal Assent, March 25, 1976.
s. 4, order 76/471.

4. **Trustee Savings Banks Act 1976.**
Royal Assent, March 4, 1976.
order 76/1054.
s. 12, sch. 5, repealed in pt.: 1976,c.4, sch.6.
s. 38, orders 76/642, 1829.

5. **Education (School-Leaving Dates) Act 1976.**
Royal Assent, March 25, 1976.

6. **Solicitors (Scotland) Act 1976.**
Royal Assent, March 25, 1976.

7. **Trade Union and Labour Relations (Amendment) Act 1976.**
Royal Assent, March 25, 1976.

8. **Prevention of Terrorism (Temporary Provisions) Act 1976.**
Royal Assent, March 25, 1976.
ss. 13, 14, sch. 3, order 76/465.
ss. 16, 18, orders 76/772, 895, 896.

9. **Water Charges Act 1976.**
Royal Assent, March 25, 1976.

10. **Post Office (Banking Services) Act 1976.**
Royal Assent, March 25, 1976.

11. **Housing (Amendment) (Scotland) Act 1976.**
Royal Assent, April 13, 1976.

12. **Statute Law Revision (Northern Ireland) Act 1976.**
Royal Assent, April 13, 1976.

13. **Damages (Scotland) Act 1976.**
Royal Assent, April 13, 1976.

14. **Fatal Accidents and Sudden Deaths Inquiry (Scotland) Act 1976.**
Royal Assent, April 13, 1976.

15. **Rating (Caravan Sites) Act 1976.**
Royal Assent, April 13, 1976.
s. 1, repealed in pt.: 1976,c.70,sch.8.

16. **Statute Law (Repeals) Act 1976.**
Royal Assent, May 27, 1976.

17. **Land Drainage (Amendment) Act 1976.**
Royal Assent, May 27, 1976.
repealed: 1976,c.70,sch.8.

18. **Licensing (Amendment) Act 1976.**
Royal Assent, May 27, 1976.

CAP.

1976—cont.

19. **Seychelles Act 1976.**
Royal Assent, May 27, 1976.
order 76/894.

20. **Education (Scotland) Act 1976.**
Royal Assent, June 10, 1976.
s. 7, order 76/925.

21. **Crofting Reform (Scotland) Act 1976.**
Royal Assent, June 10, 1976.

22. **Freshwater and Salmon Fisheries Act 1976.**
Royal Assent, June 10, 1976.

23. **Atomic Energy Authority (Special Constables) Act 1976.**
Royal Assent, June 10, 1976.

24. **Development Land Tax Act 1976.**
Royal Assent, July 22, 1976.
s. 11, amended: 1976,c.75,s.31.
s. 47, order 76/1148.

25. **Fair Employment (Northern Ireland) Act 1976.**
Royal Assent, July 22, 1976.

26. **Explosives (Age of Purchase) Act 1976.**
Royal Assent, July 22, 1976.

27. **Theatres Trust Act 1976.**
Royal Assent, July 22, 1976.

28 **Congenital Disabilities (Civil Liability) Act 1976.**
Royal Assent, July 22, 1976.

29. **Representation of the People (Armed Forces) Act 1976.**
Royal Assent, July 22, 1976.
s. 4, order 76/2044.

30. **Fatal Accidents Act 1976.**
Royal Assent, July 22, 1976.

31. **Legitimacy Act 1976.**
Royal Assent, July 22, 1976.
ss. 4, 6, amended: 1976,c.36,sch.3.
sch. 1, repealed in pt.: *ibid.*,sch.4.

32. **Lotteries and Amusements Act 1976.**
Royal Assent, July 22, 1976.

33. **Restrictive Practices Court Act 1976.**
Royal Assent, July 22, 1976.
s. 9, rules 76/1897, 1898, 1899.
s. 12, order 76/1896.

34. **Restrictive Trade Practices Act 1976.**
Royal Assent, July 22, 1976.
s. 22, rules 76/1897.
s. 45, order 76/1877.
sch. 5, repealed in pt.: 1976,c.53,sch.3.

35. **Police Pensions Act 1976.**
Royal Assent, July 22, 1976.
ss. 1, 3, 5, regs. 76/1707.

36. **Adoption Act 1976.**
Royal Assent, July 22, 1976.

37. **Food and Drugs (Control of Food Premises) Act 1976.**
Royal Assent, July 22, 1976.

38. **Dangerous Wild Animals Act 1976.**
Royal Assent, July 22, 1976.

184

Exhibit 82

d. *Current Law, Scottish Edition*. There are separate Scottish editions of the monthly Current Law, Year Books, and the Current Law

Citator. The Scottish Year Books consist of the English material in the front part on white-paper stock; coverage of statutes, statutory instruments, and cases applicable solely to Scotland are in a second part on colored-paper stock. The Current Law Consolidation (1947–1951) was not published for the Scottish edition.

3. *Mews' Digest*.[37] This is a selective digest of cases deemed by the editors to be of substantial legal interest through 1969; it then ceased publication. Case summaries are more lengthy than in other comparable works. The main set includes cases through 1924. Decennial consolidations were published for the period 1925–1945, and annual volumes were issued thereafter.

4. *The Solicitors' Journal* prints brief notes of many cases each year. Although the separate report series of Law Times and the Law Journal are no longer published, brief reports of cases appear in these periodicals also.

§24.8. Encyclopedias.

1. *Halsbury's Laws of England*.[38] A fourth edition of this comprehensive encyclopedia is in progress. The scope of the new edition includes new titles such as administrative law and foreign relations. A volume on European Communities law will complete the set. Additionally, elements of European Community law such as agricultural law or transport policy are considered in the agriculture and carriers volumes respectively.

The new edition is patterned generally after the earlier ones. Concise analyses of all aspects of law in essay format are arranged under broad subject titles. Paragraphs are numbered sequentially within each title. Considerable attention is given to statutory law. See Exhibit 83. Cases cited as authority are cross-referenced to the appropriate titles and sections of the English and Empire Digest through a table of cases. Conversely, if the case is first found in the English and Empire Digest, the related essay section in the encyclopedia can be located through the table of cases or, in the newest green-banded volumes of the Digest, through direct citations to Halsbury's Laws, third or fourth edition, depending upon the revision dates of the subject treated.

If analysis of a particular statute is wanted, it can be found easily by consulting the table of statutes which gives reference to the proper page in the volume. Halsbury's Statutes also contains references to Halsbury's Laws. In addition to the tables of statutes and cases included in each volume, consolidated tables are planned for the entire set. There is detailed subject access to each volume. There will

37. *Ibid*.
38. London, Butterworths, 1973 to date.

Since *Jefford v Gee* [1970] 2 QB 130, [1970] 1 All ER 1202, CA, it has been necessary for the courts to itemise damages under the heads of pain and suffering etc. and past and future pecuniary loss for the purpose of calculating interest, so earlier decisions, discouraging such a practice, are no longer operative. As to interest, see para. 1204, post; see also *Harris (infant) v Harris* [1973] 1 Lloyd's Rep 445, CA.

2 *Fletcher v Autocar and Transporters Ltd* [1968] 2 QB 322 at 351, [1968] 1 All ER 726 at 747, CA, per Diplock LJ. See also the dissenting judgment of Salmon LJ at 364 and 751 for the view that this factor should only be taken into account if the court was proposing to add something to the normal measure in respect of the loss of a particular amenity.

3 The Law Commission has proposed that damages should be separately assessed for non-pecuniary and pecuniary loss, and added together without adjustment for "overlap": see Report on Personal Injury Litigation—Assessment of Damages (Law Com. no. 56), paras. 193–198, 214. The same report makes other proposals for more detailed itemisation of heads of damage.

1150. Overlap between claims under the Fatal Accidents Acts and the Law Reform (Miscellaneous Provisions) Act 1934. The dependants of a deceased man killed by the negligence of another have a claim under the Fatal Accidents Acts in respect of their pecuniary loss[1], but certain benefits which they receive as a result of the death fall to be taken into account in reduction of their loss[2]. If damages awarded or likely to be awarded[3] under the Law Reform (Miscellaneous Provisions) Act 1934 for loss of expectation of life[4] are receivable by the dependants, they fall to be deducted from a claim under the Fatal Accidents Acts[5]. Where the only damages under the Act of 1934 are in respect of loss of expectation of life, the practical effect is usually small. Where, however, the deceased has survived for a period of years before his death, there may be a substantial claim under that Act, for example, for pain and suffering and loss of amenity, and whether this is taken into account against damages under the Fatal Accidents Acts depends on whether or not it is received as a result of the death[6].

1 I.e. under the Fatal Accidents Acts 1846–1959; Law Reform (Miscellaneous Provisions) Act 1971, s. 4 (1): see NEGLIGENCE. Section 4 (1) of the Act of 1971, which provides that the remarriage of a widow (or her prospects of remarriage) is not to be taken into account when assessing damages payable under the Fatal Accidents Acts, is to be strictly construed and the benefit to the children as a result of the remarriage must be considered in assessing damages payable to them: *Burlison v Official Solicitor* [1975] 125 NLJ 68. As to the "lost years" rule, see para. 1154, post.

2 The rule before the Fatal Accidents Act 1959 was that every pecuniary advantage which the dependent had received as a result of the deceased's death had to be deducted, but insurance money, national insurance or social security benefits, payments from friendly societies or trade unions, pensions and gratuities are now disregarded: see s. 2; Social Security Act 1973, s. 100 (2) (a), Sch. 27, para. 20; and NEGLIGENCE.

The Law Commission has proposed that there should be no reduction from damages awarded under the Fatal Accidents Acts in respect of any benefits received from the deceased's estate: see the Report on Personal Injury Litigation—Assessment of Damages 1973 (Law Com. no. 56), paras. 256, 262.

See also *Hay v Hughes* [1974] 1 Lloyd's Rep 475, CA, where it was held that it was correct to ignore the unpaid services of a relative when calculating the financial loss to a child as a result of its mother's death.

3 See the Law Reform (Miscellaneous Provisions) Act 1934, s. 1, and EXECUTORS; NEGLIGENCE.

4 As to such damages, see para. 1148, ante.

5 *Davies v Powell Duffryn Associated Collieries Ltd (No. 2)* [1942] AC 601, [1942] 1 All ER 657, HL.

6 *Murray v Shuter* (1970) (unreported), a decision of Shaw J (deceased survived for four years in a coma; damages awarded under the Law Reform (Miscellaneous Provisions) Act 1934 for pain and suffering and past loss of earnings; damages awarded under the Fatal Accidents Acts 1846 to 1959; damages under the Act of 1934 were deductible from damages under the Fatal Accidents Acts although the wife and children had the full use of the deceased's money and would have had the use of the damages for pain and suffering and loss or earnings, subject to the control of the Court of Protection, even if the deceased had lived). See further NEGLIGENCE.

Exhibit 83

also be a subject or descriptive-word index for the whole set. In the interim, cumulative paper indexes are issued after publication of every tenth volume.

The set is kept current while publication of the new edition is in progress by a cumulative supplement covering titles revised to date. See Exhibit 84. Annual cumulative supplements are expected thereafter, as was provided for the third edition. Paragraph numbers in the cumulative supplements are the same as in the main volumes. A current service loose-leaf binder contains tables of cases, statutes, and statutory instruments, as well as a noter-up, and a monthly review in periodical format.

Northern Ireland and Scotland are included in the coverage of Halsbury's Laws.

2. *Encyclopedia of European Community Law.*[39] Legislative sources of European Community law, annotations of those laws relevant to the United Kingdom, and decisions of the European Community and national courts are covered in this set. United Kingdom sources covered in the first volume include the European Community Act of 1972 and amendments, other related legislation of England and Wales, Scotland, and Northern Ireland, Rules and Orders (including a section on Northern Ireland Rules and Orders), and Command Papers. The second volume covers the European Community treaties. Volume 3 contains regulations, and directions of the Council and the Commission of the European Communities. Regular supplementation is made by insertion in the loose-leaf format.

§24.9. Citators reviewed.

There is no tabular English system noting the legislative and judicial treatment of statutes and judicial consideration of cases similar to Shepard's Citations, but there are other means of finding this information. All are incidental functions of some digests, encyclopedia, or tables of cases. In general, they fall within four categories: (a) those in which annotations are printed as part of a digest paragraph or syllabus and "note up" the case digested by indicating subsequent judicial action; (b) those in the form of statutory and case tables in which the citation material follows the name of the case or the date of the statute; (c) those in which citation material follows statutes listed by title; and (d) those in which the citation is part of a legal encyclopedia footnote. The citators listed below have been noted earlier in this chapter in describing the works of which they are a part; they are coordinated here for the convenience of reference.

1. *Statute citators.* Current Law Statutes Citator, updated by the Monthly Current Law, provides perhaps the most satisfactory table for the period it covers. Amendments, repeals, or restrictions and cases construing are cited for all statutes affected since 1947; cited statutes from earliest times are included. Consult Halsbury's Statutes,

39. London, Sweet & Maxwell, 1973- , 3 vols. in 8, loose-leaf.

DAMAGES

Part 1. Introduction

PARA.

1108 **Damages distinguished from costs.** NOTES 12-14.—See *Vernon & Co (Pulp Products) Ltd's Patent* [1976] RPC 625.

1115 **Damages associated with a statute.** NOTES 6, 7.—Fatal Accidents Acts 1846-59 are repealed and replaced by Fatal Accidents Act 1976.

1123 **Meaning of "compensation".** NOTE 8.—Fatal Accidents Act 1846 is repealed and replaced by Fatal Accidents Act 1976.

Part 2. The Measure of Damage; Remoteness

1135 **Continuing damages.** NOTE 3.—Limitation Act 1963, s. 1; Law Reform (Miscellaneous Provisions) Act 1971, s. 1 (1) (a) repealed: Limitation Act 1975, Sch. 2. In general, in the case of causes of action in respect of personal injuries time runs from the date of the plaintiff's knowledge if that date is later than the date on which the cause of action accrued. The date of knowledge is the date on which he had knowledge of various facts including the fact that the injury was significant: Limitation Act 1939, s. 2A; Limitation Act 1975, s. 1. See LIMITATION OF ACTIONS.

Part 3. The Measure of Damages in Tort

1150 **Overlap between claims under the Fatal Accidents Acts and the Law Reform (Miscellaneous Provisions) Act 1934.** NOTE 1.—Fatal Accidents Act 1976, s. 1 has repealed and replaced the Fatal Accidents Acts 1846-59 and Law Reform (Miscellaneous Provisions) Act 1971, s. 4 (1). See *Regan v Williamson* [1976] 2 All ER 241, [1976] 1 WLR 305 as to valuation of loss of wife's services.

NOTE 2.—Fatal Accidents Act 1959, s. 2, as amended, is repealed and replaced by Fatal Accidents Act 1976, s. 4 (2). The benefits mentioned are to be disregarded in assessing damages even if the result of so doing is to make a dependant better off than she would have been had the deceased survived: *Humphrey v Ward Engineering Services Ltd* (1975) 119 Sol Jo 461 (widow's lump sum and pension).

NOTE 6.—On appeal [1975] 3 All ER 375, [1975] 3 WLR 597, CA (damages for lost earnings not deductible).

1151 **Pecuniary loss through personal injuries.** In the case of severe injuries to children damages for future loss of earnings should be based on an estimate of the child's loss of future earnings although that estimate is necessarily speculative; the court should not award merely a conventional sum; see *Taylor v Bristol Omnibus Co Ltd* [1975] 2 All ER 1107, [1975] 1 WLR 1054, CA (child aged 3½ in accident; unemployable; awarded £16,000 for loss of future earnings, annual earnings based on yardstick of father's position, multiplier of 16 and half resulting figure deducted for immediate payment).

Exhibit 84

its Supplement, continuation volumes, and current statutes service for statutes in force which have been amended and/or construed by the courts. Amendments to statutes in force can be checked through the latest Index to the Statutes in Force, supplemented by the annual statute volume indexes to date. Lastly, to ensure currency, consult the monthly Current Law. All digests, excepting the English and Empire Digest, have tables of statutes judicially construed. The footnotes to Halsbury's Statutes of England are an additional source of cases related to a statute or section thereof.

2. *Statutory instruments citators*. The tables in the official edition of the Statutory Instruments or Rules serve as citators; or see Halsbury's Statutory Instruments' tables and its cumulative additions. Digests, excepting the English and Empire, have citator tables, covering varying periods from 1891 to date. Tables in Law Reports series and All England Law Reports show instruments judicially considered.

3. *Case citators*. All digests described in this chapter serve as case citators, the English and Empire Digest through the annotations to each digest paragraph (found through the table of cases), and other digests through alphabetical tables of cases judicially noticed. Current Law, published monthly, is the most current of the citators. For construing cases from 1947 to date (Scottish cases from 1948 to date), Current Law Citator is also the most convenient. Cited cases are of any date, that is, any case of any date which is cited by a case decided from 1947 to date is covered by case name. For cases prior to 1865, a limited amount of "noting up" appears in the English Reports Full Reprint.

§24.10. Dictionaries.

For consideration of the authority and function of law dictionaries, see Chapter 21. For an excellent historical discussion of English law dictionaries, refer to F. C. Hicks's Materials and Methods of Legal Research,[40] third edition, revised (1942).

Jowitt's Dictionary of English Law[41] is a standard source, encyclopedic in scope, and especially useful for its definitions of medieval legal terms and those from foreign languages which have come into English legal usage. A Concise Law Dictionary,[42] edited by P. Osborn, is in one volume. It reflects the law as of January 1976.

Stroud's Judicial Dictionary of Words and Phrases[43] purports to be the originator of the words and phrases approach. Definitions are

40. Rochester, Lawyers Co-op., 1942.
41. London, Sweet & Maxwell, 1959. 2 vols.
42. London, Sweet & Maxwell, 1976.
43. 4th ed., London, Sweet & Maxwell, 1971 – 1974. 5 vols.

lengthy. Cases interpreting the same statute or a particular section are arranged chronologically. Words and Phrases Legally Defined,[44] second edition, while continuing to emphasize judicial interpretations and meanings, has been broadened to include textbooks and statutory definitions. Words and phrases judicially construed are listed cumulatively in the monthly Current Law and appear also in the Current Law Year Books. See also the words-phrases segment of the English and Empire Digest. Finally, an encyclopedia, such as Halsbury's Laws of England, serves as an expanded function of a dictionary.

§24.11. Periodical indexes.

Access to important periodicals of the United Kingdom and the periodical literature of the Common Market is through Index to Legal Periodicals,[45] Index to Foreign Legal Periodicals,[46] and Annual (and Current) Legal Bibliography.[47] The first two titles mentioned afford access by author as well.

There are references to relevant periodical literature at the end of each subject section in Monthly Current Law and the Year Books. There is a cumulative list of periodicals which appeared in the 1947–1956 Year Books; thereafter consult the annual Year Books.

44. London, Butterworths, 1968–1970. 5 vols.
45. New York, Wilson. 1909 to date.
46. London, Institute of Advanced Legal Studies, 1960 to date.
47. Cambridge, Harvard Law School, 1961 to date.

25 | Canadian Materials*

§25.1. Introduction.

In many respects, Canadian legal publications parallel their English and United States counterparts. There is one difference between the United States and Canadian legislation to be noted in searching and understanding the law. Whereas in the United States, all residual powers not determined by the Constitution adhere to the states, the opposite is true in Canada. The distribution of federal and provincial powers and jurisdiction is set out in the British North American Acts. The Organization of the Government of Canada Manual is a useful source for some history and the present organization of the government and for identifying responsibility and authority of administrative agencies and commissions.

§25.2. Laws and statutes.

1. *Federal.*

a. *Slip laws.* Beginning 1974, the Canada Gazette, Part III,[1] con-

* This chapter was written by Mary L. Fisher, Law Librarian, General Electric Company, Fairfield, Conn.

1. Ottawa, Queen's Printer.

tains laws passed by Parliament. A subscription service to separate slip laws is available from the Queen's Printer. Acts receiving royal assent are designated by chapter number within a calendar year.

b. *Statutes of Canada*. Acts of the Parliament of Canada[2] are session laws, typical of their kind. Part I is devoted to Public General Acts, Part II to Local and Private Acts (excluding divorce acts, which are listed in a separate table). There is an alphabetical list of acts as well as a subject index of public general acts for the session and a list of proclamations. There is a table showing all chapters of the Revised Statutes of Canada 1970 which have been amended, with citations to them by chapter and section.

Revised Statutes of Canada 1970.[3] R.S.C. 1970 is the latest published consolidation, superseding that of 1952, and encompassing public general statutes in force through December 31, 1969. Many of the acts are consolidations of acts formerly in force but reenacted as positive law in the manner of the United States Code reenactments of certain code titles. A First Supplement covers new and changed enactments in 1970 and a schedule of acts repealed by R.S.C. 1970. The Second Supplement contains only those acts or parts thereof passed during the 1970–1971 Parliamentary session that amend acts contained in R.S.C. 1970 and the First Supplement. Other legislation that does not amend R.S.C. 1970 or the First Supplement is found in the annual volume of the Acts of Parliament. Arrangement of material is by broad subject titles. This is a bilingual edition. See Exhibit 85.

An appendix volume prints the text of constitutional acts and documents, including the British North American Acts. It includes also a history and disposal of the acts with parallel tables from the R.S.C. 1952 and subsequent Acts of the Parliament of Canada through 1969–1970. A page illustration from the subject index is shown as Exhibit 86.

To search federal law and possible amendments to it through official publications, consult first the subject index to the Revised Statutes. For amendments which may appear in the Supplements and/or in the annual Acts of Parliament, consult the Table of Public Statutes printed on colored sheets in the latest annual Acts volume. See Exhibit 87.

2. *Provincial and territorial*.

a. *Slip laws*. Separate laws of the provinces are not available on a subscription basis, nor are they regularly included in the provincial gazettes. Subscriptions to bills are available, and the text of a bill in third reading is tantamount to the text of the slip law when it receives royal assent. There is no systematic indexing of bills.

2. *Ibid*.
3. *Ibid*.

CHAPTER B-11

An Act to implement a broadcasting policy for Canada

CHAPITRE B-11

Loi ayant pour objet de mettre en œuvre, pour le Canada, une politique de la radiodiffusion

SHORT TITLE

Short title

1. This Act may be cited as the *Broadcasting Act*. 1967-68, c. 25, s. 1.

TITRE ABRÉGÉ

Titre abrégé

1. La présente loi peut être citée sous le titre: *Loi sur la radiodiffusion*. 1967-68, c. 25, art. 1.

PART I

GENERAL

Interpretation

Definitions

2. In this Act

"broadcaster" «*radiodiffuseur*» — "broadcaster" means a person licensed by the Commission to carry on a broadcasting transmitting undertaking;

"broadcasting" «*radiodiffusion*» — "broadcasting" means any radiocommunication in which the transmissions are intended for direct reception by the general public;

"broadcasting licence" «*licence...*» — "broadcasting licence" or, in Parts II and III, "licence" means a licence to carry on a broadcasting undertaking issued under this Act;

"broadcasting undertaking" «*entreprise...*» — "broadcasting undertaking" includes a broadcasting transmitting undertaking, a broadcasting receiving undertaking and a network operation, located in whole or in part within Canada or on a ship or aircraft registered in Canada;

"Commission" «*Conseil*» — "Commission" means the Canadian Radio-Television Commission established by Part II;

"Corporation" «*Société*» — "Corporation" means the Canadian Broadcasting Corporation established by Part III;

"licensee" «*titulaire*» — "licensee" means a person licensed by the

PARTIE I

DISPOSITIONS GÉNÉRALES

Interprétation

Définitions

2. Dans la présente loi

«Conseil» "*Commission*" — «Conseil» désigne le Conseil de la Radio-Télévision canadienne établi par la Partie II;

«entreprise de radiodiffusion» "*broadcasting undertaking*" — «entreprise de radiodiffusion» comprend une entreprise d'émission de radiodiffusion, une entreprise de réception de radiodiffusion et l'exploitation d'un réseau situé en tout ou en partie au Canada ou sur un navire ou un aéronef immatriculé au Canada;

«exploitation temporaire d'un réseau» "*temporary...*" — «exploitation temporaire d'un réseau» désigne l'exploitation d'un réseau en ce qui concerne une certaine émission ou une série d'émissions s'étendant sur une période d'au plus un mois;

«licence de radiodiffusion» ou «licence» "*broadcasting licence*" — «licence de radiodiffusion», ou, aux Parties II et III, «licence», désigne une licence d'exploitation d'une entreprise de radiodiffusion, attribuée en vertu de la présente loi;

«Ministre» "*Minister*" — «Ministre» désigne, dans les Parties II et III, le secrétaire d'État du Canada;

«radiocommunication» "*radiocommunication*" — «radiocommunication» désigne toute transmission, émission ou réception de signes,

Exhibit 85

b. *Annual session laws and revised statutory compilations*. These are published for each of the provinces, and ordinances for the territories. Editions of the revised statutes contain tables showing the history and disposal of laws from prior revisions and a subject index. The annual statute volumes supplement the latest revision. These volumes do not uniformly contain tables of statutes showing amendments as provided on the federal level. Each does have an alphabetical table of statutes and subject index to the volume. Provincial legislation may be traced in the following sources. The beginning date of first session law is given when known.[4]

4. When no publisher is given, the Queen's Printer may be assumed. Place of publication applicable to all official imprints is noted after the revised compilations.

Revised Statutes Index

(References are to sections)

BRITISH COLUMBIA—(cont'd)
16; Prairie Grain Advance Payments Act, R.S., c. P-18; Prisons and Reformatories Act, R.S., c. P-21, s.140; Provincial Subsidies Act, R.S., c. P-26; Transport Act, R.S., c. T-14, s.12(4); Yukon Act, R.S., c. Y-2, s.35

BRITISH COLUMBIA DIVORCE APPEALS ACT
See Divorce Act, R.S., c. D-8

BRITISH COLUMBIA GRAIN SHIPPERS' CLEARANCE ASSOCIATION
See Bank Act, R.S., c. B-1, s.2(1)

BRITISH COMMONWEALTH MERCHANT SHIPPING AGREEMENT, 1931
See Canada Shipping Act, R.S., c. S-9, s.2

BRITISH COMMONWEALTH OF NATIONS
See Canadian Citizenship Act, R.S., c. C-19, s.2; Customs Tariff Act, R.S., c. C-41; Interpretation Act, R.S., c. I-23

BRITISH HONDURAS (BELIZE)
See Customs Tariff Act, R.S., c. C-41

BRITISH MEDICAMENTARIUS
See Proprietary or Patent Medicine Act, R.S., c. P-25, s. 2(1)

BRITISH NATIONALITY ACT, 1948
See Canada Shipping Act, R.S., c. S-9

BRITISH NAVAL SHIPS
See Dry Docks Subsidies Act, R.S., c. D-9, s.20

BRITISH NORTH AMERICA ACT, 1867
See Canada Evidence Act, R.S., c. E-10, s.17; Currency and Exchange Act, R.S., c. C-39; Department of Justice Act, R.S., c. J-2, s.5; Electoral Boundaries Readjustment Act, R.S., c. E-2, s.12; Federal Court Act, R.S., c.10 (2nd Supp.), s.2, 25; Financial Administration Act, R.S., c. F-10, s.19; Members of Parliament Retiring Allowances Act, R.S., c. M-10, s.37(2); Northwest Territories Act, R.S., c. N-22, s.14(1); Oaths of Allegiance Act, R.S., c. O-1, s.2(1); Prisons and Reformatories Act, R.S., c. P-21, s.86; Provincial Subsidies Act, R.S., c. P-26, Senate and House of Commons Act, R.S., c. S-8, s.4(a); Supreme Court Act, R.S., c. S-19, s.55(1); Yukon Act, R.S., c. Y-2, s.17(1)

BRITISH PREFERENTIAL TARIFF
See Customs Tariff Act, R.S., c. C-41

BRITISH SOLOMON ISLANDS PROTECTORATE
See Customs Tariff Act, R.S., c. C-41

BRITISH TRUSTEESHIP
See Customs Tariff Act, R.S., c. C-41

BRITISH VIRGIN ISLANDS
See Customs Tariff Act, R.S., c. C-41

BROADCASTING
See Broadcasting Act, R.S., c. B-11; Department of State Act, R.S., c. S-15; Radio Act, R.S., c. R-1

BROADCASTING ACT, R.S., c. B-11*—*see also Expropriation Act, R.S., c.16 (1st Supp.), s.42(2); Radio Act, R.S., c. R-1, s.3(2) Railway Act, R.S., c. R-2, s.320(2)
Aeronautics Act
application 11(2)
Annual report 47
Application of Act 39(3)
Auditor General of Canada
accounts of Corporation, audit re 46
report re 46
Bank of Canada 45(1)
Broadcaster
defined 2
Broadcasting
defined 2
language 3(e)
policy for Canada 3
pre-emption, requirement re 18(2)
prohibitions re 28(1)
research re 18(1)
Broadcasting licence
defined 2
revocation 24(1)
Broadcasting policy 3
Broadcasting undertaking
defined 2
By-laws of Commission 13
By-laws of Corporation 44
Canada Gazette
decision of Commission, publication in 24(2)
directives of Minister, publication in 17(4)
notice, publication in 18(2), 20(1), 24(1)
order of Governor in Council, publication in 27(2)
regulation of Commission, copy, publication in 16(2)
Canadian Broadcasting Corporation 2
establishment 34(1)
Canadian broadcasting system 3(a)
control 3(b)
educational broadcasting facilities 3(i)
programming 3(d)
regulations 3(j)
supervision 3(j)
Canadian Radio-Television Commission 2, 5
Chairman
absence 8(3)
acting Chairman 8(4)
defined 4
designation 8(1)
duties and functions 8(2)
public hearing, powers re 19(4)
Clerk of the Privy Council 6(2), 34(5)
Commission
acting Chairman, powers re 8(4)
broadcasting licence, application, regulations re 21
by-laws, powers re 13
defined 2
duties and functions 15, 19, 20
establishment 5(1)
Executive Committee 4
head office 12(1)
licence,
conditions of issue, violation 24(3)
notice of application, duties re 20(1)
renewal, hearing re 19(3)
revocation, conviction re 24(1)
meetings 12(2)
by-laws re 13(a)
new hearing, powers re 23(3)
notice, publication, duties re 20(2)
objects 15
order
appeal, conditions 26(1)
appeal, delay 26(2)
effect re 25
powers 16, 19(7), 23(3)
public hearing
duties re 19
powers re 19(7)
quorum 12(3)
regulatory powers 16(1)(b)
report to Parliament 31
staff, appointment 10
Committee of Commission
establishment, by-laws re 13(b)
Corporation
accounts, audit re 46
agent of Her Majesty 40(1)
bank accounts 45(1)
by-laws, powers re 44
consultation with Executive Committee 17(2)
contract, powers re 40(2)
defined 2
Executive Vice-President, appointment 38(1)
establishment 34(1)
expenses, by-law re 37(2)
expropriation, powers re 42(1) (2)
financial transactions, audit re 46
funds, administration re 45(2)
head office 43(1)
investments 45(3)
meetings 43(2)
objects 39(1)
powers 39(1) (2)
president, appointment 34(2)
proceedings 40(4)
property 40(3)
powers re 41
staff, powers re 38
employment 38(2)

Exhibit 86

Alberta
Bills (sessional).
Statutes. 1906– .
Revised Statutes 1970. Edmonton. 6 vols.

British Columbia
Bills (weekly).
Statutes. 1871– .
Revised Statutes 1960. Victoria. 4 vols. Bound or loose-leaf edition; the latter is updated semiannually. A new edition of the Revised Statutes is in progress.

Manitoba
Bills (sessional).
Statutes. 1871– .
Revised Statutes 1970. Winnipeg. 5 vols.

New Brunswick
Acts. 1786– . Bilingual since 1974.
Revised Statutes 1973. Frederickton, 6 vols. Bilingual. Subject-matter Index to Public and Private Statutes, 1971– . Loose-leaf; bilingual.
Newfoundland
Statutes. 1864– . Annual since 1949.
Revised Statutes 1970. St. John's. 8 vols.
Northwest Territories
Ordinances.
Revised Ordinances 1974. Ottawa.
Nova Scotia
Statutes. 1758– .
Revised Statutes 1967. Halifax. 4 vols.
Ontario
Current Bills Service 1975 – . Toronto, Canada Law Book.
Statutes. (Formerly Upper Canada) 1792 –?. 1825/35 – .
Revised Statutes 1977 – . Toronto. 6 vols.
Prince Edward Island
Bills (sessional).
Statutes. 1773– .
Revised Statutes 1974– .
Charlottetown. 3 vols. & Concordance.
Québec
Les statuts provinciaux de Bas-Canada 1793/96–1833/36.
Statuts de la province. 1868– .
Statuts refondus 1964. Québec. 5 vols. Bilingual. A revision of statutes amended through 1976 is forthcoming.
Code civil, 1970– .
Code de procédure civile 1971– . Montréal, Wilson et Lafleur. Both codes are bilingual.
Saskatchewan
Bills (sessional).
Statutes 1906– .
Revised Statutes 1978. Regina.
Yukon Territory
Ordinances. 1903– .
Revised Ordinances 1975. Ottawa. 3 vols. Loose-leaf.

§25.3. Subordinate legislation.

1. *Federal regulations*. With few exceptions, Canadian regulations are made pursuant to statutory authority and have the force of law. Orders and regulations as such were first published in 1940 as Proclamations and Orders in Council. From October 1942 through 1945 they were entitled Canadian War Orders and Regulations. Since its inception in 1947, the Canada Gazette, Part II,[5] issued fortnightly,

5. Ottawa, Queen's Printer.

Table of Public Statutes

Subject	R.S., 1970 Chap.	Amendments, new Acts from 1 January, 1970, and unconsolidated Acts from 1907 to 1974-75-76
B		
Bridges *Continued—*		
Saint John Bridge and Railway Company		1952-53, c. 17
Ste-Foy-St-Nicolas Bridge		1964-65, c. 16
Second Narrows Bridge, Burrard Inlet, B.C.		1935, c. 47
Valleyfield, Bridge over St. Lawrence		1951, c. 10
Van Buren Bridge Co. Agreement with H.M.		1918, c. 48
British Columbia Boundary (*See* Provincial Boundaries)		
British Columbia Coast Steamship Service		1958, c. 7
British Columbia Indian Reserves Mineral Resources		1943-44, c. 19
British Columbia-Yukon-Northwest Territories Boundary (*See* Provincial Boundaries)		
British North America Acts (*See also* Constitutional Acts and Documents in Appendix II of R.S.C., 1970, p. 121 of Appendices Volume)		**ss. 21, 22,** 1974-75-76, c. 53, s. 1 **s. 23,** 1974-75-76, c. 53, s. 2 **s. 28,** 1974-75-76, c. 53, s. 1 **s. 51,** 1974-75-76, c. 13, s. 2, c. 28, s. 2
Broadcasting	B-11	**s. 2,** 1974-75-76, c. 49, s. 18 **s. 4,** 1974-75-76, c. 49, s. 18 **ss. 5-14** repealed, 1974-75-76, c. 49, s. 18 **s. 26,** c. 10(2nd Supp.), s. 65 (Item 2) **s. 28,** 1973-74, c. 51, s. 17 **s. 42,** c. 16(1st Supp.), s. 42 **Sch. I** repealed, 1974-75-76, c. 49, s. 18
Buffalo and Fort Erie Bridge (*See* Bridges)		
Business Profits, War Tax		1916, c. 11; 1917, c. 6; 1918, c. 10; 1919, c. 39; 1920, c. 36; 1923, c. 34; 1924, cc. 10, 37; 1926-27, c. 34; 1937, c. 19
C		
Campobello-Lubec Bridge (*See* Bridges)		
Canada Agricultural Products Standards (*See* Agricultural Products Standards, Canada)		
Canada Assistance Plan	C-1	**s. 5,** 1974-75-76, c. 58, s. 11
Canada Business Corporations (*See* Corporations, Canada Business)		
Canada Cooperative Associations (*See* Cooperative Associations, Canada)		
Canada Corporations (*See* Corporations, Canada)		
Canada Council	C-2	**s. 21,** 1970-71-72, c. 43, s. 3(2), c. 63, s. 4
Canada Dairy Products (*See* Dairy Products)		
Canada Deposit Insurance Corporation	C-3	
Canada Development Corporation		1970-71-72, c. 49 **s. 39,** 1974-75-76, c. 61, s. 29 **s. 44,** Act in force 18.11.71 *see* SOR/71-607
Canada Elections (*See* Elections, Canada)		
Canada Evidence (*See* Evidence, Canada)		
Canada Fair Employment Practices (*See* Labour Code, Canada Part I)		

Exhibit 87

prints all regulations as now redefined in the Statutory Instruments Act of 1972, c. 38, and certain other classes of documents. They are numbered consecutively through the year. However, it is to be noted that certain classes of regulations are exempt from publication by the Act. There is an index to each issue of the Gazette. See further discussion below.

Regulations are bound annually as Statutory Orders and Regulations.

a. *Statutory Orders and Regulations, Consolidation of 1977.*[6] As the title suggests, this consolidation contains regulations in force as amended through December 1977; it supersedes the prior 1955 consolidation. It is similar in organization to its English counterpart. A separate index volume is anticipated. Referral to Canada Gazette, Part II, should be made to ascertain emendations to regulations or new regulations issued beginning 1978.

b. *Canada Gazette, Part II.* This section of the Gazette contains new regulations, statutory instruments, and other documents. As such, it updates the latest consolidation and subsequent annual Statutory Orders and Regulations. Index access to the regulations is through the cumulative quarterly index to the Gazette, Part II, which carries the title, Consolidated Index of Statutory Instruments. The first table of regulations is arranged alphabetically by title of the statute. In the table following, the enabling statutes are listed, and below, the regulations authorized by the statute. See Exhibit 88. In the interval between the quarterly cumulations, one must search the indexes of the biweekly issues. See Exhibit 89.

2. *Provincial and territorial regulations.* Regulations issued by the provinces and territories vary in quality and accessibility. Form of publication and indexes are provided as known.[7]

Alberta
Gazette, Part II. Fortnightly; cumulative index.
Regulations. Edmonton.

British Columbia
Gazette, Part II. Fortnightly.
Regulations. Vancouver.
Index to Current Regulations, 1958–1975. Vancouver, Law Library Foundation.
An index of regulations is appended to the British Columbia Statute Citator.

Manitoba
Gazette, Part II. Weekly.
Manitoba Regulations 1972– .
Revised Regulations 1971. Winnipeg.

New Brunswick
Royal Gazette. Weekly.
Regulations 1964– . Fredericton.
Statutory Orders and Regulations 1963. All are bilingual.

Newfoundland
Gazette, Part II. Fortnightly.
Regulations 1973– . St. John's.

Northwest Territories
Orders and Regulations 1974– . Ottawa. 3 vols. Loose-leaf.

Nova Scotia
Rules and Regulations 1973– . Halifax.

6. *Ibid.*
7. When no publisher is given, the Queen's Printer may be assumed. Place of publication applicable to official imprints is noted after the regulations.

Ontario

Gazette. Weekly.

Revised Regulations 1970. Toronto. 4 vols. & Supplement.

Ontario Regulations. Agincourt, Carswell. Loose-leaf. The Revised Regulations filed are drawn from the official Gazette. Includes a good subject index.

Prince Edward Island

Royal Gazette. Edmonton. Weekly, with annual index.

Québec

Gazette officielle 1869– . Bilingual. A revision first issued in 1972 was discontinued the following year. A new edition may be forthcoming.

Saskatchewan

Gazette, Part II. Regina. Weekly; annual index.

Yukon Territory

Regulations, 1977– . Ottawa. 5 vols. Loose-leaf.

STATUTES Regulations and other documents	Date made	No.	Date Registered	1955 Consolidation or Canada Gazette Part II Date	Page	Com
BANKRUPTCY ACT, *RSC 1970, c. B-3*—Conc.						
Orderly Payment of Debts Regulations—Conc.						
	13/ 3/73	SOR/73-152	15/ 3/73	28/ 3/73	454	
	26/11/74	SOR/74-645	27/11/74	11/12/74	2946	
Part X of the Act Proclaimed in Force:						
Alberta, April 17, 1967		SOR/67-192		26/ 4/67	680	
British Columbia, June 1, 1970		SOR/70-239		24/ 6/70	619	
Manitoba, June 1, 1967		SOR/67-239		24/ 5/67	800	
Northwest Territories, October 1, 1972	28/ 9/72	SI/72-102	25/10/72	25/10/72	1909	
Nova Scotia, July 1, 1970		SOR/70-167		13/ 5/70	488	
Prince Edward Island, March 28, 1968		SOR/68-138		24/ 4/68	462	
Saskatchewan, April 1, 1969		SOR/69-159		23/ 4/69	544	
BELLEVILLE HARBOUR COMMISSIONERS ACT, *1952, c. 34*						
General By-law of the Belleville Harbour Commissioners		SOR/53-377		23/ 9/53	866	
BLIND PERSONS ACT, *RSC 1970, c. B-7*						
Blind Persons Regulations		SOR/60-565		28/12/60	1564	r
		SOR/62-273		8/ 8/62	788	
		SOR/64-2		8/ 1/64	4	
		SOR/65-494		10/11/65	1693	
		SOR/68-100		27/ 3/68	265	
		SOR/69-32		12/ 2/69	217	
		SOR/69-613		24/12/69	1731	
		SOR/71-95		24/ 3/71	487	
	9/11/72	SOR/72-457	10/11/72	22/11/72	2024	
	22/ 5/73	SOR/73-268	23/ 5/73	13/ 6/73	1185	
BLUE WATER BRIDGE AUTHORITY ACT, *1964, c. 6*						
Blue Water Bridge Authority Financial Reports Regulations	5/10/72	SOR/72-420	10/10/72	25/10/72	1833	n
BRETTON WOODS AGREEMENTS ACT, *RSC 1970, c. B-9*						
Canadian Dollar Par Value Order		SOR/62-168		23/ 5/62	529	n
BROADCASTING ACT, *RSC 1970, c. B-11*						
Broadcasting Information Return Regulations	23/ 6/72	SOR/72-234	29/ 6/72	12/ 7/72	983	r
Broadcasting Licence Fee Regulations		SOR/68-564		25/12/68	1579	n
	23/ 6/72	SOR/72-231	29/ 6/72	12/ 7/72	979	
CRTC Rules of Procedure		SOR/71-330		28/ 7/71	1154	r
Cable Television Regulations	14/11/75	SOR/75-665	17/11/75	26/11/75	3103	n
Direction to the Canadian Radio-Television Commission		SOR/69-590		10/12/69	1695	r
		SOR/71-33		27/ 1/71	86	
	20/ 2/75	SOR/75-102	21/ 2/75	12/ 3/75	356	
Direction to the Canadian Radio-Television Commission re Reservation of Cable Channels		SOR/70-113		8/ 4/70	381	n
Direction to the Canadian Radio-Television Commission Respecting Ineligibility to Hold Broadcasting Licences	13/ 7/72	SOR/72-261	17/ 7/72	26/ 7/72	1047	r
Order Setting Aside Certain Broadcasting Licences Issued by the Canadian Radio-Television and Telecommunications Commission	10/11/76	SI/76-153	8/12/76	8/12/76	3285	n
Radio (A.M.) Broadcasting Regulations		SOR/64-49		12/ 2/64	157	r
		SOR/64-249		8/ 7/64	643	
		SOR/64-397		14/10/64	1179	
		SOR/65-189		26/ 5/65	635	

Exhibit 88

28/9/77 Canada Gazette Part II, Vol. 111, No. 18 — **SOR/77-712—759** — **SI/77-158—174**

INDEX SOR: Statutory Instruments (Regulations)
SI: Statutory Instruments and Other Documents (Other than Regulations)

Abbreviations: n — new; r — revises; x — revokes

Regulations Statutes	Registration No.	Date	Page	Comments
Adult Occupational Training Regulations, amendment Adult Occupational Training Act	SOR/77-726	7/9/77	4194	
Airport Traffic Regulations, amendment Transport Act, Department of Government Property Traffic Act	SOR/77-729	7/9/77	4198	
Atlantic Pilotage Tariff Regulations (1977) Pilotage Act	SOR/77-732	7/9/77	4218	r
British Columbia Fishery (General) Regulations Fisheries Act	SOR/77-716	7/9/77	4098	r
Cable Television Companies Remission Order, amendment Financial Administration Act	SI/77-159	28/9/77	4249	
Calgary International Airport Zoning Regulations Aeronautics Act	SOR/77-724	7/9/77	4185	n
Canso Zone Marine Traffic Regulations, amendment Canada Shipping Act	SOR/77-725	7/9/77	4193	
Certain Sections of the Act Proclaimed in Force August 10, 1977 Canadian Human Rights Act	SI/77-168	28/9/77	4262	
Chicoutimi District Order National Housing Act	SI/77-165	28/9/77	4256	n
Chlorobiphenyl Regulations No. 1 Environmental Contaminants Act	SOR/77-734	7/9/77	4231	n
Commonwealth Law Ministers Meeting Remission Order Financial Administration Act	SI/77-158	28/9/77	4248	n
Customs Duties Reduction Regulations, amendment Customs Act	SOR/77-736	12/9/77	4232	
Food and Drug Regulations, amendment—Schedule No. 415 Food and Drugs Act	SOR/77-722	7/9/77	4183	
Food and Drug Regulations, amendment—Schedule No. 398 Food and Drugs Act	SOR/77-757	16/9/77	4244	
Food and Drug Regulations, amendment—Schedule No. 399 Food and Drugs Act	SOR/77-758	16/9/77	4245	
General Radio Regulations, Part II, amendment Radio Act	SOR/77-735	7/9/77	4231	
General Radio Regulations, Part II, amendment Radio Act	SOR/77-738	13/9/77	4235	
Hull Construction Regulations, amendment Canada Shipping Act	SOR/77-728	7/9/77	4197	
Imported Prefabricated Buildings and Structural Building Sections Remission Order, amendment Financial Administration Act	SI/77-162	28/9/77	4252	
Income Tax Regulations, amendment Income Tax Act	SOR/77-723	7/9/77	4184	
Income Tax Regulations, amendment Income Tax Act	SOR/77-731	7/9/77	4215	
Lockheed L 1011 Aircraft Remission Order, amendment Financial Administration Act	SI/77-166	28/9/77	4259	

Exhibit 89

§25.4. Treaties.

Canada Treaty Series.[8] From 1928 to date, this is a chronological collection of bilateral and multilateral treaties. It is bilingual and issued in fascicles with a long time lag in publication. If necessary, resort may be made to the Treaty Registration Section of the Department of External Affairs.

8. Ottawa, Queen's Printer.

§25.5. Law reports.

Under the three-tier system by which Canadian courts are organized, courts of the first instance and the lower appellate courts are under provincial aegis. The Supreme Court and the Federal Court are under federal control.

Decisional law is covered by conventional law reports; additionally, some legal periodicals and services print reports in full or abridged form.

1. *Canada Supreme Court*. Decisions of this court are published officially in Canada Supreme Court Reports,[9] formerly entitled Reports of the Supreme Court of Canada from 1876 through 1922, and Canada Law Reports: Supreme Court of Canada from 1923 through 1969. Each volume has a table of cases judicially construed, a subject index, and a list of unreported judgments and motions, excepting applications for leave to appeal. There is a current alphabetical subject index for the series. Supreme Court cases are included in the Dominion Law Reports for which see below.

2. *Federal Court*. Effective June 1971, the Federal Court continues the Exchequer Court of Canada as a superior court of record having civil and criminal jurisdiction and with both trial and appeal divisions. Its decisions are published in Canada Federal Court Reports,[10] 1971 to date. Each volume has tables of cases, cases judicially construed, also statutes and regulations judicially noticed.

Decisions of the Exchequer Court are found in the Reports of the Exchequer Court of Canada from 1891 through 1922, and thereafter through mid-1970, in Canada Law Reports: Exchequer Court. The Dominion Law Reports series covers the Federal Court and its predecessor.

3. *Dominion Law Reports*.[11] This set purports to include all reportable cases from all the courts of Canada and decisions of the Privy Council from 1912 to date. Through 1922 the volumes were numbered consecutively; thereafter through 1955 they were renumbered each year and cited in the manner of the English Law Reports as [1950] 3 D.L.R. 118; [1951] 1 D.L.R. 361. With the beginning of the second series in 1956, consecutive volume numbering was resumed. The third series, 1969 to date, begins a new sequential numbering. In 1968 a weekly reporting series was initiated.

There is a cumulative table of cases volume for the second series. For the third series there is an additional service volume consisting of a table of cases and, in separate parts, annotations to cases in the second and third series which serve, in effect, as comprehensive case

9. *Ibid*.
10. Ottawa, Queen's Printer, 1971 to date.
11. Agincourt, Ontario, Canada Law Book.

citators with references to all Canadian jurisdictions and published report series. To use this volume as a citator, it is necessary to determine the D.L.R. volume and page reference, under which enumeration of the annotations is organized.

4. *National Reporter.*[12] This series, begun in 1974, widens the coverage of Supreme and Federal Courts' judgments rendered. In format, it is loosely patterned after the West reporters.

5. *Atlantic Provinces Reports.*[13] Since its inception in 1975, this series contains appeal cases of New Brunswick, Nova Scotia, Prince Edward Island, Newfoundland, and other selected decisions. From 1929 through 1974 these reports carried the title, Maritime Provinces Reports. No advance parts are published.

6. *Western Weekly Reports.*[14] The series prints significant appeal cases from Alberta, British Columbia, Manitoba, Saskatchewan, and the territories, and appeals therefrom to the Supreme and Federal Courts of Canada. The earlier Western Law Reporter covered the period 1911–1916. Under the present title, the first series encompassed the years 1917 through 1950, a new series 1951 through 1970, and the current series 1971 to date. There are consolidated tables and an index for the earlier series and for the current series through the last complete calendar year. There is an additional section in the latest series index on words and phrases judicially considered.

7. *Provincial law reports of individual provinces.* Individual provincial reports are currently issued as follows. Generally these reports include appeals from the province through the Supreme Court of Canada.

Alberta Law Reports. 1st ser. 1908–1932. 2d ser. 1976– . Calgary, Burroughs.

British Columbia Law Reports. 1st ser. 1925/35–1947. New ser. 1976– . Calgary, Burroughs.

Manitoba Law Reports. 1883–1961. Calgary, Burroughs.

New Brunswick Reports. 1st ser. 1825/35–?. 2d ser. 1968– . Frederickton, Maritime Law Book.

Newfoundland and Prince Edward Island Reports. 1971– . Frederickton, Maritime Law Book.

Nova Scotia Reports. 1st ser. 1834/51–?. 1965–1969 in 4 vols. 2d ser. 1970– . Frederickton, Maritime Law Book.

Ontario Reports. 1st ser. 1882–1973 (volumes within the series numbered variously). 2d ser. 1974– . Toronto, Canada Law Book. Ontario Law Report Table of Cases, 1975, is cumulated for all series.

Québec

Recueils de jurisprudence de Québec. Cour d'appel. 1970– .

Recueils de jurisprudence de Québec. Cour supérieure. 1967– .

(From 1892 through 1969 or 1966 respectively, both were published as

12. Frederickton, Maritime Law Book, 1974 to date.
13. Frederickton, Maritime Law Book, 1975.
14. Alberta, Burroughs.

Rapports judiciaires officiels de Québec.)
Saskatchewan Law Reports. 1908–1931. Calgary, Burroughs

8. *Territorial court decisions*. Decisions of the courts of Northwest Territories and Yukon Territory can be found in the Western Weekly Reports. They are digested in Canadian Abridgment and Canadian Encyclopedic Digest (Western), second series.

§25.6. Digests.

1. *Canadian Abridgment*.[15] This is the most complete digest in terms of scope and period covered. A first edition begun in 1935 was followed by a second edition, of which bound volumes cover reports through 1964 of the Supreme and Exchequer Courts as well as the provincial and territorial courts, appeals to the Privy Council, and Québec court decisions of universal application. Arrangement is by broad subject titles with subject paragraphs consecutively numbered throughout. Cases are abridged at some length, focusing on the issues of major legal interest. See Exhibit 90. A table of cases and subject index(es) are within each volume.

A First Permanent Supplement in three volumes provides coverage through 1974; thereafter material is published in a loose-leaf cumulative supplement binder, the contents of which transfer periodically into permanent bound volumes. Material in the cumulative supplement binder is updated monthly by Canadian Current Law, for which see below. To facilitate use of both titles concurrently, the cumulative supplement binder carries, in addition to the table of cases for the binder, a supplementary case table of current decisions abridged in Canadian Current Law, with paragraph references to the latter title.

There is a consolidated table of cases with coverage through the first permanent supplementary volumes. Thereafter use the table of cases in the cumulative supplement binder. A Table of Cases Judicially Considered with coverage through 1973, supplemented by the table of cases judicially considered in a loose-leaf appendix binder, functions as a comprehensive case citator. See Exhibits 91 & 92.

Words and Phrases Judicially Considered completes the set. It consists of an alphabetical list of words and phrases considered in the reports with enumerated references to cases and the subject section(s) wherein the words are treated. See Exhibit 93. Currency of this new feature is achieved by additions printed in the appendix binder.

Beginning coverage at the end of 1975, Canadian Abridgment . . . Practice is for the practitioner, as the name implies.

15. Toronto, Carswell.

1059. Skill or judgment of seller not relied on — Sale of Goods Act, R.S.B.C. 1948, c. 294, s. 21(a). The mere fact that the vendor knows the use to which the article is intended will not raise the presumption of an implied warranty where it is apparent the skill or judgment of the seller are not relied on.

SMITH SHEET METAL WORKS LTD. v. BINGHAM & HOBBS EQUIPMENT CO., [1949] 4 D.L.R. 363 (B.C.).

1060. Warranties — Exclusion clause — Used motor vehicle — Implied conditions — Sale of Goods Act, R.S.N.B. 1952, c. 199, ss. 15(a), (b), 52. Plaintiff purchased from defendant a used motor vehicle under a conditional sales agreement which contained the following clause: "Purchaser acknowledges that this agreement constitutes the entire contract and that there are no representations, warranties or conditions, expressed or implied, statutory or otherwise, other than as contained herein." There were no warranties or representations in the agreement. Plaintiff's action for alleged non-compliance with the statutory conditions contained in s. 15(*a*) and (*b*) of the Act was dismissed. On appeal, *held*, the appeal should be dismissed. Plaintiff did not rely on defendant's skill or judgment, he examined the car himself. The sale was for a specified vehicle referred to in the contract, and the implied conditions in s. 15 did not attach to the contract. Furthermore, the exclusion clause, which was expressly permitted by s. 52 of the Act, was effective to exclude the implied conditions in s. 15 of the Act.

GODSOE v. BEATTY (1958), 44 M.P.R. 1, 19 D.L.R. (2d) 265 (N.B. C.A.).

1061. Implied condition — Breach of warranty — Action for price of goods — Sale of Goods Act, R.S.O. 1950, c. 345, s. 15. Defendant bought certain irrigating equipment for his farm from plaintiff, but after a week it failed to work properly because of the inadequacy of the water supply which was provided by a creek on defendant's farm. In an action for the price, *held*, plaintiff was entitled to succeed. (1) There was no complaint as to the quality or efficiency of the goods, but only that the system did not operate because of lack of water. Accordingly s. 15 of the Act did not assist defendant. (2) Defendant's claim that plaintiff's agent had represented that the stream in question was sufficient to supply the required water had not been made out on the evidence.

HADLEY v. COONEY, [1960] O.W.N. 101.

1062. Sale of used car — Caveat emptor. Defendant and his wife purchased a used car. The car was returned because of alleged defects. *Held*, plaintiff was entitled to the purchase price. Defendant had ample opportunity to inspect the car, and the maxim *caveat emptor* applied. Moreover, warranties of fitness were specifically excluded by the agreement which, although not enforceable by plaintiff, was not void *ab initio* and could be asserted as a defence to the counterclaim.

COHEN v. MULLIN, [1960] O.W.N. 115, 23 D.L.R. (2d) 293 (C.A.).

1063. Clause in contract excluding warranties and conditions — Defects so numerous as to render merchandise unusable — Buyer's "acceptance" of defective merchandise — Effect of exclusionary clause. Plaintiff purchased an engine for his boat from defendant. There was a written contract of sale which contained exclusionary clauses to the effect, *inter alia*, that the buyer relied solely on his own judgment that the equipment was fit for its intended purpose and that "there are no representations, warranties or conditions, express or implied, statutory or otherwise, other than those herein contained, except for the standard manufacturer's written warranty . . .". The engine never worked at full power. *Held*, plaintiff was entitled to judgment. The engine was useless for plaintiff's purposes and, therefore, the exclusionary clause did not assist defendant as he had supplied something different from that which was bargained for. Moreover, the "acceptance" of the engine did not preclude plaintiff from claiming damages.

KNOWLES v. ANCHORAGE HOLDINGS CO. (1964), 46 W.W.R. 173, 43 D.L.R. (2d) 300 (B.C.).

d. Sale of Goods under Patent or Trade Name

1064. Particular article purchased — No warranty of fitness. Per Middleton J., quoting Mellor J., in *Jones v. Just*, L.R. 3 Q.B. 197: "Where a known described and defined article is ordered of a manufacturer, although it is stated to be required by the purchaser for a particular purpose, still if the known, described, and defined thing be

Exhibit 90

CASES JUDICIALLY CONSIDERED

Apld. Jaworski v. Jaworski, [1973] 2 O.R. 420.
Consd. Cooper v. Cooper, 10 R.F.L. 184.
Apld. Storey v. Storey, 4 N. & P.E.I.R. 229.
Apld. Westmacott v. Westmacott, 10 R.F.L. 377.

Knoll v. Wright, [1945] 1 W.W.R. 552.
Apld. Mareen Homes Ltd. v. Malcher (1966), 57 W.W.R. 733.

Knoor v. Clark (1914), 27 W.L.R. 753.
Folld. Clermont v. Mid-West Steel Products Ltd., 51 D.L.R. (2d) 340.

Knott, Re, 27 W.W.R. (N.S.) 382.
Apld. Re Bohachewski, 60 W.W.R. 635.

Knott v. Knott, [1935] P. 158.
Consd. Liske v. Liske, 58 Man. R. 54.

Knott v. London County Council, [1934] 1 K.B. 126.
Apld. Stanford v. Robertson, [1946] 3 W.W.R. 767.

Knott v. Morgan, 2 Keen 213.
Consd. Brewster Tpt. Co. v. Rocky Mt. Tours Co., [1931] S.C.R. 336.

Knott v. Telegram Printing, 27 Man. L.R. 336.
Aff. 55 S.C.R. 631.

Knowlden v. R., 5 B. & S. 532.
Apld. R. v. Cooper, [1941] 2 W.W.R. 206.

Knowles, Re, 24 U.C.Q.B. 311.
Consd. Merritt v. Shaw, 15 Gr. 321.

Knowles, Re, [1938] O.R. 369.
Apld. Re Orford, [1944] 1 D.L.R. 277.
Dist. Re Eacrett, [1949] O.W.N. 10.
Consd. Re Robertson, [1952] O.R. 283.
Folld. Tolosnak v. Tolosnak, [1957] O.W.N. 273.
Consd. Re Blackwell, [1962] O.R. 832.
Apld. Re Etter, 61 W.W.R. 427.
Apld. Re Treasure Island Gdns. Ltd. and Lawson, 13 C.B.R. (N.S.) 47.

Knowles v. Anchorage Holdings Co., 46 W.W.R. 173.
Apld. Lightburn v. Belmont Sales Ltd., 69 W.W.R. 734.
Apld. Gibbons v. Trapp Motors Ltd., 9 D.L.R. (3d) 742.
Consd. Barber v. Inland Truck Sales Ltd., 11 D.L.R. (3d) 469.
Dist. Peters v. Irving Oil Co., 1 N.S.R. (2d) 861.

Knowles v. Knowles, [1970] 3 O.R. 722.
Consd. Fortese v. Fortese, [1973] 2 O.R. 143.

Knowles v. Peter, 12 W.W.R. (N.S.) 560.
Apld. U.S.A. v. Annesley, 21 W.W.R. 520.
Apld. Chauvel v. Chauvel and Montreal Trust Co., 47 W.W.R. 574.
Apld. Halpin v. Accept. Mtge. Corpn., 55 W.W.R. 636.
Apld. McMeekin v. Certified Concrete (Central) Ltd., 58 W.W.R. 56.

Knowles v. Richardson, 2 Keble 642.
Apld. Morris v. Dom. Foundries & Steel Ltd., [1947] 2 D.L.R. 840.

Knowles v. Roberts, 38 Ch. D. 263.
Folld. Transcontinental Townsite Co. v. G.T.P. Dev. Co., 25 Man. L.R. 843.
Apld. Rothschild v. Custodian, [1945] 4 D.L.R. 65.
Consd. Brydon v. Brydon, [1951] O.W.N. 369.
Apld. U.S. Fidelity and Guar. Co. v. Boland, [1957] O.W.N. 237.
Apld. Saunders v. Bank of N.S., 1 N.B.R. (2d) 897.

Knowles v. Southern Ry. Co., 52 T.L.R. 465.
Apld. Gibson v. B.C. Dist. Telegraph, [1936] 3 W.W.R. 241.

Knowlton v. H.E.P.C., 58 O.L.R. 80.
Apld. Dority v. Ottawa R.C.S.S. Trustees, 65 OL.R 360.
Folld. Fletcher v. Thomas, [1931] O.R. 195.
Folld. Gargotch v. Cohen, [1940] O.W.N. 479.
Apld. Evers v. Bay-Front Garage Ltd., [1943] O.W.N. 179.
Folld. Enridge v. Copp (1966), 55 W.W.R. 457.
Folld. McKittrick v. Byers, 58 O.L.R. 158.

Exhibit 91

SUPPLEMENT TO CASES JUDICIALLY CONSIDERED

Knatchbull v. Hallett.
See Re Hallett.

Knickle v. Tanner, 48 D.L.R. (3d) 458.
Aff. 10 N.S.R. (2d) 658.

Knight v. Eriksson, 26 W.W.R. 203.
Apld. Saskatoon v. Zarzeczny, [1976] 6 W.W.R. 107.

Knight v. Knight, [1925] 1 W.W.R. 824.
Not folld. McKay v. McKay, 19 R.F.L. 32.

Knight v. Knight, 68 W.W.R. 464.
Apld. Bertram v. Bertram, [1974] 1 W.W.R. 499.
Apld. Yanoshewski v. Yanoshewski, 40 D.L.R. (3d) 461.
Folld. Connelly v. Connelly, 9 N.S.R. (2d) 48.
Apld. Goudreau v. Bedard, [1974] Que. S.C. 350.

Knight v. Martelle, [1966] 1 O.R. 147.
Consd. Sfyras v. Kotsis, 10 O.R. (2d) 27.

Knight v. Yorkton S. Bd., Unit No. 36, 34 D.L.R. (3d) 592.
Apld. Re Melanson and Halifax Bd. of S. Commrs., 75 D.L.R. (3d) 641.

Knight (Andre) Ltd. v. Presement, [1967] 2 O.R. 289.
Dist. Whitehead v. Lach Gen. Contractors Ltd., 3 O.R. (2d) 680.

Knight Sugar Co. v. Alta. Ry. & Irrigation Co., [1938] 1 W.W.R. 234.
Dist. Richview Const. Co. v. Raspa, 11 O.R. (2d) 377.
Apld. First Nat. Mtge. Co. v. Grouse Nest Resorts Ltd., 2 B.C.L.R. 300.

Knoll v. Knoll, [1970] 2 O.R. 169.
Folld. M. v. M., 7 N.B.R. (2d) 491.
Apld. Kahn v. Kahn, 13 R.F.L. 269.
Apld. Mark v. Mark, 15 R.F.L. 73.
Apld. Shumila v. Shumila, [1975] 5 W.W.R. 697.
Apld. Rauch v. Rauch, 9 O.R. (2d) 761.
Apld. Graham v. Graham, 25 R.F.L. 107.
Apld. Wales v. Wales, 24 R.F.L. 138.

Knott v. Knott, [1935] P. 158.
Not folld. G. v. G., 22 R.F.L. 325.

Knott v. London, [1934] 1 K.B. 126.
Apld. Maynes v. Galicz, [1976] 1 W.W.R. 557.

Knowles, Re, 13 R.F.L. 76.
Apld. Burgess v. Burgess, 19 N.S.R. (2d) 689.

Knowles v. Anchorage Holdings Co., 46 W.W.R. 173.
Apld. Findlay v. Couldwell, [1976] 5 W.W.R. 340.
Apld. Burridge v. City Motors (Nfld.) Ltd., 10 N. & P.E.I.R. 451.
Apld. Mulrooney v. Greene, 12 Nfld. & P.E.I.R. 292.

Knowles v. Knowles.
See Re Knowles.

Knowles v. Peter, 12 W.W.R. 560.
Dist. Garon Realty & Ins. Ltd. v. James (George) (Collins), [1977] 1 W.W.R. 45.

Knox v. Knox, [1942] O.W.N. 462.
Dist. Bickerton v. Bickerton, 9 O.R. (2d) 333.
Dist. R. v. MacDonald, 26 R.F.L. 204.

Knudsen and Hollingsworth Invts. Ltd., Re, [1971] 3 O.R. 580.
Dist. Re Nadeau and Gallaugher, 54 D.L.R. (3d) 367.

Knuller v. D.P.P., [1973] A.C. 435.
Dist. R. v. Celebrity Enterprises Ltd., [1977] 4 W.W.R. 144.

Knupffer v. London Express Newspaper Ltd., [1944] A.C. 116.
Consd. Church of Scientology of Toronto v. Internat. News Distributing Co., 4 O.R. (2d) 408.

Kocotis v. D'Angelo, [1958] O.R. 104.
Apld. Calax Const. Inc. v. Lepofsky, 5 O.R. (2d) 259.

Koechlin v. Waugh, [1957] O.W.N. 245.
Folld. Sandison v. Rybiak, 1 O.R. (2d) 74.
Apld. Cheese v. Hardy, [1975] 1 W.W.R. 249.
Folld. Prior v. McNab, 1 C.C.L.T. 137.

Kokan v. Dales, [1970] 1 O.R. 465.
Apld. Bowlen v. R., 76 D.T.C. 6334.

Kokatt v. Melidonis, 13 Sask. L.R. 470.
Folld. Tudor Devs. Ltd. v. Van Es, 53 D.L.R. (3d) 716.
Dist. Balageorge v. McCulloch, [1977] 4 W.W.R. 195.

Kolacz v. Munzel, [1971] 5 W.W.R. 757.
Dist. Greschuk v. Bizon, 1 Alta. L.R. (2d) 163.

Kolan v. Solicitor, [1970] 1 O.R. 41; [1970] 2 O.R. 686.
Apld. Major v. Buchanan, 9 O.R. (2d) 491.

Exhibit 92

WORDS AND PHRASES

ABUSE OF PRIVILEGE
Re Shaw .... (Master and Servant) S3.55320

ABUTS
Catkey Const. (Toronto) Ltd. v. Bankes .... (Highways) S2.37755

ACCELERATED RENT
Re Sobies Ltd.; Buzzell and Farmer v. Nardelda Ltd. .... (Bankruptcy) 3.1624

ACCEPT
Scott v. Merchants Bank .... (Bills of Exch.) 4.3474

ACCEPTANCE
Re Commercial Bank; Re Claims for Interest on Debts Proved (Bills of Exch.) 4.3476
J. Materne Design & Const. Ltd. v. Gendel .... (Sale of Goods) 34.606
Slater v. Black .... (Sale of Goods) 34.627
Knowles v. Anchorage Holdings Co. .... (Sale of Goods) 34.1063
Mooney v. Huggard Equipment Co. and Huxley Cartage Ltd. (Sale of Goods) 34.2167
Burroughs Business Machines Ltd. v. Feed-Rite Mills (1962) Ltd. (Sale of Goods) S3.83245

ACCEPTANCE OF OPTION
Lawrence v. Pringle .... (Sale of Land) 34.3595

ACCEPTED
Re Toronto Beaches Election; Ferguson v. Murphy .... (Banking) 2.2803
Northern Bank v. Yuen .... (Estoppel) 14.2825
Derome v. Caisse Populaire de Bedford .... (Bills of Exch.) S1.7024

ACCEPTED (Method)
Ken Steeves Sales Ltd. v. M.N.R. .... (Income Tax) 18.2521

ACCEPTING
McKean v. Jones .... (Choses in Action) 6.262
Barber v. Inland Truck Sales Ltd. .... (Sale of Goods) 34.1983

ACCESS
Van Alstyne v. Ruck .... (Easements) 14.146
Brooking v. Brooking .... (Infants) 19.606

ACCESS VISIT
Callender v. Callender .... (Matr. Causes) S3.61191

ACCESSIBLE TO STOCK
Glenn v. Schofield .... (Animals) 2.39

ACCESSORIES
Dep. M.N.R. v. Gen. Supply Co. .... (Customs) 12.3412

ACCESSORY (Buildings)
Dobson v. Edmonton .... (Municipal Corpns.) 28.1927

Exhibit 93

2. *Canadian Current Law.*[16] This is a monthly reporting service of both reported and selective unreported decisions of the Supreme Court and provincial courts, with the restriction that Québec cases reported are limited to those of common-law interest. Its arrangement parallels that of the Canadian Abridgment second edition, which it supplements. There is also a list of recent federal and provincial statutes and proclamations with dates when they enter into force. See Exhibit 94. Tables of cases judicially considered and subject indexes cumulate in the June and December issues.

3. *Canadian Weekly Law Sheet.*[17] This is an index digest in classified arrangement of the latest cases in all areas of law. Additionally, it notes new statutes, orders and regulations, and significant periodical articles. There is a detailed quarterly cumulative subject index.

4. *The Supreme Court of Canada Reports Service.*[18] This loose-leaf service in its second edition provides brief digest notations under alphabetically arranged subject headings for cases of the highest court beginning with 1972. It includes a Current Service volume, which digests recent cases not incorporated into the three main volumes, a quarterly summary of unreported Supreme Court decisions, and an index to the complete series of Canada Supreme Court Reports for the period 1876–1977.

5. *Federal Court of Canada Service.*[19] Since 1970, this loose-leaf service annotates cases under sections of the Federal Court Act, its Rules, and relevant sections of the Income Tax Act. Arrangement is by key numbers similar to CCH paragraph numbers. There is also the standard table of cases and subject access. Cases of the predecessor court are found in Digest of Cases . . . in the Exchequer Court of Canada for the period 1922–1969.

6. *English and Empire Digest.* This set, discussed in detail at §24.7.1, includes many Canadian cases. See Exhibit 78.

7. *Dominion Report Service.*[20] This is a monthly CCH loose-leaf reporter digesting all reported Canadian cases and selected unreported cases under classified subject headings such as commercial law and contracts. Standard CCH topical indexing, case tables, and bound transfer volumes are employed, but paragraph numbering varies from the standard CCH practice. Case digests are consecutively numbered within each topic, followed by a jurisdictional symbol. To illustrate: ¶1-580 Q denotes general commercial law, specific case number, Québec. There is a statutory citator covering bankruptcy, criminal law, and parts of the Québec code.

16. Agincourt, Ontario, Carswell, 1948 to date.
17. Toronto, Butterworths, 1959 to date. Loose-leaf.
18. Toronto, Butterworths. 2 vols. Loose-leaf.
19. *Ibid.*
20. Toronto, Commerce Clearing House Canadian.

ADMINISTRATIVE LAW [1977] C.C.L. 2823

CASE LAW

The subject titles used coincide with those used in the Canadian Abridgment (2nd Edition) and are listed on the inside back cover of the January issue. The numbers in round brackets refer to the Abridgment classifications; those in square brackets refer to the title [T] and paragraph number [§] in the Canadian Encyclopedic Digest (Ontario 3rd Edition) dealing with the subject matter of the case.

ADMINISTRATIVE LAW

2818. (IV, 1, c)
Judicial review — Certiorari — Review of board's decision confirming dismissal of teachers for marihuana possession — Board addressing itself to proper questions — Education Act, R.S.N.S. 1967, c. 81, s. 76 [re-en. 1972, c. 29, s. 12; am. 1973, c. 27, s. 6]. Two teachers were dismissed by their school board, and their dismissal was confirmed by a Judge sitting as a board of appeal under s. 76 of the Act. The teachers applied for an order in the nature of *certiorari* to quash the board's decision, contending that the Judge had failed to decide whether their marihuana convictions constituted just cause for dismissal and had also failed to decide whether dismissal was a suitable disciplinary measure. *Held*, the application should be dismissed. A careful reading of the Judge's decision as a whole indicated that he did address himself to the question of whether the criminal convictions amounted to just cause. His disciplinary powers were restricted by legislation to either suspension with pay, or dismissal, and by his decision he confirmed the school board's choice of dismissal.

BECKWITH v. COLCHESTER-EAST HANTS AMALGAM. SCHOOL BD., N.S. T.D., July 14, 1977 (not yet reported).

2819. (IV, 2, c) [T3 §71]
Boards and tribunals — Party given status — Tribunal not having right to prohibit cross-examination by party — Tribunal's right to control conduct of hearings not extending to right to prohibit cross-examination by party.

RE HENDERSON AND ONT. SECURITIES COMMN. (1976), 14 O.R. (2d) 498 (H.C.).

2820. (IV, 2, d) [T3 §60]
Boards and tribunals — Quorums — Death of one of board panel of three — Tariff Board Act, R.S.C. 1970, c. T-1, s. 3(8) — Interpretation Act, R.S.C. 1970, c. I-23, s. 21(1), (2). A statute provided that, on an appeal to a tariff board, three or more board members could exercise all the powers of the board. Following the death of one of an original panel of three board members, the board referred to the Federal Court of Appeal the question whether the surviving members had jurisdiction to continue. *Held*, the panel had no jurisdiction to continue. The requirement of three members was a quorum provision and the quorum provisions of the Interpretation Act did not apply.

REFERENCE RE TARIFF BOARD (1977), 73 D.L.R. (3d) 173 (Fed. C.A.).

2821. (IV, 2, e) [T3 §60]
Judicial review — Lack of jurisdiction — Quorum — Statute requiring three or more members to sit on appeal to Tariff Board — Hearing being held before three members — One member dying before decision — Court holding two remaining members not having jurisdiction to issue declaration — Tariff Board Act, R.S.C. 1970, c. T-1.

RE TARIFF BD. ACT (1977), 15 N.R. 361 (Fed. C.A.).

2822. (IV, 2, g)
Judicial review — Natural justice — Bias — Municipal council obtaining permit from Planning Commission for gravel pit — Resident appealing to Development Appeal Board which was Municipal Council — Council dismissing appeal — Resident appealing to Court of Appeal — Court holding that obvious bias of council did not disqualify council from sitting on appeal — Planning Act, R.S.A. 1970, c. 276.

MCARTHUR v. FOOTHILLS MUN. DIST. NO. 31 (1977), 4 A.R. 30 (C.A.). See also No. 2823.

2823. (IV, 2, i)
Judicial review — Exercise of discretion — Municipal zone being restricted to 20-acre lots — Permits being available for smaller lots at discretion of Planning Commission — Municipal Council applying for permit for gravel pit — Council stating lot size 20 acres — Lot being 14 acres — Resident appealing — Court quashing granting of per-

Exhibit 94

8. *All Canada Digest System.*[21] This publication purported to digest series of Canadian reports from 1910 to 1961. For the period, it traverses the same ground as the Canadian Abridgment system although in considerably shorter compass. It was a conventional digest listing words and phrases, cases judicially noticed, and Dominion and provincial statutes judicially considered to 1957.

9. *Western Weekly Digests.*[22] During its brief existence, 1975–1976, it digested cases of the Western provinces and territories. A table of cases and a subject index for each year are included.

10. *Butterworth's Ontario Digest.* This loose-leaf service annotates all reported Ontario cases including Appeals to the Canada Supreme Court and Privy Council. Digests are classified under broad subject headings and sections by key number. Cases are numbered consecutively throughout each volume. The digest functions as a citator: subsequent history and treatment of the case by Ontario courts are given, and there is tabular notice of both Ontario and federal statutes considered in the cases digested. There is a useful subject index. The Digest of Ontario Case Law, precedent to Butterworth's Ontario Digest, serves as a summary of case law for the period 1823 to 1900.

11. *Annuaire de jurisprudence de Québec.*[23] This is a subject digest of Québec cases and of subjects relevant to Québec, beginning 1956. It is a continuation of Repertoire général de jurisprudence canadienne 1770–1913, with supplements in series through 1955.

12. There are also published digests to the provincial reports for the following provinces: Alberta, British Columbia, Manitoba, Nova Scotia, and Saskatchewan.

§25.7. Encyclopedias.

1. *Canadian Encyclopedic Digest.*[24] There are two editions of this work commonly referred to as C.E.D., the Ontario and the Western.

a. *Canadian Encyclopedia Digest (Ontario).* C.E.D. Ontario 3d 1973– , in progress, is an encyclopedia of statutory and case law with copious annotations to the case or statutory authority in which the encyclopedic commentary resides. It is arranged by broad subject titles with distinct paragraph numbering for each title. There is a detailed table of contents and a table of cases for each subject title. Currency is ensured by addition or substitution of pages in its loose-leaf binders and by supplementary releases on colored paper stock, in the manner of some Binder services.

b. *Canadian Encyclopedic Digest (Western).* C.E.D. Western 2d ed. surveys all reported decisions of Alberta, British Columbia, Mani-

21. Toronto, Canada Law Book, 1935–1962. 24 vols.
22. Calgary, Burroughs.
23. Montréal, Wilson & Lafleur.
24. Toronto, Carswell; Calgary, Burroughs.

toba, and Saskatchewan and appeals therefrom to the Canada Supreme Court. Some references are made to statutory law. The organization is similar to that of the Ontario edition. There is a 1968 permanent supplement volume and a further cumulative supplement through 1972.

2. *Halsbury's Laws of England*—Canadian Converters.[25] These function as the name implies. Note that the converter volumes are presently to Halsbury's Laws, third edition.

§25.8. Citators.

There is no single series comparable to Shepard's Citations for searching the legislative and judicial treatment of statutes and judicial consideration of cases. There are some published citators; additionally there are segments of some digests and encyclopedias which serve this function.

1. *Statute citators*. In the citators noted below, statutes are commonly listed by the short title of the original act or its consolidation. Exceptions are the Canadian criminal code and the Québec codes which are cited by code and section. Having found the desired statute and section in the citator, the searcher finds amendments, repeals, or restrictions cited first, followed by citations to cases construing the section. Since these are merely brief notations of what action the construing court took, the cases themselves must be examined.

A feature of Canadian statute citators not found in those for the United States is the notation of statutory rules and orders (corresponding to our Code of Federal Regulations) promulgated under the authority of the statutes listed, and cases interpreting them. To find the interpretation of the order, look up the basic act under the authority of which the order was issued.

a. *Canada Statute Citator*.[26] This loose-leaf service to R.S.C. 1970 is updated quarterly and may be used to search the law and possible changes in it when the title of the statute is known. Texts of amendments are printed in full as they come into force. Acts repealed are noted. New acts are noted in the alphabetical order of the volumes' arrangement by R.S.C. title, but the text of the law is not included. Proclamations and Orders in Council affecting statutes are noted, particularly proclamations directing delayed legislation into force. Cases from all published reports interpreting a statute are digested under the statute and its pertinent sections. See Exhibit 95.

b. *British Columbia Statute Citator*.[27] Citations in this loose-leaf service are geared to the province's Revised Statutes 1960. Presum-

25. Toronto, Butterworths.
26. Agincourt, Ontario, Canada Law Book, 2 vols.
27. Agincourt, Ontario, Canada Law Book. 2 vols. Loose-leaf.

BROADCASTING ACT

R.S.C. 1970, Chap. B-11
Amended R.S.C. 1970, c. 16 (1st Supp.), s. 42(2)
Amended R.S.C. 1970, c. 10 (2nd Supp.), s. 65; proclaimed in force August 1, 1972
Amended 1973-74, c. 51, s. 17; in force July 14, 1974, see s. 23
Amended 1974-75-76, c. 49, s. 18; proclaimed in force April 1, 1976
Administered by the Canadian Radio-Television Commission and the Canadian Broadcasting Corporation, both of which report to Parliament through the Secretary of State

Generally

Re Purdy et al. and The Queen (1972), 28 D.L.R. (3d) 720, 8 C.C.C. (2d) 52, 4 N.B.R. (2d) 848 *sub nom. Re Purdy* (N.B.C.A.).

Provisions of the Criminal Code made applicable to other federal statutes by virtue of s. 27(2) of the Interpretation Act must be read as they are found and cannot be applied "*mutatis mutandis*". Therefore, s. 443 of the Code conferring power to issue search warrants in respect of offences against the Code cannot apply in respect of offences against this Act since the section refers specifically to offences against the Code.

NOTE: *cf. Re Krassman and The Queen* (1972), 8 C.C.C. (2d) 45, [1972] 6 W.W.R. 374 *sub nom. Krassman v. Foster et al.* (Alta.C.A.), see Small Loans Act, *post*; and *Re Adelphi Book Store Ltd. and The Queen* (1972), 8 C.C.C. (2d) 49, 7 C.P.R. (2d) 166, [1972] 6 W.W.R. 126 *sub nom. R. v. King* (Sask.C.A.), see Copyright Act, *post*.

Section 2

Definition "Commission" repealed and the following substituted by 1974-75-76, c. 49, s. 18:

"Commission" means the Canadian Radio-television and Telecommunications Commission established by the *Canadian Radio-television and Telecommunications Commission Act*;

Definition "Minister" repealed and the following substituted by 1974-75-76, c. 49, s. 18:

"Minister" means, in Part II, the Minister of Communications, and in Part III, the Secretary of State of Canada;

Section 4

The headings preceding this section and this section repealed and the following substituted by 1974-75-76, c. 49, s. 18:

PART II

OBJECTS AND POWERS OF THE CANADIAN RADIO-TELEVISION AND TELECOMMUNICATIONS COMMISSION IN RELATION TO BROADCASTING

Interpretation

4. In this Part,

"Chairman" and "Vice-Chairman" mean the Chairman and any Vice-Chairman of the Commission designated by the Governor in Council pursuant to sub-

Exhibit 95

ably a new citator edition will follow the publication of the new statutory consolidation now in progress. In the present citator, the history and judicial interpretation of statutes and their sections are given. There is an index of regulations in the last loose-leaf binder.

c. *Ontario Statute Citator.*[28] This loose-leaf citator in two volumes to the Ontario Revised Statutes 1970 is patterned in organization after the Canada Statute Citator.

d. Statute citators in appendix binders to the Western Weekly Reports have been issued for the Western provinces. British Columbia Statutes Judicially Considered, initiated in 1961 and conforming to the R.S.B.C. 1960, and Saskatchewan Statutes Judicially Considered, initiated in 1966 and conforming to R.S.S. 1965, are current. Whether or not they will be revised to conform to the new statutory revisions of the provinces is presently unknown. Binder services for Alberta and Manitoba were discontinued when the latest statutory consolidations of those provinces were published.

2. *Case citators.*

a. *Cases judicially noticed.* These volumes of the Canadian Abridgment for the period through 1973 (see Exhibit 91), supplemented by the table of cases judicially considered in the loose-leaf appendix binder of the set and Canadian Current Law, used together are comprehensive citators.

b. *The Table of Cases volume, Dominion Law Report*, second series, together with the table of cases for the third series and annotations to cases in the second and third series fulfill a citator function — once the D.L.R. volume and page reference in which the annotation appears — is known.

c. *Butterworth's Ontario Digest and Annuaire de jurisprudence de Québec* include tables of cases in the respective jurisdictions judicially noticed.

§25.9. Subject loose-leaf services.

Special subject and regulatory loose-leaf services perform the same functions in Canada and in the same manner as those in the United States. Available services cover such topics as company law, federal labor, and taxation, and provincial aspects are analyzed as relevant. Cases reported in connection with some of the services are later bound separately to form a special-subject report series.

28. Agincourt, Ontario, Canada Law Book.

§25.10. Automated research.

QUIC-LAW[29] is a system of automated legal searching, first developed experimentally by Queen's University. It became viable commercially in 1973 as the legal segment of Q-L Systems, Ltd.

The data bases presently consist of (a) federal statutes (R.S.C. 1970, Supplements, annual statutes, and subsequent acts receiving royal assent; (b) federal regulations; (c) current statutory consolidations of British Columbia and Nova Scotia, kept current by annual statutes or a loose-leaf service; (d) headnotes from the Supreme Court Reports, Federal Court Reports, and Dominion Law Reports 2d and 3d series; (e) Hansard's oral questions (opposition queries); (f) All Canada Weekly Summaries; and (g) Weekly Criminal Bulletins. A separate tax library can also be searched. Additions now in progress include the Ontario Statutes Revised 1977 and the Saskatchewan Statutes Revised 1978.

§25.11. Dictionaries.

1. *Encyclopedia of Words and Phrases, Legal Maxims, Canada, 1825–1962*, and Supplement to 1974[30] is a standard source for legal terms.

2. *Petit dictionnaire de droit québecois et canadien*,[31] compiled by D. Page, is what the title implies.

3. Refer also to the Words and Phrases volume of the Canadian Abridgment, §25.6.1; the words and phrases section of Canadian Current Law, §25.6.2; and Western Weekly Reports, current series, §25.5.6.

§25.12. Periodical indexes.

1. *Index to Canadian Law Periodicals*.[32] This index, begun in 1961, is a locator for Canadian legal serial literature published in both English and French. It includes legal periodicals, legal articles in non-law journals, and legal festschriften. French references are made to the English-subject term under which material is indexed. There are copious cross-references, a separate author index, table of cases, and book review index.

2. *Other indexes*. There is some coverage of Canadian periodical literature duplicated in Index to Legal Periodicals. In the appendix binder to the Canadian Abridgment, there is a cumulative subject index of articles from selected Canadian legal periodicals since 1956.

29. Q-L Systems, Ltd., Kingston, Ontario.
30. Toronto, De Boos, 1963–1965. 5 vols.
31. Montréal, Fides, 1975.
32. Montreal, Canadian Association of Law Libraries, 1961 to date.

26 Australian Materials*

§26.1. Introduction.

Within the Commonwealth of Nations, Australia is a federation of six member states each with unitary constitutions originally derived from acts of the Parliament of the United Kingdom. Legal expression of the federation is found in the Australian Constitution Act 1900, as amended, and its relation to the United Kingdom in the Statute of Westminster 1931. While the parliamentary structure of its government is similar to the United Kingdom, the act of federation grants specific powers to the central government or Commonwealth, and all other powers adhere to the states.

The Commonwealth administers a few dependencies and the Capital Territory. The Northern Territory, granted self-government on July 1, 1978, has begun the transition to a de facto state.

The Commonwealth of Australia Directory, published annually, is a useful guide to Parliament, the Office of the Governor-General, Prime Minister, Cabinet, government departments, and the judiciary. It is similar in content to the U.S. Government Manual.

* This chapter was written by Mary L. Fisher, Law Librarian, General Electric Company, Fairfield, Conn.

§26.2. Laws and statutes.

From the received English law as of 1828, Australian law has developed its own statutory patterns by legislation of its states, and since 1901, federal parliament. Since the Statute of Westminster 1931, an Australian Commonwealth statute supersedes any inimical United Kingdom legislation, excepting the Australian Constitution Act and the Australian Constitution. Annotated texts of the constitutions of Australia and the states may be located in the compiled laws of the Commonwealth and of the individual states and in Constitutions of the Australian States, compiled by R. D. Lumb.[1]

1. *Commonwealth.*

a. *Slip laws.* Slip laws are issued by and are separately available from the Government Printer. They are numbered consecutively within the calendar year. With each slip law, there is a printed schedule of other acts affected.

b. *Session laws.* Acts of the Australian Parliament[2] are published annually. Volumes include alphabetical and chronological tables of the statutes passed since 1901 with the date given on which each statute came into force. There is also a subject index to the acts of that year.

c. *Compilations.* Consolidations of Commonwealth statutes in effect, pared of obsolete provisions, have been published periodically. The most recent edition is the Acts of the Australian Parliament 1901–1973[3]. To accompany it, there is a separately published Tables Relating to Acts 1901–1973, which contains a chronological table, an alphabetical table of acts passed, through the end of 1973, showing how acts have been affected by subsequent legislation or if they have been repealed, and a table of acts passed in relation to provisions of the Constitution.

A first Cumulative Supplement covering the years 1974–1975 contains principal acts passed since the consolidation, printed alphabetically by short title, and amending acts located under the short title of the principal acts which they alter. See Exhibit 96. Note that the principal act, if passed prior to December 31, 1973, is not reprinted in the supplement, but the texts of all amendments are printed fully. In instances where the principal act and its amendments have been repealed, this is stated as a headnote to the principal act. References to decisional law are made under the legislation.

d. *Index to statutes.* A detailed subject Index to Acts of Parliament has been compiled by B. M. Wicks.[4] Its present usefulness as a find-

1. 2d ed. St. Lucia, Univ. of Queensland Press, 1977.
2. Canberra, Government Printer.
3. Canberra, Gov. Pr., 1974–1975. 12 vols.
4. Canberra, Libra Books, 1976.

Customs Act 1901-1975—*continued*

2. The following provisions of the Principal Act are amended by omitting the words "of this Act", "to this Act" and "of this section" (wherever occurring):—

Sections 4 (1) (definitions of "Airport", "Narcotic substance" and "Trafficable quantity"), 35A (1A), (1B) and (2), 37 (3), 40AA (3), (4), (5) and (7), 40A (4), 40B (2), (3), (4), (5), (6), (7) and (8), 50 (4), 62, 71B (3) and (4), 97 (3), 104 (3), 119 (2), 120, 129 (3) and (4), 130A, 130B (1), 151 (5), (6) and (7), 157 (3), 162 (3), 162A (8), 167 (5), 179A (definitions of "Committee" and "licence"), 183B (5) and (6), 183D (1), 183J (3), 183M (1), 199, 226 (2), 231 (1) and (3), 233A (2), 233B (3), 235 (1) and (4) and 275A (5).

[*Formal amendments inserted, Act No.* 28, 1974, *s.* 7 *and Sch.*]

4. (1) "Customs Acts". *Omit* "the Commonwealth" (*wherever occurring*), *insert* "Australia".

[*Def. amended, Act No.* 28, 1974, *s.* 7 *and Sch.*]

"Developing country" has the same meaning as in the *Customs Tariff* 1966-1974;

[*New def., Act No.* 120, 1974, *s.* 3 (1) (a).]

"Less developed country". [*Def. omitted, Act No.* 120, 1974, *s.* 3 (1) (b).]

5. *Omit* "inclusive, of this Act", *insert* "inclusive".

[*S.* 5 *amended, Act No.* 28, 1974, *s.* 7 *and Sch.*]

6. [*Repealed, Act No.* 28, 1974, *s.* 3.]

7. *Omit* "the Commonwealth", *insert* "Australia".

[*S.* 7 *amended, Act No.* 28, 1974, *s.* 7 *and Sch.*]

13. (2) *Omit* "the Commonwealth" (*wherever occurring*), *insert* "Australia".

Omit "the nineteenth day of September, One thousand nine hundred and twelve", *insert* "19 September 1912".

[*Sub-s.* (2) *amended, Act No.* 28, 1974, *s.* 7 *and Sch.*]

35. *Omit* "through the Post Office", *insert* "by post".

[*S.* 35 *amended, Act No.* 56, 1975, *s.* 38 *and Sch.* 2.]

35A. *Omit* "the Commonwealth" (*wherever occurring*), *insert* "Australia".

[*S.* 35A *amended, Act No.* 28, 1974, *s.* 7 *and Sch.*]

45. (2) A security in respect of any duty that may be payable on goods under section 8, 9, 10 or 11 of the *Customs Tariff* (*Anti-Dumping*) *Act* 1975 shall be cancelled before the expiration of 3 months after the date of the security, or before the expiration of such longer period, not exceeding 6 months after the date of the security, as the exporter and the importer of the goods request.

[*Sub-s.* (2) *inserted, Act No.* 77, 1975, *s.* 3.]

59. *Omit* "the Commonwealth" (*wherever occurring*), *insert* "Australia".

[*S.* 59 *amended, Act No.* 28, 1974, *s.* 7 *and Sch.*]

59. [*See* Article "The Commission of Customs Offences in the Australian Territorial Sea; An Analysis and Synthesis of R. v. Bull": (1975) 49 A.L.J. 16.]

65. (2) *Omit* "the Commonwealth", *insert* "Australia".

[*Sub-s.* (2) *amended, Act No.* 28, 1974, *s.* 7 *and Sch.*]

71B. (5) Subject to sub-section (6), a permission under sub-section (1) does not authorize the delivery of goods in respect of which a quota order under sub-section (3) of section 132B is in force at any time if the Customs would have the right under sub-section (8) of that section, if the goods were entered for home consumption under sub-section (1) of section 37 at that time, to take security with respect to the goods for the protection of the revenue of the Customs.

(6) For the purposes of sub-section (5), a quota order, or a variation of a quota order, shall be deemed not to be in force unless it has been served on the person to whom the quota order applies or has otherwise been brought to the notice of that person.

[*Sub-ss.* (5) (6) *inserted, Act No.* 28, 1974, *s.* 4.]

Exhibit 96

ing tool is restricted by its end date of January 1, 1976. Revisions to restore and maintain its currency have been planned.

2. *States and territories.*

a. *New South Wales.* Session laws have been issued since 1851, annually since 1917 as Statutes of New South Wales.[5] Slip laws are also available. Acts are numbered consecutively by date of assent within the calendar year. Each annual volume includes alphabetical and chronological tables of the statutes by short title. Date of commencement of the statute is given in the chronological table only. There is a separately issued Alphabetical and Chronological Table of the Statutes, 1824–1969, with annual cumulative supplements thereafter. In addition to the contents implied by the title, it contains an alphabetical table of certified acts, that is, those reprinted under the Acts Incorporation Act, 1906 and the Acts Reprinting Act, 1972.

The Incorporated Acts,[6] referred to above, are issued annually with a schedule showing history of the act and citations to the original amending acts.

The Public Acts of New South Wales, 1824–1957,[7] commonly known as the Red Statutes, is the most recent compilation of acts in force. Amendments are, for the most part, incorporated into the statute with marginal notes added. Other amendments not incorporated are printed immediately following the act. Permanent supplements include annotations to decisional law. There is a cumulative subject index to the set. The government of New South Wales has announced that instead of a new bound consolidation set, it will reprint the statutes in force as fascicles in binder format.

b. *Queensland.* When the state separated from New South Wales in 1859, it received those laws then in force from its parent colony. Session laws of the unicameral parliament have been compiled since 1860. They are presently entitled Statutes of Queensland.[8] Arrangement of the acts is alphabetical. Appended to each annual Statutes is an annotated subject table of acts which gives the title and citation of the amending act but does not specify the sections of the principal act which it has altered.

The most recent incorporated public acts compilation is the Queensland Statutes 1828–1962,[9] encompassing the law of July 2, 1962 and selected acts to March 1963. It is in classified format with substantive amendments to original enactments printed separately, followed by annotations to the act. There is a consolidated table of acts and a subject index.

5. Sydney, New South Wales, Gov. Pr.
6. *Ibid.*
7. *Ibid.*
8. Brisbane, Queensland, Gov. Pr.
9. Brisbane, Qld., Gov. Pr. 20 vols.

c. *South Australia*. Sessional laws have been issued since 1837. They are now published annually as Acts of the South Australian Parliament[10] and are also available in slip form. Acts are arranged in numbered sequence by date of assent, excepting reprinted acts with amendments incorporated, which are printed at the end of the volumes. Each annual includes an alphabetical list of acts enhanced by the interspersing of many cross-references to related subjects, a table of acts and sections affected by amendment or judicial decision, a table of acts repealed since the last consolidation, and a table of regulations, rules, and by-laws, and proclamations, with citations to the state's Government Gazette in which they were promulgated.

The tables in the annual volumes are especially necessary because the latest consolidation is the Public General Acts of the Parliament 1837–1936.[11] There is a general subject index to the acts which are arranged alphabetically by title in the consolidation.

d. *Tasmania*. Sessional laws have been issued since 1826. Acts of Parliament[12] are now published annually; arrangement therein is in the numbered sequence of the enactments during the session. Each annual contains an alphabetical table of all acts in force to date of that annual, with references made to amendments and to other legislation which impinge upon those acts assented to since the last compilation.

The latest consolidation is the Tasmanian Statutes, 1826–1959,[13] which contains all acts in force as of December 31, 1959. Public acts are arranged alphabetically by short title. Texts of Imperial acts and instruments as they pertain to the Constitution and other related material are printed in volume 6. The last volume contains a subject index and the standard alphabetical and chronological tables. The latest consolidation is not annotated, although the preceding consolidation was and included annotations still useful in a retrospective search of statutes still in force in that form.

e. *Victoria*. Laws in force in New South Wales as of July 1, 1851 were adopted by Victoria when it separated at that time from its parent colony. Acts of Parliament[14] have been issued since 1851, following the creation of Parliament. The sole access to the annual acts is alphabetical by title. Slip laws are also available.

The latest compilation, Victorian Statutes: General Public Acts,[15] consolidates the acts in force as of September 1, 1958. Arrangement is alphabetical by short title. The last volume of the set consists of an index to the statutes and annotations of cases decided by Victorian

10. Adelaide, South Australia, Gov. Pr.
11. Adelaide, S.A., Gov. Pr. and Law Book. 9 vols.
12. Hobart, Tasmania, Gov. Pr.
13. Hobart, Tasmania, Gov. Pr. and Law Book. 9 vols.
14. Melbourne, Victoria, Gov. Pr.
15. Melbourne, Vic., Gov. Pr. and Law Book 1958–1960. 9 vols.

courts and those appealed to the High Court of Australia and the Privy Council and decisions of other federal courts related to Victorian legislation. Notations are made to the history of the legislation interpreted and references are made to the Australian Digest, first edition. Such coverage extends only through 1958 in this set.

Since publication of the 1958 consolidation, reprints have been issued by the Government Printer of several principal acts with their amendments passed prior to and since 1958.

Index to the Subject Matter of the Public General Acts in Force in Victoria[16] has been separately published annually since 1968, prior to which a subject index was bound in with the annual Acts. References are made to the latest consolidation or subsequent annual Acts of Parliament. The index includes a chronological table of unrepealed acts to date of issue.

General Public Acts of Victoria, Cumulative Supplement[17] recorded acts passed since the 1958 consolidation and provides texts of current amendments to principal acts not included in the reprints described above. See Exhibit 97.

Case annotations, printed following the acts, continue the coverage in volume 9 of the Victorian Statutes: General Public Acts (1958). There are alphabetical and chronological tables of statutes listed in the Supplement, and a table of cases.

f. *Western Australia*. The first sessional laws were printed in 1829, although those of the parliamentary government were in 1890. The laws are published annually as Acts of Parliament of Western Australia.[18] Arrangement is chronological by date of assent. There is a table of prior acts affected by enactments passed in the session.

The latest compilation is the Reprinted Acts of Western Australia, 1939–1969[19] encompassing acts in force as of January 29, 1969. Note that in relating amendments to an original act through this or earlier reprint compilations, there is sometimes variation in section numbering between the Reprint and the original text of the act.

Index to Legislation of Western Australia,[20] 1960 to date, is an annual tabular guide in binder format to the Western Australian acts and Imperial acts in force and to the regulations, orders in council, and proclamations. Arrangement of statutory material is by short title of the acts with amendments listed thereunder. See Exhibit 98. Because there is no general subject index, subject access is limited to one's prior knowledge of the titles or contents. It is, in effect, more of a citator to be used in conjunction with other finding tools.

16. Melbourne, Vic., Gov. Pr.
17. Melbourne, Vic., Law Book.
18. Perth, Western Australia, Gov. Pr.
19. Perth, WA, Gov. Pr., 1969. 22 vols.
20. Perth, WA, Gov. Pr.

g. *Territories*. Ordinances, orders, and regulations of the Capital and Northern Territories, which emanate from the Governor-General or the territorial legislatures are issued in slip form and bound annually in numbered sequence. There are periodic cumulations.

3. *Dates of statutes*. Commonwealth statutes passed by the Australian Parliament before January 1, 1938 came into effect on the date of assent unless otherwise stated. Since that date, acts come into force twenty-eight days after assent unless otherwise expressed in the statute. Other exceptions to this latter rule are acts amending the Constitution, which become effective on the date of assent, and acts reserved by the Governor-General for the Queen, which become effective on the day promulgated in the Government Gazette.

Public acts of the Commonwealth Parliament have always been designated by number and calendar year. Acts are customarily cited for convenience by short title which includes the year. Commonwealth statutes which have been amended may be cited by the short title with inclusive dates of the principal act and the date of the latest amendment, for example, the Customs Act 1901–1976.

Enactments of the parliaments of the states become effective from the day they are accorded assent, unless otherwise denoted. The Commonwealth practice of designating public acts by number and calendar year has now been adopted by all the states. The convention of short title with date is also followed. New South Wales and South Australian Statutes which have been amended bear the inclusive dates in their short title citation following the Commonwealth pattern.

§26.3. Subordinate legislation.

Delegated legislation conferred by the Commonwealth and state parliaments on a Cabinet Minister, department, or other authority, commonly issued in the form of a regulation or order, is first published or noticed in the appropriate official government gazette. Regulations may thereafter be negated within a specified time by either the Upper or Lower House except in Victoria, where both Houses must affirmatively resolve to disallow the rule, and in Queensland, which has a unicameral legislature.

1. *Commonwealth. Commonwealth Statutory Rules 1901–1956.*[21] This is the latest printed official compilation of statutory instruments, which were published initially in the Commonwealth of Australia Gazette. Arrangement of the regulations in the bound compilation is by title of the enabling legislation. The compilation contains also lists of selected proclamations, acts under which statutory rules in force

21. Canberra, Gov. Pr.

Mines Act 1958 (No. 6320). Vol. VI, p. 385; Vol. IX (annotations), col. 564.

[The Act incorporating amendments up to those effected by Act No. 7876 has been reprinted in pamphlet form (Reprint No. 2). For the text of the amendments the reprinted Act should be consulted.]

Amended by—**Companies Act 1958 (No. 6455),** s. 2 and 1st Sch. Assented to 2 Dec., 1958. Commenced, 1 Apr., 1959: Gaz. No. 20, 4 Mar., 1959, p. 496.

1959—**Statute Law Revision Act 1959 (No. 6505).** Assented to, 5 May, 1959. Commenced, 1 Apr., 1959: s. 1 (2).

1961—**Companies Act 1961 (No. 6839),** s. 4 and 1st Sch. Pt. III. Assented to, 19 Dec., 1961. Commenced, 1 July, 1962: Gaz. No. 16, 21 Feb., 1962, p. 392. **Mines (Explosives) Act 1961 (No. 6801).** Assented to, 28 Nov., 1961.

1962—**Subordinate Legislation Act 1962 (No. 6886)** s. 3 and Sch. Assented to, 8 May, 1962. Commenced, 1 Aug., 1962: Gaz No. 70, 4 July, 1962, p. 2314. **Statute Law (Further Revision) Act 1962 (No. 6961)** s. 2 and Sch. Assented to. 18 Dec., 1962.

1964—**Public Lands and Works Act 1964 (No. 7228)** s. 7, Sch. 4, Pt XXVIII. Assented to, 15 Dec., 1964. Commenced, 15 Mar., 1965: Gaz. No. 17, 11 Mar., 1965, p. 557. **Mines (Exploration Licences) Act 1964 (No. 7233).** Assented to, 22 Dec., 1964. Commenced, 11 Feb., 1965: Gaz. No. 8, 10 Feb., 1965, p. 280.

1965—**Mines (Regulations) Act 1965 (No. 7297).** Assented to, 12 Oct., 1965.

1971—**Statute Law Revision Act 1971 (No. 8181)** s. 2 (1), Sch. items 143-146. Assented to, 23 Nov., 1971.

1972—**Mines (Amendment) Act 1972 (No. 8337).** Assented to, 5 Dec., 1972. Saving provision in s. 2 (2).

1973—**Magistrates' Courts (Jurisdiction) Act 1973 (No. 8427)** s. 11 and Sch. Assented to, 17 Apr., 1973. S. 11 commenced, 3 Feb., 1975: Gaz. No. 3, 22 Jan., 1975, p. 122. **Mines (Fees) Act 1973 (No. 8469).** Assented to, 7 Nov., 1973. Commenced, 12 Dec., 1973: Gaz. No. 115, 12 Dec., 1973, p. 3972. **Mines (Amendment) Act 1973 (No. 8516).** Assented to, 18 Dec., 1973. Commenced, 17 Jan., 1974: Gaz. No. 4, 17 Jan., 1974, p. 113.

1975—**Mines (Amendment) Act 1975 (No. 8805).** Assented to, 2 Dec., 1975. Transitory provisions in s. 6 (2). Amendments effected by s. 21 (1) (2) deemed to be retrospective to commencement of principal Act: s. 21 (4).

1976—**Mines Act 1976 (No. 8920).** Assented to, 7 Dec., 1976. **Minerals and Energy Act 1976 (No. 8953).** Assented to, 16 Dec., 1976. Commencement not proclaimed at 7 Mar., 1977. Transitional provisions in s. 6.

The following Acts are relevant:

Explosives Act 1960 (No. 6715), ss. 38, 45, 58 (1), 59, 73 (1): exclusion from provisions of *Explosives Act* 1960.

Mt. Hotham Alpine Resort Act 1972 (No. 8260) s. 30: exclusion of miner's right.

National Parks Act 1975 (No. 8702), s. 40 (1): consent of Minister required to mining leases and licences.

Underseas Mineral Resources Act (No. 7095) s. 2: *Mines Act* 1958 declared to extend and apply to sea bed and its subsoil within territorial limits of Victoria and to such parts outside territorial limits to which jurisdiction and legislative power of Victoria extends.

Am., Act No. 8516 s. 3(1).

1. Table. For "Subdivision 3.—Mining Managers ss. 384-400" *substitute* "Subdivision 3.—Mine Managers ss. 384-400E".

Subst. intn., Act No. 8805 s. 2 (*a*).

3. (1) "Claim" means land pegged out as a claim under the provisions of section 15.

Am., Act No. 8039 s. 2.

"Mineral". For "platinoid minerals and mineral water" *substitute* "and platinoid minerals".

Am., Act No. 8805 s. 2 (*b*).

"Mining purposes". After "the purpose of" *insert* "prospecting for or of".

New intns., Act No. 8805 s. 2 (*c*).

"Mining Registrar" means any person for the time being holding or acting in the office of Mining Registrar or Deputy Mining Registrar under this Act.

Exhibit 97

TABLE ONE—PUBLIC GENERAL ACTS.

MINING ACT—*continued.*

Amendments to First Reprint as Principal Act:—
38 of 1932, Secs. 3, 4 and 9, proc. 1 May, 1937; *G.G.* 23 Apl., 1937, p. 580.
45 of 1932.
7 of 1933.
29 of 1937.
56 of 1937.

Amendments to Second Reprint as Principal Act—
48 of 1945.
84 of 1948 (Div. I (Secs. 313-327) and Div. II (Secs. 328-341) of Part XIII, as inserted in principal Act by Sec. 6 of this (84 of 1948) Act, commenced as follows:—
Div. I—7 Apl., 1952; *G.G.* 10 Apl., 1952, p. 900.
Div. II—1 Mar., 1954; *G.G.* 26 Feb., 1954, p. 305/306.)
26 of 1950
22 and 33 of 1952.

Amendments to Third Reprint as Principal Act—
16 of 1955.
60 of 1957

Amendments to Fourth Reprint as Principal Act—
23 of 1961.
82 of 1963.
83 of 1963 (Proc. 1 July, 1964, *G.G.* 26/6/64, p. 2526).
84 of 1963 (operative from 1 Feb., 1964).
45 of 1964.
13 of 1965.

Amendment to Fifth Reprint as Principal Act—
53 of 1968.

Amendment to Sixth Reprint as Principal Act—
17 of 1969.
33 of 1970.
2 of 1971.
56 of 1971. (Proc. 1 Jan., 1972; *G.G.* 31 Dec., 1971, p. 5467.)
1 of 1973.

Affecting Acts—
4 of 1942, Sec. 2, Mining Tenements (War Time Exemption) Act.
15 of 1945, Sec. 3, Soil Conservation Act.
24 of 1963, Sec. 3, Iron Ore (Hamersley Range) Agreement Act.

MINING DEVELOPMENT ACT, 1902. 2 Edw. VII, No. 20.
First Reprint, incl. No. 25 of 1924 in Appx. Sess. Vol. 1927.
Amendment to Mining Development Act, 1902, as Principal Act—
25 of 1924.
Amendment to First Reprint as Principal Act—
83 of 1973. (Metric Conversion Act, 1972-73; Third Sched.) (To operate from 20th Sept., 1974; see *G.G.* 20/9/74, p. 3533.)

MINING ON PRIVATE PROPERTY ACT, 62 Vict. No. 29 (1898). (Secs. 55 to 62 and Sched. only.)
First Reprint, incl. No. 15 of 1904, in Vol. 6 of Rep. Acts. Appd. 2 Apl., 1954.
Second Reprint, in Vol. 12 of Rep. Acts. Reprinted by Minister's authorisation dated 22 May, 1958.

Exhibit 98

on 31 December 1956 were promulgated, rules in force, and a table of cases construing them to date of issue. This set must be used in conjunction with subsequent annual supplemental volumes, which arrangement is by number within the year. Regulations are referred to either by number or short title. The cumulative index of rules in force in the latest annual volume should be used to determine the existence or present validity of a regulation.

The Commonwealth of Australia Gazette[22] should be consulted to affirm currency of a regulation or publication of the most recent regulations.

2. *States*. Subordinate legislation of the states is promulgated in their respective government gazettes. New South Wales, Tasmania, and Victoria compile their statutory rules and regulations annually with the standard chronological and alphabetical tables for that year as well as a locater table of those rules and regulations in force. An index to the subordinate legislation in force in Queensland appears in the latest Statutes Reprint of Queensland, that in South Australia is published in the latest annual volume of the Acts, and that in Western Australia appears in the Index to Legislation in Western Australia. See Exhibit 99. Subordinate legislation of Queensland can be traced also under the enabling legislation in Queensland Statute and Case Annotations for which see §26.8.2.

§26.4. Treaties.

Treaties to which Australia is a party are printed in Treaty Series [23] in numbered sequence. There is an index to the series, which is found not to be current. For the earlier period, one can search Australian treaties in the League of Nations Treaty Series and later the United Nations Treaty Series. World Treaty Index,[24] together with the United Nations Treaty Cumulative Index, are useful adjuncts for a retrospective treaty search.

§26.5. Law reports.

At the pinnacle of the judicial hierarchy is the High Court of Australia, which has specific original jurisdiction in matters delineated in the Constitution and by Parliament. It also hears appeals from state and territorial supreme courts and federal courts. The Australian Industrial Court, Family Court, Federal Court of Bankruptcy, and Federal Court of Australia are special federal courts. The mandate of

22. *Ibid*.
23. Canberra, Gov. Pr., 1949 to date.
24. Ed. by P. H. Rohn. Santa Barbara, Calif., Clio, 1974 to date.

TABLE FOUR.

	GG.	*Pp.*
MINING ACT, 1904, No. 15 of 1904, as amended.		
Regs. (G.G. 4/12/25.) Reprinted with amendments up to and including G.G. 4/10/68, published	29/1/69	293-400
Amendments—		
Reg. 54 Am.	3/12/71	5005
55 Am.	3/12/71	5005
84 Am.	11/6/69	1764
99 Am.	17/12/68	3883
100 Am.	5/6/70	1518
108 Sub.	5/6/70	1518
110 Sub.	5/6/70	1518
110 Am.	27/9/74	3626
129 Sub.	5/6/70	1519
147 Am.	17/12/68	3883
147 Sub.	5/6/70	1519
147A Ins.	5/6/70	1519
147B Ins.	5/6/70	1519
147C Ins.	5/6/70	1519
147D Ins.	5/6/70	1519
153 Am.	5/6/70	1520
161 Am.	17/12/68	3883
161 Am.	5/6/70	1520
161 Am.	27/9/74	3626
Sch. of Forms and Fees Am.	22/9/69	2915-6
Sched. Am.	3/12/71	5005
Sched. Am.	31/12/71	5480
Western Australian Coal Industry Tribunal Regulations, 1952 (G.G. 14/11/52 and 10/7/53) Reprinted	11/6/69	1740
Western Australian Coal Mines Advisory Board Regs. 1953 (G.G. 20/3/53) Reprinted	11/6/69	1739
Regs. for Guidance of Surveyors (Mines) (G.G. 28/11/61). Reprinted with amendments up to and including G.G. 25/6/69, published	**4/3/71**	**637-651**
Amendments—		
Published	**9/8/72**	**3020-1**
Proclamations (unless otherwise stated), as to constitution or amendment of boundaries of Goldfields, etc.—		
Black Range, Lawlers, constituted	3/6/04	1468
Malcolm, Mt. Morgans, boundaries amended	4/8/05	2403
Phillips River Goldfield and Minefield, boundaries Am.	1/6/06	1614
Coolgardie, Broad Arrow, boundaries Am.	8/6/06	1689
E. Coolgardie, N.E. Coolgardie, boundaries Am.	15/6/06	1839
Coolgardie, E. Coolgardie, N. E. Coolgardie, Mt. Magnet, Phillips River, Yilgarn, Yalgoo, Murchison, E. Murchison, Peak Hill, Pilbara, W. Pilbara, boundaries Am.	1/3/07	766
Greenbushes, boundaries Am.	22/3/07	938
Donnybrook Goldfield, abolished	6/3/08	699
East Coolgardie, East Coolgardie-Bulong-Kanowna-Kurnalpi Dists., boundaries Am.	27/3/08	843-4
O.I.C. Wardens Court, Bulong, abolished, Wardens Court, Kalgoorlie, to be Wardens Court for Bulong Dist.	27/3/08	843-4
Lawlers, boundaries Am., Wiluna Procd.	25/2/10	586
Lawlers, Wiluna, boundaries Am.	2/6/11	1775

Exhibit 99

the first mentioned is the enforcement of decisions or hearing of appeals of the Commonwealth Council and Arbitration Commission and the Trade Practices Tribunal and the interpretation of other industrial issues within the Commonwealth's purview. Interpretation of some federal law is vested also in the state courts.

In each state and territory, there is a Supreme Court with limited original and general appellate jurisdiction. In most states there are, for civil cases, intermediate courts called District Courts (in New South Wales and Queensland), or County Courts (in Victoria), which are courts of the first instance as well as appellate courts.

Prior to the Appeals from High Court Act 1975, an appeal from the High Court of Australia lay to the Judicial Committee of the Privy Council. The High Court in its recent decision in *Viro* v. *Regina* [1978] 18 A.L.J.R. 257 has further clarified the relationship of the states' Supreme Courts to the Privy Council by ruling that the High Court would not accept necessarily a Privy Council precedent as determining the law, and that when in conflict, the judgment of the High Court would bind the states' Supreme Courts as well as other courts in Australia.

However, case law of the United Kingdom continues to have an impact on Australian courts. In instances when no relevant Australian statute exists or when a relevant Australian statute does exist and no Australian case law yet exists, a decision of the Court of Appeal of the United Kingdom or of the House of Lords will be given considerable weight by the Australian judiciary. Overall, the case law of the United Kingdom is often cited in parallel with Australian case law. See §26.5.9. One should note that, as in the United Kingdom, law reports are edited by barristers, and these only may be cited with authority.

1. *Commonwealth Law Reports.*[25] These reports, begun in 1903, are considered the authorized reports of the High Court of Australia. Included also are appeal cases from the High Court to the Judicial Committee of the Privy Council through 1975. Volumes are issued in monthly parts. The parts lack a cumulative table of cases and subject access. There is an index digest to the set through 1972.

2. *Australian Law Reports.*[26] This series, initiated in 1973, continues The Australian Argus Reports or, prior to 1960, Argus Law Reports. It contains decisions of the High Court of Australia, the supreme courts of the states when exercising federal jurisdiction, other federal courts and tribunals, and selected decisions of the supreme courts of the Northern and Capital Territories. Prior to 1960, decisions of the Supreme Court of Victoria were included. Decisions are issued semimonthly as advance sheets, four to a vol-

25. Sydney, NSW, Law Book, 1904 to date.
26. Chetswood, NSW, Butterworths, 1973 to date.

ume. There is a cumulating table of cases for the volume within each issue. There are also tables of statutes and rules judicially considered and abstracts of unreported decisions of the High Court.

3. *Australian Law Journal Reports*.[27] Since 1927 the journal has served as a monthly advance service for reported decisions of the High Court of Australia and of the Privy Council on appeal from Australian courts. Since 1958 these reports have been appended to the Australian Law Journal. With folios separate from the Law Journal, these are often bound to stand under their distinctive title.

4. *Federal Law Reports*.[28] Issued bimonthly since 1956, this series reports cases of the Australian Industrial Court, Federal Court of Bankruptcy, the Family Court (since its creation in 1976), state supreme courts in their exercise of federal jurisdiction, supreme courts of the territories, and the Trade Practices Tribunal. It has absorbed the Australian Bankruptcy Cases, 1928–1964. There is a consolidated subject index, a list of words and phrases, and tables of statutes and cases for the period 1957–1973.

5. *Commonwealth Arbitration Reports*.[29] This extensive series, begun in 1905, publishes orders and awards issued by the Commonwealth Court of Conciliation and Arbitration to 1956 and thereafter of the Commonwealth Conciliation and Arbitration Commission and the Australian Industrial Court. Subject and tabular case access is to single volumes only.

6. *Commonwealth Taxation Board of Review Decisions* (new ser.).[30] These are the officially authorized reports; they continue the earlier decisions of the Boards of Review, 1921–1950. A table of cases and a subject index in each volume apply to that volume only.

7. *Australasian Tax Reports*.[31] This series, initiated in 1969, covers decisions related to income, use, and estate and gift taxes. It incorporates the Australia and New Zealand Income Tax Reports, 1944–1968, which itself had continued the Australian Income Tax Reports, 1940–1944.

8. *Local Government Reports of Australia*.[32] Decisions of the High Court of Australia and inferior courts relating to local government, land, and planning as well as the New South Wales Land and Valuation Court and Local Government Court, Queensland, have been issued since 1956 in advance parts. This series continues the New South Wales Local Government Reports. There is a comprehensive word index to the series at least through 1970.

27. Sydney, NSW, Law Book, 1958 to date.
28. Sydney, NSW, Law Book.
29. Canberra, Gov. Pr., 1906 to date.
30. Sydney, NSW Butterworths. 1902 to date.
31. Sydney, NSW, Butterworths.
32. Sydney, NSW, Law Book.

9. *All England Law Reports Reprint: Australian Extension Volumes*.[33] English cases chosen from the All England Law Reports from the period 1865 through 1935 have been selected for their particular interest or applicability to Australian law. There is a consolidated index to the set.

10. *State reports*. There are distinctive report series covering the decisions of each state's supreme court. Additionally, law reporting of Supreme Court decisions of New South Wales and Queensland includes some decisions of lower courts. The table of contents of each series volume usually includes the tables of cases for the volume, cases judicially construed, statutes and statutory instruments judicially construed, and a subject index or digest.

a. *New South Wales*. Decisions of the Supreme Court of New South Wales and the Land Valuation Court have been reported since 1971 in New South Wales Law Reports.[34] This series continues the New South Wales Reports, 1960–1970, for which there is a one-volume consolidated index and table of cases covering the decade and the earlier State Reports, New South Wales, 1901–1959.

Weekly Notes, New South Wales, 1884–1970,[35] reported all decisions of the Supreme Court and selected decisions of the District Courts; some of the latter are not found elsewhere.

b. *Queensland*. Queensland Reports,[36] initiated in 1958, continues State Reports, Queensland (with variant title) 1902–1957, and Queensland Law Journal, 1879–1901, Queensland Law Reports, 1876–1878, and Queensland Supreme Court Reports, 1860–1881 in recording decisions of the state's high court and appeals therefrom to the High Court of Australia or the Privy Council.

c. *South Australia*. Decisions of the Supreme Court of South Australia and appeals therefrom have been published since 1921 in South Australian Reports,[37] earlier in the South Australian Law Reports, 1865–1892 and 1899–1920. The last paper part of each volume of the current series includes a subject index to the volume

d. *Tasmania*. Tasmanian State Reports,[38] begun in 1941, continues Tasmanian Law Reports, 1905–1940 and the prior abbreviated coverage of Nicholls and Stops' Reports, 1897–1904. They contain decisions of the Supreme Court and appeals therefrom. There is a table of cases and a subject index for each volume, but there is no cumulative case or subject access for the period overall.

e. *Victoria*. The Victorian Reports, 1958 to date,[39] incorporates

33. Sydney, NSW, Butterworths. 16 vols.
34. Sydney, NSW, Law Book.
35. Sydney, Law Book, 1884–1970. 92 vols.
36. Brisbane, Qld., Law Book.
37. Sydney, NSW, Law Book.
38. *Ibid*.
39. Sydney, NSW, Butterworths.

Victorian Law Reports, 1875–1956 and the Australian Law Times Reports, 1879–1928 (for which volumes were numbered consecutively through 1904, thereafter by year). Prior coverage of Victorian Supreme Court decisions can be found in Australian Jurist, 1870–1874, Victorian Reports, 1870–1872 (Webb, A'Beckett and Williams) and in the earlier nominative reports, Wyatt, Webb and A'Beckett, 1864–1869, and Wyatt and Webb, 1861–1863. Decisions of the Supreme Court of Victoria were included in the Australian Law Reports until 1960.

The Victorian Reports are currently issued first monthly in paper parts, for which there is a table of cases and subject index for each bound volume. There is a consolidated table of cases volume and a two-volume consolidated subject index in classified arrangement covering the period 1861–1965. Thereafter consult Victorian Reports Consolidated Index and Table of Cases, 1966–1976, with supplements cumulating periodically.

t. *Western Australia.* Western Australian Reports.[40] This series, begun in 1960, reports the Supreme Court decisions and appeals therefrom. Prior coverage can be found in Australian Law Reports, 1898–1959. There is a consolidated index digest and table of cases for the period 1898–1969, to which supplements are anticipated.

§26.6. Digests.

Digests issued as an element of or directly related to a specific set are described above with that set.

1. *Australian Digest.*[41] Comprehensive in scope, it covers reported decisions of virtually all Australian courts and Australian appeals to the Judicial Committee of the Privy Council, superseding other fragmentary Commonwealth and state digests. The first edition, covering the period from 1825 through 1933 in the original set and through 1961 in its supplements, is undergoing a lengthy revision. The second edition, beginning coverage in 1962, encompasses Australian case law from 1825 to the last day of the year preceding the preparatory date of that volume. When completed, the second edition will entirely supersede the first edition. Until publication of the second edition is completed, a fairly detailed description of the scope and content of the segments of both editions may be helpful in using the sets effectively. See also Exhibit 100.

The format of both editions is according to subject classifications or titles with subclasses or parts and divisions. Subparts within each subject title are numbered sequentially. Cases digested within each sub-

40. *Ibid.*
41. Sydney, NSW, Law Book.

INTERIM SUPP. 2ND ED. VOLS. 1-31

Sharebroking—Custom to cross buyer's and seller's orders.]—JONES *v.* CANAVAN '72 (COMPANIES [377])

Insurance business — Cancellation of policies—Custom to credit broker with refundable premiums—To debit broker with rebate of his commission.] — *Re* COLIN WILLIAMS (INSURANCE) PTY. LTD. '75 (INSURANCE [139])

Meat export trade—No custom for buyer to open irrevocable letter of credit in seller's favour.]—LETOVSKY BROS. LTD. *v.* KREMNIZER; HUMPHREY & PEARE PTY. LTD. (THIRD PARTY) '69 (this title [8])

Common law possessory liens having their origin in custom.]—MAJEAU CARRYING CO. PTY. LTD. *v.* COASTAL RUTILE LTD. '73 (LIENS [1])

[9] MISCELLANEOUS EFFECTS OF CUSTOMS '73

Warehouseman's lien (Q.).] — MAJEAU CARRYING CO. PTY. LTD. *v.* COASTAL RUTILE LTD. '73 (LIENS [1])

CUSTOMS AND EXCISE

10.25 (2nd ed. 1825-1966)

Note: The following altered headings, which are indicated in the text by ●, appear in this title:

[42-46] Pt X. JURISDICTION AND PROCEDURE IN CUSTOMS PROSECUTIONS

[42] DIVN 1. HOW INSTITUTED AND IN GENERAL

This facilitates noting up the main work.

[1] GENERAL — CUSTOMS AND EXCISE LAWS '69 '70

Nature of excise duties — Validity of State legislation.]—WESTERN AUSTRALIA *v.* HAMERSLEY IRON PTY. LTD. '69 (CONSTITUTIONAL LAW [67])

Dumping duty — Imposition on goods which have passed out of customs' control or which have ceased to exist—Validity—Validity of Minister's notice—Specification of all goods of a class—Tariff Board's report not referring to all goods of that class—Extent to which Minister's satisfaction must accord with report of Tariff Board.]—CARMODY *v.* F. C. LOVELOCK PTY. LTD. '70 (this title [1])

[3] CUSTOMS CONTROL '72 '73

Imported goods—Goods entered for export — Manner of export.] — COMMONWEALTH *v.* STERLING NICHOLAS DUTY FREE PTY. LTD. '72 (this title [3])

Issue of customs clearance to ship — Necessity for export licence before issue—Foreign yacht in course of overseas voyage —Clearance issued without export licence —Liability of Commonwealth to co-owner abandoned in Australia by other co-owners —Conversion—Special action on the case—Negligence.]—KITANO *v.* COMMONWEALTH '73 (this title [3])

[6] IMPORTATION OF GOODS '71 '73 '74

Importation — Meaning.] — FORBES, COLLECTOR OF CUSTOMS (N.S.W.) *v.* TRADERS FINANCE CORPORATION LTD. '71 (this title [29])

Import — Meaning.]—R. *v.* BULL '74 (this title [6])

Whether ship calling in course of overseas voyage "imported".]—KITANO *v.* COMMONWEALTH '73 (this title [3])

[7] PROHIBITED IMPORTS '69 '70 '74

What constitute—Customs offences—Import of prohibited imports — Preventing seizure of prohibited imports—Assembling to prevent seizure of prohibited imports—Incidents within three-mile limit.]—R. *v.* BULL '74 (this title [6])

Indecent or obscene goods—Test of indecency or obscenity—Sale to public generally—Men's magazine.]—CHANCE INTERNATIONAL PTY. LTD. *v.* FORBES '69 (this title [7])

—— Goods unduly emphasizing matters of sex — What constitute.] — ALTMAN *v.* FORBES '70 (this title [7] (first and second notes))

[9] IMPORTATION OF GOODS — MISCELLANEOUS MATTERS '70

Dumping duty.] — CARMODY *v.* F. C. LOVELOCK PTY. LTD. '70 (this title [1])

[10] EXPORTATION OF GOODS '73 '76

Prohibition of exportation of minerals, &c., unless with written approval of Minister of State for Minerals and Energy—Constitutional validity — Discretion of Minister—Matters relevant to exercise of discretion—Environmental aspects of mining operations.]—MURPHYORES INCORPORATED PTY. LTD. *v.* COMMONWEALTH '76 (CONSTITUTIONAL LAW [37])

Issue of customs clearance to ship — Necessity for export licence before issue—Foreign yacht in course of overseas voyage —Clearance issued without export licence —Liability of Commonwealth to co-owner abandoned in Australia by other co-owners —Conversion—Special action on the case—Negligence.] — KITANO *v.* COMMONWEALTH '73 (this title [3])

[19] CUSTOMS DUTIES—VALUE FOR AD VALOREM DUTY '74 '75

Price paid or current domestic value—Seller not selling nor prepared to sell similar goods in country of export.]—CARMODY *v.* SARAH COVENTRY PTY. LTD. '74 (this title [19])

—— Applicability of current domestic value—Seller in country of export selling only to specially selected dealers on special terms.]—CATERPILLAR OF AUSTRALIA LTD. *v.* CARMODY (COMPTROLLER GENERAL OF CUSTOMS) '75 (this title [19])

Exhibit 100

class are not assigned a distinctive number; they fall collectively within the subject subclass to which they are assigned. Be forewarned that the subject classification numbers are not completely consistent between the first and second edition. In pursuing a subject search from one edition to the other, one should check the comparative table printed in each of the volumes of the second edition. The index prepared for each volume of the second edition is complementary to that of the cumulative index of the first edition. To the 20 volumes in the original set of the first edition, there is a 5-volume permanent supplement covering decisions 1933–1947 and annual supplements thereafter to date, spanning the classified contents of both editions. There are master volumes for the periods 1948–1959, 1960–1967, 1968–1972, and 1973–1976, containing the following: 1) a cumulative list of cases digested and notes of additional references to cases previously digested, 2) a list of words, phrases, and maxims with references to the case notes in the annual supplement, 3) cumulative table of cases judicially noticed in the case digests covered, 4) cumulative subject index of cases covered during the period, and 5) a key to cases. With respect to the last-mentioned category, the latest master volume contains the key to cases in subject titles in those volumes of the first edition which have not yet been superseded by the second edition. References are made to the case notes in the 5-volume supplement covering 1933–1947 and in the annual volumes following to date.

The Annual Digest in three volumes is the vehicle for keeping the Digest current. The Digest of Cases notes cases reported during the calendar year covered. Arrangement follows the classified pattern, and there is a table of cases digested therein. The Interim Supplement to the second edition (vols. 1 to 31) covers all cases reported since the cutoff date of each volume of the second edition. An abbreviated note provided for each case and citation is given to the annual Digest of Cases volume wherein the full note is printed. Thus, for subject titles already covered in the second edition, one needs to search the appropriate volume of the second edition and the Interim Supplement. The master volume is the general research aid and key to the volumes of the first edition: it is discussed more fully above. A list of subject titles used in the Digest is printed in each of the three volumes of the Annual Digest. Additionally, there is a list of subject titles in volume 1 of the first and second editions. The caveat should be restated that there is some slight variation in classification between the two editions. It is anticipated that, once the second edition is complete, a consolidated supplement will be issued to bring the work to a common end date.

Australian Legal Monthly Digest. This provides the more current references to both Commonwealth and state case law before it is elsewhere reported in full text, as well as legislative action of the Commonwealth and state Parliaments. Each monthly issue contains a cumulative square-bracket number table for each subject title under the Australian Digest classification scheme. It also includes a cumulating chronological table of statutes, tables of statutes repealed or amended, a cumulative table of cases, and a cumulative subject index. It is the monthly supplement to the Australian Digest.

2. *Australian Current Law.*[42] Published since 1963 and in loose-leaf format since 1975, this is a monthly digest service providing concise information on statutes, regulations and rules, and case law of general importance. In scope it covers the Commonwealth, all states and territories. A subject index and tables, statutory information, case annotations, and a digest of yet unreported cases and legislative commentary comprise the four sections of the service. The subject index and tables of statutes judicially interpreted, cases judicially considered, and reprinted statutes (by jurisdiction) cumulate bimonthly. Statutory information includes summaries (by jurisdiction) of statutes and delegated legislation, the latter distinguished by a variant typeface. Date of assent is given for each act with a notation of the legislation it affects. This section is useful also in identifying recently issued Law Reform reports and Parliamentary bills. Case annotations are grouped under fixed subject headings. Access to them is either through the table of cases or the subject index. Cross-references are made to the Australian Pilot to Halsbury's Laws, third edition, or to the Commentary to Halsbury's Laws insofar as it is published.

3. *Australian Law Journal.*[43] This monthly journal includes a law report digest section of case law of the Commonwealth and the states in addition to substantive subject articles and practice notes. There is a cumulative author and subject index and table of cases through 1965 and supplements thereafter. Since 1958 the Australian Law Journal Reports (see §26.5.3) have been appended to the journal but separately paginated.

4. *English and Empire Digest.* Following the United Kingdom cases, selective Australian and other Commonwealth of Nations cases are included in the Digest; the latter are printed in larger type. For fuller details on the scope and use of the Digest see §24.7.1 and Exhibit 78.

5. *Queensland Lawyer.*[44] This series, formerly the Queensland Justice of the Peace and Reports, 1907–1972, serves as a bimonthly digest of selected judgments of Queensland courts.

6. *Legislative digests.* Summaries of Commonwealth and states' legislation may be found in Australian Legal Monthly Digest and in

42. Sydney, NSW, Butterworths.
43. Sydney, NSW, Butterworths. 1974 in progress.
44. Sydney, NSW, Law Book.

Current Law. For a summary of legislation of Tasmania, refer also to the University of Tasmania Law Review, for that of Victoria see Melbourne University Law Review.

§26.7. Encyclopedia

The Australian and New Zealand Commentary on Halsbury's Laws of England, fourth edition in progress,[45] will supersede the Australian Pilot to Halsbury's Laws of England, third edition. Whereas Pilot editions to Halsbury's Laws were separately issued for Australia and New Zealand, the Commentary encompasses both countries in a single format; separate texts are anticipated in exceptional instances only. Further, whereas the Pilot editions provide simply references to the laws of Australia and New Zealand, the Commentary aspires to be something more. In encyclopedic format, it provides a limited exposition of the law of the two countries with attention given to areas where the common law of one or the other country has diverged or developed differently from that of the United Kingdom. See Exhibit 101. It is intended as a precursor of a truly self-contained encyclopedia of the laws of Australia and New Zealand to be published some years hence, paralleling Halsbury's Laws of England.

The Commentary is being issued in fascicles by chapter corresponding to the titles in Halsbury, although not in the same sequence as the publication of Halsbury's Laws, fourth edition. Cross-references are made to the third or fourth edition of the parent volume depending upon the publication scheduling of the subject at issue. Paragraphs are numbered, with addition of a C prefix, to their subject equivalents in Halsbury. In footnote references, those of the Australian Commonwealth and states precede those of New Zealand. An alphabetical table of cases and a jurisdictional table of statutes are included within each chapter. An index appended to each chapter of additional material unique to the Commentary should be used in conjunction with the indexes to Halsbury's Laws. Issues of Butterworth's Current Law serve to maintain currency of the Australian aspects of the Commentary.

§26.8. Citators.

There is no tabular system noting the legislative history and judicial treatment of statutes and judicial consideration of cases in the format of Shepard's Citations, but there are other means of finding this information. Some are auxiliary functions of digests and tables

45. Sydney, NSW, Law Book. 1973 to date.

(*a*) (WA) Charitable Trusts Act 1962 s 5, (QLD) Trusts Act 1973 s 103(2) and (3), by both of which certain recreational purposes are declared to be charitable, thus forming a fifth category.
(*b*) *eg In re Bruce, Simpson v Bruce* [1918] NZLR 16, [1918] GLR 26, CA: *Grant v Commissioner of Stamp Duties* [1943] NZLR 113, [1943] GLR 119; *In re MacDonald, Woods v Melanesian Mission Trust Board (Inc.)* [1951] NZLR 502, GLR 261.
(*c*) See C512 and C544-C547.

(2) PARTICULAR CHARITABLE PURPOSES

(i) Relief of the Aged, Impotent and Poor

C514. Purposes in preamble to be read separately.
Australia: fn (2) See *Re Clark, Perry v Salvation Army (VIC) Property Trust* [1957] VR 171; *City of Hawthorn v Victorian Welfare Association* [1970] VR 205.
fn (4) See *Re Bond; Brennan v A-G* [1929] VLR 333; *Re Chown; Teele v University of Melbourne,* [1939] VLR 443; *Re Inman (dec'd)* [1965] VR 238.

New Zealand: fn (2), (3) *In re Bingham (dec'd), Public Trustee v New Plymouth Council for Social Service Incorporated* [1951] NZLR 491, [1951] GLR 223; *Re McIntosh (dec'd)* [1976] NZLR 308.
fn (4) *In re Simmonds, Public Trustee v Stone* [1933] NZLR s 172, [1933] GLR 757 (wounded and disabled soldiers, wounded sailors). *In re Flannagan (dec'd), Beatty v A-G* [1962] NZLR 480 (non-existent convalescent ward of hospital); *In re Mitchell, Public Trustee v Salvation Army* [1963] NZLR 935, 937 (young women whose first child was born in a specified Salvation Army maternity home).

C515. Meaning of "poor", "aged" and "impotent".
Australia: A gift may be for the relief of the poor, and consequently be a charitable gift or for a charitable purpose, notwithstanding that the benefits are not confined to supplying the necessities of life to the destitute, but take the form of relieving distress occasioned by lack of money (*a*).
Dispositions in favour of aged persons are in one respect different from those in favour of the poor or the impotent. Since age does not necessarily involve disability, it may be that a gift for aged persons cannot claim to be prima facie charitable. But a gift made in relief of aged persons, in the sense that it is in relief of the needs arising from old age (such as the need for protection against the dangers and distresses incident to living alone), is charitable, unless some limitation of the class of objects deprives it of that character (*b*).
Gifts to provide hospitals and similar institutions without distinction as to the means of the patients, have been held to be charitable as in relief of impotent persons, in the sense of being in relief of needs arising from distress or other disability (*c*).
fn (2) For what is not embraced by "relief of poverty", see *A-G (NSW) v Adams* (1908) 7 CLR at 126 per Isaacs J.

(*a*) *City of Hawthorn v Victorian Welfare Association* [1970] VR at 208.
(*b*) *City of Hawthorn v Victorian Welfare Association* [1970] VR at 209; *Re Clark; Perry v Salvation Army (VIC) Property Trust* [1957] VR 171. The decisions in *NSW Nursing Service and Welfare Association for Christian Scientists v Willoughby Municipal Council* [1968] 2 NSWR 78; *Church of England Property Trust; Diocese of Canberra and Goulburn v Imlay Shire Council* [1971] 2 NSWLR 216, and *Trustees of Property for the Diocese of Newcastle,* 24 May 1973 *(unreported)* all per Else-Mitchell J, are inconsistent with *City of Hawthorn v Victorian Welfare Association,* in that while they recognise that mere old age does not provide an object of charity they ignore the significance of the relief of old age, as laid down by the

Exhibit 101

described above; others are identified as follows.

1. *Annotations to Acts and Regulations of the Australian Parliament.*[46] This loose-leaf citator digest to legislation replaces the Commonwealth Statutes Case Annotations 1903–1964 and its supplements. The replaced loose-leaf service is updated semiannually and marks changes in legislation as follows: notation of an amendment appears under the principal act and includes date that the amending section came into effect; notation of repeal also appears under the act; notation to a reenactment appears under the new title. Brief annotations and citations to case law affecting an entire act or interpreting a section are given under the appropriate section of the act. Regulations pursuant to the act are listed with the citation to the Government Gazette and appear under the enabling act.

2. *Queensland Statute and Case Annotations.*[47] As the title implies, this is a citator digest to both legislative and decisional law. It is kept current through published supplements. See Exhibit 102. In form and content it is similar to the Annotations . . . of the Australian Parliament described above. Orders in council and regulations are listed following the act under which they were created.

3. *Victorian Statutes Annotations.*[48] This service, in its fifth edition, follows the pattern described above. Cumulative supplements are published to maintain its currency.

4. *Australian and New Zealand Citator to U.K. Reports.*[49] United Kingdom decisional law from 1558 to date which has been judicially noticed by Australian and New Zealand courts since 1825 and which cases have been published in the Law Reports, Weekly Law Reports, and All England Law Reports, including the reprint volumes, can be traced through this citator. The United Kingdom cases are arranged alphabetically with citations to reports in the series listed above and are followed by citations to the Australian and New Zealand cases which have cited them. Currency of the citator is maintained by periodic cumulative supplements.

§26.9. Subject loose-leaf services.

Special subject and regulatory loose-leaf services, which report and annotate both Commonwealth and state law, cover company law, land law, trade practices, securities, text, and industrial law. Illustrative of the last mentioned is the Industrial Arbitration Service,[50] the

46. Sydney, NSW, Butterworths. 1974 to date.
47. Sydney, NSW, Butterworths. 1972 to date.
48. Sydney, NSW, Butterworths. 1968 to date.
49. Sydney, NSW, Butterworths, 1973 to date.
50. Sydney, NSW, Law Book. 2 vols. Loose-leaf.

MINING ACT 1968-1976 —

Mining Act 1968, No.51
Commenced 1 Jan. 1972 (Proc. pubd. Gaz. 13 Nov. 1971, p.1193).
Mining Act Amendment Act 1971, No.24
Mining Act Amendment Act 1971 (No.2), No.82
Metric Conversion Act 1972, No.31, Part II, First Sch.
Part II and First Schedule in relation to this Act not yet proclaimed into force.
Land Act and Other Acts Amendment Act 1973, No.41
Mining Royalties Act 1974, No.47
Commenced 18 Sep. 1974 (Proc. pubd. Gaz. 17 Sep. 1974, p.222).
Mining Act and Another Act Amendment Act 1974, No.49
Commenced 21 Sep. 1974 (Proc. pubd. Gaz. 21 Sep. 1974, p.270).
Age of Majority Act 1974, No.57
Commenced 1 Mar. 1975 (Proc. pubd. Gaz. 16 Nov. 1974, p.1083).
Mining Act Amendment Act 1976, No.15
Mining Act Amendment Act 1976 (No.2), No.50
Mining Act Amendment Act 1976 (No.3), No.75

STATUTORY ANNOTATIONS — Vols. 1968, p.396; 1971, pp.351, 1073; 1972, p.263; 1973, p.424; 1974, pp.480, 487, 582; 1976, pp.120, 478, 897

s. 3 Amended, 1971, No.24 s.2.
s. 5 Amended, 1971, No.24 s.3; Amended, 1974, No.49 s.6; Amended, 1976, No.15 s.2.
s. 7 Amended, 1971, No.24 s.4; Amended, 1971, No.82 s.2; Amended, 1974, No.49 s.7; Amended (as from 1 Jan. 1977), 1976, No.75 s.3.
s.10 Amended, 1974, No.49 s.8.
s.12 Amended, 1974, No.49 s.9.
s.13 Amended, 1974, No.49 s.10.
s.14 Amended, 1974, No.49 s.11; Amended (as from 1 Jan. 1977), 1976, No.75 s.4.
s.14A Inserted, 1976, No.50 s.2.
s.16 Amended, 1971, No.24 s.5; Amended, 1976, No.15 s.3.
s.17 Amended, 1971, No.24 s.6; Amended (as from 1 Jan. 1977), 1976, No.75 s.5.
s.18 Amended, 1971, No.24 s.7; Amended, 1971, No.82 s.3; Amended, 1974, No.49 s.12; Amended (as from 1 Jan. 1977), 1976, No.75 s.6.
s.21 Amended, 1971, No.24 s.8; Amended, 1971, No.82 s.4; Amended, 1974, No.49 s.13; Amended (as from 1 Jan. 1977), 1976, No.75 s.7.

Exhibit 102

scope of which includes the complementary New South Wales and Commonwealth arbitration systems and the relevant laws of other states and territories. Its several parts consist of an outline of the systems, a summary of the laws and regulations, a digest of cases or awards arranged by subject, and a current review summary, issued monthly. Industrial Law Service is similar in content. Commerce Clearing House publishes Australian tax, securities, trade practices, and company law (entitled Corporate Affairs) reports.

§26.10. Dictionaries.

1. Refer to the section on dictionaries in the chapter on United Kingdom Materials (§24.10) and also to the words and phrases segment of the general index to the English and Empire Digest. See also the words, phrases, and maxims section in the master volumes of the Australian Digest.

2. *Australian Commercial Dictionary*[51] includes definitions of legal words and phrases used in commercial practice.

§26.11. Periodical indexes.

1. *Current Australian and New Zealand Legal Literature Index*.[52] This is a quarterly subject list of articles, case notes, and book reviews in Australian and New Zealand law journals and in selected other English language law journals and nonlegal periodicals about Australian and New Zealand law, including some analytics of essays on other collected works. There is a separate name and index and table of cases appended to each issue. Entries are in broad classified arrangement and are numbered sequentially. Publication of the service began in 1973.

2. *Other indexes*. Subject coverage of both monographs and serial literature may be found also in Harvard Law School's Annual Legal Bibliography/Current Legal Bibliography. Use its geographical index to locate material, which is in classified arrangement.

Butterworth's Current Law includes a selective listing of periodical literature. Index to Periodical Literature provides limited coverage to Australian law journals.

51. 5th ed. Compiled by K. Yorston. Sydney, NSW, Law Book, 1972.
52. Sydney, NSW, Law Book, 1973 to date.

27 | New Zealand Materials*

§27.1. Introduction.

New Zealand legal publications are in some ways similar to those of Australia and Canada, as these countries, being constituent members of the Commonwealth of Nations, reflect their legal basis in the common law. There are, however, some intrinsic differences in the government structure and organs of the two countries. The first to be noted is that New Zealand is a unitary state.

§27.2. Laws and statutes.

From the received English law as of 1840, the legislature has created its own legislative framework. Legislation was by ordinances and orders in council until creation of the Parliament in 1853, pursuant to the New Zealand Constitution Act 1852. Since 1951 the Legislative Council has been replaced by a single House of Representatives.

1. *Session laws*. Session volumes have been published since 1854 as

* This chapter was written by Mary L. Fisher, Law Librarian, General Electric Company, Fairfield, Conn.

Statutes of New Zealand.[1] For acts amended during the calendar year of the session, the last volume of the annual set includes text of the reprinted acts with amendments incorporated. There are tables showing the effect of legislation on previous enactments and an alphabetical table by short title of acts and amendments in force at the end of the year for which the annual is issued, with reference given to the Statutes Reprint. Acts are numbered consecutively by date of assent throughout the calendar year. Date of assent is given with each act.

Notice of legislation of the current session can be found in Butterworths Current Law. For further details, see §27.6.2.

2. *Compilations*. New Zealand Statutes Reprint 1908–1957[2] is the second reprint edition, superseding that of 1908–1931. It contains all public acts of general applicability within the period covered and all acts passed prior to 1908 in force as of that date. United Kingdom Acts are excluded except for the New Zealand Constitution Act 1852 as amended. Arrangement is alphabetical by title of act. Each act is preceded by a headnote analysis. Amending acts are reprinted following the original act in chronological order, although all sections making textual amendments are not fully reproduced but are interpreted by notes. There are cross-references in the table of contents of each volume as an aid to locating subject matter. There is no general subject index; the alphabetical arrangement of titles serves in a limited way in a subject search.

3. *Dates of statutes*. Acts come into force on the date of royal assent, the date which appears following the long title of the act, unless a later date of commencement of the act appears in section 1 of the act. Acts may be cited by short title, which includes the year.

§27.3. Subordinate legislation.

Rules, regulations, and orders in council issue from the Governor-General as advised by the Prime Minister and Cabinet and as bylaws from local or other authorities. Rules and regulations have been issued since 1910, first in the New Zealand Gazette and compiled as Regulations and Bylaws, 1910–1936,[3] thereafter as Statutory Regulations.[4] These are available in slip form from the Government Printer. They are numbered consecutively throughout the year, e.g., 1976/16. Proclamations, orders in council and notices of regulations are printed in the daily New Zealand Government Gazette. Delegated

1. Wellington, Government Printer.
2. Wellington, Gov. Pr., 1958–1961. 16 vols.
3. Wellington, Gov. Pr., 1937. 13 vols.
4. Wellington, Gov. Pr.

legislation is officially brought to the notice of the House and may be brought up for question and negated by Parliament.

§27.4. Treaties.

There is a New Zealand Treaty List, 1856–1947,[5] issued by the Ministry of External Affairs. Text of a treaty during this period can be sought in Parry's Consolidated Treaty Series and in the League of Nations Treaty Series, 1920–1946. New Zealand Treaty Series,[6] which commenced in 1948, is in slip form. It is a chronological collection of bilateral and multilateral treaties to which the country is a party. For a subject or country search of a New Zealand treaty or other agreement subsequent to 1947, the United Nations Treaty Cumulative Index or World Treaty Index[7] may be used, although neither index is completely current.

§27.5. Law reports.

In the institutional hierarchy of the New Zealand courts, the Court of Appeal stands first. Decisions of that court are final unless permission is given by that court or the Judicial Committee of the Privy Council to appeal to the Privy Council. Unlike Australia, New Zealand has retained the right of appeal to the Privy Council. The Court of Appeal, comprised of the Chief Justice and two judges of the Supreme Court, hears appeals from the Supreme Court, and in certain instances, appeals from inferior courts and administrative tribunals. The Supreme Court, next in the judicial hierarchy, has some original jurisdiction and general appellate jurisdiction over Magistrates' Courts and administrative tribunals. Special courts and administrative tribunals include Workers Compensation Court, Court of Arbitration, Trade Practices and Prices Commission, and Taxation Review Authority (formerly Taxation Board of Review).

1. *New Zealand Law Reports.*[8] These contain the official reports dating from 1861 of the Judicial Committee of the Privy Council, Court of Appeal, Supreme Court, and Workers' Compensation Court. It incorporated the Gazette Law Reports, 1898–1953. Currently it is issued monthly in paper parts, each part providing a cumulative table of cases for the volume. There is a digest for the Gazette Law Reports and index digests and cumulative table of cases for the New Zealand Law Reports, but no cumulative indexes are issued on

5. Wellington, Ministry of External Affairs, 1948.
6. Wellington, Ministry of Foreign Affairs, 1948 to date.
7. Edited by P. H. Rohn. Santa Barbara, Calif., Clio, 1974 to date.
8. Wellington, Butterworths, 1884 to date.

a current basis. Each volume has a digest and an index.

2. *Magistrates' Court Decisions.*[9] This series, issued 1939 to date, reports all judgments of the named court, with the exception of those judgments of that court from which appeals are pending. It is issued in parts, with a cumulating subject index in each issue. There are a cumulative subject index and a table of cases within each bound volume.

3. *Magistrates' Court Reports.*[10] Reporting of the same court with partial overlapping coverage was provided by this series from 1906 through 1952. It was then absorbed by Magistrates' Court Decisions.

4. *Magistrates' Court Cases Index.*[11] This is a classified subject index of cases reported in Magistrates' Court Decisions from 1939 through 1969 and in Magistrates' Court Reports from 1906 until the index ceased in 1952.

5. *New Zealand Law Reports Reprint.*[12] This is a closed series reprinting completely all the various law reports earlier published in New Zealand, including the contents of New Zealand Law Reports, 1861-1961.

6. *Special court reports.* Illustrative of the law reporting of the courts having special jurisdiction are the officially issued Awards, Agreements, Orders, and Decisions made under the Industrial Relations Act, the Apprentices Act, and other Industrial Legislation 1894 to date[13] and the Tax Reports.[14] The latter series, begun in 1975, replaced the earlier New Zealand Taxation Board of Review Decisions, 1961-1974. The Tax Reports, issued monthly in paper parts, include, in addition to the decisions of the Taxation Appeal Authority, tax cases decided in the Supreme Court, Court of Appeal, and Privy Council.

7. *New Zealand Administrative Reports.*[15] This series, which began in 1976, covers selectively the decisions of all tribunals excepting the Taxation Review Authority and the Country Planning Appeal Boards. It is published periodically in parts and is in the same format as the New Zealand Law Reports.

§27.6. Digests.

Digests issued as an element of or directly related to a specific set are described above with that set.

9. Wellington, Butterworths, 1940 to date.
10. Wellington, New Zealand Times, 1906-1952.
11. Wellington, Butterworths, 1970.
12. Wellington, Butterworths.
13. Wellington, Gov. Pr., 1902 to date.
14. Wellington, Butterworths, 1976 to date.
15. *Ibid.*

1. *Abridgement of New Zealand Case Law.*[16] This is a consolidated digest covering, for the period since 1861, the decisions in the New Zealand Law Reports and the Gazette Law Reports. Patterned after the English and Empire Digest, it is in classified arrangement with entries numbered chronologically within each subject title. Each subject title begins with a listing of its classified parts and subheadings. The entry for each case includes a catchline, a brief headnote, and complete citations to all reports in which the case has been printed. Within each case digest entry, references are made to other cases which have interpreted or otherwise referred to the case at issue. See Exhibit 103. Cases relevant to more than one subject title are repeated under each subject. There are a table of cases and a concise index within each volume and a separate subject index to the set. There is an alphabetical list of annotated cases through 1973; also a list of words and phrases considered in the cases 1861–1973. A cumulative permanent supplement and periodic paper supplements maintain complete currency of the digest. See Exhibit 104.

2. *Butterworths Current Law.* This is a semimonthly containing tables of recent New Zealand legislation, regulations and rules, bills pending, and a digest of case law as well as notes on United Kingdom and Australian case law of special significance. There are periodic cumulating table of cases to the volume, and there is a cumulating subject index appended to each part. Since November 1974 it has been issued as a supplement to New Zealand Law Journal.

3. *English and Empire Digest.* This set, discussed in detail at §24.7.1, includes selective New Zealand cases.

§27.7. Encyclopedia.

The Australian and New Zealand Commentary on Halsbury's Laws of England, fourth edition in progress,[17] will supersede the New Zealand Pilot to Halsbury's Laws of England, third edition. Whereas Pilot editions to Halsbury's Laws were separately issued for Australia and New Zealand, the Commentary encompasses both countries in a single format; separate texts are anticipated in exceptional instances only. Further, whereas the Pilot editions provide simply references to the law of Australia and New Zealand, the Commentary aims to be something more. In encyclopedic format, it provides a limited exposition of the law of the two countries with attention given to areas where the common law of one or the other country has diverged or developed differently from that of the United Kingdom. See Exhibit 105. It is intended as a precursor of a truly self-contained encyclope-

16. Wellington, Butterworths.
17. Sydney, Butterworths, 1974 in progress.

dia of the laws of Australia and New Zealand to be published some years hence, paralleling Halsbury's Laws of England.

The Commentary is being issued in fascicles by chapter, corresponding to the titles in Halsbury, although not in the same sequence as the publication of Halsbury's Laws, fourth edition. Cross-references are made to the third or fourth edition of the parent volume depending upon the publication scheduling of the subject at issue. Paragraphs are numbered, with addition of a C prefix, to their subject equivalents in Halsbury. In footnote references, those of the Australian Commonwealth and states precede those of New Zealand. An alphabetical table of cases and jurisdictional table of statutes are included within each chapter. An index appended to each chapter of additional material unique to the Commentary should be used in conjunction with the indexes to Halsbury's Laws. Issues of Butterworth's Current Law serve to maintain currency of the New Zealand aspects of the Commentary.

§27.8. Citators.

There is no series strictly comparable to Shepard's Citations for searching the legislative and judicial treatment of statutes and judicial consideration of case law in New Zealand. Butterworths Annotations, as described below, partially fulfills this function; so too do the Abridgement of New Zealand Law and the Australian and New Zealand Commentary on Halsbury's Laws of England, fourth edition, and its predecessor, the New Zealand Pilot to Halsbury's Laws of England, third edition.

1. *Butterworths Case Annotations of the New Zealand Statutes Reprint*. This is a citator digest service to statutes and to case law interpreting the statutes and statutory regulations formulated under them. The title is a misnomer in the sense that it covers legislation enacted since 1957 as well as that included in the Reprint set.

Under each act found in the Statutes Reprint, 1909–1957, case citations interpreting sections of acts with a very brief summary of the finding on the issue involved are enumerated. If the act has been recently reenacted, cases decided under the earlier act are given. However, if the act has been consolidated in several reenactments with substantial case law under the earlier statutes, reference is made to the volume and page of the Annotations wherein the earlier citations may be found. Decisions reported through 1957 are included in the first two volumes of this series. Decisions reported through 1973 are covered in volume 3A together with decisions of the United Kingdom which bear on the New Zealand law. References are made in this volume to the prior two volumes where pre-1958 cases on an due under one of the before-mentioned agreements.

GOLDFINCH & CO. v. RANGITIKEI SAWMILLERS' CO-OPERATIVE ASSOCIATION LTD. (1914) 33 N.Z.L.R. 666; 16 G.L.R. 371.

Annotations:

Apld. *Nelson District Hopgrowers' Co-operative Association Ltd.* v. *McGlashen* [1932] N.Z.L.R. 308; [1932] G.L.R. 1.

Refd. *R.* v. *The Crown Milling Co. Ltd.* [1925] N.Z.L.R. 753; [1926] G.L.R. 65.

2. **Objects of company including insurance business — Capital of company under fifty thousand pounds—Refusal of Registrar to register company—Companies Act 1908, s. 331.**

Application was made for the registration of a company one of the objects of which was the carrying on of insurance business of all kinds. The Registrar refused to register the company, as its capital was under £50,000. *Held,* That the company was entitled to be registered, but could not carry on insurance business until its capital amounted to £50,000.

SCALES v. REGISTRAR OF COMPANIES [1920] N.Z.L.R. 821; [1920] G.L.R. 456.

3. **Restraint of trade—Agreement respecting sale of hops—Illegality—Company limited by guarantee—Registration—Void by statute—Trade Unions Act 1908, ss. 5, 6.**

Plaintiff, a company limited by guarantee, had entered into an agreement with defendant by which the latter agreed to deliver all hops grown by him to plaintiff for sale by the latter. He also entered into a bond with a penal sum to secure performance of the agreement. During the 1931 season defendant grew 21 bales of hops, but delivered only 11 bales to plaintiff company and sold the remaining 10 elsewhere. In an action by plaintiff on the bond for the penalty, or, in the alternative, for damages for the breach of the agreement, *Held,* That plaintiff company was a trade union within the meaning of the Trade Unions Act 1908 and therefore its registration under the Companies Act 1908 was void. The Court could, therefore, not entertain the action without contravening the express provisions of the statute. *Goldfinch* v. *Rangitikei Sawmillers' Co-operative Association Ltd.* (1914) 33 N.Z.L.R. 666; 16 G.L.R. 371, applied.

NELSON DISTRICT HOPGROWERS' CO-OPERATIVE ASSOCIATION LTD. v. McGLASHEN [1932] N.Z.L.R. 308; [1932] G.L.R. 1.

4. **Unregistered partnership exceeding ten members—Formation of, to purchase block of land to resell or to lease—Whether carrying on of business with object of acquisition of gain within Companies Act 1903, s. 5—Court's jurisdiction thereunder—Companies Act 1933, s. 372.**

In 1906 plaintiff and defendants formed a partnership of 12 persons under a syndicate agreement whereby it appeared that the members of the syndicate had purchased a block of land to be held by trustees for the benefit of the partnership with the intention of making profits from dealing with it, either by letting it, or selling it, or any part or parts of it, or by both of such methods. In an action brought by plaintiff against all other members of the partnership asking for a decree for the dissolution of the partnership, and an order for the taking of its accounts, and for the winding up of its business upon the ground that plaintiff had paid all the moneys that he was required to pay under the agreement, and that defendants had failed to pay their shares, *Held,* 1. That the partnership was formed for the carrying on of a business which had for its object the acquisition of gain and therefore came within the prohibition of s. 5 of the Companies Act 1903 (1908). 2. That the effect of the said section was to require the Court, in civil proceedings at least, to take no legal cognisance of such partnerships except to the extent required by the provisions of subss. (2) and (3) thereof. 3. That as the partnership existed when the said s. 5 was repealed by s. 372 of the Companies Act 1933, it became one that could be wound up as an unregistered company under Part XI of that Act, but that as the present action was not an appropriate proceeding to obtain a winding up order thereunder, it must be dismissed.

HERBERT v. GREATHEAD [1936] N.Z.L.R. 185; [1936] G.L.R. 143.

PART 2 — COMPANIES UNDER THE COMPANIES ACT 1955

PROMOTION AND FLOTATION

5. **Business of testator—Conversion into company—Shares to trustees in payment—Power of Court to sanction.**

Where the trustees of a will have no power to invest the trust moneys in the purchase of shares in a company, the Court has no power to sanction a sale by the trustees to a company of a business left by the testator, the trustees taking shares in the company as payment or part payment of the purchase money. *In re Morrison, Morrison* v. *Morrison* [1901] 1 Ch. 701, followed.

In re SCOULLAR, AITKEN v. SCOULLAR (1901) 21 N.Z.L.R. 89; 4 G.L.R. 156.

Annotations:

Dstd. *In re Lees, Melville* v. *Lees* (1915) 34 N.Z.L.R. 1054; 17 G.L.R. 761.

Dstd. *Wood* v. *Wood* [1917] N.Z.L.R. 152.

6. **Remuneration — Agreement to float company.**

On or about 27 June 1899 defendant placed in plaintiff's hands for flotation into a company a dredging claim on the Kawarau River. Plaintiff

Exhibit 103

earlier act or sections may be found. See Exhibit 106. Case annotations of subsequent decisions are included in annual supplements together with other material discussed below. See Exhibit 107.

Cases decided pursuant to statutory regulations were first included in volume 3A and are to be found at the end of the enabling statute.

PART 2—COMPANIES UNDER THE COMPANIES ACT 1955 [Cases 2-11]

was to receive 300 fully paid-up shares, and he undertook that the company should be floated within three weeks, or a reasonable time. In consequence of delay, defendant arranged with another person, who, in consideration of receiving 600 fully paid-up shares, underwrote the balance of the share capital, and the company was then incorporated. Plaintiff brought an action for the 300 shares or their value. *Held,* That plaintiff was not entitled to the 300 shares, as he had not shown that the company was floated through his efforts, and judgment was given for defendant, with costs.

WILLIAMSON v. PEARSON (1900) 3 G.L.R. 121.

NAME OF COMPANY AND CHANGE OF NAME

7. **Change of name—Application for approval of Court—Application opposed—Companies Act 1908, s. 160.**

The applicant company had for some time carried on business under the name of "Lewis R. Eady & Son Ltd." and it was now desired to change this name to "Lewis Eady Ltd." The necessary formalities were complied with, and the requisite certificate of the Registrar of Companies had been obtained. The application to the Court for its approval of the change was opposed by two firms carrying on separately similar businesses in the same locality under the names of "Arthur Eady Ltd." and "Kenneth Eady Ltd.," respectively. The basis of the objection was that the proposed change would tend to increase the confusion already existing in the public mind and to prejudice the objectors in the conduct of their several businesses. Reed J., after reviewing the evidence, held that the proposed change was not calculated to add to the confusion which to some extent already existed, and made an order approving of the alteration. *National Timber Co. Ltd.* v. *National Hardware, Timber & Machinery Co. Ltd.* [1923] N.Z.L.R. 1258; [1923] G.L.R. 346, referred to.

In re LEWIS R. EADY & SON LTD. [1928] N.Z.L.R. 181; [1928] G.L.R. 97.

8. **Change of name—Petition and affidavit affirming the passing of special resolution in accordance with articles of association—Omission from affidavit of particulars as to steps taken—Necessity for supplying details to Court—Companies Act 1903, s. 160.**

The applicant company, in a petiton to the Court to approve of a proposed change of name, under the provisons of s. 160 of the Companies Act 1903, set out that the necessary special resolution for the proposed change of name had been duly passed at an extraordinary general meeting of the company, duly called, and held at Auckland on 31 July 1908, and that the resolution had been duly confirmed at another extraordinary general meeting, duly called, and held on 28 August 1908. The affidavit filed in proof of this allegation stated that the meetings of the members of the company called and held for the purpose of considering the resolution set out in the petition were duly summoned in accordance with the articles of association of the company, and that the resolution had been duly carried and confirmed, as set out in the petition, without any dissentient. *Held,* That this could not be accepted as sufficient proof that the resolution had been duly passed, as the question whether or not it had been duly passed was a matter of law dependent upon proof of the various steps taken.

In re DRURY COAL CO. LTD. (1908) 28 N.Z.L.R. 105; 11 G.L.R. 237.

9. **Change of name—Private company—Special resolution—Companies Act 1908, ss. 91, 168 (6).**

A private company desiring to change its name and a shareholder who held more than one-fourth of the shares being absent from the Dominion, the company passed a special resolution complying with s. 91 of the Companies Act 1908. The company moved for the approval of the Court, to the change under s. 160 of the Act. *Held,* dismissing the motion, That the provisions of subs. (6) of s. 168 were substitutional and exclusive of s. 91 and therefore the latter section was not applicable to a private company, and that the proceedings should have been by way of petition instead of motion.

Ex parte SIMSON BROTHERS LTD. (1913) 16 G.L.R. 159.

Annotations:
Ovrd. *Pacey* v. *Premier Drapery Co. Ltd.* [1928] N.Z.L.R. 14; [1927] G.L.R. 592.
Dstd. *Dannevirke Motor Co. Ltd. Re* [1920] G.L.R. 266.

10. **Change of name—Similarity of name—Whether calculated to deceive.**

An application by a company for the approval of the Court to a change of its name to "British New Zealand Motors Limited" was opposed by a company incorporated under the name of "British Motors Limited." *Held* (dismissing the application), That the name for which approval was sought, so nearly resembled the name of the opposing company as to be calculated to deceive.

In re KINGSWAY (WANGANUI) LTD. [1931] G.L.R. 16.

11. **Change of name—Similarity—Whether deceptive or descriptive of work undertaken—Companies Act 1908, s. 27.**

An application by C. & T. Ltd., for approval of a change of name to the "Cu-Tone Precision Engineers Limited," was opposed by the Precision Engineering Co. Ltd. Both companies were engaged in the engineering business. The applicant had been engaged in making what are known as "precision tools," and in what is styled "precision work." The objecting company was engaged in manufacturing motor plates, steel shelving, lockers, and office equipment. The applicant company had decided to make "precision work" a prominent feature of its business, and adopted the term "precision" not as a fancy word, but as being descriptive of the kind of

Exhibit 103 (cont.)

In the following annual supplement, case annotations on regulations in force as of January 1970 are found under the relevant statutes.

Volumes 4 and 5 contain annotations of statutory amendments passed by Parliament since 1957. The first of these covers the years 1958–1967 for all statutes as well as statutory amendments in the

Vol 2 – Civil Aviation

PART 5 – POWERS AND DUTIES OF TRUSTEES

150 Annotation
Refd Morgan v Wellington City Corporation [1975] 1 NZLR 416 (CA).

155 Add Annotation
Refd Morgan v Wellington City Corporation [1975] 1 NZLR 416 (CA).

CIVIL AVIATION

PART 2 – CARRIAGE BY AIR

5a Add Annotation:
Flld Carr v New Zealand Refrigerating Co Ltd [1976] 2 NZLR 135.

PART 4 – OFFENCES

11 Add Annotation:
Flld Carr v New Zealand Refrigerating Co Ltd [1976] 2 NZLR 135.

COMPANIES

PART 2 – COMPANIES UNDER THE COMPANIES ACT 1955

7a Annotation:
Apld New Zealand Insurance Co Ltd v New Zealand Insurance Brokers Ltd [1976] 2 NZLR 40.
52 Annotation:
Apld Broadlands Finance Ltd v Gisborne Aero Club Inc [1974] 1 NZLR 157.
Annotation
Flld Broadlands Finance Ltd v Gisborne Aero Club Inc [1975] 2 NZLR 496 (CA).

MEMORANDUM AND ARTICLES OF ASSOCIATION

62a Alteration of objects – Shares bought by two charitable trusts – Proposed alteration to carry on business exclusively for the benefit of the trusts – Confirmation refused – Companies Act 1955, s 18 (1) (a), (e).
All the shares in a company were purchased by the trustees of two charitable trusts. The principal object of the company was to carry on business as a subdivider and seller of real property. The shareholders passed a special resolution to alter the objects of the company so that the company carried on its businesses exclusively for the benefit of the two trusts, and would obtain exemption from income tax under s 86 (1) (o) of the Land and Income Tax Act 1954. On an application under s 18 of the Companies Act 1955 for confirmation of the resolution. Held, 1 The alteration did not impose any restriction on the objects or powers in the memorandum of association within para (e) of s 18 (1) of the Companies Act 1955, but only re-defined the purpose for which the company's business was being carried on. 2 If the company were to be successful in obtaining exemption under s 86 (1) (o) of the Land and Income Tax Act 1954 it would only reflect a change in the purpose of the company's operations and could not amount to the company carrying on its business more economically within para (a) of s 18 (1). Semble, If the proposed alteration constituted the company a trustee of its income and property for the shareholders, it would be void as purporting to constitute the shareholders beneficial owners of the company's property.
RE GRASSLANDS FARMS LTD [1975] 1 NZLR 92

113 Add Annotation:
Apld Re Hodder & Tolley Ltd [1975] 2 NZLR 395.

MEMBERSHIP

122a Company separate entity from its shareholders and shareholders not directly liable for rent payable by their company.
The plaintiffs were the owners of an old building until February 1974, when they sold it. In March 1970 the plaintiffs leased the building to the first defendant for a term of 10 years, and the second defendants guaranteed to the plaintiffs the performance by the first defendants of the terms of the lease. In October 1970 the first defendant assigned its interest under the lease to BC Ltd with the consent of the plaintiffs, but without prejudice to their rights under the lease. BC Ltd paid rent until 3 May 1971 and in June 1971 went into liquidation. The rent had not been paid for the period 10 May 1971 until 19 February 1974 when the plaintiffs sold the building, and the rates had not been paid by the defendants. Held, The first defendant was a corporate entity distinct from the second defendants

Exhibit 104

(*a*) (WA) Charitable Trusts Act 1962 s 5, (QLD) Trusts Act 1973 s 103(2) and (3), by both of which certain recreational purposes are declared to be charitable, thus forming a fifth category.
(*b*) eg *In re Bruce, Simpson v Bruce* [1918] NZLR 16, [1918] GLR 26, CA: *Grant v Commissioner of Stamp Duties* [1943] NZLR 113, [1943] GLR 119; *In re MacDonald, Woods v Melanesian Mission Trust Board (Inc.)* [1951] NZLR 502, GLR 261.
(*c*) See C512 and C544-C547.

(2) PARTICULAR CHARITABLE PURPOSES

(i) Relief of the Aged, Impotent and Poor

C514. Purposes in preamble to be read separately.
Australia: fn (2) See *Re Clark, Perry v Salvation Army (VIC) Property Trust* [1957] VR 171; *City of Hawthorn v Victorian Welfare Association* [1970] VR 205.
fn (4) See *Re Bond; Brennan v A-G* [1929] VLR 333; *Re Chown; Teele v University of Melbourne,* [1939] VLR 443; *Re Inman (dec'd)* [1965] VR 238.

New Zealand: fn (2), (3) *In re Bingham (dec'd), Public Trustee v New Plymouth Council for Social Service Incorporated* [1951] NZLR 491, [1951] GLR 223; *Re McIntosh (dec'd)* [1976] NZLR 308.
fn (4) *In re Simmonds, Public Trustee v Stone* [1933] NZLR s 172, [1933] GLR 757 (wounded and disabled soldiers, wounded sailors). *In re Flannagan (dec'd), Beatty v A-G* [1962] NZLR 480 (non-existent convalescent ward of hospital); *In re Mitchell, Public Trustee v Salvation Army* [1963] NZLR 935, 937 (young women whose first child was born in a specified Salvation Army maternity home).

C515. Meaning of "poor", "aged" and "impotent".
Australia: A gift may be for the relief of the poor, and consequently be a charitable gift or for a charitable purpose, notwithstanding that the benefits are not confined to supplying the necessities of life to the destitute, but take the form of relieving distress occasioned by lack of money (*a*).
Dispositions in favour of aged persons are in one respect different from those in favour of the poor or the impotent. Since age does not necessarily involve disability, it may be that a gift for aged persons cannot claim to be prima facie charitable. But a gift made in relief of aged persons, in the sense that it is in relief of the needs arising from old age (such as the need for protection against the dangers and distresses incident to living alone), is charitable, unless some limitation of the class of objects deprives it of that character (*b*).
Gifts to provide hospitals and similar institutions without distinction as to the means of the patients, have been held to be charitable as in relief of impotent persons, in the sense of being in relief of needs arising from distress or other disability (*c*).
fn (2) For what is not embraced by "relief of poverty", see *A-G (NSW) v Adams* (1908) 7 CLR at 126 per Isaacs J.

(*a*) *City of Hawthorn v Victorian Welfare Association* [1970] VR at 208.
(*b*) *City of Hawthorn v Victorian Welfare Association* [1970] VR at 209; *Re Clark; Perry v Salvation Army (VIC) Property Trust* [1957] VR 171. The decisions in *NSW Nursing Service and Welfare Association for Christian Scientists v Willoughby Municipal Council* [1968] 2 NSWR 78; *Church of England Property Trust; Diocese of Canberra and Goulburn v Imlay Shire Council* [1971] 2 NSWLR 216, and *Trustees of Property for the Diocese of Newcastle*, 24 May 1973 *(unreported)* all per Else-Mitchell J, are inconsistent with *City of Hawthorn v Victorian Welfare Association*, in that while they recognise that mere old age does not provide an object of charity they ignore the significance of the relief of old age, as laid down by the

Exhibit 105

Companies Act 1955, No. 63. (Reprint 1968).
ss. 2, 7, 9, 14 ...... *(Refer Vol. 1, p. 154.)*

s. 16 ...... **North of England Zoological Society** *v.* **Chester Rural District Council** (Ch. D.) [1958] 3 All E.R. 535; (C.A.) [1959] 3 All E.R. 116.
Memorandum of association—Object clauses—Distinction between objects and powers—Numerous objects set out—Determination of main objects by reference to evidence of company's activities.

...... **Victory (Ex-Services) Assn. Ltd.** *v.* **Paddington Borough Council** [1960] 1 All E.R. 498.
Memorandum of association—Object clauses—Ascertainment of main object—Evidence of activities necessary only where object ambiguous.

...... **Angol Overseas Agencies Ltd.** *v.* **Green** [1960] 3 All E.R. 244.
Memorandum of association—Object clauses—Construction—Numerous objects set out in separate paragraphs—Concluding words of clause providing that objects specified in any one paragraph not to be limited by reference to terms of any other paragraph or by name of company—Main object of company export and import of goods—Whether scope of subsequent object clauses limited so as to be ancillary to main object—Whether proposed acquisition of building lease for a venture in land development *ultra vires*.

s. 17 ...... *(Refer Vol. 1, p. 154.)*

s. 18 (1) (b) *Re* **Hydraulic Mining (N.Z.) Ltd.** [1968] N.Z.L.R. 1153.
Companies under the Companies Act 1955—Application for confirmation of alteration of objects in memorandum of association—New objects completely different from old objects—Completely different business not contemplated by the legislation.

s. 18 (1) (e) ...... *Re* **Hampstead Garden Suburb Trust Ltd.** [1962] 2 All E.R. 879.
Memorandum of association—Alteration of objects—Cancellation of alteration—Alteration not one enabling company to restrict or abandon any of objects—Notice not given to debenture stockholders—Company precluded from contending that

Exhibit 106

1955–1957 annuals, which were still in force in 1957 but which do not appear in the Reprint, and have not been subsequently reprinted. Repeals of statutes during 1955–1957 are also indicated. Acts of the United Kingdom in force in New Zealand to which amendments have been made as well as those which have ceased effect can also be traced. Chronological and alphabetical tables of public acts 1958–1967 are included.

Volume 5 covers the years 1968–1973 in the scope as described above. See Exhibit 108. In addition, it contains a list of the statutory regulations 1936–1973 in force as of the end of 1973. Annotations for the years following will be found in annual supplement composites.

2. *Australian and New Zealand Citator to U.K. Reports.*[18] United Kingdom decisional law from 1558 to date, which has been judicially noticed by New Zealand and Australian courts since 1825 and which cases have been published in the Law Reports, Weekly Law Reports, and All Law Reports, including the reprint volumes can be traced through this citator. The United Kingdom cases are arranged alphabetically with citations to reports in the series listed above and are followed by citations to the New Zealand and Australian cases which have cited them. Currency of the citator is maintained by periodic cumulative supplements.

18. Sydney, Butterworths, 1973 to date.

Annotations Supplement

Companies Act 1955, No 63
Extd 1974, No 3, s 46
To Rural Banking and Finance Corporation
Excld 1974 No 27, s 25 (2)
Concerning Cornish Companies Manager's reports.
Extd and Mod 1974 No 27, s 25 (3)
To Cornish Companies Management
Ref 1974 No 70, s 2
Concerning protection of retail Customers under Chattels Transfer Act 1924.
Parts VI and VII – Excld 1974 No 27, s 25 and Second Schedule
From Cornish Companies
Part VII – Ref 1974 No 27, s 16
Concerning Cornish Companies Management
s 41 – Excld 1974 No 27, s 25 and Second Schedule
From Cornish Companies
s62 – Wallersteiner v Moir [1974] 3 All ER 217.
Liability for loss to company – Director responsible for procuring loan by company Companies Act 1948, s54 (UK).
s 101 – Ref 1974 No 27, s 13 (4) (b)
Concerning Cornish Companies Management
s 102 – Waitomo Wools (New Zealand) Ltd v Nelsons (New Zealand) Limited [1974] 1 NZLR 484 (CA).
Companies – Registration and mortages and charges – Instrument creating general possessory lien not a charge within the Companies Act 1955, s 102. Re an Application by Tileman New Zealand Ltd: John Burns and Company v C L Kemp Limited (In Liquidation) (1974) 14 MCD 70
ss 130 – 135 – Excld 1974 No 27, s 25 and Second Schedule
From Cornish companies
ss 152 – 162 – Excld 1974 No 27, s 25 and Second Schedule
From Cornish companies
s 163 – Mod 1974 No 27 s 21 (2) (b)
Concerning Cornish Companies Management
s 188 (1) – R v Newth [1974] 2 NZLR 760
Bankruptcy and Insolvency – Offences – Undischarged bankrupt "concerned in the management of a company – Offence to take a hand in the real business of a company notwithstanding that not a director.
s190 – Wallersteiner v Moir [1974] 3 All ER 217.
Loan to company wholly-owned and controlled by director – Whether loan to director – Companies Act 1948, s190 (UK).
s217 (e) – Re Bryant Investment Co Ltd [1974] 2 All ER 683.
Whether company should be deemed unable to pay its debts – Neglect to comply with demand for payment – Debt not due at date of demand – Companies Act 1948, ss222, 223 (UK).
s218 (c) – Re Bryant Investment Co Ltd [1974] 2 All ER 683.
[See s217 (e)]
s234 – Re a Company [1974] 1 All ER 256.
Jurisdiction of Court – Creditor applying for appointment of provisional liquidator after presentation of petition – Court striking out creditor's petition as abuse of process – Whether jurisdiction to appoint provisional liquidator – Companies Act 1948, s238 (UK).
Re a Company [1974] 1 All ER 256.
Power of Court to stay proceedings – Petition of creditor for stay of all litigation against company – Court then striking out creditor's petition as abuse of process – Whether Court having jurisdiction to grant stay – Companies Act 1948, s226 (UK).
s258 – Butler et anr v Broadhead et ors [1974] 2 All ER 401.
Exclusion of creditor from distribution of assets – Unjust enrichment – Sums overpaid to contributors at expense of creditor – Creditor ignorant of breach at time of distribution – Companies Act 1948, s264 (UK).
s 308 – Ref 1974 No 27, s 13 (4) (b)
Concerning Cornish Companies Management
s 308 – Mod 1974 No 41, s 51 (2)
Concerning priority of contribution deductions under New Zealand Superannuation Act

Exhibit 107

Statutory Amendments, Etc.

Commissions of Inquiry Act 1908, No. 25—*Continued*

s. 13 (3)——Am. 1968 No. 73, s. 2 (2) (a).
By omitting the words "section four", and substituting the words "subsection (1) of section 4".

s. 13 (3)——Am. 1968 No. 73, s. 2 (2) (b).
By omitting the word "Magistrate", and substituting the words "Magistrate's Court".

ss. 13-15——Excld. 1969 No. 139, s. 12 (8).
As to Appeal Tribunal under the Hotel Association of New Zealand Act 1969.

Companies Act 1955, No. 63.

Reprinted with Amendments 1959 No. 55, 1960 No. 49, 1963 No. 136, 1964 No. 42, 1965 No. 75, 1965 (No. 2) No. 129, 1966 No. 105, 1967 No. 63, to 1 July 1969 incorporated: 1968 Statutes, Vol. 3, p. 1759.

App. 1949 No. 8, s. 26A (as added by 1969 No. 49, s. 13 (1).
As to offences by companies under Physiotherapy Act 1949.

Excld. 1968 No. 25, s. 25.
Relating to claims on the Real Estate Agents Fund.

App. 1968 No. 152, s. 35A (b) and (c).
As to meaning of overseas corporation.

Ref. 1968 No. 146, s. 11.

Ref. 1968 No. 147, s. 2 (1).

Ref. 1969 No. 132, s. 3 (2).

Excld. 1969 No. 132, s. 3 (7).
As to audit of accounts of company in which Minister of Industries and Commerce has acquired shares.

App. 1970 No. 20, s. 2 (1).
In relation to meaning of "independent broker" under the Payroll Tax Act 1970.

Excld. 1964 No. 124, s. 33 (a) (as added by 1970 No. 38, s. 12).
Development Finance Corporation not a company.

App. 1970 No. 143, s. 2 (1).
As to meaning of "company" under the Pharmacy Act 1970.

App. 1971 No. 51, s. 7 (h).
Share warrant to be instrument of conveyance under the Stamp and Cheque Duties Act 1971.

Excld. 1971 No. 51, s. 11 (1).
Memorandum and articles exempt from the Stamp and Cheque Duties Act 1971.

Excld. 1971 No. 51, s. 15 (3).
As to duty on transfer of shares under the Stamp and Cheque Duties Act 1971.

App. 1971 No. 55, s. 3 (1).
As to donations by local authorities to Commonwealth Games Fund.

App. 1964 No. 124, s. 7 (1) (aa) (as added by 1971 No. 95, s. 2).
As to meaning of "subsidiary".

Excld. 1972 No. 15, s. 64 (2).
As to deposit by a company of a unit plan.

App. 1954 No. 67, s. 126B (1) (b) (as added by 1972 No. 17, s. 20 (1)).
As to gifts of money by public companies.

App. 1972 No. 3, s. 16 (3).
As to auditor for the Orton Bradley Trust Board.

App. 1963 (L.) No. 18, s. 45A.
As to purchase of shares in passenger service.

Excld. 1963 (L.) No. 18, s. 45A (1) (j) (as added by 1972 (L.) No. 12, s. 6).
As to purchase of shares in passenger service.

Exhibit 108

§27.9. Subject loose-leaf services.

Special subject loose-leaf services available from commercial publishers are similar to those for United States law. Services cover such topics as commercial and company law, industrial relations and industrial law, and taxation.

§27.10. Dictionaries.

1. *Hinde's New Zealand Law Dictionary*, second edition,[19] defines legal terms and phrases in historical and contemporary context with special reference to present applicability.

2. *Abridgment of New Zealand Case Law*, volume 18, contains a list of words and phrases judicially considered in cases reporting during the period 1861–1973. Supplements to the Abridgment add to this listing. Refer also to the section on dictionaries in the chapter on United Kingdom Materials (§24.11).

§27.11. Periodical indexes.

1. *Current Australian and New Zealand Literature Index*.[20] This is a quarterly subject list of articles, case notes, and book reviews in New Zealand and Australian law journals and in selected other English language law journals and nonlegal periodicals about New Zealand and Australian law, including some analytics of essays and collected works. A separate name index and a table of cases are appended to each issue.

2. *Index to New Zealand Legal Writing*.[21] The scope and coverage of this new publication are extensive. It indexes monograph and serial literature published from 1955 through 1977 both in New Zealand and elsewhere. It contains also references to cases not included

19. Wellington, Butterworths, 1972.
20. Sydney. Distributed by Law Book, 1973 to date.
21. Legal Research Foundation, University of Auckland School of Law, Auckland, 1978.

in New Zealand Law Reports as well as references to notes on reported decisions. Regular supplementation is anticipated.

3. *Other indexes*. Subject coverage of both monographs and serial literature may be found also in Harvard Law School's Annual Legal Bibliography/Current Legal Bibliography. Use its geographical index to locate references, which are in classified arrangement.

Butterworths Current Law includes a selective listing of periodical literature. The Index to Legal Periodicals provides limited coverage to New Zealand law journals.

20. Sydney. Distributed by Law Book, 1973 to date.

21. Legal Research Foundation, University of Auckland School of Law, Auckland, 1978.

28 | South African Materials*

§28.1. The legal system.

In recent times, there is increasing interest in African nations. The turmoil and strife, as well as the economic importance of South Africa, in particular, has stirred an interest in the legal system of that country. Since there is a dearth of information in the standard American legal research sources on South Africa, it seems appropriate here to fill that gap by providing at least a description of the basic sources for the jurisdiction.

South Africa has an interesting legal background in that Roman-Dutch law is an important element of its jurisprudence. British law and equity concepts have also had a strong influence, however, resulting in a country of mixed law. The writings and decisions of Dutch jurists of the seventeenth and eighteenth centuries are of primary importance and are considered binding authority in South African courts. During the period of British control, 1806–1910, there was a certain amount of infiltration of English common-law concepts through the enactment of statutes, particularly in the area of constitutional law, mercantile law, criminal procedure, and evidence. Additionally, the actual practice of law in South Africa added to this infiltration through the use of British treatises and law reports, which were more accessible and were more readily understandable than the writings in Dutch or Latin. Another contributing factor to this influence was the appeal to the Judicial Committee of the Privy Council

* The authors acknowledge the valuable assistance of Marlene C. McGuirl, J.D., LL.M., M.A. in L.S., Law Librarian in Washington, D.C., Chief, American-British Law Division, Law Library, Library of Congress, who compiled this chapter.

which could be taken as in the case of all English possessions. This appeal process was abolished in 1950.

The common-law principle of stare decisis is followed in South Africa, though with less rigidity than in British and, sometimes, American courts. Decisions of the Privy Council are followed in the highest court in South Africa, although it has departed from them if the court finds them in error. One further interesting factor is that Privy Council decisions even subsequent to 1950, if related to statutory construction of laws which are identical to South African statutes, have persuasive authority in South African courts. Court decisions are highly important for another reason as well. The civil-law aspect of South African jurisprudence, Roman-Dutch law, is uncodified and therefore court decisions must be consulted for determination of those principles with any degree of certainty.

Works which discuss the background and development of the legal system in detail are The Union of South Africa; the Development of its Laws and Constitution[1] by H. R. Hahlo and E. Kahn, and the South African Legal System and its Background[2] by the same authors. Another more recent work is by W. J. Hosten and is entitled Introduction to South African Law and Legal Theory.[3] A classic work on Roman-Dutch law and the influence of British common law in South Africa is Sir Johannes Wessells' History of the Roman-Dutch Law.[4] This work was based on a series of articles published in the South African Law Journal.

The historical writings of Dutch jurists, such as Hugo Grotius or Johannes Voet, are frequently quoted or cited by South African courts. Grotius' work Inleidinge tot de Hollandsche has been translated into English by Robert W. Lee under the title, The Jurisprudence of Holland.[5] This work is in two volumes with the second volume a commentary. The Selective Voet,[6] edited by J. van der Linden and translated into English by P. Gane, was published in eight volumes from 1955–1958. Another notable, though slightly outdated work, is Manfred Nathan's The Common Law of South Africa[7] which is based on Voet's writing. This four-volume set brings principles of Roman-Dutch law as stated by Voet up to 1907.

There is a further element of the law in South Africa, namely, native customary law. Although this subject is beyond the scope of this examination, it should be noted that there are a number of secondary sources discussing native law. One might refer to A Bibliog-

1. London, Stevens, 1960. Supplement, 1962.
2. Cape Town, Juta, 1968.
3. Durban, Butterworth, 1977.
4. Grahamstown, Cape Colony, African Book Company, 1908.
5. Oxford, Claredon, 1926–1936. 2 vols.
6. Durban, Butterworth, 1955–1958. 8 vols.
7. Grahamstown, Cape Colony, African Book Company, 1904–1907. 4 vols.

raphy of Native Law in South Africa, 1941–1961[8] and Jacques Vanderlinden's African Law Bibliography, 1947–1966[9] which has a section on this subject.

§28.2. The Constitution.

The South Africa Act of 1909, which was passed by the Parliament of Great Britain in that year and became effective in 1910, created the Union of South Africa. The Union was a quasi-federal form of government in that it created a unitary state with four provinces, Transvaal, Cape, Orange Free State, and Natal. Each had an elected provincial council with limited legislative powers and an appointed administrator. Following a referendum in 1960, South Africa withdrew from the Commonwealth and became a Republic on May 31, 1961. The Republic of South Africa Constitution Act of 1961 did not specifically repeal or replace the 1909 Constitution, however, but instead merely revised it in order to facilitate the transition from Dominion status to that of an independent republic. Consequently, it was essentially the same with regard to the governmental structure and operation. References to the King and the Governor-General were changed. The New Constitution which is the 1962 supplement to Hahlo's work[10] contains comparative tables of the two documents. The 1909 Constitution is found published in 9 Edw. 7, c. 9 and under the topic "Constitutional Law" in the current Statutes of the Republic of South Africa.[11] The Republic of South Africa Constitution Act of 1961 is also found in the Statutes of the Republic of South Africa. Another source of the constitution as amended is Constitutions of the Countries of the World,[12] where it appears in both Afrikaans and English, the two official languages of the Republic.

§28.3. The executive and the legislature.

The Constitution provides for a State President who is elected for a period of seven years by a majority vote of both houses of the Parliament. His duties are primarily ceremonial, for he acts on the advice of the Executive Council. The Executive Council of Ministers is appointed from members of Parliament by the President and may not exceed 18, although as many as six deputy ministers may also be appointed. The deputy ministers do not serve as part of the Council,

8. B. Kuper, A Bibliography of Native Law in South Africa, 1941–1961. 23 African Studies 155 (1964).
9. Bruxelles, Presses Universitaires de Bruxelles, 1972.
10. *Supra* note 1.
11. Durban, Butterworths, 1961– . Loose-leaf.
12. A. Blaustein & G. Flanz, eds., Constitutions of the Countries of the World. Dobbs Ferry, N.Y., Oceana Publications, 1971– . Loose-leaf.

however. There is a constitutional position of Prime Minister as well.

The Parliament consists of two chambers, the Senate and the House of Assembly. Legislative sessions are held every year for a period of five years at which time an election is held. The Parliament is, however, subject to dissolution. Legislative procedure generally follows the British system.

The acts of Parliament are published in the weekly Republic of South Africa Government Gazette,[13] as are the regulations. Although the Gazette is numbered on a weekly basis, it may in fact have several issues published bearing the same date. Annual volumes of legislative acts are called Statutes of the Union of South Africa[14] until 1910 and thereafter the Statutes of the Republic of South Africa. The yearly volumes contain both alphabetical and chronological tables. Subject arrangements of the earlier acts are found in the official publication entitled Revised Statutes of the Union of South Africa, 1910–1932.[15] A privately published compilation is Union Statutes, Classified and Annotated Reprint, 1910–1947.[16] There is a separate volume, an Index to the Statutes of the Union of South Africa (1910–1934),[17] which is "intended for use either with the Revised Statutes published in six volumes or with the ordinary annual volumes." The current set of statutes, organized by subject, is a loose-leaf set published by Butterworth, called the Statutes of the Republic of South Africa, Classified and Annotated from 1910.[18] This set has, in addition to chronological and alphabetical tables, an annual permanent supplemental volume which contains "the wording of sections, etc. prior to amendment, of the Acts included in the main work which have been amended by Acts which were either brought into force on promulgation" during the current parliamentary session or by proclamations during the current year.

Butterworth also publishes a consolidated legislation service[19] in loose-leaf form which includes important acts and implementing regulations. Each of the provinces has corresponding official gazettes and annual volumes of ordinances.[20]

13. Pretoria, Government Printer, 1902– . Previously called the Union of South Africa Government Gazette.
14. Pretoria, Government Printer, 1910– .
15. Pretoria, Government Printer, 1933–1935. 7 vols.
16. Durban, Butterworth, 1947. 13 vols.
17. Pretoria, Government Printer, 1936.
18. *Supra* note 11.
19. Durban, Butterworth, 1959– . Loose-leaf.
20. Official Gazette of the Province of Natal. Pietermaritzburg, Natal Press, 1910– ; Orange Free State Official Gazette. Bloemfontein, Dreyer Printers, 1910– ; Province of the Cape of Good Hope Official Gazette, Elsiesrivier, Nasionale Handelsdrukkery, 1910– ; Ordinances of the Province of Natal. Pietermaritzburg, Natal Press, 1911– ; Ordinances of the Province of the Orange Free State, 1911– ; Ordinances of the Province of the Cape of Good Hope. Elsiesrivier, Nasionale Handelsdrukkery, 1911– ; Ordinances of the Province of Transvaal. Pretoria, Government Printer, 1911– .

§28.4. The courts.

The judicial system consists of the Supreme Court with Provincial, Local and Appellate Divisions. The Appellate Division is the final court of appeal. There are also Income Tax Appeal Courts, Water Courts (dealing with matters related to the use of water resources), and a Patent Court on the superior court level. The inferior courts include [or included] the Magistrates' Courts, both district and regional.

From 1919–1947, Appellate Division cases were reported in the Decisions of the Supreme Court of South Africa (Appellate Division).[21] The South African Law Reports[22] began publication in 1947 and absorbed the All South Africa Law Reports, so that it includes decisions of the Supreme Court of South Africa, the South-West Africa Division, and the High Court of Rhodesia. This series includes a subject index, a table of cases and a table of "Cases Overruled, Considered, Discussed, etc." in each issue. There is also a handy listing of judges of the various courts included. A unique companion series, which no doubt underscores the importance of the Afrikaans language, is the South African Law Reports; Translation of Afrikaans Passages in Reported Cases,[23] which is published in four parts per year.

More specialized reports consist of Decisions of the Water Courts of South Africa, 1913–1946 and 1947–1969;[24] South African Tax Cases;[25] and Reports of the Native Appeal Courts.[26]

There is a subject index to reported decisions, Butterworth's Consolidated Index and Noter Up to the South African Law Reports, 1947–1972,[27] which includes an alphabetical table of cases reported, a table of statutes construed, a listing of words and phrases judicially considered and a subject index. This work is updated in the annual Butterworth's Index and Noter Up to South Africa Law Reports.[28] An index to the earlier cases of the Appellate Division is found in the Index to Decisions of the Supreme Court of South Africa, 1910–1932[29] and its supplemental volume covering 1932–1945. The supplement contains a consolidated table of cases. There is also a consolidated Index to South African Tax Cases[30] which was published in

21. Cape Town, Juta, 1947– .
22. Cape Town, Juta and Durban, Butterworth, 1947– .
23. Cape Town, Juta, 1969– .
24. Pretoria, Government Printer, 1922–1947. 4 vols.
25. Cape Town & Johannesburg, Juta, 1921– .
26. Pretoria, Government Printer, 1929– .
27. Durban, Butterworth, 1973.
28. Durban, Butterworth, 1974– .
29. T. Duncan, Index to the Appellate Division Reports, 1910–1932. Cape Town and Johannesburg, Juta, 1933; E. Egan, Index to the Appellate Division Reports, 1933–1945. Cape Town and Johannesburg, Juta, 1946.
30. Cape Town and Johannesburg, Juta, 1925– .

conjunction with the reprinting of the first 20 volumes of that title.

For digests of early South African law cases, one would consult the Digest of South African Case Law[31] with four consolidated editions covering cases for 1909–1921, 1922–1933, 1934–1945, and 1946–1949. This title is continued by Bisset and Smith's Digest of South African Case Law,[32] covering cases from 1950 on. The supplement included in the annual volumes of the current Digest contains a "Table of All Cases Overruled, Considered, Discussed, etc." and a "Table of Statutes and Ordinances Which Have Been Interpreted or Applied." It should be noted that the consolidated editions for 1922–1933 and 1934–1945 do not include the tables of cases overruled, etc., from the annual volumes of the Digest. There is also a digest of native civil-law cases by H. W. Warner covering 1894–1957, 1958–1962, and 1963–1968 in a supplement.[33]

Court rules are found in the Handbook of the Consolidated Rules of the Supreme Court by I. Isaacs, published in 1965.[34]

§28.5. Other sources.

There are many monographs and treatises on all aspects of South African law and a substantial number of periodicals and journals.

A new, and as yet incomplete, publication in the form of an encyclopedia is The Law of South Africa,[35] edited by Professor W. A. Joubert. The set, projected for 24 volumes, is intended to cover the whole span of South African law based on authoritative sources including statutes, cases, and Roman-Dutch legal writings. Two volumes have thus far been published, each including bibliographies and indexes. Volume 1 begins with the topic "Accountants," and Volume 2 starts with "Building Contracts."

Another incomplete work, comprehensive in nature, is The South African Encyclopedia of Forms and Precedents.[36] This set includes business forms as opposed to pleadings and also provides notes explaining the use of the forms and the reasons for particular expressions.

31. M. Bisset, Digest of South African Case Law . . . through the end of 1921. Consolidated ed. Cape Town and Johannesburg, Juta, 1926–1929. 6 vols.; Digest of South African Case Law from 1922–1933. Cape Town and Johannesburg, Juta, 1936. 2 vols.; Digest of South African Case Law. Cape Town and Johannesburg, Juta, 1935–1949. 2 vols.; Index and Digest of the South African Law Reports, 1946–1949. 4th Consolidated ed. Cape Town, Juta, 1951.

32. Cape Town, Juta, 1951– .

33. H. Warner, A Digest of South African Native Civil Case Law 1894–1957. Cape Town, Juta, 1961. Supplement, 1958–1962; 1963–1968.

34. Durban, Butterworths, 1965.

35. Durban, Butterworths, 1976– .

36. Durban, Butterworths, 1967– .

Rather than try to describe these general sources any further, it seems more appropriate to refer the reader to bibliographic sources. The A.A.L.S. Recommended Law Books for Libraries in number 39 on African Law and its 1974 supplement,[37] are excellent tools for identifying materials by subject. Earlier works are extensively covered in A. Roberts', A South African Legal Bibliography,[38] published in 1942. Current materials are found in the African Legal Bibliography, 1947–1966.[39] Mention should also be made of the short section on South Africa in J. Vanderlinden's An Introduction to the Sources on Contemporary African Laws,[40] which covers legislation, case law, and legal writing.

Volume 7 of A Legal Bibliography of the British Commonwealth of Nations[41] is an excellent source for statutory enactments, proclamations, and regulations as well as treatises and periodicals published up through the early 1960s.

A listing of local periodicals can be found in A. Blaustein's article, African Legal Periodicals: A Bibliography.[42] These include, among others, Acta Juridica, Speculum Juris, South African Law Journal, Annual Survey of South African Law and Comparative and International Law Journal of South Africa (see §29.9 *infra*). Most of these titles are found indexed in the Index to Foreign Legal Periodicals. These publications can also serve as a source of information about new titles.

37. South Hackensack, N.J., Fred B. Rothman, 1968.
38. Pretoria, 1942.
39. *Supra* note 9.
40. Beograd, Institute of Comparative Law, 1975–
41. London, Sweet & Maxwell, 1964.
42. 59 Law Library Journal 93 (1966).

29 | International Law[1]

§29.1. Scope of chapter.

When researching questions in international law or foreign law, the American lawyer or law student often feels unprepared to use original source material. However, research tools are available in English and many of them are well indexed. This chapter will not devote any substantial discussion to American treaties, an important source in international law, as this has been covered earlier in Chapter 6. However, selected collections of foreign treaties and international law sources published in English, as well as selected American sources, will be examined. United Nations publications have generally not been covered.

§29.2. Branches of international law.

Traditionally, there are two branches of international law. Public international law refers to relations between sovereign states. The other distinct branch refers to those matters of private litigation when the laws of two or more sovereign jurisdictions are involved. This

1. The authors acknowledge the valuable assistance of Mrs. Marlene C. McGuirl, J.D., LL.M., M.A. in L.S., Law Librarian in Washington, D.C., Chief, American-British Law Division, Law Library, Library of Congress, who compiled this chapter.

branch is called private international law. Publications in the areas of both public and private international law may well be consulted by practising attorneys in their work of advising clients and handling litigation in national and international tribunals. With the advent of international law and related courses in law schools, the student will also find that he must utilize a variety of these research tools.

§29.3. Sources of international law defined.

Sources of international law have been defined by the Statute of the International Court of Justice[2] as custom, treaties and conventions, authoritative writings, judicial decisions, and general principles of international law and equity.

§29.4. Sources of international law: custom.

Custom as a source of this body of law refers to the conduct or policy of a country or several countries arising out of necessity, business or otherwise, which is generally recognized and followed. In the bibliographic sense, publications containing the customary international law of a country may be found in the decisions of its local courts, in press releases, opinions of legal advisors, and diplomatic correspondence, among others. Digests of international law, such as Whiteman's Digest of International Law in the U.S. and the supplemental annual Digest of United States Practice in International Law (see Chapter 6) generally contain statements of a nation's policy and practices. Current material on U.S. practices is also found in the section in each quarterly issue of the American Journal of International Law[3] entitled "Contemporary Practice of the United States Relating to International Law." Two other unofficial United States sources of general practice established through common law are found in the American Law Institute's Restatement of the Law Second: the Foreign Relations Law of the United States[4] which contains public international law and the Restatement of Conflict of Laws,[5] containing a discussion of private international law.

Other countries have similar publications. One such is the British Digest of International Law,[6] containing information based on official Foreign Office archives and papers. The multivolume work covers two phases, 1860–1914 and 1914–1960. Another series, E.

2. Statute of the I.C.J., art. 38, 3 Bevans 1187 (July 26, 1945).
3. Washington, D.C., American Society of International Law, 1907– .
4. St. Paul, Minn., American Law Institute Publishers, 1965.
5. St. Paul, Minn., American Law Institute Publishers, 1971. 2 vols.
6. London, Stevens, 1965– .

Lauterpacht's British Practice in International Law,[7] covered the period 1962–67. This series was published on a semiannual basis from 1962 to 1965 and annually for 1966 and 1967 under the auspices of the British Institute of Comparative and International Law and the International Law Fund. "Canadian Practice in International Law" is found as a section in the annual publication called Canadian Yearbook of International Law.[8] Published since 1965, the Australian Year Book of International Law[9] has included a digest of that country's practices.

§29.5. Sources of international law: treaties and treaty indexes.

The second major source of international law, treaties, conventions and other agreements, is bibliographically well documented in the United States (see Chapter 6). In other countries as well, it is common to find official publications of local treaties and various index tools. An example is the texts of treaties published in the Treaty Series of Great Britain.[10] This series is prepared in the Foreign Office and each item contains a treaty series number. The year is a necessary element of the citation since the numbering annually begins anew. Treaties to which Great Britain is a party are also usually printed as Command Papers with their own Command Paper number. In this way, the documents are made public in a relatively timely fashion. An annual index to the Treaty Series, cumulated approximately every four years, is also published. It contains a numerical list with Command Paper numbers and a subject and country index. There are similar publications, also called "Treaty Series," for Canada and Australia.

A consolidated index to the British Treaty Series was published in three volumes in 1970. Clive Parry and C. Hopkins' An Index to British Treaties 1101–1968,[11] includes a chronological listing and a subject and country index for multilateral and bilateral treaties.

The European Treaty Series[12] contains the texts of treaties negotiated among members of the Council of Europe. They also appear in the annual volume of the European Yearbook.[13] The Yearbook, published under the auspices of the Council of Europe, contains a documentary section with the texts of treaties and agreements among the

7. London, British Institute of International and Comparative Law, 1963– .
8. Vancouver, University of British Columbia, 1963– .
9. Sydney, Butterworths, 1965– .
10. London, H.M.S.O., 1892– .
11. London, H.M.S.O., 1970. 3 vols.
12. Strasbourg, Council of Europe, 1949– .
13. La Haye, Nijhoff, 1955– .

various European organizations, including, for example, the Council of Europe, the Western European Union, the Nordic Council and Nordic Council of Ministers, and others. There is also a bibliographic chapter containing selected books, periodicals and pamphlets on the subject of European cooperation.

The European Treaty Series booklets are an official publication by the Secretary General of the Council, each numbered in the chronological order of their signature. The texts appear in both French and English.

The Council of Europe recently published a three-volume compilation of European treaties (1949–1970) called European Conventions and Agreements[14] which includes the text of the treaties, the number of signatory and contracting states, and information as to reservations, ratifications and accessions. (Non-member states of the Council may become parties to a European Council agreement by accession which is not preceded by a signature. A member state must sign the agreement which is then domestically ratified.)

A unique, though outdated publication, is the Soviet Treaty Series; A Collection of Bilateral Treaties, Agreements, and Conventions, etc., Concluded Between the Soviet Union and Foreign Powers.[15] Although only one volume of this work covering the period 1917–1928 was published, it is probably the most comprehensive collection of these documents translated into English that is available.

An all-inclusive treaty publication, also edited and annotated by Clive Parry, is the Consolidated Treaty Series[16] covering the period 1648–1918, which marked the beginning of the League of Nations Treaty Series. Arranged chronologically, these volumes include treaties in their original languages from all countries. If there is an English and/or a French translation available, it also is printed. If not, an English summary is frequently provided.

A number of selected compilations of treaties have also been published, including Major Peace Treaties of Modern History, 1648–1967,[17] edited by Fred L. Israel; Key Treaties for the Great Powers, 1814–1914,[18] selected by Michael Hurst; the Register of Texts of Conventions and Other Instruments Concerning International Trade Law,[19] compiled by the U.N. Commission on International Trade Law; and the H.M.S.O. publication, Hertslet's Commercial Treaties, 1820–1925.[20] For background information on United States defense commitments under security or mutual defense agreements, the

14. Strasbourg, Council of Europe, 1971. 3 vols.
15. L. Shapiro, ed., Washington, D.C., Georgetown University Press, 1950.
16. Dobbs Ferry, N.Y., Oceana Publications, 1969– .
17. New York, Chelsea House, 1967. 4 vols.
18. New York, St. Martin's Press, 1972. 2 vols.
19. New York, United Nations, 1971– .
20. London, H.M.S.O., 1827–1925. 31 vols.

Committee on Foreign Affairs of the House of Representatives published the Committee Print, "Collective Defense Treaties With Maps, Texts of Treaties, a Chronology, Status of Forces Agreements and Comparative Chart"[21] in 1969. Complete texts to which the United States is a party, as well as those to which the United States is not a party, are included. Pertinent excerpts from other defense agreements and declarations are also included.

International Legal Materials,[22] published by the American Society of International Law on a bimonthly basis since 1962, "is a collection of current documents designed to provide up-to-date information." A substantial portion of the selective material included in the ILM is not available in any other source, official or unofficial, until a much later date. There is an ILM cumulative subject, area and author index for 1962–1969.

Another helpful treaty source is Unperfected Treaties of the United States of America, 1776–1976,[23] edited by Christian Wiktor, containing the text of over 400 treaties which have not entered into force in the United States for one reason or another. Treaties which are still pending are excluded. These treaty texts have never been compiled before in a published work. The volumes are in a chronological arrangement by date of signature.

In addition to those indexes found in the official publications of treaties, there are several privately produced indexes. Those for American treaties include: United States Treaties and Other International Agreements, Cumulative Index 1776–1949.[24] This four-volume set includes indices by treaty number, chronologically, by date of signing, by country, and by subject. The U.S.T. Cumulative Index, 1950–1970,[25] is similarly arranged and also has four volumes. A supplement covering the period 1971–1975 is projected.

For international coverage of treaties one may use the five-volume computer-generated World Treaty Index.[26] This Index covering 1920–1972 includes agreements published in the League of Nations Treaty Series and the U.N. Treaty Series plus additional treaties found in the national treaty collections for 42 countries.

Another valuable tool is the Harvard Law School Library, Index to Multilateral Treaties,[27] published in 1965 and supplemented for the years 1964–1966. It is a chronological listing of international treaties to which three or more countries were parties from 1596 to 1963. Ref-

21. Washington, D.C., G.P.O., 1969.
22. Washington, D.C., American Society of International Law, 1962– .
23. Dobbs Ferry, N.Y., Oceana Publications, 1976. 3 vols.
24. I. Kavass & M. Michael, United States Treaties and Other International Agreements, Cumulative Index 1776–1949. Buffalo, N.Y., Wm. Hein & Co., 1975. 4 vols.
25. I. Kavass & A. Sprudzs. UST Cumulative Index, 1950–1970. Buffalo, N.Y., Wm. Hein & Co., 1973. 4 vols.
26. Santa Barbara, Calif., American Bibliographical Center, 1974. 5 vols.
27. Dobbs Ferry, N.Y., Oceana Publications, 1965.

erences are to a variety of text sources such as the UNTS or UST. A unique feature of this publication is the references to draft treaties. An alphabetical subject and regional arrangement is provided for those documents whose signature date is unknown.

The Cumulative List and Index of Treaties and International Agreements Registered or Filed and Recorded with the Secretariat of the United Nations December 1969–December 1974,[28] by Joseph and Rose Vambery, unofficially updates the Cumulative Indexes of the United Nations Treaty Series (usually issued after publication of every 50 volumes). This work also includes an alphabetical index arranged by subject and country.

§29.6. Sources of international law: cases.

Judicial decisions and precedents merit great weight in common-law nations such as Great Britain and the United States. In civil-law countries, however, where domestic law is not based primarily on judicial precedents, this is not the case. Mixing of these different legal traditions adds to the complexity of international law. Clearly, the domestic court decisions of one country are not considered binding precedents for other nations to follow. However, courts will "receive with respect" decisions of another nation's courts, as, if nothing else, a showing of international custom. Also, in the international judicial forum, previous court decisions are not binding on later courts and therefore the principle of stare decisis does not generally apply in international law.

Disputes between states are often settled through direct negotiation or through diplomatic means, sometimes resulting in a treaty or other agreement. However, in cases when an agreement cannot be negotiated, such disputes may be submitted to an adjudicatory body or settled through arbitration by an institution organized specifically for that purpose. One such institution is the Permanent Court of Arbitration which was created at the First Hague Peace Conference in 1899.

The Jay Treaty of 1794 between Great Britain and the United States is generally considered to be the beginning of modern arbitration since it provided that disputes not settled by negotiation be submitted to arbitral commissions. The Washington Treaty of 1871 further encouraged arbitration, as it was the basis of the Alabama Claims Arbitration of 1872 by which the British government was assessed $15,500,000 in damages.

The Permanent Court of Arbitration is not a judicial body in the traditional sense, but consists of a permanent panel of jurists whose members may be selected to serve on arbitral tribunals. The awards

28. Dobbs Ferry, N.Y., Oceana Publications, 1977. 2 vols.

of the Court and the International Commission of Inquiry are published in the two volumes entitled The Hague Court Reports,[29] 1st series, 1916, and 2d series, 1932. This series was continued by the United Nations publication, Reports of International Arbitral Awards,[30] which publishes the awards in English and French but has no cumulative index or table of cases. Volumes 1 to 11 of this set retrospectively covered 1902–1941. A comprehensive listing is found in the Survey of International Arbitrations, 1794–1970[31] which is a chronological arrangement of arbitrations showing the decision or other disposition of the case. Two appendices provide information on ad hoc settlements as well as certain European regional tribunals and the military tribunals of Nürenberg and Tokyo. J. B. Moore compiled another selective publication, History and Digest of the International Arbitrations to Which the United States Has Been a Party . . . ,[32] in six volumes.

The first formal international court, universal in nature, was the Permanent Court of International Justice. It was created in 1920 in conjunction with (though not a part of) the League of Nations and continued its activities from 1922–1940. Six series of publications were issued by the Permanent Court, as follows: A.—Judgments; B.—Advisory Opinions; C.—Acts and Documents Relating to Judgments and Opinions; D.—Acts and Documents Concerning the Organization of the Court; E.—Annual Reports; F.—Indexes. A four-volume annotated compilation of the decisions and advisory opinions of the Permanent Court, 1922–1942 was edited by Manley O. Hudson and is entitled World Court Reports, 1922–1942.[33]

The present International Court of Justice, the principal judicial organ of the United Nations, was established by the Charter of that organization. It operates independently under its own statute, contrary to the other main organs of the United Nations. To assure judicial continuity and that the decisions of the Permanent Court would be available to the Court of Justice, there is a particular reference in the ICJ Statute to the Statute of the Permanent Court. The ICJ handles few cases and while their decisions are not binding as precedent, except on the parties to the case, there is no appeal. If, however, there is new evidence, the parties may request a revision of the judgment. The Court may render advisory opinions on any legal question submitted to it by the U.N. General Assembly, Security Council or other specialized U.N. agencies. There are five series of publications

29. New York, Oxford University Press, 1916, 1932. 2 vols.

30. New York, United Nations, 1948– .

31. A. Stuyt, Survey of International Arbitrations, 1794–1970. Dobbs Ferry, N.Y., Oceana Publications, 1972.

32. Washington, D.C., G.P.O., 1898. 6 vols.

33. Washington, D.C., Carnegie Endowment for International Peace, 1934–1943. 4 vols.

of the ICJ: 1. Reports of Judgments, Advisory Opinions and Orders; 2. Pleadings, Oral Arguments, Documents; 3. Acts and Documents Concerning the Organization of the Court: 4. Yearbook; 5. Bibliography.

The first series is issued at the outset in the form of advance sheets and then as an annual bound volume which has an index. The fourth series has information on the ICJ itself, such as organization, finances and biographical information on judges. The Bibliography has only been issued as a fifth series since 1964, since prior to that time it was included as a part of the Yearbook. A separate series, designated D, which is carried over from the Permanent Court, includes the rules of the Court. One should remember, however, that there are no series A, B or C in the publications of the ICJ.

Digests of the ICJ opinions have been privately published. One by Edvard Hambro is entitled Case Law of the International Court,[34] which includes passages taken from the court's decisions. Another, edited by K. Marek, is called A Digest of the Decisions of the International Court.[35] Volume 1 of this last title contains summaries of essentially all cases brought before the Permanent Court, giving the facts and listing the main issues raised in each case.

There are also other international tribunals associated with regional cooperative organizations such as the Court of Justice of the European Communities (discussed at §29.10 *infra*), and the European Commission and Court of Human Rights.[36] This latter organization, established by the European Convention for the Protection of Human Rights and Freedoms, is a court of last resort when human rights complaints cannot be settled by the Commission. Decisions of the Court, though few in number, are selectively published or summarized in the Yearbook of the European Convention on Human Rights[37] since 1955. The decisions appear in both English and French. A mimeographed series of the decisions is also issued by the Court in Series A — Judgments and Decisions and Series B — Pleadings, Oral Arguments, Documents. These series appear on a much

34. E. Hambro & A. W. Rovine, The Case Law of the International Court. Leiden, Sijthoff, 1952– . Volume 1 covers cases up to 1952; volume 2 covers the period 1952–1958; volume 3 contains individual and dissenting opinions, 1947–1958; volumes 4 and 5 contain excerpts from the majority of the Court as well as from dissenting and separate opinions, 1959–1963 and 1964–1966; volume 6 covers judgments, advisory opinions and orders of the Court including dissenting and separate opinions for the period 1967–1970; volume 7, in two books, covers the period 1971–1972.

35. The Hague, Nijhoff, 1974– .

36. A new international Court patterned after the European Court of Human Rights was created by a treaty which came into force in 1978. Called the Inter-American Court of Human Rights, it will have seven judges elected from the Organization of American States Assembly and will usually hear cases brought by the Inter-American Commission on Human Rights. Eleven nations, excluding the United States, have thus far ratified this treaty.

37. The Hague, Nijhoff, 1955– .

more timely basis than the Yearbook which is often two years late. A complementary publication is the Digest of Case-Law Relating to the European Convention on Human Rights[38] (1955–1967) which contains summaries or extracts from the "more important" decisions of the Commission, Court, and Committee of Ministers for this period.

A significant part of the corpus juris of international law is also found in local decisions of the courts in various countries. A comprehensive, though selective, publication of many of these decisions is Lauterpacht's International Law Reports,[39] which was preceded by the Annual Digest and Reports of Public International Law Cases[40] covering 1919–1949. This set is current in over 50 volumes. Decisions of many international tribunals as well as international courts are included. There are separate consolidated indexes to volumes 1–35 (1919–1967) in 2 volumes and volumes 36–45 (1968–1972) in a single volume. These indexes are arranged by country and by court or tribunal and also have consolidated tables of cases and treaties.

Publications of individual national collections of international law cases are few in number. A recent contribution is Francis Deak's American International Law Cases, 1783–1968.[41] Published in 18 volumes, the set has full reprints of cases from both federal and state courts, but not decisions of administrative agencies. They are arranged under the major branches of public international law. The cases included are selective in that the "editor omitted cases which do not contain any real discussion of international law." There is a table of cases in each volume, and a separate index volume is projected.

The British counterpart is British International Law Cases,[42] edited by the scholar Clive Parry, and is complete in 9 volumes. Six volumes cover 1607–1950, and the three supplementary volumes cover 1950–1970. Coverage is limited to decisions of courts in the British Isles and the Judicial Committee of the Privy Council. Conflicts and prize cases have been generally omitted, as have cases on war and neutrality. The arrangement follows the classification scheme of Lauterpacht's International Law Cases set. Each volume has an index, and there are also a cumulative index and a table of cases in the final volume.

An extension of the above British work, also edited by Clive Parry, is entitled Commonwealth International Law Cases.[43] The editor has described this set as "something between a collection and a selection

38. Heule, Belgium, Editions Administratives, 1970.

39. London, Butterworths, 1919– . E. Lauterpacht became editor beginning with volume 25 in 1958.

40. *Id.* Title of earlier volumes varies. From 1919–1932, it was Annual Digest of Public International Law Cases.

41. Dobbs Ferry, N.Y., Oceana Publications, 1971–1978. 20 vols.

42. London, Stevens, 1964–1970. 9 vols.

43. C. Parry and J. Hopkins, Commonwealth International Law Cases. Dobbs Ferry, N.Y., Oceana, 1974–

of decisions having reference to questions of international law, of courts of countries at any time belonging to the Commonwealth overseas." However, no cases in this series were published in the more comprehensive International Law Cases. Extradition practice and immigration cases are also omitted. The volumes issued to date have no indexes.

§29.7. Sources of international law: authoritative writings.

Writings of scholars or authorities in the area of international law are found in secondary sources such as treatises, periodicals, yearbooks and others. They serve the functions of defining the state of the law and also of influencing its development.

There are a number of classic authoritative texts in this field including, from Great Britain, International Law[44] by Lassa F. Oppenheim, published in 1905 originally, but now in its 8th edition, or Charles Hyde's International Law: Chiefly as Interpreted and Applied by the United States[45] in three volumes. The second revised edition was published in 1945 and reprinted in 1951. A good introductory one-volume work is James Brierly's Law of Nations.[46] The last edition was published in 1963. Private international law is covered in great detail in the British work by Dicey and Morris on The Conflict of Laws[47] and in O. Kahn-Freund's General Problems of Private International Law.[48] The Dicey work is particularly useful to the practitioner for its lucid statements of rules or propositions, comments and illustrations from leading cases. "Private International Law" is also covered in volume 3 of the International Encyclopedia of Comparative Law.[49] The sources in Chapter 2 are particularly useful.

A rather current treatise on American international conflicts of law is a two-volume work by Albert Ehrenzweig and Erik Jayme on Private International Law.[50] This title is comparative in its approach, presenting comments on civil and common law in the various countries as well as the 50 American states. This work also contains an extraordinary number of references to books and articles on a worldwide basis. The sixth edition of a Manual of International Law[51] by Professor Georg Schwarzenberger is a "presentation of the rules of

44. 8th ed., New York, Longmans, Green, 1955.
45. 2d rev. ed., Boston, Little, Brown, 1945. 3 vols.
46. 6th ed., New York, Oxford University Press, 1963.
47. 9th ed., London, Stevens, 1973. 1976 Supplement.
48. Leyden, Sijthoff, 1976.
49. Published under the auspices of the International Association of Legal Science, Tübingen, J. C. B. Mohr, 1971– .
50. Leyden, Sijthoff, 1967. 2 vols.
51. G. Schwarzenberger & E. D. Brown, A Manual of International Law. 6th ed., Milton, Professional Books Limited, 1976.

international, judicial and Anglo-American practice." This volume is particularly good for its extensive bibliographic references and its "Glossary of Terms and Maxims." It also contains "Study Outlines" for more in-depth reading on various subjects. The same author has provided a more voluminous study in his International Law as Applied by International Courts and Tribunals,[52] of which volumes I to III have thus far been published.

§29.8. Bibliographies.

In addition to those bibliographies found in treatises themselves, there are numerous individual bibliographies, many of them specialized, which list materials including texts, treaties and articles. One of the most comprehensive and current on public international law is Ingrid DeLupis' Bibliography of International Law.[53] This work is intended as a guide for students and practitioners. It generally excludes works prior to 1920 or later than 1974 except those described by the author as "classics" or "semiclassics" or "works on particularly important cases, treaties or incidents." Books and articles in many languages are arranged in a highly detailed classification scheme. Brief annotations are sometimes given, though not often.

Another relatively recent bibliography, comprehensive in scope, is by Jacob Robinson and is entitled International Law and Organization; General Sources of Information.[54] This publication, also devoted to public international law, differs from DeLupis in that the introductory notes preceding each subject section are more extensive and the frequency of annotations is greater. Citations to reviews of the latest edition of the work are also given. A unique feature is the information given on periodicals and other serials, as well as information on the history of international law societies and other organizations. There is an index of persons, areas and subjects.

A new bibliographic publication in the field of public international law began in 1976 and has been compiled by collaborators of the Max Planck Institute based on the holdings of their library. Public International Law: A Current Bibliography of Articles[55] serves the purpose of providing an extensive bibliography in specialized areas and facilitates "through its computer-produced index, the retrieval of literature from the whole field of public international law." There are two issues per year.

The African Law Bibliography, 1947–1966,[56] also has sections

52. 3d ed., London, Stevens, 1957.
53. London, Bowker, 1975.
54. Leiden, Sijthoff, 1967.
55. New York, Springer-Verlag New York, Inc., 1976– .
56. Bruxelles, Presses Universitaires de Bruxelles, 1972.

devoted to both public and private international law including books and articles relevant to African countries. Supplementation is found in the Annual Survey of African Law.[57]

There are other related and subject bibliographies which deserve mention. In 1972 the American Society of International Law encouraged and supported the publication of Social Science Literature: A Bibliography for International Law[58] due to the indication of practitioners and professors "that they would like to make use of the findings of social scientists that are relative to their work." Both articles and books with annotations from 1955–1965 (with a few more current entries) are included and arranged by social science research concepts. The Association of American Law School's Law Books Recommended for Libraries[59] includes in number 46 and its 1976 supplement an annotated listing of books and documents recommended for law school collections in the public international law field. In this publication, social science literature has been expressly omitted. Foreign and comparative law materials are covered in the comprehensive bibliography on "non-common law legal systems" compiled by Charles Szladits. A Bibliography on Foreign and Comparative Law: Books and Articles in English[60] consists of four volumes in five books, covering 1790–1971, with three annual supplemental paperback volumes for 1972–1974. Current materials are found in the winter issue of the American Journal of Comparative Law.[61] It is, therefore, intended to be a continuing series. This work contains a section on private international law and gives evaluative annotations in many instances.

Specialized subject bibliographies in any field are useful because of their in-depth surveys of the literature which may produce obscure, but helpful, sources. The international law field has several such tools. Two relatively current ones include The International Bibliography of Air Law, 1900–1971[62] and its 1972–1976 supplement. It should be noted that this work excludes references to titles relating to "space law, case law, legislation, treaty texts, or unpublished manuscripts." Criminal law as established through rules of international custom and agreement as well as domestic law is the subject of Dr. Bart de Schutter's Bibliography on International Criminal Law.[63]

57. London, F. Cass, 1967– .

58. W. Gould & M. Barkun, Social Science Literature: A Bibliography for International Law. Princeton, Princeton University Press, 1972.

59. South Hackensack, N.J., Fred B. Rothman, 1968.

60. Dobbs Ferry, N.Y., published for the Parker School of Foreign and Comparative Law, Columbia University, 1953– .

61. Berkeley, University of California, 1952– . Quarterly.

62. W. Heere, International Bibliography of Air Law, 1900–1971. Leyden, Sijthoff, 1972. Supplement 1972–1976. Leyden, Sijthoff, 1976.

63. Leiden, Sijthoff, 1972.

This 1972 work lists over 5000 items in all languages and is particularly strong in its materials on military war crimes and extraterritorial jurisdiction.

§29.9. Journals and yearbooks.

Most major countries have one or more significant periodical publications in the international law field. Many of them are found indexed in the Index to Legal Periodicals, the Index to Foreign Legal Periodicals, Harvard's Current Legal Bibliography, or in indexes such as the Canadian Index to Legal Periodical Literature.

The leading American periodical is the American Journal of International Law[64] which has been referred to earlier. This Journal contains not only substantive articles and editorials but case notes and book reviews and a summary of current United States policy and practice. Great Britain has the International and Comparative Law Quarterly[65] published by the British Institute of International and Comparative Law and also the Bulletin of Legal Developments; A Fortnightly Survey of U.K., European, Foreign, Commonwealth and International Legal Events.[66] The Comparative and International Law Journal of Southern Africa,[67] a relative newcomer, is published by the Institute of Foreign and Comparative Law at the University of South Africa.

Numerous American law schools and professional associations also publish periodicals with an international law emphasis. Examples include: Cornell International Law Journal, Law and Policy in International Business, Vanderbilt Journal of Transnational Law, Lawyer of the Americas, Journal of World Trade Law, and others. A list, though not complete, is found in Part II of A.A.L.S.'s Law Books Recommended for Libraries. Some of the law school periodicals have special features which may be especially useful. The Journal of International Law and Economics published by the National Law Center at George Washington University, beginning with Volume 11 (1976), contains a section called "Research Sources on International Law: Bibliographic Notes." This is a helpful tool aimed at bibilographically describing materials of practical value to practising attorneys.

Many national yearbooks on international law also provide information in the form of articles, reports on proceedings or conferences, pertinent documents or simply factual information about interna-

64. *Supra* note 3.
65. London, 1952– . Quarterly.
66. London, British Institute of International and Comparative Law, 1966– . Biweekly.
67. Pretoria, Institute of Foreign and Comparative Law, University of South Africa, 1968– . Three issues per year.

tional organizations. One of the oldest is the British Yearbook of International Law [68] which began publication in 1920. In addition to the substantive articles and notes found in this annual publication, there are sections devoted to decisions of British courts involving public and private international law, decisions of the European Commission and Court of Human Rights and, finally, the Court of Justice of the European Communities.

The Canadian Yearbook of International Law[69] published under the auspices of The Canadian Branch, International Law Association, contains information on Canadian practice in international law. There is also a useful digest of important domestic cases in the field of public and private international law. The Australian Year Book of International Law[70] is similar to those previously discussed, and there are many others including those for Italy, Japan, the Philippines, Poland, the Netherlands, and the Soviet Union.

Although not a yearbook in the traditional sense, the Annual Survey of South African Law[71] contains chapters on public international law and conflicts of law which summarize both legislative and decisional developments in that country. The Annual Proceedings published by the American Society of International Law may also be considered a type of yearbook containing papers and discussion from its yearly conference, which comment upon current international law developments.

Another useful yearbook of a factual nature is the Yearbook of International Organizations.[72] Governmental and non-governmental organizations the world over are described in this publication with information as to their addresses, objectives, structure, finance, publications, meetings and membership.

The Hague Academy of International Law also publishes a unique type of yearbook entitled Recueil des Cours.[73] It contains the lectures of leading international lawyers offered during the annual six-week sessions by the Academy. There are presently over 170 volumes in this series.

§29.10. European Communities laws and legal system.

Following World War II, six Western European countries, Belgium, France, the German Federal Republic, Italy, Luxembourg, and the Netherlands, took steps toward political and economic integration.

68. London, Oxford University Press, 1920/21– .
69. Vancouver, University of British Columbia, 1963– .
70. Sydney, Butterworths, 1965–.
71. Cape Town, Juta, 1948– .
72. Brussels, Union of International Associations, 1948– .
73. Académie de Droit International, Recueil des Cours. Leiden, Sijthoff, 1923– .

Three European organizations, referred to as Communities, were formed by those countries under separate treaties but with certain common organs for coordination of policies. The three Communities are: the European Coal and Steel Community (ECSC), created by a treaty effective July 25, 1952; the European Economic Community (EEC or Common Market) and the European Atomic Energy Community (EURATOM), the latter two created by treaties effective January 1, 1958. Two organs or institutions are common to all three Communities: the Court of Justice and the European Parliamentary Assembly. Prior to the Merger Treaty which came into force on July 1, 1967, each of the Communities had its own executive institution. The merger, however, created a single Council of Ministers and a single Commission which now serve all three organizations. Several other bodies have also been established which assist in the work of the Communities. These include the Economic and Social Committee, a Consultative Committee, a Monetary Committee, a Budgetary Policy Committee, and others. The European Investment Bank was also created by the 1957 EEC Treaty.

Under the provisions of the basic treaties other European states may join each Community if they receive the unanimous consent of all member States. Since 1973, Denmark, Ireland, and the United Kingdom have joined; and other countries, including Greece and Turkey and certain African nations, have become associated with the Communities by special conventions. For an introductory discussion of the framework and laws of the Communities, one may refer to A Guide to European Community Law by P. Mathijsen[74] or Lasok and Bridges' An Introduction to the Law and Institutions of the European Communities.[75]

1. *Basic Documents*. The primary law of the Communities is found in the treaties which created them and their amending documents. The language of the basic treaties is the original four languages, French, German, Dutch and Italian. (Danish and English, as official languages, were added in 1973.) Official publication of the original treaties can be found in the national treaty series of the original member states and in a publication issued by the Official Publications Office of the European Communities, entitled Treaties Establishing the European Communities; Treaties Amending These Treaties; Documents Concerning the Assession.[76] This title is available in the original languages and in English, Irish and Danish. The three basic treaties were also published as Command Papers (Cmnd. 5179 and 5189).

74. 2d ed., London, Sweet and Maxwell, 1975.

75. D. Lasok & J. Bridge, An Introduction to the Law and Institutions of the European Communities. 2d ed., London, Butterworth, 1976.

76. Luxembourg, Official Publications Office, 1973.

Additionally, there are unofficial publications which include the basic documents in English. One such publication is the 3d edition of Sweet & Maxwell's European Community Treaties,[77] which includes the texts as amended by the Merger, Budgetary and Assession Treaties. The Encyclopedia of European Community Law,[78] edited by K. R. Simmonds, contains in its B volume the translated text of the basic treaties, as well as the numerous treaties entered into by the Communities with non-member states, and those relevant treaties entered into among member states themselves. Other volumes in this Encyclopedia include United Kingdom sources and regulations, directives and other secondary legislation of the Communities.

2. *The Parliament*. The European Parliamentary Assembly is composed of 198 members chosen from the member states on a proportional representation basis and meets several times a year. It is part of the legislative process, though it is not in fact the legislature. Matters frequently discussed by the Assembly include budgets for Committees, reports submitted, and political problems or disputes between members. Parliamentary debates are published in an Annex or supplement to the Official Journal of the European Communities Series C (Communications et Informations). Other important parliamentary matters included in series C are the minutes of proceedings and the working documents which contain the reports of Parliamentary committees and also legislative proposals. This supplement includes an annual subject and member index and also contains a list of the working documents dealt with by the Parliament. Annual indexes of parliamentary questions by subject and author are issued, and the texts of all Resolutions passed by the Parliament in a sessional year are printed in a separate publication.

Since 1968 the Official Journal of the European Communities[79] has been issued in two parts as Series C and Series L. Series L contains the regulations and directives. It should be noted that regulations are the more important since they are binding on all member states. The Official Journal as the major publication of the Communities is published on a daily basis in the original four languages plus Danish and English since 1973. Each part is color-coded so that those in lilac are in English, while those in blue are in French. Pagination of the Official Journal is separate for each issue since July 1, 1967, and therefore citations must include the number of the issue and its date.

77. London, Sweet & Maxwell, 1977.

78. London, Sweet & Maxwell, 1973– . Loose-leaf. Volume A, United Kingdom Sources is in one loose-leaf binder; volume B, European Community Treaties, is in three binders; and volume C, Community Secondary Legislation, is in five binders.

79. European Communities, Journal Officiel. Luxembourg, 1958– . (Vols. 1–15, 1958–1972 in French, German, Dutch and Italian only; the English edition begins with vol. 16, 1973.)

A Special Edition of the Official Journal has been officially published in Danish and English covering the period 1952–1972 in two series. The first series is an official translation and includes all items in force on January 1, 1973. For items not in force on that date, one would have to consult an unofficial translation or one of the non-English versions of the Official Journal. The second series of the Special Edition is a subject arrangement of the secondary legislation for 1952–1970. There is also an alphabetical Subject Index and Numerical List[80] to the Special Edition published by H.M.S.O. The Special Edition contains references to the number and page of the text as found in the original language versions of the Official Journal.

Since 1975, a monthly alphabetical index to both Series L and Series C of the Official Journal has been issued in all 6 languages. An Annual Index for 1973 and 1974 is also available in English from the Official Publications Office.

The work of the Parliament is reviewed annually since 1959 in its yearbook entitled Annuaire.[81] This work also contains biographical information about the representative members. Its organization and procedures are described in the 1973 publication by B. Cocks, The European Parliament.[82]

3. *Council of Ministers and the Commission*. The Council of Ministers is composed of a representative from each member state and is the final policy-making body. The decisions of the Council, however, are made, based on proposals from the Commission, usually unanimously. The Commission is composed of representatives from all member states and has assumed the former powers of the High Authority of the ECSC and of the Commissions of the EEC and EURATOM. The Commission has a President and five Vice-Presidents. Its duties are to recommend and implement the policies of the Communities and generally supervise the common market, acting only as individuals and not as representatives of their respective countries. The Commission makes an annual report to the Parliamentary Assembly. The Council of Ministers also publishes an annual report. Both of these annual reports are available through the Publications Office.

The Secretariat of the Commission also issues a monthly Bulletin of the European Communities[83] with supplements which give information about the work of the Communities, draft legislation, a publications list, a listing of documents published in the Official Journal, and the docket of the Court of Justice. The supplements, which are

80. London, 1973.
81. Annuaire-manuel. Luxembourg, 1958/59– .
82. London, H.M.S.O., 1973.
83. Luxembourg, Secretariat of the Commission, 1968– . Monthly. This supersedes the European Economic Community Bulletin and the European Coal and Steel Community Bulletin.

not published with each issue, are important as they print significant reports or studies, speeches and selected draft legislation and regulations. There is an annual index to both the Bulletin and its Supplements. Proposals for legislative acts of the Council are published in Series C of the Official Journal.

4. *The Court of Justice.* The judicial function of the Communities is performed by the Court of Justice which was established on October 7, 1958. This Court serves only the Communities with regard to resolving disputes between member states or between institutions of the Communities or cases where the Communities sue or are sued in tort or contract. The Court will also hear matters referred to it by national courts concerning the interpretation of Community law. The law which it applies is generally the law of the treaties rather than domestic or international law, since it is the separate applicable treaty provisions that are the jurisdictional basis by which the Court serves the three Communities. There are nine judges on the Court, appointed for six years, who are assisted by four advocates-general. The advocates-general render detailed documented opinions or conclusions on cases submitted to the Court and therefore are an important source of Community law. A distinctive feature which distinguishes this Court from the previously mentioned international courts is the fact that any judgment against a party who is not a member state is enforceable as a local court judgment in the party's state. As for member states, there are provisions for sanctions in the Treaty ranging from fines to loss of rights under the Treaty. Although not bound by precedent, the Court generally follows its prior judgments. An interesting and current introductory work on the Court, describing its jurisdiction and procedures, is by L. Neville Brown, The Court of Justice of the European Communities.[84]

Decisions of the Court and submissions of the advocates-general were published officially in the four original languages, beginning in 1954, in Recueil de la Jurisprudence de la Cour.[85] Since 1973 there has also been an English translation called Reports of Cases Before the Courts. An English translation of cases from 1962–1968 has also been published by the Official Publications Office. The annual volume of the current reports includes a subject index and an index of legal provisions judicially considered. There is also a 1973 Compendium of Case Law Relating to the European Communities[86] which contains summaries of Court decisions and decisions of domestic courts applying Community law, compiled by H. Sperl and H. J.

84. L. N. Brown & F. Jacobs, The Court of Justice of the European Communities. London, Sweet & Maxwell, 1977.

85. Luxembourg, 1954– . Also published in German, Dutch, and Italian.

86. H. Sperl & H. Eversen. Compendium of Case Law Relating to the European Communities, 1973–1975. Amsterdam, Elsevier North Holland, 1975. English edition by J. A. Usher. 3 vols.

Everson, and translated by J. A. Usher into English in 1975. A work which contains English translations of decisions from 1958 to 1962 is The Court of Justice of the European Communities[87] by D. G. Valentine. Volume 1 of Valentine's work is a comprehensive study of the history, jurisdiction, and procedures of the Court. The Common Market Law Reports[88] contains selected decisions of the Court in English from 1962 and also contains English translations of domestic court cases concerning Community law. The Commerce Clearing House three-volume loose-leaf service, Common Market Reporter,[89] also contains the text of selected Court decisions in English. This service is updated biweekly and also includes regulations, treaties, and summaries of the pertinent national legislation of the European members. Other works useful in locating case materials, as well as other information, include Common Market Law[90] by A. Campbell, which is a comprehensive treatise covering all aspects from treaties to legislation to case law. The main work and its supplements cover the period up to 1973. Beginning in 1973 the European Law Digest[91] has provided an analytical summary of the major Court decisions, domestic court decisions, national legislation, and Community directives and regulations.

Court rules are found in the publication, Selected Instruments Relating to the Organization, Jurisdiction and Procedure of the Court.[92] Other information about the Court is available in the pamphlet issued by the Court, entitled The Court of Justice of the European Communities.[93] The Court also issued a Bibliography of Works on European Integration[94] with supplements from 1966–1974 and in 1965 a Bibliography of European Case Law[95] with supplementation from 1967 through 1973.

Analytical comments on current developments in Community law can be found in several secondary sources. There are at least two periodicals which emphasize the common market and Community law. The European Law Review[96] issues have regular article coverage of the Communities with a "Current Survey" of legal develop-

87. London, Stevens, 1965. 2 vols.
88. Edinburgh, T. Nelson, 1962– . Monthly.
89. Chicago, Commerce Clearing House, 1965– . Loose-leaf. 3 vols. Biweekly.
90. London, Longmans, 1969–1973. 3 vols.
91. London, Common Law Reports, 1973– .
92. 2d ed., rev., Luxembourg, Official Publications Office. 1965.
93. Luxembourg, Official Publications Office, 1975.
94. Court of Justice of the European Communities. Publications juridiques concernant l'intégration européenne, 1952–1966. The Hague, Documentation Service of the Court of Justice, 1966. Supplements for 1967, 1968, 1971, 1974.
95. Court of Justice of the European Communities. Bibliography of European Case Law, Comprising Judicial Decisions Relating to the Treaties Establishing the European Communities. The Hague, Documentation Service of the Court of Justice, 1965. Supplements for 1967, 1968, 1969, 1970, 1973.
96. Andover, Eng., Sweet & Maxwell, 1975– . Six issues per year.

ments in the Communities and member states. The British Institute of International and Comparative Law has, since 1963, published the Common Market Law Review.[97] This quarterly publication contains, in addition to substantive articles, information on Court of Justice decisions and Community legislation.

An extensive bibliography of publications is a Catalog of the Collection of the European Economic Community,[98] in the Northwestern University School of Law Library. This compilation, assembled by M. Pryjma, is an excellent guide to basic documents as well as secondary sources.

97. London, Stevens, 1963– . Quarterly.
98. Chicago, Northwestern University School of Law Library, 1975.

30 Coordinating the Research Techniques

§30.1. Approaches to finding the law.

Finding the law may be compared to playing golf. Seldom does a player make a hole in one or cover the course by use of a single club. Similarly, most legal research problems require the use of more than one source and index to the law. Seldom is one approach a sufficient safeguard upon either the scope or the completeness of a search. The skillful and imaginative interplay of the various means of finding the law is the mark of the successful searcher. Since the various techniques involved in finding and evaluating specific legislation and cases have been described in the preceding chapters, a knowledge of them is assumed here. The aim of this chapter, accordingly, is to suggest some of the many possibilities of combining techniques in the solution of typical problems.

As explained in Chapter 1, the aim of all legal research is to find mandatory and persuasive authority in an efficient and thorough fashion. Lawyers are chiefly concerned with the discovery of mandatory authority. In particular, they seek mandatory authority which cannot be factually distinguished from their case. In the absence of clear mandatory authority, however, they rely heavily upon persuasive authority which will support their case. A lawyer's legal research techniques should be shaped in accordance with these goals.

This book presents, below, six approaches to legal research. To a large degree, a person's decisions regarding research techniques are a matter of personal taste and judgment. You should acquaint yourself with these techniques outlined below but feel free to develop your own method of combining various research tools. More important than following any step-by-step procedure is the development of thorough and efficient research habits and a familiarity with the variety of research tools so that you accomplish your goal efficiently without sacrificing thoroughness.

1. *Table of cases approach*. This is a common and extremely significant approach to discovering the case law. Case tables are found in almost every publication which prints, discusses or cites reported cases. A case in point is the chief aim of most searches. Once a case in point is found, some of the other approaches may usually be abandoned or modified. Through a digest, one case in point leads to other cases in point or to a detailed analysis of that and similar cases in a treatise, law review or annotation.

a. *Utility of case tables in the search for the law: Information supplied*. Case tables supply the page number in the volume or advance sheet of law reports, casebook, periodical, treatise or annotation where a particular case is printed or discussed. They provide parallel case citations from one set of reports to another printing the same case. Tables lacking the volume and page citation of the case, but referring to the place in a book where the case is printed or discussed, lead by this one additional step to the full citation. Usually the full citation appears on the page where the case is printed or referred to in the work served by the table. The case table in a digest lists the digest topic or topics and the section numbers under which a case is digested. (If the Reporter is available to the searcher, it should be consulted for the topic and section or the Key Number given in the headnote of the report.) In some way, the searcher has found a case or the name of a case in point and wants to read similar cases. The digest table of cases supplies the topics and section numbers under which these are digested.

Similarly, the case table may lead to the place in a treatise, legal periodical or annotation where a case is discussed. Treatises commonly provide case tables. Case tables may also be found in the Index to Legal Periodicals and the A.L.R. Digests (leading to an A.L.R. annotation). General legal encyclopedias and annotated statutes commonly lack tables of cases, however. Thus, the table of cases approach is not available for most legal encyclopedias and annotated statutes.

b. *Alphabetizing case tables*. The alphabetizing practices in case tables lack uniformity and consistency. Some frequently applied principles are described below, but the searcher must always be prepared to find that a particular case table does not apply them. Thus, searchers must always exercise ingenuity in order to find particular cases in a table of cases. The material below follows the presentation order, though not the content, of the very full Explanatory Notes at pages v and vi of the table of cases volume of the A.L.R. Permanent Digest.

(1) Corporations, associations and partnerships. Alphabetizing is by full corporate or partnership name, as *American Brake Shoe Co.* v. *Bowles*. However, where a name begins with the name of a person, as *E. I. Du Pont de Nemours & Co.*, there are three variant practices. (a) Index exactly as written above. (b) Place the initials at the end of the surname, and index by the surname: *Du Pont de Nemours (E. I.)* & Co. (c) Cross-reference from (a) above: *E. I. Du Pont de Nemours & Co.* See *Du Pont de Nemours (E. I.) & Co.*

(2) Railroads, street railways, insurance companies. The common practice here is to spell out the first word of the title and to give the full name in abbreviated form. *Chicago, R. I. & P. R. Co.* v. *New York L. Ins. Co.*

(3) Cities, counties, states, territories. There is no consistency among indexes here. "City of New Orleans" in one table may be filed under "City," in another as "New Orleans." Most case tables are fairly liberal with cross-references from one form to the other.

(4) *Ex rel., Use of.* Usually there is a cross-reference from the relator's name. Thus, *State of New York ex rel. Zagayko* v. *Pechefsky* is filed under State of New York, but cross-referenced from *Zagayko* v. *Pechefsky*. *Use-of* cases are similarly treated. Titles beginning with "State . . . ex rel." are alphabetized by relator and are filed at the end of other "State" cases. Thus, *State* v. *Zolantikis* precedes *State ex rel. Adams* v. *Lee*.

(5) *Ampersand* (&). This is alphabetized as "and" in most tables. In some, however, titles containing it are filed after all others bearing the words preceding it. Thus, *Borden's Will, Re* precedes *Borden & Co.* in such tables.

(6) *Abbreviations.* These are treated as though spelled out: Ft.— Fort; St.— Saint; Mt.— Mount. M', Mc, Mac are usually all treated as though spelled "Mac" and so alphabetized. Some tables, however, file by the letters with a cross-reference from "Mac."

(7) *Ex parte, In re, Matter of, Estate of.* All are filed under the party's name with a cross-reference from the prefix.

(8) *Numerals.* These are filed as though spelled out. Numbers (principally dates and street numbers) which are commonly expressed in hundreds are filed as follows:

1690 Longfellow Ave.	Sixteen hundred ninety
1676 Claremont Ave.	Sixteen hundred seventy-six
1942 Chevrolet Motors Co.	Nineteen hundred forty-two
19 Rector St. Corp.	Nineteen Rector St.Corp.
1935 East 71st St. Corp.	Nineteen hundred thirty-five Seventy-first St. Corp.

Although this results in case names being filed out of numerical order, numerals are filed in this fashion in many case tables.

(9) *Filing by "letter" or by "word."* Filing according to the exact succession of letters, regardless of any ensuing word division, is called "filing by letters." "Filing by words" recognizes the word division and thus results in a different filing order. It is the system employed by telephone directories. The two systems are illustrated below.

By Letters	*By Words*
N. E. Wentworth Co.	N. E. Wentworth Co.
Newhart Mfg. Co.	New Haven
New Haven	New York
Newman	Newhart Mfg. Co.
New York	Newman

(10) "De," "Du," "Van," "Von." Most case tables treat the prefix as an integral part of the name. Thus, "De Groot," "Dennis," "Devlin," "De Witt," "Van Cott," "Vancouver," "Van de Carr," are filed in that order.

c. *Plaintiff-defendant tables.* This is the usual type of table of cases. Except in digest case tables, the only information commonly given in such tables is the page where the listed case is printed or referred to in the work containing the table — except that parallel citations to all standard reports of the case are also given. Generally, citations appear in the following order: official, National Reporter System, and selective cases system (A.L.R.). In a digest table, the information usually includes not only the parallel citations but also the direct classification topics and sections under which the digest of the case is found. In many digests it also includes certain citator information concerning the history of the case — i.e., whether the case has been affirmed, reversed, etc., on appeal within the period of time covered by the table. Sometimes a digest table of cases fails to record the A.L.R. citation of a case because the case was not printed in A.L.R. until after the digest table of cases was compiled. A surer parallel citation guide is in Shepard's Citations. A typical digest table of cases entry is Exhibit 109, from the seventh Decennial Digest table of cases.

Harrington v. State, TexCivApp, 385 SW2d 411, rev 407 SW2d 467, cert den 87 SCt 977—Admin Law 385; App & E 837(2), 970(2), 1041(2), 1047(4), 1051(1); Atty Gen 7; Const Law 303; Costs 69, 101, 237; Crim Law 1214; Discov 46; Evid 28, 65, 150; Mines 92.8, 92.15, 92.23, 92.42, 92.56, 94, 97, 100; Penalties 4, 32, 33; Plead 34(3), 248(15), 251, 290(3); Statut 223.2(1); Trial 71, 194(9, 20), 215, 216, 219, 283, 350(1, 3, 8).

Exhibit 109

Some digests omit the names of cases for which no printed opinion is given in the report because there is nothing to digest. Most digests, however, include the names of even memorandum cases which are not digested. The Decennial Digests list such a case when the memorandum decision is connected with another case which is digested.

d. *Defendant-plaintiff tables*. These tables, a comparatively recent development in case tables, frequently supply less information than the plaintiff-defendant tables. Often they refer only to the plaintiff-defendant entry, which must then be searched in its table for the full information. The value of these tables is that when only the defendant's name is known, the case can still be found by case name.

e. *Popular-name tables*. Where the only available reference to a case is by some title such as *Hot Oil Case* or *Nitro-Glycerine Case*, a popular-name table is essential. Shepard's Acts and Cases by Popular Names, Federal and State, gives parallel citations to all standard report series for such cases. Beginning with the Second Decennial Digest and ending with the Sixth Decennial Digest, each Decennial has had such a table in the Table of Cases volume, as do many of the regional and local digests. In some, such as the Digest of the United States Supreme Court Reports, L. Ed., the popular name appears with a cross-reference in the regular plaintiff-defendant table. Thus: *Hot Oil Case*. See *Panama Refining Co.* v. *Ryan*.

f. *Official-to-Reporter and Reporter-to-Official citation tables*. Where only the official or Reporter citation is known, parallel citations may be found in the appropriate Shepard's Citations unit. The transfer tables in the National Reporter System Blue Book and Blue and White Books, as described in §14.5.2a, b, perform the same function.

g. *Patents and trademark tables*. Tables of adjudicated patents and trademarks are found under "Patents" and "Trademarks," respectively, in the Decennial Digests, the Modern Federal Practice Digest (and its precursor, the Federal Digest), and in the Federal Supplement, Federal Reporter, and Supreme Court Reporter. Shepard's United States Citations, Patents and Trademarks has a similar table, as does the digest of the United States Patents Quarterly.

h. *American Digest System case tables*. By far the most complete tables of American cases are those in the units of the American Digest System. This system purports to list every case digested or connected with a case which is digested in all standard report series covered, from 1658 to date. If the case date is unknown, it may be necessary to search in all Decennial units. All cases from 1658 to 1906 are listed in volumes 21 to 25 of the First Decennial Digest. From 1906, each succeeding Decennial has its own table. Each monthly pamphlet and bound volume of the supplementing General Digest has its table of cases, which will cumulate into the next Decennial table. A complete table of cases search may comprise all of these units. Citation information given may include notice of affirmance, reversal, certiorari grant or refusal, dismissal, rehearing, and several other court actions on the listed case within the decennium. Beginning with the Second Decennial Digest and ending with the Sixth Decennial Digest, there has also been a table of cases by popular name printed in the table of cases volume for cases digested in each decennium. For some new topics, such as "Workman's Compensation," special tables of cases are provided which embrace all case names from the earliest digest topics now included in the new ones. The proper use of such tables is described in §16.5.

i. *Legal periodicals case tables*. Since 1917, cases discussed in law reviews have been listed in the Index to Legal Periodicals. Since 1928, case comments in the Legal Periodical Digest have been listed. Individual legal periodicals in both annual and cumulative indexes, commonly list case comments.

j. *Loose-leaf services case tables*. Most loose-leaf services have case tables, which are plainly tabbed as such so that they can be found easily.

k. *English and Canadian tables of cases*. These are described in Chapters 24 and 25.

1. *Statutes through the case approach*. Even when a statute is involved in a legal problem, the searcher usually searches for a case in point interpreting that statute and uses that case as a rallying point. The searcher wants to know how the courts have construed legislation applicable to the legal issue involved. A statute must be evaluated through judicial construction, which may be discovered not only through annotated statutes and citators but also through digests and other case indexes. Digests do not afford a direct lead to the construction of specific statutes (with a few exceptions such as the Table of Statutes Construed in the regional Reporter digests and similar tables in the Digest of the Supreme Court Reports, L. Ed.). However, cases construing statutes are digested by subject matter in the usual fashion. Whenever a statute is involved in a decision, it is cited in a headnote paragraph. This often leads searchers to statutes, the applicability of which was unsuspected by them. Thus the case approach can function as an important step in statutory construction.

2. *Key Number approach*. Since the Key Number in the Decennial Digests leads to other cases in point, once you have found a relevant Reporter case, you can easily locate in its headnote a pertinent digest paragraph or paragraphs and Key Numbers without further ado. As noted in §16.5, where an older digest topic has been expanded later or a new topic is created, the original Key Number has been discarded, and an additional step is necessary to find the presently applicable numbers.

The discovery of one pertinent Key Number should not lull the searcher into believing that all pertinent cases may be discovered through the use of that single Key Number. Frequently, case language concerning the same analytical topic will be assigned different Key Numbers or even different topics. Thus, for example, the requirement that married women assume their husband's surnames can be profitably explored in Names ⚷ 20 and Automobiles ⚷ 132 (surname requirement for driver's license); and just exploring Names ⚷ 20 would result in missing a significant case in point: *Whitlow* v. *Hodges*, 539 F.2d 582 (6th Cir. 1976).

In order to assure thoroughness, searchers should extract significant legal and factual elements from their problems. Each of these elements should be independently explored in the index to the various digests. The searcher should then examine all digest topics which appear relevant in order to determine if additional Key Numbers will be helpful. Because headnotes traditionally distill only the most important aspects of a court opinion, frequently relevant dicta (e.g., a dissenting opinion) will not be found through the use of Key Numbers. Although it contains these inherent limitations, the Key Number system functions as an efficient and invaluable research tool for those who use it wisely.

3. *Annotated Reports System approach*. Once an A.L.R. or Lawyers' Edition case in point is found, the searcher almost always has available an annotation on a point of law involved in it. In the annotation the publishers aim to examine all primary authority and significant secondary authority, so that a reader will find a comprehensive discussion of all cases in which this point of law has been adjudicated. The editor carefully analyzes the cases and comments on the various rules extracted from them. Annotations thus provide a great deal of preliminary information to the searcher.

4. *Fact or descriptive-word index approach*. This approach is described in §16.6.1b, under Digests. While usually associated with digests, it is by no means confined to them. Every statutory index uses the fact approach (including the indexes in the Federal Register System and its state counterparts for administrative regulations).

Annotated statutes combine a fact approach to the statutes (through their general subject indexes) with a similar and more direct approach to the cases interpreting many individual sections of the statutes. Special subject indexes to cases construing a particular statutory section are provided when that section contains a large number of digest paragraphs. That is, the mass of digest paragraphs for that section is arranged according to a subject classification. Then the digest paragraphs are indexed by catchword references to such minute subtopics as "change of basis," "death," "exhaustion," "severance damages," etc. An example from the United States Code

Ch. 2 **COURTS OF BANKRUPTCY** **11 § 11**

Notes of Decisions

III. RECEIVERSHIP IN STATE OR OTHER COURT

Subdivision Index

141. Generally

As a general rule where the appointment of a receiver is relied on as an act of bankruptcy, and bankruptcy proceedings are duly instituted, the jurisdiction

11 § 11
Note 149

149. Stockholder's or officer's suit

Stockholders of bankrupt corporation, by virtue of stock purchased in building corporation, held equitable interest in rents which court of equity could protect through receivership. Wolf v. De Wolf & Co., Inc., C.C.A.Ill.1931, 53 F.2d 990.

Receivership in stockholder's action, wherein receiver did not get possession of the assets before petition in bankruptcy, did not prevent jurisdiction of bankruptcy court from attaching. In re Hollywood Bond & Mortgage Co., D.C.Fla. 1931, 51 F.2d 255, 17 Am.Bankr.Rep.N.S. 616.

Pendency of stockholders' suit in state court and receiver's possession of corporate property does not deprive creditors of superior right to bankruptcy proceedings. In re Bartlett Oil & Gas Corporation, D.C.Okl.1930, 44 F.2d 616, 16 Am. Bankr.Rep.N.S. 512.

Exhibit 110

Annotated is shown in Exhibit 110. Note that in this example there are both a combined fact index for the entire title and one for each subtopic.

The descriptive-word index approach is also applicable to case reporters, encyclopedias, treatises, loose-leaf services, legal periodicals, and A.L.I. Restatements. Most A.L.R. 2d and 3d annotations are preceded by a fact index referring to the respective sections of the annotation. For example, the annotation to *Henningsen* v. *Bloomfield Motors*, 32 N.J. 358, 161 A.2d 69, 74 A.L.R.2d 1 (1960), on privity of contract as an element in products liability, has a three-page descriptive-word index in addition to a one-page table of jurisdictions represented. The subjects treated in the annotation, as listed in the index, range from "Abrasive wheel" to "Worm in canned food."

5. *Analytical or topic approach*. This approach has been discussed in detail in Chapters 16 and 17. Statutory compilations also make use of this approach. The analysis preceding the text of various titles and subtitles saves much time in arriving at the applicable section. See Exhibits 47 and 48.

6. *Words and phrases approach*. This approach, described in Chapter 21, is used in nearly all digests and encyclopedias. The West Publishing Company's Words and Phrases is a dictionary of common words and legal words of art as they have been judicially defined. In most other similar works an alphabetical index refers to the page where the listed word is defined. This approach is commonly used when the definition of a word or term is a significant factor.

7. *Treatises approach*. The following simple problem illustrates the function of treatises in leading the searcher to other sources of authority and in clarifying the points of law involved in a case in your casebook.

Your torts casebook has the case of Mrs. X, who purchased at her butcher shop a sealed package of sausages manufactured by the Y company. Although no negligence on the part of the manufacturer was found, the sausages were contaminated. This contamination resulted in the death of Mr. X, the husband. Mrs. X sues both the retailer and manufacturer. Your casebook points out the possible grounds for the action and defenses to it, but you are still somewhat at sea and wish a considerably fuller discussion of the issues (particularly concerning privity of contract and warranty between the consumer and the supplier of the product).

You are familiar with a typical student book, Prosser, Handbook of the Law of Torts.[1] The table of contents seems to indicate the pertinence of Chapter 16, Liability of Contracting Parties to Third Persons. Because that is a long chapter, however, you try a shorter approach: the subject index. You look under "Food," but find nothing there. Generally, the list of subjects and topics used in a treatise is

1. 6th ed., Mineola, New York, Foundation Press (1976).

not as extensive as in some other legal publications. After checking "Consumer" and "Privity of Contract" you find a lead under "Supplier of Chattels." Under "Supplier of Chattels—Liability to third person—food and drink," you are referred to page 653, where the various ramifications of the topic are discussed.

Desiring even more detailed discussions of the topic, with the latest cases in point and with indications of the jurisdictional trends, you consult a practitioners' book, such as Frumer and Friedman, Products Liability.[2] There, under the tab "Food and Beverages" in volume 1, a long chapter discusses the subject in minute detail and provides numerous citations to cases and to annotations.

§30.2. Order of search.

Although the mode of search in each case involves subjective judgment and varies somewhat with the fact situations, the following outline is suggested as a checklist of factors to bear in mind. The order given is logical, but often the circumstances of the search will dictate a different attack and the omission of some of the steps. All the steps in the outline below are necessary at one time or another, but seldom are all of them required in the solution of any single problem.

Do not underestimate the value of analyzing the problem and undertaking a preliminary review of the subject matter. A thorough analysis and review can frequently reduce the amount of time and energy expended in a search. Analysis often exposes hidden issues of which you were previously unaware. Secondary literature may provide helpful commentary on previous cases and may clarify the issues involved. The use of secondary literature, however, is never an effective substitute for first-hand examination of the case law.

1. *Suggested outline of search.*
   a. *Analysis of the problem.* Separate the problem into the various aspects involved. What are the substantive issues and facts? Are there procedural questions?
   b. *Preliminary review of the subject matter.* Examine secondary literature (periodicals, treatises, encyclopedias, Restatements, etc.) which will be helpful in providing an orientation to the problem and references to significant primary authority.
   c. *Search of statutes and administrative regulations involved.*
      (1) Federal statutes.
      (2) Home state statutes.
      (3) Other state statutes: collections and indexes across state lines; persuasiveness of cases construing.
      (4) Administrative regulations implementing statutes.
      (5) Finding legislative intent where helpful.

2. Albany, N.Y., Matthew Bender & Co., Inc. (1960), 2 vols. loose-leaf.

d. *Search for cases in point.*
   (1) Reading cases and orders cited by annotated statutes, periodicals, treatises, etc.
   (2) Finding additional cases through digests.
      (a) Through Key Numbers in Reporter cases read.
      (b) Table of cases approach.
      (c) Analytical or topical approach.
      (d) Fact approach.
      (e) Words and phrases approach.

e. *Search of secondary literature.* Look through periodicals, treatises, encyclopedias, etc., to refresh your memory, to supply additional cases, and to find analysis of the subject matter.

f. *Search of loose-leaf services.* If loose-leaf services are available in your problem area (especially in tax and regulatory fields), use them to coordinate and update your research.

g. *Search of miscellaneous materials.* Study A.L.I. Restatements, form books, government publications, etc.

h. *Completing the search.* Make certain that the latest editions and supplements have been consulted, including the digest portions of the National Reporter System advance sheets covering later cases than the General Digest.

i. *Appraising the authorities found.* Shepardize statutes and cases.

The accompanying search checklist has been found useful by the students of Professor Albert P. Blaustein, Rutgers University School of Law, South Jersey Division. With his permission it is reproduced here as Exhibit 111.

2. *Resourcefulness.* Since few extended legal searches progress smoothly, a most important weapon of searchers is resourcefulness. In the use of indexes they must remember that perhaps the indexer had a point of view different from theirs. Thus they must cast about for other words or terms under which their fact situations might have been listed. The same is true of the analytical approach. Often, what seems to the searcher a perfectly obvious classification for his or her point of law did not seem so at all to the digester, who may have a broader view of the whole topic. Even when a substantial number of cases on point have been found, searchers can seldom be certain that other cases just as applicable are not lurking under other entries or classifications. It does not pay to be either too easily discouraged or too quickly satisfied.

3. *Other factors to be considered.* Digest paragraphs, text expositions, or annotations are not the law; the cases should always be read. Note the parties involved, how the case arose, the pertinent statutes,

LEGAL BIBLIOGRAPHY CHECK LIST

Researcher ....
Memorandum for ....
Research: begun .... completed ....

Topic: ....

STATUTORY DATA

State Stat. Ann.	U.S.C.S.
State Code	U.S.C.A.
State Session Laws	U.S.C.C.A.N.
Current Legis. Serv.	Fed. Legis. Hist.
State Legis. Hist.	C.F.R.
State Adm. Code	and Fed. Reg.
and Reg./Bull.	Fed. Rules
State and Court Rules	Treaties
Uniform L. Ann.	Eng. Stat.
Municipal Ord.	Canadian Stat.

LATEST SOURCES Checked

	Name	Date
Pocket part		
Pocket		
Pamphlet Supp.		

DIGESTS

State	5th Gen. Digest
Regionals	8th Decennial
Sup. Ct.	7th Decennial
Mod. Fed. Pract. 2d	6th Decennial
Mod. Fed. Pract.	5th Decennial
Federal	4th Decennial
	3d Decennial
	2d Decennial
Eng. & Empire	Decennial
Canadian	Century

CATCH-WORD & PHRASES Checked

KEY-NUMBERS Checked

LATEST SOURCES Checked

	Name	Date
Digest pocket part		
Digest pocket part		
Advance Sheets		
Advance Sheets		
Descriptive Word Indexes		
General Digest: Vol. .... Month .... Year		

ANNOTATED REPORTS

ALR 3d	ALR Fed. pocket parts
ALR 3d pocket parts	L.Ed. 2d
ALR 2d	L.Ed. 2d p.p.
ALR	
ALR Federal	

ANNOTATIONS Checked

LATEST SOURCES Checked

	Date
ALR First Service	
ALR 2d & 3d Quick Index	
ALR 2d Later Case Service	
ALR 2d Digest	
ALR 2d Word Index	
ALR Red Books (Desk Book)	
ALR Blue Book	
ALR Permanent Digest	
ALR Federal Quick Index	
L.Ed. 2d Later Case Service	

MISCELLANEOUS

State Practice Books	Restatements
State Encyclopedias	Loose-leaf services
C.J.S.	Index to Legal Periodicals
Am. Jur. 2d New Topic Svc.	Shepards Citations
Am. Jur. 2d	Treatises
Am. Jur. Proof of Facts, 2d	Lexis
Am. Jur. Trials	Westlaw
Words and Phrases	

LEGAL PERIODICALS

Articles Checked — Topics Checked

TREATISES Checked (Pages and §§)

LATEST SOURCES Checked

	Name	Date
Index to Legal Periodicals		
Shepards		
Shepards		
Loose-leaf Service		
Loose-leaf Service		
Other		

NOTES

3030—Legal bibliography checklist 1-78

Exhibit 111

etc. Most of the references found must be discarded. In case work there is much chaff and little wheat.

4. *Care and accuracy*. The searcher should utilize a checklist or reminder of things to examine in the search in order to ensure completeness and accuracy. The Blaustein checklist reproduced above is a good one.

Prominent in any list should be an admonition to *copy citations and other data accurately and with sufficient fullness to be clear*—to you or to anybody else reading them. More time has probably been lost by lawyers and students because of inaccurate and incomplete copying of various data during searches than in any other way. That cryptic notation of yours which saves a few seconds in recording and seems initially so crystal clear to you will probably be incomprehensible at your desk later on when you wish to incorporate it in your brief or memorandum of law. Write it down as though you expected somebody else to have to decipher it.

Copy with reasonable fullness. Although this advice sounds unnecessary, its importance is clear to efficient legal researchers. Copying down a complete statute or case citation (including all parallel references) provides a significant check on accuracy. Thus: *Cohen* v. *Wypiski*, 599 N.Y. 301, 201 N.E.2d 518, 275 N.Y.S. 93, 201 A.L.R.2d (1970), instead of only 599 N.Y. 301. The more parallel references you have, the more chances there are that one or more of them will be correct. Care should be taken that all necessary units — including supplements, advance sheets, etc. — of a publication consulted are covered. In this connection, the careful searcher will *preserve a precise record of each publication and part thereof covered in a search*, as a measure of the completeness of the search and a safeguard against having to search the same publication twice.

§30.3. Illustrative problem involving statutes.

1. *The problem stated*. Your client, executor of the estate of a deceased partner, wishes to know his rights and duties. The partnership agreement contained a clause providing for the continuation of the business by the remaining partners after the death or retirement of one of them. There are also questions regarding the tax treatment of the partnership income. Thus, the following issues are involved: the rights, duties, and personal liabilities of the executor; the rights of the deceased partner's estate; the rights of the partners; and the tax liability to the federal and state governments. No question of procedure is involved.

2. *Preliminary review of the subject matter*. Through an elementary treatise or legal encyclopedia you learn that in the United States, legal issues regarding partnership, income taxation, and the liabilities of an executor are largely regulated by statute. You therefore begin by examining the statutes.

3. *Search of applicable federal and home state statutes*.

a. *Federal statutes: Partnership income tax*. Although this is a matter of both federal and state jurisdiction, only the federal taxation is considered for the purpose of this problem. The subject index of the United States Code leads to Title 26, where a reading of the law shows the tax of partners to be covered by Section 702. The annotations in the U.S.C.A. and the U.S.C.S. digest several promising cases which you read in full, including *Guaranty Trust Co. of N.Y.* v.

Commissioner, 303 U.S. 493, 58 S.Ct. 673, 82 L. Ed. 975 (1938).

b. *Continuing the partnership business*. The subject index of the annotated statutes of your state leads to the applicable sections covering your problem. The absence of case annotations shows that your courts have never construed these sections.

c. *Executor's personal liabilities*. The search here might begin with the annotated statutes of your state, with a local book on executors and administrators, or with a loose-leaf service on wills, trusts, and estates. You use the same techniques elaborated above in uncovering your state's answer to this question.

4. *Search of the statutes and decisions of other states*. You wonder if states other than your own have similar statutes which their courts have construed. If so, do their decisions have any weight as precedent in your state? You remember that there are numerous collections and indexes of statutes across state lines and that one of them is the Uniform Laws Annotated. From volume 7, Partnership, you learn that your state statute is copied from the Uniform Partnership Act.

a. *Authority of the decisions of other states*. You learn from the discussion in the topic "Statutes" in Am. Jur. or C.J.S. or a legal encyclopedia for your state that where a question of statutory construction is one of first impression in a state, the courts will generally consider the construction of similar statutes in other states by their courts. You therefore return to the Uniform Laws Annotated, where the index leads to Section 41 or Section 42 as probably covering the continuation of a partnership after the death of a partner. You observe that in searching the statute (as well as other search books), it is advisable to examine the material of more than one possibly applicable provision. In practice your problems are rarely pinpointed so that you can focus on one section alone.

The annotations turn up several cases reasonably in point, from different states. One, *Froess* v. *Froess*, 289 Pa. 69, 137 Atl. 124 (1927), seems especially promising, and you read it.

5. *Search of other indexes*. Since there is so much overlapping of subject matter in the law, there may be applicable cases not digested under the exact statutory section which, in your opinion, logically covers the matter. Also, some points raised by apparently inconsistent cases are not clear to you, so you decide to search other indexes to the law.

6. *Digest search*.

a. *Key Number approach*. Your reading of the *Froess* and *Guaranty Trust* cases in the Atlantic Reporter and the Supreme Court Reporter has given you some applicable headnotes with their pertinent Key Numbers. You then proceed directly to any appropriate West digest employing the Key Number classification. Sometimes the Key

Number classification has been expanded, or a new title has been added to the classification since the publication of your case. If your case headnote has been placed in a new classification or title, the Key Number found in the headnote of your case as published years ago no longer applies. Thus, in the American Digest System, the original Internal Revenue 🔑 7(3) of the *Guaranty Trust* case has been changed to Internal Revenue 🔑 834, following the great expansion of the Internal Revenue title after the adoption of the Internal Revenue Codes of 1939 and 1954. How to find the current Key Number classification in such cases is discussed in §16.5.

b. *Table of cases approach*. This approach is described in §26.1. No matter what digest is consulted, the table of cases will note all classification numbers under which a case is digested. In the American Digest System, knowing the date of decision is a time-saving lead to the proper table of cases unit. Otherwise, the searcher must check each decennial unit.

c. *Fact and analytical approaches*. Our partnership problem presents no special difficulties meriting full discussion. In the income tax aspect, however, the Key Number found (Internal Revenue 834) turns up a case in point, *Heiner* v. *Mellon*, 304 U.S. 271, 58 S.Ct. 926, 82 L. Ed. 1337 (1938). Note that this case was decided not under the Internal Revenue Code §182, but under a section of the Revenue Act of 1918 not in the Code at all. This shows that even in searching statutes, the digest subject analysis often leads to cases in point involving unsuspected applicable statutes or sections.

d. *Words and phrases approach*. Our problem does not seem to hinge in any way upon the judicial definition of a word or term.

7. *Annotated reports search*. Your task may have been partly performed for you if you can find your problem treated in an A.L.R. annotation. Accordingly, you turn to the A.L.R. and A.L.R.2d–3d Quick Indexes and to the Word Indexes to Annotations, where you find several annotations on partnership taxation. One in particular, "Construction of §42 of the Uniform Partnership Act as to the rights of parties where business is continued after a partner retires or dies," in 2 A.L.R.2d 1084 seems exactly in point. In it, the cases are analyzed from various aspects, including the effect of consent on continuation of the business (§2 of the annotation), and the effect of particular agreements (§4). The A.L.R.2d Supplement Service lists several later cases in point on these precise sections.

8. *Search of secondary literature*. After reading the cases and treatises found through the above means, you are still uncertain as to some aspects of your client's problem. In particular, *Guaranty Trust* and *Heiner* seem inconsistent, and you are not certain that they can be inconsistent, and you are not certain that they can be reconciled with one another. You know that legal periodicals provide a forum of

discussion of legal theory and that, in addition, specific cases are often discussed in detail. A search of the Index to Legal Periodicals reveals at least six leading articles dealing with various aspects of your problem. Weyher and Flom, Death and Income Taxes—The Demise of a Partner, 52 Colum. L. Rev. 695 (1952), sounds particularly good. You find in it that your cases and others in point are analyzed and the issues discussed at length. As is common in law review articles, this one gives in its footnotes a rather extensive review of the earlier literature. The Index to Legal Periodicals, under the heading of "Partnership," lists law review comments upon several other cases in point.

9. *Loose-leaf service or reporter search.* Because your problem involves both tax and estate matters, the loose-leaf publications described in Chapter 23 are particularly applicable.

10. *Appraising the value of authorities found.* Before writing your brief or memorandum of law, you Shepardize all cases and statutes on which you will rely. You realize that citing an overruled case for authority is a serious error; therefore you search *all* supplements in order to make sure that the authority on which you rely has not been overruled. For statutes, do not forget the Statutes Construed tables, because they may give you a later case than you have found elsewhere.

§30.4. Illustrative problem involving administrative law.

1. *The problem stated.* Your client has purchased a dairy farm and dairy which, until the purchase, had distributed general milk products in the New York marketing area. Desiring to add a line of frozen desserts, your client asks whether this new activity affects his legal status. You consider only the federal aspect of his question.

2. *Analysis of the problem.* This problem involves the production, processing, and marketing of milk and milk products in a given area. One possible issue is whether this marketing activity is regulated by federal legislation.

3. *Search of statutes and administrative regulations involved.*

a. *Federal statutes.* Because this is a matter of "public, general and permanent interest," you believe that the subject may be incorporated into the United States Code. You examine the index to the Code, where, under "Milk and Cream," you note several entries which lead you to 7 U.S.C. §608c. The text of §608c(5) suggests that your client, because of the new marketing activity, may be subject to federal regulation as a "handler" of milk products. Case annotations in both the U.S.C.A. and U.S.C.S. turn up cases close to the point, but you are still doubtful as to whether processors of their own milk into frozen desserts are "handlers" under the statute. Hoping that the regulations of the government agency concerned are more explicit, you search them.

b. *Administrative regulations.* Administrative regulations and the agency decisions implementing them change so rapidly that any outline of problem solving through them must describe only means and procedures. What follows, therefore, while typical of the procedures employed, may not be accurate as you now read it as to the designations of specific C.F.R. regulations in point, and is to be regarded only as showing a typical search, by way of example.

The United States Government Manual, described in §7.3.4, reveals that the regulatory body involved in our problem is the Agricultural Marketing and Consumer Service of the Department of Agriculture. You know, therefore, that the regulations you seek will be in the Code of Federal Regulations, Title 7, "Agriculture." Since this is an enormous title, you consult the annual General Index of the C.F.R. under "Milk and Milk Products," which refers you to Title 7, Parts 1001 to 1137. You then discover that for your convenience, Title 7 has been split into numerous "use units," one of which (covering the "Eastern Region") prints Regulations 7:1000 to 1029. A table in the front of this small volume tells you that New York regulations are in Part 1002. The separate and detailed table of contents for this Part tells you that "Handler" is treated in Part 1002.7, and "Frozen desserts" in Part 1002.114. Nothing in the pamphlet you have consulted covers references beyond January 1, 1977. You may examine two more tables to determine if the form of your two regulations has changed since that date: the List of C.F.R. Sections Affected, issued monthly, and the cumulative List of C.F.R. Parts Affected in the latest daily edition of the Federal Register (see §7.3.2b above). Through these, you check down to yesterday the present form of the two regulations in which you are interested.

Another way to find this regulation is through the parallel table leading from the United States Code sections to the corresponding regulations of the C.F.R. This table is found in the C.F.R. Index volume as described in §7.3.2c. Here the entry under 7 U.S.C. §608c (the section covering federal regulation of milk and cream) cites the regulations issued under authority of the statute. Checking (1) the C.F.R. latest pamphlet, (2) the List of C.F.R. Sections Affected, and (3) the cumulative List of C.F.R. Parts Affected in the Federal Register, you find that the regulation has not been renumbered or changed in text since 1977 and is still in the form in which it was printed in the 1977 revision of Title 7.

4. *Agency and judicial rulings search.* Because your question is a Department of Agriculture matter, your search leads to the Agriculture Decisions of the Department of Agriculture. This is a series of

reports printing both agency and court rulings construing both the above statute and the regulations issued under it. Each volume of Agriculture Decisions has an elaborate cumulative citator (by both federal statute and departmental regulation construed, and by subject) covering all court and agency decisions under the act with which you are concerned. The agency rulings give both the agency interpretation of "handler" and citations to Congressional hearings, reports, etc., indicating the legislative intent. Such citators, however, are found in few reports of administrative rulings. Constructions of such regulations must ordinarily be sought indirectly through digests, loose-leaf services, or Shepard's U.S. Administrative Citations. This Shepard's unit covers only a few of the many administrative agencies issuing decisions. For example, the Department of Agriculture decisions are not covered by this Shepard's unit.

5. *Remainder of the search*. The rest of the search follows the outline already given above. Note, however, that since this case involves the judicial definition of what constitutes a milk "handler," the words and phrases approach is available. Several cases are listed in digests under this word. Although the statute here and the court decisions construing it can be Shepardized in the usual manner, the regulations are not directly covered by Shepard's Citations. But if the regulations have been construed by federal courts, they will be listed in the Statutes Construed Tables of the Federal Supplement and the Federal Reporter. These tables, however, do not cumulate from volume to volume.

§30.5. Illustrative problem involving a treaty – state law conflict.

1. *The problem stated*. A, B, and C, brothers residing and doing business in your state, were killed in an accident and left wills bequeathing their personal property situated in your state to their mother, a national and resident of Denmark. A was an American citizen; *B* was a national of Denmark; and C was a national of Belovia, a newly constituted political entity. Your state inheritance tax imposes a discriminatory tax on personal property passing to alien nonresident beneficiaries. Your client, the mother, resists this tax.

2. *Analysis of the problem*. Consider only the state inheritance tax aspect. (a) The personal property passing is physically within the state, but is to be removed to Denmark. (b) A was an American citizen but *B*, C and their mother were aliens. (c) There was a mother/son relationship between the parties. (d) Is the state law valid, and does it affect all parties alike?

3. *Preliminary review of the subject matter*. You are uncertain

whether a state in which the decedent's property is situated may discriminate in inheritance taxation against alien beneficiaries. Your preliminary research in legal periodicals, treatises, and legal encyclopedias uncovers a recent decision by your state's highest court upholding the constitutionality of such discrimination. Although a constitutional attack is foreclosed, there is a caveat to the effect that the right to discriminate has been impaired to a considerable degree by treaty. Through encyclopedias and annotations on the relation of treaties to state and federal laws, in 4 A.L.R. 1377; 134 A.L.R. 882, 835; 3 A.L.R.2d 484; and 14 A.L.R.2d 992 (this final annotation is 242 pages in length), you learn that where there is a conflict between a treaty and a state constitution or statute, the treaty provisions are controlling, regardless of whether the state provisions were enacted prior to or subsequent to the making of the treaty. (If there is a conflict between a federal statute and a treaty, the later enactment is controlling.)

4. *Federal statutes search*. Although this is a state tax matter, the treaty caveat sends you in search of an applicable treaty between the United States and Denmark. Through the means described in Chapter 6 you find and read the Treaty of April 26, 1826, with Denmark on friendship, commerce, and consular rights, 8 Stat. 340 T.S. 65, 3 Miller 239, 1 Malloy 373. Article 7 of that treaty, concerning inheritance taxation and the removal of property from one country by resident nationals of the other country, seems repugnant to your state inheritance tax statute, but you seek judicial construction.

In practice, at this time, you would now skip several steps in the search outline in §30.2 and Shepardize this treaty to see if the United States Supreme Court has ever construed it. This Shepardization procedure for treaties is outlined in Chapter 6. You discover that the Court has construed this section three times, and you read the cases. Two of them, *Nielsen* v. *Johnson*, 279 U.S. 47, 49 S. Ct. 233, 73 L. Ed. 607 (1929), and *Petersen* v. *Iowa*, 245 U.S. 170, 38 S. Ct. 109, 62 L. Ed. 225 (1917), both involving Iowa statutes, seem to be in point. Since treaties are uncodified, this one is not covered by the annotations in U.S.C.A.; but U.S.C.S. has a special volume covering uncodified federal laws (including treaties), and the above cases are noted in the annotations to treaties in this special volume.

5. *Home state statute search*. A search of the annotated statutes of your state reveals that, except for its constitutionality, the inheritance tax provision which we are considering has not been construed by your state courts. You therefore seek a similar statute in another state, which has been construed.

6. *Other state statute search*. Statutes in point and their construction by the respective state courts may be found in at least four ways. Since this problem involves state inheritance taxation, the first and speediest solution is through loose-leaf services covering the topic for

all states. Here a uniform classification scheme for state statutes leads to the appropriate section for each state having inheritance taxes discriminating against aliens. In the services, all the law (federal and state, statutory and case) relevant to this problem is collected in one place.

Second, treatises frequently cite the pertinent statutory provisions. Third, and most difficult, the statutes of the various states may be checked, one by one. Finally, as in our problem, if a treaty is involved, the cases found by Shepardizing cite the state statutes construed.

An Iowa statute is cited in the two cases above, but one of them is Section 1467 of the Iowa Code of 1907, and the other includes Sections 7311, 7313, and 7315 of the Iowa Code of 1927. This makes it necessary to translate these sections of older codes into those for the current edition, so that you can compare all with your state statute. Transferring into the present Iowa citation form can be done through the Iowa Code Annotated subject index, or more exactly through the elaborate parallel transfer tables from earlier to corresponding statute forms. Both of these methods lead to Sections 450.10 and 450.11 of the present Iowa Code. You find that Section 450.11, exactly in point as discussed in the Supreme Court decisions, has been repealed (probably as a result of those decisions).

In addition, a History and Source of the Law note affords another check on the correspondence of the 1907 and 1927 sections to the present form by citing all earlier forms of that section. Furthermore, Iowa Law Review comments in point are listed (as they are in Shepard's Iowa Citations also). The transfer table technique enables you to convert the 1907 and 1927 Code sections into the later forms as found in the current Shepard's Iowa Citations, where all cases construing all forms of the statute presently in force are listed.

7. *Other cases in point search: Reading the cases found*. From the digest paragraphs in their headnotes, the *Petersen* and *Nielsen* cases seem irreconcilable. A careful reading of the full reports, however, indicates that Section 7 of the treaty seems to protect the estate of the transferor who was a national of the country to which the property was to be transferred (Denmark here), rather than the transferee (the mother). Therefore it would seem that the estate of A, the American citizen, is not protected. Because he is not a national of Denmark seeking to remove property, the transfer of his property by succession is subject to the discriminatory tax. The estate of *B*, a national of Denmark, is protected, and *B*'s property is not subject to the tax because *B*'s estate seems to fall within the protective parameters of the treaty. The estate of C, with whose country the United States has not yet concluded such a treaty as is here involved, has no such transfer protection.

8. *Remainder of the search*. The remainder of the search follows con-

ventional lines. The major Key Number covering the topic, as noted in the *Nielsen* case headnote, is Treaties ⚷ 11, "Operation as to laws inconsistent with or repugnant to treaty provisions," where such cases are digested. Because the treaty has been thoroughly Shepardized by you, it is doubtful that more cases reasonably in point will be found. To make certain, however, you consult the Statutes Construed tables in the Federal Supplement, Federal Reporter, and the appropriate state or regional Reporter advance sheets.

31 Automated Legal Research

§31.1. Automated legal research: purpose and function.

The impressive developments of computer technology since the Second World War have only recently been applied to the storage and retrieval of legal documents. That such an application of computer technology was long overdue is obvious. Legal bibliography includes everything from state and federal statutory law, trial court and appellate court opinions, administrative regulations and decisions, to treaties and treatises, congressional hearings and municipal codes, restatements and encyclopedias. It is, therefore, especially suited to central computer data bank storage which involves less space than conventional volumes and which eliminates the need for duplication of legal libraries. More importantly, however, our common-law system demands that statutes, regulations, and decisions be searched so that laws and regulations which govern, and cases which are on point, are found in order to resolve legal issues. If programmed and instructed properly, computer systems are far better equipped than human researchers to search *all* documents stored to find *every* case or statute which may have a bearing on the legal problem being researched.

Automated legal research does not, however, replace the critical function of the lawyer. Only the searcher can finally evaluate the value of a case as precedent and its factual and legal relevance to the case at hand. Ideally, the primary functions performed by the computer, then, are to dispense with much of the time-consuming preliminary search for possibly appropriate statutes and cases and to ensure thorough and complete searches of all available documents.

Two legal computer systems, LEXIS and WESTLAW, are presently commercially available to perform these functions. Because they are in their infancy and have limited data bases, neither system perfectly performs the intended function of computerized legal research to search all relevant documents. Further, each system has its own built-in problems of programming and language which result in the retrieval of too few, too many, and/or inapposite documents. Nonetheless, with an awareness of their proper use as well as of their limitations, the searcher can use LEXIS and WESTLAW to shorten research time while, at the same time, expanding the scope of search. What follows is an explanation of the scope and use of each system and a discussion of the advantages and disadvantages of each. For more background information to LEXIS and WESTLAW, the reader is urged to consult James A. Sprowl's A Manual for Computer Assisted Legal Research.[1]

§31.2. LEXIS.

LEXIS is a full-text document retrieval computer system. A pre-prototype of LEXIS was initiated by OBAR (Ohio State Bar Association Automated Research Corporation) which organized in 1967. Building on some of the fundamental ideas developed by OBAR in conjunction with other interested bar groups, Mead Data Central developed LEXIS as a sophisticated on-line, rapidly interactive, computer-assisted system for legal research.

1. *Scope*. Located in Dayton, Ohio, the LEXIS data base stores the full text of legal documents. By mid-1978, these documents included the United States Code, Supreme Court decisions from 1938, Courts of Appeals decisions from 1959, and United States District Court decisions from 1970. Securities law documents in the data bank were Title 15 of the United States Code, sections 77a–80b; Supreme Court, Circuit Court, and District Court securities law decisions from 1936, 1935, and 1934 respectively; SEC rules, regulations, and interpretative releases contained in 17 C.F.R. Chapter 2; No-Action Letters from 1971; selected administrative decisions from 1933; Federal Reserve Board regulations G, T, U, and X; and House, Senate, and Conference Reports for the 1933 and 1934 Acts and the amendments to them. Tax law materials stored were the Internal Revenue Code; final, temporary, and proposed Internal Revenue Service Regulations; Revenue Rulings, Executive Orders, and other materials from the Cumulative Bulletin starting with C.B. 54-1; Cumulative Bulletin Finding List tables from 1954; Cumulative Bulletin Commissioner's

1. American Bar Foundation, Chicago, 1976.

Acquiescence and Non-Acquiescence tables from 1942; Cumulative Bulletin announcements from 1972; private rulings released to the public from 3/14/1977 to date; Tax Court opinions and memorandum decisions from 1942; Board of Tax Appeals opinions from 1924 to 1942; Supreme Court tax decisions from 1913; Court of Appeals tax decisions from 1945; District Court tax decisions from 1960; Court of Claims tax decisions from 1942; and Public Laws and House, Senate, and Conference Reports for the 1954 Code and its amendments. The LEXIS trade regulation library contained Supreme Court trade decisions from 1890; Court of Appeals and District Court trade decisions from 1945 and 1950 respectively; Federal Trade Commission opinions from 1950; and Federal Trade Commission Consent Orders from 1970. A Federal Patent, Trademark and Copyright library contains: pertinent cases in the Supreme Court from 1850, and in the Court of Appeals and the District Courts from 1945 and 1950 respectively; cases in the Court of Claims from 1977, and in the U.S. Court of Customs and Patent Appeals from 1952. Cases from Arizona, California, Florida, Georgia, Illinois, Kansas, Kentucky, Massachusetts, Michigan, Minnesota, Missouri, New Jersey, New York, Ohio, Pennsylvania, Texas, Virginia, and Washington; and statutes from Kansas, Missouri, New York, and Ohio are already part of the LEXIS data base. All states are scheduled to be added by 1980.

Stored in the LEXIS data bank are the full texts of all the decisions, statutes, orders, etc., included in its libraries. This means that the computer, if requested, not only searches names and/or official headnotes, but the entire text of a stored document. In addition to published opinions, slip opinions and recently enacted legislation are included in the LEXIS data bank.

2. *Organization*. All of the documents in the LEXIS data bank are grouped into "libraries." The federal library contains the United States court decisions and United States Code. State libraries encompass an individual state's case law and statutes. Specialized libraries have been established to cover federal agency materials. These include tax, securities, and trade regulation. In addition, Delaware corporation case law is contained in a separate library.

Internally, each document within a library is assigned a number. The document itself is broken down into numbered segments. With the exception of articles, conjunctions, and superfluous legalese ("thereto," "hereinafter," etc.) every word has been given a number. Each word is entered in the library data base with its document number, segment number, and position number. The LEXIS computer can then determine the exact location, both in terms of document and position within a document, of every significant word in every document stored in a library. From this numbering, the searcher writes a set of words-and-logic specifications for language that may occur in the documents.

3. *Use*. In order to search LEXIS documents for texts containing the words or phrase desired, it is necessary for the searcher to learn how to formulate a request so that the computer will understand it and carry it out. For most requests, this is quite simple. The language which must be used is based on Boolean logic. Connecting two words with the word "AND" will retrieve all documents where both words appear. The request "cat AND dog" will retrieve all documents containing both words. The command "cat OR dog," however, will retrieve the same documents *and* all documents where either word appears. The command "AND NOT" retrieves, to continue the example, all documents with the word "cat" which do not contain the word "dog." A search for a phrase or sentence containing both words is formulated by "cat W/8 dog." This command tells the computer to search for the word "cat" within the same segment and to retrieve it only when it is within eight words (not counting insignificant non-indexed words) before or after the word "dog." A request to search a segment is "cat W/SEG dog" and one to search for a word coming within these significant words before another word is "cat PRE/8 dog." Along with the use of "BUT NOT," "AFT.," "BEF.," parentheses, and various combinations of the commands, precise and sophisticated requests can be made of the LEXIS computer.

In order to formulate commands that yield documents which are relevant but which do not produce an unwarranted number of irrelevant documents, the searcher must be familiar with the problem to be searched. It is necessary to know how a court is likely to phrase its opinion. It is essential that the searcher be more than merely acquainted with legal terminology used in the designated area. General background reading in legal encyclopedias and/or treatises will aid in promoting familiarity. It will also aid the searcher in preparing and analyzing commands before the LEXIS system is used and in preventing costly and fruitless searches.

With the commands mastered, preliminary research complete, and commands in hand, the searcher logs on the LEXIS terminal, indicates the library desired, and types in the command. The television monitor connected to the terminal will then display the text of a document which fulfills the request. The most recent text of the highest court will be displayed first. The key words which initiated the retrieval will be highlighted. The searcher then reads or skims the document and determines its value. If it is found valuable, a "hard" copy can be typed, if the searcher wishes, at the printout machine located near the terminal. The searcher then calls for the next document and repeats the process, until all documents fulfilling the command have been displayed.

To save time, the searcher can use a KEY WORD IN CONTEXT (KWIC) display. Requesting KWIC, the searcher will get the highlighted words with approximately 20 words before or after those words. If the KWIC looks promising, the searcher, by pressing the "EXP KWIC" button on the terminal, may get progressively more of the text.

4. *Advantages*. LEXIS has always stored the full text of documents and recent slip opinions. This has meant not only that the full text of an opinion can be obtained as a printout upon request but that the entire text of an opinion can be searched for legal phrases. Because retrieval is based solely on words and word order, the searcher can judge the value of the opinion without having to rely on the possibly mistaken significance given it by a digester. Full-text retrieval means that unique factual situations that might be ignored or overlooked by a headnote writer can be researched and found.

Because it includes statutes and administrative materials, LEXIS's data base is frequently more valuable in researching issues involving statutes or administrative law than WESTLAW's, which is comprised solely of case headnotes and opinions.

5. *Disadvantages*. LEXIS's strengths give rise to its greatest weaknesses. Other than being arranged into libraries, LEXIS documents have not been subject-indexed. The possibility of irrelevant documents being retrieved is great. Even more serious, however, is the danger of a document being missed because a court or agency has used different terminology from that in the searcher's request. In addition, a poorly formulated command can easily result in too few or too many documents. Finally, because there is no ranking (other than chronological) of the LEXIS documents retrieved, it is impossible to avoid or curtail lengthy searches because all documents must at least be skimmed.

In using the LEXIS system, the searcher must be well-informed and capable of judging the significance of a document which has been retrieved. With this kind of sound preparation and legal judgment, the weaknesses of LEXIS can largely be avoided.

§31.3. WESTLAW.

West Publishing Company has been collecting, digesting, and publishing federal and state appellate court decisions for over 100 years in its National Reporter System. A computer-based retrieval system was a natural development from the National Reporter System and its key-numbered headnotes. West's computer system, WESTLAW, became operational during the early 1970s and has expanded significantly since then.

1. *Scope*. Originally, only the West summary headnote digests of cases and their key numbers were included in the data base. Digests of all current cases were automatically fed into the data base while, at the same time, the digests of earlier cases were systematically being included, the most recent cases being stored first. By 1977, the headnotes from all federal court opinions from 1961, and all state appellate court decisions from 1967, had become part of the WESTLAW system.

In 1978, the WESTLAW data base was expanded to include the full text of opinions, including those from the Military Justice Reporter. The full text of all current opinions published by West, as well as their digest headnotes, become part of the WESTLAW system as soon as they are available. The full text of opinions of United States Supreme Court, United States Circuit Courts of Appeals, and United States District Courts from 1961 were also made part of the data base.

2. *Organization*. Like LEXIS documents, WESTLAW cases and their headnotes are grouped into libraries. WESTLAW libraries correspond to the Reporter Series from which they were taken—e.g., North Eastern Reporter, Pacific Reporter, Federal Supplement, Federal Reporter, Supreme Court Reporter, etc.

Before the inclusion of the full text of opinions into the WESTLAW data base, each WESTLAW headnote had its own document number. The headnote was then divided into segments which included the topic heading number and key number, the topic heading, the key number and definition, the court and year, the headnote text, the case title, and the West citation to the case. Significant words in each segment were indexed. A request would initiate a search among the headnotes; and individual headnotes, each fulfilling the request, would be retrieved. This meant that isolated rules of law were retrieved and the searcher's ability to evaluate the factual relevancy of the case was limited because only headnotes fulfilling the request were displayed.

When the full texts of opinions were added to the WESTLAW data base, document numbers were changed. Each case was assigned a document number, and each case subdivided into fields. These fields are the case's full title and citations; the West synopsis; the court, year, and judge; the topics and key numbers; the topic headings; headnotes without topics and key numbers; the full text of the opinions of the court (if included), and the digest (headnotes with their topic and key number). Each significant word or number within a field is assigned a number.

3. *Use*. The WESTLAW user logs onto a computer terminal, connected by phone to the computer in St. Paul, Minnesota, by entering a WESTLAW identification number. The monitor then displays the libraries stored in the data base, and the library needed is indicated.

The searcher can then indicate a field of search — opinion, digest, key number topic, etc. — desired by entering "@" and the field. A command is then entered.

As in LEXIS, Boolean-type commands can be formulated to retrieve WESTLAW data. There are differences between the two languages which can be readily learned. The LEXIS "AND," for example, is WESTLAW's "&", and WESTLAW's "%" is the LEXIS "AND NOT." Two words with no connecting symbol are equivalent to two words connected by the LEXIS "OR." WESTLAW proximity terms are "/S" or within the same sentence, and "/P" or within the same paragraph. The command "cat +S dog" limits the search to sentences where cat comes before dog and "cat +P dog" requires cat to appear before dog in the same paragraph. The use of Boolean commands and, particularly, of proximity terms is advised when doing searches of the full text of opinions so that unresponsive data is not retrieved.

WESTLAW requests are not limited to artificial language formulations. The searcher can ask, for example,

> Does the business judgment rule bar a stockholder derivative suit for director-mismanagement?

The WESTLAW computer will break this request into individual words, eliminating insignificant words. It will then match these words against words appearing in each entry and rank them accordingly. The entry with the most correspondence of different search words appearing the greatest number of times will be displayed first. The one with the second greatest correspondence of different words will be displayed second. If more than one document has the same number of different search words appearing the same number of times, the most recent document will be shown first.

Natural language requests like the one above might produce a headnote or opinion about a "business" which was subject to "judgment" because of an "obsolete rule of law" which, three pages later, refers to "directors" who are also "stockholders." Even proximity terms such as "business +S judgment +S rule" can yield an irrelevant entry such as "his business was unsound, and a judgment lien was ruled appropriate." By phrasing the request

> "business judgment rule"

the searcher can ask the computer to retrieve headnotes or cases with the phrase "business judgment rule." Once the text has been retrieved in response to the significant words in the request, the WESTLAW computer will then review the text for any insignificant words. The computer will display only phrases which exactly match the request.

Among the most valuable WESTLAW commands are those based on the fact that cases have been already digested and, therefore, indexed by the rules of law found in them. The searcher can ask for a particular key number and topic and specify particular key words or a phrase and/or a particular jurisdiction and/or certain years. A similar search in the General Digest could be extremely time-consuming and, in work hours, very costly. WESTLAW greatly reduces both time and cost.

Because WESTLAW headnotes have been indexed for their legal content, there is less chance of missing important cases with WESTLAW digest search than with LEXIS because of a poor command. Even so, advance preparation for the use of WESTLAW is advisable and prudent. The searcher should always determine what key numbers might be relevant to the issue being researched and what terms and phrases are likely to be used in the summary digests. As with LEXIS searches, full-text WESTLAW searches must be made with advance knowledge of the legal issue and the words likely to be used by courts.

Once a request has been entered and the computer has done its search, an entry is displayed on the monitor. Before the words initiating a search are shown, the searcher is given the case name and the West synopsis of the case. The request words which initiated the search are then shown and highlighted. If desired, a printout of the headnote or opinion can be made. The computer indicates how many headnotes and/or cases have been retrieved and will be displayed. Once promising headnotes are found in a digest search, the searcher should read the other headnotes of the case and opinion to insure that the headnote is accurate and reflects holding, not dicta. If the full text of the headnote is part of the WESTLAW data base, the searcher may ask to have it displayed. If not, it is necessary for the searcher to find the case in its bound form. If there is more than one responsive headnote or case, the searcher then asks for the next headnote which will have fewer instances of the search words.

4. *Advantages*. WESTLAW has two distinct advantages over LEXIS. First, cases in the WESTLAW data are indexed according to the rules of law which they contain. By employing West's key number indexing system in commands, the searcher can be sure of retrieving cases which, if not on point, at least relate to the issue of law being researched. Totally irrelevant cases are not likely to be displayed. Second, WESTLAW's flexibility means that the searcher is not required to learn the intricacies of Boolean commands, their meaning and use, in order to retrieve data. For persons not thoroughly familiar with the legal issue being researched or not acquainted with artificial language commands, WESTLAW digest searches are more likely to yield successful first results. Inclusion of the full text of opin-

ions in the WESTLAW data base means, at the same time, that searches are not limited to digests, which are not always accurate, and that unique factual situations, not likely to be reflected in the digests, can be researched.

5. *Disadvantages*. When it has incorporated the entire National Reporter System into its data base, WESTLAW, because of its key number indexing, will have an extremely comprehensive and valuable case law library. The fact, however, that it does not include legislative materials and, particularly, administrative regulations and decisions will continue to limit its value to the specialist who must have access to such materials. For the antitrust, securities, and tax lawyer and for lawyers from states whose statutes are covered by LEXIS in addition to cases, LEXIS will probably be the preferred system.

§31.4. Other legal research computer systems.

Other computer systems for the storage and retrieval of legal documents have also been developed in recent years. For the most part, these are limited access systems which serve particular users. Some, like LEXIS, are programmed for Boolean commands; others, like WESTLAW, employ both artificial and natural language requests. What follows is a brief description of some of these systems. For a more detailed discussion of other systems, the reader should refer to Automated Law Research,[2] published by the A.B.A.

1. *JURIS*. JURIS was developed by the Department of Justice in cooperation with West Publishing Company for use by Justice Department attorneys both in Washington and in state federal attorneys' offices throughout the United States. The JURIS data bank also includes West headnotes which, as in the WESTLAW system, are considered part of one document number for each case.

2. *FLITE*. Sponsored by the United States Department of Defense through the Air Force, FLITE — Federal Legal Information Through Electronics — is a full-text computer system which was first developed in the 1960s. It is available only to Department of Defense personnel and to other subscribing federal agencies. The FLITE data base reflects the needs of its users and includes such things as the United States Code, Court of Claims decisions, Defense Department international law materials, court martial reports. User requests are made to FLITE staff attorneys who, in turn, process the requests and feed them into the computer. The need for the individual user to learn Boolean commands is, therefore, eliminated.

2. American Bar Association Standing Committee on Law and Technology, Chicago, 1973.

3. *QUIC/LAW*. Developed by Queens University, QUIC/LAW is a computerized system comprising Canadian federal case law, as well as the decisions of some provincial courts, and federal legislation and administrative regulations. Requests can be formulated in either natural language or Boolean commands. The full text of documents is stored, and every significant word is indexed.

4. *DATUM*. To meet the special needs of bilingual Quebec, Documentation Automatique des Textes juridiques de l'Université de Montréal or DATUM was developed. The data base includes the French and English texts of decisions from the province of Quebec.

§31.5. Mechanical aids to legal research.

Along with the development of computerized legal research, other technical developments have led to mechanical devices which shorten research time and reduce valuable storage space.

Auto-Cite. As the publisher of the American Law Reports, American Jurisprudence, and the United States Code service, the Lawyers Co-operative makes use of computerized data banks. One of its own systems is available to commercial users as Auto-Cite.

Auto-Cite permits the user to verify the accuracy of a legal citation. By typing a citation into the Auto-Cite computer, the user can determine the name of a case, the year of decision, parallel citations, and the nature of and citation to subsequent court action. If a citation is incorrect, the computer might respond "NO CASE STARTS ON PAGE GIVEN" and suggest the correct citation. Auto-Cite can be used, with economy of time, by non-legal as well as legal personnel to check the accuracy of citations in briefs and other legal writings before they are submitted to the court and opposing counsel, and to update such citations before oral arguments.

32 Standard Legal Citation Forms[1]

§32.1. Function and construction of a good citation.

A legal citation has only one purpose: to lead its reader to the material cited without necessitating the use of an additional source of information for data which should be given in the citation itself. The aim of this chapter is to provide citation rules and examples that will enable the user to combine utility with good form so that this sole purpose is fulfilled.

1. This chapter is abridged from Price, A Practical Manual of Standard Legal Citations (2d ed. 1958), by permission of the copyright owner, Oceana Publications, Inc.

A good case citation possesses the following elements: the name of the case, the official citation, the parallel citation (if any), and the date. If not evident from the report, a notation of the court deciding the case should be made. The citation includes the volume number, the recognizable abbreviation for the reporter, and the page number. The date is both a check against citation errors, which are unbelievably frequent, and a means of appraising the cited reference. The parallel citation serves the dual purpose of a check against error and an assurance that the reader will have one of the cited forms available. The additional time and space expended in providing parallel citations are justified in light of the trouble resulting from an insufficient or inaccurate reference.

In compiling this chapter on citation forms, approximately 600 briefs and opinions, about evenly divided among federal and state courts and federal administrative agencies, have been examined for form. The output of approximately 40 different law reviews has been scrutinized. In addition, courts, attorneys general, and administrative agencies have cooperated by supplying forms of citations preferred by them. The United States Government Printing Office Style Manual has been the arbiter of citation form and style, wherever pertinent, and any departures from it have been noted.

Law review practice, as formulated in A Uniform System of Citation,[2] though it agrees in the great majority of respects with the rules laid down in this chapter for briefs, is often more complicated. The practices among law book publishers are not uniform. For example, the rules regarding the italicizing of the titles of books and periodical articles, observed by the publisher of this book, differ in some details from those advocated in this chapter. For written work in law schools and for briefs in law practice, however, the rules presented in this chapter are believed to be those applied by the great majority of lawyers and legal departments; they are acceptable in all law courts.

§32.2. Section and chapter designations in statute citations.

1. *In general.* There is little uniformity in the treatment of chapter, article, and section designations in statute citations, either in abbreviation or capitalization, but the forms given below follow the preferred practice.

2. *Suggested form.*

a. *Quotations:* Follow copy quoted as to section designations.

b. *Main text:* Spell out and capitalize "section" if it is the first word of a sentence and in references to a specific section and act.

2. Cambridge, Mass. The Harvard Law Review Assn.

Section 321 of the Act provides . . .
It was provided in Section 321 of the Act . . .
It was provided (Section 321) that . . .

The word "section" should not be capitalized and may be replaced by the "§" in casual main text references to a section formerly cited:

This provision, 58 Stat. 631, §8, that . . .
. . . of this statute, 58 Stat. 631, §8.
This provision (58 Stat. 631, §8), that . . .
. . . does not constitute reversible error. Rev. Civ. Code, §2414.

c. *Footnotes.* Spell out "section" as the first word of a sentence; otherwise use "§" except in comment on a specific section, when the same form as for text references should be used.

3. *Section references to the United States Code.* Use the style of 28 U.S.C. §18, even in the main text. The Supreme Court preference for this style is reflected in its opinions.

4. *Chapter and clause designations.* For chapter, use "c." The plural of "c" is "cc." Clause is abbreviated "cl." and should not be capitalized except as the first word of a sentence or as a proper noun, e.g., "Commerce Clause."

5. *"Sec."* Uncapitalized, "sec." is seldom found except in quotations. "Sec." capitalized is more common. The majority rule follows the forms suggested above, however.

6. *Quoting the statute in a footnote.* Where the cited provisions are short, copy them in a footnote when cited for the first time. Thereafter refer to them by section number.

[1]The pertinent provisions are as follows:
"Sec. 5(a) [quoting the section]."
"Sec. 15 [quoting the section]."

§32.3. Constitutions.

1. *General Considerations.* Constitutions are cited by article, section, and clause (if given). In footnotes and in text references, when set off by parentheses or by commas, the symbol "§" should be used to designate the particular section. The date of the United States Constitution is not given in citations. According to the prevailing rule, the date of adoption of other constitutions should be given only if it is not presently in force or if it has been significantly amended since the date of adoption, e.g., N.Y. Const., art. 2, §1 (1847). One should refer to "the Constitution" only if the reference is to the United States Constitution; otherwise, one should specify the consti-

tution to which the writer is referring, i.e., "the Constitution of Indiana."

"Constitution" is capitalized only when used as a proper name, i.e., when a particular constitution is clearly specified. Conservative practice is to capitalize "article," "section," and "clause" (or their abbreviations) only when they form the first word of a sentence, or in headings. Amendment citations or citations of particular clauses by name are spelled out in full except in parenthetical or footnote references, but parts of the United States Constitution are not capitalized when the writer includes a direct reference to the Constitution. Parts of the Constitution are frequently capitalized when the Constitution is not explicitly mentioned. For further capitalization rules, see §32.19.

2. *Text references.*

> the various state constitutions.
> the Constitution [meaning of the United States].
> the United States Constitution.
> Article V, section 18, of the Constitution of Indiana.
> The fourteenth amendment of the Constitution provides.
> The Fourteenth Amendment provides.
> the commerce clause of the Constitution
> the Commerce Clause
> The Constitution provides (Art. I, §8, cl. 8) for a patent system.
> The Constitution provides for patents. Art. I, §8, cl. 8.

3. *Footnote references.*

> U.S. Const., Art. I, §8, cl. 8.
> U.S. Const., Amend. XVII.
> Ind. Const., Art. IV, §5.
> N.Y. Const., Art. 2, §1 (1847). [Suggested form.]
> N.Y. Const., Art. 2, §1. [Prevailing practice.]

§32.4. Congressional bills, resolutions, and publications.

1. *Congressional bills.*

House and Senate bills	H.R.	S.
House and Senate resolutions	H. Res.	S. Res.
Concurrent resolutions	H. Con. Res.	S. Con. Res.
Joint resolutions	H. J. Res.	S.J. Res.

Note that when the abbreviation consists of two single letters (such as H.R.), no space is left between the individual components; when one component has more than a single letter, a space is left (e.g., H. Res.).

H.R. 70, 81st Cong., 1st Sess. (1949), p. 3.
S. 1201, 81st Cong., 1st Sess. (1949), p. 2. [Dates and page references are usually omitted in bills.]
. . . hereinafter cited as H.R. 70. [form for repeating citations].

2. *Enacted Congressional Resolutions.*

Joint resolutions	Cited as a slip law until publication in Statutes at Large.
Concurrent resolutions	Cited to Congressional Record until publication in Statutes at Large.
Simple resolutions	Cited to Congressional Record.

H. Con. Res. 49, 80th Cong., 1st Sess., 61 Stat. 1023 (1947).
S. Res. 218, 83d Cong., 2d Sess., 100 Cong. Rec. 2972 (1.54).

3. *Congressional hearings.*

Hearings before Senate Committee on H.R. 5327 (Import Duty on Virgin Copper), 81st Cong., 1st Sess. (1949), p. 56.

4. *Congressional committee reports and documents.*
A title for the report or documentary may be given if desirable. If a title is given, the author should be specified. The writer should utilize the following abbreviations:

H.R. Rept. No.	S. Rept. No.
H.R. Doc. No.	S. Doc. No.
H.R. Exec. Doc. No.	S. Exec. Doc. No.
H.R. Misc. Doc. No.	

H.R. Rept. No. 19, 81st Cong., 1st Sess. (1949), p. 25.
S. Exec. Doc. No. 23, 81st Cong., 1st Sess. (1949), p. 19.

5. *Bulletin or report bearing a document number.*

Parking Lots in the District of Columbia. Report . . . (S. Doc. No. 209, 81st Cong., 2d Sess. (1949)), p. 56.

6. *Congressional debates and proceedings.*
a. *Annals of Congress* ("Debates and Proceedings in the Congress of the United States"), 1789–1824.

18 Annals of Cong. 1763 (1819).

b. *Register of Debates* ("Gales and Seaton") (1824–1837).

11 Reg. Deb. 127 (1835).

c. *Congressional Globe* 1833–1873. Cite by Congress and session.

Cong. Globe, 41st Cong., 1st Sess. (1869), p. 499.

d. Congressional Record, 1873 to date. The page numbers of the daily edition and of the bound edition do not match. Cite the bound volume if available. In citing the daily edition, give the full date.

Bound volume: 94 Cong. Rec. 9761 (1948).
Daily edition: 94 Cong. Rec. 9917 (Aug. 4, 1948). [The same material.]

§32.5. Congressional legislation.

1. *Current or slip laws*. Give the public or private law number, the Congress and (before the 83d Congress, 1957) session, and date of approval. The Statutes at Large citation is now printed in the margin of the official slip laws and may be added to the slip law citation, for convenience in future reference. Beginning with the Eighty-third Congress, the session designation is omitted.

Pub. L. No. 101, 80th Cong., 1st Sess. (June 23, 1947). [Pre-1957 form.]
Pub. L. 83-315 (Sept. 9, 1957). [1957 to date form.]

2. *Statutes at large*. As soon as the Statutes at Large form is published, cite it instead of the law number.

47 Stat. 1470 (1933), 11 U.S.C. §909 (1958 ed.).

Here the Code is cited only for added convenience. Because the Code is only prima facie the law, researchers should always consult the language in the Statutes at Large. Even in the event that there is no discrepancy between the language found in the Statutes at Large and the Code, the Statutes at Large citation should be given. However, for those Code titles reenacted into positive law, it is neither necessary nor proper to cite the Statutes at Large, except for historical purposes, since they are no longer in force in that form. The proper citation, therefore, is simply by title, section, and edition of the Code. For further discussion, see §32.5.3a, b, c, d, below.

In citing the Statutes at Large, it is customary to cite also the act from which the Statute is derived, by date, unless it can be readily identified from the context. Where footnotes are employed, the name and section of the act generally appear in the main text, and the volume and page references are footnoted. Where the section number of the Code is cited as part of the complete footnote citation, the section number of the act normally appearing in the text is usually omitted in order to avoid needless repetition.

a. *Dating Statutes at Large citations.* When the Statute citation alone is given, it should be dated, as 61 Stat. 37 (1947). Where the date of the Statute and the date of the cited edition of the United States Code are the same, give only the latter when citing both forms; otherwise give both dates.

47 Stat. 1470 (1933), 11 U.S.C. §908 (1958 ed.).
60 Stat. 89, 47 U.S.C. §506 (1946 ed.). [A 1946 act.]

b. *Citing an untitled act.*

Act of July 23, 1947, c. 302, 61 Stat. 413. [Date is in the act here.]
The act for payment of fees, 61 Stat. 413 (1947), provided . . . [Context identifies the statute.]

c. *Citing a particular section or page.*

The Second Decontrol Act of 1947, Section 6(a), 61 Stat. 321, 323, empowered . . . [The reference to page 321, where the act begins, is usually omitted. In a footnoted brief, 61 Stat. 321, 323 would appear as a footnote.]

d. *Citing an amended act.*

Act of March 4, 1934, c. 84, §7, 48 Stat. 460, as amended Aug. 2, 1946, c. 753, §601(a), 60 Stat. 850.

e. *Citing an act by popular name.*

The Labor Management Relations Act, 1947 (Taft-Hartley Act), Act of June 23, 1947, c. 120, 61 Stat. 136 hereinafter cited as LMRA (or, the Act). [With footnotes, only the title would appear in the main text.]

3. *The United States Code.* Include the original act in citations, except where a Code title has been reenacted into positive law and thus the original act from which the Code title is derived has been repealed. As explained in §32.5.2, the original act governs in the event of a discrepancy in language between the Code and the act unless the Code has been enacted as positive law.

As of the end of 1978, the following Code titles have been enacted as positive law: 1, 3–6, 9, 10, 13, 14, 17, 18, 28, 35, 37–39, and 44.

Federal statutes are usually cited to the United States Code (U.S.C.). If material appears in unofficial services, then the United States Code Annotated (U.S.C.A.) and the United States Code Service (U.S.C.S.) may be cited.

a. *Code citation to the latest edition, with supplement citations.* In the citations below, if the "Act" citation is omitted, date the Statutes at Large citation. In citing the supplement, give the supplement number also. A writer should use the date conspicuously given on the title page of the supplement. If none is given, use the copyright date.

Act of June 29, 1959, Pub. L. 86-72, 73 Stat. 155, 49 U.S.C. §1112 (Supp. I, 1959), hereinafter cited as Code §1112.

b. *Code citation where original act has been amended once.*

Act of June 8, 1938, c. 328, §1(c), 52 Stat. 633, as amended Sept. 5, 1940, c. 715, §11, 54 Stat. 876, 23 U.S.C. §10b (1958 ed.).

c. *Code citation where original act has been amended several times.*

Act of Nov. 9, 1921, c. 199, §11, 42 Stat. 214, as amended 23 U.S.C. §12 (1958 ed.).

d. *Code citation of legislation of current year.* The unofficial United States Code Annotated and United States Code Service pamphlet supplements may be cited when covering a period for which there is as yet no official supplement. Cite both the month and the year of the pamphlet.

63 Stat. 98, 18 U.S.C.A. §3771 (Aug. 1961 pam.).

e. *Internal Revenue Code.* The edition date should form part of the citation.

Int. Rev. Code of 1939, §811 (g) (Sec. 404, Revenue Act of 1942).

Although in the above citation the Revenue Act of 1942 is no longer in force as to Section 404, it is cited for convenience.

Treasury Department briefs have an appendix in which the provisions of the Internal Revenue Code relied upon are quoted in full.

f. *Code titles reenacted into positive law.*

28 U.S.C. §41.

28 U.S.C. §41 as amended Oct. 31, 1951, c. 655, §34, 65 Stat. 723. [If subsequently amended, use this citation form.]

4. *United States Revised Statutes.* The edition is a necessary part of the citation (1875; or second, 1878). Do not cite "1873" as the date of the first edition. Chapter and page references are omitted. "U.S." is omitted, except in states which themselves have "Revised Statutes." Then it should be included to avoid ambiguity. In briefs, the usual abbreviation is R.S.; in legal periodicals, Rev. Stat., but either is acceptable in briefs.

Congress expressly provided, R.S. §1 (1875), 1 U.S.C. 1 (1958 ed.) . . .

§32.6. Treaties.

Treaties before 1950 are cited in briefs as Statutes at Large because until then they were printed in the Statutes at Large. The last volume containing treaties is Volume 64. Beginning with 1950 (printing

T.I.A.S. No. 2010), treaties and executive agreements of international import are published in the new series, United States Treaties and Other International Acts. The component parts of a treaty or executive agreement citation should ordinarily include the short title or a paraphrase thereof, the type of agreement (i.e., treaty, convention, etc.), subject (peace, commerce), countries signing, and date of signature, *not* of Senate approval, the designated "effect date," or the date proclaimed.

1. *Cited as a Statute at Large in a brief.*

 Treaty of Peace with Romania, Feb. 10, 1947, Part II, 61 Stat. 1757, 1801 (1947).

2. *Cited as United States Treaties and other International Acts.*

 1 UST 1 (1952).

3. *Cited in a periodical.*

 Treaty of Friendship, Commerce and Consular Rights, with Germany, Dec. 8, 1923.[1] [Text.]

 [1]44 Stat. 2132, U.S. Treaty Ser. 725, 4 Trenwith 4191. [Footnote.]

§32.7. Subordinate legislation: Administrative rules and regulations.

1. *Federal Register: The official chronological reporter.*

 14 Fed. Reg. 6190 (1949).

2. *Code of Federal Regulations: The official codification.* The date of the revision should be given. The form "CFR" is common, but "C.F.R." should be used.

 24 C.F.R. §202.13 (1959).

3. *Presidential proclamations and executive orders.* Generally these are cited to C.F.R. with a parallel citation to a section of U.S.C., if printed herein. If, however, a C.F.R. page number is not available, cite to Fed. Reg.

 Exec. Order No. 11, 230, 3 C.F.R. 320 (1964–1965 compilation) reprinted in 3 U.S.C. §301 (Supp. I, 1954).
 Proc. No. 2855, 14 Fed. Reg. 5413 (1949).

4. *Rules of practice.* In briefs intended for courts, the initial citation should make the name of the agency clear. Agencies themselves frequently cite the Federal Register or Code of Federal Regulations form of a rule.

 Patent Office, Rule 122 (Patents 1949).

F.T.C. Rules of Practice, Rule 7(c), 16 C.F.R. §2.7(c) (1949).

5. *Administrative regulations*. Begin the citation with the agency's name or abbreviation and give the date of publication. Federal administrative regulations, except for Treasury Regulations, can generally be found in and should be cited to C.F.R. if possible.

U.S. Treas. Regs. 105, §81.24 (1943). [Footnote form.]
Bureau of Land Management, Classification Order, Aug. 24, 1949, 14 Fed. Reg. 5245.

6. *Court rules*. The citations below are from official briefs.

Federal Rules of Criminal Procedure, Rule 18.
General Orders in Bankruptcy, No. 26.
Admiralty Rules, No. 54 (as amended July 21, 1948).
Mich. Court Rules, No. 51.
Rules, No. 51 (318 Mich. XII). [Giving place of publication.]
Ill. Sup. Ct. Rule 49.

§32.8. State legislation.

1. *Legislative history*.

1 Cal. Senate Jour. 317, 56th Sess. (1945).
Neb. Legis. Jour., 68th Sess. (1947), p. 793.

2. *Miscellaneous documents*. Reports of state departments, when cited by numbered volume, follow the form of volume and page citation of law reports and periodicals; where not numbered by volume, the page citation follows the date and is preceded by a comma or follows the same form as the multivolume citation, as desired.

Louisiana Revenue Code Comm., *Project of a Revenue Code* . . . (1949), p. 916.
N.Y. Law Revision Comm., *Act, Recommendations and Study* . . . Legis. Doc. No. 65(F) (1949).

3. *Dating state session law and statute citations*. Statute citations should include the date of compilation. Session laws (except perhaps in Ohio, where the volumes are numbered consecutively and are often so cited), are always dated.

a. *Dating session laws*. Session laws should be dated in the middle with no comma between the title and date.

Wash. Laws 1941, c. 1, §9, p. 8.

b. *Dating statutes*.

S.C. Code of Laws, §53-252 (1952).

4. *Slip laws and session laws*.

a. *General form.*

Me. Laws 1945, P. & S., c. 96.
Mass. Resolves 1945, c. 35. [For Acts: Stat. 1938, c. 136.]
Tenn. Private Acts 1945, c. 69.
Ohio Laws 1947, c. 119, 113 O.L. 179.

b. *Extra sessions.* These should be clearly indicated.

Ala. Laws, 2d E.S. 1947, No. 16.
Ga. Laws, E.S. Nov. 1948, No. 2.

c. *Advance sheet citations.* These should be shown if available.

N.Y. Laws 1950, c. 11 (1950 N.Y. Sess. L. Serv. 91).

d. *Earlier editions of session laws.* Some of these reprints are cited by the name of their editor, and by volume and page.

N.Y. Laws 1779, c. 25, 1 Laws of New York 26 (Greenleaf, 1792).
Va. Acts of Assembly 1647; Act II, 1 Laws of Virginia 341 (Hening, 1823).

5. *State statutes.* Where they exist, the latest official editions of statutes (as amended by session laws) are usually cited in briefs, rather than the unofficial annotated editions, even when the latter bear a much later publication date. This is because the official edition is still the "best evidence" of the law. In legal writing generally, however, the tendency is to cite the unofficial, if later. A good and safe practice is to cite both the official and the unofficial in parallel, in both a brief and a memorandum of law.

Recommended standard form for state statutes. In briefs addressed to your own state courts, follow their preferred form, as found in the judicial opinions of the forum; in citing statutes of other states, the standard citation form below is advised.

Ore. Rev. Stat. §551.010 (1953), as amended by . . .
N.J. Stat. Ann. §54:10 A-32 (West, 1960).
Kan. Gen. Stat. 1949, §10-801 (Supp. 1959).
Conn. Gen. Stat. Ann. 1959, §9-174 (West, 1960).

Statutory citation forms will vary with time because editions constantly change. A Uniform System of Citation[3] (beginning with the twelfth edition) offers a helpful table of citation forms for all state statutes.

§32.9. English and Canadian statutory material.

1. *Parliamentary debates.* In some fashion, these are published

3. Cambridge, Mass. The Harvard Law Review Assn.

from 1066 to date. The series name, volume, page number, and the date are parts of the citation.

> 7 Parl. Hist. of Eng. 356 (Hansard's 1716).
> 118 Parl. Deb. 678 (Hansard's 3d Ser. 1891).
> 230 H.C. Deb. 721 (Hansard's 5th Ser. 1929).

2. *English statutes and court rules.*

a. *Session laws.* Cite by title (if any), regnal year, date, chapter, section and schedule (if any). Unofficial editions of the statutes (as Halsbury's) are not cited as such.

> Supreme Court of Judicature Act, 1925, c. 49, s. 226, Sched. 6.

Where the title of the statute is not otherwise given, add the date in parentheses.

> 19 & 20 Geo. V, c. 34, s. 2(2) (1929).

In tabular citations, by year, the title is enclosed in parentheses.

> 12 & 13 Geo. VI, c. 38 (Companies Act, 1948), s. 101
> 12 & 13 Geo. VI, c. 58 (Criminal Justice Act, 1948), s. 38(2).

b. *Statutory rules and orders and Instruments.* Cite by year, number, volume and page.

> S.R. & Order 1914 (No. 1629).
> S.I. 1948 (No. 2357) I, p. 101 [in which I is the volume number].

c. *Supreme Court rules.*

> R.S.C., Ord. 46, r. 5.

3. *Canadian statutes and court rules.*

a. *Statutes.* Citation of Canadian statutes is generally similar to the citation of English statutes. In Canada, as in the United States, however, revised statutes are the rule, and these are cited very much as here. The citations below are from official opinions.

> Section 37(24) of the Interpretation Act, 1927 R.S. Canada, c. 1, as amended by . . .
> Ontario Rev. Stat. (1937), c. 18, as amended, 1939 Stats. c. 25.
> Farm Security Act (Sask. 2d Sess.), c. 39, as amended 1945 (Sask.)

b. *Supreme Court rules.*

> Rules of the Supreme Court, Order IV, rule 1 (Alberta).

§32.10. Case material.

1. *Case names.*

a. *Omissions.* Use only the surnames of individuals rather than their full names. Do not, however, omit portions of an individual's name when the name identifies a corporation. Give only so much of the case name as is necessary to identify the parties clearly. Thus, *Gryer* v. *Burke*, not *Francis Joseph Gryer, Petitioner* v. *C. J. Burke, Warden, Eastern State Penitentiary*.

Omit the following extraneous material: (1) omit *et al.*, *et ux.*, *deceased;* (2) when there is a title containing both "Co." and "Inc." or "Ltd.," retain only "Co."; (3) omit the description of the position occupied by a party; and (4) omit "City of" and "State of" unless necessary to avoid confusion.

Examples

Brown Co. v. *Jones—not Brown Co., Inc.* v. *Jones*
Durkee Foods, Inc. v. *Harrison* [omitting "Collector of Internal Revenue"]

City of Washington v. *Hodges*	*Washington* v. *Oregon*
Coyle v. *New York*	*Morral* v. *City of New York*

b. *Abbreviations*. Do not abbreviate the first word of a case name. Abbreviate "United States" only when it forms part of the name of a government vessel. In legal writing, the initials of government administrative agencies and organizations (such as labor unions), commonly known by initials, may be substituted for the complete name when there is no danger of confusion. You should remember, however, that many such initials, although perfectly clear at one time, are not clear at a later date. Legal periodicals and frequently the agencies themselves omit periods in these titles.

Examples

United States v. *Maryland & Va. Milk Assn.*
The U.S.S. Texas
NLRB v. *Hearst Publications*
NAACP v. *Button*

The following are commonly abbreviated in case titles except when they form the first word of the name of a party.

Administrator	(Admr.)	Federal	(Fed.)
Association	(Assn.)	Government	(Gov.)
Board	(Bd.)	Incorporated	(Inc.)
Commissioner	(Commr.)	Limited	(Ltd.)
Committee	(Comm.)	Manufacturing	(Mfg.)
Company	(Co.)	National	(Natl.)
Corporation	(Corp.)	Railroad	(R.R.)
Department	(Dept.)	Railway	(Ry.)
Division	(Div.)	Transportation	(Transp.)

c. *Corporate titles beginning with an initial*. Give the corporate name in full; alphabetize in indices under *both* initial and surname.

> *H. J. Heinz Co.* v. *NLRB*

d. *Case name changed on appeal*. Where the name has been changed or altered, it is cited as follows:

> *Colver* v. *Skeffington*, 265 F.2d 17 (2d Cir. 1945), reversed sub nom. *Skeffington* v. *Katzoff*, 387 U.S. 467 (1946).

The "sub nom." device need not be used (1) where certiorari has been denied under another name; and (2) where one of the parties was an official, replaced by another by the time the case on appeal is argued. For example, if Robertson were replaced by Ooms as Commissioner of Patents, *Jones* v. *Robertson*, would become on appeal *Ooms* v. *Jones*.

e. *Popular name case citations*. Capitalize "case" only when it is part of the official title. Once a case has been fully cited, later text references may be made by short title.

> *Slade's Case*. [Official title.]
> *Slaughter-House* cases. [Popular title.]
> *Williams* v. *North Carolina* . . . the *Williams* case

2. *General considerations in case citation*.

a. *Dating case report citations*. Case citations should be dated because, other things being equal, the value of a recent case as authority is likely to be greater than that of earlier cases. Dating the citation provides an important element of appraisal. It is also a check upon error in citations. For unpublished decisions, both the docket number and the exact date are given.

Place the date citation in parentheses at the end of the citation. Where report volumes are dated but not numbered, the date precedes the series designation.

> *People* v. *Roth*, 128 Misc. 550, 220 N.Y. Supp. 167 (Gen. Sess. 1937).
> 1927 C.D. (Patents) 193. [An unnumbered but dated series.]
> *Wade* v. *Major*, no.40, U.S. S.Ct., June 14, 1948. [Unpublished.]

b. *Designating the court deciding the case*. Clearly indicate the court deciding the case when any chance of ambiguity exists. The court is indicated in parentheses at the end of the citation, preceding the date. In parallel citations, indicate the court only once.

> *Application of Jacoby*, 33 N.Y.S.2d 621 (Sup. Ct. 1942).
> *Brady* v. *Brooklyn*, 1 Barb. 584 (N.Y. Sup. Ct. 1847).
> *De Bekker* v. *Stokes*, 219 N.Y. 573, 114 N.E. 1064 (1916).

c. *Named reporters*. Because most "nominatives" have been renumbered as parts of consecutively numbered series, cite the official reporter with the nominative parenthetically.

Supreme Court reports.

> *Watts* v. *Waddle*, 31 U.S. (6 Pet.) 164 (1932).

Lower federal courts to 1880. Cite as federal cases, omitting reporter's name.

State nominative reports. Generally cite as Supreme Court nominatives. If the nominative reports have been incorporated as part of the official series and the pagination differs, give parallel cites to the official reprint and the nominative report.

> *Jones* v. *Andover*, 23 Mass. 58, 6 Pick. 59 (1827).

3. *Citing judicial opinions of federal courts*. It is customary to cite only the official report in federal courts if the official report has been published. For United States Supreme Court decisions, if the United States report (— U.S. —) is not available, then refer to the Supreme Court reports (— S.Ct. —), the United States Law Weekly (— U.S.L.W. —) or other loose-leaf service, in that order of preference. If none of these are available, then cite the case as an unreported decision.

For the first 90 volumes of the United States reports, cite by the reporters' names.

Examples of citation form for Supreme Court decisions.

> *United States* v. *United Shoe Machinery Co*., 247 U.S. 62 (1918).
> *United States* v. *Capital Transit Co*., 70 S.Ct. 115 (1949). [U.S. reports are unavailable.]
> *General Electric* v. *Smith*, 46 U.S.L.W. 4050 (U.S. December 17, 1976). [Neither the U.S. reports nor the Supreme Court reports have been published.]
> *Jones* v. *Smith*, 49–152, U.S. S.Ct., Jan. 10, 1950. [Unreported decision.]
> *Smith* v. *Orton*, 21 How. 241 (1858).
> *In re Rosenberg*, 346 U.S. 313 (1953) (order by Douglas, J., sitting as a Circuit Judge). [This is the form for citing a case in which a Supreme Court Justice sits as a circuit judge.]

4. *Special citation forms for lower federal court reports*.

a. *Early circuit courts (abolished June 1, 1912)*. Cite the district but not the division thereof.

> *Micon* v. *Lamar*, 1 Fed. 14 (C.C. S.D. N.Y. 1880).
> *Smith* v. *Jones*, 21 Fed. Cas. 770, No. 12,505 (C.C. D. Pa. 1812).

b. *District courts*.

> *Edwards* v. *Brown*, 85 F. Supp. 290 (N.D. W.Va. 1949).

c. *Circuit Courts of Appeals (to August 31, 1948).* Cite by circuit number and date.

> *Smith* v. *Brown*, 143 F.2d 531 (9th Cir. 1944). [The abbreviation "C.C.A. 9th" has been largely superseded by "9th Cir."]

d. *Courts of Appeals (beginning Sept. 1, 1948).* Cite by circuit number and year.

> 171 F.2d 281 (9th Cir. 1948). [The abbreviation "C.A. 9th" has been largely superseded by "9th Cir."]

e. *United States District Court of Appeals for the District of Columbia Circuit.* The separate reporter, until November 10, 1941 (volumes 1 to 74), was known as Appeal Cases, but is better known as United States Court of Appeals, District of Columbia. Cite the Federal Reporter, however, except when citing to the court itself (because of the superior availability of the Federal Reporter to most readers).

> 61 F.2d 404 (D.C. Cir. 1932). [Formerly cited as "App. D.C. 1932."]

The court itself prefers its own reporter.

> *Bacon* v. *Bacon*, 83 U.S. App. D.C. 313 (1948).

f. *Emergency Court of Appeals.*

> *Herman* v. *Woods*, 175 F.2d 781 (Em. App. 1949).

g. *Court of Claims.*

> *Joseph Meltzner, Inc.* v. *United States*, 111 Ct. Cl. 389 (1949). [More often cited as 77 F. Supp. 1018 (Ct. Cl. 1949) because of the superior availability of the Federal Supplement.]

h. *Court of Customs and Patent Appeals.* These reports are in two series. In Supreme Court briefs, cite the official reports if available; briefs to the Court of Customs and Patent Appeals itself usually give parallel citations, if available.

> *In re Lobdell*, 35 C.C.P.A. (Patents) 1091 (1948).
> *United States* v. *Field*, 12 C.C.P.A. (Customs) 1202, 111 F.2d 902 (1940).

i. *Federal Rules Decisions.*

> *Ratner* v. *Paramount Pictures*, 6 F.R.D. 618 (S.D. N.Y. 1942).

5. *Citation forms for state court reports.* Every state court citation should indicate the date of decision, the court and the jurisdiction. When available, both the official and unofficial reporters should be

cited. When the official or unofficial reports do not clearly indicate the court and the jurisdiction, include this information as a parenthetical. If no state court is specified, either parenthetically or within the title of the state reporter itself, the writer implicitly refers to the highest court of the jurisdiction. If only the unofficial report prints the opinion, then cite as follows.

> *Blank* v. *Blank*, 59 Hun. 1000, opinion in 5 N.Y.S. 200 (Sup. Ct. 1889).

Examples of citation form for state court decisions.

> *Lively* v. *Munday*, 201 Ga. 409, 40 S.E.2d 62 (1946). [If both official and unofficial reporters are available. By implication, the writer has informed us that the highest state court in Georgia has rendered this decision.]
>
> *Lively* v. *Munday*, 201 Ga. 409, 410, 40 S.E.2d 62, 63 (1946). [Citation to a particular page.]
>
> *Lipman* v. *Martin*, 39 N.W.2d 69 (Mich. 1949). [If only the unofficial reporter is available. The highest state court in Michigan has rendered this decision.]
>
> *Sharpe* v. *Hayes*, 43 Del. 494 (Super. Ct. 1946). [Case is found only in the official reporter. The court rendering the decision is added parenthetically because it is not the highest court of Delaware.]

6. *Miscellaneous case citation matters.*

a. *Annotated reports series.* These are not cited in federal court briefs or in law reviews as case reports, but often they are in state courts. They should be preceded by "See" if cited for their notes.

> *Lively* v. *Munday*, 201 Ga. 409, 40 S.E.2d 62, 173 A.L.R. 1295 (1946).

b. *Federal administrative agency rulings as cited by the agencies themselves.* Tables of typical modes of citation by federal agencies of their rulings are printed in Price and Bitner, *Effective Legal Research* (1953), pp. 342–345, and in Price, *A Practical Manual of Standard Legal Citations* (2d ed. 1958), pp. 43–51.

c. *Administrative material cited from legal newspapers.* Give the exact date of decision and docket number if available.

> *In re Transportation Activities of Midwest Transfer Co.*, 18 U.S.L.W. 2002, I.C.C. June 13, 1949.
>
> *In re Ryan Aeronautical Co.*, 85 N.L.R.B. No. 200, decided Sept. 6, 1949, 24 L.R.R.M. 1547.

d. *Loose-leaf and other services.* Cases or administrative rulings for which no official report exists may often be found only in unofficial loose-leaf or other services. In this event, or when the official report is not readily accessible to lawyers, cases may be cited to the unofficial service. See §32.14.19 for citation form of loose-leaf services.

7. *Punctuation in case citation.*

a. *Commas.* Commas separate the case name from the volume, page and date citation, but are not used in the volume and page element itself except in multipage references.

> *Doe* v. *Roe*, 154 F.2d 859 (9th Cir. 1946).
> *SEC* v. *Bourbon*, 47 F. Supp. 70, 73 (W.D. Ky. 1942).

Comma use in the main text depends upon the number, locations, and completeness of the citations to be set off. Note the punctuation below.

> These objections prevailed. Brown v. Coumanis, 135 F.2d 163 (9th Cir. 1943).
> These objections prevailed in Brown v. Coumanis.[1] [Text.]
> [1]135 F.2d 163 (9th Cir. 1943). [Footnote.]

b. *Parentheses.* The parenthesis at the end of a citation is a significant device for imparting information. Writers should use this device whenever they feel additional information concerning the cited case would be helpful to the reader.

In the middle of a sentence. Use a comma only if it would have been necessary if the parentheses were not there.

> The case cited (401 Ill. 262) is not in point.
> The case cited (401 Ill. 262), not being in point, is . . .

If a complete citation is given in the middle of a sentence, writers should set off the citation by commas rather than employing parentheses.

> These objections prevailed, *Brown* v. *Coumanis*, 135 F.2d 163 (9th Cir. 1943), but that case is not in point.

Parenthetical matter closing a sentence. Place the period outside and after the final parenthesis, with no comma preceding the parenthetical matter.

> These objections prevailed (*Brown* v. *Coumanis*, 135 F.2d 163).

In a separate sentence. Place the period before the final parenthesis.

> These objections prevailed. (*Brown* v. *Coumanis* is not applicable.)

Miscellaneous comments. Except with "semble" and "passim," brief comments made upon a case but not bearing upon its authority as precedent may be enclosed in parentheses.

Bridges v. *Wixon*, 326 U.S. 135 (1945) (deportation).
Wood Paper Co. v. *Heft*, 75 U.S. (8 Wall.) 333 (1869).
See *Gulf Oil Corp.* v. *Gilbert* (Mr. Justice Black dissenting, 330 U.S. 501, 512 (1947)).

c. *Semicolons*. These are used to set off citations in a string.

Hargrave v. *Turbeville*, 114 F.2d 33, 36 (2d Cir. 1940); *Salmon* v. *Leverett*, 201 Fed. 99, 100 (2d Cir. 1912).

8. *English law reports citation*.

a. *Indicating the court deciding the case*. The court should be included except in report series where the court is plainly indicated in the series title. In the Law Reports series the title usually indicates the court, but Court of Appeal cases (C.A.) and Judicial Committee of the Privy Council cases (P.C.) are exceptions.

Comber v. *Jones*, 3 Bos. & Pull. 114, 127 Eng. Rep. 62 (C.P. 1802).
Fyfe v. *Garden*, [1946] 1 All E.R. 366 (H.L.).

b. *Dating English case decisions*. Put dates in parentheses at the end of the citation. Exceptions are those Law Reports beginning in 1891, and the All England Reports, in which the date, in brackets, is an integral part of the citation, preceding the series volume and page notation.

Bain v. *Central Vermont Ry. Co.*, [1921] 2 A.C. 412.
Fyfe v. *Garden*, [1946] 1 All E.R. 366 (H.L.).

When the actual *decision* date differs in year from the bracketed *publication* or imprint date, then the decision date is added, in parentheses, at the end of a bracketed date citation.

Petrie v. *Mac Fisheries, Ltd.*, [1940] 1 K.B. 258 (C.A. 1939).

c. *Volume numbers*. For cases since 1891, be certain to cite both the bracketed date and the volume number of the Law Reports, as each series renumbers annually.

Hill v. *Regem*, [1945] 1 K.B. 329.

d. *Parallel citations of English cases*. There has never been a system of "official" reporting in England. Even the Law Reports are not official. American practice is to give parallel citations for reports up to the Law Reports (through 1865); after that date, cite only the Law Reports if the case is printed therein. If the case is

The Law Reports, 1865 to Date

Reporter	*1865-1875*	*1876-1881*	*1881-1891*	*1891-1926*	*1926-date*
Admiralty and Ecclesiastical Cases	L.R.A. & E.				
Chancery Appeal Cases	L.R. Ch. App.				
Chancery Division		1 Ch. D.	16 Ch. D.	L.R. [1891] Ch.	[1926] Ch.
Common Pleas Cases	L.R.C.P.	1 C.P.D.			
Crown Cases Reserved	L.R.C.C.				
English and Irish Appeal Cases	L.R.H.L.				
Equity Cases	L.R. Eq.				
Exchequer Cases	L.R. Ex.	1 Ex. D.			
Privy Council Appeal Cases					
House of Lords Cases	L.R.P.C.	1 App. Cas.	6 App. Cas.	[1891] App. Cas.	[1926] App. Cas.
Privy Council Cases					
Probate and Divorce Cases	L.R.P. & D.	1 P.D.	6 P.D.	L.R. [1891] P.	[1926] P.
Queen's Bench Cases	L.R.Q.B.				
Queen's Bench Division (inc. Crown Cases Reserved)		1 Q.B.D.	6 Q.B.D.	L.R. [1891] 2 Q.B.	
King's Bench Division				L.R. [1902] 2 K.B.	[1926] 2 K.B.

not printed in the Law Reports, cite other reports in parallel, if any.

Parallel citations in original report and English Report, Full Reprint. This series collected nearly all the early cases and reprinted them in 176 volumes and a two-volume table of cases. The parallel citation to the original report is found with the head-note of the reprint and should be given.

Campbell v. *French*, 6 T.R. 200, 101 Eng. Rep. 510 (K.B. 1795).

e. *Citing the Law Reports.* Citation is rather complicated. In the accompanying chart, note particularly the use or omission of "L.R." as part of the citation, the use of brackets for dates, and, since 1891, the renumbering of volumes each year when there is more than one volume in any series for that year. English practice for cases after 1891 places the date in brackets at the beginning of the series citation. For cases prior to 1891 the date is in parentheses at the end of the citation.

Hargrave v. *Turbeville*, L.R. 2 Ex. 130 (1867).
Leverette v. *Salmon*, L.R. 2 Ch. App. 100 (1866).
Stonaker v. *Fiodalisi*, 7 Ch. D. 680 (1877).
Breuer v. *Bloomfield*, L.R. 6 Q.B. 130 (1870).
Borner v. *Nolan*, [1946] 1 K.B. 480.

Cite the present Queen's Bench Division reports as Q.B., not Q.B.D., as was done from 1876 to 1891. The "D" was dropped in 1891 for Probate and Chancery Division citations also.

f. *Law Journal, Law Times, Times Law, and All England Reports.* With the exception of the All England Reports, these have ceased publication, but are still cited.

Rex v. *Knockaloe Camp*, 87 L.J.K.B. (N.S.) 46 (1918).
Beard v. *Beard*, 174 L.T.R. (N.S.) 65 (C.A. 1845).
Lemon v. *Lardeur*, [1946] 2 All E.R. 329 (C.A.).

g. *Court of Appeal cases.* There is no such report series, though there is such a court.

Milmo v. *Carreras*, [1946] 1 K.B. 306 (C.A.).
Lemon v. *Lardeur*, [1946] 2 All E.R. 329 (C.A.).

h. *Appeals Cases.* Do not confuse the House of Lords and Judicial Committee of the Privy Council cases with the Court of Appeal cases above.

9. *Canadian law reports.* Canadian case citation form, as employed in law reports, differs from the United States style in that the decision date precedes (rather than follows) the series citation. Where, as in the Canada Law Reports beginning with

1923, and in the Dominion Law Reports, volumes are numbered anew each year instead of in a consecutive series, the date is in brackets (identical with the English Law Reports style). Where the numbering is consecutive, the date is in parentheses.

> [1926] S.C.R. 412. [1926 has only one volume.]
> [1951] 3 D.L.R. 86; *but*
> (1906) 23 R.P.C. 66
> (1951) 3 W.W.R. (N.S.) 169.

It is suggested, in the interest of uniformity, that when cited in the United States, the last two citations above read

> 23 R.P.C. 66 (1906).
> 3 W.W.R. (N.S.) 169 (1951).

10. *Civil law citations*. While there is no uniform citation for all Civil Law countries, the following forms are suggested to the American user by Dr. Bruno H. Greene, formerly of the Vienna Bar, Professor of Law and Law Librarian of the University of Minnesota.

a. *Statutes*. Cite: (1) country, (2) the word "Law," (3) exact date, (4) number of official gazette or collection in which published.

> *France:* Law, July 14, 1819, Sec. VII B [Bulletin des Lois] 294.
> *Germany:* Law, March 30, 1892, R. Ges. Bl. 369.

b. *Codes*. Cite: (1) country, (2) article or section, (3) code name. If the edition is important, add date in parentheses at end of the citation.

> *Italy*: Art. 54, Cod. di Commercio.

c. *Law reports*. Cite: (1) country, (2) the word "Decision," (3) name of court and/or place (if given), (4) date, (5) docket number (if given), (6) name and number of collection in which case is contained. Parties' names are usually omitted.

> *Belgium:* Decision, Bruxelles, April 5, 1913, Pas[icrisie Belge], 1013, II, 334.
> *Austria:* Decision, March 17, 1914, R II 64 G[lasier] U[nger] 6865.

d. *Periodicals*. Cite: (1) author, (2) country (in parentheses), (3) title of article, (4) volume number, (5) name of periodical, (6) date, (7) number of issue, (8) page or other subdivision.

> Pogoda, Benon (Poland), *Niesluszne Zbogacenie*, 62 Gazeta Sadvowa Warszawska, Jan. 29, 1934, n. 5, pp. 65–67.
> Braun, Rudolf (Austria), *Zur Frage der Reformbeduerftigkeit des Drit-*

ten Rueckstellungsgesetzes, J[uristische] Bl[aetter], Jan. 7, 1950, n. 1, pp. 1–3.

e. *Treatises and commentaries*. Cite: (1) author, (2) title, (3) place of publication, (4) date, (5) volume, (6) page or other subdivision.

Demogue, *Les Notions Fondamentales du Droit Privé*, Paris, 1911, I, n. 246.

§32.11. Table of signals.

Briefs often confine themselves to noting that a cited authority has affirmed or reversed, was dismissed on appeal, or was a square holding or dictum, or should be compared with another authority. In much theoretical writing, however, a more elaborate system is employed to indicate shades of authority. In using signals, it is wise to refer to the particular page or section number to which the signal refers.

No signal	This (1) indicates direct support for the stated proposition or (2) identifies the source of a quotation.
Accord	The cited authority supports directly the previous authority cited but is in some respect distinguishable from it.
Cf.	The cited authority supports an analogous proposition arising from substantially different facts.
See	The cited authority either (1) contains dicta in support of a proposition or (2) *implicitly* supports the stated proposition.
Contra	The cited authority directly contradicts the proposition. Compare with "no signal."
But see	The cited authority (1) contains dicta in contradiction to the proposition or (2) implicitly contradicts the stated proposition. Compare with "*See*."
But cf.	The cited authority contradicts an analogous proposition arising from substantially different facts. Compare with "*cf.*"
Compare . . . with . . .	Comparison of the cited authorities will illustrate a proposition.
E.g.; see, e.g.,	The cited authority is representative of many cases or authorities which are not cited. When using *e.g.*, always (1) begin a new citation sentence, (2) italicize, and (3) follow it with a comma.

See generally	The cited authority provides useful background information but does not support the proposition made.
See also	The cited authority provides background information which is analogous to that examined in the text and which will be profitable to the reader.

Examples

no signal, *accord*	Failure to provide the patient with necessary information constitutes malpractice. *Doctors' Hospital* v. *Amos*, 126 Conn. 432, 436, 25 A.2d 429, 431 (1943); *accord*, *Lowe* v. *Rose*, 212 Minn. 514, 2 N.W.2d 426 (1942).
Cf.	*Cf. Thomas* v. *Collins*, 232 U.S. 516, 540 (1945). *But cf. Bailey* v. *Alabama*, 219 Ala. 220 (1911).
See	*See Wright* v. *Cummins*, 109 Kan. 667, 668, 196 Pac. 246, 247 (1921).
Contra	*In re La Porte*, 54 F. Supp. 911 (W.D.N.Y. 1943); *contra*, *In re Danby* [giving citation].
See, e.g.,	*See, e.g.*, Scanlon, *A Theory of Freedom of Expression*, 1 Phil. & Pub. Aff. 204, 207–208 (1972).

§32.12. Citation order.

Primary authority is cited before secondary authority; higher courts before lower courts in the same jurisdiction; a statute before a case interpreting it. In citing secondary authority, the descending order is from a book to a leading article, to a note, to a case comment.

1. *Primary authority*.

Statutes: Cite in chronological order from earlier to later forms.

> Act of March 3, 1873, c. 234, §1, 17 Stat. 567, 38 U.S.C. §155 (1958 ed.).

Cite a statute which is positive law before one which is not.

> 49 Stat. 499 (1935), 29 U.S.C. §151 (1958 ed.).

In parallel citations, cite the official before the unofficial.

> Ohio Law of October 14, 1931, 114 O.L. 843, General Code of §3294 (Throckmorton, 1940).

Cite the statute before the case interpreting it. Separate the statute from the case with a comma.

N.Y. Decedent Estate Law §78, *Stark* v. *National City Bank*, 278 N.Y. 388, 16 N.E.2d 376 (1938).

Case citations: Cite the official, National Reporter System unit (e.g., Atlantic), and A.L.R. (if reference to A.L.R. is desired), in that order.

2. *Secondary authority: Purpose signals*. Unless the material cited is in support of a settled point of law, a proper signal should precede the citation of such material. Utilize the signals discussed in §32.11.

§32.13. Repeating citations.

Legal writers have adopted such devices as *ibid.*, *id.*, *supra*, *infra*, *op. cit. supra*, etc. (always italicized) as shortcuts. They are to be used with great caution so that confusion is avoided.

1. *Text references*. Once a case has been fully cited in the main text (or cited there by name with appropriate footnote reference to the reporter) it may thereafter be referred to by short title only. Employ such short titles only if the second reference is reasonably proximate to the first reference so that the reader can easily determine the full title. If a particular page is referred to in the later reference, the full name must be given.

In the *Hot Oil* case, the court said . . .
As noted in *Halvey* v. *Halvey*, *supra* at 613 . . .

a. *Supra*. Use *supra* to refer to a case previously cited on the same or preceding page, but if more pages than that intervene, repeat the citation in full.

Halvey v. *Halvey*, *supra*.

b. *Quotation containing a citation*. Where the citation to a case in the text is in a quotation, cite the case fully in further references.

c. *Ibid.*, *Id*. Where (in a text or footnote reference) there is a complete case citation and another reference is made to that case without intervening citations (in footnotes, in succeeding notes), "*ibid*." is sufficient. Where the citation is to a different page, cite "*id*. at page 119." This shortcut is restricted to references on the same or the opposite page of the text so that both references are visible to the reader at the same time. Note the punctuation below.

"For this Court has declared in *Guaranty Trust Co.* v. *York*, 326 U.S. 99, 109, that a right without a remedy is not a right. . . . The York case says this precludes a resort to the Federal court . . . *ibid.*, so that Bullington's chance to get to the Federal court on such a basis was practically nil. *Id*. at 109."

In a footnoted brief, the volume and page citation above and the "*ibid*." and "*id*." following would be footnotes.

> [1]326 U.S. 99, 108 (1946).
> [2]*Ibid*.
> [3]*Id*. at 109.

2. *Footnote references*. When an authority is cited in a footnote relative to a statement in the main text but has not been mentioned in the text directly, repeat the citation in full in a later text reference to it.

If a case has been cited in a footnote and is referred to again in the same footnote, the case name, with *supra*, is sufficient. Indicate dictum by the usual means for a spot citation.

> *Quigg* v. *Newgrass Co.*, *supra*.
> *Quigg* v. *Newgrass Co.*, *supra* at 900, 286 N.Y. Supp. at 928.

In a footnote reference to a single case cited in the footnote immediately preceding, the case name is sufficient.

> [17]*Halvey* v. *Halvey*, *supra* note 16.

3. *Secondary material citations*. A limited use of "*op. cit. supra*" is permissible, but the device should never be employed where ambiguity is possible, as when two different works by the same author have been cited.

> *Robertson*, *op. cit. supra* note 3, at 15.

4. *Shortened citation to avoid full repetition*.

> *Hearings before Senate Committee on Finance on H.R. 5327 (Import Duty on Virgin Copper)*, 81st Cong., 1st Sess. (1949), p. 56 (hereinafter cited as *Hearings on H.R. 5327*).

5. *Punctuation*. *Id*. at, *supra* at, *infra* at, *supra* note 17 at, require no comma following the italicized words.

§32.14. Treatises, reports, periodicals, etc.

1. *Generally*. The material is cited by volume (if more than one), author (personal or corporate), title, page or section, edition, editor (when important), and date.

> 2 Pomeroy, Equity Jurisprudence 428 (5th ed., Symonds, 1941). [5th ed. 1941, if no editor is named, omitting commas.]

2. *Page or section references*. See §32.16.

3. *Author entry*. Authors are personal (as Wigmore, Powell), or corporate (as Columbia University, Department of State, New York Law

Revision Commission). Many works (as monographs in series) have both kinds. The table below shows these forms.

Volume	*Author*	*Title*	*Edition, date, etc.*
6	Williston	*Contracts*	(rev. ed. 1936)
	American Jewish Congress	*Survey of . . . Admissions*	(1947)
33	U.S. Dept. of Labor	Annual Report [no italics]	(1945)
	A.B.A. Special Committee on Assistance to Lawyers	Report	(1944)
6	N.Y. Judicial Council	Annual Report	(1940)

a. *Personal author*. Legal citation practice omits given names or initials unless their inclusion is necessary for clarity: Wigmore, but T. R. Powell, R. R. B. Powell.

> Steiber, *Ten Years of Minnesota Labor Relations Act* (1949), p. 9. [Text or footnote reference.]
>
> Steiber, Jack W., *Ten Years of Minnesota Labor Relations Act* (Bull. No. 9, University of Minnesota Industrial Relations Center 1949), p. 9. [Index to brief.]

b. *Corporate author*. Many reports and pamphlets lack a personal author. Cite the significant author, whether personal or corporate, first. Note that in the table above, all but Williston are corporate authors.

Occasionally a report which is better known by title than by the agency producing it is cited by title. This is not recommended, however. Both title and author should be given in all situations in order to provide the reader with necessary information for finding the publication.

> *Investment Trusts and Investment Companies:* Part 5, *Conclusions and Recommendations* (SEC 1942).

c. *Both a personal and a corporate author*. Generally cite by the personal author, with a parenthetical reference to the publishing agency.

> Walton Hamilton, *Patents and Free Enterprise* (TNEC Monograph No. 31, 1941), p. 19. [Note that the author's name is not inverted.]

4. *Title*. Cite in full the title as on the title page with "A", "An," or "The," unless unduly long or complicated. "Treatise on" is usually omitted. Do not cite as "Williston on Contracts," unless that is the exact title. Cite as "Williston, *Contracts*."

a. *Editor's name as part of the title*. Cite by the editor's name only when it has become better known than the original author's.

Brannan, *Negotiable Instrument Law* (7th ed., Beutel, 1948), but *Medina's Bostwick's Forms*.

b. *Annual reports*.

6 N.Y. Jud. Council Ann. Rept. 17 (Leg. Doc. No. 48, 1940).

5. *Edition*. Note the capitalization and punctuation below.

Gray, *Rule against Perpetuities* (4th ed., Roland Gray, 1942).
Williston, *Contracts* (rev. ed. 1936). [No comma.]
Walker, Patents *(Deller's* ed. 1937). [No comma here.]

6. *Translators*. These are shown in parentheses.

Hatschek, *An Outline of International Law* (Manning trans. 1930).

7. *Periodic reports*. Cite by agency and title. The tradition of citing the publications of the Attorney General of the United States by title (Ops. Atty. Gen.) is still too strong to break, however.

A periodic report is cited as is a law report, with the title not italicized.

a. *If the volumes are numbered*.

73 A.B.A. Rept. 207 (1948).
33 Dept. of Labor Ann. Rept. 19 (1948).

b. *If the volumes are not numbered*.

1947 Attorney Gen. Ann. Rept. 49.

8. *Numbered bulletins lacking a personal author*.

a. *If cited singly*.

Characteristics of Company Unions (U.S. Bureau of Labor Statistics, Bull. No. 634, 1935), p. 37.

b. *If cited as one of several*.

Bull. No. 634 *(Characteristics of Company Unions*, 1935), p. 37.
Bull. No. 770 [giving title, etc.].

9. *Collected essays*.

a. *Collected essays of one author*.

Bohlen, *Landlord and Tenant*, in his *Studies in the Law of Torts* (1926), p. 202.

b. *Collected essays of several authors*.

Corwin, *Judicial Review in Action*, in 1 *Selected Essays in Constitutional Law* 449 (1938).

10. *American Law Institute publications*. For citation purpose in briefs the Restatements should be assimilated to statutes, and not italicized.

21 A.L.I. Proceedings 157 (1944).
A.L.I. Restatement, Torts §18 (1934).
A.L.I. Restatement, Agency §390, comment (1933).
A.L.I. Model Code of Evidence, Rule 399 (1942).
Uniform Commercial Code §76 (1949).

11. *Legal encyclopedias*. Cite to volume, page, topic, section and note, and date. Providing the date takes care of the problem of replacement volumes of C.J.S. and Am. Jur.

43A C.J.S. 712, Injunctions, Section 321 (1978) [Main text.]
43A C.J.S. 712, Injunctions, Section 321 (1978) [Footnote.]
43A C.J.S., Injunctions, Section 156 (Ann. Cum. Part 1978).
36 Am. Jur., Mechanics' Liens §206 (Cum. Supp. 1957).
53 Am. Jur. 2d, Mechanics' Liens §206 (Cum. Supp. 1978).

When omitting the subject heading:

47 C.J. 644, n. 30; 36 Am. Jur. 136.

12. *Briefs*. Parts of the briefs, transcript of the record below, etc., are usually cited in parentheses in other briefs. Do not italicize the references. Examples of citations in briefs are given below.

The formula in Appellant's brief (p. 4) is inoperable.
The Appellant's formula is alleged to contain kaolin (Br. 4).
It is alleged that this is operable (Appellant's Brief 17), but . . .
Brief for the United States as *amicus curiae*, p. 17, *Smith* v. *Jones* . . .
Brief for Appellees, pp. 17, 27 *Doe* v. *Roe*, 300 N.Y. 19 (1948).
Transcript of Record, p. 10, *Jackson* v. *Clayton & Durante*, 60 F.2d 18 (1932).
The Appellant is licensed to do business in Canada (R. 17).
Appellant does business in Canada (R. 17) and in . . .
Appellant argues (Br. 53) that . . .
The agreement (Appellant's Exhibit 19, not printed in the record) was . . .
. . . were assigned against Defendant (Defendant's Exhibit 27, R. 29, f. 1).
Is it true that Defendant's formula contains kaolin? (R. 21).

13. *Department of State publications*. Routine publications are cited by series number and title.

Dept. of State Pub. No. 1288, *Communications to the Mexican Ambassador at Washington* (1939).

More important publications may be cited by title.

United States Relations with China . . . (U.S. Dept. of State Pub. No. 3673, Far Eastern Series No. 30, 1949).

Foreign Relations of the United States (a series).

Foreign Rel. U.S. 1912 (Dept. of State 1937), p. 616.

2 Foreign Rel. U.S. 1932, at 473 (Dept. of State 1947). [There were two volumes of the series this year.]

Department of State Bulletin.

20 Dept. of State Bull. 577 (1949).

14. *Press releases*. These are usually cited by title; if mimeographed, the citation should so indicate.

Proposed New Rules of Practice, Treasury Dept. Press Release No. 793, Nov. 27, 1949 (mimeographed).

15. *Law reviews*.

a. *Volume and page references*.

49 Colum. L. Rev. 344 (1949).

1948 Wis. L. Rev. 528. [Where volumes are unnumbered.]

b. *Leading articles*. Cite by author, title, volume, periodical, and page. In the main text, the author's name may be copied in full. In footnote references cite as below, with initials given only when their omission might cause uncertainty.

Browder, *Testamentary Conditions Against Contest* . . . 49 Colum. L. Rev. 321, 327 (1949). [Spotting material on page 327, of an article beginning on page 321.]

W. A. Hamilton, *Safety in Airline Maintenance*, 9 J. Air L. 275 (1938). [Where there is more than one Hamilton.]

c. *Notes*. As distinguished from case comments, these are variously called by law reviews "notes," "Comments," "Notes and Comments," etc. When citing, follow the periodical's own nomenclature. Notes are cited with or without title.

Note, 34 Va. L. Rev. 944 (1948). [Footnote style.]

Note, *Constitutionality of Proposed Legislation*, 34 Va. L. Rev. 944 (1948).

Notes, 49 Colum. L. Rev. 363 (1949), 27 Tex. L. Rev. 337 (1949). [In consecutive notes from different reviews, all are designated as "Notes."]

d. *Legislation notes*.

Legis., *Merger and Consolidation in Iowa*, 34 Iowa L. Rev. 67 (1948).

e. *Case comments*. Cite either by volume and page alone or by the case commented upon. In the latter instance, the case comment citation is given as a parallel citation to the case itself. Give both the law review publication date and the decision date if they differ. Follow the review's own nomenclature.

Recent Decisions, 47 Mich. L. Rev. 109 (1948).
Pope v. *Garrett*, 204 S.W.2d 867 (1947), 37 Ky. L. Rev. 113 (1948).

16. *Newspapers*. Cite by title, page, column and date. When there are several sections not continuously paged, add the section number before the page number.

Smith v. *Jones*, U.S. Sup. Ct., New York Times, Feb. 5, 1950, p. 6, col. 3.
Krock, *How the Super-Bomb Was Disclosed*, New York Times, Feb. 2, 1950, p. 26, col. 5. [A signed article.]

17. *Capitalization of titles of leading articles and notes*. Capitalize first words, nouns, pronouns, adjectives, adverbs and verbs. Do not capitalize, except as first words, articles, conjunctions or prepositions.

Bargain and Sale under Power in Deeds of Trust.
Distress and Execution in Pennsylvania.

18. *Government periodicals*. Cite as any other periodical.

94 Cong. Record 9761 (1948).

19. *Loose-leaf services*. Loose-leaf services are cited by volume, name and publisher, subdivision, and date. Generally, refer to a section number within the service. If section numbers are not provided, refer to page numbers. The date to be given is the date of decision (if reference is to a case), the date of enactment (if to a statute), or the date of the publication of the page on which the cited material appears (if the cited material itself is undated).

1976 12 Lab. L. Rep. (CCH) 3010.

§32.15. Page citations.

1. *Multivolume works*. Where the reference is to sections rather than pages, the same principles govern as in page citations. No comma should separate the title of the reporter, treatise or document from either the page or section designation.

330 U.S. 219 (1948).
49 Colum. L. Rev. 927 (1949).
4 Walker, *Patents* 28 (Deller's ed. 1947).
6 Fed. Res. Bd. Ann. Rept. 36 (1919).
8 Wigmore, Evidence §2195 (3d ed. 1940).

2. *Single-volume works*.
a. *Law reports*. Pages are referred to in the same manner as in multivolume works.

Gilbert v. Cooley, Walk. Ch. 494 (Mich. 1844).

b. *Unnumbered treatises, bulletins, reports, etc.*

S. Rept. No. 1631, 77th Cong., 2d Sess. (1942), p. 51.
Prosser, *Torts* (2d ed. 1955), p. 193. [Or pp. 193–198.]
Prosser, *Torts* (2d ed. 1955), §95.
Secretary of Labor Ann. Rept. (1946), p. 40.

3. *Citations to more than one page.*

Where numbers are consecutive: 69–83. [Or pp. 69–83.]
Where numbers are not consecutive: 69, 70, 73. [Or pp. 69, 70, 73.]
Where numbers are consecutive and above 100: 169–173, *not* 169–73.

4. *Spot page references.*

a. *Law reports. Edmonds* v. *Heil,* 333 Ill. App. 497, 77 N.E.2d 863 (1948), is to the entire case beginning on the pages noted. A citation to 333 Ill. App. 497, 501, 77 N.E.2d 863, 866 (1948), is to the matter on pages 501 and 866 of the reporters cited.

b. *"At" in spot page references.* This convention is now usually confined to one of the following situations so that the use of "p." or "page" as a part of a citation is avoided.

In case citation. Further references to a different page of a case already cited may be made as follows. Note punctuation.

297 N.Y. 315
Id. at 319.
Jones v. *Smith, supra* at 321.

In further citation to a different page. Where a treatise or periodical article has already been fully cited, "at" may be used as follows. Note the punctuation.

4 Wigmore, *op. cit. supra* note 23, at 18.
4 Wigmore, *op. cit. supra* note 23, §2817. Since the section symbol is necessary here anyway, no purpose is served by adding "at."

c. *Annotations.* The citation is to the first page and a page reference of the *annotation*, not to the case.

Annot. 157 A.L.R. 315, 321 (1945).

5. *Parenthetical page citations.* If the citation is a sentence by itself, the period in the parenthetical sentence is inside the parenthesis.

The formula is copied from Appellant's brief. (See p. 17.)

If a page citation at the end of a sentence is a part of that sentence, the period follows the parenthesis.

This was cited in the Appellant's brief (p. 17).

If the page citation occurs in the middle of a sentence, cite as follows:

The case cited (401 Ill. 262) is not in point.
The case cited (401 Ill. 262), not being in point, is not . . . .

Where there is more than one parenthetical page reference in a sentence, cite as follows.

The court held (p. 319) as the State claims, but the Appellant's brief denies it (p. 2).

Where the parenthetical citation follows a question, avoid possible ambiguity by citing as follows.

Did the formula in Appellant's brief contain kaolin? (See pg. 4.)

6. *Briefs*. For page references in briefs, see §32.17.2.

7. *Statutes*. Except in some state session laws and in the United States Statutes at Large, statutes are seldom cited by page.

a. *United States Statutes at Large*. Cite by volume and page, plus either the title of the act, the chapter, section, or a specific page, if the context does not identify the reference.

38 Stat. 730 (1914). [Alone, it is insufficient.]
The Clayton Act, 38 Stat. 730 (1914), identifies the act by name.
Section 6 of the Clayton Act, 38 Stat. 731 (1914), refers to the exact page where the section is printed.
38 Stat. 731, §6 (1914).

b. *United States Code*. Page citations are rare.

c. *State session laws*. See §32.8.

§32.16. Numerals.

1. *Cardinal and ordinal*. One, two, six are cardinals; first, second, sixth are ordinals. The contractions 1st, 2d, 6th, etc., are not abbreviations, and need no following period except when they close a sentence.

2. *Figures*.

a. *Serial numbers*. Cite in figures.

Bulletin 725 Document 71 pages 352–357, *not* 352–57.

b. *Dates, quantities, and measurements are expressed in figures*.

June 1935, *not* June, 1935 March 6 to April 15, 1935
1st day of May [in forms] *but* the last of May 6 acres

c. Isolated numbers of 10 or more are expressed in figures.

50 ballots 10 times as large about 40 persons

d. *Percent*. Use figures with "percent."

3. *Numbers spelled out*.

a. *At the beginning of a sentence*. Spell out.
b. *In a sentence in the main text*.

> Eighty-first Congress, *but* in a statute or report, 81st Cong., 1st Sess.

c. *Numbers less than ten are spelled out*.

> six horses eight times as large *but* 3½ cans

d. *Fractions standing alone*. Generally, these should be spelled out.

> three-fourths of an inch *but* ½ to 1¾ cans

§32.17. Quotations in briefs.

1. *In general*. Quoted matter is reproduced verbatim, even to errors in spelling, etc. Some matter, however, is usually deleted in a quotation, page references may be added, emphasis supplied, and obvious errors noted (but not corrected). Whenever any of these actions is taken, it should be precisely indicated.

2. *Citing the source: Cases*. In quoting from an opinion not previously cited, the quotation is preceded or followed by a citation to the quoted source, including the exact page upon which the quotation begins.

> "It is likewise generally recognized law . . . that negligence exists toward a pedestrian using a passive path. . . . " *Erie Railroad Co.* v. *Tompkins*, 304 U.S. 64, 70 (1938).

Generally, page references should precede the quotation.

> Mr. Justice Holmes stated in his dissent (page 273) that the doctrine was outmoded: [quoting].

3. *Short quotations*. Set off in the main text by quotation marks.

> The defendant contended "that by the common law . . . the only duty owed to the plaintiff was to refrain from willful or wanton injury" (*id*. at 80).

4. *Long quotations*. A quotation of more than three or four lines becomes cumbersome in the body of a brief and should be set off by itself, by a wide indention on both sides. The quotation is dropped two spaces and is typed single space, with double spaces between the paragraphs quoted. Omit quotation marks.

> Mr. Justice Reed in his dissent discussed the application of *Swift* v. *Tyson* (p. 9):.
>
> > The "doctrine of *Swift* v. *Tyson*," as I understand it, is that the words, "the laws," as used in §34, line one, of the Federal

> Judiciary Act of September 24, 1789, do not include in their meaning "the decisions of the local tribunals." Mr. Justice Story, in deciding that point, said . . .

To decide the case now before us and to "disapprove" the doctrine of *Swift* v. *Tyson* [continuing the quotation].

5. *Quotation within a quotation.* Where a quotation appears within a quotation, the primary quotation is enclosed by double marks, the secondary one by single marks.

> "In support of the above statement, the court quoted from the case of *State ex rel. Gwin* v. *Spencer*, 220 Ind. 337, 339, 43 N.E.2d 724 (1942), as follows:
>
> " 'Jurisdiction over the case must necessarily be in some court . . . for the protection of the rights of the parties litigant.' "

6. *Omissions from quoted matter.* It is customary and permissible to quote selectively, being careful that the meaning of the matter quoted is in no way altered and that the original text is not garbled. Whenever something is omitted from a quotation, the omission should be indicated by three periods or by asterisks.

a. *Omissions within a sentence.* An omission is indicated by the three dots or asterisks located one space apart and separated by one space from the rest of the quoted matter.

> We do not question the . . . holding of this court . . . that "the laws of the several states . . . do not include state court decisions as such."

b. *Omission of words at the beginning of a sentence.* Formerly this was always done by prefacing the omission by three dots or asterisks, as: He declared ". . . the operation of the writs has extended." Increasingly popular, however, is the formerly impermissible use of brackets instead of dots. Thus: "[T]he operation of the writs has extended."

c. *Omission of an entire sentence.* At the beginning of a quotation this is indicated by a sentence beginning with a capitalized word.

> . . . There is no federal common law.

d. *When the final sentence of the quotation is incomplete.* Show this by four dots, with one space before the first dot.

e. *When an omission occurs following a complete sentence.* Give the complete sentence its usual period, followed by the three dots indicating the omission.

> Jones alleged he was not there. . . . However, he was there.

7. *In the main text.* When the quoted matter is made a part of the sentence but is not itself a sentence, only the quotation marks are necessary.

> The doctrine assumes "a transcendental body of law . . . " and is therefore inadequate.

b. A *longer quotation*. Where this is set off by itself by wide indention, the three dots are necessary when the quotation does not begin with the first word of a sentence. "This court said in part (p. 82) that . . . as a general rule this court [continuing quotation]."

8. *Dropping a paragraph in a quotation*. Indicate by using five dots to separate the paragraphs actually quoted, to take the place of the one or ones not quoted. Double space between the five dots and the paragraphs above and below.

. . . . .

9. *When the quoted matter itself has dropped matter*. Indicate by using "*sic*."

> Mr. Justice Butler quoted Mr. Justice Holmes to the effect that "a court of the United States was bound . . . [*sic*] before the state courts had rendered an authoritative decision."

10. "*Sic*." *Sic*, a complete word, requires no period except at the end of a sentence. It is italicized. Indicate errors in quoted matter by using "*sic*" (placed in brackets) following the error.

> The statutes was [*sic*] held vaid [*sic*].

11. *Editorial interpolations*. Extraneous matter supplied by the commentator is placed in brackets, and within the quotation marks. Such matter (as page citations, for example), when outside the quotation marks, is placed in parentheses. When using both brackets and parentheses together, brackets are always used outside the parentheses.

12. *Emphasis*. Matter italicized in the quoted matter is of course italicized when quoted. In order to emphasize quoted matter not italicized in the original text, italicize the quoted matter to be emphasized. At the end of the quotation, or in a footnote, use the form below.

> [Emphasis supplied.] [Italics supplied.]

13. *Position of punctuation marks, relative to quotation marks*. The United States Government Printing Office rule is: The comma and the final period will be placed inside the quotation marks. Other punctuation marks should be placed inside the quotation marks only if they are a part of the quotation.

> Mr. Justice Holmes said, "I dissent from the decision. . . . "
> Was it "just one of those things"?
> Who asked, "Why?" [A question part of the quotation.]
> The appellant said, "No!"
> He said that belonged to "The Star"; that it was his.

14. *Citing the source: Statutes.*

a. *In the main text.* Casual reference to the statutory language is frequently made within sentences of the text.

> Section 303 requires notice "in writing."

b. *In parenthetical citations in the main text.* Whether set off by parentheses or commas, or as a separate citation at the end of the sentence, employ the form of designation (Sec., sec., §) used in printing the act itself.

> According to that section (Sec., sec., §303) "notice is required to be in writing."
> ". . . notice is required to be in writing" (Sec. 303).
> ". . . notice is required to be in writing." (Sec. 303.)

c. *A verbatim quotation from a statute in the main text.* Where this requires more than three or four lines, it is blocked off by wide indentions on both sides and dropped two spaces below the preceding text. In federal briefs, when first referring to a statute, writers commonly quote verbatim in a footnote the relevant portions of the statute. Thereafter, previously quoted sections of the statute are referred to only by section. In such footnote citations, quotation marks for the cited matter are the rule.

> The pertinent provisions are as follows:
> "Sec. 5(a). Unfair methods of competition [quoting] 52 Stat. 111-112, 15 U.S.C. §15(a) (1958 ed.)."

Where several rather lengthy sections are to be quoted, a common federal brief practice is to place them together (without using quotation marks) in an appendix.

> APPENDIX I
>
> Relevant provisions of Sec. 5, Sec. 12, and Sec. 15 of the Federal Trade Commission Act (Act of September 26, 1914, 38 Stat. 717, as amended by Act of March 21, 1938, 52 Stat. 111-115, and by Sec. 1107(f) of Act of June 23, 1938, 52 Stat. 1028, 15 U.S.C. Sec. 45, Sec. 52, and Sec. 55):
>
> Sec. 5(a). Unfair methods of competition [quoting].
> Sec. 12(a). It shall be unlawful [quoting].
> Sec. 15. For the purposes of section 12 [quoting].

§32.18. Indexes to briefs.

1. *Scope.* The so-called index is really (a) a table of contents followed by (b) a résumé of counsel's argument, and (c) a list of authorities cited. Exhibits are best listed in the table of contents, which

should list the contents of the brief in the order of presentation in the brief.

2. *Capitalization*. The first word of each new entry is capitalized. Thereafter capitalize only those words which would be capitalized in the brief itself. Section, chapter and clause references, however, are not capitalized except in tabular citations. (See the Fair Labor Standards Act in the index on page 507, compared with other statutory citations there.)

3. *Table of authorities cited*.

a. *Cases*. List alphabetically, in the same form as in the brief. Court action (usually certiorari granted or denied, or affirmance of appeal) is noted. If certiorari is pending, give the case docket number and the term of court. Dates and a notation of the court deciding are sometimes omitted. Pages in the brief where the case is cited are noted in the right-hand column. Case names are italicized in the brief itself.

Alphabetizing case names. Alphabetize by significant name, ignoring corporate initials, *ex parte*, *in re*, etc., but make cross-references as needed.

b. *Federal Constitution and statutes*. List the Constitution, then statutes chronologically.

> Act of June 23, 1947, c. 120, 61 Stat. 136, 29 U.S.C. (1958 ed.) (Labor Management Relations Act of 1947).

Most federal agency briefs list acts by title, if any. Note the Fair Labor Standards Act of 1938, under "Authorities Cited," below.

c. *State constitutions and statutes*. List constitutions alphabetically by states, followed by statutes listed alphabetically by states.

d. *Miscellaneous material*. List alphabetically by author or title. Follow the form used in the brief itself. It is common to give the author's full name in the index, even though cited only by surname in the brief.

4. *Typography*. Follow the form used in the brief itself. Briefs printed all in roman, except the case names, are common in all courts.

INDEX

AUTHORITIES CITED

H.R. 5711, 75th Cong., 1st Sess. 39
Webster's New International Dictionary (2d ed. 1939) 31

§32.19. Capitalization.

1. *In general.* The tendency of most writers is to capitalize too often. When in doubt as to whether a letter should be capitalized, be conservative.

2. *Proper names and their derivatives.* Capitalize unless the derivative has acquired an independent meaning no longer closely identified with the original.

> Italy, Italian, *but* italics.
> Rome, Roman, *but* roman type.

3. "*The.*" Capitalize part of an official name.

> *The Queen Mary* [in a case name].
> the Attorney General.

4. *Names of organized bodies.*

> Congress, House, Senate.
> Committee of the Whole, *but* the committee.
> Virginia Assembly, the assembly.
> State Highway Commission, the highway commission.

5. *First words of an independent clause or sentence.*

> The question is, Shall the bill pass?

a. *Following a colon, exclamation point, or interrogation point.* The first word after punctuation is not capitalized if merely a supplementary remark follows.

> Revolutions are not made: they come.

b. *Where the first word following a colon is an independent passage or sentence or where it is tabular matter.*

> The decision was as follows: That Jones is liable.
> Section 8 provides for these things:
> 1. For a notice in writing.
> 2. For a hearing.
> 3. For an appeal.

6. *Suggested capitalization of words frequently used.*

Act: The Merrill Act, Section 13 of that Act; *but* the act, an act of Congress.
Bill: Bill of Rights; *but* the Ives bill, a Congressional bill.
Brief: Brief for Respondent; *but* as said in Appellant's brief.
Circuit: The Fifth Circuit: *but* the circuit courts.

Clause: as a heading or title: the Commerce Clause; *but* the commerce clause of the Constitution.

Court: The Supreme Court of the United States, the Court; *but* the Court of Appeals, the court.

District: United States Court for the Southern District of New York; *but* the district courts.

Ex parte in a case name: *Ex parte Smith*; *but* an *ex parte* hearing.

Federal: capitalize only when part of a proper name: Federal Constitution; *but* federal courts, federal judges.

Ibid., *id.*: capitalize at beginning of sentence.

In re (no period): Capitalize only when part of a case report: *In re Perkins*.

Law: as a heading or title: Public Law No. 1

Number: only as a heading or as part of a title: House Document number 17, page 3; *but* H. Doc. No. 17, 81st Cong., 1st Sess.

Report: only as a title or a proper name: Attorney General's Report, House Report No. 18; *but* the report of the Attorney General for 1949.

Session: as part of a title: Eighty-first Congress, first session, 81st Cong., 1st Sess.; *but* a special session of Congress.

Volume: as a heading only: Volume 2: Rule against perpetuities; *but* volume 2 of Williston, *supra*.

§32.20. Abbreviations.

1. *Caution*. In employing the shortcut which abbreviations provide, the legal writer must never lose sight of the sole object of a citation to lead its reader to the work cited, without error, ambiguity, or the necessity of consulting additional conversion tables or tables of cases for data which the citation itself should have provided. There is never a legitimate choice between brevity and time-saving for the writer on the one hand and clarity for the citation-user on the other.

2. *Contractions*. Distinguish contractions from abbreviations. Dep't, adm'r, Ass'n, are examples of contractions. They are not followed by a period unless they close a sentence. A contraction begins and ends with the same letter as the full word; an abbreviation often ends on a different letter: Rev., Stat., La., Wis., etc., are examples. Abbreviations are the preferred style.

3. *Spacing abbreviations*.

a. *Omit spacing between elements generally*. But insert space between elements of abbreviations consisting of more than one letter; the ampersand (&) is considered a multiliteral abbreviation.

301 U.S. 15	175 S.E. 81	*NLRB* v. *Jones*
C.C. S.D. N.Y.	Sup. Ct.	Fed. Cas.

b. *Space the following*. The initials of a personal name; before and after unabbreviated words or abbreviations of more than one letter.

United States v. *H. J. Heinz Co.* *S.D. Ohio*

4. *Second series of law reports.* Most law reports series have gone into their second series, some of which are differently abbreviated from the first series: Fed., F.2d; Atl., A.2d; N.Y. Supp., N.Y.S.2d; Pac., P.2d, etc. When the abbreviation unit next to the figures is multiliteral, space: So. 2d, *not* So.2d.

135 F.2d   69 S.W.2d   13 So. 2d

Unofficial reports often designate their second series as "new series."

29 P.U.R. (N.S.) 18 (1948).

5. *Periods.* With a few exceptions, every abbreviation which stands for a single word is followed by a period.

N.Y.   Ind. App.   App. Div.   LL.B.

The exceptions are:

R.R. (for railroad, a single word): S.S. (for steamship);
WGY (radio call letters); SOS (distress signal);
NLRB, ICC, FTC, CIO (for government agencies and labor unions).

6. *Words not abbreviated.* Some words are not abbreviated in legal writing. A few of them follow:

day	mount	fort	point	Senator	port
March	April	May	June	July	Figure
Alaska	Hawaii	Idaho	Iowa	Ohio	Utah

7. *Corporate, firm, and railway names.*

a. *Corporate titles beginning with an initial.* Give the name in full; alphabetize under both the initial and the surname in the index.

H. J. Heinz Co. v. *NLRB*

b. *Railroads' first names.* Spell out the first name in title of railroad, but the rest may commonly be abbreviated. The ampersand (&) should be used for "and" where it is part of the corporate title. Do not abbreviate geographical designations within railroad names.

Chicago, R.I. & P.Ry. Co. v. *Chicago, M. & St. P.R.R. Co.*

8. *Ampersand* (&). Use this in place of "and" only where it is part of the corporate or firm name, as found in legal documents (incorporation) or partnership papers, etc.) or letterheads.

9. *Table of frequently used American abbreviations.* A full table from abbreviation to complete word is found in Price and Bitner, Effective Legal Research (1953), pp. 511–620. An abridged table is included as Appendix III in this book.

§32.21. Typography.

The type styles recommended below are intended for use in briefs and in student papers which conform to the style of briefs. They are the styles most commonly found in printed briefs. Publishers of law books, however, vary in their typographical practices, and each issues its own manual of them for use by its authors. The type styles of the publisher of this book do not always agree with those prescribed in this chapter, particularly as to italicizing titles of books and periodical articles.

1. *Function of type styles*. The great majority of briefs print only the case names except the "v." in italics (whether in text, footnotes, or index references) with everything else in roman. A brief so printed is acceptable in any court or quasi-judicial tribunal. This is a simple rule which reduces the possibility of error.

The use of italics to make more vivid on the printed page the titles of cited secondary material is growing in briefs, however, especially in those presented to federal agencies and courts. This is the style adopted in this chapter. The only problem involved is the determination of what, for the purposes of italics, is a title. Some suggested rules are stated below. In typing, italics are indicated by underlining the words to be italicized.

2. *Statutes and session laws*. All references to section, article, chapter, clause, session laws, statutes, etc., are customarily printed in roman in most legal writing, without large and small caps. In quoting a statute, the typographical style of the matter quoted is adopted. Law review footnote style is to print the titles of session laws in roman ("New York Laws 1942, c. 387"), but titles of statutes in large and small caps ("CONST.," not "Const."; "STAT.," not "Stat."; "INT. REV. CODE," not "Int. Rev. Code"). This book follows the more usual style of printing both session laws and statutes in roman without small caps. (Large and small caps are indicated in manuscript by double-underscoring the letters to be set in small caps.)

3. *Case reports: Case names*. Except for the "v.," italicize case names, whether in the main text, footnotes, or index references. Law reviews italicize case names—including the "v."—in the main text but not in footnotes.

a. *Initials standing for persons*. "A," "B," etc., standing for persons, are capitalized and italicized: *A*, *B*.

b. *Ex parte*, *ex rel.*, *Matter of*. In briefs which italicize case names in text or footnotes, these terms are also italicized. If case names are not italicized, the Latin terms (but not the English "Matter of") are italicized. *Ex rel.* (an abbreviation) requires a period. *In re* (complete words) does not.

Law reviews differentiate Latin elements of case names typographically from the rest. Thus, Ex parte *Sterba* in the text becomes *Ex parte* Sterba in the footnote; *United States* ex rel. *Greathouse* v. *Smith* in the text becomes United States *ex rel.* Greathouse v. Smith in the footnote. Briefs seldom are so complex in their typography.

4. *Case reports: Subsequent history of a case.* When noting that a cited case was later *affirmed, reversed, reversed on other grounds, affirmed* or *reversed sub nom.*, or that *certiorari* or *rehearing* was *denied* or *granted*, the significant words may be italicized. Briefs practically never do this, however. Thus:

> *Joseph A. Holpuch Co.* v. *United States*, 104 Ct. Cl. 67, 67 F. Supp. 949 (1945), certiorari granted sub nom. *United States* v. *Joseph A. Holpuch Co.*, 327 U.S. 772, reversed, 328 U.S. 237 (1946).

5. *Treatises, bulletins, reports.* Most briefs print the entire entry, author and title, in roman type, which is simple and acceptable to courts. Many government briefs, however, following the usual scholarly practice, italicize the title (not including the edition and editor's name), with the rest of the entry in roman. This book recommends the government style.

> Gray, *Rule against Perpetuities* (4th ed., Roland Gray, 1942).

Where the title is that of a periodic report or of a publication assimilated to a statute, print the whole entry in roman; that is, do not italicize "Report," "Annual Report," "Restatement," etc.

> 1947 Atty. Gen. Ann. Rep. 19
> A.L.I. Restatement, Agency §18 (1933).

Where the title of a series, other than a periodical, forms part of a citation, print in roman.

> Walton Hamilton, *Patents and Free Enterprise* (TNEC Monograph No. 31, 1941), p. 19.

6. *Periodicals and newspapers.* Cite the name of the author of a cited article in roman type, whether the author is a person or an impersonal agency. The majority of briefs cite the title in roman, properly enclosed in quotation marks. A substantial number of government briefs, however, italicize the title whether it appears in the text, footnotes, or the index. That form is recommended. No confusion can result as to the title of the article, as sometime results with other type styles.

> Lathrop, *The Racial Covenant Cases*, 1948 Wis. L. Rev. 509.

Everything in a newspaper citation is printed in roman, except that the title of a signed article is italicized, as in a periodical article.

7. *Congressional publications.* Titles of hearings, committee

reports with titles other than "Report," Congressional documents, etc., are italicized.

8. *Italics*. For the use of italics in case names, treatises, periodicals and Congressional publications, see the material immediately preceding this paragraph.

a. *Capital letters indicating persons*.

> *A* went to see *B* about it.

b. *Conventional expressions in legislation and legal documents*.

> *Whereas*, *Resolved*, *Provided*, *Ordered*, *Be it enacted*

c. *Latin and other foreign words and phrases*. Few foreign legal words or phrases are now italicized, as most of them have been taken over into the language and it is an unnecessary affectation to italicize.

Words not to be italicized.

ad valorem	in toto	nisi	res judicata
bona fide	in transitu	nolle	stare decisis
certiorari	ipso facto	pendente lite	subpoena
circa	laissez faire	post mortem	sub nom.
contra	mandamus	pro rata	ultra vires
habeas corpus			

Words to be italicized.

ab initio	*ex parte*	*infra*	*loc. cit.*
a fortiori	*ex rel.*	*in limine*	*nunc pro tunc*
amicus curiae	*ibid.*	*in loco parentis*	*op. cit.*
ante	*id.*	*in re*	*sic*
coram nobis	*idem*	*in rem*	*sua sponte*
e.g.	*i.e.*	*inter se*	*sui generis*
et seq.	*in extenso*	*inter sese*	*supra*

Appendix I | Standard Form of Appellate Brief[1]

[COVER TITLE.]

No. 387

Supreme Court of the United States

October Term, 1951

Jones & Company, *Petitioner,*

v.

Smith Corporation, *Respondent*

ON WRIT OF CERTIORARI TO THE UNITED STATES COURT OF APPEALS FOR THE EIGHTH CIRCUIT

BRIEF FOR PETITIONER

John Jones Smith,
Attorney for Petitioner

1. This form is reprinted here by permission of a prominent law firm. It is the form supplied to its own attorneys for use by them in writing briefs. It is, of course, only an outline of a complete brief.

INDEX

CITATIONS

[FIRST PAGE OF BRIEF]

Supreme Court of the United States

October Term, 1951

No. 387

Jones & Company, *Petitioner,*

v.

Smith Corporation, *Respondent*

ON WRIT OF CERTIORARI TO THE UNITED STATES COURT OF APPEALS FOR THE EIGHTH CIRCUIT

BRIEF FOR PETITIONER

OPINIONS BELOW

The opinion of the District Court (R. 202) is unreported. The opinion and dissenting opinion in the Court of Appeals (R. 276) are reported at 182 F.2d 841.

JURISDICTION

This is an action for breach of contract, brought in the District Court of the United States for the Western District of Missouri. The District Court had jurisdiction under 28 U. S. Code Sec. 1332, the plaintiff Smith Corporation being organized under the laws of the State of Missouri (R. 36), the defendant Jones & Company being a partnership all of whose members are citizens of the State of Oklahoma (R. 48), and the matter in controversy exceeding the sum of $3,000 exclusive of interest and costs (R. 171).

The final judgment of the District Court, in favor of the plaintiff for the sum of $4,325.76 and costs, was entered on January 16, 1949 (R. 204). Notice of appeal to the United States Court of Appeals for the Eighth Circuit was filed on March 3, 1949 (R. 207), that Court having jurisdiction of the appeal under 28 U. S. Code Sec. 1291.

The final judgment of the Court of Appeals affirming the judgment of the District Court was entered on August 24, 1951 (R. 282). The petition for a writ of certiorari was filed on October 14, 1951, and was granted on November 20, 1951. The jurisdiction of this Court rests on 28 U. S. Code Sec. 1254(1).

QUESTIONS PRESENTED

* * * *

STATUTE INVOLVED

The pertinent provisions of the Missouri Sale of Goods Law, Missouri Revised Code, Sections 4226-4240 (1936), are set out in full in Appendix A to this brief, pp. i-iii, *infra.*

* * * *

STATEMENT

* * * *

History of the Litigation

* * * *

Findings of Fact and Judgment

* * * *

SPECIFICATION OF ERRORS TO BE URGED

* * * *

SUMMARY OF ARGUMENT

* * * *

ARGUMENT

* * * *

I

THIS CASE "INVOLVES OR GROWS OUT OF A LABOR DISPUTE" AND THEREFORE IS GOVERNED BY THE NORRIS-LAGUARDIA ACT

Section 1 of the Norris-LaGuardia Act is plain and unambiguous:

> ". . . no court of the United States . . . shall have jurisdiction to issue any restraining order or temporary or permanent injunction in a case involving or growing out of a labor dispute, except in a strict conformity with the provisions of this Act. . . ."

The "labor dispute" involved in this case consists primarily of three fundamental issues, etc., etc., etc.

* * * *

A. VIOLENCE AGAINST CUSTOMERS IS NEITHER CHARGED, PROVED NOR FOUND

* * * *

1. THE FINDING THAT THE POLICE WERE UNABLE AND UNWILLING TO FURNISH ADEQUATE PROTECTION MUST BE SET ASIDE

* * * *

a. Upon This Record the District Court Was Clearly Wrong in Finding that any Effort by Plaintiffs to Settle the Dispute Would Have Been Impossible, Useless, or Unreasonable, and upon the Basis of this Finding, in Excusing the Making of any Effort

* * * *

II

All clauses of the decree enjoining use or threats of fraud must be reversed

* * * *

A. DISCRIMINATION AGAINST THE INTERNATIONAL

* * * *

1. Findings required by Section 7(a)

* * * *

a. Speed-up System

* * * *

CONCLUSION

Wherefore, it is respectfully submitted that the judgment of the court below should be reversed and the cause remanded with instructions to grant the motion to dismiss the complaint.

August 1, 1953

Respectfully submitted,

John Jones Smith,
Attorney for Petitioner

APPENDIX A

Pertinent Provisions of Statutes

1. AGRICULTURAL ADJUSTMENT ACT OF MAY 12, 1933, C. 25, 48 STAT. 31, AS AMENDED, 48 STAT. 676, 49 STAT. 48, 770, 1739, 7 U.S.C. § 617 (1946)

Sec. 17 (a) Upon the exportation to any foreign country (and/or to the Philippine Islands, the Virgin Islands, American Samoa, the Canal Zone, and the island of Guam) of any product processed wholly or partly from a commodity with respect to which product or commodity a tax has been paid or is payable under this title, the tax due and payable or due and paid shall be credited or refunded. Under regulations prescribed by the Commissioner of Internal Revenue, with the approval of the Secretary of the Treasury, the credit or refund shall be allowed to the consignor named in the bill of lading under which the product is exported or to the shipper or to the person liable for the tax provided the consignor waives any claim thereto in favor of such shipper or person liable for the tax. In the case of rice, a tax due under this title which has been paid by a tax-payment warrant shall be deemed for the purposes of this subsection to have been paid; and with respect to any refund authorized under this section, the amount scheduled by the Commissioner of Internal Revenue. . . .

* * * *

2. INTERNAL REVENUE CODE, § 1112

In any proceeding involving the issue whether the petitioner has been guilty of fraud with intent to evade tax, the burden of proof in respect of such issue shall be upon the Commissioner.

* * * *

APPENDIX B

Legislative History

1. REPORT OF THE HOUSE COMMITTEE ON WAYS AND MEANS, H. REPT. NO. 2475, 74TH CONG., 2D SESS. (1934), p. 13.

It is the purpose of Section 601 of Title IV to reenact into law certain sections of the Agricultural Adjustment Act.

Appendix II Memorandum of Law[1]

Question Presented

Under the terms of a will governed by Rhode Island law, does a gift in trust to the testator's daughter for life with a testamentary power of appointment and a gift to "her own right heirs, of my blood" in default of appointment mean that the daughter's heirs take *per stirpes* or *per capita* upon the death of the daughter failing to exercise the power of appointment?

Conclusion

The Rhode Island cases indicate that the gift would be construed to require a stirpital division.

Facts

Joseph Paul Jones died a resident of the State of Rhode Island, and his will was proved on February 15, 1911. By the terms of his will, the testator after making certain specific bequests gave the residue of his estate to trustees in trust. He directed that the corpus be divided into five equal shares, one such share to be held in trust for each of his two sons and each of his two daughters, and one share to be held in trust for his wife. The share for each daughter was to be held for her for life, and upon her death, as she might appoint by her will, and in default of such appointment, "to her own right heirs, of my blood." One of the daughters of Joseph Paul Jones died failing to exercise the

---

1. An important function of the junior attorneys in a law firm is to submit memoranda of law to seniors, on request. The one here reproduced is an actual memorandum from such a junior to his senior, reproduced here by permission. It shows the form and style desired, though it is somewhat shorter and simpler than most memoranda. Note that the conclusion is given immediately following the statement of the problem, not at the end of the memorandum. The same form and techniques may profitably be employed by law students in their written work.

power of appointment. The question arises, do the heirs of the daughter take *per stirpes* or *per capita*.

Applicable Statutes

The applicable provisions of the Rhode Island statute of descent and distribution are found in Rhode Island General Laws 1938, ch. 567.

Course of Descent

§1. Whenever any person having title to any real estate or inheritance shall die intestate as to such estate, it shall descend and pass, in equal portions to his kindred, in the following course:

First. To his children or their descendants, if any there be.

Second. If there be no children nor their descendants, then to the parents in equal shares, or to the surviving parent of such intestate.

Third. If there be no parent, then to the brothers and sisters of such intestate, and their descendants, or such of them as there be. (As amended by ch. 1283, Public Laws 1943.)

Section 2 of ch. 567 makes provisions for the event that there be no parent nor brother nor sister.

Inheritance by Descendants

§5. The descendants of any person deceased shall inherit the estate which such person would have inherited had such person survived the intestate, subject to the express provisions of these canons of descent.

Distribution of Surplus Property Not Bequeathed

§9. The surplus of any chattels or personal estate of a deceased person, not bequeathed, after the payment of his just debts, funeral charges, and expenses of settling his estate, shall be distributed by order of the probate court which shall have granted administration in manner following:

First. — The sum of $3,000.00 from said surplus and one-half of the remainder to the widow or surviving husband forever, if the intestate died without issue.

Second. — One-half of said surplus to the widow or surviving husband forever, if the intestate died leaving issue.

Third. — The residue shall be distributed among the heirs of the intestate in the same manner real estates descend and pass by this chapter but without having any respect to the life estate and discretionary allowance provided by section 4 of this chapter. (As amended by ch. 1283, Public Laws 1943.)

Case Law

From this it can be seen that the statute itself provides in section 7 for stirpital provision. The descendants are to inherit the share which their deceased ancestor would have taken. However, this statutory direction can be overcome if the will of the person making a gift to "heirs" indicates an intent that the division be *per capita*. For example, in *Oulton* v. *Kidder*, — R.I. —, 128 Atl. 674 (1925), where a testatrix gave the residue of her estate to her brother for life, and upon his death "to Helen E. Oulton and my legal heirs," it was held that Helen Oulton and the legal heirs of the testatrix took *per capita* and not *per stirpes*. The Court said, at 128 Atl. 675,

> The general rules controlling whether a gift to "legal heirs" is to be distributed per capita or per stirpes had been considered at length in *Branch* v. *DeWolf*, 38 R.I. 395, 95 A. 857, and *Turbitt* v. *Carney*, 43 R.I. 582, 114 A. 134. The court said: "heirs at law" commonly not only designated the beneficiaries as those who would inherit in case of intestacy but the quantum of interest each should take. This is determined per stirpes and not per capita, unless a contrary intention appears. If Helen E. Oulton had not been interjected into the residuary clause, there would be good ground for the application of the usual rules calling for a per stirpes distribution. Does the will show any facts indicating a contrary intention?

The Court answers its own question in the affirmative, and finds that the testatrix intended the distribution to be *per capita*. Helen E. Oulton received a specific gift under a separate clause of the will, and the Court found no intention to prefer her, through a stirpital division of the residue, to other nephews and nieces.

Another case in which a gift to "heirs" was held to require a *per capita* division is *Dodge* v. *Slate*, 71 R.I. 191, 43 A.2d 242 (1945). The testator left his entire estate to "my heirs now living, share and share alike." The Court says at 43 A.2d 244,

> In both sentences which constitute clause "First" of the will, the testator leaves the estate to his "heirs." Although there are decisions to the contrary, it is generally held that, in the absence of language in the will indicating a different intention, a devise or bequest to a testator's "heirs" without qualification, designates not only the persons who are to take, but also the manner in which the estate shall be distributed, both being in accordance with the statute of intestate succession. The determining issue on this point therefore is whether the testator intended a distribution to his estate to be different from the one prescribed by such statute.

By singling out the words "share and share alike" and "equally among the heirs," the Court finds an intention that the estate be distributed to the heirs *per capita*. Great stress is laid on the word "among" as indicative of an intention that the distribution be *per capita*.

The will of Joseph Paul Jones appears to contain not the slightest hint of an intention that the distribution to the heirs of his daughter should be other than that provided by the statute, that is, stirpital. It is assumed, that at the time the will was executed, the daughters of the testator were unmarried and childless, consequently it cannot be argued that there were any particular individuals in mind when he used the word "heirs." It would seem that here, the general rule of a *per stirpes* provision should apply. No significance can be attached to the word "right" or the words "of my blood" used in the phrase "to her own right heirs, of my blood." These words in no way connote a *per capita* provision. The words "right heirs" are synonymous with "legal heirs," or just "heirs," *Starrett* v. *Botsford*, 64 R.I. 1, 9 A.2d 871 (1931). The cases of *Oulton* v. *Kidder*, *supra*, and *Dodge* v. *Slate*, *supra*, which found an intention that there be a *per capita* distribution are clearly distinguishable on their facts from the situation at hand.

A recent case, *Powers* v. *Dossett*, — R.I. —, 81 A.2d 275 (1951), held that a gift to heirs at law required a *per stirpes* distribution. In this case a testatrix established by her will a trust for her father-in-law and mother-in-law for life, and upon the death of the survivor directed her trustee "to pay over to my heirs at law all [the] trust estate." In a construction proceeding, the Court said,

> In construing the meaning of heirs at law as used in the instant will, we find nothing therein to show clearly that the testatrix intended that those answering such description should be determined at a time other than at her death. We therefore apply the general rule to the will before us and decide that the testatrix' heirs at law are those to whom her estate and property would pass immediately upon her death by operation of law under the statutes of descent and distribution of this state. It follows that our answer to the first question is that the balance of the trust estate should be distributed among the heirs at law of the testatrix *per stirpes*.

As previously said, no intention can be found in the will of Joseph Paul Jones that the distribution to the heirs of his daughter should be other than *per stirpes*. His daughter's heirs will naturally be ascertained at the time of her death.

February 10, 1953

Appendix III | Abbreviations Commonly Used in Anglo-American Law

Scope of definitions. The abbreviations defined in this list are those which law students are most likely to encounter in their course work. No attempt is made at such complete coverage as is required for extensive research.

The present list aims to include practically all United States — federal and state — law reports; all United Kingdom law reports of general interest, the principal Australian, Canadian, and New Zealand law reports of general interest, and some Scottish, Irish, English and Canadian election, bail, bankruptcy and ecclesiastical reports.

Legal periodical abbreviations included are those referring to periodicals of general interest in law school instruction. Where the abbreviation is self-explanatory, it is not defined in this list: where some doubt as to its meaning may exist, the abbreviation is defined. Thus, Georget. L.J. is not defined, but Geo. L.J. is.

Alphabetical arrangement. In order to follow the forms of abbreviations as found in the literature, the abbreviations are listed herein in three different sequences for each initial letter.

1. Abbreviations of which the *first* element is a single letter and the *second* element is not an ampersand (&). Thus:

A.B.C. A.R.R. A.Ins.Co. A.T.&T.Co.

2. Next come abbreviations of which the *first* element is a single letter and the *second* is an ampersand. Thus:

A.&B. A.&E. A.&E.Pat.Cas.

3. Last come abbreviations, the *first* element of which is composed of two or more letters, as:

Ab.Eq.Cas. Am.L.Rev. Ad.&El.

Abbreviations employed in the definitions. In the definitions themselves in this list, certain standard abbreviations are sometimes employed, among which are the following:

A.	Annotated	Ex.	Exchequer
Admin.	Administration	H. L.	House of Lords
Annot.	Annotated	Jour.	Journal
Cas.	Cases	K.B.	King's Bench
Ch.	Chancery	N.P.	Nisi Prius
Cir.	Circuit	P.C.	Privy Council
C.P.	Common Pleas	Pr.R.	Practice Reports
Comm.	Commission	Q.B.	Queen's Bench
Cr. Cas. Res.	Crown Cases Reserved	R.C.	Rolls Court
Crim.	Criminal	Rep.	Reports
Ct.	Court	Rev.	Review
Dec.	Decisions	Sup.	Supreme
Dist.	District	Super.	Superior
Div.	Division	UN	United Nations
Eq.	Equity	Y.	Yearbook

A. Abbott
Alabama
American
Arkansas
Atlantic Reporter
Louisiana Annuals

A.2d Atlantic Reporter, Second Series

AAA Agricultural Adjustment Admin., *U.S.*

AALS Proc. Association of American Law Schools Proceedings

A.B. Anonymous Rep. at end of Benloe, *Eng.*

A.B.A.J. American Bar Assn. Jour.

A.B.A. Rep. American Bar Assn. Rep.

A.B.C. Australian Bankruptcy Cas.

A.B.C. Newsl. International Assn. of Accident Boards and Commissions Newsletter

A.B.F. Research Reptr. J. American Bar Foundation Research Jour.

A.C. Advance Cal. Rep.
Appeal Cas., *Can.*
Law Rep. Appeal Cas., *Eng.*
Law Rep. Appeal Cas., Third Series, *Eng.*

A.C.A. Advance Cal. Appellate Rep.

A.C.L.J. American Civil Law Jour.

A.C.L.U. Leg. Action Bull. American Civil Liberties Union Legislative Action Bulletin

A.C.M. Court-Martial Rep. Air Force Cas.

A.C.M.S. Special Court-Martial Air Force, *U.S.*

A.C.R. American Criminal Rep.

ACTR Australian Capitol Terr. Rep.

A.D. Agriculture Dec., American Dec., *U.S.*
New York Sup. Ct. App. Div. Rep.

A.E.C. Atomic Energy Comm., *U.S.*

A.E.L.J. Atomic Energy Law Jour.

A.E.L.R. All England Law Rep.

A.F.L.R. Air Force Law Rev.

A.F. Rep. Alaska Fed. Rep.

AFTR American Fed. Tax Rep. (P–H)

A.G. Attorney General's Opinions, *U.S.*

A.G.O. Same as above

AGO Adjutant General's Office, *U.S.*

A.I.D. Accident/Injury/Damages

A.J. American Jurist

A.J.R. Australian Juris Reports

A.K. Marsh. A. K. Marshall (8–10 Ky.)

A.L.C. (or ALC) American Labor Cas. (P–H)

A.L.I. American Law Institute

A.L.J. Albany Law Jour.

A.L.J.R. Australian Law Journ. Rep.

A.L.R. American Labor Cas. (P–H)
American Law Rep., Annot.
Argus Law Rep.

A.L.R. 2d Same as above, Second Series

A.L.R. 3d Same as above, Third Series

A.L.R. Fed. American Law Reports Federal

A.L. Rec. American Law Record

A.L. Reg. (N.S.) American Law Register, New Series

A.L. Reg. (O.S.) American Law Register, Old Series

A.L.T. Australian Law Times

A.M.C. American Maritime Cas.

AMS Agricultural Marketing Service, *U.S.*

A.M.S., P.&S. Agricultural Marketing Service, P.&S. Docket, *U.S.*

A. Moo. A. Moore Rep., in 1 Bosanquet & Puller, *Eng.*

A.M.&O. Armstrong, Macartney & Ogle N.P., *Ir.*

A.N.C. Abbott's New Cas., *N.Y.*
American Negligence Cas.

A.N.R. American Negligence Rep.

A.O. Admin. Order, *U.S.*
A.O.C. Newsl. Administrative Office of the Courts Newsletter
A.R. American Rep. Atlantic Rep.
A. Rep. American Rep. Atlantic Rep.
A.R.C. American Ruling Cas.
A.R.M. Appeals & Review Memorandum Committee (I.R. Bulletin)
A.R.R. Appeals & Review Recommendation (I.R. Bulletin)
A.S.B.C.A. Armed Services Board of Contract Appeals
A.S.R. American State Rep.
A.T. Alcohol Tax Unit (I.R. Bulletin)
A.T.C. Australian Tax Cas.
A.T.D. Australian Tax Dec.
A.T.L.A.J. American Trial Lawyers Assn. Jour.
A.T.R.R. Antitrust and Trade Regulation Reporter (BNA)
A.&E. Admiralty and Ecclesiastical, *Eng.*; Adolphus & Ellis, W.B. Rep., *Eng.*
A.&E. Anno. Cas. American and English Annot. Cas.
A.&E. Anno. Same as above
A.&E. Cas. Same as above
A.&E. Corp. Cas. American & English Corporation Cas.
A.&E. Corp. Cas. (N.S.) Same as above, New Series
A.&E. Enc. L.&Pr. American & English Encyclopedia of Law and Practice
A.&E. Ency. American & English Encyclopedia of Law
A.&E. Ency. Law Same as above
A.&E. (N.S.) Adolphus & Ellis, New Series, *Eng.*
A.&E.P.&Pr. American & English Pleading and Practice
A.&E.R. Cas. American & English Railroad Cas.
A.&R. Cas. (N.S.) Same as above, New Series
A.&E.R.R. Cas. American & English Railroad Cas.
A.&E.R.R. Cas. (N.S.) Same as above, New Series
A.&H. Arnold & Hodges, Q.B. Rep., *Eng.*
Ab. (N.S.) Abstracts, Treasury Dec., New Series
Abb. Abbott, Cir, and Dist. Ct. Rep., *U.S.*
Abb. Adm. Abbott's Admiralty Rep., *U.S.*
Abb. App. Dec. Abbott Ct. of Appeals Dec., *N.Y.*
Abb. C.C. Abbott's Cir. Ct. Rep., *U.S.*
Abb. Ct. App. Abbott's Ct. of Appeals Dec., *N.Y.*
Abb. Dec. Same as above
Abb. Dict. Abbott's Dictionary
Abb. N.Cas. Abbott's New Cas., *N.Y.*
Abb. N.Y. App. Abbott's Ct. of Appeals Dec., *N.Y.*
Abb. Pr. Abbott's Practice Rep., *N.Y.*
Abb. Pr. (N.S.) Same as above, New Series
Abb. U.S. Abbott's Cir. Ct. Rep., *U.S.*
A'Beck. Res. Judg. A'Beckett's Reserved Judgments, *Victoria*
Abs. Abstracts, Treasury Dec., Ohio Law Abstract
Acad. Pol. Sci. Proc. Academy of Political Science Proceedings
Acq. Acquiescence by Commissioner in Tax Court or Board of Tax Appeals Dec., *U.S.*
Act. Acton Prize Cas., P.C., *Eng.*
Acta Cancelariae English Chancery Rep., *Eng.*
Acta Jur. Acta Juridica
Acton Acton Prize Cas., P.C., *Eng.*
Act. P.C. Acts of P.C. (Dasent), *Eng.*
Act. P.C. (N.S.) Same as above,

New Series
Act. Pr. C. Acton's Rep., Prize Cas., *Eng*.
Ad.&El. Adolphus & Ellis, K.B. Rep., *Eng*.
Ad.&El. (N.S.) Same as above, New Series
Adams Adams' Rep. (41, 42 Me.) Adams' Rep. (1 N.H.)
Add. Addison's Rep. (Pa. Sup. Ct.)
Add. Eccl. Rep. Addam's Ecclesiastical Rep., *Eng*.
Add. Pa. Addison's County Ct. Rep., *Pa*.
Add. Penn. Addison, *Pa*.
Add. Rep. Same as above
Ad.L. Administrative Law
Ad.L.2d Same, Second Series
Ad.L.Rev. Admin. Law Review
Adelaide L.Rev. Adelaide Law Review
Adm.&Ecc. Law Rep., Admiralty and Ecclesiastical, *Eng*.
Adol.&El. Adolphus & Ellis, Q.B. Rep., *Eng*.
Adol.&El. (N.S.) Same as above, New Series
Advocate The Advocate
Af.L. Studies African Law Studies
Agri. Dec. Agriculture Dec.
Aik. Aiken's Rep., *Vt*.
Air L.R. Air Law Rev.
Akron L. Rev. Akron Law Rev.
Al. Alabama
Aleyn, K.B. Rep., *Eng*.
ALA. Alabama
Ala. Alabama Sup. Ct.
Minor's Ala Rep. 1820–26
Ala. App. Alabama Appeals Rep.
Ala. Law. Alabama Lawyer
Ala. L. Rev. Alabama Law Rev.
Ala. (N.S.) Alabama Rep., New Series, 1840–date
Ala. Sel. Cas. Alabama Select Cas. (and in 37–39 Ala.)
Ala. St. B. Found. Bull. Alabama State Bar Foundation Bulletin
Alaska Alaska Rep.
Alaska B.J. Alaska Bar Jour.
Alaska Fed. Alaska Fed. Rep.
Alaska L.J. Alaska Law Jour.
Alb. L.J. Albany Law Jour.
Alb. L.Q. Alberta Law Quarterly
Alb. L.R. Alberta Law Rep.
Alb. L. Rev. Albany Law Rev.
Alberta Law Rev.
Alc.&N. Alcock & Napier, K.B., *Ir*.
Ald. Alden's Condensed Rep., *Pa*.
Alexander Alexander's Rep. (66–72 Miss.)
Aleyn Aleyn's K.B. Rep., *Eng*.
ALI–ABA Course M.J. American Law Institute–American Bar Assn. Course Materials Jour.
All E.R. All England Law Rep. (formerly All England Law Rep. Annot.)
All India Crim. Dec. All India Criminal Dec.
All India Rep. All India Reporter
All Pak. Leg. Dec. All Pakistan Legal Dec.
Allen Allen's Rep. (83–96 Mass.)
Allen's Rep.
(6–11 New Brunswick)
Allen's Rep.
(1–2 Washington Terr. 1854–85)
Allin. Allinson's Pa. Super. and Dist. Ct. Rep.
Alison Pr. Alison Practice, *Sc*.
Alta L. Alberta Law
Alta. L.Q. Alberta Law Quarterly
Alta. L.R. Alberta Law Rep.
Alta. L.Rev. Alberta Law Review
Am. A. Psych. L. Bull. American Academy of Psychiatry & the Law Bulletin
Am. Acad. Matri. Law. J. American Academy of Matrimonial Lawyers Jour.
Am. B. A. American Bar Association
Am. B.R. American Bankruptcy Rep.
Am. B.R.(N.S.) Same as above, New Series
Am. Bank. Rev. American

Bankruptcy Rev.
Am.Bankr. L.J. American Bankruptcy Law Jour.
Am.Bankr.Reg. American Bankruptcy Register
Am. Bus. L.J. American Business Law Jour.
Am. Corp. Cas. American Corporation Cas.
Am.Cr.Rep. American Criminal Reports
Am. Crim. L.Q. American Criminal Law Quarterly
Am. Crim. L.Rev. American Criminal Law Rev.
Am.Dec. American Dec.
Am.Dig. American Digest
Am. Elect. Cas. American Electrical Cas.
Am. Fed. Tax R. American Fed. Tax Rep. (P–H)
Am. Hist. Rev. American Historical Rev.
Am. Ind. L.R. American Indian Law Rev.
Am. Ins. Rep. American Insolvency Rep.
Am. Insolv. Rep. American Insolvency Rep.
Am. J. Comp. Law American Jour. of Comparative Law
Am. J. Crim. L. American Jour. of Criminal Law
Am. J. Int. L. American Jour. of International Law
Am. J. Jurisprud. American Jour. of Jurisprudence
Am. J. of Law & Med. American Jour. of Law & Medicine
Am. J. Legal Hist. American Journal of Legal History
Am.Jud.Soc. American Judicature Soc. (Bulletins or Jour.)
Am. Jur. American Jurisprudence American Jurist
Am. L. J. American Law Jour., *Pa.*
Am. L.J.(N.S.) Same as above, New Series
Am. L. Rec. American Law Record, *Ohio*
Am. L. Reg. American Law Register
Am. L. School Rev. American Law School Rev.
Am. L. T. Bankr. Rep. American Law Times Bankruptcy Rep.
Am. Lab. Cas. American Labor Cas. (P–H)
Am. Lab. Arb. Cas. American Labor Arbitration Cas.
Am. Lab. Leg. Rev. American Labor Legis. Rev.
Am. Law Rec. American Law Record
Am. Law Reg. American Law Register
Am. Mar. Cas. American Maritime Cas.
Am. Neg. Cas. American Negligence Cas.
Am. Neg. Rep. American Negligence Reports
Am. Pat. L.A. Bull. American Patent Law Assn. Bulletin
Am. Pol. Sci. Rev. American Political Science Rev.
Am. Pr. Rep. American Practice Rep., *D.C.*
Am. Prob. Rep. American Probate Rep.
Am. Prob. Rep. (N.S.) Same as above, New Series
Am. R. American Rep.
Am. R.&C. Rep. American Railroad & Corporation Rep.
Am. R. Rep. American Railway Rep.
Am. Railw. Cas. American Railway Cas. (Smith & Bates)
Am. Rep. American Rep.
Am. Ry. Rep. American Railway Rep.
Am. Soc. Int. L. Proc. American Society of International Law Proceedings.
Am. St. P. American State Papers
Am. St. Rep. American State Rep. (Annot. Cas. System)

Am. St. R.D. American Street Railway Dec.
Am. Tr. M. Cas. American Trade Mark Cas. (Cox)
Am.&E. Corp. Cas. American & English Corporation Cas.
Am.&E. Corp. Cas. (N.S.) Same as above, New Series
Am. &E.R. Cas. American & English Railroad Cas.
Am.&E.R. Cas. (N.S.) Same as above, New Series
Am.&Eng. Ann. Cas. American & English Annot. Cas.
Am.&Eng. Eq. D. American & English Dec. in Equity
Am.&Eng. Pat. Cas. American & English Patent Cas.
Am. J.L. Rev. American Jour. Law Rev.
Am. Tax Q. American Taxpayer's Quarterly
Am. Them. American Themis
Am.U.Int.L.Rev. American University Intramural Law Review
Amb. Ambler's English Ch. Rep.
Amer. American; Amerman's Rep. (111–115 Pa.)
Amer. Fed. Tax Rep. American Federal Tax Reporter (P–H)
Amer. Jur. American Jurist
Amer. Law Reg. American Law Register (U. Pa. L. Rev.)
Ames Ames' Rep. (1 Minn.)
Ames' Rep. (4–7 R.I.)
Ames, K.&B. Ames, Knowles & Bradley (8 R.I.)
An. Anonymous, at end of Benloe Rep., *Eng.*
An. B. Anonymous Rep. at end of Benloe, or Benlow (1661), *Eng.*
And. Anderson's C.P. Rep. *temp.* Eliz., *Eng.*
Andrews' K.B. Rep., *Eng.*
Andr. Andrews' K.B. Rep., *Eng.*
Ang. Angell's Rep., *R.I.*
Angell & Durfee Rep. (1 R.I.)
Ang.&Dur. Same as above
Ang.&A.L. Rev. Anglo & American Law Rev.
Ann. Cunningham's Rep. *temp.* Hardwicke, K.B., 7–10 Geo. II, *Eng.*
Ann. Cas. American and English Annot. Cas.
American Annot. Cas.
New York Annot. Cas.
Ann. Dig. Annual Digest and Rep. of International Law Cas.
Ann. Law Reg. Annual Law/Register
Ann. Leg. Forms Mag. Annotated Legal Forms Magazine
Ann. Tax Cas. Annotated Tax Cas.
Annals Annals of the American Academy of Political and Social Sciences
Annaly Lee's K.B. Rep. *temp.* Hardwicke, Annaly ed., *Eng.*
Anst. Anstruther's Rep., Ex., *Eng.*
Anth. Anthon's N.Y. N.P. Rep.
Anth. N.P. Same as above
Antitrust Bull. Antitrust Bulletin
Antitrust L.&Econ. Rev. Antitrust Law and Economics Rev.
Antitrust L.J. Antitrust Law Jour.
Ap. Bre. Breese's *Ill.* Rep., Appendix
App. Appleton's Rep. (19, 20 Me.)
Ohio Appellate Rep.
App. Bd. O.C.S. Office of Contract Settlement, Appeal Board Dec., *U.S.*
App. Cas. Law Rep., Appeal Cas., *Eng.*
App. Cas. 2d Same as above, Second Series
App. D.C. Appeal Cases, District of Columbia
App. Div. Appellate Div. Rep., N.Y.
App. Div. 2d . Same as above, Second Series
App. N.Z. Appeal Reports, *New Zealand*
App. N.Z. 2d Same as above, Second Series

App. Rep. Ont. Ontario Appeal Rep.
Appleton Appleton's Rep. (19, 20 Me.)
Arb. J. Arbitration Jour.
Arb. J. (N.S.) Same as above, New Series
Arb. L. Dig. Arbitration Law: A Digest of Court Dec.
Arb. Schools Arbitration in the Schools
Archer Archer's Rep. (2 Fla.)
Archer & H. Archer & Hogue, *Fla.*
Archer & Hogue Archer & Hogue (2 Fla.)
Argus L.R. Argus Law Rep., *Aust.*
Ariz. Arizona
Ariz. B.J. Arizona Bar Jour.
Ariz. L. Rev. Arizona Law Rev.
Ariz. St. L.J. Arizona State Law Jour.
Ark. Arkansas
Ark. L.J. Arkansas Law Jour.
Ark. L. Rev. Arkansas Law Rev.
Ark. Law. The Arkansas Lawyer
Armour Manitoba Q.B. Rep. *temp.* Wood
Arms. Con. Elec. Armstrong's Contested Elections, *N.Y.*
Arn. Arnold's Rep., C.P., *Eng.*
Arn.&H. Arnold & Hodges' Q.B. Rep., *Eng.*
Arn.&Hod. Same as above
Arnold Arnold C.P., *Eng.*
Art & Law Art and the Law
Ash. Ashmead Pa. Rep. 1808–41
Asp. Aspinall's Maritime Cas., *Eng.*
Asp. Cas. Same as above
Asp. M.C. Same as above
Asp. M.L.C. Aspinall's Maritime Law Cas., *Eng.*
Aspin. Aspinall's Maritime Cas., *Eng.*
Atk. Atkyn's Ch. Rep., *Eng.*
Atl. Atlantic Reporter
Atl. Comm. Q. Atlantic Community Quarterly
Atl. P.R. Altantic Province Rep., *Can.*
Atty. Gen. Op. Attorney General's Opinions
Atw. Atwater's Rep. (1 Minn.)
Auck. U.L. Rev. Auckland Univ. Law Rev.
Aust. Bus. L.R. Australian Business Law Rev.
Aust. L.J. Australian Law Jour.
Aust.&N.Z.J. Crim. Australian & New Zealand Jour. of Criminology
Aust. Y. Int. L. Australian Yearbook of International Law

B. Barbour's N.Y. Rep.
Weekly Law Bulletin, *Ohio*
B. Bar Bench and Bar
B.C. Bail Ct.
Bankruptcy Cas.
British Columbia Rep.
B.C.A. Board of Contract Appeals Dec., *U.S.*
B.C.C. Bail Court Cas., *Eng.*
B.C. Ind.&Com. L.R. Boston College Ind. & Com. Law Rev.
B.C.R. British Columbia Rep.
B.Ch. Barbour's Ch. Rep., *N.Y.*
B. Current L. Butterworth's Current Law
B.D.&O. Blackham, Dundas & Osborne, N.P., *Ir.*
BIS Bank for International Settlements
BLS Bureau of Labor Statistics, *U.S.*
B.M. Burrow's Rep. *temp.* Mansfield, *Eng.*
B. Mon. Ben Monroe Rep. (40–57 Ky.)
B. Moore Moore C.P. Rep., *Eng.*
B.N.A. Bureau of National Affairs (unofficial), *U.S.*
B.N.A. Sec. Reg. Securities Regulation & Law Rep.
B.N.C. Bingham's New Cas., C.P., *Eng.*
Brook's New Cas., K.B., *Eng.*
Busbee's Rep. (44, 45 N.C.)
B.P.N.R. Bosanquet & Puller, New

Rep., C.P., *Eng.*

B.R. Bancus Regis (K.B.), *Eng.*
Bankruptcy Rep.
Bankruptcy Register
Board of Review, U.S. Army

B.R.C. British Ruling Cas.

B.R.H. Cases *temp.* Hardwicke, K.B., *Eng.*

B.R.&J.C. (Army) Board of Review and Judicial Council of the Army

B.T.A. Board of Tax Appeals, *U.S.*

B.U.L. Rev. Boston Univ. Law Rev.

B.W.C.C. Butterworth's Workmen's Compensation Cas., *Eng.*

B.&A. Barnewall & Adolphus' K.B. Rep., *Eng.*
Barnewall & Alderson's K.B. Rep., *Eng.*

B.&Ad. Barnewall & Adolphus K.B. Rep., *Eng.*

B.&Ald. Barnewall & Alderson, K.B. Rep., *Eng.*

B.&Arn. Barron & Arnold Election Cas., *Eng.*

B.&Aust. Barron & Austin Election Cas., *Eng.*

B.&B. Broderip & Bingham's C.P. Rep., *Eng.*
Ball & Beatty's Chancery, *Ir.*

B.& Bar Bench and Bar

B.&C. Barnewall & Cresswell, K.B. Rep., *Eng.*

B.&C.R. Reports of Bankruptcy & Companies Winding up Cas., *Eng.*

B.&D. Benloe & Dalison's C.P., Rep., *Eng.*

B.&F. Broderip & Freemantle's Ecclesiastical, *Eng.*

B.&G. Brownlow & Goldesborough's N.P. Rep., *Eng.*

B.&H. Blatchford & Howland Dist. Ct. Rep., *Eng.*

B.&H. Cr. Cas. Bennet & Heard's Criminal Cas., *Eng.*

B.&H. Crim. Cas. Same as above

B.&L. Browning & Lushington's Admiralty Rep., *Eng.*

B.&M. Browne & MacNamara's Rep., *Eng.*

B.&P. Bosanquet & Puller C.P., Ex. and H.L. Rep., *Eng.*

B.&P.N.R. Bosanquet & Puller, New Rep., *Eng.*

B.&S. Best & Smith's Q.B. Rep., *Eng.*

Bac. Abr. Bacon's Abridgement, *Eng.*

Bac. Dec. Bacon's Dec. (Ritchie), *Eng.*

Bach Bach's Rep. (19–21 Mont.)

Bagl. Bagley's Rep. (16 Cal.)

Bagl.&H. Bagley & Harman, *Cal.*

Bagl.&Har. Bagley & Harman Rep. (17–19 Cal.)

Bai. Bailey's Law Rep., *S.C.*

Bai. Eq. Bailey's Eq. Rep., *S.C.*

Bail. Bailey's Eq. or Law Rep., *S.C.*

Bail Ct. Cas. Bail Ct. Cas. (Lowndes & Maxwell), *Eng.*

Baild. Baildon's Select Cas. in Ch., *Eng.*

Bailey Bailey's Rep., *S.C.*

Bal. Ann. Codes Ballinger's Annot. Codes & Statutes, *Wash.*

Bald. Baldwin's Rep., Cir. Ct., *U.S.*

Bald. App. Appendix to 11 Peters, *U.S.*

Bald. C.C. Baldwin's Cir. Ct. Rep., *U.S.*

Balf. Pr. Balfour's Practice, *Sc.*

Ball &B. Ball & Beatty Ch., *Ir.*

Balt. C. Rep. Baltimore City Rep.

Balt. L.T. Baltimore Law Transcript

Ban. & A. Banning & Arden Patent Cas., *U.S.*

Bank. & Ins. R. Bankruptcy & Insolvency Rep., *Eng.*

Bank. Cas. Banking Cas.

Bank. Ct. Rep. Bankrupt Ct. Rep.

Bank. L.J. Banking Law Jour.

Banking L.J. Same as above

Bankr. L. Rep. Bankruptcy Law

Reporter (CCH)
Bankr. Reg. National Bankruptcy Register, *N.Y.*
Banks Banks Rep. (1–5 Kan.)
Bann. Bannister's C.P. Rep., *Eng.*
Bann. Br. Bannister's O. Bridgman's C.P. Rep., *Eng.*
Bann. &A. Banning & Arden's Patent Cas., *U.S.*
Bar. Barbour Rep., *N.Y.*
Barnardiston, Ch. and K.B. Rep., *Eng.*
Bar. &Ad. Barnewall & Adolphus' K.B. Rep., *Eng.*
Bar. &Al. Barnewall & Alderson, K.B. Rep., *Eng.*
Bar. & Arn. Barron & Arnold, Election Cas., *Eng.*
Bar. & Aust. Barron & Austin, Election Cas., *Eng.*
Bar. & Cr. Barnewall & Cresswell, K.B. Rep., *Eng.*
Barb. Arkansas Rep. (14–42 Ark.)
Barbour's N.Y. Sup. Ct. Rep.
Barbour's Ch. Cas. (Contracts), *Eng.*
Barb. Ch. Barbour's N.Y. Ch. Rep.
Barb. S.C. Barbour's N.Y. Sup. Ct. Rep.
Barber Barber's Rep. (14–42 Ark.)
Barn. Barnardiston, Ch. and K.B. Rep., *Eng.*
Barn. Ch. Barnardiston's Ch. Rep., *Eng.*
Barn. K.B. Barnardiston's K.B. Rep., *Eng.*
Barn. & A. Barnewall & Adolphus' K.B. Rep., *Eng.*
Barnewall & Alderson, K.B. Rep., *Eng.*
Barn. & C. Barnewall & Cresswell, K.B., *Eng.*
Barn. & Cr. Barnewall & Cresswell, K.B. Rep., *Eng.*
Barn. & Cress. Same as above
Barnes Barnes Practice Cas., *Eng.*
Barnes' Notes Barnes' Notes, *Eng.*
Barnet Barnet's Rep., C.P., *Eng.*
Barnf. & S. Barnfield & Stiness' Rep. (20 R.I.)
Barr. Barr Rep. (1–19 Pa.)
Barrows' Rep. (18 R.I.)
Barr. Ch. Pr. Barroll Ch. Practice, *Md.*
Barr. Mss. Barradall's Manuscript Rep., *Va.*
Bart. Elec. Cas. Bartlett's Election Cas.
Bates Bates' Del. Ch. Rep.
Bates Ch. Bates Ch., *Del.*
Batty Batty, K.B., *Ir.*
Bax. Baxter's Rep. (60–68 Tenn.)
Bay Bay's Rep. (1–3, 5–8 Mo.)
Bay's S.C. Rep.
Baylor L. Rev. Baylor Law Rev.
Beasl. Beasley's N.J. Eq. Rep.
Beav. Beavan Rolls Ct., *Eng.*
Beav. R.&C. Cas. Beavan, Railway & Canal Cas., *Eng.*
Beav.& W. Ry. Cas. Beavan & Walford's Railway & Canal Cas., *Eng.*
Beaw. Lex. Mer. Beawes Lex Mercatoria, *Eng.*
Beck Beck's Col. Rep.
Bedell Bedell's Rep. (163–191 N.Y.)
Bee Bee's Dist. Ct. Rep., *U.S.*
Bee Adm. Bee's, *U.S.*
Bee Alm. Bee's Dist. Ct. Rep., *U.S.*
Bee C.C.R. Bee's Crown Cas. Res., *Eng.*
Bel. Bellewe's K.B. Rep., *Eng.*
Bel. Ca.*t*.H.VIII Bellewe's Cas. *temp.* Henry VIII (Brooke's New Cas.), *Eng.*
Bell Bell's Crown Cas. Res., *Eng.*
Bellewe's K.B. Rep., *Eng.*
Bellinger's Rep. (4–8 Ore.)
Bell App. Cas. Bell's Appeal Cas., H.L., *Sc.*
Bell C.C. T. Bell's Crown Cas. Res., *Eng.*
Bell Cas. Bell's Cas., *Sc.*
Bell. Cas.*t*.H.VIII Brooke's New Cas., *Eng.*
Bell. Cas.*t*.R.II Bellewe's Cas.,

temp. Richard II, *Eng*.
Bell Comm. Bell's Commentaries, *Eng*.
Bell Cr. Cas. Bell's Crown Cas. Res., *Eng*.
Bell H.L. Bell's H.L. Cas., *Eng*.
Bell P.C. Bell's Parliament Cas., *Sc*.
Bell Sc. Cas. Bell's Scotch Ct. Sessions Cas.
Bell Ses. Cas. Same as above
Bellewe Bellewe's Cas. *temp*. Rich II, *Eng*.
Bellewe *t*.H.VIII Brooke's New Cas., *Eng*.
Bellinger Bellinger's Rep. (4–8 Ore.)
Belt Bro. Brown's Ch. Cas., by Belt, *Eng*.
Belt's Sup. Belt's Supplement to Vesey Senior's Ch. Rep., *Eng*.
Belt Ves.Sen. Belt's ed. of Vesey Senior's Ch. Rep., *Eng*.
Ben. Benedict's Dist. Ct. Rep., *U.S*.
Benloe's C.P. and K.B. Rep., *Eng*.
Ben Monroe Ben Monroe's Rep. (40–57 Ky.)
Ben.&Dal. Benloe & Dalison's C.P. Rep., *Eng*.
Ben. & H.L.C. Bennett & Heard Leading Criminal Cas., *Eng*.
Bendl. *See* Benloe
Bened. Benedict's Dist. Ct. Rep., *U.S*.
Benl. *See* Benloe
Benl. & D. Benloe & Dalison C.P., *Eng*.
Benl. in Keil. Benloe in Keilway Rep., *Eng*.
Benl. K.B. Benloe's K.B., *Eng*.
Benl. New Benloe's K.B. and C.P. Rep. 1661 ed., *Eng*.
Benl. Old Benloe & Dalison C.P. Rep., *Eng*.
Benl. & Dal. Benloe & Dalison's C.P. Rep., *Eng*.
Benloe Benloe's K.B. & C.P. Rep., *Eng*.
Benn. Bennett's Rep. (1 Cal.)
Bennett's Rep., *Dak*.
Bennett's Rep. (16–21 Mo.)
Benne. Modern Rep., v.7, *Eng*.
Bennett *See* Benn.
Bent. Bentley's Ch., *Ir*.
Ber. Berton's New Brunswick Rep.
Berks Berks County Law Jour., *Pa*.
Berry Berry's Rep. (1–28 Mo. App.)
Bert. Berton's New Brunswick Rep.
Best &Sm. Best & Smith's Q.B. Rep., *Eng*.
Betts. Dec. Blatchford & Howland Dist. Ct. Rep., *U.S*.
Olcott's Dist. Ct. Rep., *U.S*.
Bibb Bibb's Rep. (4–7 Ky.)
Bibl. Cott. Cotton MSS.
Bick. Bicknell & Hawley's Rep. (10–20 Nev.)
Bick. & Hawl. Bicknell & Hawley's Rep. (10–20 Nev.)
Big. Ov. Cas. Bigelow's Overruled Cas.
Big. Plac. Bigelow's Placits Anglo-Normanica, *Eng*.
Bill of Rights J. Bill of Rights Jour.
Bin. Binney's Rep. (Pa. 1799–1814)
Bing. Bingham's C.P. Rep., *Eng*.
Bing. N.C. Bingham's New Cas., *Eng*.
Binn. Binney's Rep., *Pa*.
Birk. J. Birkenhead's Judgments (H.L. 1919–22), *Eng*.
Bis. Bissell's Cir. Ct. Rep., *U.S*.
Bitt. Rep. in Ch. Bittleson's Reports, Q.B., *Eng*.
Bitt. W.&P. Bittleson, Wise & Parnell Practice Cas.
Bk. Black's Sup. Ct. Rep. (66, 67 U.S.)
Bl. Same as above
Blackford's Ind. Rep. (1817–47)
Blackstone's Commentaries
Henry Blackstone's C.P. Rep., *Eng*.
Blatchford's Cir. Ct. Rep., *U.S*.
Bl.C.C. Blatchford's Cir. Ct. Rep., *U.S*.

Bl. Comm. Blackstone's Commentaries
Bl.H. Henry Blackstone's C.P., *Eng*.
Bl.(N.S.) Bligh's H.L. Rep., New Series, *Eng*.
Bl.Pr.Cas. Blatchford's Prize Cas., *U.S*.
Bl.R. William Blackstone's K.B. Rep., *Eng*.
Bl.W. Same as above
Bl.&H. Blake & Hedges' Rep. (2, 3 Ind.)
Blatchford & Howland's Dist. Ct. Rep., *U.S*.
Bl.&How. Blatchford & Howland's Admiralty Rep., *U.S*.
Bla. Same as above
Bla. Ch. Bland's Ch. Rep., *Md*.
Bla.H. Henry Blackstone's C.P. Rep., *Eng*.
Bla.W. William Blackstone's K.B. Rep., *Eng*.
Black Black's Rep. (30–53 Ind.)
Black's Sup. Ct. Rep. (66, 67 U.S.)
Black L.J. Black Law Jour.
Black. Blackford's Rep. (Ind. 1817–47)
Henry Blackstone's C.P. Rep., *Eng*.
William Blackstone's K.B., *temp*. Geo. II, III; C.P. *temp*. Geo. III, *Eng*.
Black. Cond. Rep. Blackwell's Condensed Rep., *Ill*.
Black. D.&O. Blackham, Dundas & Osborne, N.P., *Ir*.
Black. H. Henry Blackstone's C.P., Rep., *Eng*.
Black. Jus. Blackerby's Justices' Cas., *Eng*.
Black R. *See* Black
Black. W. William Blackstone's K.B. Rep., *Eng*.
Blackf. Blackford's Rep. (Ind. 1817–47)
Blackst. Blackstone's Rep., K.B., *temp*. Geo. II, III; C.P., *temp*. Geo. III, *Eng*.
Blackw. Cond. Blackwell's Condensed Rep., *Ill*.
Blair Co. L.R. Blair County Law Rep., *Pa*.
Blake Blake's Rep. (1 Mont.)
Blake & H. Blake & Hedges' Mont. Rep.
Bland Bland's Ch. Rep. (Md. 1811–32)
Blatch. Blatchford's Cir. Ct. Rep., *U.S*.
Blatch. Pr. Cas. Blatchford's Prize Cas., *U.S*.
Blatch. & H. Blatchford & Howard's Dist. Ct. Rep., *U.S*.
Bleck. Bleckley's Rep. (34, 35 Ga.)
Bli. Bligh's Rep., H.L., *Eng*.
Bli. (N.S.) Same as above, New Series
Bligh. *See* Bli.
Bliss Delaware County Rep., *Pa*.
Bloom. Man. Bloomfield's Manumission Cas., *N.J*.
Blm. Neg. Bloomfield's Negro Cas., *N.J*.
Blue Sky L. Rep. Blue Sky Law Reporter (CCH)
Bluett Bluett's Isle of Man Cas.
Bond Bond's Cir. Ct. Rep., *U.S*.
Bond Md. App. Proceedings of Court of Appeal of Maryland (in American Legal Records, v.1)
Book of Judg. Book of Judgments, *Eng*.
Boor. Booraem's Rep. (6–8 Cal.)
Booth Chester Palatine Courts 1811, *Eng*.
Bos. Bosworth's Super. Ct. Rep., *N.Y*.
Bos. Pol. Rep. Boston Police Rep.
Bos. & P. Bosanquet & Puller's C.P. Rep., *Eng*.
Bos. & Pul. N.R. Bosanquet & Puller's New Rep., C.P., *Eng*.
Bost. L.R. Boston Law Reporter
Boston B.J. Boston Bar Jour.
Bosw. Bosworth's N.Y. Sup. Ct. Rep.
Bott Poor Law Cas. Bott's Poor

Laws Settlement Cas., *Eng.*
Bott's Set. Cas. Same as above
Bould. Bouldin, *Ala.*
Bouv. Bouvier Law Dictionary
Bov. Pat. Cas. Bovill's Patent Cas.
Bow. Bowler & Bowers (U.S. Comptroller's Dec., v.2, 3)
Boyce Boyce's Rep. (24–30 Del.)
Br. Bracton; Bradford; Bradwell; Brayton; Breese; Brevard; Brewster; Bridgman; British; Brockenbrough; Brooke; Brown; Browne; Brownlow
Br. Abr. Brooke's Abridgement, *Eng.*
Br. C.C. British Crown Cas.
Br. N.C. Brook's New Cas., K.B., *Eng.*
Br. P.C. Brown's Ch. Cas., *Eng.*
Br. & B. Broderip & Bingham's C.P. Rep., *Eng.*
Br. & Col. Pr. Cas. British and Colonial Prize Cas.
Br. & F.Ecc. Broderick & Freemantle's Ecclesiastical Cas., *Eng.*
Br.&G. Brownlow & Goldesborough's C.P. Rep., *Eng.*
Br. & L. Browning & Lushington's Admiralty Rep., *Eng.*
Br. &R. Brown & Rader's Rep., *Eng.*
Bra. Bracton's De Legibus Angliae, *Eng.*
Bract. Same as above
Brad. Bradford's Rep. (Iowa, 1838–41)
Bradford's N.Y. Surrogate Rep.
Bradford's Somerset Star Chamber, *Eng.*
Bradwell's Rep. (1–20 Ill. App.)
Bradb. Bradbury's Pleading and Practice Rep., *N.Y.*
Bradf. *See* Brad.
Bradf. Surr. Bradford's Surrogate Ct., *N.Y.*
Bradl. Bradley, *R.I.*
Bradw. Bradwell's Ill., Appellate Rep.
Brame Brame's Rep. (66–72 Miss.)
Branch Branch's Rep. (1 Fla.)
Brant. Brantley's Rep. (80–116 Md.)
Breese Breese's Rep. (1 Ill.)
Brev. Brevard's Rep. (2, 3 S.C.)
Brew. Brewer's Rep. (19–26 Md.)
Brewer's Md. Rep.
Brewster's Rep. (Pa. 1856–73)
Bridg.J. J. Bridgman's C.P. Rep., *Eng.*
Bridg. O. O. Bridgman's C.P. Rep., *Eng.*
Brief Brief of Phi Delta Phi
Brigham Young U.L. Rev. Brigham Young Univ. Law Rev.
Bright. Brightly's N.P. Rep., *Pa.*
Bright. N.P. Same as above
Brightly El. Brightly's Leading Election Cas., *Pa.*
Brisbin Brisbin's Rep. (in 1 Minn.)
Brit. J. Criminol. British Jour. of Criminology, *Eng.*
Brit. Tax Rev. British Tax Review
Brit. Y. Int.L. British Year Book of International Law
Bro. Brooke. *See* Brooke
Brown's English Ch. Rep.
Brown's Parliamentary Cas., *Eng.*
Brown's Mich. N.P. Rep.
Brown's Rep. (53–65; 80–136 Mo.)
Browne's Rep. (Pa. 1801–14)
Bro. A. & R. Brown's Dist. Ct. (Admiralty and Revenue) Rep., *U.S.*
Bro. Ab. Brooke's Abridgement, *Eng.*
Bro. Adm. Brown's Admiralty Rep., *U.S.*
Bro. C. C. W. Brown's Ch. Rep., *Eng.*
Bro. Ch. Brown's Ch. Rep., *Eng.*
Bro. Eccl. Brown's Ecclesiastical, *Eng.*
Bro. Just. Brown's Justiciary, *Sc.*
Bro. N. C. R. Brooke's New Cas., *Eng.*

Bro. N. P. Brown's Mich. N.P. Rep.
Bro. P. C. J. Brown's Cas. in Parliament, *Eng*.
Bro. Pa. Browne's Pa. Rep.
Bro. & F. Broderick & Freemantle's Eccles. Cas., *Eng*.
Bro. & Fr. Same as above
Bro. & G. Brownlow & Goldesborough's C.P. Rep., *Eng*.
Bro. & H. Brown & Hemingway's Rep. (53–65 Miss.)
Bro. & L. Browning & Lushington's Admiralty Cas., *Eng*.
Brock. Brockenbrough's Marshall's Dec., U.S. Cir. Ct.
Brock. Cas. Brockenbrough's Va. Cas.
Brock. & H. Brockenbrough & Holmes Va. Cas.
Brod. & Bing. Broderip & Bingham's C.P. Rep., *Eng*.
Brod. & F. Ecc. Cas. Broderick & Freemantle's Ecclesiastical Cas., *Eng*.
Brodix Am. & F. Pat. Cas. Brodix American & English Patent Cas.
Brook Abr. Brook's Abridgement, *Eng*.
Brooke Brooke's New Cas., K.B., *Eng*.
Brooke N.C. Brooke's New Cas., *Eng*.
Brooke (Petit) Brooke's New Cas., *Eng*.
Brooklyn J. Int.L. Brooklyn Jour. of International Law
Brooklyn L. Rev. Brooklyn Law Rev.
Brooks Brooks' Rep. (106–119 Mich.)
Brown Brown's Dist. Ct. Rep., *U.S.*
Brown's Ch. Rep., *Eng*.
Brown's Rep. (97–109 Mass.)
Brown's Rep. (Mich. N.P.)
Brown's Rep. (53–65 Miss.)
Brown's Rep. (4–25 Neb.)
Brown's Parliamentary Cas., *Eng*.
Brownlow & Goldesborough's C.P. Rep. *Eng*.
Brown A. & R. Brown's Dist. Ct. Rep. (Admiralty and Revenue Cas.), *U.S.*
Brown Adm. Brown's Admiralty Rep.
Brown C. Brown's Ch. Cas. *temp.* Lord Thurlow, *Eng*.
Brown Dict. Brown's Law Dictionary
Brown Ecc. Brown's Ecclesiastical, *Eng*.
Brown N.P. Brown's Mich. N.P. Rep.
Brown Parl. Cas. Brown's H.L. Cas., *Eng*.
Brown. & Gold. Brownlow & Goldesborough's C.P. Rep., *Eng*.
Brown &H. Brown & Hemingway's Rep. (53–58 Miss.)
Brown. & Lush. Browning & Lushington's Rep., Admiralty, *Eng*.
Brown & MacN. Brown & MacNamara, Railway Cas., *Eng*.
Brown & R. Brown & Rader, *Mo*.
Browne Browne, *Mass*.
Browne C.P., *Pa*.
Browne's Civil Procedure Rep., *N.Y.*
Browne's Rep. (Pa. 1801–14)
Browne Bank Cas. Browne's National Bank Cas.
Browne & Gray Browne & Gray's Rep. (110–114 Mass.)
Browne & H. Browne & Hemingway, *Miss*.
Brownl. Brownlow & Goldesborough's C.P. Rep., *Eng*.
Bruce Bruce, *Sc*.
Brunn. Coll. Cas. Brunner's

Collected Cas., *U.S.*
Bt. Benedicts, *U.S.*
Buch. Buchanan's Rep. (71–85 N.J.)
Buchan. *See* Buch.
Buchanan *See* Buch.
Buck Buck's Rep. (7–8 Mont.)
Buck. Dec. Buckner's Dec. (in Freeman's Miss. Ch. Rep. 1839–43)
Buff. Super. Ct. Buffalo N.Y. Sup. Ct. Rep., Sheldon
Buffalo L. Rev. Buffalo Law Rev.
Bull. Bulletin
Weekly Law Bulletin, *Ohio*
Bull. Can. Welfare Law Bulletin of Canadian Welfare Law
Bull. Cr. Soc. Bulletin Copyright Soc. of U.S.A.
Bull. JAG Bulletin of Judge Advocate General of Army, *U.S.*
Bull. N.P. Buller's N.P., *Eng.*
Bull. N.T.A. Bulletin of the National Tax Association
Bull. O. Weekly Law Bulletin, *Ohio*
Buller N.P. Buller's N.P., *Eng.*
Bulst. Bulstrode's K.B. Rep., *Eng.*
Bunb. Bunbury's Ex. Rep., *Eng.*
Bur. Burnett's Rep. (Wis. 1841–43)
Burnett's K.B. Rep., *Eng.*
Bur. M. Burrow's Rep. *temp.* Mansfield, *Eng.*
Bur.S.C. Burrow's Settlement Cas., *Eng.*
Burf. Burford's Rep. (6–18 Okla.)
Burgess Burgess' Rep. (46–51 Ohio)
Burk Burk, *Va.*
Burlesque Rep. Skillman's N.Y. Police Rep.
Burn High Commission Ct. 1865, *Eng.*
Burnett Burnett's Rep. (Wis. 1841–43)
Burr. Burrow's K.B. Rep. *temp.* Mansfield, *Eng.*
Burr. S. Cas. Burrow's Settlement Cas., *Eng.*
Burr. *t*.M. Burrow's Rep. *temp.* Mansfield, *Eng.*
Burrell Burrell's Admiralty Rep., *Eng.*
Burrnett Burrnett's Rep. (20–22 Ore.)
Bus. Law The Business Lawyer
Busb. Busbee's Law Rep. (44 N.C.)
Bus. Eq. Busbee's Equity Rep. (45 N.C.)
Bush Bush's Rep. (64–77 Ky.)
Butt's Sh. Butt's Shower's K.B. Rep., *Eng.*
Buxton Buxton's Rep. (123–29 N.C.)

C. Cowen's N.Y. Rep.
C.A. Court of Appeal; Court of Appeals
Customs Appeals Rep., *U.S.*
U.S. Ct. of Appeals
C.A.A. Civil Aeronautics Admin., *U.S.*
Civil Aeronautics Authority Rep.
C.A.A.J. Civil Aeronautics Jour.
C.A.A.Op. Civil Aeronautics Authority Opinions, *U.S.*
C.A.B. (or CAB) Civil Aeronautics Board, *U.S.*
C.A.D. Canadian Annual Digest
C.A.R. Criminal Appeal Rep., *Eng*
Commonwealth Arbitration Reports, *Aus.*
C.App. R. Same as above
C.B. Common Bench Rep. (Manning, Granger & Scott), *Eng.*
Cumulative Bulletin, Internal Revenue Service, *U.S.*
C.B.C. Colliers Bankruptcy Cases
C.B.(N.S.) Common Bench Rep., New Series, *Eng.*
C.B.R. Canadian Bankruptcy Rep.
C.C. Cases in Ch., *Eng.*
Coleman's N.Y. Cas.
Ohio Cir. Ct. Rep.
C.C.A. Cir. Ct. of Appeals, *U.S.*

County Ct. Appeals
Ct. of Crim. Appeal, *Eng*.
C.C.C. Canadian Crim. Cas.
Central Crim. Ct. (Old Bailey), *Eng*.
Choyce Cas. In Ch., *Eng*.
Cox's Crim. Cas., *Eng*.
C.C.Ct. Cas. Central Crim. Ct. Cas., *Eng*.
C.C.E. Caine's Cas. In Error, *N.Y.*
Caines' N.Y. Term Rep.
CCF Federal Contract Cas. (CCH)
CCH Commerce Clearing House
CCH Atom. En. L. Rep. Atomic Energy Law Reporter
CCH Comm.Mkt.Rep. Common Market Reporter
CCH Fed. Banking L.Rep. Federal Banking Law Reporter
CCH Fed. Sec. L. Rep. Federal Securities Law Reporter
CCH Inh. Est. & Gift Tax Rep. Inheritance, Estate, and Gift Tax Reporter
CCH Lab. Arb. Awards Labor Arbitration Awards
CCH Lab. Cas. Labor Cas.
CCH Lab. L. Rep. Labor Law Reporter
CCH Stand. Fed. Tax Rep. Standard Federal Tax Reporter
CCH State Tax Cas. Rep. State Tax Cas. Reporter
CCH Tax Ct. Mem. Tax Court Memorandum Dec.
CCH Tax Ct. Rep. Tax Court Reporter
C.C.N.S. Cir. Ct. Rep., *N.S.*
C.C.P.A. Ct. of Customs and Patent Appeals, *U.S.*
C.C.R. Cir. Ct. Rep.
City Courts Rep.
County Courts Rep.
Crown Cas. Res., *Eng*.
C.C. Supp. City Ct. Rep. Supplement, *N.Y.*
C.D. Ch. Div.
Commissioner's Dec., U.S. Patent Office
Customs Ct. Dec., *U.S.*
Customs Dec. (U.S. Treasury Dept.)
C.E.D. Canadian Encyclopedic Digest
C.E. Gr. Green's Rep. (16–27 N.J. Eq.)
C.F.R. (or CFR) Code of Fed. Regulations, *U.S.*
C.G.O. Comptroller General's Op., *U.S.*
CGR Coast Guard Regulations, *U.S.*
C.H. &A. Carro, Hamerton & Allen's New Session Cas., *Eng*.
CIA Central Intelligence Agency, *U.S.*
C.J. Corpus Juris
C.J. Ann. Corpus Juris Annotations
C.J. Can. Corpus Juris Canonici
C.J. Civ. Corpus Juris Civilis
C.J.S. Corpus Juris Secundum
C.L. Common Law Rep.
C.L. Ch. Common Law Chamber Rep., *Ont*.
C.L.J. Canada Law Jour.
Central Law Jour.
Chicago Law Jour.
C.L.J. (N.S.) Canada Law Jour., New Series
C.L.J. (O.S.) Canada Law Jour., Old Series
C.L.L.C. Canadian Labour Law Cas.
C.L.N. Chicago Legal News
C.L.R. Canada Law Rep.
Columbia Law Rev.
Common Law Rep.
Commonwealth Law Reports, *Aus*.
C.L.R. Can. Canada Law Rep.
Common Law Rep., *Can*.
C.L. Rec. Cleveland Law Record
C.L. Reg. Cleveland Law Register

C.L. Rep. Cleveland Law Reporter
C.L.T. Canadian Law Times
CM Ct. Martial Rep. Army Cas., *U.S.*
C.M.O. U.S. Judge Advocate General (Navy) Compilation of Ct. Martial Orders
CMR Ct. Martial Rep., Judge Advocates General of the Armed Forces and the U.S. Ct. of Military Appeals
CMR(AF) Court-Martial Rep., Air Force
C.M.&R. Crompton, Meeson & Roscoe's Ex. Rep., *Eng.*
C.N. Conf. Cameron & Norwood's Conference Rep., *N.C.*
C.P. C.P. Rep., Upper Canada Law Rep., C.P. Series
C.P.C. C.P. Cooper's Prac. Cas., *Eng.*
C.P.C.*t*.BR. C.P. Cooper's Ch. Rep. *temp*. Brougham, *Eng.*
C.P.C.*t*. Cott. C.P. Cooper's Ch. Rep. *temp*.Cottenham, *Eng.*
C.P.D. Law Reports, C.P. Div., *Eng.*
C.P.R. Canadian Patent Reporter
C.P. Rept. Common Pleas Rep., *Pa.*
C.P.U.C. Upper Canada C.P. Rep.
C.R. Canadian Rep., Appeal Cas.
Ch. Rep. *temp*. Car. I to Queen Anne
Central Reporter
Criminal Rep.
C.R. (date) A.C. Canadian Appeal Cas.
C.R.C. Criminal Rep.
Canadian Railway Cas., *Can.*
C.R. (N.S.) Code Rep., New Series, *N.Y.*
C.R.T.C. Canadian Railway & Transport Cas.
C.Rob. Robinson's Admiralty Rep., *Eng.*
C.S. Supreme Ct. Rep., *Quebec*
CSAB Contract Settlement Appeal Bd., *U.S.*
C.S.A.B. Civil Service Arbitration Awards, *U.S.*
C.S.C.R. Cincinnati Super. Ct. Rep.
CSJAG Opinion of Judge Advocate General, U.S. Army
CSJAGA Military Affairs Div., Judge Advocate of U.S. Army
CSJAGE Assistant Judge Advocate General for Procurement (Army); Contract Div., Office of Judge Advocate General of Army
C.S.T. Capital Stock Tax Div. (I.R. Bulletin)
C.T. Carriers Taxing Ruling (I.R. Bulletin)
C.T.C. Canada Tax Cas.
C. Tax C. Canadian Tax Cas.
C.*t*.K. Macnaghten's Select Ch. Cas. *temp*. King, *Eng.*
C.*t*.N. Eden's Ch. Rep. *temp*. Northington, *Eng.*
C.*t*.T. Cas. *temp*. Talbot, Ch., *Eng.*
C.W. Dud. Dudley's Rep.Law or Eq., *S.C.*
Ct. Conn.
CZO Canal Zone Order
C.Z. Rep. Canal Zone Rep., *U.S.*
C.&A. Cooke & Alcock, K.B. & Ex., *Ir.*
C.&C. Case and Comment
Coleman & Caines' N.Y. Cas.
C.&D. Corbett & Daniel's Election Cas., *Eng.*
Crawford & Dix's Abridged Cas., *Ir.*
C.&D.A.C. Crawford & Dix's Abridged Cas., *Ir.*
C.&D.C.C. Crawford & Dix's Cir. Cas., *Ir.*
Crawford & Dix's Criminal Cas., *Ir.*
C. & E. Cababé & Ellis Rep., *Eng.*
C.&F. Clark & Finnelly's H.L. Cas., *Eng.*

C.&J. Crompton & Jervis Ex. Rep., *Eng.*
C.&K. Carrington & Kirwan's N.P. Rep., *Eng.*
C.&L. Connor & Lawson's Ch., *Ir.*
C. & L.C.C. Cane & Leigh's Crown Cas., *Eng.*
C. & M. Carrington & Marshman's N.P. Rep., *Eng.*
Crompton & Meeson Ex. Rep., *Eng.*
C. & Marsh. Carrington & Marshman's N.P. Rep., *Eng.*
C. & N. Cameron & Norwood's Conference Rep., *N.C.*
C. & P. Carrington & Payne's N.P. Rep., *Eng.*
Craig & Phillips' Ch. Rep., *Eng.*
C. & R. Cockburn & Rowe's Election Cas.
C. & S. Clarke & Scully's Drainage Cas., *Ont.*
Ca. *temp*. F. Cas. *temp*. Finch, *Eng.*
Ca. *temp*. H. Cas. *temp*. Hardwicke, *Eng.*
Ca. *temp*. Holt Cas. *temp*. Holt, *Eng.*
Ca. *temp*. K. Cas. in Ch. *temp*. King, *Eng.*
Ca. *temp*. Talb. Cas. in Ch. *temp*. Talbot, *Eng.*
Cab. & E. Cababé & Ellis Rep., Q.B.D., *Eng.*
Cadwalader Cadwalader's Dist. Ct. Cas. (E.D. Pa.)
Cai. Caines' N.Y. Term Rep.
Cai. Cas. Caine's Cas. in Error, N.Y.
Cai. R. Caines' Rep.
Cai. T. R. Caines' Term Rep., N.Y.
Cal. Caldecott's K.B. Rep., *Eng.*
California Law Rep.
Calthrop K.B. Rep., *Eng.*
Cal. App. California Appeals Rep.
Cal. App. 2d California Appeals Rep., Second Series
Cal. App. Dec. California Appellate Dec.
Cal. Dec. California Dec.
Cal. Ind. Acct. Dec. California Industrial Accidents Dec.
Cal. Jur. California Jurisprudence
Cal. Jur. 2d California Jurisprudence, Second Edition
Cal. Leg. Rec. California Legal Record
Cal. Prac. California Practice
Cal. Rptr. California Reporter (West)
Cal. S.B.J. California State Bar Jour.
Cal. Sup. California Super. Ct. Rep.
Cal. Unrep. Cas. California Unreported Cas.
Calcutta W.N. Calcutta Weekly Notes
Cald. Caldwell's Rep. (25–36 W. Va.)
Cald. J.P. Caldecott's Magistrates' Cas., *Eng.*
Cald. M. Cas. Same as above
Cald. Mag. Cas. Same as above
Cald. S.C. Caldecott's Settlement Cas., *Eng.*
Cald. Sett. Cas. Same as above
Calif. L. Rev. California Law Rev.
Calif. W. Int. L.J. California Western International Law Jour.
Calif. Western L. Rev. California Western Law Rev.
Call Call's Rep. (5–10 Va.)
Calth. Calthrop's K.B. Rep., *Eng.*
Cam. Cameron's Rep., *Upper Canada*
Cam. Cas. Cameron's Sup. Ct. Cas., *Can.*
Cam. Op. Cameron's Legal Opinions, *Can.*
Cam. Prac. Cameron's Sup. Ct. Practice, *Can.*
Cam. Scacc. Camera Scaccarii (Ex. Chamber), *Eng.*
Cam. Stell. Camera Stellate (Star Chamber), *Eng.*
Cam. & N. Cameron & Norwood's

N.C. Conference Rep.
Camb. L. J. Cambridge Law Jour.
Cameron *See* Cam.
Cameron Pr. Cameron's Practice, *Can.*
Camp Camp's Rep. (1 N.D.)
Camp. Campbell's N.P. Rep., *Eng.*
Campbell's Rep. (26–58 Neb.)
Camp. Dec. Taney's U.S. Cir. Ct. Dec. by Campbell
Camp. N.P. Campbell's N.P. Rep., *Eng.*
Campb. Campbell, *Neb.*
Campbell's N.P., *Eng.*
Camp. L.G. Campbell's Legal Gazette, *Pa.*
Campbell Campbell's Legal Gazette (27–58 Neb.)
Campbell's N.P. Rep., *Eng.*
Taney's Cir. Ct. Dec., *U.S.*
Can. Abr. Canadian Abridgement
Can. App. Cas. Canadian Appeal Cas.
Can. B.A.J. Canadian Bar Association Jour.
Can. B.J. Canadian Bar Jour.
Can. B.R. Canadian Bar Rev.
Can. B. Rev. Same as above
Can. Bankr. Ann. Canadian Bankruptcy Rep., Annot.
Can. Bankr. Ann.(N.S.) Same as above, New Series
Can. Com. R. Canadian Commercial Law Rep.
Can. C. C. Canada Crim. Cas. Annot.
Can. Cr. Cas. Canadian Criminal Cas.
Can. Crim. Criminal Rep., *Can.*
Can. Crim. Cas. Same as above
Can. Crim. Cas. Ann. Canadian Criminal Cas. Annot.
Can. Exch. Rep. Ex. Ct., *Can.*
Can. J. Correction Canadian Jour. of Correction
Can. Gaz. Canadian Gazette
Can. L. J. Canada Law Jour.
Can. L. J. (N.S.) Same as above, New Series
Can. L. R. Canada Law Rep.
Can. L. T. Occ. N. Canadian Law Times Occasional Notes
Can. Mun. J. Canadian Municipal Jour.
Can. R. A. C. Canadian Rep., Appeal Cas.
Can. R. Cas. Canadian Railway Cas.
Can. Ry. Cas. Same as above
Can. S. C. Rep. Canada Sup. Ct. Rep.
Can. Sup. Ct. Same as above
Can. Tax App. Bd. Canada Tax Appeal Board
Can. Tax Cas. Ann. Canada Tax Cas. Annot.
Can. Tax. J. Canadian Tax Jour.
Can. Y. B. Int. Law Canadian Yearbook of International Law
Cane & L. Cane & Leigh's Crown Cas. Res., *Eng.*
Capital U. L. Rev. Capital Univ. Law Rev.
Car. H. & A. Carrow, Hamerton & Allen Session Cas., *Eng.*
Car. L. Rep. Carolina Law Respository (4 N.C.)
Car. & K. Carrington & Kirwan, N.P., *Eng.*
Car. & Kir. Carrington & Kirwan's N.P. Rep., *Eng.*
Car. & Mar. Carrington & Marshman's N.P. Rep., *Eng.*
Car. & P. Carrington & Payne's N.P. Rep., *Eng.*
Carey M. R. Carey's Manitoba Rep. *temp.* Wood
Carl. Carleton's New Brunswick Rep.
Carp. Carpenter, *Cal.*
Carp. P. C. Carpmael Patent Cas., *Eng.*
Carpenter Carpenter's Rep. (52, 53 Cal.)
Cart. Carter's Rep., C.P., *Eng.*
Carter's Rep. (1, 2 Ind.)
Cart. B. N. A. Cartwright's Constitutional Cas., *Can.*
Carter Carter's C.P. Rep., *Eng.*

Carter's Rep. (1, 2 Ind.)
Carth. Carthew's K.B. Rep., *Eng.*
Cartwr. Cas. Cartwright's Cases, *Can.*
Cary Cary's Ch. Rep., *Eng.*
Cas. Casey's Rep. (25–36 Pa.)
Cas. App. Cas. of Appeal to H. L., *Eng.*
Cas. Arg. & Dec. Cas. Argued and Decreed in Ch., *Eng.*
Cas. B.R. Cas. Banco Regis *temp.* Wm. III (12 Modern Rep.), *Eng.*
Cas. C. L. Cas. in Crown Law, *Eng.*
Cas. C. R. Cas. *temp.* Wm. III (12 Modern Rep.)
Cas. Ch. (or Cas. in Ch.) Cases in Ch. 1660–88, *Eng.*
Cas. in Ch. 1660–97, *Eng.*
Select Cas. in Ch., *Eng.*
Cas. in Ch. *temp.* Car. II, *Eng.*
Cas. Eq. Gilbert's Cas. in Eq., *Eng.*
Cas. L. Eq. Cas. in Law & Eq. (10 Modern Rep.), *Eng.*
Cas. F. T. Cas. in Ch., *temp.* Talbot, by Forester, *Eng.*
Cas. H. L. Cas. in the H.L., *Eng.*
Cas. in Ch. See Cas. Ch.
Cas. K. B. Cas. in K.B. (8 Modern Rep.), *Eng.*
Cas. K. B. *t.* H. Cas. *temp.* Hardwicke (Kelynge's K.B. Rep.), *Eng.*
Cas. P. Cas. in Parliament, *Eng.*
Cas. Prac. C. P. Cas. of Practice, C.P., *Eng.*
Cas. R. Casey's Rep. (25–36 Pa.)
Cas. *t.* Ch. II Rep. in Ch., Cas. *temp.* Charles II, *Eng.*
Cas. *t.* F. Ch. Cas. *temp.* Finch, *Eng.*
Cas. *t.* Geo. I. Ch. Cas. *temp.* Geo. I (8, 9 Modern Rep.), *Eng.*
Cas. *t.* H. K.B. Cas. *temp.* Hardwicke, *Eng.*
Ch. Rep. *temp.* Hardwicke (West), *Eng.*
K.B. Rep. *temp.* Holt (7, 11 Modern Rep.), *Eng.*
Cas. *t.* Holt Cas. *temp.* Holt, K.B., *Eng.*
Cas. *t.* K. Ch. Cas. *temp.* King, *Eng.*
Ch. Rep. *temp.* King (Mosley), *Eng.*
Cas. *t.* Mac. Cas. *temp.* Macclesfield (10 Modern Rep.), *Eng.*
Cas. *t.* Northington Cas. *temp.* Northington, Ch. Rep., *Eng.*
Cas. *t.* Q. Anne (11 Modern Rep.), *Eng.*
Cas. *t.* Talb. Ch. Cas. *temp.* Talbot, *Eng.*
Cas. *t.* Wm. III Cas. *temp.* Wm. III (12 Modern Rep.), *Eng.*
Cas. Tak. & Adj. Cas. Taken and Adjudged (Rep. in Ch., First Edition), *Eng.*
Cas. *temp.* *See* Cas. *t.*
Cas. Wm. I Cas., Wm. I to Rich. I (Bigelow), *Eng.*
Case W. Res. J. Int. L. Case Western Reserve Jour. of International Law
Case W. Res. L. Rev. Case Western Reserve Law Rev.
Case & Com. Case and Comment
Casey Casey's Rep. (25–36 Pa.)
Cass. Prac. Cas. Cassels' Practice Cas., *Can.*
Cass. S. C. Cassels' Supreme Ct. Dec.
Cates Cates' Rep. (109–127 Tenn.)
Catholic Law The Catholic Lawyer
Catholic U.L. Rev. Catholic Univ. of America Law Rev.
Cent. Crim. C.R. Central Crim. Ct. Reg., *Eng.*
Cent. Dig. Century Digest
Centr. L.J. Central Law Jour.
Cert. Certiorari
Ch. Law Rep., Ch., *Eng.*
Law Rep. Ch. Div., Third Series

Ch. App. Law Rep. Ch. Appeals, *Eng.*
Ch. App. Cas. Same as above
Ch. Cal. Calendar of Proceedings in Ch., *Eng.*
Ch. Cas. Cas. in Ch. 1660–88, *Eng.*
Select Cases in Ch. *temp.* King, *Eng.*
Ch. Ch. Upper Canada Ch. Chambers Rep.
Ch. Cham. Same as above
Ch. Col. Op. Chalmer's Colonial Opinions
Ch. D. Law Rep., Ch. Div., *Eng.*
Ch. D. 2d Same as above, Second Series
Ch. Pre. Precedents in Ch., *Eng.*
Ch. R. Chitty's K.B. Rep., *Eng.*
Rep. in Ch. 1615–1712, *Eng.*
Upper Canada Ch. Chambers Rep.
Ch. R.M. R.M. Charlton's Ga. Rep. (1811–37)
Ch. Rep. See Ch. R.
Ch. Rob. Christopher Robinson's Admiralty Rep., *Eng.*
Ch. Sent. Ch. Sentinel, *U.S.*
Ch. T.U.P. T.U.P. Charlton's Ga. Rep.
Cha. App. Ch. Appeal Cas. English Law Rep.
Cham. Chambers' Upper Canada Rep.
Chamb. Rep. Chambers' Ch. Rep., *Ontario*
Chan. Chaney's Rep. (37–58 Mich.)
Chand. Chandler's Rep. (20, 38–44 N.H.)
Chandler's Rep. (Wis. 1849–52)
Chaney Chaney's Rep. (37–58 Mich.)
Charley Pr. Cas. Charley's Practice Cas., *Eng.*
Charl. R.M. R. M. Charlton's Ga. Rep.
Charl. T.U.P. T.U.P. Charlton's Ga. Rep.
Chase Chase's Cir. Ct. Dec., *U.S.*
Chest. Co. Rep. Chester County Rep., *Pa.*
Chev. Cheves' Rep. (S.C. 1839–40)
Chev. Ch. Cheves' Eq. Rep. (S.C. 1839–40)
Chev. Eq. Same as above
Chi. Kent L. Rev. Chicago-Kent Law Rev.
Chi. Leg. N. Chicago Legal News, *Ill.*
Chic. L.T. Chicago Law Times
Chicago L.B. Chicago Law Bulletin
Chicago L.J. Chicago Law Jour.
Chicago L. Rec. Chicago Law Record
Chicano L. Rev. Chicano Law Rev.
Chil. Rts. Rep. Children's Rights Rep.
Chip. Chipman's Rep., *New Brunswick*
Chipman's Rep. (Vt. 1789–1824)
Chip. D. D. Chipman's Vt. Rep.
Chip. N. N. Chipman's Vt. Rep.
Chit. Chitty's Bail Ct., *Eng.*
Chit. B.C. Same as above
Chitt. Same as above
Chitt. L.J. Chitty's Law Jour.
Cho. Ca. Ch. Choyce Cas. in Ch., *Eng.*
Chr. Rep. Chamber's Rep., *Upper Canada*
Chr. Rob. Christopher Robinson's Admiralty Rep., *Eng.*
Chy. Chrs. Upper Canada Ch. Chambers Rep.
Cin. L. Rev. Cincinnati Law Rev.
Cin. Law Bull. Weekly Law Bulletin, *Ohio*
Cin. Mun. Dec. Cincinnati Municipal Dec.
Cin. Rep. Cincinnati Super. Ct. Rep.
Cin. S.C. Rep. Same as above
Cin. L. Bull. Cincinnati Law

Bulletin
Cin. Sup. Ct. Same as above
Cincinnati Law Bull. Weekly Law Bulletin
Cir. Ct. Dec. Ohio Cir. Ct. Dec.
City Ct. R. Supp. New York, City Ct. Rep. Supplement
City Ct. Rep. New York, City Ct. Rep.
City H. Rep. City Hall Reporter, *N.Y.*
City Hall Rec. City Hall Recorder, *N.Y.*
Civ. Lib. Rptr. Civil Liberties Reporter
Civ. Pr. Rep. Civil Procedure Rep., *N.Y.*
Civil Lib. Dock. Civil Liberties Docket
Cl. *See* Clark; Clarke
Cl. App. Clark's H.L. Appeal Cas., *Eng.*
Cl. Ch. Clarke's Ch. Rep., *N.Y.*
Clark Col. Law Clark Colonial Law
Cl. & Fin. Clark & Finnelly's H.L. Cas., *Eng.*
Cl. & Fin. (N.S.) Same, New Series
Clark Clark's H.L. Cas., *Eng.*
Clark (Pa.) Clark's Pa. Law Jour. Rep.
Clark & Fin. See Cl. & Fin.
Clarke Clarke's N.Y. Ch. Rep.
Clarke's Rep. (19–22 Mich.)
Clarke's Rep. (Pa. 1842–52)
Clarke Ch. Clarke's N.Y. Ch. Rep.
Clarke & S. Dr. Cas. Clarke & Scully's Drainage Cas., *Ont.*
Clay. Clayton's Rep. and Pleas of Assizes at York, 1631–50, *Eng.*
Clayton Same as above
Clem. Clemens' Rep. (57–59 Kan.)
Clev. B.A.J. Cleveland Bar Association Jour.
Clev. St. L. Rev. Cleveland State Law Rev.
Cleve. L. Rec. Cleveland Law Record, *Ohio*
Cleve. L. Reg. Cleveland Law Register
Cleve. L. Rep. Cleveland Law Reporter, *Ohio*
Cleve. Law R. Cleveland Law Reporter, *Ohio*
Cleve. Law Rec. Cleveland Law Record, *Ohio*
Cleve. Law Reg. Cleveland Law Register, *Ohio*
Cleve. Mar. L. Rev. Cleveland-Marshall Law Rev.
Clif. South. El. Cas. Clifford, Southwick Election Cas.
Cliff. Clifford's First Cir. Rep., *U.S.*
Clk. Mag. Clerk's Magazine, *London*
Rhode Island Clerk's Magazine
Co. Coke's Institutes
Coke's K.B. Rep., *Eng.*
Co. Cr. Cas. County Ct. Cas., *Eng.*
Co. Ct. Chr. County Ct. Chronicle, *Eng.*
Co. Ct. Rep. Pennsylvania County Ct. Rep.
Co. Cts. Coke's Courts (4th Institute), *Eng.*
Co. Ent. Coke's Entries, *Eng.*
Co. G. G. Coke's Practice Rep., *Eng.*
Cooke's Practice Rep., *Eng.*
Co. Inst. Coke's Institutes, *Eng.*
Co. Litt. Coke on Littleton, *Eng.*
Co. Mass. Pr. Colby Mass. Practice
Co. on Courts Coke's 4th Institute, *Eng.*
Co. P.C. Coke's Pleas of the Crown, *Eng.*
Co. Rep. New York City Code Reporter
Coke's K.B. Rep., *Eng.*
Cobb Cobb's Rep. (121 Ala; 4–20 Ga.)
Coch. Cochran's Nova Scotia Rep.
Cochr. Cochran's Nova Scotia

Rep.
Cochran's Rep. (3–10 N.D.)
Cochran Same as Coch.
Cockb. &R. Cockburn & Rowe's Election Cas., *Eng.*
Cocke Cocke's Rep. (16–18 Ala.; 14, 15 Fla.)
Code Rep. New York City Code Reporter
Code Rep. (N.S.) New York Code Reporter, New Series
Coffey Coffey's Probate Dec., *Cal.*
Coke *See* Co.
Col. Coldwell's Rep. (41–47 Tenn.)
Coleman's Rep., *Ala.*
Colorado Rep.
Colonial
Columbia
Col. App. Colorado Appeals Rep.
Col. C.C. Collyer's Ch. Cas., *Eng.*
Col. Cas. Coleman's Practice Cas., *N.Y.*
Col. L. Rep. Colorado Law Reporter
Col. L. Rev. Columbia Law Rev.
Col. N.P. Colorado N.P. Dec.
Col. & Cai. Cas. Coleman & Caines' Cas., *N.Y.*
Cold. Coldwell's Rep. (41–47 Tenn.)
Cole. Coleman's Rep., *Ala.*
Colem. Cas. Coleman's Cas., *N.Y.*
Coll. C.R. Collyer's Ch. Rep., *Eng.*
Coll. & E. Bank. Collier's & Eaton's American Bankruptcy Rep.
Colles Colles Cas. in Parliament, *Eng.*
Colo. Colorado
Colo. App. Colorado Appeals Rep.
Colo. Dec. Colorado Dec.
Colo. L. Rep. Colorado Law Reporter
Colo. N.P. Dec. Colorado N.P. Dec. 1900–02
Colq. Colquit's Rep. (1 Modern Rep.), *Eng.*
Coltm. Coltman Registration Appeal Cas., *Eng.*
Colum. Columbia
Colum. Human Rights L. Rev. Columbia Human Rights Law Rev.
Colum. J. Env. L. Columbia Jour. of Environmental Law
Colum. J. L. & Soc. Prob. Columbia Jour. Law & Soc. Problems.
Colum. J. Transnat. L. Columbia Jour. of Transnational Law
Colum. L. Rev. Columbia Law Rev.
Colum. Soc. Int. L. Bull. Columbia Society of International Law Bulletin
Colum. Survey Human Rights L. Columbia Survey of Human Rights Law
Com. Blackstone's Commentaries
Comberbach's Rep., K.B., *Eng.*
Comstock's Rep. (1–5 N.Y.)
Comyns' Rep. K.B., C.P., Ex., *Eng.*
Com. B. Common Bench Rep. 1845–65, *Eng.*
Com. B. (N.S.) Common Bench Rep., New Series, *Eng.*
Com. Cas. Commerical Cas. Since 1895, *Eng.*
Com. Dec. Commissioners' Dec. (Patent)
Com. L. Commercial Law, *Can.*
Com. L. J. Commercial Law Jour.
Com. L. R. Common Law Rep. 1853–55, *Eng.*
Com. L. Rep. Same as above
Com. P. Reptr. Common Pleas Reporter (Scranton)
Com. Pl. Div. Law Rep. C.P. Div., *Eng.*
Com. & Mun. L. Rep. Commercial & Municipal Law

Reporter
Comb. Comberbach's K.B. Rep., *Eng.*
Comb. B. Common Bench (Manning, Granger & Scott), *Eng.*
Comm. Mkt. L. R. Common Market Law Rep.
Comm. Mkt. L. Rev. Common Market Law Rev.
Commw. Arb. Commonwealth Arbitration Rep.
Commw. L. R. Commonwealth Law Rep.
Comp. Dec. Comptroller of the Treasury Dec., *U.S.*
Comp. Gen. Comptroller General's Dec., *U.S.*
Comp. Jurid. Rev. Comparative Juridical Rev.
Comp. L. S. Comparative Law Series
Comp. Rev. Compensation Rev.
Comp. &Int. L. J. S. Afr. Comparative and International Law Jour. of South Africa
Computer L. & T. Rep. Computer Law & Tax Rep.
Comst. Comstock's Rep. (1–4 N.Y.)
Comyns Comyns' K.B. Rep., *Eng.*
Comyns Dig. Comyns Digest, *Eng.*
Con. Conover's Rep., *Eng.*
Connoly's Crim. Rep., *N.Y.*
Con. Sur. Connoly's Surrogate's Rep., *N.Y.*
Condit. Sale-Chat. Mort. Rep. Conditional Sale–Chattel Mortgage Rep. (CCH)
Conf. North Carolina Conference Rep. (Cameron & Norwood)
Cong. Deb. Congressional Debates, *U.S.*
Cong. Dig. Congdon's Digest, *Can*
Cong. Rec. Congressional Record, *U.S.*
Conn. Connecticut
Connecticut Reports
Connolly's N.Y. Surrogate's Rep.
Conn. B. J. Connecticut Bar Jour.
Conn. L. Review Connecticut Law Rev.
Conn. S. Connecticut Supplement
Connolly Connolly's Surrogate's Rep., *N.Y.*
Conover Conover's Rep. (16–153 Wis.)
Const. Constitutional Rep. by Harper, Mill, Treadway, *S.C*
Const. (N.S.) Same as above, New Series
Const. R. S. C. Constitutional Rep. of S.C. by Treadway
Const. Rep. Constitutional Rep., *S.C.*
Const. Rev. Constitutional Review
Const. S. C. South Carolina Constitutional Rep., New Series
Convey. Conveyancer
Convey. (N.S.) Conveyancer & Property Lawyer, New Series
Cook Vice-Adm. Cook's Vice-Admiralty, *Lower Can.*
Cooke Cooke's Practice Rep., C.P., *Eng.*
Cooke's Rep. (3 Tenn.)
Cooke C.P. Cooke's C.P. Rep., *Eng.*
Cooke & A. Cooke & Alcock K.B., *Ir.*
Cooley Cooley's Rep. (5–12 Mich.)
Coop. Cooper's Ch. Rep., *Eng.*
Cooper's Ch. Rep. *temp.* Cottenham, *Eng.*
Cooper's Rep. (21–24 Fla.)
Cooper's Tennessee Ch. Rep.
Coop. C.C. Cooper's Ch. Cas. *temp.* Cottenham, *Eng.*
Coop. Ch. Cooper's Tenn. Ch. Rep.
Coop. Ch. Pr. Cooper's Ch. Practice Rep., *Eng.*
Coop. G. G. Cooper's Ch. Rep., *Eng.*
Coop. Pr. Cas. C. P. Cooper's Ch.

Practice Cas., *Eng*.
Coop. *t*. Brough. Cooper's Cas. *temp*. Brougham, Ch., *Eng*.
Coop. *t*. Cott Cooper's Cas. *temp*. Cottenham Ch., *Eng*.
Coop. *t*. Eldon Cooper's Rep. *temp*. Eldon Ch. *Eng*.
Coop. Tenn. Ch. Cooper's Tenn. Ch. Rep.
Cooper Cooper's Tenn. Ch. Rep.
Cope Cope's Rep. (63–73 Cal.)
Copp Min. Dec. Copp's Mining Dec., *U.S.*
Corb. & D. Corbett & Daniels Election Cas., *Eng*.
Cornell Int. L. J. Cornell International Law Jour.
Cornell L. Q. Cornell Law Quarterly
Cornell L. Rev. Cornell Law Rev.
Corp. J. Corporation Jour.
Corp. Pract. Comment Corporate Practice Commentator
Corp. Reorg. Corporate Reorganizations
Corp. Reorg. & Am. Bank. Rev. Corporate Reorganization & American Bankruptcy Rev.
Corp. Rep. Pennsylvania Corp. Reporter
Counsellor The Counsellor
Count. Cts. Chron. County Courts Chronicle
Coup. Couper's Justiciary, *Sc*.
Court Cl. Court of Claims, *U.S.*
Court. & MacL. Courtennay & MacLean, *Sc*.
Cout. Coutlee's Unreported Cas., *Can*.
Cout. S. C. Notes of Unreported Cas., Sup. Ct. of Canada (Coutlee)
Coutlee Coutlee's Supreme Ct. Cas.
Cow. Cowen's N.Y. Rep. 1823–29
Cowper's K.B. Rep., *Eng*.
Cow. Cr. Rep. Cowen's Crim. Rep., N.Y.
Cowp. Cowper's K.B. Rep., *Eng*.
Cowp. Cas. Cowper's Cas., Ch., *Eng*.
Cox Cox's Ch. Rep., *Eng*.
Cox's Crim. Cas., *Eng*.
Cox's Rep. (25–27 Ark.)
Cox Am. T.M. Cas. Cox's American Trade Mark Cas.
Cox C. C. Cox's Crim. Law Cas., *Eng*.
Cox Ch. Cox's Ch. Cas., *Eng*.
Cox Cr. Ca. Cox's Crim. Cas., *Eng*.
Cox Eq. Cox's Eq.
Cox J. S. Cas. Cox's Joint Stock Cas., *Eng*.
Cox & Atk. Cox & Atkinson Registration Appeals, *Eng*.
Coxe Coxe's Rep. (1 N.J. Law)
Cr. Cranch's Sup. Ct. Rep. (5–13 U.S.)
Cranch's Cir. Ct. Rep., *U.S.*
Cr. App. Criminal Appeals, *Eng*.
Cr. Cas. Res. Crown Cas. Res., *Eng*.
Cr. M. & R. Crompton, Meeson & Roscoe Rep., *Eng*.
Cr. & J. Crompton & Jervix Ex. Rep., *Eng*.
Cr. & M. Crompton & Meeson's Ex. Rep., *Eng*.
Cr. & Ph. Craig & Phillips Ch. Rep., *Eng*.
Crabbe Crabbe's Dist. Ct. Rep., *U.S.*
Craig & Ph. Craig & Phillips Ch. Rep., *Eng*.
Cranch Cranch's Sup. Ct. Rep. (5–13 U.S.)
Cranch C. C. Cranch's Cir. Ct. Rep.
District of Columbia App. Cas. (v.1–5)
Cranch D. C. Same as above
Cranch Pat. Dec. Cranch's Patent Dec., *U.S.*
Crane Crane's Rep. (22–29 Mont.)
Craw. Crawford's Rep. (53–69,

72–191 Ark.)
Crawf. & D. Abr. Cas. Crawford & Dix's Abridged Cas., *Ir*.
Crawf. & Dix Crawford & Dix Cir. Cas,, *Ir*.
Crawford & Dix Criminal Cas., *Ir*.
Creighton L. Rev. Creighton Law Rev.
Crim. App. Criminal Appeal Rep.
Crim. App. Rep. Cohen's Criminal Appeals Rep., *Eng*.
Crim. J. J. Criminal Justice Jour.
Crim. L. Bull. Criminal Law Bulletin
Crim. L. Mag. Criminal Law Magazine, *N.J*.
Crim. L. Q. Criminal Law Quarterly
Crim. L. Rec. Criminal Law Recorder
Crim. L. Rep. Criminal Law Reporter
Crim. L. Rev. Criminal Law Rev.
Criminal Law Rev., *Eng*.
Crim. L. Rptr. Criminal Law Reporter
Crim. Rec. Criminal Recorder, *Pa*.
Criminal Recorder, *London*
Criminal Recorder (1 Wheeler's N.Y. Criminal Rep.)
Crim. Rep. (N.S.) Criminal Rep., New Series
Crime & Del. Crime & Delinquency
Cripp Ch. Cas. Cripp's Church & Clergy Cas.
Critch. Critchfield's Rep. (5–21 Ohio)
Cro. Croke's K.B. Rep., *Eng*.
Keilway's K.B. Rep. 1496–1531, *Eng*.
Cro. Car. Croke's K.B. Rep. *temp*. Car. I, *Eng*.
Cro. Eliz. Croke's Rep. *temp*. Eliz., *Eng*.
Cro. Jac. Croke's K.B. Rep. *temp*. James (Jacobus) I, *Eng*.
Crockford Crockford's Maritime Law Rep., *Eng*.
Croke *See* Cro.
Crom. Crompton's Star Chamber Cas., *Eng*.
Cromp. Ex. R. Crompton's Ex. Rep., *Eng*.
Cromp. M. & R. Crompton, Meeson & Roscoe's Ex. Rep., *Eng*.
Cromp. & Jerv. Crompton & Jervis' Ex. Rep., *Eng*.
Cromp. & Mees. Crompton & Meeson's Ex. Rep., *Eng*.
Crosw. Pat. Cas. Croswell's Collection of Patent Cas., *U.S*.
Crounse Crounse's Rep. (3 Neb.)
Crumrine Crumrine's Rep. (116–146 Pa.)
Pittsburgh Rep., ed. Crumrine
Ct. Cl. Ct. of Claims, *U.S*.
Ct. Cl. N.Y. Ct. of Claims Rep., *N.Y*.
Ct. Cls. Ct. of Claims, *U.S*.
Ct. Com. Pl. Ct. of C.P.
Ct. Crim. App. Ct. of Criminal Appeals, *Eng*.
Ct. Cust. App. Ct. of Customs Appeals, *U.S*.
Ct. Cust. & Pat. App. Court of Customs & Patent Appeals
Ct. Errors & App. Court of Errors & Appeals
Ct. Just. Court of Justiciary
Ct. Rev. Court Rev.
Cum. Bull. Cumulative Bulletin, Internal Revenue Service, *U.S*.
Cum. L. Rev. Cumberland Law Rev.
Cum.-San. L. Rev.
Cumberland-Sanford Law Rev.
Cummins Cummins' Rep. (Idaho 1866–67)
Cun. Cunningham's K.B. Rep., *Eng*.
Cur. Curtis' Cir. Ct. Rep., *U.S*.
Cur. Dec. Curtis' Edition, U.S. Sup. Ct. Rep.
Cur. Leg. Thought Current Legal Thought
Cur. Ov. Ca. Curwen, Overruled

Cas., *Ohio*
Cur. Reg. R. Curia Regis Rolls, *Eng.*
Current L. Current Law
Current L.Y. Current Law Yearbook
Current Legal Prob. Current Legal Problems
Current Med. Current Medicine for Attorneys
Curry Curry's Rep. (6–19 La.)
Curt. Curtis Cir. Ct. Rep., *U.S.*
Curtis' Edition, U.S. Sup. Ct. Rep.
Curt. C.C. Curtis' Cir. Ct. Rep., *U.S.*
Curt. Cond. Curtis' Edition, U.S. Sup. Ct. Rep.
Curt. Dec. Same as above
Curt. Eccl. Curtis Ecclesiastical, *Eng.*
Curtis Curtis' Cir. Ct. Rep., *U.S*
Curtis' Edition, U.S. Sup. Ct. Rep.
Curw. Ov. Cas. Curwen's Overruled Ohio Cas.
Cush. Cushing's Rep. (55–66 Mass.)
Cushing Same as above
Cushman Cushman's Rep. (23–29 Miss.)
Cust. App. United States Customs Appeals
Cust. Bull. Customs Bulletin
Cust. Ct. Customs Ct. Rep., *U.S.*
Cut. Pat. Cas. Cutler's Trademark and Patent Cas., *U.S.*
Cust. Pen. Dec. Customs Penalty Decisions
Cyc. Cyclopedia of Law & Procedure

D. Dallas' U.S. Sup. Ct. Rep. (1–4 U.S.)
Dallas' Pa. Rep. 1754–1806
Delaware Rep.
Denio's Rep., *N.Y.*
Denison's Crown Cas., *Eng.*
Dictionary
Dixbury
Digest, Justinian's
Dowling. *See* Dow
Dyer's Rep., *Eng.*
Disney's Ohio Sup. Ct. Rep.
D.B. Domesday Book
D.C. District Ct.; District of Columbia
Treasury Department Circular, *U.S.*
(no.) Bull. Memo. U.S. Internal Revenue Service, Cumulative Bulletin, Treasury Dept. Circular
D.C.A. Dorion's Q.B. Rep., *Can.*
D.C. App. District of Columbia Appeals Rep.
D. Chip. D. Chipman's Rep. (Vt. 1789–1824)
D. Ct. District Ct. (usually U.S.)
D.F.&J. DeGex, Fisher & Jones' Ch. Rep., *Eng.*
D.J.&S. DeGex, Jones & Smith's Ch. Rep., Eng.
D.L.R. Dominion Law Rep., *Can.*
D.M.&G. DeGex. Macnaghten & Gordon Ch. Rep., Eng.
D.(N.S.) Dow, New Series (H.L. Cas.), *Eng.*
D.P.R. Porto Rico Reports (Spanish ed.)
D.R.S. Dominion Rep. Service (CCH), *Can.*
D.T.C. Dominion Tax Cas.
D.&B. Dearsley & Bell's Crown Cas., *Eng.*
Devereux & Battle's Rep. (18–20 N.C.)
D.&C. Dist. and County Rep., *Pa.*
Dow & Clark's Parliamentary Cas., *Eng.*
D.&E. Durnford & East's K.B. Rep. (Term Rep.), *Eng.*
D.&J. DeGex & Jones' Ch. Rep., *Eng.*
D.&M. Davison & Merivale's Q.B. Rep., *Eng.*
D.&P. Dearsley & Pearce's Crown Cas., *Eng.*

D.&R. Dowling & Ryland's K.B. Rep., *Eng*.
D.&R.N.P. Dowling & Ryland's N.P. Cas., *Eng*.
D.&S. Drewry & Smale's Ch. Rep., *Eng*.
Dak. Dakota
Dak. L. Rev. Dakota Law Rev.
Dal. Dalison's C.P. Rep., *Eng*.
Dallas' U.S. Sup. Ct. Rep., *Eng*.
Dallas' Pa. Rep. 1754–1806
Dale Dale's Rep. (2–4 Okla.)
Dale Ecc. Dale's Ecclesiastical, Eng.
Dale Leg. Rit. Dale's Legal Ritual, *Eng*.
Dalhousie L.J. Dalhousie Law Jour.
Dall. Dallam's Dec.
Dallam's Tex. Sup. Ct. Dec.
Dallas' Pa. Rep. 1754–1806
Dallas' U.S. Sup. Ct. Rep. (1–4 U.S.)
Dall. in Keil. Dallison's Rep. in Keilway's K.B. Rep., *Eng*.
Dall. S.C. Dallas' U.S. Rep.
Dallas *See* Dall.
Dalr. Dalrymple's Dec., *Sc*.
Daly Daly's N.Y.C.P. Rep.
Dan. Dana's Rep. (31–39 Ky.)
Daniell's Ex. Eq., *Eng*.
Danner's Rep. (42 Ala.)
Dan. & Ll. Danson & Lloyd's Mercantile Cas., *Eng*.
Dana Dana's Rep. (31–39 Ky.)
Dane Abr. Dane's Abridgement, *Eng*.
Dann. Dann's Rep. (1 Ariz.)
Dann's Rep. (in 22 Cal.)
Danner's Rep. (42 Ala.)
Danner Danner's Rep. (42 Ala.)
Dans. & Ll. Danson & Lloyd's Mercantile Cas., *Eng*.
Danv. Danvers' Abridgement, *Eng*.
Das. Common Law Rep., v.3, *Eng*.
Dass. Ed. Dassler's Edition, Kansas Rep.
Dauph. Co. Rep. Dauphin County Rep., *Pa*.
Dav. Daveis Dist. Ct. Rep. (v.2 of Ware), *U.S*.
Davis' Dist. Ct. Rep.
Davies' Abridgement of Coke's Rep., *Eng*.
Davis' Hawaiian Rep., *Eng*.
Dav. Coke Same as above
Daveis Same as above
Daveis or Davis Davis K.B., *Ir*.
Dav. & Mer. Davison & Merivale's Q.B. Rep., *Eng*.
Davis Rep. Davis' Hawaiian Rep.
Davys Davys K.B.
Day Day's Rep. Conn. 1802–1813
Dayton Dayton (Laning) Rep., *Ohio*
Dayton Term Rep. Idding's Term Rep., *Ohio*
Dea. Deady's Cir. and Dist. Ct. Rep., *U.S*.
Deady Deady's Cir. and Dist. Ct. Rep., *U.S*.
Deac. Deacon, Bankruptcy Rep., *Eng*.
Deac. & C. Deacon & Chitty, Bankruptcy, *Eng*.
Deane Deane's Rep. (24–26 Vt.)
Deane & Swabey's Probate and Divorce Rep., *Eng*.
Deane's Blockade Cas., *Eng*.
Dears. C.C. Dearsly's Crown Cas., *Eng*.
Dears. & B.C.C. Dearsly & Bell's Crown Cas., *Eng*.
Deas & A. Deas & Anderson, *Sc*.
Dec. Com. Pat. Dec. of Commissioner of Patents
Dec. Dig. Decennial Digest
Dec. O. Ohio Dec.
Dec. Rep. Ohio Dec. Reprint
Dec. *t*.H.&M. Admiralty Dec. *temp*. Hay and Marriott, *Eng*.
Dec. U.S. Compt. Gen. Dec. of U.S. Comptroller General
Decalogue Decalogue Jour.
Defense L.J. Defense Law Jour.
DeG.F.&J. DeGex, Fisher & Jones

Ch. Rep., *Eng.*
DeG.J.&S. DeGex, Jones & Smith Ch. Rep., *Eng.*
DeG.M.&G. DeGex, Macnaghten & Gordon Ch. Rep., *Eng.*
DeG.&J. DeGex & Jones' Ch. Rep., *Eng.*
DeG.&Sm. DeGex & Smale's Ch. Rep., *Eng.*
DeGex DeGex' Bankruptcy Rep., *Eng.*
Del. Delaware Rep.
Del. Ch. Delaware Ch. Rep.
Del. Co. R. Delaware County (Pa.) Rep.
Del. Cr. Cas. Houston's Criminal Cas., Del.
Del. J. Corp. L. Delaware Jour. of Corporate Law
Delane Delane's Revision Courts Dec., *Eng.*
Delehanty New York Miscellaneous Rep.
Dem. Demarest's Surrogate Rep., N.Y.
Den. Denio's N.Y. Rep.
Denis' Rep. (32–46 La.)
Denison's Crown Cas. Res., *Eng.*
Den. C. C. Same as above
Den. L. J. Denver Law Jour.
Den. & P. Denison & Pearce's Crown Cas., *Eng.*
Denio Denio's N.Y. Rep.
Denis Denis' Rep. (32–46 La. Annual)
Denver J. Int. L. & Policy Denver Jour. of International Law and Policy
Denver L. N. Denver Legal News
DePaul L. Rev. DePaul Law Rev.
Dept. State Bull. Department of State Bulletin, *U.S.*
Des. Desaussure's Eq. Rep., *S. C.*
Desaus. Eq. Same as above
Det. Coll. L. R. Detroit College of Law Rev.
Det. L. Rev. Detroit Law Rev.
Det. Leg. N. Detroit Legal News
Dev. Devereux' Rep. (N.C. Law and Eq.)
Devereux' Ct. of Claims Rep., *U.S.*
Dev. Ct. Cl. Devereux' Ct. of Claims Rep., *U.S.*
Dev. Eq. Devereux' Rep. (16, 17, N.C. Eq.)
Dev. L. Devereux' Rep. (12–15 N.C. Law)
Dev. & Bat. Devereux & Battle's Rep. (17–20 N.C. Law)
Devereux & Battle's Rep. (21, 22 N.C. Eq.)
Dew. Dewey's Rep. (60–70 Kan.)
Dewey's Kan. Ct. of Appeal Rep.
DeWitt DeWitt's Rep. (24–42 Ohio)
Dice Dice's Rep. (71–99 Ind.)
Dick. Dickens' Ch, Rep., *Eng.*
Dickinson's Rep. (46–66 N.J. Eq.)
Dick. L. R. Dickinson Law Rev.
Dicta Dicta of the Denver Bar Assn.
Dill. Dillon's Cir. Ct. Rep., *U.S.*
Dirl. Dec. Dirleton's Dec., *Sc.*
Disn. Disney's Ohio Super. Ct. Rep.
Div. Ct. Divisional Ct.
Doct. & St. Doctor and Student, *Eng.*
Dod. Dodson's Admiralty Rep., *Eng.*
Donaker Donaker's Rep. (154 Ind.)
Donn. Donnelly's Ch. Rep., Eng.
Donnelly Same as above
Donnelly's Irish Land Cas.
Dorion Dorion's Q.B. Rep., *Quebec*
Doug. Douglas' K.B. Rep., *Eng.*
Douglas' Rep. (Mich., 1843–47)
Doug.K.B. Douglas' K.B. Rep., *Eng.*
Dougl. El. Cas. Douglas Election Cas., *Eng.*
Dow Dow's H.L. Rep., *Eng.*
Dow & Clark's H.L. Cas., *Eng.*
Dow & Cl. Same as above

Dow. Dowling's Practice Cas., *Eng.*
Dow. P. C. (N.S.) Dowling Practice Cas., New Series, *Eng.*
Dow. & L. Dowling & Lowndes' Bail Ct., *Eng.*
Dow. & Lownd. Dowling & Lowndes' Practice Cas., *Eng.*
Dow. & Ry. Dowling & Ryland's K.B. Rep., *Eng.*
Dowling & Ryland's N.P. Cas., *Eng.*
Dow. & Ry. N.P. Dowling & Ryland's N.P. Rep., *Eng.*
Down. & Lud. Downton & Luder's Election Cas., *Eng.*
Dr. Drewry's Vice-Chancellors' Rep., *Eng.*
Dr. & Sm. Drewry & Smale's Vice-Chancellors' Rep., *Eng.*
Dra. Draper, *Upper Can.*
Draper's K.B. Rep., *Can.*
Drake L. Rev. Drake Law Rev.
Drew. Drewry's Ch., *Eng.*
Drew's Rep. (13 Fla.)
Drewry's Vice-Chancellors' Rep., *Eng.*
Drew. & Sm. Drewry & Smale's Ch. Rep., *Eng.*
Drink. Drinkwater's C.P. Rep., *Eng.*
Drug Abuse L. Rev. Drug Abuse Law Rev.
Drury Drury's Ch., *Ir.*
Dublin U. L. Rev. Dublin University Law Rev.
Dud. Dudley's Ga. Rep. 1830–33
Dud. Ch. Dudley's S.C. Eq. Rep. 1837–38
Dud. L. Dudley's S.C. Law Rep. 1837–38
Duer Duer's Super. Ct. Rep., *N.Y.*
Dug. Orig. Dugdale's Origines Juridiciales
Dugd. Same as above
Duke B. A. J. Duke Bar Assn. Jour.
Duke L. J. Duke Law Jour.
Duke's Charitable Uses Duke's Charitable Uses, *Eng.*
Dunc. Ent. Cas. Duncan Entail Cas., *Sc.*
Dunc. N.P. Duncombe N.P.
Dunn. Dunning's K.B. Rep., *Eng.*
Duquesne U. L. Rev. Duquesne Univ. Law Rev.
Durf. Durfee's Rep. (2 R.I.)
Durie Durie's Ct. Ses. Cas., *Sc.*
Durn. & E. Durnford & East's (Term) Rep., *Eng.*
Dutch. Dutcher's Rep. (25–29 N.J. Law)
Duv. Duvall's Rep. (62, 63 Ky.)
Duval's Reports, *Can.*
Dy. Dyer's K.B. Rep., *Eng.*

E. East's Rep., *Eng.*
E.B.&E. Ellis, Blackburn, & Ellis' Rep., *Eng.*
E.C. English Ch.
E.D. Ex. Div.
E.D. Smith E. D. Smith's C.P. Rep., *N.Y.*
E.E. Eq. Ex.
E.E.R. English Ecclesiastical Rep.
E.G.L. Encyclopedia of Georgia Law
E.L.&Eq. English Law & Eq. Rep.
E.L.R. Eastern Law Rep., *Can.*
E.O. Presidential Executive Order, *U.S.*
E.P.C. East's Pleas of the Crown, *Eng.*
E.P.D. Employment Practices Decisions (CCH)
E.R. East's K.B. Rep., *Eng.*
Election Rep., *Ont.*
English Rep., Full Reprint
E.R.C. English Ruling Cas.
Environmental Reporter Cases (BNA)
E. School L. Rev. Eastern School Law Rev.
E.T. Estate and Gift Tax Ruling, (IRS)
E.&A. Ecclesiastical & Admiralty Rep. (Spinks), *Eng.*

Upper Canada Error & Appeal Rep.
E.&A.R. Same as above
E.&A.W.C. Grant's Error & Appeal Rep., *Ontario*
E.&B. Ellis & Blackburn's Q.B. Rep., *Eng.*
E.&E. Ellis & Ellis' Q.B. Rep., *Eng.*
E.&I. English & Irish Appeals, H.L., *Eng.*
E.A.S. Executive Agreement Series, *U.S.*
E.Afr.L.R. East Africa Law Rep.
Ea. East's K.B. Rep., *Eng.*
Eag.T. Eagle's Commutation of Tithes, *Eng.*
Eag.&Y. Eagle & Young's Tithe Cas., *Eng.*
East Same as above
Eastern Law Reporter, *Can.*
East. L.R. Eastern Law Reporter, *Can.*
East P.C. East's Pleas of the Crown, *Eng.*
East. Rep. Eastern Law Reporter, *Can.*
Eastern Reporter, *U.S.*
East. T. Eastern Term, *Eng.*
Ebersole Ebersole's Rep. (59–80 Iowa)
Eccl. & Adm. Spink's Ecclesiastical & Admiralty, *Upper Canada*
Eccl. R. Ecclesiastical Rep., *Eng.*
Ecology L. Q. Ecology Law Quarterly
Ed. Eden's Ch. Rep., *Eng.*
Ed. Bro. Brown's Ch. Rep., *Eng.*
Ed. C.R. Edward's Ch. Rep., *N.Y.*
Ed.L.J. Edinburgh Law Jour.
Eden Eden's Ch. Rep., *Eng.*
Edg. Edgar, *Sc*
Edinb.L.J. Edinburgh Law Jour.
Edm. Sel. Cas. Edmonds' Select Cas., *N.Y.*
Edw. Edwards' Admiralty Rep., *Eng.*
Edwards' N.Y. Ch. Rep.
Edwards' Rep. (2, 3 Mo.)
Edw. Abr. Edwards' Abridgement P.C.
Edwards Abridgement Prerogative Ct. Cas., *Eng.*
Edw. Ch. Edward's Ch. Rep., *N.Y.*
Edw. Lead. Dec. Edwards' Leading Dec. in Admiralty
Edw. P.C. Edwards' Prize Cas., *Eng.*
Edw. Pr. Ct. Cas. Edwards' Prerogative Ct. Cas., *Eng.*
Efird Efird Rep. (46–51 *S.C.*)
El. Elchies' Dec., *Sc.*
El.B.&E. Ellis, Blackburn & Ellis' Q.B. Rep., *Eng.*
El.&Bl. Ellis & Blackburn's Q.B. Rep., *Eng.*
El. Cas. Election Cas.
Elchies Elchies' Dec., *Sc.*
Elect. Cas. Election Cas. Armstrong, *N.Y.*
Elect. Rep. Election Rep., *Ontario*
Ell.B.&S. Ellis, Best & Smith's Q.B. Rep., *Eng.*
Ell.Bl.&Ell. Ellis, Blackburn & Ellis' Q.B. Rep., *Eng.*
Ell.&Bl. Same as El.&Bl.
Els. W. Bl. Elsley's Edition of Wm. Blackstone's K.B., *Eng.*
Em.App. Emergency Ct. of Appeals, *U.S.*
Emory L.J. Emory Law Jour.
Enc.Pl.&Pr. Encyclopedia of Pleading & Practice.
Enc. U.S. Sup. Ct. Rep. Encyclopedia of United States Sup. Ct. Rep.
Eng. English's Rep. (6–13 Ark.)
Eng. Adm. English Admiralty
Eng. C.C. English Crown Cas.
Eng. C.L. English Common-Law Rep.
Eng. Ecc.R. English Ecclesiastical Rep.
Eng. Hist. Rev. English Historical Rev.

Eng. Ir. App. Law Rep. English & Irish Appeals
Eng. Judg. English Judges, *Sc*.
Eng. L. & Eq. English Law & Eq. Rep.
Eng. Pr. Cas. Roscoe's English Prize Cas.
Eng. Rep. English Rep., Full Reprint
Eng. Ru. Cas. English Ruling Cas.
Eng. Ry.&C. Cas. English Railway and Canal Cas.
Eng. Sc. Ecc. English & Scotch Ecclesiastical Rep.
English English's Rep. (6–13 Ark.)
Env. L. Environmental Law
Env. L. Rev. Environmental Law Rev.
Env. L. Rptr. Environmental Law Reporter
Eq. Cas. Equity Cases in 9, 10 Modern Rep., *Eng*.
Eq. Rep. Equity Rep. 1835–55, *Eng*.
Gilbert's Eq. Rep., Eng.
Harper's Rep. (S.C. Eq. 1824)
Erie Co. L.J. Erie County Law Jour., *Pa*.
Err. & App. Error & Appeals Rep., *Upper Canada* (Grant)
Ersk. Dec. Erskine's U.S. Cir. Ct. Dec. (in 35 Ga.)
Esp. Espinasse's N.P. Rep., *Eng*.
Estee Estee's Dist. Ct. of Hawaii Rep., *U.S*.
Euer Euer Doctrina Placitandi, *Eng*.
Europ. T.S. European Treaty Series
Evans Evans, Washington Territory Rep.
Lord Mansfield's Dec., *Eng*.
Ex. Exchequer Rep. 1848–56, *Eng*.
Ex.C.R. Canada Ex. Ct. Rep.
Canada Law Rep. (Ex. Ct.)
Ex. D. Law Rep., Ex. Div., *Eng*.
Ex. Div. Same as above
Exch. Same as above
Ex. Rep. (Welsby, Hurlstone & Gordon), *Eng*.
Exch. C. Canada Law Rep. Ex. Ct.
Exch. C.R. Ex. Ct. Rep., *Can*.
Exch. Can. Same as above
Exch. Div. Law Rep. Ex. Div., Eng.
Exch. Rep. English Ex. Rep., Reprint
Ex. Rep. (Welsby, Hurlston & Gordon), *Eng*.
Exec. Order Presidential Executive Order, *U.S*.
Exter. Ca. Lobingier's Extraterritorial Cas., U.S. Ct. for China
Extra. Ca. Same as above
Eyre Eyre's K.B. Rep. *temp*. Wm. III, *Eng*.

F. Federal Reporter, *U.S*.
F. (Ct. Sess.) Fraser's Ct. of Sessions Cas., *Sc*.
F.2d Federal Reporter, Second Series
F.A.D. Federal Anti-Trust Dec., *U.S*.
FAO Food & Agriculture Organization, *UN*
F.B.C. Fonblanque's Bankruptcy Cas., *Eng*.
FBILEB F.B.I. Law Enforcement Bulletin
F.C. Faculty Collection of Dec., *Sc*.
Federal Cases, *U.S*.
F.C.A. Farm Credit Admin., *U.S*.
Federal Code Annotated
F.C.C. (or FCC) Federal Communications Comm., *U.S*.
FDA Food & Drug Admin., *U.S*.
F.D. Cosm. L. Rep. Food, Drug, Cosmetic Law Reporter (CCH)
FEA Foreign Economic Admin., *U.S*.
FEB Fair Employment Bd., *U.S*.
FEP Fair Employment Practice Cases (BNA)

F.H.L. Fraser, H.L., *Sc*.
F.L.J. Canada Fortnightly Law Jour.
F.L.P. Florida Law and Practice
F.L.R. Family Law Reporter
Federal Law Reports, *Aus*.
F.L.R.C. U.S. Federal Labor Relations Council Decisions and Interpretations
F.P.C. Federal Power Comm., *U.S*.
F.R. Federal Register, *U.S*.
FRB Federal Reserve Bd., *U. S*.
FRES Federal Regulation of Employment Service (Lawyers Co-op. Pub. Co.)
F.R.S. Federal Reserve System, *U.S*.
Federal Rules Service
FSA or F.S.A. Farm Security Admin., *U.S*.
Federal Security Agency, *U.S*.
F. Supp. Federal Supplement, *U.S*.
FTC Federal Trade Comm., *U.S*.
F.&F. Foster & Finlason's N.P. Rep., *Eng*.
Fac.L.Rev. Faculty Law Rev., *Toronto*
Fairfield Fairfield's Rep. (10–12 Me.)
Falc. Falconer's Ct. of Session Cas., *Sc*.
Falc.&F. Falconer & Fitzherbert's Election Cas., *Eng*.
Fam. Law Rep. Family Div., *Eng*.
Family L.Q. Family Law Quarterly
Far. Farresley (7 Modern Rep.), *Eng*.
Farresley Farresley's Rep. (7 Modern Rep.), *Eng*.
Holt's K.B. Rep. (Farresley Cas.), *Eng*.
Fawc. Fawcett's Ct.of References Rep., *Eng*.
Fed. Federal Reporter, *U.S*.
The Federalist
Fed. 2d Federal Reporter, Second Series, *U.S*.
Fed. Anti-Tr. Dec. Federal Anti-Trust Dec., *U.S*.
Fed. B.A.J. Federal Bar Assn. Jour.
Fed. B.J. Federal Bar Jour.
Fed. Cas. Federal Cas., *U.S*.
Fed. Com. B.J. Federal Communications Bar Jour.
Fed. Est. & Gift Tax Rep. Federal Estate and Gift Tax Reporter (CCH)
Fed. Juror Federal Juror
Fed. L. Rep. Federal Law Rep.
Fed. L. Rev. Federal Law Rev., *Aus*.
Fed. R. Federal Ct. Rep., *Can*.
Fed. R.D. Federal Rules Dec., *U.S*.
Fed. Reg. Federal Register
Fed. Ins. Counsel Q. Federation of Insurance Counsel Quarterly
Fed. Rep. Federal Reporter, *U.S*.
Fed. Rules Serv. Federal Rules Service
Fed. Rules Serv., 2d Same as above, Second Series
Fed. Supp. Federal Supplement, *U.S*.
Fam. Family, *Eng*.
Ferg. Cons. Fergusson's Consistory (Divorce), *Sc*.
Fergusson Fergusson (of Kilkeran), *Sc*.
Fid. L. Chron. Fiduciary Law Chronicle
Fin. Finch's Ch. Rep., *Eng*.
Fin. H. H. Finch's Ch. Rep., Eng.
Finch Finch's Ch. Rep., *Eng*.
Finch's Precedents in Ch., *Eng*.
Fire & Casualty Cas. Fire and Casualty Cas. or (CCH)
Fish. Fisher's Prize Cas., Dist. Ct., *U.S*.
Fish. Pat. Cas. Fisher's Patent Cas., *U.S*.
Fish. Pat. Rep. Fisher's Patent Rep., *U.S*.
Fish. Pr. Cas. Fisher's Prize Cas., Dist. Ct., *U.S*.
Fitz. Fitzgibbon's K.B. Rep., *Eng*.

Fitzh. Fitzherbert's Abridgement, *Eng.*
Fitzh. Abr. Fitzherbert's Abridgement, *Eng.*
Fitzh. N.B. Fitzherbert's New Natura Brevium, *Eng.*
Fl. Fleta, *Eng.*
Fla. Florida
Fla. B.J. Florida Bar Jour.
Fla. Jur. Florida Jurisprudence
Fla. L.J. Florida Law Jour.
Fla. Supp. Florida Supplement
Fla. & K. Flanagan & Kelly, Rolls, *Ir.*
Flan. & Kel. Flanagan & Kelly, Rolls, *Ir.*
Flip. Flippin's Cir. Ct. Rep., *U.S.*
Fogg Fogg's Rep. (32–37 N.H.)
Fonbl. N.R. Fonblanque's Cas. in Ch., *Eng.*
For. Forrest's Ex. Rep., *Eng.*
Forrester's Ch. Rep. *temp.* Talbot, *Eng.*
For. Aff. Foreign Affairs
Forbes Forbes, *Sc.*
Ford. Urban L.J. Fordham Urban Law Jour.
Fordh. L. Rev. Fordham Law Rev.
Forman Forman's Rep. (1 Scammon, 2 Ill.)
Forr. Ch. Cas. *temp.* Talbot, *Eng.*
Forrest's Ex. Rep., *Eng.*
Fort. Fortescue's K.B. Rep., *Eng.*
Fort. de Laud. Fortesque, De Laudibus Legum Angliae, *Eng.*
Fortes. Rep. Fortescue's K.B. Rep., *Eng.*
Fortn. L.J. Fortnightly Law Jour.
Forum Forum: Bench and Bar Rev.
Forum Law Rev.
Forum, Dickinson School of Law
Fost. Foster's Crown Cas., *Eng.*
Foster's Legal Chronicle Rep., *Pa.*
Foster's Rep. (21–31 N.H.)
Foster's Rep. (5, 6, 8 Hawaii)
Fost. & Fin. Foster & Finlason's N.P., Rep., *Eng.*
Fount. Dec. Fountainhall's Dec., *Sc.*
Fox Fox's Cir. and Dist. Ct. Dec., *U.S.*
Fox's Patent, Trade Mark, Design and Copyright Cas., *Can.*
Fox's Registration Cas., *Eng.*
Fox Pat. Cas. Fox's Patent, Trade Mark, Design and Copyright Cas., *Can.*
Fox & S. Fox & Smith's K.B., *Ir.*
Fr. Freeman's K.B. and Ch. Rep., *Eng.*
Fr. Chy. Freeman's Ch. Rep., *Eng.*
France France's Rep. (3–11 Colo.)
Fraser Fraser Ct. of Session Cas., *Sc.*
Free. Freeman's Ch. Rep., *Eng.*
Freeman's K.B. Rep., *Eng.*
Freeman's Rep. (31–96 Ill.)
Free. Ch. Freeman's Ch. Rep., *Eng.*
Freeman's Rep. (Miss. Ch. 1839–43)
Freem. Freeman's Rep. (31–96 Ill.)
Freeman's Rep. (Miss. Ch.)
Freem. C.C. Freeman's Ch. Cas., *Eng.*
Freem. Ch. Freeman's Ch. Rep., *Eng.*
Freem. K.B. Freeman's K.B. and C.P. Rep., *Eng.*
French French's Rep. (6 N.H.)
Fuller Fuller's Rep. (59–105 Mich.)

G. Gale's Ex. Rep., *Eng.*
Georgia
GA General Assembly, *UN*
G.A. General Appraisers' Dec., *U.S.*
G.A.O. General Accounting Office, *U.S.*
GATT/CP General Agreement Tariffs and Trade, Contracting Parties, *U.S.*
G.C.M. General Counsel's Memorandum, Internal Revenue Service, *U.S*

G.E.R.R. Govt. Employees Relations Rep. (BNA)
G.Gr. G. Green's Rep. (Iowa 1847–54)
G.L.R. Gazette Law Rep., *N.Z.*
G.M. Dud. Dudley's Rep. (Ga. 1830–33)
GSA General Services Admin., *U.S.*
G.S.R. Gongwer's State Rep., *Ohio*
G. & G. Goldsmith & Guthrie's Rep. (36–37 Mo. App.)
G. & J. Gill & Johnson's Rep., *Md.*
Glyn & Jameson's Bankruptcy, *Eng.*
G. & R. Geldert & Russell's Nova Scotia Rep.
Ga. Georgia
Ga. App. Georgia Appeals Rep.
Ga. B.J. Georgia Bar Jour.
Ga. Bus. Law Georgia Business Lawyer
Ga. Dec. Georgia Dec.
Ga. J. Int. & Comp. L. Georgia Jour. of International & Comparative Law
Ga. L. Georgia Lawyer
Ga. L. J. Georgia Law Jour.
Ga. L. Rep. Georgia Law Reporter
Ga. L. Rev. Georgia Law Rev.
Ga. St. B.J. Georgia State Bar Jour.
Ga. Supp. Lester's Supplement to 33 Ga.
Gal. & Dav. Gale & Davison's Q.B. Rep., *Eng.*
Galb. & M. Galbraith & Meek's Rep. (12 Fla.)
Galbraith Galbraith's Rep. (9–12 Fla.)
Gale Gale's Ex. Rep., *Eng.*
Gale's New Forest Dec., *Eng.*
Gale & Dav. Gale & Davison's Q.B. Rep., *Eng.*
Gall. Gallison's Cir. Ct. Rep., *U.S.*
Gard. N.Y. Rep. Gardiner's N.Y. Reporter
Gardenhire Gardenhire's Rep. (14, 15 Mo.)
Gay. Gayarre's Rep. (25–38 La.)
Gayarre Same as above
Gaz. Weekly Law Gazette, Cincinnati
Gaz. L.R. Gazette Law Rep.
Geld. & M. Geldart & Maddock's Ch., *Eng.*
Geld. & Ox. Geldert & Oxley's Nova Scotia Dec.
Geld. & R. Geldert & Russell's Nova Scotia Rep.
Geldart Geldart & Maddock's Ch. Rep. (6 Maddock), *Eng.*
Gen. Dig. General Digest
Geo. Georgia
Geo. Coop. G. Cooper's Ch. Cas. *temp.* Eldon, *Eng.*
Geo. Dec. Georgia Dec.
Geo. L.J. Georgetown Law Jour.
Geo. Wash. Law Rev. George Washington Law Rev.
George George's Rep. (30–39 Miss.)
Gibbons Gibbons' Surrogate's Rep., *N.Y.*
Gibbs Gibbs' Rep. (2–4 Mich.)
Giff. Giffard's Ch. Rep., *Eng.*
Giff. & H. Giffard & Hemming's Ch. Rep., *Eng.*
Gil. Gilbert's Cas. in Law and Eq., *Eng.*
Gilbert's Ch. Rep., *Eng.*
Gilman's Rep. (6–19 Ill.)
Gilmer's Rep. (21 Va.)
Gilb. Gilbert's Cas. in Law and Eq., *Eng.*
Gilb. C.P. Gilbert's C.P., *Eng.*
Gilb. Cas. Gilbert's Cas. in Law and Eq.
Gilb. Ch. Gilbert's Ch. and Ex. Rep., *Eng.*
Gilb. Eq. Rep. Gilbert's Ch. and Eq. Rep., *Eng.*
Gilb. Rep. Gilbert's Ch. Rep., *Eng.*
Gildersleeve Gildersleeve's Rep. (1–10 N.M.)
Gilfillan Minnesota Rep., Gilfillan ed.
Gill. Gill's Rep. (Md. App.)

Gill & Johns. Gill & Johnson's Md. Rep.
Gilm. Gilman's Rep. (6–10 Ill.)
Gilmer's Rep. (21 Va.)
Gilm. & Falc. Gilmour & Falconer, *Sc.*
Gilmer Gilmer's Rep. (21 Va.)
Gilp. Gilpin's Dist. Ct. Rep., *U.S.*
Gl. & J. Glyn & Jameson's Bankruptcy Cas., *Eng.*
Glanv. Glanville's De Legibus et Consuetudinibus Regni Angliae, *Eng.*
Glanv. El. Cas. Glanville's Election Cas., *Eng.*
Glendale L.R. Glendale Law Rev.
Glenn Glenn's Rep. (16–18 La.)
Goldb. Goldbolt's K.B. Rep., *Eng.*
Gold. & G. Goldsmith & Guthrie's Rep. (36, 37 Mo. App.)
Golden Gate L. Rev. Golden Gate Law Rev.
Gonzaga L. Rev. Gonzaga Law Rev.
Gordon Gordon's Rep. (24–26 Colo.)
Gordon's Rep. (10–13 Colo. App.)
Gottschall Gottschall, *Ohio*
Gouldsb. Gouldsborough's K.B. Rep., *Eng.*
Gouldsborough's Q.B. Rep., *Eng.*
Gour. Gourick's Patent Digest 1889–91, *U.S.*
Gov. Cont. Rep. Government Contracts Reporter (CCH)
Gow Gow's N.P. Rep., *Eng.*
Gr. Grant's Upper Canada Ch. Rep.
Grant's Pa. Cas. 1814–63
Green's Rep. (N.J. Law and Eq.)
Greenleaf's Rep. (1–9 Me.)
Gr. Eq. Green's Rep. (16–27 N.J. Eq.)
Gra. Graham's Rep. (98–139 Ga.)
Granger Granger's Rep. (22, 23 Ohio)
Grant Grant's Upper Canada Ch. Rep.
Grant E. & A. Grant's Ontario Error and Appeal Rep.
Grat. Grattan's Rep. (42–74 Va.)
Gray Gray's Rep. (67–82 Mass.)
Gray's Rep. (112–22 N.C.)
Graya Graya (periodical)
Green Green's Rep. (N.J. Law and Eq.)
Green's Rep. (1–9 Me.)
Green's Rep. (1 Okla.)
Green's Rep. (11–17 R.I.)
Green Bag Green Bag., Boston
Green Cr. Green's Criminal Law, *Eng.*
Green C.E. Green's Rep. (16–27 N.J. Eq.)
Green Ch. H. W. Green's Rep. (2–4 N.J. Eq.)
Green L. Green's Rep. (13–15 N.J. Law)
Greenl. Ov. Cas. Greenleaf's Rep. Overruled Cas.
Grein. Pr. Greiner La. Practice
Griffith Griffith's Rep. (117–32 Ind.)
Griffith's Rep. (105 Ind. App.)
Grisw. Griswold's Rep. (14–19 Ohio)
Guild Prac. Guild Practitioner
Gunby Gunby's Dist. Ct. Rep. (La. 1885)
Guthrie Guthrie's Rep. (33–83 Mo. App.)
Gwill. T. Cas. Gwillim's Tithe Cas., *Eng.*

H. Hare's Ch. Rep., *Eng.*; Hill N.Y. Rep. 1841–44; Howard Sup. Ct. Rep. (42–65 U.S.)
H.B. House of Representatives Bill
H. Bl. H. Blackstone's C.P. Rep., *Eng.*
H. Con. Res. House of Representatives Concurrent Resolution
H. Doc. House of Representatives Document
H.J. Res. House of Representatives Joint Res.
H.L. House of Lords; Clark's H.L.

Cas., *Eng.*
H.L. Cas. Same as above
H.L.R. Harvard Law Rev.
HOLC Home Owner's Loan Corp., *U.S.*
H.P.C. Hale's Pleas of the Crown, *Eng.*
H.R. House of Representatives Bill House Roll, *U.S.*
H.R. Rept. House of Representatives Report
H. Res. House of Representatives Resolution
H.W. Gr. H. W. Green's Rep. (2–4 N.J. Eq.)
H. & B. Hudson & Brooke's K.B., *Ir.*
H. & C. Hurlstone & Coltman's Ex. Rep., *Eng.*
H. & G. Harris & Gill's Md. Rep. 1826–29
Hurlstone's & Gordon's Rep., *Eng.*
H. & H. Harrison & Hodgin's Municipal Rep., *Upper Can.*
Horn & Hurlstone's Ex. Rep., *Eng.*
H. & J. Harris & Johnson's Rep. (Md. App.)
H. & M. Hemming & Miller's Vice-Chancellor's Rep., *Eng.*
Henning & Munford's Rep. (11–14 Va.)
H. & McH. Harris & McHenry's Md. Rep.
H. & N. Hurlstone & Norman's Ex. Rep., *Eng.*
H. & R. Harrison & Rutherford's C.P. Rep. *Eng.*
H. & S. Harris & Simrall's Rep. (49–52 Miss.)
H. & T. Hall & Twell's Ch. Rep., *Eng.*
H. & W. Harrison & Wollaston's K.B. Rep., *Eng.*
Hurlstone & Walmsley's Ex. Rep., *Eng.*
H. Bl. Henry Blackstone's C.P., *Eng.*
H.L. Cas. H.L. Cas., *Eng.*
Ha. Hare's Vice-Chancery, *Eng.*
Hare's Vice-Chancellor's Rep., *Eng.*
Ha. & Tw. Hall & Twell's Ch. Rep., *Eng.*
Had. Hadley's Rep. (45–48 N.H.)
Hadd. Haddington MSS Rep., *Sc.*
Hadley Hadley's Rep. (45–48 N.H.)
Hag. Hagan's Rep. (1–5 W. Va.)
Haggard's Admiralty Rep., *Eng.*
Hag. Adm. Same as above
Hag. Con. Haggard's Consistory Rep., *Eng.*
Hagan Hagan's Rep. (1, 2 Utah)
Hagans Hagans' Rep. (1–5 W. Va.)
Hagn. & Mill. Hagner & Miller's Rep. (2 Md. Ch.)
Hailes Dec. Haile's Dec., *Sc.*
Hal. Law Halsted's Rep. (6–12 N.J. Law)
Hale Hale, *Cal.*; Hale's Common Law, *Eng.*
Hale P.C. Hale's Pleas of the Crown. *Eng.*
Hall Hall's Rep. (56, 57 N.H.)
Hall's Rep. (1, 2 N.Y. Super.)
Hallett's Rep. (1, 2 Colo.)
Hall N.H. Hall's Rep. (56, 57 N.H.)
Hall & Tw. Hall & Twell's Ch. Cas., *Eng.*
Hallett Hallett's Rep. (1, 2 Colo.)
Hals. Halsted's Rep. (6–12 N.J. Law)
Hals. Ch. Halsted's Rep. (5–8 N.J. Eq.)
Ham. Hammond's Rep. (1–9 Ohio)
Hamlin Hamlin's Rep. (81–99 Me.)
Hammond Hammond's Rep. (36–45 Ga.)
Hammond's Rep. (1–9 Ohio)
Hammond & Jackson Hammond & Jackson's Rep. (45 Ga.)
Ham. A. & O. Hamerton, Allen & Otter, New Session Cas., *Eng.*
Han. Handy's Ohio Rep. (12 Ohio

Dec.)
Han. N.B. Hannay's Rep., *New Brunswick*
Hand Hand's Rep. (40–45 N.Y.)
Handy Handy's Ohio Rep. (12 Ohio Dec.)
Hans. Deb. Hansard's Parliamentary Debates, *Eng.*
Hansb. Hansbrough's Rep. (76–90 Va.)
Har. Harrington, *Del.*; Harrington's Ch., *Mich.*; Harrison, *La.*; Harrison's Ch., *Mich.*
Har. Del. Harrington's Rep. (1–5 Del.)
Har. St. Tr. Hargrave's State Trials, *Eng.*
Har. & Gil. Harris & Gill's Rep. (1826–29 Md.)
Har. & John. Harris & Johnston's Rep. (Md. App.)
Har. & McH. Harris & McHenry (Md. Gen. Ct.)
Har. & Ruth. Harrison & Rutherfurd's C.P. Rep., *Eng.*
Harc. Harcarse, Dec., *Sc.*
Hard. Hardin's Rep. (3 Ky.); Hardres' Ex. Rep., *Eng.*; Kelyngs (W.), Ch. Rep., *Eng.*
Hardes. Hardesty's Rep. (Del. Term)
Hardin Hardin, *Ky.*
Hardres Hardres' Ex., *Eng.*
Hardw. Cases *temp.* Hardwicke, Lee's, *Eng.*
Cases *temp.* Hardwicke, Ridgeway's, *Eng.*
Hare Hare's Vice-Chancellors' Rep., *Eng.*
Hare & W. American Leading Cas., Hare & Wallace
Harg. Hargrove's Rep. (68–75 N.C.)
Hargrave's State Trials, *Eng.*
Hargrove Hargrove's Rep. (68–75 N.C.)
Harm. Harmon's Rep. (13–15 Cal.)
Harmon's Upper Can. C.P. Rep.
Harp. Con. Cas. Harper's Md. Conspiracy Cas.
Harp. Eq. Harper's Rep. (1824 S.C. Eq.)
Harp. L. Harper's Rep. (1823–30 S.C. Law)
Harr. Harrington's Rep. (1–5 Del.); Harrington's Ch. Rep. (Mich. 1836–42); Harris' Rep. (13–24 Pa.); Harrison's Rep. (15–17, 23–29 Ind.); Harrison's Rep. (16–19 N.J. Law)
Harr. Ch. Harrison's Ch., *Eng.*
Harrington's Mich. Ch. Rep.
Harr. Con. La. R. Harrison's Condensed La. Rep.
Harr. N.J. Harrison's Rep. (16–19 N.J. Law)
Harr. & G. Harris & Gill's Rep. (Md. 1826–29)
Harr. & H. Harrison & Hodgins Municipal Rep., *Upper Can.*
Harr. & J. Harris & Johnson's Rep. (Md. 1800–26)
Harr. & M. Harris & McHenry, *Md.*
Harr. & Ruth. Harrison & Rutherfurd's C.P. Rep., *Eng.*
Harr. & Sim. Harris & Simrall's Rep. (49–52 Miss.)
Harr. & W. Harrison & Wollaston's K.B., *Eng.*
Harrison's Rep. (16–19 N J. Law)
Harring. Harrington's Rep. (1–5 Del.)
Harrington's Mich. Ch. Rep.
Harris Harris' Rep. (13–24 Pa.)
Harris & Sim. Harris & Simrall's Rep. (49–52 Miss.)
Harrison Harrison's Rep. (15–17, 23–29 Ind.)
Harris & G. Harris & Gill, *Md.*
Hartley Hartley's Rep. (4–10 Tex.)
Hartley & Hartley Rep. (11–21 Tex.)
Harv. Bus. Rev. Harvard Business Rev.
Harv. Civ. Rts.–Civ. Lib L. Rev.

Harvard Civil Rights–Civil Liberties Law Rev.
Harv. Ed. Rev. Harvard Ed'l Rev.
Harv. Env. L. Rev. Harvard Environmental Law Rev.
Harv. Int. L.J. Harvard International Law Jour.
Harv. J. Legis. Harvard Jour. on Legislation
Harv. L. Rev. Harvard Law Rev.
Hasb. Hasbrouk, *Idaho*
Hask. Haskell's Rep. for U.S. Courts in Maine (Fox's Dec.)
Hast. Hastings' Rep. (69, 70 Me.)
Hast. Int. & Comp. L. Rev. Hastings' Int'l & Comparative Law Rev.
Hast. L.J. Hastings Law Jour.
Havil. Haviland, *Prince Edward Island*
Haw. Hawkins' Pleas of the Crown, *Eng.*
Hawkins' Rep. (19–24 La. Annual)
Hawaii (Sandwich Islands) Rep.
Hawley's Rep. (10–20 Nev.)
Hawaii Hawaii Rep.
Hawarde Hawarde's Star Chamber Cas., *Eng.*
Hawarde St. Ch. Same as above
Hawk. Hawkins' Louisiana Annual
Hawk. P.C. Hawkins' Plea of the Crown, *Eng.*
Hawkins Same as above; Hawkins' Rep. (19–24 La. Annual)
Hawks Hawks' Rep. (8–11 N.C.)
Hawley Hawley's Rep. (10–20 Nev.)
Hay Haywood's Rep. (4–6 Tenn.)
Hay's Scotch Dec., *Sc.*
Hay & H. Hay & Hazelton, *U.S.*
Hay & M. Hay & Marriott's Admiralty, *Eng.*
Hayes Hayes' Ex., *Ir.*
Hayes & J. Hayes & Jones' Ex., *Ir.*
Hayw. Haywood's Rep. (2, 3 N.C.)
Haywood's Rep. (4–6 Tenn.)
Hayw. Tenn. Haywood's Rep. (4–6 Tenn.)
Hayw. & H. Hayward & Hazelton's District of Columbia Rep. 1840–63.
Haz. Reg. Hazard's Register, *Pa.*
Head Head's Rep. (38–40 Tenn.)
Heath Heath's Rep. (36–40 Me.)
Hedges Hedges' Rep. (2–6 Mont.)
Heisk. Heiskell's Rep. (48–59 Tenn.)
Helm Helm's Rep. (2–9 Nev.)
Hem. Bl. H. Blackstone's C.P., Rep., *Eng.*
Hem. & M. Heming & Miller's Ch. Rep., *Eng.*
Heming. Hemingway's Rep. (53–65 Miss.)
Hemp. Hempstead's Cir. Ct. Rep., *U.S.*
Hen. & Mun. Hening & Munford's Rep. (11–14 Va.)
Hennepin Law. Hennepin Lawyer
Hepb. Hepburn's Rep. (3, 4 Cal.); Hepburn, *Colo.*
Het. Hetley's C.P. Rep., *Eng.*
Hibb. Hibbard's Rep. (67 N.H.)
Higgins Higgins Rep. (Tenn. Civil App.)
Hight Hight's Rep. (57–58 Iowa)
Hil. T. Hilary Term, *Eng.*
Hill Hill's N.Y. Rep., 1841–44
Hill's Rep. (S.C. Law 1883–37)
Hill Eq. Hill's Rep. (S.C. Eq.)
Hill S.C. Hill's Rep. (S.C. Law or Eq.)
Hill & Den. Hill & Denio Supplement (Lalor) 1842–44, N.Y.
Hillyer Hillyer's Rep. (20–22 Cal.)
Hilt. Hilton's N.Y. C.P. Rep.
Hines Hines' Rep. (83–98 Ky.)
Ho. L. Cas. Clark's H.L. Cas., *Eng.*
Hob. Hobart's C.P. & Ch., *Eng.*; Hobart's K.B. Rep., *Eng.*
Hodg. Hodges' C.P. Rep., *Eng.*
Hodg. El. Hodgin's Election, *Upper Can.*
Hoff. Hoffman's N.Y. Ch. Rep.

Hoff. Ch. Same as above
Hoff. L.C. Hoffman's Land Cas., U.S. Dist. Ct.
Hoff. N.Y. Hoffman's N.Y. Ch. Rep.
Hoffm. Ch. Same as above
Hog. Hogan's Rolls Ct., *Ir.*
Hogue Hogue's Rep. (1–4 Fla.)
Holl. Hollinshead's Rep. (1 Minn.)
Holm. Holmes' Cir. Ct. Rep., *U.S.* Holmes' Rep. (15–17 Ore.)
Holt Holt's Eq. Rep., *Eng.*; Holt's K.B. Rep., *Eng.*; Holt's N.P. Rep., *Eng.*
Holt Adm. W. Holt's Rule of the Road Cas. (Admiralty), *Eng.*
Holt Eq. W. Holt's Eq. Rep., *Eng.*
Holt K.B. John Holt's K.B. Rep., *Eng.*
Holt N.P. F. Holt's N.P. Rep., *Eng.*
Home Home MSS. Dec., Ct. of Session, *Sc.*
Hook. Hooker's Rep. (25–62 Conn.)
Hop. Hopkins
Hope Dec. Hope's Dec., *Sc.*
Hopk. Adm. Hopkinson's Judgments in Admiralty (Pa. 1779–89)
Hopk. Adm. Dec. Hopkinson's Admiralty Dec. (*See* Gilpin's U.S. Dist. Ct. Rep.)
Hopk. Ch. Hopkins' N.Y. Ch. Rep.
Hopw. & C. Hopwood & Coltman's Registration Appeal Cas., *Eng.*
Hopw. & P. Hopwood & Philbrick's Registration Appeal Cas., *Eng.*
Horn & H. Horn & Hurlstone's Ex. Rep., *Eng.*
Horner Horner's Rep. (11–28 S.D.)
Horw. Y.B. (Horwood) Y. of Edward I
Hosea Hosea's Rep., *Ohio*
Hoskins Hoskins' Rep. (2 N.D.)
Houghton Houghton's Rep. (97 Ala.)
Houst. Houston's Rep. (6–14 Del.); Houston, *Del.*
Houst. L. Rev. Houston Law Rev.
Hov. Hovenden's Supplement, Vesey's Ch., *Eng.*
How. Howard's Rep. (2–8 Miss.) Howard's N.Y. Practice Rep. Howard's Rep. (42–65 U.S.) Howell Rep. (22–26 Nev.)
How. App. Howard's Appeal Cas. (N.Y. 1847–48)
How. Cas. Same as above
How. Ch. Howard's Ch., *Ir.*
How. Cr. Tr. Howison's Crim. Trials (Va. 1850–51)
How. L.J. Howard Law Jour.
How. (N.S.) Howard's N.Y. Practice Rep., New Series
How. Pr. Howard's N.Y. Practice Rep.
How. St. Tr. Howell's State Trials, *Eng.*
How. & Beat. Howell & Beatty's Nev. Rep.
How. & N. Howell & Norcross, *Nev.*
Howard S.C. U.S. Sup. Ct. Rep. (42–65 U.S.)
Howell N.P. Howell's N.P. Cas. (Mich. 1868–84)
Hu. Hughes
Hubbard Hubbard's Rep. (45–51 Me.)
Hud. & B. Hudson & Brooke's K.B., *Ir.*
Hugh. Hughes' Cir. Ct. Rep., *U.S.*; Hughes' Rep. (1 Ky.)
Hughes Hughes, *Ky.*; Hughes, *U.S.*
Hum. Humphrey's Rep. (20–30 Tenn.)
Human Rts. J. Human Rights Jour.
Hume Hume's Dec., *Sc.*

Humph. Humphrey's Rep. (20–30 Tenn.)
Hun New York Sup. Ct. Rep. Hun's N.Y. Appellate Div. Rep.
Hunt. Torrens Hunter's Torrens Cas.
Hurl. & Colt. Hurlstone & Coltman's Ex. Rep., *Eng.*
Hurl. & Gord. Hurlstone & Gordon's Rep. (10, 11 Ex. Rep.), *Eng.*
Hurl. & Nor. Hurlstone & Norman's Ex. Rep., *Eng.*
Hurl. & Walm. Hurlstone & Walmsley's Ex. Rep., *Eng.*
Hut. Hutton's C.P. Rep., *Eng.*
Hutch. Hutcheson's Rep. (81 Ala.)
Hutt. Hutton's C.P. Rep., *Eng.*
Hy.Bl. Henry Blackstone's C.P. Rep., *Eng.*

ICAO International Civil Aviation Organization, *UN*
I.C.C. Pract. J. I.C.C. Practitioners' Jour.
I.C.J. International Ct. of Justice Rep.
I.C.J.Y.B. Y. of the International Ct. of Justice
I.C. Rep. Interstate Commerce Commission Rep., *U.S.*
I.D. Interior Department Dec., *U.S.*
I.J. Irish Jurist
I.L.E. Indiana Law Encyclopedia
ILO International Labor Organization, *UN*
I.L.P. Illinois Law and Practice
I.L.R. Insurance Law Reporter, *Can.*
I.L.T. Irish Law Times
I.O.C.C. Bull. Interstate Oil Compact Comm. Bulletin
I.R. Internal Revenue Dec.
I.R.B. Internal Revenue Bulletin, *U.S.*
I.R.C. Internal Revenue Code, *U.S.*
ISL L. Rev. ISL Law Review (International School of Law)
I.T. Income Tax Div. Ruling (U.S. Internal Revenue Service)
ITO International Trade Organization, *UN*
I.T.R. Irish Term Rep. (Ridgeway)
ITU International Telecommunication Union, *UN*
I.&N. Immigration and Nationality Laws Administrative Dec. (Justice Dept.), *U.S.*
I.&N.S. Immigration and Naturalization Services, *U.S.*
Ia. Iowa
Ia.L.Rev. Iowa Law Rev.
Id.L.J. Idaho Law Jour.
Ida. Idaho
Idaho Idaho Rep.
Iddings T.R.D. Iddings' Dayton (Ohio) Term Rep.
IDEA Pat. Tradem., & Copyr. J. of Research & Ec.
Ill. Illinois
Ill. App. Illinois Appellate Ct. Rep.
Ill. App. 2d Same as above, Second Series
Ill. B.J. Illinois Bar Jour.
Ill. Cir. Illinois Circuit Ct.
Ill. Cont.L.Ed. Illinois Continuing Law Education
Ill.Ct.Cl. Illinois Ct. of Claims
Ill.L.B. Illinois Law Bulletin
Ill.L.Q. Illinois Law Quarterly
Ill.L. Rev. Illinois Law Rev.
Immig.B. Bull. Immigration Bar Bulletin, *Ind.*
Ind. Indiana
Ind. App. Indiana Appellate Rep.
Ind.L.J. Indiana Law Jour.
Ind. L. Rev. Indiana Law Rev.
Ind. Legal F. Indiana Legal Forum
Ind. Rel. J. Econ. & Soc. Industrial Relations: Jour. of Economy and Society
Ind. S.C. Indiana Super. Ct.
Ind. Super. Wilson's Ind. Super. Ct. Rep. 1871–74
Ind. T. Indian Territory

Ind. & L. Rel. Rev. Industrial and Labor Relations Rev.
India Crim. L. J. R. Criminal Law Jour. Rep.
India S. Ct. India Supreme Ct. Rep.
Ind. J. Int. L. Indian Journal of Int'l Law
Indian L.R. Indian Law Rep.
Indian Rul. Indian Rulings
Indian Terr. Indian Territory Rep.
Ins. Counsel J. Insurance Counsel Jour.
Ins. L.J. Insurance Law Jour.; Insurance Law Jour., *Pa.*
Ins. L. Rep. Insurance Law Reporter (CCH)
Inst. Coke's Institutes, *Eng.* Justinian's Institutes
Inst. Min. L. Inst. on Mineral Law, *La.*
Int. Aff. International Affairs
Int. Arb. J. International Arbitration Jour.
Int. Com. Com. Interstate Commerce Comm., *U.S.*
Int. Com. Rep. Interstate Commerce Comm. Rep., *U.S.*
Int. J. Pol. International Jour. of Politics
Int. Jurid. Assn. Bull. International Juridical Association Bulletin
Int. L. Q. International Law Quarterly
Int. Law. The International Lawyer
Int. Legal Materials International Legal Materials
Int. Rev. Code of 1954 Internal Revenue Code of 1954
Int. Rev. Rec. Internal Revenue Record
Int. Tax Jour. International Tax Jour.
Int. Trade L.J. International Trade Law Jour.
Int. Woman L. International Woman Lawyer
Int. & Comp. L.Q. International and Comparative Law Quarterly
Inter-Am. L. Rev. Inter-American Law Rev.
Interior Dec. United States Interior Department Dec.
Interst. Com. R. Same as Int. Com. Rep.
Intramural L. Rev. Intramural Law Rev.
Iowa Iowa Rep.
Iowa L. B. Iowa Law Bulletin
Iowa L. Rev. Iowa Law Rev.
Ir. Law Reports, *Ir.*
Ir. C.L. Irish Common Law
Ir. Ch. Irish Ch. Rep.
Ir. Cir. Irish Circuit Rep.
Ir. Eccl. Irish Ecclesiastical Rep.
Ir. Eq. Irish Equity
Ir. Jur. Irish Jurist
Ir. L. & Eq. Irish Law & Equity
Ir. L.T.R. Irish Law Times Rep.
Ir. R. Irish Rep.
Ir. R.C.L. Irish Reports Common Law
Ir. R. Eq. Irish Reports Eq.
Ired. Iredell's Rep. (23–35 N.C. Law)
Ired. Eq. Iredell's Rep. (36–43 N.C. Eq.)
Irish L.T. Irish Law Times
Irv. Just. Irvine's Justiciary, *Sc.*
Israel L. Rev. Israel Law Rev.

J. Johnson's Cas. or Rep., *N.Y.*
JAG Bull. JAG Bulletin (USAF)
JAGA Military Affairs Div., Office of Judge Advocate General, U.S. Army
JAGJ JAG Jour.
J.A.M.A. Jour. of the American Medical Association
J. Account. Jour. of Accountancy
J. African L. Jour. of African Law
J. Air L. & Com. Jour. of Air Law and Commerce
J. Am. Jud. Soc. Jour. of American Judicature Soc.
J. Am. Soc. C.L.U. Jour. of the

American Society of Chartered Life Underwriters
J.B. Assn. D.C. Jour. of the Bar Assn. of the District of Columbia
J. Assn. L. Teachers Jour. of the Association of Law Teachers
J.B. Assn. St. Kan. Jour. of the Bar Association of the State of Kansas
J.B. Moo. J. B. Moore's C.P. Rep., *Eng.*
J. Bridg. J. Bridgman's C.P. Rep., *Eng.*
J. Bus. L. Jour. of Business Law
J.C. Johnson's Cas. or Rep., *N.Y.*
J.C.L. & I.L. Jour. of Comparative Legislation and International Law
J.C.R. Judicial Council Rep.
J.Can.B.Assn. Jour. of the Canadian Bar Association
J.Ch. Johnson's Ch. Rep., *N.Y.*
J. Church S. Jour. of Church and State
J.Coll.&U.L. Jour. of College and University Law
J.Comp.Leg. Jour. of Society of Comparative Legislation
J.Comp.Leg.&Int. Law Jour. of Comparative Legislation and International Law
J. Crim. L. Jour. of American Institute of Criminal Law and Criminology
Jour. of Criminal Law, *Eng.*
J.Crim.L.&Crim. Jour. of Criminal Law and Criminology
J.Crim.L.,C.&P.S. Jour. of Criminal Law, Criminology and Police Science
J.Fam.L. Jour. of Family Law
J.Fin. Jour. of Finance
J.For.Med. Jour. Forensic Medicine
J.For.Sci. Jour. Forensic Science
J.For.Sci.Soc. Jour. of the Forensic Science Society
J.H. Jour. House of Representatives, *U.S.*
J.Int.L.&Econ. Jour. of International Law and Economics
J.Int.L.&Pol. Jour. of International Law and Politics
J.J.Mar. Marshall's Rep. (24–30 Ky.)
J.Jur. Jour. of Jurisprudence
J.Juv.L. Jour. of Juvenile Law
J.Kel. John Kelyng's Crown Cas., *Eng.*
J.L.Soc. Jour. of the Law Society of Scotland
J. Land &Pub. Util. Econ. Jour. of Land and Public Utility Economics
J. Law &Econ. Jour. of Law and Economics
J. Law &Econ.Dev. Jour. of Law and Economic Development
J.Law &Ed. Jour. of Law and Education
J.Law Reform Jour. of Law Reform
J.Leg.Ed. Jour. of Legal Education
J.Leg.Med. Jour. of Legal Medicine
J.Leg.Prof. Jour. of the Legal Profession
J.Mar. Law &Com. Jour. of Maritime Law and Commerce
J.Mo.Bar Jour. of the Missouri Bar
J.P. Justice of the Peace
J.P.L. Jour. of Public Law
J.P.O.S. Jour. of the Patent Office Society
J.P.Sm. J. P. Smith's K.B. Rep., *Eng.*
J.Pl.L. Jour. of Planning Law
J.Pub. L. Jour. of Public Law
J.R. Johnson's Rep., *N.Y.*
J.Radio L. Jour. of Radio Law
J.S.Gr. J.S. Green's Rep. (13–15 N.J. Law)
J.Soc.Pub.Teach. Law Jour. of the Society of Public Teachers of Law
J.Soc.Pub.Teach. Law (N.S.) Same as above, New Series
J. Space L. Jour. of Space Law

J.Tax. Jour. of Taxation
J. Urban L. Jour. of Urban Law
J. World Tr.L. Jour. of World Trade Law
J.&C. Jones & Cary's Ex., *Ir.*
J.&H. Johnson & Hemming's Ch., *Eng.*;
Johnson & Hemming's Vice-Ch. Rep., *Eng.*
J.&L. Jones & La Touche's Ch., *Ir.*
J.&S. Jones & Spencer's Rep. (33–61 N.Y. Super.)
J.&W. Jacob & Walker's Ch. Rep., *Eng.*
Jac. Jacob's Ch. Rep., *Eng.*
Jac.L.Dict. Jacob's Law Dictionary
Jac.&W. Jacob & Walker's Ch. Rep., *Eng.*
Jack. Jackson, *Ga.*
Jack. Tex. App. Jackson's Rep. (1–29 Tex. Ct. of Appeals Rep.)
Jackson Jackson's Rep. (46–58 Ga.)
Jackson's Rep. (1–29 Tex. App.)
Jackson & Lumpkin Jackson & Lumpkin's Rep. (59–64 Ga.)
James James' Rep. (2 Nova Scotia)
James. & Mont. Jameson & Montagu's Bankruptcy, *Eng.*
Jebb Jebb's Crown Cas., *Ir.*
Jebb & B. Jebb & Bourke's Q.B., *Ir.*
Jebb & S. Jebb & Symes' Q.B., *Ir.*
Jeff. Jefferson's Rep. (Va. Gen. Ct.)
Jenk. Jenkins' Rep. 1220–1623, *Eng.*
Jenk. Cent. Same as above
Jenks Jenks' Rep. (58 N.H.)
Jenn. Jennison's Rep. (14–18 Mich.)
Jo.T. T. Jones' K.B. Rep., *Eng.*
John. Johnson's Rep. (Md. Ch.)
Johnson's Rep. (N.Y. Sup. or Ch.)
Chase's Cir. Ct. Dec. ed., by Johnson, *U.S.*
Johnson's Vice-Ch. Rep., *Eng.*
John Mar.J.Prac.&Proc. John Marshall Jour. of Practice and Procedure
John Marsh.L.J. John Marshall Law Jour.
John Marsh.L.Q. John Marshall Law Quarterly
John.&H. Johnson & Hemming Ch. Rep., *Eng.*
Johns. Cas. Johnson's Cas. (N.Y. 1799–1803)
Johns.Ch. Johnson's Md. Ch. Dec.
Johnson's Ch. Rep. (N.Y. 1814–23)
Johnson's Vice-Ch. Rep., *Eng.*
Johns.Ct.Err. Johnson's Rep., (N.Y. Ct. of Errors)
Johns.Dec. Johnson's Ch. Dec., *Md.*
Johns.Eng.Ch. Johnson's Ch. Rep., *Eng.*
Johns.N.Z. Johnson's New Zealand Rep.
Johns.Rep. Johnson's Rep. (N.Y. Sup. or Ch.)
Johns.U.S. Chase's Cir. Ct. Dec., ed. by Johnson, *U.S.*
Johns.V.C. Johnson's Vice-Ch. Rep., Eng.
Johns.&Hem. Johnson & Hemming's Ch. Rep., *Eng.*
Jon. T. Jones' K.B. and C.P. Rep., *Eng.*
Jones Jones' Ex., *Ir.*
Jones' Law or Eq.
Jones' Rep. (43–46, 52–57, 61, 62 Ala.)
Jones' Rep. (22–30 Mo.)
Jones' Rep. (11, 12 Pa.)
Jones' Rep. (N.C. Law or Eq.)
Jones' Upper Canada C.P. Rep.
Jones 1 W. Jones' K.B. Rep., *Eng.*
Jones 2 T. Jones' K.B. Rep., *Eng.*
Jones B.&W. (Mo.) Jones, Barclay & Whittelsey (Mo.)
Jones, Barclay & Whittlesey (31 Mo.)
Jones Eq. Jones' Rep. (54–59 N.C. Eq.)
Jones N.C. Jones' Rep. (46–53 N.C. Law)
Jones Pa. Jones' Rep. (11, 12 Pa.)

Jones T. (or 2) T. Jones' K.B. Rep., *Eng.*
Jones W. (or 1) W. Jones' K.B. Rep., *Eng.*
Jones & C. Jones & Cary's Ex., *Ir.*
Jones & McM. Jones & McMurtrie's Pa. Sup. Ct. Rep.
Jones & Sp. Jones & Spencer's Rep. (33–61 N.Y. Super.)
Jos. Joseph's Rep. (21 Nev.)
Josephs Josephs, *Mo.*
Jud. Chr. Judicial Chronicle
Jud. Rep. Judicial Repository, *N.Y.*
Judd Judd's Rep. (4 Hawaii)
Judg. U.B. Judgments of Upper Bench, *Eng.*
Judge Advoc. J. The Judge Advocate Jour.
Judge's J. Judge's Jour.
Judicature Jour. of the American Judicature Society
Jur. Jurist, *Eng.*
Jur. (N.S.) Jurist, New Series
Jurid. Rev. Juridical Rev.
Jurimetrics J. Jurimetrics Jour.
Jurispr. The Jurisprudent
Just. Cas. Justiciary Cas.
Just. L.R. Justices' Law Reporter, *Pa.*
Just. Peace Justice of the Peace
Juv. Ct. Judges J. Juvenile Ct. Judges' Jour.
Juv. Just. Juvenile Justice

K. Keyes' Ct. of Appeals Rep. (40–43 N.Y.)
Kenyon's K.B. Rep., *Eng.*
K.B. Law Rep. K.B., *Eng.*
Law Rep., K.B. Div., *Eng.*
KBP Q. Kappa Beta Phi Quarterly
K.B.U.C. Upper Canada K.B. Rep.
K.C.R. Reports *temp.* King, *Eng.*
K. Counsel King's Counsel
K.&G. Keane & Grant's Registration Appeal Cas., *Eng.*
K.&J. Kay & Johnson's Ch. Rep., *Eng.*
Kames Dec. Kames' Dec., *Sc.*
Kames Elucid. Kames' Elucidation, *Sc.*
Kames Rem. Kames' Remarkable Dec., *Sc.*
Kames Sel. Dec. Kames' Select Dec., *Sc.*
Kan. Kansas
Kan App. Kansas Appeals Rep.
Kan. B. Assn. J. Kansas Bar Assn. Jour.
Kan. City L. Rep. Kansas City Law Reporter
Kan. City L. Rev. Kansas City Law Rev.
Kan. L. J. Kansas Law Jour.
Kan. L. Rev. University of Kansas Law Rev.
Kan. St. L.J. Kansas State Law Jour.
Kans. App. Kansas Appeals Rep.
Kay Kay's Ch. Rep., *Eng.*
Kay's Vice-Ch., *Eng.*
Kay & John. Kay & Johnson's Vice Chancellors' Rep., *Eng.*
Keane & G.R.C. Keane & Grant's Registration Appeal Cas., *Eng.*
Keb. Keble's K.B. Rep., *Eng.*
Keen Keen's Rolls Ct., *Eng.*
Keil. Keilway's K.B. Rep., *Eng.*
Keilw. Same as above
Keith Ch. Pa. Registrar's Book, Keith's Ct. of Ch., *Pa.*
Kel. John Kelyng's Crown Cas. Rep., *Eng.*
Kel. 1 (or J.) John Kelyng's Crown Cas., *Eng.*
Kel. 2 (or W.) W. Kelyng's Rep., *Eng.*
Kel. C.C. Kelyng's Crown Cas., *Eng.*
Kel. Ga. Kelly's Rep., (1–3 Ga.)
Kel. J. Same as Kel. 1
Kel. W. Same as Kel. 2
Kellen Kellen's Rep. (146–55 Mass.)
Kelly Kelly's Rep. (1–3 Ga.)
Kelly & Cobb Kelly & Cobb's Rep. (4, 5 Ga.)

Kelyng J. Kelyng's Crown Cas., *Eng.*
Ken. Kenyon's K.B. Rep., *Eng.*
Ken. Dec. Kentucky Dec., Sneed, *Ky.*
Ken. L.J. Kentucky Law Jour.
Ken. L.R. Kentucky Law Reporter
Ken. Opin. Kentucky Opinions 1864–86
Kenan Kenan's Rep. (76–91 N.C.)
Keny. Kenyon's K.B. Rep., *Eng.*
Keny. Ch. Ch. Cas. (v.2 of Notes of K.B. Cas.), *Eng.*
Keny. Chy. (3 Keny.) Ch. Rep. at end of 2 Kenyon, *Eng.*
Kenya L.R. Kenya Law Rep.
Kern. Kern's Rep. (100–116 Ind.)
Kernan, *Md.*
Kernan's Rep. (11–14 N.Y.)
Kerr Kerr's Rep. (18–22 Ind.)
Kerr's Rep. (27–29 N.Y. Civil Procedure Rep.)
Key. Keyes' Rep. (40–43 N.Y.)
Keyl. Keilway's English Bench Rep.
Kilk. Kilkerran's Dec., *Sc.*
King King's Civil Practice Cas., *Colo.*
King's Rep. (5, 6 La. Annual)
Select Cas., *temp.* King, Ch., *Eng.*
King's Conf. Ca. King's Conflicting Cas. (Tex. 1840–1911)
Kir. Kirby's Rep. and Supplement (Conn. 1785–89)
Kn. Knapp's P.C. Cas., *Eng.*
Kn. A.C. Knapp's Appeal Cas., P.C., *Eng.*
Kn. P.C. Knapp's P.C. Cas., *Eng.*
Kn.&Moo. 3 Knapp's P.C. Rep., *Eng.*
Knapp Knapp's P.C. Rep., *Eng.*
Knapp &O. Knapp & Ombler's Election Cas., *Eng.*
Knight's Ind. Knight's Industrial Rep.
Knowles Knowles' Rep. (3 R.I.)
Knox Knox, S.W.
Knox &Fitz. Knox & Fitzhardinge, *N.S.W.*
Kreider Kreider's Rep. (1–23 Wash.)
Kress Kress's Rep. (166–194 Pa.)
Kress's Rep. (2–12 Pa. Super.)
Kulp Kulp's Luzerne Legal Register Rep., *Pa.*
Ky. Kentucky
Ky.Comment'r Kentucky Commentator
Ky.Dec. Sneed's Ky. Dec. (2 Ky.)
Ky.L.J. Kentucky Law Jour.
Ky.L.Rep. Kentucky Law Reporter
Ky.Op. Kentucky Ct. of Appeals Opinions
Ky.St.B.J. Kentucky State Bar Jour.

L. Lansing's Select Cas. in Ch. (N.Y. 1824, 1826)
L.A.C. Labour Arbitration Cas.
L.Abr. Lilly's Abridgement, *Eng.*
LC Labor Cases (CCH)
L.C. Lord Chancellor; Lower Canada
L.C.D. Ohio Dec. (Lower)
L.C.J. Lower Canada Jurist
L.C.L.J. Lower Canada Law Jour.
L.C.R. Lower Canada Rep.
L.C.Rep.S.Qu. Lower Canada Rep. Seignorial Questions
L. Comment. Law Commentary
L.D. Land Office Dec., *U.S.*
L.Ed. Lawyers' Edition, U.S. Sup. Ct. Rep.
L.Ed.2d Same as above, Second Series
L.G. Law Glossary
L.Guard. Law Guardian
L.I. Legal Intelligencer, *Pa.*
L. In Trans.J. Law in Transition Jour.
L.Inst.J. Law Institute Jour.
L.Inst.J.Vict. Law Institute Jour. of Victoria
L.J. Law Jour.; Hall's Law Jour.; H.L. Jour.; New York Law Jour.
L.J.Adm. Law Jour. Rep., Admiralty, *Eng.*

L.J.App. Law Jour. Rep., New Series, Appeals
L.J.Bankr. Law Jour. Bankruptcy, *Eng.*
L.J.C. Law Jour. Rep., New Series, C.P., *Eng.*
L.J.C.C.R. Law Jour. Rep., New Series, Crown Cas. Res., *Eng.*
L.J.C.C.R.(N.S.) Same as above, New Series
L.J.C.P. Law Jour. Rep., C.P., *Eng.*
L.J.C.P.(O.S.) Law Jour. Common Pleas, Old Series, *Eng.*
L.J.C.P.D. Law Jour. Rep., New Series, C.P. Dec., *Eng.*
L.J.Ch. Law Jour. Rep., New Series, Ch., *Eng.*
L.J.Ch.(O.S.) Law Jour. Rep., Ch., Old Series, *Eng.*
L.J.D.&M. Law Jour. Rep., New Series, Divorce and Matrimonial, *Eng.*
L.J.Eccl. Law Jour. Ecclesiastical Cas., *Eng.*
L.J.Ex.D. Law Jour. Rep., New Series, Ex. Div., *Eng.*
L.J.Ex.Eq. Law Jour., Ex. in Eq., *Eng.*
L.J.Exch. Law Jour. Rep., New Series, Ex., *Eng.*
L.J.Exch.(O.S.) Law Jour. Ex., Old Series, *Eng.*
L.J.H.L. Law Jour. Rep., New Series, H.L., *Eng.*
L.J.K.B. Law Jour. Rep., K. B., *Eng.*; Law Jour. K.B., Old Series, *Eng.*
L.J.L.C. Law Jour., *Lower Canada*
L.J.M.C. Law Jour. Magistrates' Cas., New Series, *Eng.*
L.J.M.C.(O.S.) Law Jour. Magistrates' Cas., Old Series, *Eng.*
L.J.M.P.A. Law Jour. Rep., Matrimonial, Probate and Admiralty, *Eng.*
L.J.Mag. Law Jour., New Series Common Law, Magistrates' Cas. (discontinued)
L.J.Mat.Cas. Law Jour. Rep., New Series, Divorce and Matrimonial, *Eng.*
L.J.N.C. Law Jour. Notes of Cas., *Eng.*
L.J.(O.S.) Law Jour., Old Series, *Eng.*
L.J.P. Law Jour. Rep., New Series, P.C., *Eng.*
Law Jour. Rep., Probate, Divorce and Admiralty, *Eng.*
L.J.P.C. Law Jour. Rep., P.C., *Eng.*
L.J.P.C.(N.S.) Law Jour. Rep., New Series, P.C., *Eng.*
L.J.P.D.&A. Law Jour. Rep., New Series, Probate, Divorce, and Admiralty, *Eng.*
L.J.P.&M. Law Jour. Probate & Matrimonial, *Eng.*
L.J.P.M.&A. Law Jour. Rep., New Series, Probate, Matrimonial, & Admiralty, *Eng.*
L.J.Q.B. Law Jour. Rep., New Series, Q.B., *Eng.*
L.J.Q.B.D. Law Jour. Rep., New Series, Q.B. Div., *Eng.*
L.J.R. Law Jour. Rep., *Eng.*
L.J.Rep.(N.S.) Law Jour. Rep., New Series (from 1831), *Eng.*
L.J.U.C. Law Jour. of Upper Canada
L. Jo. Law Jour. (newspaper), *Eng.*
L.L.J. Law Library Jour.
L.Lib.J. Law Library Jour.
L.M.&P. Lowndes, Maxwell & Pollock's Bail Cas., *Eng.*
L.N.T.S. League of Nations Treaty Series
L.O. Legal Observer Solicitor's Law Opinion (U.S. Internal Revenue Service)
L.Q.Rev. Law Quarterly Rev.
L.R. Law Recorder, *Ir.*; Law Rep., *Eng.*; Louisiana Rep.; Ohio Law Reporter
L.R.(N.S.) Irish Law Recorder, New Series
L.R.A. Lawyers' Rep. Annot.

L.R.A.(N.S.) Lawyers' Rep. Annot., New Series, *Eng.*
L.R.A.C. Law Reports, Appeal Cas., *Eng.*
L.R.A.&E. Law Rep., Admiralty & Ecclesiastical Cas., *Eng.*
L.R.App. Law Reports, Appeal Cas., H.L., *Eng.*
L.R.A.(N.S.) Lawyers' Rep. Annot., New Series, *U.S.*
L.R.C.C.R. Law Rep., Crown Cas. Res., *Eng.*
L.R.C.P. Law Rep., C.P., *Eng.*
L.R.C.P.D. Law Rep., C.P. Div., *Eng.*
L.R.Ch. Law Rep., Ch. Appeal Cas., *Eng.*
L.R.Ch.D. Law Rep., Ch. Div., *Eng.*
L.R.E.&I.App. Law Rep., H.L. (English & Irish Appeals)
L.R.Eq. Law Rep. Eq., *Eng.*
L.R.Ex. Law Rep., Ex., *Eng.*
L.R.Ex.Div. Law Rep., Ex. Div., *Eng.*
L.R.H.L. Law Rep., English & Irish Appeals & Peerage Claims, H.L., *Eng.*
L.R.H.L.Sc. Law Rep., H.L. (Scotch Appeal Cas.)
L.R. Indian App. Law Rep., Indian Appeals, *Eng.*
L.R.Ir. Law Reports, *Ir.*
L.R.K.B. Law Reports, K.B. Div., *Eng.*
L.R.Misc.D. Law Reports, Miscellaneous Div., *Eng.*
L.R.N.S.W. Law Rep., *New South Wales*
L.R.P. Law Rep., Probate Div., *Eng.*
L.R.P.C. Law Rep., P.C., *Eng.*
L.R.P.Div. Law Rep., Probate, Divorce & Admiralty Div., *Eng.*
L.R.P.&D. Law Rep., Probate, Divorce, *Eng.*
L.R.P.&M. Law Rep., Probate, Matrimonial, *Eng.*
L.R.Q.B. Law Rep., Q.B., *Eng.* Quebec Rep., Q.B.
L.R.Q.B.D. Law Rep., Q.B. Div., *Eng.*
LRR Labor Relations Reporter (BNA), *U.S.*
LRRM Labor Relations Reporter; Labor-Management Relations (BNA), *U.S.*
L.R.S.A. Law Rep., *South Australia*
L.R.Sess.Cas. Law Rep., Session Cas., *Eng.*
L.Rep.Mont. Law Reporter, *Montreal*
L.Repos. Law Repository
L.Rev.&Quart.J. Law Rev. and Quarterly Jour.
L.S. Law Student
L.S.G. Law Society Gazette, *Eng.*
L.Soc.J. Law Society Jour.
L.T. Law Times (Luzerne Law Times, Pa.)
L.T.(N.S.) Law Times Rep., New Series, *Eng.*
L.T.(O.S.) Law Times Rep., Old Series, *Eng.*
L.T.J. Law Times Jour. (newspaper), *Eng.*
L.T.R. Law Times Rep., *Eng.*
L.V.Rep. Lehigh Valley Law Reporter (Pa. 1885–87)
L.&B.Bull. Weekly Law & Bank Bulletin, *Ohio*
L.&C. Lefroy and Cassels' Practice Cas., *Ont.*
Leigh & Cave's Crown Cas., *Eng.*
Leigh & Cave's Crown Cas. Reserved, *Eng.*
L.&E. English Law & Eq. Rep., *Boston*
L.&E.Rep. Law & Equity Reporter, *N.Y.*
L.&M. Lowndes & Maxwell's Practice Cas., *Eng.*
L.&W. Lloyd & Welsby's Mercantile Cas., *Eng.*
L.&Welsb. Lloyd & Welsby's

Commercial & Mercantile Cas., *Eng.*
La. Lane's Ex. Rep., Eng.; Louisiana
La.A. Louisiana Ct. of Appeals, *Orleans*
Louisiana Annual Rep.
La.Ann. Louisiana Annual Rep.
La.App. Louisiana Courts of Appeal Rep.
La.App.(Orleans) Orleans Ct. of Appeals Rep., by Teissier (La. 1903–17)
La.B.J. Louisiana Bar Jour.
La.L.J. Louisiana Law Jour.
La.L. Rev. Louisiana Law Rev.
La.T.R. Louisiana Term Rep. (Martin)
Lab. Labatt's Dist. Ct. Rep. (Cal. 1857–58)
Lab.Arb. Labor Arbitration Rep. (BNA)
Lab.L.J. Labor Law Jour.
Lac.Jur. Lackawanna Jurist, *Pa.*
Lack.Leg.N. Lackawanna Legal News, *Pa.*
Lack.Leg.R. Lackawanna Legal Record, *Pa.*
Ladd. Ladd's Rep. (59–64 N.H.)
Lalor Lalor's Supplement to Hill & Denio's N.Y. Rep.
Lamar Lamar Rep. (25–42 Fla.)
Lamb Lamb's Rep. (103–105 Wis.)
Lanc.Bar Lancaster Bar (Pa. 1869–83)
Lanc.L.Rev. Lancaster Law Rev. (Pa. 1883–date)
Land Dec. Land Dec., *U.S.*
Land.Est.C. Landed Estate Ct., *Eng.*
Land U.Pl.Rep. Land Use Planning Rep.
Land & WaterL.Rev. Land & Water Law Rev.
Lane Lane's Ex. Rep., *Eng.*
Lans. Lansing, *Mich.*
Lansing's Sup. Ct. Rep. (N.Y. 1869–73)
Lans.Ch. Lansing's Select Cas., Ch. (N.Y. 1824, 1826)
Lans.Sel.Cas. Same as above
Lat. Latch's K.B. Rep., *Eng.*
Lath. Lathrop's Rep. (115–145 Mass.)
Law Cas.Wm.I. Law Cas. William I to Richard I, *Eng.*
Law Chr. Law Chronicle
Law Chr.&Jour.Jur. Law Chronicle & Jour. of Jurisprudence
Law.Ed. Lawyers' Edition, U.S. Sup. Ct. Rep.
Law Gaz. Law Gazette
Law. Guild Rev. Lawyers' Guild Rev.
Law Inst.J. Law Institute Jour.
Law J. Law Jour. Rep. For various series *see* L.J.
Law Jour. Same as above
Law Q.Rev. Law Quarterly Rev.
Law Reg. Law Register, *Chicago*
American Law Register, *Philadelphia*
Law Rep. Law Rep. *See* abbreviations under L.R.
Law Reporter (Ramsey & Morin), *Can.*
Law Reporter, *Eng.*
Law Rep.(N.S.) Monthly Law Reporter, New Series
Law Repos. Carolina Law Repository
Law Rev.&Qu.J. Law Rev. & Quarterly Jour.
Law Soc.Gaz. Law Society's Gazette (London or Regina)
Law Soc.J. Law Society Jour., *N.S.W.*
Law Society of Massachusetts Jour.
Law T.Rep.(N.S.) Law Times Rep., New Series, *Eng.*
Law T.Rep.(O.S.) Law Times Rep., Old Series, *Eng.*
Law Times Law Times (London; Scranton, Pa.)

Law.&Bank. Lawyer and Banker, *New Orleans*
Lawyers' & Bankers' Quarterly, *St. Louis*
Law &Bk.Bull. Weekly Law and Bank Bulletin, *Ohio*
Law &Contemp.Prob. Law & Contemporary Problems
Law. &L.N. Lawyer & Law Notes
Law &Pol.Int.Bus. Law & Policy in International Business
Law &Soc.Ord. Law and the Social Order, Arizona State Law Jour.
Law &Soc.Rev. Law and Society Rev.
Lawr. Lawrence, *Ohio*
Lawrence Lawrence's Reports (20 Ohio)
Lawrence Comp.Dec. Lawrence's Comptroller's Dec.
Lawyer & Banker Lawyer & Banker & Central Law Jour.
Lawyer's Med.J. Lawyers' Medical Jour.
Lay Lay's Ch. Rep., *Eng.*
Ld.Birk. Lord Birkenhead's Judgments, H.L., *Eng.*
Ld.Ken. Lord Kenyon's K.B. Rep., *Eng.*
Ld.Raym. Lord Raymond's K.B. & C.P. Rep., *Eng.*
Le.&Ca. Leigh & Cave's Crown Cas. Res., *Eng.*
Lea Lea's Rep. (69–84 Tenn.)
Leach Leach's Crown Cas., *Eng.*
League of Nations Off.J. League of Nations Official Jour.
Lee Lee's Rep. (9–12 Calif.)
Lee Eccl. Lee's Ecclesiastical, *Eng.*
Lee *t.*Hard. Lee's Cas. *temp.* Hardwicke, in K.B. & Ch., *Eng.*
Leese Leese, *Neb.*; Leese's Rep. (26 Neb.)
Leg.Chron. Legal Chronicle (Foster's Pa. Rep.)
Leg.Gaz.Rep. Campbell's Legal Gazette Rep. (Pa. 1869–71)
Leg.Int. Legal Intelligencer, *Philadelphia*
Leg. News Legal News (Montreal; Sunbury, Pa.; Toledo, Ohio)
Leg.Op. Legal Opinion (Harrisburg, Pa.)
Leg.Rec. Legal Record, *Detroit*
Leg.Rec.Rep. Legal Record Rep. (1–2 Schuylkill County, Pa.)
Leg.Rep. Legal Reporter, *Tenn.*
Leg.Rev. Legal Rev., *Eng.*
Leg.&Ins.R. Legal & Insurance Reporter, *Pa.*
Legal Adv. Legal Advertiser, *Chicago*
Lehigh Co.L.J. Lehigh (Pa.) Law Jour.
Lehigh Val.L.Rep. Lehigh Valley (Pa.) Law Reporter
Leigh Leigh, *Pa.*; Leigh's Rep. (28–39 Va.)
Leigh &C. Leigh & Cave's Crown Cas., *Eng.*
Leo. Leonard's K. B. Rep., *Eng.*
Leon. Leonard's K.B., C.P. Ex. Rep., *Eng.*
Lest.P.L. Lester's Public Land Dec.
Lester Lester's Reports (31–33 Ga.)
Lester Supp. Supplement to 33 Ga. Rep.
Lester &B. Lester & Butler's Supplement, *Ga.*
Lev. Levinz's K.B. & C.P. Rep., *Eng.*
Lev.Ent. Levinz's Entries, *Eng.*
Lew. Lewin's Crown Cas. Res., *Eng.*; Lewis' Rep. (29–35 Mo. App.); Lewis' Rep. (1 Nev.)
Lew.C.C. Lewin's Crown Cas. Res., *Eng.*
Lewis Lewis' Kentucky Law Reporter
Lewis' Reporters (1 Nev.)
Lewis's Rep. (29–35 Mo. App.)
Kentucky Law Reporter
Ley Ley's K.B. Rep., *Eng.*
Ley's Ct. of Wards Rep., *Eng.*
Lib.Ass. Liber Assisarum, Year Books, 1–51 Edw. III, *Eng.*

Life Cas. Life (Health & Accident) Cas. (CCH)
Life Cas.2d Same as above, Second Series
Lil. Lilly's Assize Rep., *Eng.*
Lill. Ent. Lilly's Entries, *Eng.*
Lilly Lilly's Cas. in Assize, *Eng.*
Lincoln L. Rev. Lincoln Law Rev.
Lit. Littell's Rep. (11–15 Ky.) Littleton's C.P. Rep., *Eng.*
Lit.Brooke Brooke's New Cas., K.B., *Eng.*
Litt. Littleton's C.P. Rep., *Eng.*
Littell Littell's Rep. (11–15 Ky.)
Little Brooke Brooke's New Cas., *Eng.*
Liv.Cas. Livingston's Cas. in Error, *N.Y.*
Liv.Jud.Op. Livingston's Judicial Opinions, *N.Y.*
Ll.L.Pr.Cas. Lloyd's List Prize Cas., *Eng.*
Ll.L.Rep. Lloyd's List Law Rep., *Eng.*
Ll.List.L.R. Same as above
Ll. & G.*t*.Pl. Lloyd & Goold *temp.* Plunkett, Ch., *Ir.*
Ll. & G.*t*.S. Lloyd & Goold *temp.* Sugden, Ch., *Ir.*
Ll. & W. Lloyd & Welsby's Mercantile Cas., *Eng.*
Lloyd,L.R. Lloyd's List Law Rep., *Eng.*
Lloyd List Lloyd's List, *Eng.*
Lloyd's Pr.Cas. Lloyd's Prize Cas. Rep., *Eng.*
Lloyd's Rep. Lloyd's List Law Rep., *Eng.*
Lobin. Lobingier's Extraterritorial Cas., U.S. Ct., for China
Local Gov. Local Government & Magisterial Rep.
Local Gov.R.Aust. Local Government Rep. of Australia
Lock.Rev.Cas. Lockwood's Reversed Cas., *N.Y.*
Lofft Lofft's K.B. Rep., *Eng.*
Lond.Gaz. London Gazette, *Eng.*
Lond.Jur. London Jurist Rep., *Eng.*
Long &R. Long & Russell's Election Cas., *Mass.*
Longf. &T. Longfield & Townsend's Ex., *Ir.*
Loss &Dam.Rev. Loss & Damage Rev.
Lou. Louisiana. *See* La.
Lou.L.J. Louisiana Law Jour.
Lou. L. Rev. Louisiana Law Rev.
Lou. Leg. N. Louisiana Legal News
Louisville Law. Louisville Lawyer
Low. Lowell's Dist. Ct. Rep. (U.S., D. Mass.)
Low.C.Seign. Lower Canada Seignorial Rep.
Low.Can. Lower Canada Rep.
Low.Can.Jur. Lower Canada Jurist
Low.Can.L.J. Lower Canada Law Jour.
Low.Can.R. Lower Canadian Rep.
Low.Can.Rep. Lower Canada Rep.
Low.Can.Rep.S.Q. Lower Canada Rep., Seignorial Questions
Lowell Lowell, *U.S.*
Lower Ct.Dec. Ohio Lower Ct. Dec.
Loyola Dig. Loyola Digest
Loyola L.Rev. Loyola Law Rev.
Loyola U.Chi.L.J. Loyola University of Chicago Law Jour.
Loyola U.L.A.L.Rev. Loyola University of Los Angeles Law Rev.
Luc. Lucas' Rep. (Modern Rep., pt. X), *Eng.*
Lucas Same as above
Ludden Ludden's Rep. (43, 44 Me.)
Lumpkin Lumpkin's Rep. (59–77 Ga.)
Lush. Lushington's Admiralty Rep., *Eng.*
Lut.E. Lutwyche's Entries & Rep., C.P., *Eng.*
Lutw.Reg.Cas. Lutwyche's Registration Cas.
Luz.L.J. Luzerne Law Jour., *Pa.*
Luz.L.T. Luzerne Law Times, *Pa.*

Luz.Leg.Obs. Luzerne Legal Observer, *Pa.*
Luz.Leg.Reg. Luzerne Legal Register, *Pa.*
Luz.Leg.Reg.Rep. Luzerne Legal Register Rep., *Pa.*
Lynd. Lyndwoode, Provinciale, *Eng.*
Lyne Lyne's Ch., *Ir.*

M. Maine; Manitoba; Maryland; Massachusetts; Michigan; Minnesota; Mississippi; Missouri; Montana; Miles' Pennsylvania Rep.; New York Miscellaneous Rep.
M' *See* Mac and Mc.
MA Maritime Admin., *U.S.*
M.A. Missouri Appeals Rep.
M.B. Miscellaneous Branch, Internal Revenue Service, *U.S.*
M.C. Mayor's Ct.
M.C.C. Interstate Commerce Comm. Rep.,
Motor Carrier Cas., *U.S.*
Moody's Crown Cas. Res., *Eng.*
Mixed Claims Comm. Motor Carriers' Cas. (I.C.C.)
M.C.D. Magistrates' Courts Dec., *N.Z.*
M.C.J. Michigan Civil Jurisprudence
M.C.R. Magistrates' Courts Rep., *N.Z.*
M.D. Master's Dec. (Patents)
M.D.&D. (or DeG.) Montagu, Deacon & DeGex's Bankruptcy Rep., *Eng.*
MLB Maritime Labor Board, *U.S.*
M.L.E. Maryland Law Encyclopedia
M.L.J. Memphis Law Jour.
M.L.P. Michigan Law & Practice
M.L.R. Maryland Law Record; Montreal Law Rep.; Modern Law Rev.
M.L.R.Q.B. Montreal Law Rep., Q.B.
M.L.R.S.C. Montreal Law Rep., Super. Ct.
M.O.JAGA Memorandum Opinions, Judge Advocate General of the Army, *U.S.*
M.P.C. Moore's P.C. Cas., *Eng.*
M.P.R. Maritime Provinces Rep., *Can.*
M.R. Manitoba Law Rep.
Master of the Rolls, *Eng.*
MSA Mutual Security Agency, *U.S.*
MT Miscellaneous Branch Ruling International Revenue Service, *U.S.*
M.U.L.R. Melbourne University Law Rev.
M.&A. Montague & Ayrton's Bankruptcy, *Eng.*
M.&Ayr. Same as above
M.&B. Montague & Bligh's Bankruptcy, *Eng.*
M.&C. Montague & Chitty's Bankruptcy, *Eng.*
M.&G. Macnaghten & Gordon's Ch. Rep., *Eng.*
Maddock & Geldart's Ch. Rep., *Eng.*
Manning & Granger's C.P. Rep., *Eng.*
M.&Gel. Maddock & Geldart's Ch. Rep., *Eng.*
M.&Gord. Macnaghten & Gordon's Ch. Rep., *Eng.*
M.&H. Murphy & Hurlstone's Ex. Rep., *Eng.*
M.&K. Mylne & Keen's Ch. Rep., *Eng.*
M.&M. Moody & Malkin's N.P. Rep., *Eng.*
M.McA. Montague & McArthur's Bankruptcy, *Eng.*
M.&P. Moore & Payne's C.P. Rep., *Eng.*
M.&R. Maclean & Robinson's Appeal Cas., *Sc.*
Manning & Ryland's K.B., *Eng.*
Moody & Robinson's N.P., *Eng.*

M.&R.M.C. Manning & Ryland's Magistrates' Cas., K.B., *Eng*.
M.&Rob. Moody & Robinson's N.P., *Eng*.
M.&S. Manning & Scott's Rep. (9 Common Bench), *Eng*.
Maule & Selwyn's K.B. Rep., *Eng*.
Moore & Scott's C.P. Rep., *Eng*.
M.& Scott Moore & Scott's C.P. Rep., *Eng*.
M.&W. Meeson & Welsby's Ex. Rep., *Eng*.
M.&W.Cas. Mining & Water Cas. (Annot.)
M.&Y. Martin & Yerger's Rep. (8 Tenn.)
Mac. *See also* Mc
Mac.&G. Macnaghten & Gordon's Ch. Rep., *Eng*.
Macall. McAllister's Cir. Ct. Rep., *U.S*.
MacAr. McArthur's District of Columbia
MacAr.&M. MacArthur & Mackey's District of Columbia Sup. Ct.
MacAr.Pat.Cas. MacArthur's Patent Cas., *D.C*.
MacArth. MacArthur, *D.C.*; MacArthur's Patent Cas., *D.C*. MacArthur's Rep. (8–10 D.C.)
MacArth.&M. MacArthur & Mackey, *D.C*.
MacArthur & Mackey's Rep. (11 D.C.)
MacFarl. MacFarlane, Jury Ct., *Sc*.
MacG.C.C. MacGillivray's Copyright Cas., *Eng*.
Mackey Mackey's Rep. (12–20 D.C.)
Macl. McLean's Cir. Ct. Rep. *U.S*.
MacL.&R. Maclean & Robinson's H.L., *Eng*.
Macn. Macnaghten's Select Cas. Ch. *temp*. King, *Eng*.
Macn.Sel.Cas. Same as above
Macn.&G. Macnaghten & Gordon Ch. Rep., *Eng*.
Macph. Macpherson, Ct. of Session, *Sc*.
Macph.L.&B. Macpherson, Lee & Bell, *Sc*.
Macph.S.&L. Macpherson, Shireff & Lee, *Sc*.
Macq. Macqueen's Scotch Appeal Cas.
Macr. Macrory's Patent Cas., *Eng*.
Mad. Maddock's Ch. Rep., *Eng*.; Maddock's Rep. (9–18 Mont.)
Mad.&B. Maddox & Bach's Rep. (19 Mont.)
Mad.&Gel. Maddock & Geldart's Ch. Rep., *Eng*.
Madd. Maddock's Ch. Rep., *Eng*.; Maddox's Rep. (9–18 Mont.)
Madd.&B. Maddock & Bach, *Mont*.
Madd.&G. Maddock & Geldart's Ch. Rep., *Eng*.
Mag. Magruder's Rep. (1, 2 Md.)
Mag.Cas. Magisterial Cas.
Magruder Same as Mag.
Maine Maine Rep.
Maine L. Rev. Maine Law Rev.
Mait. Maitland's Select Pleas of the Crown, *Eng*.
Maitland *See also* Mait.
Maitland's Pleas of the Crown 1221, *Eng*.
Maitland's Select Pleas of the Crown, *Eng*.
Malone Heiskell's Rep. (6, 9, 10 Tenn.)
Malloy Malloy's Ch., *Ir*.
Man. Manitoba
Manning Rep., Revision Ct., *Eng*.
Manning Rep. (1 Mich.)
Man.B.News Manitoba Bar News
Man.Bar News Same as above
Man.Gr.&S. Manning, Granger, & Scott's Common Bench Rep., Old Series, *Eng*.
Man.L.J. Manitoba Law Jour.
Man.L.R. Manitoba Law Rep.
Man.R. Same as above
Man.R.*t.*Wood Manitoba Rep., *temp*. Wood

Man.Unrep.Cas. Manning's Unreported Cas., *La*.
Man.&G. Manning & Granger's C.P. Rep., *Eng*.
Man.&Ry. Manning & Ryland's K.B. Rep., *Eng*.
Man.&Sc. Manning & Scott's Common Bench Rep., Old Series, *Eng*.
Manb.Coke Manby's Abridgement of Coke's Rep.
Mann. Manning's Rep. (1 Mich.)
Mann.&G. Manning & Granger's C.P., *Eng*.
Manning Manning's Rep. (1 Mich.)
Manning (La.) Manning's Unreported Cas., *La*.
Mans. Mansfield's Rep. (49–52 Ark.)
Manson Manson's Bankruptcy, *Eng*.
Manum.Cas. Bloomfield's Manumission Cas., *N.J*.
Mar. Maritime; March's K.B. Rep., *Eng*.; Marsden's Admiralty, *Eng*.; Martin's Rep. (1 N.C.); Martin's Rep. (La. 1809–30); Marshall's Cir. Ct. Rep.; Marshall's Rep. (24–30 Ky.)
Mar.Br. March's Brooke's New Cas., *Eng*.
Mar.Cas. Maritime Law Cas., *Eng*.
Mar.L.C. Maritime Law Rep. (Crockford), *Eng*.
Mar.L.C.(N.S.) Maritime Law Cas., New Series, by Aspinall, *Eng*.
Mar.L.Cas.(N.S.) Maritime Law Cas., New Series
Mar.L.Rec. Maryland Law Record
Mar.L.Rev. Maryland Law Rev.
Mar.(La.) Martin's Rep., *La*.
Mar.N.C. Martin's Rep. (1 N.C.)
Mar.(N.S.) Martin's Rep., New Series, *La*.
Mar.R. Maritime Law Rep., *Eng*.
March March's K.B. & C.P. Rep., *Eng*.
March N. March's New Cas., K.B. & C.P., *Eng*.
March N.C. March's New Cas., K.B., *Eng*.
Marijuana Rev. The Marijuana Rev.
Marks & Sayre Marks & Sayre's Rep. (108 Ala.)
Marq.L.Rev. Marquette Law Rev.
Marr. Hay & Marriott's Admiralty Dec., *Eng*.
Marsh. Marshall's Cir. Ct. Dec., *U.S*.
Marshall's C.P. Rep., *Eng*.
Marshall's Rep. (8–10, 24–30 Ky.)
Marshall's Rep. (4 Utah)
Marsh.A.K. A.K. Marshall's Rep. (8–10 Ky.)
Marsh.C.P. Marshall's C.P. Rep., *Eng*.
Marsh.Dec. Marshall's Cir. Ct. Dec., by Brockenbrough, *U.S*.
Marsh.J.J. J.J. Marshall's Rep. (24–30 Ky.)
Mart.Ark. Martin's Dec. in Eq., Matthews, *Ark*.
Mart.Cond.La. Martin's Condensed Rep., *La*.
Mart.Dec. (1 N.C.; contains U.S. Cir. Ct. Rep. for N.C.)
Mart.Ga. Martin's Rep. (21–30 Ga.)
Mart.Ind. Martin's Rep. (54–70 Ind.)
Mart.La. Martin's Rep. (La., Old & New Series)
Mart.N.C. Martin's Rep. (1N.C.)
Mart.(N.S.) Martin's La. Rep., New Series
Mart.(O.S.) Martin's La. Rep., Old Series
Mart.U.S.C.C. Martin's Cir. Ct. Rep. in 1 N.C.
Mart.&Yerg. Martin & Yerger's Rep.
Martin *See also* Mart.
Martin's Rep. (21–30, 54–70 Ga.)
Martin's Rep. (La. 1809–30)
Martin's Rep. (1 N.C.)

Martin Mining Martin Mining Cas.
Marvel Marvel's Rep. (15, 16 Del.)
Maryland Maryland Rep.
Mas. Mason's Cir. Ct. Rep., *U.S.*
Mass. Massachusetts Rep.
Mass.App.Div. Massachusetts Appellate Div. Rep. 1935–date
Mass.L.Q. Massachusetts Law Quarterly
Mast. Master's Sup. Ct. Rep., *Can.*
Math. Mathieu's Quebec Rep.
Matson Matson's Rep. (22–24 Conn.)
Matthews Matthews' Rep. (75 Va.)
Matthews' Rep. (6–9 West Va.)
Mau.&Sel. Maul & Selwyn's K.B. Rep., *Eng.*
M'Cl. M'Clelland's Ex. Rep., *Eng.*
M'Cle. Same as above
M'Cl.&Y. M'Clelland & Younge's Ex. Rep., *Eng.*
M'Cl.&Yo. Same as above
M'Mul.Ch.S.C. M'Mullan's Eq. Rep. (S.C. 1840–42)
M'Mul.L.S.C. M'Mullan's Law Rep. (S.C. 1840–42)
Mc *See also* Mac
McAl. McAllister's Cir. Ct. Rep., *U.S.*
McAll. Same as above
McBride McBride, *Mo.*
McCah. McCahon's Rep., (Kan. 1858–68)
McCahon Same as above
McCart. McCarter's Rep. (14, 15 N.J. Eq.)
McCarty's N.Y. Civil Procedure Rep.
McCarter McCarter's Ch., *N.J.*
McCl. McClelland's Ex. Rep.
McCl.&Y. *See also* M'Cl.&Y; McClelland & Younge's Ex. Rep., *Eng.*
McClel. *See* McCl.
McCook McCook's Rep. (1 Ohio)
McCord McCord's Rep. (S.C. Law 1821–28)
McCord Ch. McCord's Rep. (S.C. Eq. 1825–27)
McCord Eq. Same as above
McCorkle McCorkle's Rep. (65 N.C.)
McCr. McCrary's Cir. Ct. Rep., *U.S.*
McGl. McGloin's Ct. of Appeal Rep., *La.*
McL. McLean's Cir. Ct., Rep., *U.S.*
McMul. McMullan's Rep. (S.C. Law 1840–42)
McMul.Eq. McMullan's Rep. (S.C. Eq. 1840–42)
McNagh. *See* Macn.
McWillie McWillie's Rep. (73–78 Miss.)
Md.B.J. Maryland Bar Jour.
Md.Ch. Maryland Ch.; Maryland Ch. Rep.
Md.L.Rec. Maryland Law Record
Md.L.Rep. Maryland Law Reporter
Md.L.Rev. Maryland Law Rev.
Me.L.Rev. Maine Law Rev.
Means Means, *Kan.*
Med. Legal J. Medico-Legal Jour.
Med.Sci.&L. Medicine, Science and the Law
Med. Trial Tech.Q. Medical Trial Technique Quarterly
Meddaugh Meddaugh's Rep. (13 Mich.)
Mees.&Ros. Meeson & Roscoe's Ex. Rep., *Eng.*
Mees.&Wels. Meeson & Welsby's Ex. Rep., *Eng.*
Meg. Megone Company Cas., *Eng.*
Meigs Meigs' Rep. (19 Tenn.)
Melanesian L.J. Melanesian Law Jour., *Papua and New Guinea*
Melb.U.L.Rev. Melbourne University Law Rev.
Mem.L.J. Memphis Law Jour. (Tenn.)
Memphis St.U.L.Rev. Memphis State University Law Rev.
Menken Menken's Rep. (9 N.Y. Civil Procedure Rep.)
Mer. Merivale's Ch. Rep., *Eng.*

Mercer B.L. Rev. Mercer Beasley Law Rev.
Mercer L.Rev. Mercer Law Rev.
Meriv. Merivale's Ch., *Eng.*
Met. Metcalf's Rep. (42–54 Mass.)
Metcalf's Rep. (3 R.I.)
Metcalfe's Rep. (58–61 Ky.)
Metc.Ky. Metcalfe's Rep. (58–61 Ky.)
Metc.Mass. Metcalf's Rep. (42–54 Mass.)
Mews The Reports (1893–95), *Eng.*
Mews' Digest of English Case Law
Miami L.Q. Miami Law Quarterly
Mich. Michigan; Michaelmas Term
Mich.Jur. Michigan Jurisprudence
Mich.L.Rev. Michigan's Law Rev.
Mich.N.P. Brown's or Howell's Michigan N.P. Rep. or Cas.
Mich.St.B.J. Michigan State Bar Jour.
Mich.T. Michaelmas Term, *Eng.*
Michie's Jur. Michie's Jurisprudence of Va. & W. Va.
Mil.L.Rev. Military Law Rev.
Miles Miles' Dist. Ct. Rep. (Philadelphia 1825–41)
Milw. Milward's Ecclesiastical, *Ir.*
Mill Mill's Constitutional Rep., S.C.
Mill. Miller's Rep. (1–5 La.); Miller's Rep. (3–18 Md.)
Mill Const. Mill's S.C. Constitutional Rep.
Mill. Dec. Miller's Cir. Ct., Dec. (Woolworth's), *U.S.*
Miller's U.S. Sup. Ct. Dec. (condensed, continuation of Curtis)
Mill.La. Miller's Rep. (1–5 La.)
Mill.Md. Miller's Rep. (3–18 Md.)
Mill.Op. Miller's Cir. Ct. Dec. (Woolworth), *U.S.*
Miller Miller's Rep. (1–5 La.)
Miller's Rep. (3–18 Md.)
Mills Mills' Surrogate Rep., *N.Y.*
Mills' Surr.Ct. Same as above
Min. Minor's Rep. (Ala. 1820–26)
Minn. Minnesota
Minn.Cont.L.Ed. Minnesota Continuing Legal Education
Minn.Cont.Legal Ed. Same as above
Minn.L.Rev. Minnesota Law Rev.
Minor Minor's Institutes
Minor's Rep. (Ala. 1820–26)
Misc. Miscellaneous Rep. (N.J., N.Y.)
Misc. Dec. Ohio Miscellaneous Dec. (Gottschall 1865–73)
Miss. Mississippi
Miss.L.J. Mississippi Law Jour.
Miss.L.Rev. Mississippi Law Rev.
Miss.St.Ca. Morris' Miss. State Cas. (1818–72)
Mister Mister's Rep. (17–32 Mo. App.)
Mo. Missouri; Modern Reports 1669–1732, *Eng.*; Moore's C.P. Rep., *Eng.*; Moore's K.B. Rep., *Eng.*; Moore's P.C., *Eng.*
Mo.App. Missouri Appeals Rep.
Mo.App.Rep. Same as above
Mo.B.J. Missouri Bar Jour.
Mo.Dec. Missouri Dec.
Mo.F. Francis Moore's K.B. Rep., *Eng.*
Mo.J.B. J.B. Moore's C.P. Rep., *Eng.*
Mo.Jur. Monthly Jurist
Mo.L.Rev. Missouri Law Rev.
Mo.P.C. Moore's P.C. Rep., *Eng.*
Mo.W.Jur. Monthly Western Jurist
Mo.&P. Moore & Payne's C.P. Rep., *Eng.*
Mo.&R. Moody & Robinson's N.P. Rep., *Eng.*
Mo.&S. Moore & Scott's C.P. Rep., *Eng.*
Moak Eng.Rep. Moak's English Rep.
Mod. Modern Rep. 1699–1732, *Eng.*
Style's K.B. Rep., 1646–55, *Eng.*
Mod.Cas. Modern Cas. (6 Modern Rep.), *Eng.*

Mod.Cas.L.&Eq. Modern Rep., pts. 8, 9, Eq., *Eng*.
Mod.Cas. per Far.(*t*.Holt) Modern Cas., *temp*. Holt, by Farresby (6, 7 Modern Rep.)
Mod.L.Rev. Modern Law Rev.
Mod.Pract.Comm. Modern Practice Commentator
Mod.Rep. Modern Rep. 1669–1732, *Eng*.
Style's K.B. Rep., *Eng*.
Moll. Molloy's Ch., *Ir*.
Moly. Molyneaux's Rep. *temp*. Car. I, *Eng*.
Mon. Monaghan's Unreported Cas. (Pa. Super.)
T.B. Monroe's Rep. (17–23 Ky.)
Montana
Mon.B. Monroe's Rep. (40–57 Ky.)
Mon. T.B. T.B. Monroe's Rep. (17–23 Ky.)
Mon.W.J. Monthly Western Jurist
Monag. Monagham's Rep. (147–65 Pa.)
Monaghan's Rep. (Pa. 1888–90)
Monr. Monroe. *See* Mon.
Mont. Montana; Montana Rep.
Mont.Co.L.Rep. Montgomery County (Pa.) Law Reporter
Mont.L.R. Montreal Law Rev.
Mont.L.Rev. Montana Law Rev.
Mont.Leg.News Montreal Legal News
Mont.&Ayr. Montagu & Ayrton's Bankruptcy, *Eng*.
Mont.&M. Montagu & McArthur's Bankruptcy, Eng.
Month.L.J. Monthly Jour. of Law, *Wash*.
Month.L.Mag. Monthly Law Magazine, *London*
Month.L.Rep. Monthly Law Reporter, *Boston*
Monthly Law Rep., *Can*.
Month.L.Rev. Monthly Law Rev.
Month.Leg.Exam. Monthly Legal Examiner, *N.Y*.
Month.West.J. Monthly Western Jour., *Bloomington*
Montr.Cond.Rep. Montreal Condensed Rep.
Montreal L.R.Q.B. Montreal Law Rep., Q.B.
Montreal L.R.S.C. Montreal Law Rep., Super. Ct.
Moo. Moody's Crown Cas. Res., *Eng*.
F. Moore's K.B. Rep., *Eng*.
J.B. Moore's C.P. Rep., *Eng*.
Moo.A. Moore's Reports (1 Bosanquet & Puller after p. 470)
Moo.C.C. Moody's Crown Cas. Res., *Eng*.
Moo.C.P. J.B. Moore's C.P. Rep., *Eng*.
Moo.Cr.C. Moody's Crown Cas. Res., *Eng*.
Moo.F. F. Moore's K.B. Rep., *Eng*.
Moo.J.B. J.B. Moore's C.P. Rep., *Eng*.
Moo.K.B. Moore's K.B. Rep., *Eng*.
Moo.P.C. Moore's P.C. Cas., *Eng*.
Moo.P.C.C.(N.S.) Moore's P.C. Cas., New Series, *Eng*.
Moo.&Mal. Moody & Malkin's N.P. Rep., *Eng*.
Moo.&P. Moore & Payne's C.P. Rep., *Eng*.
Moo.&Rob. Moody & Robinson's N.P. Rep., *Eng*.
Moo.&S. Moore & Scott's C.P. Rep., *Eng*.
Mood. Moody's Crown Cas. Res., *Eng*.
Mood.C.C. Same as above
Mood.&M. Moody & Malkin's N.P. Rep., *Eng*.
Mood.&R. Moody & Robinson's N.P. Rep., *Eng*.
Moon Moon's Rep. (133–144 Ind.; 6–14 Ind. App.)
Moore *See also* Moo.; Moore's C.P. Rep., *Eng*.; Moore's K.B. Rep., *Eng*.; Moore's P.C. Rep., *Eng*.; Moore's Rep. (67 Ala.); Moore's Rep. (28–34 Ark.); Moore's Rep. (22–24 Tex.)

Moore A. Moore's Rep. (1 Bosanquet & Puller after p. 470), *Eng*.
Moore C.P. Moore's C.P. Rep., *Eng*.
Moore K.B. F. Moore's K.B. Rep., *Eng*.
Moore P.C. Moore's P.C. Rep., *Eng*.
Moore P.C.(N.S.) Moore's P.C. Rep., New Series, *Eng*.
Moore Q.B. F. Moore's Q.B. Rep., *Eng*.
Moore Indian App. Moore's Indian Appeals, *Eng*.
Moore &P. Moore & Payne's C.P. Rep., *Eng*.
Moore &S. Moore & Scott's C.P. Rep., *Eng*.
Moore & Walker Moore & Walker's Rep. (22–24 Tex.)
Mor.Ia. Morris' Rep. (Iowa 1839–46)
Mor.Miss. Morris' Rep. (43–48 Miss.)
Mor.St.Ca. Morris' State Cas. (Miss. 1818–72)
Morg. Morgan's Ch. Acts & Orders, *Eng*.
Morr. Morrill's Bankruptcy Cas., *Eng*.
Morris (Cal.; Iowa; Miss.; Ore.)
Morr.Trans. Morrison's Transcript U.S. Supreme Ct. Dec.
Morris Morris' Rep. (5 Cal.)
Morris' Rep. (Iowa 1839–46)
Morris' Rep. (23–26 Ore.)
Morrissett's Rep. (80–98 Ala.)
Morrow Morrow, *Ore*.
Morse Exch.Rep. Morse's Ex. Rep.
Mos. Moseley's Ch. Rep., *Eng*.
Moult.Ch. Moulton's Ch. Practice, *N.Y.*
Ms. Manuscript Rep. or Dec.
Ms.D. Manuscript Dec., Commissioner of Patents, *U.S.*
Manuscript Dec., Comptroller General, *U.S.*
Mu.L.J. Municipal Law Jour.
Mun. Munford's Rep. (15–20 Va.)
Mun.Atty. Municipal Attorney
Mun.Corp.Cas. Municipal Corporation Cas.
Mun.L.Ct.Dec. Municipal Law Ct. Dec.
Mun.L.J. Municipal Law Jour.
Mun.Ord.Rev. Municipal Ordinance Rev.
Mun.Rep. Municipal Rep., *Can*.
Munf. Same as Mun.
Munic.&P.L. Municipal & Parish Law Cas., *Eng*.
Mur. Murphey's Rep., (5–7 N.C.)
Murray's New South Wales Rep.
Murray's Scotch Jury Ct. Rep.
Mur.&Hurl. Murphy & Hurlstone's Ex. Rep., *Eng*.
Murph. Murphey's Rep. (5–7 N.C.)
Murr. Murray's Scotch Jury Ct. Rep.
Murr.Over.Cas. Murray's Overruled Cas.
My.&Cr. Mylne & Craig's Ch. Rep., *Eng*.
My.&K. Mylne & Keen's Ch. Rep., *Eng*.
Myer Fed.Dec. Myer's Federal Dec.
Myl.&Cr. Mylne & Craig's Ch. Rep., *Eng*.
Myl.&K. Mylne & Keen's Ch. Rep., *Eng*.
Myr. Myrick's Probate Rep. (Cal. 1872–79)
Mry.Prob. Same as above

N. Nebraska; Nevada
NACCA Law Jour., National Assn. of Claimants' Compensation Attorneys
NATO North Atlantic Treaty Organization
N. Atlantic Reg.Bus.L.Rev. North Atlantic Regional Business Law Rev.
N.B. New Brunswick; New Benloe (or Bendloe) K.B. Rep., *Eng*.

N.B.Eq. New Brunswick Equity
N.B.J. National Bar Jour.
N.B.Rep. New Brunswick Rep.
N.Benl. New Benloe's K.B. Rep., *Eng.*
N.C. North Carolina Rep.
N.C.C. New Ch. Cas., *Eng.*
N.C.C.A. Negligence & Compensation Cas., Annot.
N.C.Cent.L.J. North Carolina Central Law Jour.
N.C.Conf. North Carolina Conference Rep.
N.C.L.Rev. North Carolina Law Rev.
N.C. Law Repos. North Carolina Law Repository
NCM Navy Board of Rev. Dec., *U.S.*
Ct. Martial Rep., Navy Cas.
N.C.T.Rep. North Carolina Term Rep. (4 N.C.)
N.Car. North Carolina
N.Cent. School L.Rev. North Central School Law Rev.
N.Ch.R. Nelson's Ch. Rep., *Eng.*
H. Finch's Ch. Rep., 1673–81, *Eng.*
N.Chip. North Chipman's Rep. (Vt. 1789–91)
N.D. North Dakota
N.D.L.Rev. North Dakota Law Rev.
N.E. North Eastern Reporter
N.E.2d Same as above, Second Series
N.Eng.L.Rev. New England Law Rev.
N.F. Newfoundland
N.H. New Hampshire
N.H.L.Rep. New Hampshire Law Reporter
N.H.R. New Hampshire Rep.
N.I.R.A. National Industrial Recovery Act, *U.S.*
N.Ir.L.Q. Northern Ireland Legal Quarterly
N.Ir.L.R. Northern Ireland Law Rep.
N.J. New Jersey
N.J.Eq. New Jersey Eq. Rep.
N.J.L. New Jersey Law Rep.
N.J.L.J. New Jersey Law Jour.
N.J.L.Rev. New Jersey Law Rev.
N.J.Misc. New Jersey Miscellaneous Rep.
N.J.St.B.J. New Jersey State Bar Jour.
N.J.Super. New Jersey Super. Ct. Rep.
NL Lutwych's C.P. Rep. (Nelson), *Eng.*
N.L.G.Q. National Lawyers' Guild Quarterly
N.L.R.B. National Labor Relations Bd., *U.S.*
N.L.Rev. Northeastern Law Rev.
N.M. New Mexico
NMB National Mediation Bd.
N.Mex.L.Rev. New Mexico Law Rev., *U.S.*
NOLPE NOLPE School Law Jour.
N.P. Nisi Prius
N.P.C. Nisi Prius Cas.
N.P.&G.T.Rep. Nisi Prius & General Term Rep., *Ohio*
N.P.(N.S.) Ohio N.P. Rep., New Series
N.P. Ohio Ohio N.P. Rep.
N.P.R. Nisi Prius Rep.
N.R. Bosanquet & Puller's New Rep., *Eng.*
The New Rep., 1862–65, *Eng.*
NRA National Recovery Admin., *U.S.*
N.R.A.B. (4th Div.) National Railroad Adjustment Bd. Awards
N.R.B.P. Bosanquet & Puller's New Rep., *Eng.*
NRCI Nuclear Regulatory Commission Issuances
N.S. New Series; Nova Scotia
N.S. Dec. Nova Scotia Dec.
N.S.L.R. Nova Scotia Law Rep.
N.S.R. Nova Scotia Rep.
N.S.W. New South Wales State Rep.

N.S.W.L.R. Law Reports, New South Wales; New South Wales Law Rep., *Aus*.
N.S.W.St.R. Same as above
N.S. Wales New South Wales
N.S. Wales L. New South Wales Law
N.S. Wales L. R. Eq. New South Wales Law Rep. Eq.
N.Sc. Dec. Nova Scotia Dec.
N.T.A. Proceedings National Tax Assn. Proceedings
N.T. Rep. New Term Rep., Q.B., *Eng*.
N.W. North Western Reporter
N.W.2d Same as above, Second Series
N.W. Law Rev. Northwestern Law Rev.
N.W.T.R. North-West Territories Rep., *Can*.
N.W. Terr. Northwest Territories Sup. Ct. Rep.
N.W.U.L. Rev. Northwestern University Law Rev.
N.Y. New York
N.Y. Anno. Cas. New York Annot. Cas.
N.Y. Anno. Dig. New York Annot. Digest
N.Y. App. Dec. New York Ct. of Appeals Dec.
New York Appellate Div. Dec.
N.Y.C.B.A. Bull. Bulletin of the Assn. of the Bar of the City of New York
N.Y. Cas. Err. Caines' N.Y. Cas. in Error
N.Y.Ch. Sent. Chancery Sentinel, N.Y.
N.Y. City Ct. Rep. New York City Ct. Rep.
N.Y. City Ct. Supp. New York City Ct. Supplement
N.Y. City H. Rec. New York City Hall Recorder
N.Y. Civ. Proc. R. New York Civil Procedure Rep.
N.Y. Civ. Proc. R. (N.S.) Same as above, New Series
N.Y. Code Reptr. New York Code Reporter
N.Y. Code Reptr. (N.S.) Same as above, New Series
N.Y. Cond. New York Condensed Rep. 1881–82
N.Y. County Law. Assn. B. Bull. New York County Lawyers Assn. Bar Bulletin
N.Y.Cr.R. New York Crim. Rep. 1878–1924
N.Y. Ct. App. New York Ct. of Appeals (highest court)
N.Y. Daily L. Gaz. New York Daily Gazette
N.Y. Daily L. Reg. New York Daily Law Register
N.Y. Dept. R. New York Department Rep.
N.Y. Elec. Cas. New York Election Cas.
N.Y. Jud. Rep. New York Judicial Repository
N.Y. Jur. New York Jurisprudence; New York Jurist
N.Y.L. Cas. New York Leading Cas.
N.Y.L.F. New York Law Forum
N.Y.L.J. New York Law Jour.
N.Y.L. Rec. New York Law Record
N.Y.L. Rev. New York Law Rev.
N.Y.L.S. Rev. New York Law School Rev.
N.Y. Law Gaz. New York Law Gazette
N.Y. Law J. New York Law Jour.
N.Y. Law Rev. New York Law Rev.
N.Y. Leg. N. New York Legal News 1880–82
N.Y. Leg. Obs. New York Legal Observer
N.Y. Leg. Reg. New York Legal Register 1850
N.Y. Misc. New York Miscellaneous Rep.
N.Y. Misc. 2d Same as above,

Second Series
N.Y. Month. L. Bull. New York Monthly Law Bulletin
N.Y. Month. L. Rep. New York Monthly Law Rep.
N.Y. Mun. Gaz. New York Municipal Gazette
N.Y. Pr. New York Practice Rep.
N.Y. Rec. New York Record
N.Y. Rep. New York Rep. (Ct. of Appeals)
N.Y. Reptr. New York Reporter (Gardenier 1820)
N.Y.S. New York State Reporter; New York Supplement
N.Y.S.2d Same as above, Second Series
N.Y.S.D.R. New York State Dept. Rep.
N.Y. Spec. Term Rep. Howard's Practice Rep., *N.Y.*
N.Y.St.B.J. New York State Bar Jour.
N.Y.St.R. New York State Rep. 1886–96
N.Y. Super. New York Super. Ct. (various reporters)
N.Y. Supp. New York Supplement
N.Y. Supr. Ct. Rep. New York Sup. Ct. Rep.
N.Y.T.R. New York Term Rep. (Caines)
N.Y. Trans. New York Transcript 1861
N.Y. Trans. (N.S.) New York Transcript Rep., New Series
N.Y. Trans. Rep. New York Transcript Rep.
N.Y.U. Conf. Charitable New York University Conference on Charitable Foundations Proceedings
N.Y.U. Conf. Lab. New York University Conference on Labor
N.Y.U. Inst. on Fed. Tax. New York University Institute on Federal Taxation
N.Y.U. Intra. L. Rev. New York Intramural Law Rev.
N.Y.U.J. Int. Law & Pol. New York University Jour. of International Law and Politics
N.Y.U.L. Center Bull. New York University Law Center Bulletin
N.Y.U.L.Q. Rev. New York University Law Quarterly Rev.
N.Y.U.L. Rev. New York University Law Rev.
N.Y.U. Rev. Law & Soc. New York University Rev. of Law and Social Change
N.Y. Wkly Dig. New York Weekly Digest
N.Z.L.J. New Zealand Law Jour.
N.Z.L.R. New Zealand Law Rep.
N.Z.U.L. Rev. New Zealand Universities Law Rev.
N. & H. Nott & Huntington's Rep. (1–7 U.S. Ct. of Claims)
N. & Hop. Nott & Hopkins' Rep. (8–29 U.S. Ct. of Claims)
N.&M. Nevile & Manning's K.B. Rep., *Eng.*
N. & Macn. Nevile & Macnamara Railway & Canal Cas., *Eng.*
N.&Mc. Nott & McCord's Rep. (S.C. Law)
N.&P. Nevile & Perry's K.B. Rep., *Eng.*
N.&P.E.I.R. Newfoundland and Prince Edward Island Rep.
N. Bruns. New Brunswick Rep.
N.Ch.R. Nelson's Ch. Rep., *Eng.*
Nacca L.J. Nacca Law Jour., National Assn. of Claimants' Compensation Attorneys
Napton Napton's Rep. (4 Mo.)
Narcotics Control Dig. Narcotics Control Digest
Narr. Mod. Narrationes Modernae (Style's K.B. Rep. 1646–55), *Eng.*
Nat. Bankr. Reg. National Bankruptcy Register, *U.S.*
Nat. Civic Rev. National Civic Rev.
Nat. Corp. Rep. National Corporation Reporter

Nat. L. Rep. National Law Reporter
Nat. L. Rev. National Law Rev.
Nat. Law Guild Q. National Lawyers' Guild Quarterly
Nat. Legal Mag. National Legal Magazine
Nat. Mun. Rev. National Municipal Rev.
Nat. Reg. National Register (by Mead)
Nat. Rept. Syst. National Reporter System
Nat. School L. Rptr. National School Law Reporter
Nat. Tax J. National Tax Jour.
Nat. U.L. Rev. National University Law Rev.
Natural L.F. Natural Law Forum
Natural Resources J. Natural Resources Jour.
Nd. Newfoundland
Neb. Nebraska
Neb. L.B. Nebraska Law Bulletin
Neb. L. Rev. Nebraska Law Rev.
Neb. St. B.J. Nebraska State Bar Jour.
Neb. Unoff. Nebraska Unofficial Rep. 1901–04
Neg. Cas. Bloomfield's Manumission (or Negro) Cas., *N.J.*
Negl. Cas. Negligence Cases (CCH)
Negl. & Comp. Cas. Ann. Negligence & Compensation Cas., Annot.
Nel. Nelson's Ch. Rep., *Eng.*
H. Finch's Ch. Rep., *Eng.*
Nel. C.R. Nelson's Ch. Rep., *Eng.*
Nels. Nelson's Ch. Rep., *Eng.*
H. Finch's Ch. Rep., *Eng.*
Nels. Abr. Nelson's Abridgement, *Eng.*
Nev. Nevada
Nev. St. Bar J. Nevada State Bar Jour.
Nev. & M.K.B. Nevile & Manning's K.B. Rep., *Eng.*
Nev. & Man. Same as above
Nev. & P. Nevile & Perry's K.B. Rep., *Eng.*
New. Newell's Rep. (49–90 Ill. App.)
New B. Eq. Ca. New Brunswick Eq. Cas.
New Benl. Benloe's K.B. Rep. 1531–1628, *Eng.*
New Br. New Brunswick Rep.
New L.J. New Law Jour.
New Rep. New Reports 1862–65, *Eng.*
Bosanquet & Puller's New Rep. (4, 5 Bosanquet & Puller)
New Sess. Cas. New Sessions Cas. (Carrow, Hamerton, Allen), *Eng.*
New Term Rep. New Term Rep. (East), *Eng.*
Dowling & Tyland's K.B. Rep., *Eng.*
New York *See* N.Y.
Newb. Newberry's Admiralty Rep., *U.S.*
Newell Newell's Rep. (48–90 Ill. App.)
Newf. Newfoundland
Newf. S. Ct. Newfoundland Sup. Ct. Dec.
Newfld L.R. Newfoundland Law Rep.
Nigeria L.R. Nigeria Law Rep.
Noble Noble's Current Ct. Dec., *N.Y.*
Nolan Nolan, Magistrates' Cas., *Eng.*
Nonacq. (*or* NA) Nonacquiescence by Commissioner in Tax Ct. or Bd. of Tax Appeals Dec., *U.S.*
Norc. Norcross' Rep. (23, 24 Nev.)
Norris Norris' Rep. (82–96 Pa.)
North. Eden's Ch. Rep., *Eng.*; North, *Ill.*; Northington's Ch., *Eng.*; Rep. *temp.* Northington, by Eden, *Eng.*
North. Co. Northampton County Legal News, *Pa.*
North. Co. Rep. Northampton

County Reporter, *Pa*.
North & G. North & Guthrie's Rep. (68–80 Mo. App.)
Northam. Northampton Law Reporter, *Pa*.
Northam. L. Rep. Same as above
Northum. Northumberland County Legal News, *Pa*.
Northum. Co. Leg. N. Same as above
Northumb. L.N. Northumberland Legal Jour., *Pa*.
Notes of Cas. Notes of Cas., *Eng*.
Notre Dame Law. Notre Dame Lawyer
Nott &Hop. Nott & Hopkins' Rep. (8–15 U.S. Ct. of Claims)
Nott &Hunt. Nott & Huntington's Rep. (1–7 U.S. Ct. of Claims)
Nott &McC. Nott & McCord's Rep. (S.C. Law)
Nov. Sc. Nova Scotia
Nov. Sc. Dec. Nova Scotia Dec.
Nov. Sc.L.R. Nova Scotia Law Rep.
Nova L.J. Nova Law Jour.
Noy Noy's K.B. Rep., Eng.
Nw. U.L. Rev. Northwestern University Law Rev.
Nye Nye's Rep. (18–21 Utah)

O. Ohio; Oklahoma; Oregon; Ontario
Otto's Rep. (91–107 U.S.)
Solicitor's Law Opinion (U.S. Internal Revenue Service)
O.A. Ohio Appellate
O.A.G. Opinions of Attorney General, *U.S*.
O.A.R. Ontario Appeal Rep.
Ohio Appeals 1913–date
OAS Organization of American States
O.B.&F.N.Z. Oliver, Bell & Fitzgerald's New Zealand Rep.
O. Ben. Old Benloe C.P. Rep., *Eng*.
O. Bridg. Carter's Rep. *temp*. Bridgman, C.P. Rep., *Eng*.
Orlando Bridgman's C.P. Rep., *Eng*.
O.C.A. Ohio Courts of Appeal Rep. 1915–22
O.C.C. Ohio Cir. Ct. Rep. or Dec.
O.C.C. (N.S.) Ohio Cir. Ct. Rep., New Series 1903–17
O.C.D. Ohio Cir. Ct. Dec. 1901–18
O.C.S. Office of Contract Settlement, *U.S*.
O.D. Office Decision (U.S. Internal Revenue Service)
Ohio Dec. 1894–1920
O.D.C.C. Ohio Dec., Cir. Ct.
ODM Office of Defense Mobilization, *U.S*.
O. Dec. Rep. Ohio Dec. Reprint
O.E.M. Office of Emergency Management
O.F.D. Ohio Federal Dec.
O.G. (or O.G. Pat. Off.) Official Gazette, U.S. Patent Office
O. Jur. Ohio Jurisprudence
O.L.Abs. Ohio Law Abstract
O.L.B. Ohio Law Bulletin
O.L.D. Ohio Lower Ct. Dec.
O.L.J. Ohio Law Jour.
O.L.N. Ohio Legal News
O.L.R. Ontario Bar Reporter
Ontario Law Rep.
O.L.R.B. Ontario Labour Relations Bd. Monthly Rep.
O.L. Rep. Ohio Law Reporter
O. Legal News Ohio Legal News
O. Lower D. Ohio Lower Ct. Dec.
O.N.P. Ohio N.P. Rep. 1894–1901
O.N.P. (N.S.) Ohio N.P. Rep., New Series, 1903–1913
O.O. Ohio Opinions
OPA Office of Price Admin., *U.S*.
O.P.R. Ontario Practice Rep.
O.P.S. Office of Price Stabilization, *U.S*.
O.R. Ontario Rep., 1882–1900; 1931 to present
O.S. Ohio State Rep.; Upper Canada Q.B. Rep., Old Series
OSAHRC Occupational Safety

and Health Review Commission
OSHR Occupational Safety & Health Rep. (CCH)
O.S.C.D. Ohio Sup. Ct. Dec., Unreported Cas.
OSS Office of Strategic Services, *U.S.*
O.S.U. Ohio Sup. Ct. Dec., Unreported Cas.
O.St. Ohio State Rep.
O. Supp. Ohio Supplement
OWM Office of War Mobilization, *U.S.*
O.W.N. Ontario Weekly Notes, 1909–1932; 1933–1962
O.W.R. Ontario Weekly Reporter
O'Brien O'Brien's Upper Canada Rep.
Odeneal Odeneal's Rep. (9–11 Ore.)
Off. Brev. Officina Brevium
Off. Gaz. Official Gazette Patent Office
Off. Gaz. Pat. Off. Official Gazette, U.S. Patent Office
Officer Officer's Rep. (1–9 Minn.)
Ogden Ogden's Rep. (12–15 La.)
Oh. Ohio Rep. (1821–1852)
Oh.A. Ohio Court of Appeals
Oh.Dec. (Reprint) Ohio Dec. (Reprint)
Oh.F.Dec. Ohio Federal Dec.
Oh.Jur. Ohio Jurisprudence
Oh.L.Bul. Ohio Law Bulletin
Oh.L.Ct.D. Ohio Lower Court Dec.
Oh.L.J. Ohio Law Jour.
Oh.L.Rep. Ohio Law Reporter
Oh.St. Ohio State Rep.
Ohio Bar Ohio State Bar Assn. Rep.
Ohio C.C. Ohio Cir. Ct. Rep.
Ohio C.C. Dec. Ohio Cir. Ct. Dec.
Ohio C.C.(N.S.) Ohio Cir. Ct. Rep., New Series
Ohio Cir. Ct. (N.S.) Same as above
Ohio Cir. Ct. R. Ohio Cir. Ct. Rep.
Ohio Cir. Dec. Ohio Cir. Ct. Dec.
Ohio Dec. Ohio Dec. 1894–1920
Ohio Jur.2d Ohio Jurisprudence, Second Edition
Ohio L.Abs. Ohio Law Abstract
Ohio L.R. Ohio Law Reporter
Ohio Law Abst. Ohio Law Abstract
Ohio Law Bull. Ohio Law Bulletin
Ohio Leg. N. Ohio Legal News
Ohio Misc. Ohio Miscellaneous Rep.
Ohio Misc. Dec. Ohio Miscellaneous Dec.
Ohio N.P. Ohio N.P. Rep.
Ohio N.P. (N.S.) Ohio N.P. Rep., New Series
Ohio Op. Ohio Opinions
Ohio Prob. Ohio Probate Rep. by Goebel
Ohio R. Cond. Ohio Rep. Condensed
Ohio S.L.J. Ohio State Law Jour.
Ohio St. Ohio State Rep.
Ohio St. L.J. Ohio State Law Jour.
Ohio St. (N.S.) Ohio State Rep., Annot., New Series
Ohio Sup. &C.P. Dec. Ohio Super. C.P. Dec.
Ohio Supp. Ohio Supplement
Ohio Unrept. Cas. Ohio Unreported Cas. (Pollock)
Oil & Gas Compact Bull. Oil and Gas Compact Bulletin
Oil & Gas Inst. Oil & Gas Institute
Oil & Gas J. Oil & Gas Jour.
Oil & Gas Rptr. Oil & Gas Reporter
Oil & Gas Tax Q. Oil & Gas Tax Quarterly
Okla. Ap. Ct. Rep. Oklahoma Appellate Ct. Reporter
Okla. B. Assn. J. Oklahoma Bar Assn. Jour.
Okla. C.U.L.R. Oklahoma City University Law Rev.
Okla. Crim. Oklahoma Criminal Rep.

Okla. L. J. Oklahoma Law Jour.
Okla. L. Rev. Oklahoma Law Rev.
Okla. S.B.J. Oklahoma State Bar Jour.
Olc. Olcott's Dist. Rep., *U.S.*
Olc.Adm. Same as above
Old. Oldright's Rep. (5, 6 Nova Scotia)
Old Ben. Benloe in Benloe & Dalison's C.P. Rep., *Eng.*
Oliv. B. & L. Oliver, Beaven & Lefroy Railway & Canal Cas., *Eng.*
Olliv. B. & F. Olliver, Bell & Fitzgerald, *New Zealand*
O'M. & H. El. Cas. O'Malley & Hardcastle Election Cas., *Eng.*
Ont. Ontario
Ont. App. Ontario Appeal Rep.
Ont. El. Cas. Ontario Election Cas.
Ont. L.J. Ontario Law Jour.
Ont. L.J. (N.S.) Same as above, New Series
Ont. L. Rep. Ontario Law Rep.
Ont. Pr. Rep. Ontario Practice Rep.
Ont. R. Ontario Rep.
Ont. W.N. Ontario Weekly Notes
Ont. W.R. Ontario Weekly Rep.
Op. Sol. Dept. Opinions of the Solicitor, U.S. Dept. of Labor
Ops. A.G. Opinions, Attorney General
Ops. J.A.G. Opinions, Judge Advocate General, U.S. Army
Or. Oregon
Ore.L.Rev. Oregon Law Rev.
Ore.St.B.Bull. Oregon State Bar Bulletin
Orl. Bridgman Orlando Bridgman's C.P. Rep., *Eng.*
Orl. T.R. Martin's Orleans Term Rep., *La.*
Orleans App. Orleans Appeals, *La.*
Orleans Tr. Orleans Term Rep., *La.*
Ormond Ormond's Rep. (19–107 Ala.)
Osaka U.L.R. Osaka University Law Rev.
Osgoode Hall L.J. Osgoode Hall Law Jour.
Otago L. Rev. Otago Law Rev.
Ottawa L. Rev. Ottawa Law Rev.
Otto Otto's Sup. Ct. Rep. (91–107 U.S.)
Out. Outerbridge's Rep. (97–110 Pa.)
Over. Overton's Rep. (1–2 Tenn.)
Ow. Owen's K.B. Rep., *Eng.*; Owen's C.P. Rep., *Eng.*
Oxley Young's Vice Admiralty Dec. (by Oxley, *Novia Scotia)*

P. Law Rep., Probate, Divorce, & Admiralty, since 1890, *Eng.*; Law Rep. Probate, Divorce & Admiralty Div., Third Series; Pacific Reporter; Pennsylvania; Peter's U.S. Sup. Rep. (26–41 U.S.); Pickering (18–41 Mass.)
P.2d Pacific Reporter, Second Series
P.A.D. Peters' Admiralty Dec., *U.S.*; Phi Alpha Delta
P.C. Pleas of the Crown; Parliamentary Cas.; Patent Cas.; Practice Cas.; Prize Cas.; Privy Council; Probate Ct.; Precedents in Ch.; Price Control Cas. (CCH)
P.C.A. Acts of the P. C., *Eng.*
P.C.App. Law Rep. P.C. Appeals, *Eng.*
P.C.C. Privy Council Cas., *Eng.* Peters' Cir. Ct. Rep., *U.S.*
PCIJ Permanent Ct. of International Justice
P.C.L.J. Pacific Coast Law Jour.
P.C.R. Parker's Crim. Rep., *N.Y.* Pennsylvania Corporation Rep., *Eng.*
P.C.Rep. Privy Council Rep., *Eng.*
P.Cas. Prize Cas. 1914–22, *Eng.*
P. Coast L.J. Pacific Coast Law Jour.
P.D. Law Reports, Probate Div.,

Eng.
P.D.A. Probate, Divorce & Admiralty, *Eng.*
P.E.A.L.Q. Publishing Entertainment & Allied Fields Quarterly
P.E.I. Prince Edward Island Rep.
P.F.S. P. F. Smith's Rep. (51–81 Pa.)
P.-H. Prentice-Hall
PHA Public Housing Admin., *U.S.*
P.-H.Am.Lab.Arb. Awards American Labor Arbitration Awards
P.-H.Am.Lab.Cas. American Labor Cas.
P.-H.Cas. American Federal Tax Rep.
P.-H.Corp. Corporation
P.-H.Est.Plan. Estate Planning
P.-H.Fed.Taxes Federal Taxes
P.-H. Fed. Wage & Hour Federal Wage & Hour
P.-H. Ind. Rel., Lab. Arb. Industrial Relations, American Labor Arbitration
P.-H.Ind.Rel., Union Conts. Industrial Relations, Union Contracts and Collective Bargaining
P.-H.Soc.Sec. Taxes Social Security Taxes
P.-H.State & Local Taxes State & Local Taxes
P.-H.Tax Ct.Mem. Tax Court Memorandum Dec.
P.-H.Tax Ct. Rep. & Mem. Dec. Tax Court Reporter & Memorandum Dec.
P.-H.Unrep.Tr.Cas. Prentice-Hall Unreported Trust Cas.
P.Jr.&H. Patton, Jr., & Heath's Rep. (Va. Special Ct. of Appeals)
P.L. Public Law
P.L.E. Pennsylvania Law Encyclopedia
PLO Public Land Order
P.L.R. Pennsylvania Law Record
P.N.P. Peake's N.P. Cas., *Eng.*
P.R. Ontario Practice Rep.; Pacific Reporter; Parliamentary Rep., *Eng.*; Pennsylvania Rep. (Penrose & Watts); Philadelphia Rep. (Pa. 1850–51); Philippine Islands Rep.; Pittsburgh Rep. (Pa. 1853–73); Press Release (U.S. Gov. Departments); Probate Rep.; Pyke's Rep., *Can.*; Porto Rico (*now* Puerto Rico)
P.R.C.P. Practical Register, C P., *Eng.*
P.R.Ch. Practical Register in Ch., *Eng.*
P.R.&D.El.Cas. Power, Rodwell & Dew's Election Cas., *Eng.*
P.R.R. Porto Rico Sup. Ct. Rep. (*now* Puerto Rico)
P.R.S.C.R. Same as above
P.R.U.C. Upper Canada Practice Rep.
P.S.C. Public Service Comm.
P.S.C.U.S. Peters' U.S. Sup. Ct. Rep. (26–41 U.S.)
P.S.R. Pennsylvania State Rep.
P.T. Processing Tax Div. (U.S. Internal Revenue Service)
P.U. Fort. Public Utilities Fortnightly
P.U.R. Public Utilities Rep., *U.S.*
P.U.R.(N.S.) Public Utilities Rep., New Series
P.U.R.3d Same as above, Third Series
P.W. Peere Williams' Ch. & K.B. Rep., *Eng.*
P.Wms. Same as above
P.&B. Pugsley & Burbridge's New Brunswick Rep.
P.&C. Prideaux & Cole's New Session Cas., *Eng.*
P.&D. Perry & Davison's Q.B. Rep., *Eng.*
Law Reports, Probate & Divorce Series, *Eng.*
P.&F. Pike & Fischer's Administrative Law
Pike & Fischer's Federal Rules

Service
Pike & Fischer's OPA Price Service
P.&F. Radio Reg. Radio Regulation Reporter
P.&H. Patton, Jr., & Heath's Rep. (Va. Special Ct. of Appeals)
P.&K. Perry & Knapp Election Cas., *Eng*.
P.&M. Law Rep., Probate & Matrimonial Cas., *Eng*.
P.&T. Pugsley & Trueman's New Brunswick Rep.
P.&W. Penrose & Watts' Rep. (Pa. 1829–32)
Pa. Paine's Cir. Ct. Rep., *U.S.*
Pennsylvania
Pennsylvania State Rep.
Pa.B. Assn. Q. Pennsylvania Bar Association Quarterly
Pa.B. Brief Pennsylvania Bar Brief
Pa.C.P. Common Pleas Reporter
Pa.Cas. Penn. Sup. Ct. Cas. (Sadler)
Pa.Co.Ct.R. Pennsylvania County Ct. Rep.
Pa.Corp. Rep. Pennsylvania Corporation Reporter
Pa.D.&.C. Pennsylvania Dist. & County Rep.
Pa.D.&C.2d Same as above, Second Series
Pa.Dist.R. District Rep. (Pa. 1892–1921)
Pa.Dist.&C.Rep. Pennsylvania Dist. & County Rep.
Pa.Fid. Pennsylvania Fiduciary Reporter
Pa.L.J. Pennsylvania Law Jour.
Pennsylvania Law Jour. Rep. (1842–52)
Pa.L.J.R. Clark's Pennsylvania Law Jour. Rep.
Pa.L.Rec. Pennsylvania Law Record
Pa.Misc. Pennsylvania Miscellaneous Rep.
Pa.Rep. Pennsylvania Rep.
Pa.St. Pennsylvania State Rep. (1845–date)
Pa.Super.Ct. Pennsylvania Super. Ct. Rep.
Pac. Pacific Reporter
Pac. Law Reptr. Pacific Law Reporter
Pac. Leg. N. Pacific Legal News
Pacific L.J. Pacific Law Jour.
Pai. Paige's New York Ch. Rep.
Pai.Ch. Paige's New York Ch. Rep.
Paine C.C. Paine's Cir. Ct. Rep., *U.S.*
Pal. Palmer's K.B. Rep., *Eng*.
Palmer's Palmer's K.B. Rep., *Eng*.
Palmer's Rep. (53–60 Vt.)
Pan-Am.T.S. Pan-American Treaty Series
Papua &N.G. Papua & New Guinea Law Rep.
Papy Papy's Rep. (5–8 Fla.)
Par. Parker's Ex. Rep., *Eng*.
Parker's N.Y. Crim Cas. 1823–68
Par. Dec. Parsons' Dec. (from 2–7 Mass.)
Par.Eq.Cas. Parson's Select Eq. Cas. (Pa. 1842–51)
Park. Parker's Ex. Rep., *Eng*.; Parker's N.Y. Crim. Cas. 1823–68; Parker's N.H. Rep.
Park.Exch. Parker's Ex. Rep., *Eng*.
Park.Ins. Parker's Insurance
Park.N.H. Parker's New Hampshire Rep.
Parker Parker's Ex. Rep., *Eng*.
Parker's New Hampshire Rep.
Parker's New York Criminal Cas.
Parl.Cas. Parliamentary Cas., H.L. *Eng*.
Parl.Deb. Parliamentary Debates (Cobbett, Hansard)
Pars.Dec. Parson's Dec. (from 2–7 Mass.)
Pars.Eq.Cas. Parson's Select Eq. Cas. (Pa. 1842–51)
Pasc. Paschal or Easter Term
Paschal's Rep. (Supp. to 25, 28–31 Tex.)
Paschal Same as above
Pat.Cas. Reports of Patent, Design

& Trade Mark Cas.
Pat.Dec. Dec., Commissioner of Patents, *U.S.*
Pat.L.Rev. Patent Law Rev.
Pat.Off.Gaz. Official Gazette, U.S. Patent Office
Pat.T.M.&Copy.J. Patent Trademark & Copyright Jour.
Pat.&H. Patton, Jr., & Heath's Rep. (Va. Special Ct. of Appeals)
Pat.&T.M.Rev. Patent & Trademark Rev.
Pater.Ap.Cas. Paterson's Appeal Cas., *Sc.*
Paton App.Cas. Paton's Appeal Cas., *Can.*
Pea. Peake's N.P. Rep., *Eng.*
Pea.Add.Cas. Peake's N.P. Rep. (v.2 of Peake)
Peab.L.Rev. Peabody Law Rev.
Peake N.P. Peake's N.P. Rep., *Eng.*
Pearce C.C. Pearce's (Dearsley's) Crown Cas., *Eng.*
Pears. Pearson's Rep. (Pa.1850–80)
Peck Peck's Rep. (24–30 Ill.)
Peck's Rep. (7 Tenn.)
Peck.El.Cas. Peckwell's Election Cas., *Eng.*
Peeples Peeples' Rep. (78, 79 Ga.)
Peeples & Stevens (80–97 Ga.)
Peere Wms. Peere Williams' Ch. & K.B. Cas., *Eng.*
Pen. Pennington's Rep. (2, 3 N.J. Law)
Pen.N.J. Same as above
Pen.&W. Penrose & Watts' Rep. (Pa. 1829–32)
Penn. Pennsylvania. *See also* Pa.; Pennington's Rep. (2, 3 N.J. Law); Pennypacker's Rep. (Pa. 1881–84)
Penn.B.A.Q. Pennsylvania Bar Association Quarterly
Penn.Co.Ct.Rep. Pennsylvania County Ct. Rep.
Penn.Corp.Rep. Pennsylvania Corporation Reporter
Penn.Del. Pennewill, *Del.*
Penn.L.G. Pennsylvania Legal Gazette
Pennsylvania Legal Gazette Rep. (Campbell)
Pennewill Pennewill's Rep. (17–23 Del.)
Penning. Pennington's Rep. (2, 3 N.J. Law)
Penny. Pennypacker's Rep. (Pa. Unreported, or Colonial Cas.)
Pennyp.Col.Cas. Pennypacker's Colonial Cas.
Penr.&W. Penrose & Watts' Rep. (Pa. 1829–32)
Per.C.S. Perrault's Conseil Supérieur, *Can.*
Per.P. Perrault's Preévosté de Québec
Per.&Dav. Perry & Davison's Q.B. Rep., *Eng.*
Perrault Perrault's Quebec Rep.
Perrault's Conseil Supérieur, *Can.*
Perrault's Prévosté de Québec
Pers. Finance L.Q. Personal Finance Law Quarterly Rep.
Pers.Inj.Comment. Personal Injury Commentator
Pet. Peters; Peters' Admiralty Rep., Dist. Cts., U.S.; Peters' U.S. Sup.Ct. Rep. (26–41 U.S.); Peters' Prince Edward Island Rep.; Peters' Cir. Ct. Rep.
Pet.Ab. Petersdorf's Abridgement
Pet.Br. Bellewe's Cas. *temp.* Henry VIII, *Eng.*
Pet.C.C. Peters' U.S. Sup. Ct. Rep., Dist. Courts, *U.S.*
Pet.S.C. Peters' U.S. Sup. Ct. Rep. (26–41 U.S.)
Peters Adm. Peters' Admiralty Rep., U.S. Dist. Courts, *U.S.*
Petit Br. Brooke's New Cas., 1515–58, *Eng.*
Pheney Rep. Pheney's New Term Rep., *Eng.*
Phi Delta Delta Phi Delta Delta (periodical)
Phil. Phillips' Ch. Rep., *Eng.*
Phillips' Rep. (152–245 Ill.)

Philipps' Rep. (61–64 N.C.)
Philippine Rep.
Phil.El.Cas. Phillips Election Cas., *Eng.*
Phil.Eq. Phillips Rep. (62 N.C. Eq.)
Phil.L.J. Philippine Law Jour.
Phil.L.Rev. Philippine Law Rev.
Phil.Law Phillips' Law Rep. (61 N.C.)
Phil.N.C. Phillips' Law Rep. (61 N.C.)
Phil.St.Tr. Phillipps' State Trials
Phila. Philadelphia, *Pa.*
Philadelphia Rep. (Pa. 1850–91)
Phila.Leg.Int. Philadelphia Legal Intelligence
Phill. *See* Phil.
Phillim. Phillimore Ecclesiastical, *Eng.*
Phillips *See* Phil.
Pick. Pickering's Rep. (18–41 Mass.)
Pickle Pickle's Rep. (85–108 Tenn.)
Pig.&R. Pigott & Rodwell's Registration Cas., *Eng.*
Pike Pike's Rep. (1–5 Ark.)
Pike &F.Adm.Law Pike & Fischer's Administrative Law
Pike &F.Fed.Rules Ser. Pike & Fischer's Federal Rules Service
Pin. Pinney's Rep. (Wis. Reprint)
Pitts.L.J. Pittsburgh Legal Jour.
Pitts.L.Rev. University of Pittsburgh Law Rev.
Pitts.Leg.J.(N.S.) Pittsburgh Legal Jour., New Series
Pitts.Rep. Pittsburgh Rep. (Pa. 1853–73)
Pittsb. *See* Pitts.
Pittsb.Leg.J. Pittsburgh Legal Jour., *Pa.*
Pl. Ang.-Norm. Placita Anglo-Normannica Cas. (Bigelow)
Pl.C. Placita Coronae (Pleas of the Crown), *Eng.*
Plan.&Comp. Planning & Compensation Rep.
Plan. Zoning &E.D. Inst. Planning, Zoning & Eminent Domain Institute
Plow. Plowden's Reports (and Queries), *Eng.*
Pol. Pollexfen's K.B. Rep., *Eng.*
Pol.Sci.Q. Political Science Quarterly
Police L.Q. Police Law Quarterly
Poll. Pollack's Ohio Unreported Judicial Dec. (Prior to 1823)
Pollution Abs. Pollution Abstracts
Pomeroy Pomeroy, *Cal.*
Pop. Popham's K.B. Rep., *Eng.*
Poph. Same as above
Port. Porter's Rep. (Ala. 1834–39)
Porter Same as above
Portia L.J. Portia Law Jour.
Portland U.L.Rev. Portland University Law Rev.
Porto Rico Fed.Rep. Porto Rico Federal Rep.
Posey Unrep.Cas. Texas Unreported Cas. (1879–84)
Post Post's Rep. (23–26 Mich.)
Post's Rep. (42–64 Mo.)
Potter Potter's Rep. (4–7 Wyo.)
Powers Powers' New York Surrogate Ct. Rep.
Pr. Practice Rep. (various jurisdictions)
Price's Ex. Rep., *Eng.*
Pr.Dec. Kentucky Dec. (Sneed, 2 Ky.)
Pr.Div. Law Rep., Probate Div., *Eng.*
Pr.Edw.I. Prince Edward Island Rep.
Pr.Exch. Price's Ex. Rep., *Eng.*
Pr.R. Practice Rep. (various jurisdictions)
Pr.R.Fed. Porto Rico Federal Rep. (*now* Puerto Rico)
Pr.Reg.B.C. Practical Register, Bail Ct., *Eng.*
Pr.Reg.C.P. Practical Register C.P., *Eng.*
Pr.Reg.Ch. Practical Register Ch., *Eng.*
Pr. &Div. Law Rep., Probate &

Divorce, *Eng*.
Pract.Law. Practical Lawyer
Prec.Ch. Precedents in Ch., *Eng*.
Pri. Price's Ex. Rep., *Eng*.
Price Same as above
Price's Mining Commissioner's Cas., *Ont*.
Price Pr.Cas. Price's Notes of Practice Cas., *Ont*.
Prickett Prickett's Rep. (1 Idaho)
Prison L.Rptr. Prison Law Reporter
Priv.C.App. Privy Council Appeals, *Eng*.
Priv.J. Privacy Jour.
Priv.R. Privacy Report
Prob. Law Rep., Probate Div., *Eng*.
Prob.Ct.Rep. Probate Ct. Rep.
Prob.Div. Law Rep., Probate Div., *Eng*.
Prob.Rep. Probate Rep.
Probate Rep., *Ohio*
Prob.&Adm.Div. Law Rep., Probate & Admiralty Div., *Eng*.
Prob.&Div. Law Rep., Probate & Divorce Div., *Eng*.
Prob.&Prop. Probate & Property
Proc. Proclamation
Prop.&Comp. Property & Compensation Rep.
Prouty Prouty's Rep. (61–68 Vt.)
Prt.Rep. Practice Rep.
Psych.&M.L.J. Psychological & Medico-Legal Jour.
Pub.Adm.Rev. Public Administrative Rev.
Pub. Contract L.J. Public Contract Law Jour.
Pub. Employee Rel.Rep. Public Employee Relations Rep.
Pub.L. Public Law
Pub. Land &Res.L.Dig. Public Land & Resources Law Dig.
Pub.Util.Fort. Public Utilities Fortnightly
Pug. Pugsley's Rep. (14–16 New Brunswick)
Pugs.&Bur. Pugsley & Burbridge Rep. (17–20 New Brunswick)
Pugs.&T. Pugsley & Trueman, *New Brunswick*
Pulsifer Pulsifer's Rep. (35–68 Me.)
Py.R. Pyke's Lower Canada Rep., K.B.
Pyke Same as above

Q. Year Books, part IV, *Quebec*
Q.B. Queen's Bench; Adolphus & Ellis' Q.B. Rep., New Series, *Eng*.; Law Rep., Q.B., from 1891, *Eng*.; Q.B. Rep., *Quebec*; Q.B. Rep., *Upper Canada*
Q.B.D. Queen's Bench Div. Law Rep., Q.B. Div., *Eng*.
Q.B.L.C. Queen's Bench Rep., *Lower Canada*
Q.B.R. Queen's Bench Rep. (Adolphus & Ellis, New Series), *Eng*.
Q.B.U.C. Queen's Bench Rep., *Upper Canada*
Q.L.J. Queensland Law Journal and Reports
Q.L.R. Quebec Law Rep.
Queensland Law Reports
Q.R.K.B.(or Q.B.) Quebec King's or Queen's Bench Rep.
Rapports Judiciaires de Québec, Cour du Banc du Roi
Q.R.S.C. Rapports Judiciaires de Québec, Cour Supérieure
Q.S.C.R. Queensland Supreme Court Reports
Q.W.N. Queensland Weekly Notes
Qd. R. Queensland Rep.
Que.K.B. (or Q.B.) Quebec King's or Queen's Rep.
Que.L.R. Quebec Law Rep.
Que.Q.B. or Que.K.B. Quebec Official Reports (Queen's Bench or King's Bench) 1892–1941
Que.Rev.Jud. Quebec Revised Judicial
Que.S.C. Quebec Super. Ct. Rep.
Queb.Pr. Quebec Practice Rep.

Queensl. (or Qd. R.) Queensland Rep.
Queensl.J.P. Queensland Justice of the Peace
Queensl.L. Queensland Law
Queensl.L.J. Queensland Law Jour.
Queensl.S.C.R. Queensland Supreme Ct. Rep.
Queensl.St.Rep. Queensland State Rep.
Queensl.W.N. Queensland Weekly Notes
Quin. Quincy (Mass.) Superior Ct. of Judicature Rep.

R. Rawle's Rep. (Pa. 1828–35)
The Reports (1893–95), *Eng.*
Kentucky Law Reporter (1880–1908)
R.A.C. Ramsay's Appeal Cas., *Can.*
RB Renegotiation Bd.
R.C. Revue Critique de Législation et de Jurisprudence de Canada
Ruling Cas.
R.C.L. Ruling Case Law (encyclopedia)
R.C.&C.R. Revenue, Civil and Criminal Reporter
R.deD. Revue de Droit, *Que.*
R.deJ. Revue de Jurisprudence, *Can.*
R.deL. Revue de Législation et de Jurisprudence, *Can.*
REA Rural Electrification Admin., *U.S.*
R.E.D. Russell's Eq. Dec., *Nova Scotia*
RFC Reconstruction Finance Corp., *U.S.*
R.G. Regulae Generales of Ontario
R.I. Rhode Island
R.I.B.J. Rhode Island Bar Jour.
R.J.Q. Rapports Judiciaires, *Que.*
R.J.R. Quebec Revised Rep. (Mathieu)
R.J.R.Q. Same as above
R.L. Revue Légale, *Can.*
R.L.B. U.S. Railroad Labor Bd. Dec.
R.L.(N.S.) Revue Légale, New Series, *Can.*
R.L.(O.S.) Revue Légale, Old Series, *Can.*
R.L.Q.B. Revue Légale Rep., Q.B., *Can.*
R.L.S.C. Revue Légale Rep., Q.B., *Can.*
R.L.&S. Ridgeway, Lapp & Schoales, K.B., *Ir.*
R.L.&W. Robert, Leaming & Wallis County Ct., *Eng.*
R.M.C.C. Ryan & Moody's Crown Cas., *Eng.*
R.M.Ch. R. M. Charlton's Rep. (Ga. 1811–37)
R.P. Restrictive Trade Practice Rep., *Eng.*
R.P.&W. Rawle, Penrose & Watts' Rep. (Pa. 1828–40)
R.R. Revised Rep., *Eng.*
Pike & Fischer's Radio Regulations
RRB Railroad Retirement Bd., *U.S.*
R.S. Revised Statutes (various jurisdictions); Rolls Series
R.S.C. Revised Statutes of Canada
Rules of the Sup. Ct., *Eng.*
R.*t*.F. Rep., *temp.* Finch, Ch., *Eng.*
R.*t*.H. Rep. *temp.* Hardwicke, *Eng.*
Ridgway's Ch. and K.B. Rep., *temp.* Hardwicke, *Eng.*
R.*t*.Q.A. Rep., *temp.* Queen Anne (11 Modern Rep.), *Eng.*
R.*t*.W. Manitoba Rep. *temp.* Wood
R.1Cro. Croke, Elizabeth
R.2Cro. Croke, James I.
R.3Cro. Croke, Charles I.
R.&C. Russell & Chesley's Nova Scotia Rep.
R.&Can.Cas. Railway & Canal Cas., *Eng.*
R.&Can.Tr. Railway & Canal Traffic Cas., *Eng.*
R.&G. Russell & Geldert's Nova Scotia Rep.
R.&G.N.Sc. Same as above

R.&M. Russell & Mylne's Ch. Rep., *Eng.*
Ryan & Moody's N.P. Rep., *Eng.*
R.&M.C.C. Ryan & Moody's Crown Cas. Res., *Eng.*
R.&M.N.P. Ryan & Moody's N.P. Rep., *Eng.*
R.&My. Russell & Mylne's Ch. Rep., *Eng.*
R.&R. Russell & Ryan's Crown Cas. Res., *Eng.*
R.&R.C.C. Same as above
Race Rel.L.Rep. Race Relations Law Reporter
Race Rel.L.Survey Race Relations Law Survey
Rader Rader's Rep. (138–163 Mo.)
Ram. Ramsey's Quebec Appeal Cas.
Ram.&Mor. Ramsey & Morin's Montreal Law Reporter
Rand Rand, *Ohio*
Rand. Randall's Rep. (62–71 Ohio)
Randolph's Rep. (21–56 Kan.)
Randolph's Rep. (7–11 La.)
Randolph's Rep. (22–27 Va.)
Raney Raney's Rep. (16–20 Fla.)
Raw. Rawle's Rep. (Pa. 1828–35)
Rawle Rawle's Rep. (Pa. 1828–35)
Rawle Pen.&W. Rawle, Penrose & Watts' Rep. (Pa. 1828–40)
Raym.Ent. Lord Raymond's Entries, *Eng.*
Raym.Ld. Lord Raymond's K.B. Rep., *Eng.*
Raym. Sir T. T. Raymond's K.B. Rep., *Eng.*
Raymond Raymond's Rep. (81–99 Iowa)
Re.deL. Revue de Législation et de Jurisprudence, *Montreal*
Real Est.L.Rep. Real Estate Law Report
Real Est.Rev. Real Estate Rev.
Real Prop.Prob. & Trust J. Real Property, Probate & Trust Jour.
Reapp.Dec. Reappraisement Dec., U.S. Treasury
Rec.Dec. Vaux' Recorders Dec. (Pa. 1841–45)
Record of N.Y.C.B.A. Record of the Assn. of the Bar of the City of N.Y.
Red. Redfield's N.Y. Surrogate's Ct. Rep.
Redington's Rep. (31–35 Me.)
Redf. Redfield's N.Y. Surrogate's Ct. Rep.
Redf.Surr. Same as above
Redf.&B. Redfield & Bigelow's Leading Cas., *Eng.*
Redington Redington's Rep. (31–35 Me.)
Reese Reese, Heiskell's, *Tenn.*
Reeve Eng.L. Reeve's English Law
Ref.J. Referees' Jour. (Jour. of National Assn. of Referees in Bankruptcy)
Reg. Daily Register, *N.Y.*
Reg.Deb. Gales & Seaton's Register of Debates in Congress, 1824–37
Rel.&Pub. Order Religion and the Public Order
Remy Remy's Rep. (145–162 Ind.; 15–33 Ind. App.)
Rep. Report or Reports; Reporter
Coke's K.B. Rep. (commonly known as "The Reports"), *Eng.*
Knapp's P.C. Rep., *Eng.*
Rep. Atty. Gen. Attorneys General's Rep., *U.S.*
Rep.Cas.Eq. Gilbert's Ch. Rep., *Eng.*
Rep.Ch. Rep. in Ch. 1615–1710, *Eng.*
Rep.Const.Ct. South Carolina Constitutional Ct. Rep.
Rep.Eq. Gilbert's Rep. in Eq., *Eng.*
Rep.Pat.Cas. Reports of Patents, Designs & Trade-Mark Cas., *Eng.*
Rep.Q.A. Rep., *temp.* Queen Anne (11 Modern Rep.), *Eng.*
Rep.*t.*Finch Finch's Ch. Rep., *Eng.*
Rep.*t.*Hard. Lee's Rep. *temp.* Hardwicke, K.B., *Eng.*

Rep.*t.*Holt Settlement Cas., Rep. *temp*. Holt, *Eng*.
Rep.*t.*O.Br. C.P. Rep. *temp*. O. Bridgman, by Carter, *Eng*.
Rep.*t.*Q.A. Rep., *temp*. Queen Anne (11 Modern Rep.)
Rep.*t.*Talb. Ch. Rep. *temp*. Talbot, *Eng*.
Rep.*t.*Wood Manitoba Rep. *temp*. Wood
Reports Coke's K.B. Rep.
Reprint English Rep., Full Reprint
Res. Resolution
Res. Gamma Eta Gamma Rescript of Gamma Eta Gamma
Res Ipsa Res Ipsa Loquitur
Res.&Eq.Judgm. Reserved & Equity Judgments, *N.S. Wales*
Restric.Prac. Rep. of Restrictive Practices Cas.
Rettie Rettie, Crawford & Melville's Session Cas., *Sc*.
Rev.Crit. Revue, Critique, *Montreal*
Rev.Crit. de Légis. et Jur. Revue Critique de Législation et de Jurisprudence, *Montreal*
Rev. de Jur. Revue de Jurisprudence, *Que*.
Rev. de Leg. Revue de Législation et de Jurisprudence, *Montreal*
Rev. du B. Revue du Barreau de la Province de Québec
Rev. du Dr. Revue du Droit, *Que*.
Rev. du Not. Revue du Notariat, *Que*.
Rev.Gen.Reg. Revised General Regulation, General Accounting Office, *U.S*.
Rev.C.Abo.Pr. Revista de Derecho del Colegio de Abogados de Puerto Rico
Rev.D.P.R. Revista de Derecho Piertorriqueno
Rev.Jur.U.P.R. Revista Jurídica, Universidad de Puerto Rico
Rev.Leg. Revue Légale, *Montreal*
Rev.Rep. Revised Rep. (Reprint), *Eng*.
Rev.Sec.Reg. Rev. of Securities Regulation
Rev.Sel. Code Leg. Rev. of Selected Code Legislation
Rev.Stat. Revised Statutes (various jurisdictions)
Reyn. Reynolds, Miss.
Rice Rice's Rep. (S.C. Law 1838–39)
Rice Eq. Rice's Rep. (S.C. Eq. 1838–39)
Rich. Richardson's Rep. (S.C. Law)
Richardson's Rep. (3–5 N.H.)
Richardson's Rep. (18 U.S. Ct. of Claims)
Rich.C.P. Richardson's Practice, C.P., *Eng*.
Rich.Ch. Richardson's Rep. (S.C. Eq.)
Rich.Ct.Cl. Richardson's Ct. of Claims
Richardson's Rep. (18 U.S. Ct. of Claims)
Rich.Eq. Richardson's Rep. (S.C. Eq.)
Rich. Law Richardson's Rep. (S.C. Law)
Rich.N.H. Richardson's Rep. (3–5 N. H.)
Rich.(N.S.) Richardson's Rep., New Series (S.C. Law and Eq. 1850–68)
Rich.&H. Richardson & Hook's Street Railway Dec.
Rich.&W. Richardson & Woodbury's Rep. (2 N.H.)
Ridg. Ridgeway's Rep. *temp*. Hardwicke, Ch. & K.B., *Eng*.
Ridg.Ap. Ridgeway's Appeals Parliament Cas., *Ir*.
Ridg.Cas. Ridgeway's Rep. *temp*. Hardwicke, Ch. & K.B., *Eng*.
Ridg.*t.*H. Same as above
Ridg.&Hard. Same as above
Ried. Riedell's Rep. (68, 69 N.H.)
Ril. Riley's Rep. (Law & Eq. S.C.)
Riley's Rep. (37–42 W. Va.)
Ril.Harp. Harper's Rep., ed. Riley (S.C. Law and Eq.)

Rin. Riner's Rep. (2 Wyo.)
Ritch.Eq.Rep. Ritchie's Eq. Rep., *Nova Scotia*
Ro. Rolle's Abridgement
Rob. Robards's Rep. (12, 13 Mo.); Roberts' Rep. (29–31 La.); Robertson's Rep. (1 Hawaii); Robertson's Marine Ct., *N.Y.* Robinson's Admiralty Rep., *Eng*.; Robinson's Rep. (38 Cal.); Robinson's Rep. (2–9, 17–23 Colo. App.); Robinson's Rep. (1–4 La.; Sup. Ct. La. 1841–46); Robinson's Rep. (1 Nev.); Robinson's Rep. (40, 41 Va.); Robinson's Rep. (1–8 Ontario); Robinson's Upper Canada Rep.
Rob.Adm. Robinson's Admiralty Rep., *Eng*.
Rob.Cal. Robinson's Rep. (38 Cal.)
Rob.Chr. Chr. Robinson's Admiralty Rep., *Eng*.
Rob.Colo. Robinson's Rep. (2–9, 17–23 Colo. App.)
Rob.Consc.Cas. Robards' Conscript Cas., *Tex*.
Rob. Eccl. Robertson's Ecclesiastical, *Eng*.
Rob. Hawaii Robinson's Rep. (1 Hawaii)
Rob.Jun. Wm. Robinson's Admiralty Rep., *Eng*.
Rob.La. Robinson's Rep. (1–4 La.; La. Sup. Ct. 1841–46)
Rob.Mo. Robard's Rep. (12, 13 Mo.)
Rob.N.Y. Robertson's Rep. (24–30 N.Y. Sup. Ct.)
Rob.Nev. Robinson's Rep. (1 Nev.)
Rob.Ont. Robinson's Rep. (1–8 Ont.)
Rob.Super.Ct. Robertson's (24–30 N.Y. Super. Ct.)
Rob.U.C. Robinson's Rep., *Upper Can*.
Rob.Va. Robinson's Rep. (40, 41 Va.)
Rob.Wm.Adm. Wm. Robinson's Admiralty Rep., *Eng*.
Rob.&J. Robard's & Jackson's Rep. (26, 27 Tex.)
Robertson & Jacob's Marine Ct., *N.Y.*
Rob.L.&W. Roberts, Leaming & Wallis' County Ct. Rep., *Eng*.
Robards Robards' Conscript Cas. (Tex. 1862–65)
Robards Rep. (12, 13 Mo.)
Robards & Jackson (26, 27 Texas Rep.)
Robb. Robbins' Rep. (67–70 N.J. Eq.)
Robert.App.Cas. Robertson's Appeal Cas., *Sc*.
Roberts Roberts' Rep. (29–31 La.)
Robertson *See also* Rob.; Robertson's Rep., *Hawaii;* Robertson's Rep., N.Y. Marine Ct.; Robertson's Rep. (24–30 N.Y.)
Robertson's Rep. (24–30 N.Y. Super. Ct.)
Robin.App.Cas. Robinson's Appeal Cas. (H.L.), *Sc*.
Robinson Chr. Robinson's Admiralty Rep.; W. Robinson's Admiralty Rep., *Eng*.; Robinson's Rep. (38 Cal.); Robinson's Rep. (17–23 Colo.); Robinson's Rep. (La. 1841–46); Robinson's Rep. (1 Nev.); Chr. Robinson's Rep., *Ontario;* J. L. Robinson's Upper Canada Rep.; Robinson's Rep. (40–41 Va.)
Robt. *See* Robertson
Rocky Mt.L.Rev. Rocky Mountain Law Rev.
Rocky Mt.Min.L.Inst. Rocky Mountain Mineral Law Institute
Rocky Mt.Miner.L.Rev. Rocky Mountain Mineral Law Rev.
Rodm. Rodman (78–82 Ky.)
Rog.C.H.R. Rogers' City Hall Recorder (N.Y. 1816–22)
Rog.Rec. Rogers' New City Hall Recorder
Rogers Rogers' Rep. (47–51 La.)
Rol. Rolle's Abridgement, *Eng*.
Rolle's K.B. Rep., *Eng*.

Roll.Rep. Same as above
Rolle Same as above
Rolle Abr. Rolle's Abridgement, *Eng*.
Rolls Ct.Rep. Rolls Ct. Rep.
Rom.Cas. Romilly's Notes of Chancery Cas., *Eng*.
Root Root, *Conn*.; Root's Rep. (Conn. 1774–89)
Rose Rose Bankruptcy, *Eng*.
Rose's Notes Rose's Notes on U.S. Rep.
Ross Lead.Cas. Ross Leading Cas., *Eng*.
Rot.Chart. Rotulus Chartarum (The Charter Roll)
Rot.Claus. Rotuli Clause (The Close Roll)
Rot.Parl. Rotuli Parliamentarum
Rot.Pat. Rotuli Patenes
Rot.Plac. Rotuli Placitorum
Rotuli Curiae Reg. Rotuli Curiae Regis, *Eng*.
Rowe Rowe's Rep., *Eng*.; Rowe, Parliament & Military Cas., *Eng*.
Rowe's Rep. Rowe's Rep., *Eng*.
Rowell Rowell's Rep. (45–52 Vt.)
Rowell El.Cas. Rowell Election Cas., *U.S*.
Rucker Rucker's Rep. (43–46 W. Va.)
Ruff. Statutes at Large, Ruffhead's Ed., *Eng*.
Ruffin & Hawks' Rep. (8 N.C.)
Ruff.&H. Ruffin & Hawks' Rep. (8 N.C.)
Runn. Runnell's Rep. (38–56 Iowa)
Runnell Runnell's Rep. (38–56 Iowa)
Rus. *See* Russ
Russell's Election Cas., *Nova Scotia*
Russ. Russell's Ch. Rep., *Eng*.
Russ.El.Cas. Russell's Election Rep., *Can*.
Russell's Election Cas., *Mass*.
Russ.Eq.Cas. Russell's Equity Cas., New Series
Russ.*t*.Eld. Russell's Ch. Cas. *temp*. Eldon, *Eng*.
Russ.&Geld. Russell & Geldert
Russ.&M. Russell & Mylne's Ch. Rep., *Eng*.
Russ.&Ry. Russell & Ryan's Crown Cas. Res., *Eng*.
Russell Russell's Ch., *Eng*.
Russell (N.S.) Russell's Nova Scotia Eq. Dec.
Rutg.L.Rev. Rutgers Law Rev.
Rutgers J. Computers & Law Rutgers Jour. of Computers and the Law
Rutgers-Camden L.J. Rutgers-Camden Law Jour.
Ry.&M. Ryan & Moody's N.P. Rep.
Ry.&M.N.P. Same as above
Ry.M.C.C. Ryan & Moody Crown Cas., *Eng*.
Ryde Ryde's Rating Appeals, *Eng*.

S. Senate Bill; New York Supplement; Quebec Sup. Ct. Rep.; Shaw, Dunlop & Bell, *Sc*.; Shaw's Appeal Cas., H.L., *Sc*.; Southern Reporter
S.Afr.L.J. South African Law Jour.
S.Afr.L.R. South African Law Rep.
S.Afr.L.R.App. South African Law Rep. Appellate
S.Afr. Tax South African Tax Cas.
S.Aust.L. South Australian Law
S.Austl. South Australia State Rep.
S.Austl.L.R. South Australia Law Rep.
S.C. Same Case; Ct. of Session Cas., *Sc*.; Superior Ct.; Supreme Ct.; South Carolina; Supreme Ct. Reporter
S.C.D.C. Supreme Ct. Rep., *District of Columbia*
S.C.D.C.(N.S.) Same as above, New Series
S.C.Eq. South Carolina Eq. Rep.
S.C.L. South Carolina Law Rep.
S.C.L.Q. South Carolina Law Quarterly
S.C.L.Rev. South Carolina Law Rev.

S.C.R. Canada Sup. Ct. Rep; Canada Law Rep.; Sup. Ct. South Carolina Rep.; Sup. Ct. Rep., Canada (1876–1922)
S.Car. South Carolina
S.Con.Res. Senate Concurrent Resolution
S.Ct. Supreme Ct.; Supreme Ct. Reporter
S.Ct.Rev. Supreme Ct. Rev.
S.D. South Dakota
S.D.L.Rev. South Dakota Law Rev.
S.D.St.B.J. South Dakota State Bar Jour.
S.D.B.Jo. South Dakota Bar Jour.
S.D.R. New York State Dept. Rep.
S.Dak. South Dakota
S.Doc. Senate Document
S.E. South Eastern Reporter
S.E.2d Same as above, Second Series
S.E.C. Securities and Exchange Comm., *U.S.*
S.E.C.Jud.Dec. Securities & Exchange Comm. Judicial Dec. 1937–39, *U.S.*
S.F.L.J. San Francisco Law Jour.
S.J. Solicitors' Jour.
S.J.Res. Senate Joint Resolution
S.L.C. Stuart's Appeal Cas., *Lower Can.*
S.L.R. Saskatchewan Law Rep.; Scottish Law Reporter; Scots Law Rev.; Southern Law Rev.
S.L.R.B. State Labor Relations
S.L.T. Scots Law Times; Scots Law Times Rep.
S.M. Solicitor's Memorandum, Internal Revenue Service, *U.S.*
S.R. Solicitor's Recommendation Internal Revenue Service, *U.S.*; New York State Reporter; Supreme Ct. of Quebec Rep.
S.R.C. Stuart's Lower Canada Rep.
S.R.&O. Statutory Rules & Orders, *Eng.*
S.Rept. Senate Report
S.Res. Senate Resolution
S.S. Silvernail's N.Y. Sup. Ct. Rep. Synopsis Series, U.S. Treasury Dec.
S.S.C. Sandford's Super. Ct. Rep., *New York City*
S.S.R. Social Security Tax Ruling, Internal Revenue Service, *U.S.*
S.T. Sales Tax Div., Internal Revenue Service
S.T.C. State Tax Cas. (CCH)
S.T.D. Synopsis Dec., U.S. Treasury
S.T.L.J. Southern Tex. Law Jour.
S.Tex.L.J. South Texas Law Jour.
S.W. South Western Reporter
S.W.2d Same as above, Second Series
S.W.L.J. South Western Law Jour. (Nashville)
S.W.L.Rev. Southwestern Law Rev.
S.&B. Smith & Batty's K.B., *Ir.*
S.&C. Saunders & Cole's Bail Ct., *Eng.*
Swan & Critchfield, Rev. Stat., *Ohio*
S.&D. Shaw, Dunlop & Bell's 1st Series, *Sc.*
S.&G. Smale & Giffard's Vice-Ch. Rep., *Eng.*
S.&L. Schoales & Lefroy's Ch., *Ir.*
S.&M. Shaw & Maclean's H.L. Cas., *Eng.*
Smedes & Marshall's Rep. (9–22 Miss.)
S.&M.Ch. Same as above
S.&Mar. Smedes & Marshall's Rep. (9–22 *Miss.*)
S.&R. Sergeant & Rawles' Rep. (Pa. 1824–28)
S.&S. Sausse & Scully's Rolls Ct., *Ir.*
Simons & Stuart's Vice-Ch. Rep., *Eng.*
Sad.Pa.Cas. Sadley's Cas. (Pa. 1885–88)
Sadler Sadler's Cas., *Pa.*
St. John's L.Rev. St. John's Law Rev.

St. Louis L.Rev. St. Louis Law Rev.
St. Louis U.L.J. St. Louis University Law Jour.
St. Mary's L.J. St. Mary's Law Jour.
Sal. Salinger's Rep. (88–117 Iowa)
Salk. Salkeld's K.B. Rep., *Eng.*
San. Sandford's Rep. (59 Ala.)
San Diego L.Rev. San Diego Law Rev.
San Fran.L.J. San Francisco Law Jour.
Sand. Sandford's Rep. (3–7 N.Y. Super. Ct.)
Sand.Ch. Sandford's Rep. (N.Y. Ch. 1843–47)
Sand I. Rep. Sandwich Islands (Hawaiian) Rep.
Sandf. Sandford's Rep. (3–7 N.Y. Super. Ct.)
Sandf.Ch. Sandford's Rep. (N.Y. Ch.)
Sanf. Sanford's Rep. (59 Ala.)
Santa Clara Law. Santa Clara Lawyer
Sar.Ch.Sen. Saratoga Ch. Sentinel
Sask. Saskatchewan
Sask.L.R. Saskatchewan Law Rep.
Sask.L.Rev. Saskatchewan Law Rev.
Sau.&Sc. Sausse & Scully, Rolls Ct., *Ir.*
Sauls. Rep. time of Saulsbury (5, 6 Del.)
Saund. Saunders' K.B. Rep., *Eng.*
Saund. & Cole Saunders & Cole, Bail Ct., *Eng.*
Sav. Savile's C.P. Rep., *Eng.*
Saw. Sawyer's Cir. Ct. Rep., *U.S.*
Sax. Saxton's Rep. (1 N.J. Eq.)
Say. Sayer's K.B. Rep., *Eng.*
Sc. Scammon's Rep. (2–5 Ill.)
Sc.Jur. Scottish Jurist
Sc.L.T. Scots Law Times
Sc.N.R. Scott's New Rep., C.P., *Eng.*
Sc.Sess.Cas. Scotch Ct. of Session Cas.
Scam. Scammon's Rep. (2–5 Ill.)
Scher. Sherer's Rep. (22–47 N.Y. Miscellaneous)
Schm.L.J. Schmidt's Law Jour.
Schuyl.Leg.Rec. Schuylkill Legal Record, *Pa.*
Sch.&Lef. Schoales & Lefroy, Eq., *Eng.*
Sco. Scott's C.P. Rep., *Eng.*
Sco.N.R. Scott's New Rep., C.P., *Eng.*
Scot. Scotland; Scots; Scottish
Scot.Jur. Scottish Jurist
Scot.L.J. Scottish Law Jour.
Scot.L.M. Scottish Law Magazine
Scot.L.Rep. Scottish Law Rep.
Scot.L.Rev. Scottish Law Rev.
Scot.L.T. Scots Law Times
Scots L.T.R Scots Law Times Rep.
Scott Scott's C.P. Rep., *Eng.* Scott's Rep. (25, 26 N.Y. Civil Procedure)
Scott N.R. Scott's New C.P. Rep., *Eng.*
Scr.L.T. Scranton (Pa.) Law Times
Search & Seizure Search and Seizure Bulletin
Sea.&Sm. Searle & Smith's Probate and Divorce Rep., *Eng.*
Searle &Sm. Same as above
Sec.&Ex.C. Securities and Exchange Comm., *U.S.*
Sec.L.Rev. Securities Law Rev.
Sec.Reg.&Trans. Securities Regulation and Transfer Rep.
Sec.Reg.L.J. Securities Regulation Law Journ.
Seign.Rep. Lower Canada Seigniorial Rep.
Sel.Cas.Ch. Select Cases in Ch., *Eng.*
Sel.Cas.N.Y. Yates' Select Cas., *N.Y.*
Sel.Serv.L.Rptr. Selective Service Law Reporter
Seld. Selden's Notes, *N.Y.* Selden's Rep. (5–10 N.Y.)
Seld.Soc Selden Society
Selden *See* Seld.

Selw.N.P. Selwyn's N.P., *Eng.*
Selw.&Barn. Barnewall & Alderson's K.B. Rep., 1st part, *Eng.*
Sen.Doc. Senate Document
Sen.Jo. Senate Jour.
Sen.Rep. Senate Report
Serg.&Lowb. English Common Law Rep., ed. Sergeant and Lowber
Serg.&Rawl. Sergeant & Rawle's Rep. (Pa. 1814–28)
Sess.Cas. Sessions Cas., K.B., *Eng.*;
Ct. of Session Cas., *Sc.*
Seton Hall L.Rev. Seton Hall Law Rev.
Sex.L.R. Sexual Law Reporter
Sex Prob.Ct.Dig. Sex Problems Ct. Digest
Sh. Shand's Rep. (11–41 S.C.); G. B. Shaw's Rep. (10, 11 Vt.); W. G. Shaw's Rep. (30–35 Vt.); Sheldon's Rep. (Buffalo, N.Y., Super. Ct.); Shepherd's Ala. Rep.; Shepley's Rep. (13–18, 21–30 Me.); Shipp's Rep. (66, 67 N.C.); Shirley's Rep. (49–55 N.H.); Shower's K.B. Rep., *Eng.*
Shad. Shadford's Victoria Rep.
Shan. Shannon's Unreported Cas., *Tenn.*
Shand Shand's Rep. (11–41 N.C.)
Shaw G. B. Shaw's Rep. (10, 11 Vt.); W. G. Shaw's Rep. (30–35 Vt.); Shaw Appeal Cas., English H.L. from Scotland; Shaw, Scotch Justiciary Cas.; Shaw, Scotch Teind Rep. Ct. of Session
Shaw (Vt.) G. B. Shaw's Rep. (10, 11 Vt.)
W. G. Shaw's Rep. (30–35 Vt.)
Shaw (W.G.) W.G. Shaw's Rep. (30–35 Vt.)
Shaw App. Shaw Appeal Cas., *Sc.*
Shaw Crim.Cas. Shaw's Criminal Cas., Justiciary Ct., *Sc.*
Shaw, D.&B. Shaw, Dunlop, & Bell's Ct. of Session, 1st series, *Sc.*
Shaw, Dunlop & Bell's Session Cas., *Sc.*
Shaw, D.&B.Supp. Shaw, Dunlop & Bell's Supplement, H.L. Dec., *Sc.*
Shaw Dec. Shaw's Dec. in Scotch Ct. of Session
Shaw &D. Shaw & Dunlop, *Sc.*
Shaw & Dunl. Same as above
Shaw &M. Shaw & MacLean Appeals, H.L., *Sc.*
Shaw &MacL. Same as above
Shaw, Dunl.&B. Shaw, Dunlop & Bell's Session Cas., *Sc.*
Shaw, W.&C. Shaw, Wilson & Courtnay, H.L.
Sheld. Sheldon's Rep. (Buffalo, N.Y., Super. Ct.)
Shep. Shepherd's Rep., *Ala.*
Select Cas. (in 37–39 Ala.)
Shepley's Rep. (13–18, 21–30 Me.)
Shep.Abr. Sheppard's Abridgement
Shep.Touch. Sheppard's Touchstone, *Eng.*
Shepley Shepley's Rep. (13–18, 21–30 Me.)
Sher.Ct.Rep. Sheriff Ct. Rep., *Sc.*
Shingle The Shingle, Philadelphia Bar Association
Shipp. Shipp's Rep. (66–67 N.C.)
Shirl.L.C. Shirley's Leading Crown Cas., *Eng.*
Shirley. Shirley's Rep. (49–55 N.H.)
Show. Shower's K.B. Rep., *Eng.*
Show.K.B. Shower's K.B. Rep., *Eng.*
Show.P.C. Shower's Parliamentary Cas., *Eng.*
Sick. Sickel's Ct. of Appeals, *Eng.*
Sickels' Rep. (46–85 N.Y.)
Sick.Min.Dec. Sickels' U.S. Mining Laws and Dec.
Sid. Siderfin's K.B., C.P. and Ex. Rep.
Sil. Silver Tax Div., I.R. Bulletin

Silv. Silvernail's Rep. (N.Y. 1886–92)
Silvernail's Rep. (9–14 N.Y. Crim. Rep.)
Silvernail's Sup. Ct. Rep. (N.Y. 1889–90)
Silv.A. Silvernail's Appeals, *N.Y.*
Silv.Unrep. Silvernail's Unreported Cas., *N.Y.*
Sim. Simmons' Rep. (99 Wis.)
Simons' Ch. Rep., *Eng.*
Sim.(N.S.) Simons' Ch. Rep., New Series, *Eng.*
Sim.&C. Simmons & Conover's Rep. (99–100 Wis.)
Sim.&St. Simons & Stuart's Ch. Rep., *Eng.*
Sir J.S. Sir John Strange's Rep., *Eng.*
Sir T.J. Sir Thomas Jones' Rep., K.B. and C.P., *Eng.*
Sir T. Ray. T. Raymond's K.B. Rep., *Eng.*
Skill.Pol.Rep. Skillman's N.Y. Police Rep.
Skin. Skinner's K.B. Rep., *Eng.*
Skinker Skinker's Rep. (65–79 Mo.)
Slade Slade's Rep. (15 Vt.)
Sloan Leg.Reg. Sloan's Legal Register, *N.Y.*
Sm. Smith
Sm. C.C.M. Smith's Cir. Courts-Martial Rep., Me., *U.S.*
Sm.Cond.Ala. Smith's Condensed Ala. Rep.
Sm.E.D. E.D. Smith's C.P. Rep., *N.Y.*
Sm.Eng. Smith's K.B. Rep., *Eng.*
Sm.Ind. Smith's Rep. (1–4 Ind.)
Sm.K.B. Smith's K.B. Rep., *Eng.*
Sm.Me. Smith's Rep. (61–84 Me.)
Sm.&G. Smale & Giffard's Ch. Rep., *Eng.*
Smith & Guthrie's Rep. (81–101 Mo. App.)
Sm.&M. Smedes & Marshall's Rep. (Miss. Ch. 1840–45)
Smedes & Marshall's Rep. (9–22 Miss.)
Sm.&M.Ch. Same as above
Smed.&M. Smedes & Marshall's Miss. Ch. Rep.
Smith J. P. Smith's K.B. Rep., *Eng.*; Smith's Rep. (54–62 Cal.); Smith, E. B. (21–47 Ill.); Smith's Rep. (1–4 Ind.); Smith's Rep. (61–64 Me.); Smith's Rep. (81–101 Mo. App.); Smith's Rep. (N.H. 1796–1816); E. D. Smith's Rep. (N.Y. C.P.); E. H. Smith (147–162 N.Y.); E. P. Smith's Rep. (15–27 N.Y.) (47–62 N.Y.); Smith's Rep. (51–81 Pa.); Smith's Rep. (2–4 S.D.); Smith's Rep. (1–11 Wis.); Smith's Rept. (7, 12 Tenn.)
Smith C.C.M. Smith Circuit Courts-Martial, *Me.*
Smith Cond. Smith's Condensed Ala. Rep.
Smith E.D. E. D. Smith's Rep. (N.Y. C.P.)
Smith J.P. J. P. Smith's K.B. Rep., *Eng.*
Smith K.B. Same as above
Smith L.J. Smith's Law Jour.
Smith Lead.Cas., Smith's Leading Cas., *Eng.*
Smith Me. Smith's Rep. (61–64 Me.)
Smith N.H. Smith's Rep. (N.H. 1796–1816)
Smith N.Y. E. P. Smith's Rep. (15, 27, 47–62 N.Y.)
Smith P.F. P. F. Smith's Rep. (51–81 Pa.)
Smith Reg.Cas. Smith's Registration Cas., *Eng.*
Smith Wis. Smith's Rep. (1–11 Wis.)
Smith &B. Smith & Batty, K.B., *Ir.*
Smith &B.R.C. Smith & Bates, American Railway Cas.
Smith &G. Smith & Guthrie's Rep. (81–101 Mo. App.)
Smith &H. Smith & Heiskell (1–11 Tenn.)

Smy. Smythe C.P., *Ir.*
Sneed Sneed's Ky. Dec. (2 Ky.)
Sneed's Rep. (33–37 Tenn.)
Sneed Dec. Sneed's Ky. Dec. (2 Ky.)
Snow Snow's Rep. (3 Utah)
So. Southern Reporter
So.2d Same as above, Second Series
So.Calif.L.Rev. Southern California Law Rev.
So.Car. South Carolina
So.Car.Const. South Carolina Constitutional Rep. by Treadway, Mill, or Harper
So.Car.L.J. South Carolina Law Jour.
So.East.Rep. South Eastern Reporter
So.L.J. Southern Law Jour.
So.L.Q. Southern Law Quarterly
So.L.Rev. Southern Law Rev., *Tenn.*
Southern Law Rev., *Mo.*
So.L.Rev.(N.S.) Southern Law Rev., New Series, *Mo.*
So. Law. Southern Lawyer
So. Law T. Southern Law Times
So.Rep. Southern Reporter
So.Tex.L.J. South Texas Law Jour.
So.U.L.Rev. Southern University Law Rev.
So.West.Rep. South Western Reporter
Sol. The Solicitor
Sol.J. Solicitors' Jour.
Sol.Op. Solicitors' Opinion
Som.L.J. Somerset Legal Jour. (Pa. 1920–date)
South. Southern Reporter
Southard Southard's Rep. (4–5 N.J. Law)
Southwestern L.J. Southwestern Law Jour.
Sp. Spear's Rep. (S.C. Law 1842–44)
Sp.C.M. Special Court-Martial (U.S. Navy)
Sp.Eq. Spear's Rep. (S.C. Eq.)
Spaulding Spaulding Rep. (71–80 Me.)
Spears Spears' Rep. (S.C. Law of Equity)
Spears Eq. Spears' Rep. (S.C. Eq.)
Speers *See* Spears
Spencer Spencer's Rep. (10–20 Minn.)
Spencer's Rep. (20 N.J. Law)
Spinks Spinks Ecclesiastical and Admiralty Rep., *Eng.*
Spinks Eccl.&Adm. Same as above
Spooner Spooner's Rep. (12–15 Wis.)
Spottis. Spottiswoode, *Sc.*
Spottis. C.L.&Eq. Spottiswoode's Common Law and Eq. Rep., *Eng.*
Spottis.Eq. Spottiswoode's Eq., *Sc.*
Spr. Sprague's Dist. Ct. and Admiralty Dec., *U.S.*
St. Story's Cir. Ct. Rep., *U.S.*
St.Ab. Statham's Abridgement, *Eng.*
St.Ch.Cas. Star Chamber Cas., *Eng.*
St.Inst. Statutory Instruments, Eng.
St.P. State Papers
St.Pl.Cr. Staundford's Pleas of Crown, *Eng.*
St.Rep. State Reports
St.Rep.N.S.W. State Reports, *New So. Wales*
St.Tr. Howell's State Trials
Stafford Stafford's Rep. (69–71 Vt.)
Stair Stair, *Sc.*
Stan.J.Int'lStud. Stanford Jour. of International Studies
Stan.L. Rev. Stanford Law Rev.
Stan.Pa.Prac. Standard Pennsylvania Practice
Stanford Staundford's Pleas of the Crown, *Eng.*
Stanton Stanton's Rep. (11–13 Ohio)
Star. Starkie's N.P. Rep., *Eng.*

Star Ch.Ca. Star Chamber Cas., *Eng.*
Stark. Starkie's N.P. Rep., *Eng.*
Stark.N.P. Same as above
Stat. Statutes; Statutes at Large; Statutes Revised
Stat. at L. Statutes at Large
Stat. Realm Statutes of the Realm, *Eng.*
State Gov't. State Government
State Tr. State Trials (Howell), *Eng.*
State Tr. (N.S.) State Trials, New Series, ed. Macdonell, *Eng.*
Stath.Abr. Statham's Abridgement
Staund.Pl. Staundford's Pleas of the Crown, *Eng.*
Staundforde Same as above
Stevens &G. Stevens & Graham's Rep. (98–139 Ga.)
Stew. Stewart's Rep. (Ala. 1827–31)
Stewart's Rep. (28–45 N.J. Eq.)
Stewart's Rep. (1–10 S.D.)
Stew.Adm. Stewart's Nova Scotia Admiralty Rep.
Stew.Eq. Stewart's Rep. (28–45 N.J. Eq.)
Stew.N.Sc. Stewart's Nova Scotia Admiralty Rep.
Stew.V.A. Same as above
Stew.&P. Stewart & Porter's Rep. (Ala. 1831–34)
Stewart *See* Stew.
Stiles Stiles Rep. (22–29 Iowa)
Still.Eccl.Cas. Stillingfleet's Ecclesiastical Cas., *Eng.*
Stiness Stiness' Rep. (20–34 R.I.)
Sto. Story's Cir. Ct. Rep., *U.S.*
Sto.C.C. Same as above
Stock.Adm. Stockton's Vice-Admiralty Rep., *Can.*
Stockton's Rep. (9–11 N.J. Eq.)
Stockton's New Brunswick Rep.
Stockett Stockett's Rep. (27–79 Md.)
Stockt.Ch. Stockton's Rep. (9–11 N.J. Eq.)
Story Story's Cir. Ct. Rep., *U.S.*
Story Eq.Jur. Story on Equity Jurisprudence
Str. Strange's K.B. Rep., *Eng.*
Stra. Strange; *see* Str.
Strahan Strahan's Rep. (19 Ore.)
Stran. Strange; *see* Str.
Strange *See* Str.
Stratton Stratton's Rep. (12–14, 19 Ore.)
Stringfellow Stringfellow's Rep. (9–11 Mo. App.)
Strob. Strobhart's Rep. (S.C. Law)
Strob.Eq. Strobhart's Rep. (S.C. Eq.)
Struve Struve's Rep. (Washington Territory 1854–88)
Stuart Stuart's Lower Canada K.B. Rep.
Stuart K.B. Same as above
Stuart Vice-Adm. Stuart's Vice-Admiralty, *Lower Canada*
Student Law. Student Lawyer
Student Law.J. Student Lawyer Jour.
Stu.M.&P. Stuart, Milne & Peddie, *Sc.*
Sty. Style's K.B. Rep., *Eng.*
Suffolk U.L.Rev. Suffolk University Law Rev.
Sum. Sumner's Cir. Ct. Rep., *U.S.*
Summerfield Summerfield's Rep. (21 Nev.)
Sumn. Sumner's Cir. Ct. Rep., *U.S.*
Sup.Ct. Supreme Court; Supreme Court Reporter
Super. Superior Court
Super.Ct.Rep. Superior Court Rep. (N.Y., Pa., etc.)
Supp.Ves.Jun. Supplement to Vesey, Junior Rep.
Susq.L.C. Susquehanna Law Chronicle, *Pa.*
Sw. Swabey's Admiralty Rep., *Eng.*
Swan's Rep. (31, 32 Tenn.)
Swanston's Ch. Rep., *Eng.*
Sweeney's N.Y. Super. Ct. Rep.

Sw.L.J. Southwestern Law Jour.
Sw.U.L.Rev. Southwestern University Law Rev.
Sw.&Tr. Swabey & Tristram's Probate and Divorce Rep., *Eng.*
Swab. Swabey's Admiralty Rep., *Eng.*
Swan. Swan's Rep. (31, 32 Tenn.)
Swanston's Ch. Rep., *Eng.*
Swan.Ch. Swanston's Ch. Rep., *Eng.*
Swans. Same as above
Sween. Sweeny's N.Y. Super. Ct. Rep.
Swin. Swinton's Registration Appeal Cas., *Sc.*
Sydney L.Rev. Sydney Law Rev.
Syl. The Syllabi (legal periodical)
Syme Syme's Justiciary Cas., *Sc.*
Syn.Ser. Synopsis Series, Treasury Dec., *U.S.*
Syracuse L.Rev. Syracuse Law Rev.

T. Tappan's C.P. Rep., Ohio
Tobacco Div. (I.R. Bull.)
T.B.M. Advisory Tax. Bd. Memorandum (U.S. Internal Revenue Service)
T.B.Mon. T. B. Monroe's Rep. (17–23 Ky.)
T.B.R. Advisory Tax Bd. Recommendation (U.S. Internal Revenue Service)
T.B.&M. Tracewell, Bowers & Mitchell, Comptroller's Dec., *U.S.*
T.C. Tax Ct. of the U.S.; Trade Cas. (CCH); U.S. Trusteeship Council
TCM Tax Ct. Memorandum Dec. (CCH)
T.C.Memo. Tax Ct. Memorandum Dec. (P–H)
T.D. Treasury Dec. (U. S. Treasury Dept.)
T.I.A.S. Treaties and Other International Acts
T.Jo. T. Jones' K.B. and C.P. Rep., *Eng.*
T.L.R. Times Law Rep., *Eng.*
T.M.Bull. Trade Mark Bulletin, New Series
T.M.M. Tax Management Memorandum (BNA)
T.M.Rep. Trade Mark Reporter
T.N.E.C. Temporary National Economic Committee
T.R. Term Rep. (Durnford & East), *Eng.*
Caine's Term Rep., *N.Y.*
T.R.(N.S.) Term Rep., New Series (East), *Eng.*
T.Raym. T. Raymond's K.B. Rep., *Eng.*
T.S. Treaty Series, *U.S.*
T.U.P.Charlt. T. U. P. Charlton, *Ga.*
Tait Tait's Manuscript Dec., *Sc.*
TVA Tennessee Valley Authority
T.&G. Tyrwhitt's & Granger's Ex. Rep., *Eng.*
T.&M. Temple & Mew's Crim. Appeal Cas., *Eng.*
Temple & Mew's Crown Cas., *Eng.*
T.&P. Turner & Phillips' Ch., *Eng.*
T.&R. Turner & Phillips' Ch. Rep., *Eng.*
Tal. Chancery Cas. *temp.* Talbot, *Eng.*
Tamlyn Tamlyn's Ch., *Eng.*
Tam. Tamlyn's Rolls Ct. Rep., *Eng.*
Tan. Taney's Cir. Ct. Rep., *U.S.*
Tanner Tanner's Rep. (8–14 Ind.)
Tanner's Rep. (13–17 Utah)
Tapp. Tappan's Ohio C.P. Rep.
Tas.L.R. Tasmania Law Rep., *Aus.*
Tas.S.R. Tasmanian State Rep., *Aus.*
Tas.U.L.R. Tasmania University Law Rev., *Aus.*
Taun. Taunton's C.P. Rep., *Eng.*
Tax A.B.C. Canada Tax Appeal Bd. Cas.
Tax. Acct. Taxation for Accountants
Tax Adm'rs News Tax Administrators News

Tax Advisor The Tax Advisor
Tax Cas. Tax Cas., *Eng*.
Tax Coun.Q. Tax Counselor's Quarterly
Tax Exec. Tax Executive
Tax L.Rep. Tax Law Reporter
Tax L. Rev. Tax Law Rev.
Tax Law. The Tax Lawyer
Tax Mag. Tax Magazine
Tax Man. Tax Management
Tax.R. Taxation Rep.
Taxes Taxes, The Tax Magazine
Tay. Taylor; Taylor's K.B. Rep., *Can*.
Taylor's Rep. (1 N.C.)
Tay.J.L. J.L. Taylor's Rep. (1 N.C.)
Tay.N.C. Same as above
Tayl.N.C. Taylor's Rep. (1 N.C.)
Taylor Taylor's K.B. Rep., *Can*.
Taylor's Rep. (1 N.C.)
Temp.L.Q. Temple Law Quarterly
Temp. Wood Manitoba Rep. *temp*. Wood
Temp.&M. Temple & Mew's Crown Cas., *Eng*.
Temp. Geo. II Cas. in Ch. *temp*. Geo. II., *Eng*.
Tenn. Tennessee
Tenn.App. Tennessee Appeals; Tennessee Appellate Bulletin; Tennessee Civil Appeals Rep.
Tenn.C.C.A. Tennessee Ct. of Civil Appeals
Tenn.Cas. Shannon's Unreported Cas. (Tenn. 1847–94)
Tenn.Ch. Tennessee Ch. Rep. (Cooper)
Tenn.Ch.App. Tennessee Ch. Appeals (Wright)
Tenn.L.Rev. Tennessee Law Rev.
Tenn.Leg.Rep. Tennessee Legal Reporter
Term. Term Rep. (Durnford & East K.B.), *Eng*.
Term N.C. Term Rep. (Taylor, 4 N.C.)
Term Rep. Term Rep. (Durnford & East), *Eng*.
Terr. Terrell's Rep. (52–71 Tex.)
Terr.L.R. Territories Law Rep., *Can*.
Terr.&Walk. Terrell & Walker's Rep. (38–51 Tex.)
Tex. Texas
Tex.A.Civ.Cas. White & Wilson's Civil Cas., *Tex*.
Tex.A.Civ.Cas. (Wilson) Texas Ct. of Appeal Civil Cas.
Tex.App. Texas Civil Appeals Cas.; Texas Ct. of Appeals Cas.; Texas Crim. Appeals Rep.
Tex.B.J. Texas Bar Jour.
Tex.Civ.App. Texas Civil Appeals
Tex.Civ.Rep. Same as above
Tex.Com.App. Texas Comm. Appeals
Tex.Cr.App. Texas Crim. Appeals Rep.
Tex.Cr.R. Texas Crim. Rep.
Tex.Ct.App.R. Texas Ct. of Appeals Rep.
Tex.Ct.Rep. Texas Ct. Reporter (1900–08)
Tex.Dec. Texas Dec.
Tex.Int.L.Forum Texas International Law Forum
Tex.Int.L.J. Texas International Law Jour.
Tex.Int'l L.F. Same as Tex.Int.L.Forum
Tex.Jur. Texas Jurisprudence
Tex.Jur.2d Same as above, Second Series
Tex.L.J. Texas Law Jour.
Tex.L.Rev. Texas Law Rev.
Tex.S.Ct. Texas Supreme Ct. Reporter
Tex.So.U.L.Rev. Texas Southern University Law Rev.
Tex.Supp. Texas Supplement to 25 Tex. Rep.
Tex.Tech.L.Rev. Texas Tech Law Rev.
Tex.Unrep.Cas. Texas Unreported Cas. (Posey)
Texas L.Rev. Texas Law Rev.
Th.C.C. Thacher's Crim. Cas. (Mass. 1823–42)

Th.&C. Thompson & Cook's Rep. (N.Y. Sup. Ct. 1873–75)
Thac.Cr.Cas. Thacher's Crim. Cas. (Mass. 1823–42)
Thayer Thayer's Rep. (18 Ore.)
The Rep. The Reporter, Phi Alpha Delta
The Rep., Coke's Rep., *Eng.*
Thém. La Thémis, Montreal, *Que.*
Thémis La Revue Juridique Thémis
Thom. Thomas Rep. (1 Wyo.)
Thomson's Nova Scotia Rep.
Thom.Dec. Thomson's Dec. (1 Nova Scotia)
Thom.Rep. Thomson's Rep. (3 Nova Scotia)
Thom.&Fr. Thomas & Franklin's Rep. (1 Md. Ch.)
Thomas Thomas' Rep. (1 Wyo.)
Thomp.Cal. Thompson's Rep. (39, 40 Cal.)
Thomp.Tenn.Cas. Thompson's Unreported Cas. (Tenn. 1847–69)
Thomp.&C. Thompson & Cook's N.Y. Sup. Ct. Rep.
Thompson Thompson's Rep. (39, 40 Cal.)
Thomson Thomson's Rep. (Nova Scotia)
Thor. Thorington's Rep. (107 Ala.)
Thorpe Thorpe's Rep. (52 La.)
Tiffany Tiffany's Rep. (28–39 N.Y.)
Tillman Tillman's Rep. (68, 69, 71, 73, 75 Ala.)
Times L.R. Times Law Rep., *Eng.*
Tinw. Tinwald, *Sc.*
Title News Title News
Tobey Tobey's Rep. (9, 10 R.I.)
Tot. Tothill's Ch. Rep., *Eng.*
Toth. Same as above
Tr.App. Transcript Appeals (N.Y. 1867–68)
Tr. Law.Guide Trial Lawyer's Guide
Tr.Law.Q. Trial Lawyers' Quarterly
Tr.&Est. Trusts & Estates
Tr.&T.T. Trial and Tort Trends
Tr.&H.Pr. Troubat & Haly's Practice, *Pa.*
Trace.&M. Tracefell & Mitchell (Comptroller's Dec.), *U.S.*
Trade Cas. Trade Cas. (CCH)
Trade Reg.Rep. Trade Regulation Reporter (CCH)
Trade Reg.Rev. Trade Regulation Rev.
Trademark Bull. Trademark Bulletin
Trademark Bull.(N.S.) Same as above, New Series
Trademark Rptr. Trademark Reporter
Trans.Ap. Transcript Appeals (N.Y. 1867–68)
Tread. Treadway's Rep. (S.C. Constitutional)
Treas.Dec. Treasury Dec., *U.S.*
Trem. Tremaine's Pleas of the Crown, *Eng.*
Trem.P.C. Same as above
Trial Trial
Trin. Trinity Term
Tripp Tripp's Rep. (5, 6 Dak.)
Tru. Trueman's New Brunswick Rep.
True. Same as above
Tru.Railw.Rep. Truman, American Railway Rep.
Truem.Eq.Cas. Trueman's New Brunswick Eq. Cas.
Trust Bull. Trust Bulletin
Trust Terr. Trust Territory Rep.
Trusts & Es. Trusts & Estates
Tuck. Tucker's Rep., *D.C.*
Tucker's Rep. (156–175 Mass.)
Tucker's N.Y. Surrogate Rep.
Tuck. Sel. Cas. Tucker's Select Cas., *Newf.*
Tuck. Surr. Tucker's N.Y. Surrogate Rep.
Tuck. & Cl. Tucker & Clephane's Rep. (21 D.C.)
Tul. L. Rev. Tulane Law Rev.
Tul. Tax Inst. Tulane Tax Institute

Tulsa L.J. Tulsa Law Jour.
Tup. App. Tupper's Appeal Rep., *Ont.*
Tupper Same as above
Tur. & Rus. Turner & Russell's Ch. Rep., *Eng.*
Turn. & P. Turner & Phillips' Ch., *Eng.*
Turner Turner's Rep. (35–48 Ark.) Turner's Rep. (99–101 Ky.)
Tuttle Tuttle's Rep. (23–32, 41–51 Cal.)
Tuttle & Carp. Tuttle & Carpenter's Rep. (52 Cal.)
Tyl. Tyler's Rep. (Vt. 1800–03)
Tyng Tyng's Rep. (2–17 Mass.)
Tyr. Tyrwhitt's Ex. Rep., *Eng.*
Tyr. & Gr. Tyrwhitt & Granger's Ex. Rep., *Eng.*
Tyrw. Tyrwhitt, Tyr.

U. Utah
U.B.C.L. Rev. University of British Columbia Law Rev.
U.C. Upper Canada
U.C. (O.S.) Upper Canada K. (or Q.) Rep., Old Series
U.C. App. Upper Canada Appeal
U.C.C. Law Letter Uniform Commercial Code Law Letter
U.C.C.P. Upper Canada C.P. Rep.
U.C.C.P.D. Upper Canada C.P. Div.
U.C.C. Rep. Serv. Uniform Commercial Code Reporting Service
U.C. Ch. Upper Canada Ch. Rep.
U.C. Cham. Upper Canada Chambers Rep.
U.C. Chan. Upper Canada Ch. Rep.
U.C.D.L. Rev. University of California at Davis Law Rev.
U.C.E.&A. Upper Canada Error and Appeal Rep.
U.C.Err.& App. Same as above
U.C.I.S. Unemployment Compensation Interpretation Service, Benefit Series
Unemployment Compensation Interpretation Service, Federal Series
Unemployment Compensation Interpretation Service, State Series
U.C. Jur. Upper Canada Jurist
U.C.K.B. Upper Canada K.B. Rep., Old Series
U.C.L.A.-Alaska L. Rev. U.C.L.A.-Alaska Law Rev.
U.C.L.A. Intra. L. Rev. U.C.L.A. Intramural Law Rev.
U.C.L.A.L. Rev. U.C.L.A. Law Rev.
U.C.L.J. Upper Canada Law Jour.
U.C.L.J. (N.S.) Same as above, New Series
U.C.P.R. Upper Canada Practice Rep.
UCMJ Uniform Code of Military Justice, *U.S.*
U.C.Q.B. Upper Canada Q.B. Rep.
U.C.R. Upper Canada Rep.
U.Chi.L. Rec. University of Chicago Law School Record
U. Chi. L. Rev. University of Chicago Law Rev.
U. Cin. L. Rev. University of Cincinnati Law Rev.
U. Colo. L. Rev. University of Colorado Law Rev.
U. Dayton L. Rev. University of Dayton Law Rev.
U. Det. L. J. University of Detroit Law Jour.
U. Fla.L. Rev. University of Florida Law Rev.
U. Ill. L. F. University of Illinois Law Forum
U. Ill. L. Forum Same as above
U. Kan. City L. Rev. University of Kansas City Law Rev.
U.L.A. Uniform Law Annot.
U.M.K.C.L.R. University of Missouri at K.C. Law Rev.
U. Md. L. F. University of Maryland Law Forum

U. Miami L. Rev. University of Miami Law Rev.
U. Mich. J. Law Reform University of Michigan Jour. of Law Reform
U. Mo. Bull. L. Ser. University of Missouri Bulletin Law Series
U. Mo. K.C.L. Rev. University of Missouri at Kansas City Law Rev.
UN United Nations
U.N.B.L.J. University of New Brunswick Law Jour.
UNESCO United Nations Educational, Scientific, and Cultural Organization
UNICEF United Nations International Children's Emergency Fund
U.N.T.S. United Nations Treaty Series
U. New So. Wales L.J. University of New South Wales Law Jour.
U. Newark L. Rev. University of Newark Law Rev.
U. Pa. L. Rev. University of Pennsylvania Law Rev.
U. Pitt. L. Rev. University of Pittsburgh Law Rev.
U. Queens. L. J. University of Queensland Law Jour.
U. Rich. L. Rev. University of Richmond Law Rev.
U.S. United States or U.S. Sup. Ct. Rep.
U.S. & Can. A.R. United States and Canada Aviation Reports
U.S. App. United States Appeals (Cir. Courts or Courts of Appeals)
U.S. App. D.C. United States Ct. of Appeals for District of Columbia beginning with v. 75
U.S. Av. R. United States Aviation Rep.
U.S.C. United States Code
U.S.C. (Supp.) United States Code, Supplement
U.S.C.C.A. United States Cir. Ct. of Appeals Rep.
U.S.C.C.&A.N. United States Code Congressional and Administrative News
U.S.C. Govt. Rep. University of South Carolina Governmental Rev.
USCMA Official Rep., U.S. Court of Military Appeals
U.S.C.S. United States Code Service
U.S. Ct. Cl. United States Ct. of Claims
USDA United States Dept. of Agriculture
U.S. Daily United States Daily, Washington, D.C.
U.S. Dist. of Haw. District Ct., Hawaii
USHA United States Housing Authority
U.S.I.C.C.V.R. United States Interstate Commerce Comm. Valuation Rep.
U.S. Jur. United States Jurist
U.S.L. Ed. United States Sup. Ct. Rep., Lawyers' Edition
U.S.L.J. United States Law Jour.
U.S.L.Mag. United States Law Magazine
U.S.L.W. United States Law Week
U.S.M.C. United States Marine Corps
United States Maritime Comm.
U.S.P.Q. United States Patents Quarterly
U.S. Rep. United States Rep.
U.S.S.B. United States Shipping Bd. (Dec.)
U.S.S.C. Rep. United States Sup. Ct. Rep.
U.S. Sup. Ct. (L. Ed.) United States Sup. Ct. Rep., Lawyers' Edition
U.S. Sup. Ct. Rep. United States Sup. Ct. Reporter
U.S.T. United States Treaties and Other International Agreements 1950–date
USTC United States Tax Cas. (CCH)

U.S.T.D. United States Treaty Development
U.S.T.I.T. Same as U.S.T.
U.S. Treas. Reg. United States Treasury Regulations
U.S. Treaty Ser. United States Treaty Series
U.S.V.A.A.D. United States Veterans Administration Administrator's Dec.
U.S.V.B.D.D. United States Veterans Bureau Directors Dec.
U. San Fernando V.L. Rev. University of San Fernando Valley Law Rev.
U. San Fran. L. Rev. University of San Francisco Law Rev.
U. Tasm. L. Rev. University of Tasmania Law Rev.
U. Toledo L. Rev. University of Toledo Law Rev.
U. Tor. L. Rev. University of Toronto School of Law Rev.
U. Toronto L.J. University of Toronto Law Jour.
U.W. Austl. L. Rev. University of Western Australia Law Rev.
U.W.L.A.L. Rev. University of West Los Angeles School of Law, Law Rev.
U. Wash. L. Rev. University of Washington Law Rev.
U. Windsor L. Rev. University of Windsor Law Rev.
U. of P.L. Rev. University of Pennsylvania Law Rev.
Udal Fiji Law Rep., *Fiji*
Un. Prac. News Unauthorized Practice News
Unempl. Ins. Rep. Unemployment Insurance Reporter (CCH)
Unof. Unofficial Rep.
Up. Ben. Pr. Upper Bench Precedents *temp.* Car. I, Eng.
Urban Law. Urban Lawyer
Urban Law Ann. Urban Law Annual
Utah Utah
Utah, 2d Same as above, Second Series
Utah B. Bull. Utah Bar Bulletin
Utah L. Rev. Utah Law Rev.
Util. L. Rep. Utilities Law Reporter (CCH)

V. Vermont; Victoria; Virginia
VA Administrator of Veterans' Affairs, *U.S.*
V.A.D. Veterans' Affairs Dec., Appealed Pension and Civil Service Retirement Cas., *U.S.*
V.B. Veterans' Bureau, *U.S.*
V.C. Rep. Vice-Chancellor's *(Eng.; Canadian)*
V.I. Virgin Islands Rep.
V.I.B.J. Virgin Islands Bar Jour.
V.L.R. Victoria Law Rep., *Aus.*
V.N. Van Ness' Prize Cas., *U.S.*
V.R. Vermont Rep.; Virginia Rep.
Valuation Rep., Interstate Commerce Comm.
Victoria Rep., *Aus.*
Va. Virginia; Virginia Rep.
Va. Bar. News Virginia Bar News
Va. Cas. Virginia Cas. (Brockenbrough & Holmes)
Virginia Crim. Cas. (3, 4 Va.)
Va. Ch. Dec. Wythe's Ch. (Va. 1788–99)
Va. Col. Dec. Virginia Colonial Dec. (Randolph & Barradall)
Va. J. Int'l L. Virginia Jour. of International Law
Va. L.J. Virginia Law Jour.
Va. L. Reg. Virginia Law Register
Va. L. Reg. (N.S.) Same as above, New Series
Va. L. Rev. Virginia Law Rev.
Va. R. Virginia Rep.
Val. Rep. I.C.C. Valuation Rep., Interstate Commerce Comm.
Val. U.L. Rev. Valparaiso University Law Rev.
Van K. Van Koughnet's Rep. (15–21 Upper Canada C.P. Rep.)
Van N. Van Ness' Prize Cas., U.S. Dist. Ct., Dist. of N.Y.
Vand. J. Transnat'l Vanderbilt Jour. of Transnational Law

Vand. L. Rev. Vanderbilt Law Rev.
Vaugh. Vaughan's C.P. Rep., *Eng.*
Vaux Vaux's Recorder's Dec. (Pa. 1841–45)
Ve. *See* Ves.
Ve. & B. Vesey & Beames' Ch. Rep., *Eng.*
Veazey Veazey's Rep. (36–44 Vt.)
Vent. Ventris' C.P. and K.B. Rep., *Eng.*
Ver. Vermont
Verm. Vermont
Vern. Vernon's Ch. Rep., *Eng.*
Vern. & S. Vernor & Scriven, K.B., *Ir.*
Ves. Vesey, Senior's Ch. Rep., *Eng.*
Ves. Jr. Vesey, Junior's Ch. Rep., *Eng.*
Ves. Jun. Supp. Vesey, Junior, Supp. Ch., *Eng.*
Ves. Sen. Vesey, Senior's Ch. Rep., *Eng.*
Ves. & Bea. Vesey & Beames' Ch. Rep., *Eng.*
Vez. Vezey's Ch. Rep. *temp.* Hardwicke, *Eng.*
Vict. Victoria
Vict. Admr. Victorian Admiralty
Vict. Eq. Victorian Equity
Vict. L. Victorian Law
Vict. L.R. Victorian Law Rep.
Vict. L.R. Min. Victorian Law Mining Rep.
Vic. L.T. Victorian Law Times
Vict. Rev. Victorian Rev.
Vict. St. Tr. Victorian State Trials
Vict. U.L. Rev. Victoria University Law Rev.
Vict. U. Well. L. Rev. Victoria University of Wellington Law Rev.
Vilas Vilas' Rep. (1–5 N.Y. Crim. Rep.)
Vil. & Br. Vilas & Bryant's Ed. Rep., *Wis.*
Vill. L. Rev. Villanova Law Rev.
Vin. Abr. Viner's Abridgement of Law and Eq.
Vin. Supp. Supplement to above
Virg. Virginia; Virginia Cas. (Brockenbrough & Holmes)
Virgin Virgin's Rep. (52–60 Me.)
Virgin Is. Virgin Islands
Vr. Vroom's Rep. (30–85 N.J. Law)
Vroom Same as above
Vroom (G.D.W.) Vroom, G. D. W., 36–85 N.J. Law
Vroom (P.D.) Vroom, P. D., 30–35 N.J. Law
Vt. Vermont
Vt. L. Rev. Vermont Law Rev.

W. Watt's P. Rep., *Pa.*; Wendell's Rep. (N.Y., 1826–41); Wheaton's Rep. (14–25 U.S.); Wisconsin Rep.; Wright's Ohio Rep. (1831–1834); Wyoming Rep.
W.A'B. & W. Webb, A'Beckett & Williams, *Victoria, B.C.*
W. Afr. App. West African Ct. of Appeal Rep.
W.A.L.R. (*or* W.A.R.) Western Australia Law Reports
W. Austl. Ind. Gaz. Western Australia Industrial Gazette
W. Austl. J.P. Western Australia Justice of the Peace
W. Austl. L.R. (*or* W.A.R.) Western Australia Law Rep.
W. Bl. William Blackstone's K.B. Rep., *Eng.*
W.C. Ins. Rep. Workmen's Compensation & Insurance Rep.
W.C.L.J. Workmen's Compensation Law Jour.
W.C. Ops. Workmen's Compensation Opinions, U.S. Dept. of Commerce
W.C. Rep. Workmen's Compensation Rep.
W. Coast Rep. West Coast Reporter
W.H. Cas. Wage & Hour Cas. (BNA)
WHO World Health Organization, *UN*

W.H.R. Wage & Hour Reporter (BNA)
W.H.R. Man. Wage & Hour Reference Manual (BNA)
W.H. & G. Welsby, Hurlstone & Gordon's Ex. Rep., *Eng.*
W. Jo. William Jones' K.B. Rep., *Eng.*
W. Kel. William Kelynge's Ch. Rep., *Eng.*
W.L.B. Weekly Law Bulletin, *Ohio*
W.L.G. Weekly Law Gazette, *Ohio*
W.L.J. Western Law Jour.
W.L. Jour. Weekly Law Jour.
W.L.M. Western Law Monthly, *Ohio*
W.L.R. Washington Law Reporter, *D.C.*
Weekly Law Rep., *Eng.*
Western Law Reporter
W.L.T. Western Law Times and Reporter
W.N. Weekly Notes (of English Law Rep.)
W.N. (N.S.W.) Weekly Notes New South Wales, *Aus.*
W. Ont. L. Rev. Western Ontario Law Rev.
W.R. Weekly Rep.; Wendell's Rep. (N.Y. 1826–41); West's Ch. Rep., *Eng.*; Wisconsin Rep.
W.R.L.R. Women's Rights Law Reporter
W. Rep. West's Rep. *temp.* Hardwicke, *Eng.*
W. Rob. William Robinson's Admiralty Rep., *Eng.*
W.T.B.R. War Trade Bd. Rulings, *U.S.*
W. Ty. R. Washington Territory Rep. 1854–88
W. Va. West Virginia
W. Va. L.Q. West Virginia Law Quarterly
W. Va. L. Rev. West Virginia Law Rev.
W.W. Harr. W. W. Harrington, Del.
W.W. Harr. Del. W. W. Harrington's Rep. (31–39 Del.)
W.W.R. Western Weekly Rep., *Can.*
W.W.R. (N.S.) Same as above, New Series
W. & C. Wilson & Courtenay's Appeal Cas.
W. & M. Woodbury & Minot's Ct. Rep., *U.S.*
W. & S. Watts & Sergeant's Rep. (Pa. 1841–45)
W. & W. White & Webb's Victorian Rep.
White & Wilson's Tex. Civil Cas., Ct. of Appeals
W.W. & D. Willmore, Wollaston & Davison's Q.B. Rep., *Eng.*
W.W. & H. Willmore, Wollaston & Hodges' Q.B. Rep., *Eng.*
Wa. Watts' Rep. (Pa. 1832–40); Wage & Hour Reporter
Wage & Hour Cas. Wage & Hour Cas., *BNA*
Wal. Wallace, usually abbreviated as Wall.
Wal. By L. Wallis, Irish Ch. (By Lyne)
Wal. Jr. Wallace Junior, *U.S.*
Walk. Walker
Walk. Ch. Walker's Mich. Ch. Rep.
Walk. Mich. Same as above
Walk. Miss. Walker's Rep. (1 Miss.)
Walk. Pa. Walker's Rep. (Pa. 1855–85)
Walk. Tex. Walker's Rep. (22–25, 38–51, 72–88 Tex.; 1–10 Civil Appeals Tex.)
Walker Walker's Rep. (96, 109 Ala.); Walker's Mich. Ch. Rep.; Walker's Rep. (1 Miss.); Walker's Rep. (Pa. 1855–85); Walker's Rep. (22–25, 38–51, 72–88 Tex.; 1–10 Civil Appeals Tex.)
Wall. Wallace; Wallis; Wallace's Cir. Ct. Rep., *U.S.*; Wallace's Philadelphia Rep.,(Pa. 1855–85); Wallace's U.S. Sup. Ct. Rep. (68–90 U.S.)
Wall. C.C. Same as above
Wall. Jr. J. W. Wallace's Cir. Ct. Rep., *U.S.*

Wall. Rep. Wallace, The Reporters (treatise)
Wallace's U.S. Sup. Ct. Rep. (68–90 U.S.)
Wall. S.C. Wallace's U.S. Sup. Ct. Rep. (68–90 U.S.)
Wall. Sen. J. B. Wallace's Cir. Ct. Rep., *U.S.*
Wallis Wallis' Ch., *Ir.*
Walsh Walsh's Registry Cas., *Ir.*
Walter (14–16 N. M.)
War Dep. B.C.A. United States War Department, Dec. of Bd. of Contract Adjustment
War Trade Reg. War Trade Reg., *U.S.*
Ward. Warden's Rep. (2, 4 Ohio)
Warden Same as above
Warden & Smith (3 Ohio Rep.)
Warden's Law & Bk. Bull. Weekly Law & Bank Bulletin, *Ohio*
Ware Ware's Dist. Ct. Rep., *U.S.*
Wash. Washburn; Washington
Washington's Rep. (16–23 Vt.)
Washington's Rep. (1, 2 Va.)
Washington's Cir. Ct. Rep., *U.S.*
Washington Territory or State Rep.
Wash. C.C. Washington's Cir. Ct. Rep., *U.S.*
Wash. Co. R. Washington County Rep., *Pa.*
Wash. L. Rep. Washington Law Reporter, *D.C.*
Wash. L. Rev. Washington Law Rev.
Wash. Ter. (N.S.) Allen's Washington Territory Rep., New Series
Wash. Terr. Washington Territory Opinions 1854–64
Wash. Ty. *See* Wash. Terr.
Wash. U.L.Q. Washington University Law Quarterly
Wash. Va. Washington's Rep. (1, 2 Va.)
Wash. & Haz. P.E.I. Washburton & Hazard's Rep., *Prince Edward Island*
Wash. & Lee L. Rev. Washington & Lee Law Rev.
Washburn Washburn's Rep. (18–23 Vt.)
Washburn L.J. Washburn Law Jour.
Watts Watts' Rep. (Pa. 1832–40); Watts' Rep. (16–24 W.Va.)
Watts & Serg. Watts & Sergeant's Rep. (Pa. 1841–45)
Wayne L. Rev. Wayne Law Rev.
Webb Webb's Rep. (6–20 Kan.)
Webb's Rep. (11–20 Tex. Civil App.)
Webb A'B. & W. Webb, A'Beckett & Williams Rep., *Aust.*
Webb & Duval Webb & Duval's Rep. (1–3 Tex.)
Webs. Pat. Cas. Webster's Patent Cas., *Eng.*
Week. Cin. L.B. Weekly Cincinnati Law Bulletin, *Ohio*
Week. Dig. Weekly Digest, *N.Y.*
Week. Jur. Weekly Jurist, *Ill.*
Week. L. Gaz. Weekly Law Gazette, *Ohio*
Week. L. Rec. Weekly Law Record
Week. Law Bul. Weekly Law Bulletin, *Ohio*
Week. No. Weekly Notes of Cas. (Law Rep.)
Week. No. Cas. Weekly Notes of Cas., *London*
Weekly Notes of Cas. (Pa. 1874–99)
Week. Rep. Weekly Reporter, *Eng.*
Week. Trans. Rep. Weekly Transcript Rep., *N.Y.*
Weekly L.R. Weekly Law Reports, *Eng.*
Weekly Notes Weekly Notes (of Law Rep.), *Eng.*
Welfare L. News Welfare Law News
Welsb. H. & G. Welsby, Hurlstone & Gordon's Ex. Rep., *Eng.*
Welsh Welsh's Registry Cas., *Ir.*
Wend. Wendell's Rep. (N.Y. 1826–41)
Wenz. Wenzell's Rep. (60–72 Minn.)

West. West's Ch. Rep., *Eng.*; Weston's Rep. (11–14 Vt.)
West. Austl. Western Australian Rep.
West. Chy. West's Ch. Rep. *temp.* Hardwicke, *Eng.*
West H.L. West's Rep. H.L., *Eng.*
West. Jur. Western Jurist, *Des Moines*
West. L. Gaz. Western Law Gazette, *Ohio*
West. L.J. Western Law Jour.
West. L.M. Western Law Monthly, *Ohio*
West. L.R. Western Law Reporter, *Can.*
West. L. Rev. Western Law Rev.
West. R. Western Reporter
West. Res. Law Rev. Western Reserve Law Rev.
West. School L. Rev. Western School Law Rev.
West. St. U.L. Rev. Western State University Law Rev.
West *t.* Hrdw. West's Ch. Rep. *temp.* Hardwicke, *Eng.*
West Va. West Virginia
West. Week. Rep. Western Weekly Rep., *Can.*
Western Ont. L. Rev. Western Ontario Law Rev.
Western Res. L. Rev. Western Reserve Law Rev.
Westm. L.J. Westmoreland Law Jour., *Pa.*
Westmoreland Co. L.J. Westmoreland County Law Jour. (Pa. 1911–date)
Weston Weston's Rep. (11–14 Vt.)
Weth. U.C. Wethey's Rep., Upper Canada Q.B.
Wh. Wharton's Rep. (Pa. 1835–41)
Wheaton's U.S. Sup. Ct. Rep. (14–25 U.S.)
Wh. Cr. Cas. Wheeler's Crim. Cas., *N.Y.*
Whar. Wharton's Rep. (Pa.1835–41)
Whart. Law Dic. Wharton's Law Lexicon
Whart. Pa. Same as above
Whart. St. Tr. Wharton's State Trials, *U.S.*
Wheat. Wheaton's U.S. Sup. Ct. Rep. (14–25 U.S.)
Wheel. Wheelock's Rep. (32–37 Tex.)
Wheeler's Crim. Cas., *N.Y.*
Wheel. Cr. Cas. Same as above
Wheeler Abr. Wheeler's Abridgement
Whit. Pat. Cas. Whitman's Patent Cas.
White White's Rep. (31–44 Tex. App.)
White's Rep. (10–15 W.Va.)
White & T. Lead. Cas Eq. White & Tudor's Leading Cas. in Eq., *Eng.*
White & W. White & Willson's Rep. (Tex. Civil Cas., Ct. of Appeals)
White & W. Civ. Cas. Ct. App. Same as above
Whitm. Lib. Cas. Whitman's Libel Cas., *Mass.*
Whittlesey Whittlesey's Rep. (32–41 Mo.)
Wight Wight's Election Cas., *Sc.*
Wight. Wightwick's Ex. Rep., *Eng.*
Wightw. Same as above
Wil. Williams, abbreviated as Will.; Wilson, abbreviated as Wils.
Wilc. Cond. Rep. Wilcox's Condensed Rep. (1–7 Ohio, Reprint)
Wilcox Wilcox's Rep. (10 Ohio)
Wilcox's Lackawanna County (Pa.) Rep.
Wilk. Wilkinson's Rep., Tex. Ct. of Appeals and Civil Appeals
Will. Willes' C.P. Rep., *Eng.*
Will. Mass. Williams' Rep. (1 Mass.)
Will. P. Peere Williams' Ch. Rep., *Eng.*
Will. Vt. Williams Rep. (27–29 Vt.)
Will. Woll. & D. Willmore, Wollaston & Davison's Q.B. Rep., *Eng.*

Will. Woll & Hodg. Willmore, Wollaston & Hodges' Q.B. Rep., *Eng*.
Willamette L.J. Willamette Law Jour.
Willes Willes' C.P. Rep., *Eng*.
Williams Peere Williams' Ch. Rep., *Eng*.
Williams' Rep. (1 Mass.)
Williams' Rep. (10–12 Utah)
Williams' Rep. (27–29 Vt.)
Williams P. Peere Williams Ch. Rep., *Eng*.
Williams & Bruce Ad. Pr. Williams & Bruce's Admiralty Practice
Willm. W. & D. Willmore, Wollaston & Davison's Q.B. Rep., *Eng*.
Willm. W. & H. Willmore, Wollaston & Hodges' Q.B. Rep., *Eng*.
Willson Willson's Rep., Tex. Appeals
Willson Civ. Cas. Ct. App. White & Willson's Rep. (Tex. Civil Cas., Ct. of Appeals)
Wilm. Wilmot's Notes, *Eng*.
Wils. G. Wilson's Rep., K.B. and C.P., *Eng*.
Wils. Ch. Wilson's Ch. Rep., *Eng*.
Wils. Exch. Wilson's Ex., *Eng*.
Wils. Ind. Wilson's Rep., Ind. Super. Ct.
Wils. K.B. Wilson's K.B. Rep., *Eng*.
Wils. Minn. Wilson's Rep. (48–59 Minn.)
Wils. Oreg. Wilson's Rep. (1–3 Ore.)
Wils. P.C. Wilson's P.C., *Eng*.
Wils. & S. Wilson & Shaw, H.L., *Sc*.
Wilson Wilson's Ch. Rep.; Wilson's K.B. and C.P. Rep., *Eng*.; Wilson's Ex. in Eq. Rep., *Eng*.; Wilson's Rep. Ind. Super. Ct.; Wilson's Rep. (48–59 Minn.); Wilson's Rep. (1–3 Ore.)
Win. Winch's C.P. Rep., *Eng*.
Winer's Unreported Opinions (N.Y. Sup. Ct., Erie County)
Winston's Rep. (60 N.C.)
Win. Eq. Winston's Rep. (60 N.C.)
Winch Winch's C.P. Rep., *Eng*.
Winst. Winston's Rep. (60 N.C.)
Wis. Wisconsin
Wis. B. Bull. Wisconsin Bar Bulletin
Wis. L.N. Wisconsin Legal News
Wis. L. Rev. Wisconsin Law Rev.
Withrow Withrow's Rep. (9–21 Iowa)
Wm. Bl. William Blackstone's K.B. Rep., *Eng*.
Wm. Mitchell L. Rev. William Mitchell Law Review
Wm. Rob. William Robinson's Admiralty Rep., *Eng*.
Wm. & Mary L. Rev. William & Mary Law Rev.
Wms. Williams, commonly abbreviated as Will.
Wms. Mass. Williams' Rep. (1 Mass.)
Wms. Peere Peere Williams' Ch. Rep., *Eng*.
Wms. Vt. Williams' Rep. (27–29 Vt.)
Wol. Wolcott's Rep. (7 Del. Ch.)
Wollaston's English Bail Ct. Rep., *Eng*.
Wolf. & B. Wolferstand & Bristow's Election Cas., *Eng*.
Wolf. & D. Wolferstan & Dew's Election Cas., *Eng*.
Woll. Wollaston's English Bail Ct. Rep.
Women Law. J. Women Lawyer's Jour.
Women Lawyer's J. Same as above
Women's L. Rptr. Women's Law Reporter
Women's Rights L. Rptr. Women's Rights Law Reporter
Wood. Woodbury & Minot's Cir. Ct. Rep.
Wood. & M. Same as above
Wood's R. Wood's Manitoba Rep., (1875–83)
Woods Wood's Cir. Ct. Rep., *U.S.*

Woods C.C. Same as above
Woodw. Dec. Woodward's Dec. (Pa. 1861–74)
Wool. Woolworth's Cir. Ct. Rep., *U.S.*
Wool. C.C. Same as above
Woolw. Same as above
Wright Wright's Rep. (Ohio 1831–34)
Wright's Rep. (37–50 Pa.)
Wright Ch. Wright's Rep. (Ohio 1831–34)
Wright N.P. Wright's N.P. Rep., *Ohio*
Wy. Wythe's Ch. Rep. (Va. 1788–99)
Wyoming Rep.
Wy. & W. Wyatt & Webb, *Victoria*
Wy., W. & A'Beck. Wyatt, Webb & A'Beckett, *Victoria*
Wyo. Wyoming
Wyo. L.J. Wyoming Law Jour.
Wyo. T. Wyoming Territory
Wythe Wythe's Ch. Rep. (Va. 1788–99)

Y. Yearbook; Yeates Rep. (Pa. 1791–1808); Yukon
Y.A.D. Young's Vice-Admiralty Dec., *Can.*
Y.B. Year Books; The Year Books are usually cited by the year of each King's reign, the initial letter of his name, and the folio and number of the *placita*, *e.g.*, 34 H. VI, 25.3)
Y.B. Eur. Conv. on Human Rights Yearbook of the European Convention on Human Rights
Y.B. Int. L. Comm. Yearbook of the International Law Comm.
Y.B. Sch. L. Yearbook of School Law
Y.L.R. York Legal Record (Pa. 1880–date)
Y. & C. Younge & Collyer's Ch. or Ex. Eq. Rep., *Eng.*
Y. & C. Ex. Younge & Collyer's Ex. in Eq. Rep., *Eng.*
Y. & J. Young & Jervis' Ex. Rep., *Eng.*
Yale L.J. Yale Law Jour.
Yale Rev. Law & Soc. Act. Yale Rev. of Law and Social Action
Yates Sel. Cas. Yates' Select Cas. (N.Y. 1809)
Yea. Yeates' Rep. (Pa. 1791–1808)
Year Books *See* Y.B.
Yeates *See* Yea. above
Yel. Yelverton's K.B. Rep.
Yelv. Same as above
Yerg. Yerger's Rep. (9–18 Tenn.)
Yo. Younge's Ex. in Eq. Rep., *Eng.*
York Leg. Rec. York Legal Record, *Pa.*
Yorke Ass. Yorke Assizes (Clayton)
You. Younge's Ex. in Eq. Rep., *Eng.*
You. & Coll. Ch. Younge & Collyer's Ch. Rep., *Eng.*
You. & Coll. Ex. Younge & Collyer's Ex. in Eq. Rep., *Eng.*
You. & Jerv. Younge & Jervis' Ex. Rep., *Eng.*
Young Young's Rep. (21–47 Minn.)
Young Adm. Dec. Young's Nova Scotia Vice-Admiralty Dec.
Young Naut. Dict. Young's Nautical Dictionary
Younge Younge's Ex. Rep., *Eng.*
Younge & Coll. Ch. Younge & Collyer's Ch. or Ex. Eq. Rep., *Eng.*
Younge & Coll. Ex. Younge & Collyer's Ex. in Eq. Rep., *Eng.*
Younge & Jerv. Younge & Jervis' Ex. Rep., *Eng.*
Younge M.L. Cas. Younge Maritime Law Cas., *Eng.*

Zab. Zabriskie's Rep. (21–24 N.J. Law)
Zam. L.J. Zambia Law Jour., *Africa*
Zane Zane's Rep. (4–9 Utah)

Index